THE WORLD OF THE
Huns

THE WORLD OF THE

Studies in Their History and Culture

By OTTO J. MAENCHEN-HELFEN

EDITED BY MAX KNIGHT

University of California Press | Berkeley | Los Angeles | London | 1973

University of California Press
Berkeley and Los Angeles, California
University of California Press, Ltd.
London, England

Copyright © 1973, by
The Regents of the University of California

Library of Congress Catalog Card Number : 79-94985
International Standard Book Number : 520-01596-7
Designed by James Mennick
Printed in the United States of America

Contents

v

List of Illustrations

Foreword

FEW SCHOLARS would care to risk their reputation in taking on the monumental task of straightening out misconceptions about the Huns, and incidentally about the many peoples related to them, allied with them, or confused with them. At the foundation there are philological problems of mindboggling proportions in languages ranging from Greek to Chinese; above that, an easy but solidly professional familiarity with primary sources for the history of both Eastern and Western civilizations in many periods is required; finally, a balanced imagination and a prudent sense of proportion are needed to cope with the improbabilities, contradictions, and prejudices prevailing in this field of study. The late Professor Otto Maenchen-Helfen worked on this immense field of research for many years, and at his death in 1969 left an unfinished manuscript. This is the source of the present book.

Maenchen-Helfen differed from other historians of Eurasia in his unique competence in philology, archaeology, and the history of art. The range of his interests is apparent from a glance at his publications, extending in subject from "Das Märchen von der Schwanenjungfrau in Japan" to "Le Cicogne di Aquileia," and from "Manichaeans in Siberia" to "Germanic and Hunnic Names of Iranian Origin." He did not need to guess the identities of tribes, populations, or cities. He knew the primary texts, whether in Greek or Russian or Persian or Chinese. This linguistic ability is particularly necessary in the study of the Huns and their nomadic cognates, since the name "Hun" has been applied to many peoples of different ethnic character, including Ostrogoths, Magyars, and Seljuks. Even ancient nomadic people north of China, the Hsiung-nu, not related to any of these, were called "Hūn" by their Sogdian neighbors. Maenchen-Helfen knew the Chinese sources that tell of the Hsiung-nu, and thus could evaluate the relationship of these sources to European sources of Hunnic history.

His exceptional philological competence also enabled him to treat as human beings the men whose lives underlie the dusty textual fragments that allude to them, and to describe their economy, social stratifications, modes of transportation and warfare, religions, folklore, and art. He could create a reliable account of the precursors of the Turks and Mongols, free of the usual Western prejudice and linguistic limitations.

Another special competence was his expertise in the history of Asian art, a subject that he taught for many years. He was familiar with the newest archaeological discoveries and knew how to correlate them with the available but often obscure philological evidence.

To define distinctive traits in the art of a people as elusive as the Huns requires familiarity with the disjointed array of archaeological materials from the Eurasian steppe and the ability to separate materials about the Huns from a comparable array of materials from neighboring civilizations. To cite only one example of his success in coping with such thorny problems, Maenchen-Helfen's description of technical and stylistic consistencies among metal articles from Hunnic tombs in widely separated localities dispels the myth of supposed Hunnic ignorance of metal-working skills.

Archaeological evidence also plays a critical role in the determination of the origin of the Huns and their geographical distribution in ancient and early medieval times, as well as the extent of Hunnic penetration into eastern Europe and their point of entry into the Hungarian plain. Maenchen-Helfen saw clearly how to interpret the data from graves and garbage heaps to yield hypotheses about the movements of peoples. "He believed in the spade, but his tool was the pen," he once said about another scholar — a characterization that perfectly fits Maenchen-Helfen himself. Burial practices of the Huns and their associates indicate that Hunnic weapons generally originated in the east and were transmitted westward, while the distribution of loop mirrors found in association with artificially deformed skulls — a Hunnic practice — gives proof of Hunnic penetration into Hungary from the northeast. (An unpublished find of a sword of the Altlussheim type recently discovered at Barnaul in the Altai region, east Kazakhstan SSR, now in the Hermitage Museum, is a forceful argument in favor of Maenchen-Helfen's assumption about the eastern connections of this weapon. See A. Urmanskiĭ, "Sovremennik groznogo Attily," *Altaĭ* 4 [23], Barnaul 1962, pp. 79-93.) His findings define and bring to life the civilization of one of the most shadowy peoples of early medieval times.

Maenchen-Helfen's account opens *in medias res*, with a tribute to that admirable Roman historian Ammianus Marcellinus, whose view of the Hunnic incursions was, despite his prejudices, in some respects clearer than that of Western historians. Abrupt as this beginning may seem, the author perhaps intended the final version of his book to begin with such a striking evaluation of a basic text. In so doing, he underlined the necessity for sharp and well-reasoned criticism of the sources of the history of the Huns. From the beginning these people were denigrated and "demonized" (to use his own term) by European chroniclers and dismissed as avatars of the eternal but faceless barbarian hordes from the east, against whom vigilance was always necessary, but whose precise identity was of little importance. The bulk of the book discusses the history and civilization of the "Huns proper," those so familiar — and yet so unfamiliar — to Europeans. (Here we use the term "civilization" purposefully, since reports of this folk have tended to treat them as mere barbaric destroying agents — "vandals" spilling blood across the remnants of the declining Roman Empire. Maenchen-Helfen saw them with a clearer vision.)

The style is characteristically dense with realia. Maenchen-Helfen had no need to indulge in generalizations (read "unfounded guesses"). But he was not absorbed in details to the exclusion of a panoramic view. He saw, and presents to us here, the epic character of the great drama that took place on the Eurasian stage early in our era, the clash of armies and the interaction of civilizations. The book is a standard treatise not likely to be superseded in the predictable future.

GUITTY AZARPAY
PETER A. BOODBERG
EDWARD H. SCHAFER

Editor's Note

IN EARLY January 1969 Professor Otto Maenchen-Helfen brought a beautifully typed manuscript from the Central Stenographic Bureau of the university to the University of California Press. It seemed to represent the final result of his monumental study of the Huns, to which he had devoted many years of research and travel. A few days later, on January 29, he died. In the memorial speeches at the Faculty Club in Berkeley, several friends mentioned that he had truly completed his lifework, and that his manuscript was ready to go to press.

The impression that the delivered manuscript pages constituted the complete manuscript turned out to be erroneous. Mr. Maenchen had brought only the first of presumably two batches of manuscript. The chapters representing that second batch were not in final form at the time of his death, the bibliography was missing, footnotes were indicated but the sources not stated, an introduction and a complete preface were lacking, the illustrations were scattered in boxes and desk drawers and not identified. There was no table of contents, and the chapters were not numbered; although some groupings of chapters are suggested in the extant part of the author's preface, it was not clear in what order he intended to arrange his work.

On Mrs. Maenchen's suggestion I searched the author's study and eventually found a tentative draft of a contents page. It was of unknown age, and contained revisions and emendations that required interpretation. On the basis of this precious page, the "Rosetta Stone of the manuscript," the work was organized.

Several chapters mentioned in this page were not in final form. But three-ring folders in the author's study, neatly filed on shelves, bore the names of most missing chapter headings. The contents of these folders were in various stages of completion. Those that appeared to be more or less finished except for final editing were incorporated into the manuscript; also sections which, although not representing complete chapters but apparently in final form, were included and placed where they seemed to fit mostly logically. In several instances, different drafts of the same subject were found, and it was necessary to decide which was the most recent one. Occasionally, also, only carbon copies of apparently finished sections were in the folders.

Errors in judgment in these editorial and compiling activities cannot be ruled out, but wherever doubts existed about the preferred version or the placement of a fragment the material was excluded. Many notes, isolated pages, and drafts (frequently written by hand, with various kinds of emendations) remain in the author's study, including undoubtedly valuable research results.

In retyping the parts of the manuscript that existed only in draft form with many emendations and hand-written corrections, every effort was made not to introduce errors, such as misspellings of foreign words, especially in the notes and bibliography. For errors that undoubtedly slipped in nevertheless, the author is not responsible.

Although the work addresses itself to specialists, it is of interest to a broader range of educated readers who cannot, however, be expected to be familiar with some of the events, persons, institutions, and sources the author takes for granted. For these readers Professor Paul Alexander has provided an introduction; in deference to the author it was placed as "background" at the end of the book, but it may usefully be read first, as a preparation for the text.

The editorial preparation of the manuscript required the help of an unusually large number of persons, reflecting the wide range of the author's competence. The Russian references were checked by the author's friend, the late Professor Peter A. Boodberg, who delivered the corrected pages just a few days before his death in the summer of 1972. The Chinese references were checked or supplied by Professor Edward H. Schafer, also a friend of the author. The Latin and Greek passages were translated by Professor J. K. Anderson and Dr. Emmy Sachs; Mr. Anderson also faithfully filled lacunae in the footnotes and unscrambled mixups resulting from duplicated or omitted footnote numbers. Professors Talat Tekin and Hamid Algar checked and interpreted Turkish references. Professor Joachim Werner of Munich counseled on the Altlussheim sword. Questions about Gothic, Iranian, Hungarian, Japanese, and Ukrainian references or about historical (ancient and medieval) and many other aspects of the text that needed interpretation were answered by a long list of scholars contributing their services to the cause.

Miss Guitty Azarpay (to whom the author used to refer fondly as his favorite student) selected and painstakingly identified the illustrations. She also verified references with angelic patience.

The formidable task of compiling a bibliography on the basis of an incomplete set of cards and of the text itself was performed by Mrs. Jane Fontenrose Cajina. The author's working cards, assembled over many years, were not yet typed in uniform style, many entries were missing, and many lacked essential information. For Russian transcriptions in the bibliography and bibliographical footnotes (but not in the text), the Library of Congress system was used.

The map was drawn by Mrs. Virginia Herrick under the supervision of Professor J. K. Anderson. The index was prepared by Mrs. Gladys Castor.

The editor is indebted to all these many competent and sympathetic helpers; clearly, without their devotion the conversion of the Maenchen papers into the present volume would not have been possible.

MAX KNIGHT

Fragments from the
Author's Preface

[*Among the author's papers were several fragments, partly written in pencil, bearing the notation "for the preface," and evidently intended to be worked into a final draft. He may have wished to say more; all we found is presented below.—Ed.*]

THE AUTHOR of the present volume, in his early seventies, may make use of the privilege, usually granted to men in the prime of their senility, to say a few words about himself, in this case the sources of his interest in the Huns. All my life I have been fascinated by the problems of the frontier. As a boy I dug Roman copper coins along the remnants of the earthen walls that, as late as the seventeenth century, protected Vienna, my native town, from the East. Two blocks from the house in which I was born there still stood in my youth a house above whose gate a Turkish stone cannon ball from the siege of 1529 was immured. My grandfather spent a year in jail for fighting in 1848 with the revolutionaries against the Croatian mercenaries of the Habsburgs. My doctoral dissertation dealt with the "barbarian" elements in Han lore. In 1929 I lived for months in the tents of Turkish-speaking nomads in northwestern Mongolia, where the clash between "higher civilization," represented by Tibetan Lamaism, and the "primitive" beliefs of the Turks was strikingly visible. In Kashmir, at Harwan, I marveled at the artificially deformed skulls on the stamped tiles of Kushan times, those skulls that had impressed me so much when I first saw them in the museum in Vienna and that I had measured as a student. In Nepal I had another chance to see the merging of different civilizations in a borderland. I spent many days in the museum at Minusinsk in southern Siberia studying the "Scythian" bronze plaques and cauldrons. In Kabul I stood in awe before the inscription from Surkh Kotal: it brought back to me the problems of the barbarians at China's border about which I had written a good deal in previous years. Attila and his avatars have been haunting me as far back as I can recall.

In the history of the Western world the eighty years of Hun power were an episode. The Fathers assembled in council at Chalcedon showed a sublime indifference to the barbarian horsemen who, only a hundred miles away, were ravaging Thrace. They were right. A few years later, the head of Attila's son was carried in triumphal procession through the main street of Constantinople.

Some authors have felt that they had to justify their studies of the Huns by speculating on their role in the transition from late antiquity to the Middle Ages. Without the Huns, it has been maintained, Gaul, Spain, and Africa would not, or not so soon, have fallen to the Germans. The mere existence of the Huns in eastern Central Europe is said to have retarded the feudalization of Byzantium. This may or may not be true. But if a historical phenomenon were worth our attention only if it shaped what came after it, the Mayans and Aztecs, the Vandals in Africa, the Burgundians, the Albigenses, and the crusaders' kingdoms in Greece and Syria would have to be wiped off the table of Clio. It is doubtful that Attila "made history." The Huns "perished like the Avars" — "sginuli kak obry," as the old Russian chroniclers used to say when they wrote about a people that had disappeared forever.

It seems strange, therefore, that the Huns, even after fifteen hundred years, can stir up so much emotion. Pious souls still shudder when they think of Attila, the Scourge of God; and in their daydreams German university professors trot behind Hegel's *Weltgeist zu Pferde*. They can be passed over. But some Turks and Hungarians are still singing loud paeans in praise of their great ancestor, pacifier of the world, and Gandhi all in one. The most passionate Hun fighters, however, are the Soviet historians. They curse the Huns as if they had ridden, looting and killing, through the Ukraine only the other day; some scholars in Kiev cannot get over the brutal destruction of the "first flowering of Slavic civilization."

The same fierce hatred burned in Ammianus Marcellinus. He and the other writers of the fourth and fifth centuries depicted the Huns as the savage monsters which we still see today. Hatred and fear distorted the picture of the Huns from the moment they appeared on the lower Danube. Unless this tendentiousness is fully understood — and it rarely is — the literary evidence is bound to be misread. The present study begins, therefore, with its reexamination.

The following chapters, dealing with the political history of the Huns, are not a narrative. The story of Attila's raids into Gaul and Italy need not be told once more; it can be found in any standard history of the declining

Roman Empire, knowledge of which, at least in its outlines, is here taken for granted. However, many problems were not even touched on and many mistakes were made by Bury, Seeck, and Stein. This statement does not reflect on the stature of these eminent scholars, for the Huns were on the periphery of their interests. But such deficiencies are true also for books which give the Huns more room, and even for monographs. The first forty or fifty years of Hun history are treated in a cursory manner. The sources are certainly scanty though not as scanty as one might believe; for the invasion of Asia in 395, for instance, the Syriac sources flow copiously. Some of the questions that the reign of Attila poses will forever remain unanswered. Others, however, are answered by the sources, provided one looks, as I have, for sources outside the literature that has been the stock of Hunnic studies since Gibbon and Le Nain de Tillemont. The discussions of chronology may at times tax the patience of the reader, but that cannot be helped. Eunapius, who in his *Historical Notes* also wrote about the Huns, once asked what bearing on the true subject of history inheres in the knowledge that the battle of Salamis was won by the Hellenes at the rising of the Dog Star. Eunapius has his disciples in our days also, and perhaps more of them than ever. One can only hope that we will be spared a historian who does not care whether Pearl Harbor came before or after the invasion of Normandy because "in a higher sense" it does not matter.

The second part of the present book consists if monographs on the economy, society, warfare, art, and religion of the Huns. What distinguishes these studies from previous treatments is the extensive use of archaeological material. In his *Attila and the Huns* Thompson refuses to take cognizance of it, and the little to which Altheim refers in *Geschichte der Hunnen* he knows at second hand. The material, scattered through Russian, Ukrainian, Rumanian, Hungarian, Chinese, Japanese, and latterly also Mongolian publications, is enormous. In recent years archaeological research has been progressing at such speed that I had to modify my views repeatedly while I was working on these studies. Werner's monumental book on the archaeology of Attila's empire, published in 1956, is already obsolete in some parts. I expect, and hope, that the same will be true of my own studies ten years from now.

Although aware of the dangers in looking for parallels between the Huns and former and later nomads of the Eurasian steppes, I confess that my views are to a certain, I hope not undue, degree influenced by my experiences with the Tuvans in northwestern Mongolia, among whom I spent the summer of 1929. They are, or were at that time, the most primitive Turkish-speaking people at the borders of the Gobi.

I possibly will be criticized for paying too little attention to what Robert Göbl calls the Iranian Huns: Kidara, White Huns, Hepthalites, and Hunas. In discussing the name "Hun" I could not help speculating on their names. But this was as far as I dared go. The literature on these tribes or peoples is enormous. They stand in the center of Altheim's *Geschichte der Hunnen*, although he practically ignores the numismatic and Chinese evidence, on which Enoki has been working for so many years. Göbl's *Dokumente zur Geschichte der iranischen Hunnen in Baktrien und Indien* is the most thorough study of their coins and seals and, on this basis, of their political history. And yet, there remain problems to whose solution I could not make a meaningful contribution. I have neither the linguistic nor the paleographic knowledge to judge the correctness of the various, often entirely different, readings of the coin legends. But even if someday scholars wrestling with this recalcitrant material do come to an agreement, the result will be relatively modest. The Huna Mihirakula and Toramana will remain mere names. No settlement, no grave, not so much as a dagger or a piece of metal exists that could be ascribed to them or any other Iranian Huns. Until the scanty and contradictory descriptions of their life can be substantially supplemented by finds, the student of the Attilanic Huns will thankfully take cognizance of what the students of the so-called Iranian Huns can offer him; but there is little he can use for his research. A recently discovered wall painting in Afrosiab, the ancient Samarkand, seems to show the first light in the darkness. The future of the Hephthalite studies lies in the hands of the Soviet and, it is hoped, the Chinese archaeologists. Ἐν βυθῷ γὰρ ἡ ἀλήθεια.

I am aware that some chapters are not easy reading. For example, the one on the Huns after Attila's death draws attention to events seemingly not worth knowing, to men who were mere shadows; it jumps from Germanic sagas to ecclesiastical troubles in Alexandria, from the Iranian names of obscure chieftains to an earthquake in Hungary, from priests of Isis in Nubia to Middle Street in Constantinople. I will not apologize. Some readers surely will find the putting together of the scattered pieces as fascinating as I did, and I frivolously confess to an artistic hedonism which to me is not the least stimulus for my preoccupation with the Dark Ages. On a higher level, to pacify those who, with a bad conscience, justify what they are doing — Historical Research with capital letters — may I point out that I fail to see why the history of, say, Baja California is more respectable than, say, that of the Huns in the Balkans in the 460's. *Sub specie aeternitatis*, both dwindle into nothingness.

Anatole France, in his *Opinions of Jérôme Coignard*, once told the wonderful story of the young Persian prince Zémire, who ordered his scholars to write the history of mankind, so that he would make fewer errors as a monarch enlightened by past experience. After twenty years, the wise men appeared before the prince, king by then, followed by a caravan composed of twelve camels each bearing 500 volumes. The king asked them for a shorter version, and they returned after another twenty years with three camel loads, and, when again rejected by the king, after ten more years with a single elephant load. After yet five further years a scholar appeared with a single big book carried by a donkey. The king was on his death bed and sighed, "I shall die without knowing the history of mankind. Abridge, abridge!" "Sire," replied the scholar, "I will sum it up for you in three words: *They were born, they suffered, they died!*"

In his way, the king, who did not want to hear it all, was right. But as long as men, stupidly perhaps, want to know "how it was," there may be a place for studies like the present one. *Dixi et salvavi animam meam* . . . .

O. M.-H.

Author's Acknowledgments
(Fragments)

[The author left some pencil jottings of names on several slips of paper under headings indicating that he wished to acknowledge them in the preface. Some are not legible, others lack initials. They are consolidated here, initials added when known, and the spelling of unidentified names as close as the handwriting permitted. Within the various countries, the order is random; the list of country names includes France, Rumania, Taiwan, and Korea, but the names of the scholars whom the author undoubtedly intended to acknowledge under these headings are lacking. The fragments include acknowledgments of help received from the East Asiatic Library and the Interlibrary Borrowing Service of the University of California. The notes must have been written at various times throughout the years, and it is obvious that the list is not complete.—Ed.]

In Austria: R. Göbl, Hančar.

In England: Sir Ellis Minns, E. G. Pulleyblank.

In Germany: J. Werner, K. Jettmar, Tauslin.

In Hungary: Z. Takáts, L. Ligeti, D. Czallány, Gy. Moravcik, K. Cségledy, E. Lipták.

In Italy: M. Bussagli, P. Daffinà, L. Petech.

In Japan: Namio Egami, Enoki, Ushida.

In Soviet Union: K. V. Golenko, V. V. Ginsburg, E. Lubo-Lesnichenko, C. Trever, A. Mantsevich, M. P. Griaznov, L. P. Kyzlasov, I. A. Zadneprovsky, I. Kozhomberdiev, M. Saratov, A. P. Okladnikov, S. S. Sorokin, B. A. Litvinsky, I. V. Sinitsyn, Gumilev, Belenitsky, Stavisky.

In Sweden: B. Karlgren.

In Switzerland: K. Gerhart, I. Hubschmid.

In United States: P. Boodberg, E. Schafer, R. Henning, A. Alföldi, R. N. Frye, E. Kantorowicz, L. Olschki, K. H. Menges, N. Poppe, I. Ševčenko.

THE WORLD OF THE

Huns

I. The Literary Evidence

THE CHAPTER on the Huns written by the Roman historian Ammianus Marcellinus (330-400 A.D.) is an invaluable document.* Coming from the pen of "the greatest literary genius which the world has seen between Tacitus and Dante,"[1] it is also a stylistic masterpiece. Ammianus' superiority over the other writers of his time who could not help mentioning the Huns becomes evident from their statements about the first appearance of the savage hordes in the northern Balkan provinces. They tell us in a few scanty words that the Goths were driven from their sites by the Huns; some add the story of a doe which led the Huns across the Cimmerian Bosporus. And this is all. They did not care to explore the causes of the catastrophe of Adrianople, that terrible afternoon of August 9, 378, when the Goths annihilated two-thirds of the Roman army, else they would have found that "the seed and origin of all the ruin and various disasters"[2] were the events that had taken place in the transdanubian barbaricum years before the Goths were admitted to the empire. They did not even try to learn who the Huns were and how they lived and fought.

It is instructive to compare the just quoted words of Ammianus with the following passage by the historian-theologian Paulus Orosius (fl. 415 A.D), St. Augustine's disciple:

> In the thirteenth year of the reign of Valens, that is, in the short interval of time that followed the wrecking of the churches by Valens and the slaughtering of the saints throughout the East, that root of our miseries simultaneously sent up a very great number of shoots. The race of the Huns, long shut off by inaccessible mountains, broke

---

* For historical and cultural background see Chapter XII by Paul Alexander.
1 Stein 1959, 331.
2 Ammianus XXXI, 2, 1.

out in a sudden rage against the Goths and drove them in widespread
panic from their old homes."[3]

If the Arian heresy of Valens was the root of all evils and the attack of
the Huns on the Goths only a shoot, then it was clearly a waste of time
and effort to occupy oneself with the Huns. There was even the danger
that by looking too closely at *gesta diaboli per Hunnos* one might lose
sight of the devil himself. Orosius pays attention only to supernatural
agents, God or the demons. Unconcerned about the antecedents of a
happening or its consequences unless they could be used for theological
lessons, Orosius, and with him all the Christian authors in the West, showed
no interest in the Huns. Ammianus called the battle of Adrianople another
Cannae.[4] He never doubted, even when all seemed lost, that every Han-
nibal would find his Scipio, convinced that the empire would last to the
end of the world:[5] "To these I set no boundary in space or time; unlimited
power I have given them." (*His ego nec metas rerum nex tempora pono:
imperium sine fine dedi*.[6]) Among the Christians, Rufinus was the only
one who could say that the defeat of Adrianople was "the beginning of
the evil for the Roman Empire, then and from then on."[7] The others
saw in it only the triumph of orthodoxy, indulging in lurid descriptions
of the way in which the accursed heretic Valens perished. Orosius adduced
the death of the unfortunate emperor as proof for the oneness of God.

DEMONIZATION

Possibly the lack of interest in the Huns had still another reason: the
Huns were demonized early. When in 364 Hilary of Poitiers predicted
the coming of the Antichrist within one generation,[8] he repeated what
during the two years of Julian's reign many must have thought. But
since then Christ had conquered, and only an obdurate fanatic like Hilary
could see in the emperor's refusal to unseat an Arian bishop the sign
of the approaching end of the world. Even those who still adhered to
the chiliasm of the pre-Constantine church, and took the highly respected
Divinae institutiones of Lactantius as their guide to the future, did not
expect to hear themselves the sound of Gabriel's trumpet. "The fall and
ruin of the world will soon take place, but it seems that nothing of the
kind is to be feared as long as the city of Rome stands intact."[9]

---

[3] *Hist. adv. Pagan.* VII, 33, 9-10.
[4] XXXI, 13, 19.
[5] Christ 1938, 68-71.
[6] Virgil, *Aen.* I, 278.
[7] *Hist. eccles.* XI, 13.
[8] *Contra Arianos* V, *PL* 10, 611.
[9] *Div. Inst.* VII, 25.

The change set in early in 387. Italy had not been invaded by barbarians since Emperor Aurelian's time (270-275). Now it suddenly was threatened by an "impure and cruel enemy." Panic spread through the cities; fortifications were hastily improvised.[10] Ambrose, who shortly before had lost his brother Saturus, found consolation in the thought that he was "taken away that he might not fall in the hands of the barbarians. . . . that he might not see the ruin of the whole earth, the end of the world, the burial of relatives, the death of fellow-citizens." It was the time which the prophets had foreseen, "when they felicitated the dead and lamented the living" (*gratulabantur mortuis et vivos plangent*).[11] After Adrianople, Ambrose felt that "the end of the world is coming upon us." War, pestilence, famine everywhere. The final period of the world's history was drawing to its close. "We are in the wane of the age."[12]

In the last decade of the fourth century, an eschatological wave swept over the West from Africa to Gaul. The Antichrist already was born, soon he would come to the throne of the empire.[13] Three more generations, and the millennium would be ushered in, but not before untold numbers would have perished in the horrors which preceded it; the hour of judgment drew nearer, the signs pointing to it became clearer every day.[14]

Gog and Magog (Ezekiel 38:1-39:20) were storming down from the north. The initial letters suggested to some people, said Augustine, who himself rejected such equations, identification with the Getae (Goths) and Massagetae.[15] Ambrose took the Goths to be Gog.[16] The African bi-

---

[10] Ambrose, *De excessu fratris* I, 1, 31. The date, February 378, has been definitely established by O. Faller, ed., *CSEL* 73, *81-*89.

[11] Lactantius, *Div. Inst.* VII, 16; *Epitome* 66.

[12] Ambrose, *Expositio evangelii sec. Lucam* X, 10-14, *CSEL* 32, 458. Composed at the end of 378 (Rauschen 1897, 494; Palanque 1935, 534, 535: Dudden 1925, 693).

[13] "There is no doubt that the Antichrist has already been born; firmly established already in his early years, he will, after reaching maturity, achieve supreme power." (*Non est dubium, quin antichristus malo spiritu conceptus iam natus esset, et iam in annis puerilibus constitutus, aetate legitima sumpturus imperium.*) St. Martin *apud* Sulpicius Severus, *Dialogus* I (II), 14, 4, *CSEL* 1, 197.

[14] Q. Julius Hilarianus, *De cursu temporum* (written in 397), *PL* 13, 1097-1106; Paulinus of Nola, *Ep.* XXXVIII, 7, *CSEL* 29, 330 written in 397 (Reinelt 1903, 59). In the East such fears (and hopes) rarely were expressed. Cf. John Chrysostom, *In Ioannem homil.* XXXIV, *PG* 59, 197-198, delivered in Antioch about 390 A.D.

[15] Augustine, *De civ. Dei* XX, 11. "Of course those people, whom he calls Gog and Magog, are not to be understood as if they were barbarians settled in some part of the earth or Getae and Massagetae as some presume because of the initial letters of their names..." (*Gentes quippe istae, quas appellat Gog et Magog, non sic sunt accipiendae, tamquam sint aliqui in aliqua parte terrarum barbari constituti, siue quos quidam suspicantur Getas et Massagetas propter litteras horum nominum primas*, etc.)

[16] Ambrose, *De fide* II, 16.

shop Quodvultdeus could not make up his mind whether he should identify Magog with the Moors or the Massagetae.[17] Why the Massagetae? There were no Massagetae in the fifth century. But considering that Themistius, Claudian, and later Procopius called the Huns Massagetae,[18] it seems probable that those who identified Magog with the Massagetae thought of the Huns. In the Talmud, where the Goths are Gog,[19] Magog is "the country of the kanths" (Sogdian *kant*), that is, the kingdom of the white Huns.[20]

Jerome did not share the chiliastic fears and expectations of his contemporaries. In reshaping Victorinus of Poetovio's *Commentary on the Revelation* he substituted for the last part, full of chiliastic ideas, sections from Tyconius.[21] But when in 395 the Huns broke into the eastern provinces, he, too, feared that "the Roman world was falling,"[22] and the end of Rome meant the end of the world.[23] Four years later, still under the impression of the catastrophe, he saw in the Huns the savage peoples kept behind the Caucasus by the iron gates of Alexander.[24] The *ferae gentes* were Gog and Magog of the Alexander legend. Flavius Josephus (37/8-100 A.D.), the first to speak of Alexander's gates,[25] equated the Scythians and Magog.[26] Jerome, who followed him,[27] identified Herodotus' Scythians with the Huns,[28] in this oblique way equating the Huns and Magog. Orosius did the same; his "inaccessible mountains" behind which the Huns had been shut off were those where Alexander had built the wall to hold back

---

[17] *Liber de promissionibus et praedicationibus Dei, PL* 51, 848.

[18] See footnotes 40, 51, 52.

[19] L. Ginzburg 1899, 58, 468.

[20] O. Klima, *Archiv Orientální* 24, 1956, 596-597.

[21] *CSEL* 49, 138-153. Without naming Ambrose—he spoke only of him as "a distinguished contemporary" (*vir nostrae aetatis haud ignobilis*)—Jerome rejected his identification of Gog and Magog (*Hebraicae quaestiones in libro geneseos* 10, 21).

[22] *Romanus orbis ruit.* (See *Ep.* LX, 6.)

[23] "At the end of the world, when the empire of the Romans must be destroyed" (*In consummatione mundi, quando regnum destruendum est Romanorum*). See *Comm. in Danielem* VII, 8, *PL* 25, 531.

[24] *Ep.* LXXVII, 8. For Syriac versions of the legend, see F. Pfister, *Abh. Berlin* 3, 1956, 30-31, 36-39; N. V. Pigulevskaia, *Orbeli Anniversary Volume*, 423-426.

[25] *BJ* VII, 7, 4.

[26] *AJ* I, 6, 123.

[27] *Hebraicae quaestiones in libro geneseos* X, 21, written in 391. Cf. Cavallera 1922, 1, 146-147; 2, 28.

[28] *Ep.* LXXVII, 8-9. In quoting Herodotus I, 104-106, Jerome made two mistakes: Cyaxares instead of Darius, and twenty instead of twenty-eight years. His knowledge of ethnographic literature was poor. Cf. Luebeck 1872, 21. Isidorus (*Etym.* IX, 2, 66) copied Jerome.

Gog and Magog. In the sixth century, Andreas of Caesarea in Cappadocia still held the view that Gog and Magog were those Scythians in the north "called Hunnica by us" ἅπερ καλοῦμεν Οὐννικά.[29] If even the sober Jerome was inclined, for a time, to see in the Huns the companions of the apocalyptic horsemen, one can easily imagine how the superstitious masses felt.[30]

After 400, the chiliastic fears were somewhat abated.[31] But behind the Huns the devil still was lurking. The curious story in Jordanes[32] about their origin almost certainly is patterned on the Christian legend of the fallen angels:[33] The unclean spirits "bestowed their embraces on the sorceresses and begot this savage race." The Huns were not a people like other peoples. These fiendish ogres,[34] roaming over the desolate plains beyond the borders of the Christian œcumene, from which they set out time and again to bring death and destruction to the faithful, were the offspring of *daemonia immunda*. Even after the fall of Attila's kingdom, the peoples who were believed to have descended from the Huns were in alliance with the devil. They enveloped their enemies in darkness ὑπό τινας μαγείας.[35] The Avars, whom Gregory of Tours called Chuni, "skilled in magic tricks, they made them, that is, the Franks, see illusionary images and defeated them thoroughly" (*magicis artibus instructi, diversas fantasias eis*, i.e., *Francis ostendunt et eos valde superant*).[36]

To be sure, this demonization of the Huns alone would not have prevented the Latin historians and ecclesiastic writers from exploring the past of the Huns and describing them as Ammianus did. But the smell of sulphur and the heat of the hellish flames that enveloped the Huns were not conducive to historical research.

EQUATIONS

How did the Eastern writers see the Huns? One should expect the Greek historians to have preserved at least some of the ethnographic curiosity of Herodotus and Strabo. But what we have is disappointing.

---

[29] *Commentarius in apocalypsin* ch. LXIII, *PG* 106, 416c.

[30] The tendency to identify the enemies of the Christians with Gog or Magog led sometimes to strange results. Vincent of Beauvais turned Qaghan into Gog Chan (Rockhill 1900, 21, n. 1, and 108, n. 1).

[31] E. Ch. Bahut, *Revue d'hist. et de litt. religieuses*, N. S. 1, 1920, 532.

[32] *Getica* 121-122.

[33] Maenchen-Helfen 1945c, 244-248.

[34] "Ogre"<Hongre, Hungarian.

[35] John of Antioch, fr. 151, *EI* 145.

[36] *Hist. Franc.* IV, 29.

Instead of facts they serve us with equations. The Latin chroniclers of the fifth century, in calling the Huns by their proper name, were less guided by the intention to be precise than forced to be factual by their ignorance of literature. They knew next to nothing about the Scythians, Cimmerians, and Massagetae, whose names the Greek authors constantly interchanged with that of the Huns. However, even at a time when there still existed a Latin literature worthy of its illustrious past, the Latin writers, both prosiasts and poets, shunned the circumlocutions and equations in which the Greeks indulged. Ausonius rarely missed an opportunity to show how well read he was, yet he refrained from replacing the real names of the barbarians with whom Gratian fought by those he knew from Livy and Ovid.[37] Ambrose, too, avoided the use of archaic or learned words. The Huns, not the Massagetae, attacked the Alans, who threw themselves upon the Goths, not the Scythians.[38] In Ambrose, the former *consularis*, Roman soberness and aversion to speculation were as much alive as in Ausonius, the rhetor from Bordeaux. A comparison of Pacatus' panegyric on Theodosius with the orations of Themistius is revealing: The Gaul called the Huns by their name;[39] the Greek called them Massagetae.[40]

As in the West, many writers in the East lacked interest in the invaders. They looked on them as "bandits and deserters,"[41] or they called them Scythians, a name which in the fourth and fifth centuries had long lost its specific meaning. It was widely applied to all northern barbarians, whether they were nomads or peasants, spoke Germanic, Iranian, or any other tongue. Nevertheless, in the vocabulary of the educated the word retained, however attenuated, some of its original significance. The associations it called forth were bound to shape the way in which the barbarians were seen. That makes it at times difficult to decide whom an author means. Are Priscus' "Royal Scythians" the dominating tribe as in Herodotus, or are they the members of the royal clan, or simply noblemen?

---

[37] *Praecatio consulis designati pridie Kal. Ian. fascibus sumptis* 31-35; *Epigr.* XXVI, 8-10; *Ephemeris* 7 (8), 18.

[38] *Expositio evangelii secundum Lucam* X, 10.

[39] XI, 4.

[40] *Or.* XV, Harduin 1684, 207c : "The stubbornness of the Scythians, the recklessness of the Alans, the madness of the Massagetae." Except *Or.* IX, 121b, and *Or.* XIV, 181b, where "Scythians" means all transdanubian barbarians, the Scythians are the Goths *Or.* VIII, 114c; X; XVI, 210d, 211b; XVIII, 219b; XIX, 229b, c).

In *Or.* XI, 146b, Athanaric is called Σχύθης ἤ Γέτης. The Alans are called by their proper name in *Or.* XXXIV, 8. The Massagetae, the third of the peoples who in the 380's devastated the northern Balkans, must, therefore, be the Huns. In *Or.* XXXIV, 24, Themistius makes a sharp distinction between Scythians and Massagetae.

[41] For instance, Basil the Great, *Ep.* 268.

It is not enough to say that the phrase is merely one of the several instances of Priscus' literary debt to Herodotus. It certainly is. But it would be strange if the man who used this and other expressions of the great historian would not, here and there, have succumbed to the temptation to see the Huns as the ancients had seen the Scythians.

The Greek historians equated the Huns and the Cimmerians, Scythians, and other peoples of old not just to display their knowledge of the classics or to embellish their accounts,[42] but first of all because they were convinced that there were no peoples which the wise men of the past had not known. And this, in turn, was not so much narrow-minded traditionalism—it was that, too—as, to use a psychological term, a defense mechanism. Synesius of Cyrene (ca. 370—412), in his "Address on Kingship," explained why there could not be new barbarians:

> Now it was not by walling off their own house that the former rulers prevented the barbarians either of Asia or Europe from entering it. Rather by their own acts did they admonish these men to wall off their own by crossing the Euphrates in pursuit of the Parthians, and the Danube in pursuit of the Goths and Massagetae. But now these nations spread terror amongst us, crossing over in their turn, assuming other names, and some of them falsifying by art even their countenances, so that another race new and foreign may appear to have sprung from the soil.[43]

This is carrying the thesis of the identity of the old and new barbarians to absurdity. But it is, after all, what so many Roman generals said so many times on the eve of a battle: our fathers conquered them, we shall conquer them again. The ever recurring οἱ πάλαι serves the same purpose. It deprives the unknown attacker of his most frightening feature: he *is* known and, therefore, needs not be feared.

In the equation of the Huns and the peoples of former times both motives, the emotionally conditioned *reductio ad notum* and the intention of the learned historian to show his erudition, play their role, whereby the former, I believe, is more often in the service of the latter than is usually assumed. With which of the known peoples an author identified the Huns depended on his information, the circumstances under which he wrote, and the alleged or real similarity between the known and the barely known. The result was invariably the same. All speculations about the origin of the Huns ended in an equation.

---

[42] See Agathias III, 5, ed. Bonn 147, on his reasons for calling the fortress St. Stephen by its former name Onoguris.

[43] *De regno* XI; Fitzgerald 1930, 1, 27.

Philostorgius, in his *Ecclesiastical History* written between 425 and 433, "recognized" in them the Neuri.[44] A well-read man, he may have come across a now lost description of the Neuri which reminded him of what he had heard of the Huns. One could think that Philostorgius, less critical than Herodotus, believed the werewolf stories told about the Neuri.[45] Synesius[46] and Jerome[47] were probably not the only ones to compare the Huns with wolves. It was not beyond Philostorgius to identify the "wolf- ish" Huns with the werewolves of Scythia. But the most likely expla- nation of his belief is the location of the Neuri: They were the northern- most people, the Huns came from the extreme North—*ergo* the Huns were the Neuri. To say that they lived along the Rhipaean Mountains, as Phil- ostorgius did, was merely another way of placing them as far north as possible; since the legendary Aristeas[48] the Rhipaean Mountains were regarded as the region of the eternal snow, the home of the icy Boreas.

Procopius' identification of the Huns with the Cimmerians[49] is neither better nor worse than his assertion that the Goths, Vandals, and Gepids were in former times called Sauromatae.[50] As a rule Procopius, like The- mistius and Claudian,[51] equated the Huns and the Massagetae.[52] The later Byzantine writers repeated monotonously the formula: the former *x*, the present *y*.

There is finally the historian Eunapius of Sardes (ca. 345—420). The following fragment from him shows (in Vasiliev's opinion) what a conscien- tious historian Eunapius was:

> Although no one has told anything plainly of whence the Huns came and by which way they invaded the whole of Europe and drove out the Scythian people, at the beginning of my work, after collecting the accounts of ancient writers, I have told the facts as seemed to me reliable; I have considered the accounts from the point of view of their exactness, so that my writing should not depend merely on probable statement and my work should not deviate from the truth. We do

---

[44] *Hist. eccles.* IX, 17, Bidez 1960, 123.

[45] Herodotus IV, 107.

[46] The "wolf" in the *Egyptian Tale* is "the Hun." Cf. Grützmacher 1913, 59; Ch. Lacombrade *RÉA* 48, 1946, 260-266.

[47] *Ep.* LX, 16.

[48] According to Müllenhoff, *DA* 3, 24, the source of Damastes, quoted by Stepha- nus Byzantinus 630, 6; doubted by Rostovtsev 1913, 24, n.2.

[49] VIII, 5, 1.

[50] III, 22, 2.

[51] The Massagetae in *In Ruf.* I, 310, correspond to the Chuni in *Cons. Stil.* I, iii.

[52] The passages are listed in Moravcsik, *BT* 2, 183; Evagrius III, 2; Bidez 1960, 100 9-11.

not resemble those who from their childhood live in a small and poor house, and late in time, by a stroke of good fortune, acquire vast and magnificent buildings, and none the less by custom love the old things and take care of them. . . . But we rather resemble those who first using one medicine for the treatment of their body, in the hope of help, and then through their experience finding a better medicine, turn and incline towards the latter, not in order to neutralize the effect of the first one by the second but in order to introduce the truth into erroneous judgment, and, so to speak, to destroy and enfeeble the light of a lamp by a ray of the sun. In like manner we will add the more correct evidence to the aforesaid, considering it possible to keep the former material as an historical point of view, and using and adding the latter material for the establishment of the truth.[53]

All this talk about medicines and buildings, the pompous announcement of what he is going to write on the Huns, is empty. Eunapius' description of the Huns is preserved in Zosimus.[54] It shows what a windbag the allegedly conscientious historian was. One half of it Eunapius cribbed from Ammianus Marcellinus;[55] the other half, where he "collected the accounts of the ancient writers," is a preposterous hodgepodge. Eunapius calls the Huns "a people formerly unknown,"[56] only to suggest in the next line their identity with Herodotus' Royal Scythians. As an alternative he referred to the "snub-nosed and weak people who, as Herodotus says, dwell near the Ister [Danube]." What he had in mind was Herodotus V, 9, 56, but he changed the horses of the Sigynnae, "snub-nosed and incapable of carrying men," into "snub-nosed and weak people" (σιμοὺς καὶ ἀδυνάτους ἄνδρας φέρειν into σιμοὺς καὶ ἀσθενέας ἀνθρώπους).[57]

AMMIANUS MARCELLINUS

Seen against this background of indifference, superstition, and arbitrary equations, Ammianus' description of the Huns cannot be praised too highly. But it is not *eine ganz realistische Sittenschilderung*, as Rostovtsev called it.[58] For its proprer evaluation one has to take into account

[53] *ES* 84-85, translated by Vasiliev 1936, 24-25.
[54] Moravcsik, *BT* 1, 577.
[55] Maenchen-Helfen 1955b, 392. I have not been convinced by A. F. Norman (*CQ* 7, 1957, 133, n. 1) that Eunapius and Ammianus used the same sources.
[56] Zosimus IV, 20, 3.
[57] This has long been recognized by Satterer 1798, 4. Thompson (1948, 17, n. 2) erroneously refers to Herodotus IV, 23.
[58] Rostovtsev 1931, 103.

the circumstances under which it was written, Ammianus' sources of information, and his admiration for the *styli veteres*.

He most probably finished his work in the winter 392/3,[59] that is, at a time when the danger of a war between the two *partes* of the empire was steadily mounting. In August 392, the powerful general Arbogast proclaimed Eugenius emperor of the West. For some time Theodosius apparently was undecided what to do; he may have thought it advisable to come to an agreement with the usurper who was "superior in every point of military equipment."[60] But when he nominated not Eugenius but one of his generals to hold the consulship with him, and on January 23, 393, proclaimed his son Honorius as Augustus, it became clear that he would go to war against Eugenius as he had against Maximus in 388. There can be little doubt that the sympathies of Ammianus, the admirer of Julian, lay from the beginning not with the fanatic Christian Theodosius but with the learned pagan Eugenius.[61] Ammianus must have looked with horror at Theodosius' army, which was Roman in name only. Although it cannot be proved that the emperor owed his victory over Maximus to his dare-devil Hun cavalry,[62] they certainly played a decisive role in the campaign. Theodosius' horsemen were "carried through the air by Pegasi";[63] they did not ride, they flew.[64] No other troops but the Hun auxiliaries could have covered the sixty miles from Emona to Aquileia in one day.[65] Ammianus had all reasons to fear that in the apparently inevitable war a large contingent of the Eastern army would again consist of Huns. It did.[66]

Ammianus hated all barbarians, even those who distinguished themselves in the service of Rome:[67] He called the Gallic soldiers, who so gallantly fought the Persians at Amida, *dentatae bestiae*;[68] he concluded his work with an encomium for Julius, *magister militiae trans Taurum*, who, on learning of the Gothic victory at Adrianople, had all Goths in his territory massacred. But the Huns were the worst. Both Claudian[69] and

---

[59] Maenchen-Helfen 1955a, 399.

[60] Orosius, *Hist. adv. Pagan.* VII, 35, 2.

[61] Ensslin 1923, 9.

[62] As assumed by Gibbon 3, 165, followed by Seeck, *Geschichte* 5, 213-21 .

[63] Pacatus XXXIX, 5.

[64] *Non cursus est, sed volatus (ibid.* XXXIX, 1).

[65] *Ibid.* XXXIX, 2. Only cabinet scholars reject the " hyperboles " of the orator (Galletier 1949, 57 n. 6).

[66] John of Antioch, fr. 187, *EI* 119.

[67] Ensslin 1923, 31-32.

[68] XIX, 6, 3.

[69] *In Ruf.* I, 324-325.

Jordanes[70] echoed Ammianus when they called the Huns "the most infamous offspring of the north," "fiercer than ferocity itself." Even the headhunting Alans were "in their manner of life and their habits less savage" than the Huns.[71] Through long intercourse with the Romans, some Germans had acquired a modicum of civilization. But the Huns were still primeval savages.

Besides, Ammianus' account is colored by the bias of his informants. He went to Rome sometime before 378 where, except for a short while in 383, he spent the rest of his life. The possibility that he met there some Hun or other cannot be entirely ruled out,[72] but it is inconceivable that a Hun who at best understood a few Latin orders could have told Ammianus how his people lived and how they fought the Goths. The account of the war in South Russia and Rumania is based largely on reports which Ammianus received from Goths. Munderich, who had fought against the Huns, later *dux limitis per Arabias*,[73] may have been one of his informants. One could almost say that Ammianus wrote his account from a Gothic point of view. For example, he described Ermanaric as a most warlike king, dreaded by the neighboring nations because of many and varied deeds of valor;[74] *fortiter* is a praise which Ammianus did not easily bestow on a barbarian. Alatheus and Saphrax were "experienced leaders known for their courage."[75] Ammianus names no less than eleven leaders of the Goths,[76] but not one of the Huns. They were a faceless mass, terrible and subhuman.

Ammianus' description is distorted by hatred and fear. Thompson, who believes almost every word of it, accordingly places the Huns of the later half of the fourth century in the "lower stage of pastoralism."[77] They lived, he says, in conditions of desperate hardship, moving incessantly from pasture to pasture, utterly absorbed by the day-long task of looking after the herds. Their iron swords must have been obtained by barter or capture, "for nomads do not work metal." Thompson asserts that even after eighty years of contact with the Romans the productive power of the

---

[70] *Getica* 12.

[71] Ammianus XXXI, 2, 21.

[72] In *De Tobia* I, 39, *CSEL* 32, 540 (written about 389: Palanque 1935, 528; Dudden 1925, 696, suggests probably later than 385 ; cf. also Rauschen 1897, 432, n. 2), Ambrose mentions a Hun " who was known to the Roman emperor."

[73] XXXI, 3, 5.

[74] *Ibid.*, 3, 1.

[75] *Ibid.*, 3, 3.

[76] Ermanaric, Vithimir, Viderich, Alatheus, Saphrax, Athanaric, Munderich, Lagarimanus, Alaviv, Fritigern, and Farnobius.

[77] Thompson 1948, 41-43.

Huns was so small that they could not make tables, chairs, and couches. "The productive methods available to the Huns were primitive beyond what is now easy to imagine." To this almost unimaginable primitive economy corresponds an equally primitive social structure, a society without classes, without a hereditary aristocracy; the Huns were amorphous bands of marauders. Even the Soviet scholars, who still hate the Huns as the murderers of their Slavic ancestors, reject the notion that the economy and society were in any way primitive.[78]

Had the Huns been unable to forge their swords and cast their arrowheads, they never could have crossed the Don. The idea that the Hun horsemen fought their way to the walls of Constantinople and to the Marne with bartered and captured swords is absurd. Hun warfare presupposed a far-reaching division of labor in peacetime. Ammianus emphasizes so strongly the absence of any buildings in the country of the Huns that the reader must think they slept the year round under the open sky; only in passing does Ammianus mentions their tents and wagons. Many may have been able to make tents, but only a few could have been cartwrights.

The passage which, more than any other, shows that Ammianus' description must not be accepted as it stands is the following, often quoted and commented on: *Aguntur autem nulla severitate regali; sed tumultuario primatum ductu contenti, perrumpunt quidquid inciderit.*[79] In Rolfe's translation, "They are subject to no royal constraint, but they are content with the disorderly government of their important men, and led by them they force their way through every obstacle." It is not very important that this statement is at variance with Cassiodorus-Jordanes' account of the war between the Goths and Balamber, king of the Huns, who later married Vadamerca, the granddaughter of the Gothic ruler Vinitharius;[80] whoever Balamber was, Cassiodorus would not have admitted that a Gothic princess could have become the wife of a man who was not some sort of a king. More important is the discrepancy between Ammianus' statement and what he himself tells about the deeds of the Huns. Altough the cultural level of Ermanaric's Ostrogoths and the cohesion of his kingdom must not be overrated, its sudden collapse under the onslaught of the Huns would be inexplicable if the latter were nothing but an anarchic mass of howling savages. Thompson calls the Huns mere marauders and plunderers. In a way, he is right. But to plunder on the scale the Huns did was impossible without a military organization, commanders who planned a campaign and coordinated the attacking forces, men who gave

[78] See, for example, Pletneva, *SA* 3, 1964, 343.

[79] XXXI, 2, 7.

[80] *Getica* 130, 248, 249.

orders and men who obeyed them. Altheim defines *tumultarius ductus* as *eine aus dem Augenblick erwachsene, improvisierte Führung,*[81] which renders Ammianus' words better than Rolfe's "disorderly government." However, the warfare of the Huns reveals at no time anything that could be called improvised leadership.[82]

For some time the misunderstanding of the Hunnic offensive tactics— sudden, feigned flight and renewed attack—was, perhaps, inevitable.[83] But Ammianus wrote the last books fourteen years after Adrianople. He must by then have known or, at least, suspected that the early reports on the Huns' improvised leadership were not true. Yet he stuck to them, for those biped beasts had only "the form of men."[84] He maintained that their missiles were provided with sharp bone points.[85] He may not have been entirely wrong. But the tanged Hun arrowheads of which we know are all made of iron. Ammianus made the exception the rule.

In describing the Huns, Ammianus used too many phrases from earlier authors. Because the Huns were northern barbarians like the Scythians of old and because the *styli veteres* wrote so well about the earlier bar- barians, Ammianus, the Greek from Antioch, thought it best to paraphrase them. One of the authors he imitated was the historian Trogus Pompeius, a contemporary of the emperor Augustus. Ammianus wrote: "None of them ever ploughs or touches a colter. Without permanent seats, without a home, without fixed laws or rites, thye all roam about, always like fu- gitives. . . restless roving over mountains and through woods. They cover themselves with clothes sewed together from the skins of forest rodents." (*Nemo apud eos arat nec stivam aliquando contingit. Omnes sine sedibus fixis, absque lare vel lege aut ritu stabili dispalantur, semper fugientium similes. . . vagi montes peragrantes et silvas. Indumentis operiuntur ex pellibus silvestrium murum consarcinatis.*)[86] This clearly is patterned on

---

[81] Altheim and Stiehl 1954, 259.

[82] It is not quite impossible that Ammianus *concluded* from the impetuosity of Hun warfare that the savages *aguntur nulla severitate regali.* He may have thought of what Hippocrates said about the courage of the Europeans, who were more warlike than the Asiatics because they had no kings, οὐ βασιλεύονται. " Where there are kings there must be the greatest cowards. For men's souls are enslaved, and refuse to run risks readily and recklessly to increase the power of somebody else. But independent people, taking risks on their own behalf and not on behalf of others, are willing and eager to go into danger, for they themselves enjoy the prize of victory " (*De aere,* ch. 23, *Loeb* 132-133).

[83] Harmatta 1952, 289.

[84] XXXI, 2, 3.

[85] *Ibid.,* 2, 9.

[86] *Ibid.,* 2. 10. Cf. XIV, 4, 3, on the Saracens, and XXI, 8, 42, on the Alans and Costobocae.

Trogus' description of the Scythians: "They do not till the fields. They have no home, no roof, no abode. . . used to range through uncultivated solitudes. They use the skins of wild animals and rodents." (*Neque enim agrum exercent. Neque domus illis ulla aut tectum aut sedes est. . . per incultas solitudines errare solitis. Pellibus ferinis ac murinis utuntur.*)[87]

It could be objected that such correspondences are not so very remarkable because the way of life of the nomads throughout the Eurasian steppes was, after all, more or less the same. But this cannot be said about other statements of Ammianus which he took from earlier sources. "From their horses," he wrote, "by day and night every one of that nation buys and sells, eats and drinks, and bowed over the narrow neck of the animal relaxes in a sleep so deep as to be accompanied by many dreams."[88] His admiration of Trogus here got the better of him. He had read the following description of the Parthians: "All the time they let themselves be carried by their horses. In that way they fight wars, participate in banquets, attend public and private business. On their backs they move, stand still, carry on trade, and converse." (*Equis omni tempore vectantur; illis bella, illis convivia, illis publica et privata officia obeunt; super illos ire, consistere, mercari, colloqui.*)[89] Ammianus took Trogus too literally; he rendered "all the time" (*omni tempore*) by "day and night" (*pernox et perdiu*) and had, therefore, to keep the Huns on horseback even in their sleep.

Ammianus' description of the eating habits of the Huns is another example of his tendency to embroider what he read in old books. The Huns, he says, "are so hardy in their form of life that they have no need of fire nor of savory food, but eat the roots of wild plants and the half-raw flesh of any kind of animals whatever, which they put between their thighs and the backs of their horses, and thus warm it a little."[90] This is a curious mixture of good observation and a traditional topos. That the Huns ate the roots of wild plants is quite credible; many northern barbarians did. Ammianus' description of the way the Huns warmed raw meat while on horseback has been rejected as a misunderstanding of a widespread nomad custom; the Huns are supposed to have used raw meat for preventing and healing the horses' wounds caused by the pressure of the saddle.[91] However, at the end of the fourteenth century, the Bavarian soldier, good Hans Schiltberger, who certainly had never heard

---

[87] Justin II, 11. Cf. Rostovtsev 1931, 95.
[88] XXXI, 2, 6.
[89] Justin XLI, 3, 4.
[90] XXXI, 2, 3.
[91] Solymossy 1937, 134-140. I retract my consent to Solymossy's view (Maenchen-Helfen 1945b, 233).

of Ammianus Marcellinus, reported that the Tatars of the Golden Horde, when they were on a fast journey, "took some meat and cut it into thin slices and put it into a linen cloth and put it under the saddle and rode on it. . . . When they felt hungry, they took it out and ate it."[92]

The phrase "Their mode of living is so rough that they eat half-raw meat" (*ita uictu sunt asperi, ut semicruda carne uescantur*) is taken from the geographer Pomponius Mela (fl. 40 A.D.), who described the Germans as "Their mode of living is so rough and crude that they even eat raw meat" (*uictu ita asperi incultique ut cruda etiam carne uescantur*).[93] The Cimbri, too, were said to eat raw meat.[94] *Syroyadtsy*, a Russian word for the Tatars, possibly means "people who eat raw [meat]," *syroedtsy*.[95] Like so many northern peoples, the Huns may, indeed, have eaten raw meat. Ammianus, however, goes one step further; he maintains that the Huns did not cook their food at all, which is disproved by the big copper cauldrons for cooking meat, one of the leitmotifs of Hunnic civilization. But Ammianus felt he had to force the Huns into the cliché of the lowest of the barbarians.[96]

All this is not meant to dismiss Ammianus' account as untrustworthy. It contains a wealth of material which is repeatedly confirmed as good and reliable by other literary testimony and by the archaeological evidence. We learn from Ammianus how the Huns looked and how they dressed. He describes their horses, weapons, tactics, and wagons as accurately as any other writer did.

CASSIODORUS, JORDANES

In his Hunnophobia, Ammianus was equaled by Cassiodorus (487-583), of whose lost *Gothic History* much has been preserved in Jordanes' *The Origin and Deeds of the Getae*, commonly called *Getica*. But Cassiodorus had to explain why the Huns could make themselves the lords of his heroes,

---

[92] Schiltberger 1885, 62.

[93] III, 3, 2. Like everything he says about the Huns, Jerome's assertion that the Huns, *Hunorum nova feritas*, live on half raw meat (*Adv. Iovinian.* II, 7, *PL* 23, 295) goes back to Ammianus. He wrote the invective in 393; cf. Cavallera 1922, 2, 157.

[94] Cf. Norden 1921, 13-14.

[95] Spuler 1947, 440.

[96] How even such a careful observer as Procopius fell victim to the topos is illustrated by two passages on the Moors. They have, he says in IV,6 , 13, " neither bread nor wine nor any good things [Ammianus' *saporati cibi*] but they take grain, either wheat or barley, and without boiling it or grinding it to flour or barley meat, they eat it in a manner not a whit different from that of animals. " A few pages later (IV, 7, 3), Procopius tells of a Moorish woman who " crushed a little grain, and making it a very thin cake, threw it into the hot ashes on the hearth. For this is the custom of the Moors to bake their loaves. "

the Ostrogoths, and rule over them for three generations. His Huns have a wicked greatness. They are greedy and brutal, but they are a courageous people. Attila was a cruel and voluptuous monster, but he did nothing cowardly; he was like a lion.[97] According to Ammianus,[98] the Huns "furrowed the cheeks of children with the iron from their very birth," words which Cassiodorus copied. But whereas Ammianus continued "in order that the growth of hair, when it appears at the proper time, may be checked by the wrinkled scars," Cassiodorus wrote "so that before they receive the nourishment of milk they must learn to endure wounds."[99]

In his account of the early history of the Goths, Jordanes followed Cassiodorus, though not always verbatim. For the proper evaluation of the Gothic tradition about the struggle against the Huns in South Russia, one has to keep in mind that it has come down to us in an expurgated and "civilized" form. In Ostrogothic Italy the memory of the great wars fought side by side with the Huns and against them must still have been alive. Cassiodorus' sources were songs, *cantus maiorum, cantiones, carmina prisca,* and stories, some of them told "almost in the way historical events are told" (*pene storico ritu*). The *pene* must not be taken seriously. Cassiodorus wrote his *Gothic History* "to restore to the Amal line the splendor that truly belonged to it." He wrote for an educated Roman public whose taste would have taken offense at the crude, cruel, and bloody aspects of early Germanic poetry. A comparison of the *Getica* with Paul the Deacon's *History of the the Langobards* shows to what extent Cassiodorus purged the tradition of his Gothic lords all of barbaric features.

But this is not all. The *Origo gentis Langobardorum,* written about 670, one of Paul's sources, is full of pagan lore. More than two hundred years after the conversion of the Danes to Christianity, the old gods, scantily disguised as ancient kings, still were wandering through the pages of *Saxo Grammaticus.* In the 530's when Cassiodorus wrote his history, there still were alive men whose fathers, if not they themselves in their youth, had sacrificed to the old gods. The Gothic "Heldenlieder" were certainly as pagan as those of the Danes and Langobards. The original breaks through in a single passage in the *Getica,* taken over from Cassiodorus: "And because of the great victories the Goths had won in this region, they thereafter called their leaders, by whose good fortune they seemed to have conquered, not mere men but demigods, that is, *ansis.*"[100] Even here Cassiodorus euhemerized the tradition. Everywhere else the pagan elements are radi-

---

[97] *Getica* 181, 212, 259.
[98] XXXI, 2,2.
[99] *Getica* 127.
[100] *Ibid.,* 78.

cally discarded. The genealogy of the Amalungs, which in the *carmina* and *fabulae* was almost certainly full of gods, goddesses, murder, and homicide, reads like a legal document.

Where, as in the account of the war between the Ostrogoths and the Huns, Cassiodorus-Jordanes and Ammianus differ, Ammianus' version is, without the slightest doubt, the correct one. We cannot even be sure that Cassiodorus' quotations from Priscus are always exact. However, because so much of our information on the Huns is based on these quotations, they have to be taken as they are. Occasionally (as, for instance, in the story of Attila and the sacred sword, or in the description of Attila's palace) Cassiodorus renders the Priscus text better than the excerpts which the scribes made for Constantine Porphyrogenitus in the tenth century. And for this alone we must be grateful to the stammering, confused, and barely literate Jordanes. But to elevate him to the ranks of the great historians, as some years ago Giunta tried, is a hopeless undertaking.[101]

---

[101] Giunta 1952. Momigliano (1955, 207-245) tried to prove that Cassiodorus finished his *Gothic History* in Constantinople in 551; Jordanes, a Gothic bishop of Italy, is supposed to have summarized it in agreement with Cassiodorus in order to reach a larger public which was to be won over to a policy of conciliation between the Goths and the Romans. Momigliano's arguments are unconvincing. It is inconceivable that anyone in Constantinople would have read more than a page of a book written in such atrocious Latin as the *Getica*.

II. History

The first chapters of Ammianus Marcellinus' last book contain the only extant coherent account of the events in South Russia before 376. From his Gothic informants Ammianus learned that the Huns "made their violent way amid the rapine and slaughter of the neighboring peoples as far as the Halani."[1] Who those peoples were obviously no one could tell him, and the *monumenta vetera* supplied no information about them; they were among those "obscure peoples whose names and customs are unknown."[2] Ammianus' actual information begins with the Hun attack on the Alans: The Huns overran "the territories of those Halani (bordering on the Greuthungi [Ostrogoths]) to whom usage has given the surname Tanaitae [Don people]."

This passage has been variously interpreted.[3] How far to the east and west did the "Don people" live? In one passage Ammianus locates all Alans—and that would include the Tanaitae—"in the measureless wastes of Scythia to the east of the river,"[4] only to say a few lines later that the Alans are divided between the two parts of the earth, Europe and Asia,[5] which are separated by the Don.[6] The Greuthungi-Ostrogoths[7] were the western neighbors of the Tanaitae, but in another passage Ammianus puts the Sauromatae, not the Greuthungi, between the Don and

---

[1] Ammianus, XXXI, 2, 12.

[2] XXII, 8, 38.

[3] See, *e.g.*, the articles in Rosenfeld 1956 and 1957a, and Altheim 1956a and 1956b.

[4] XXXI, 2, 13.

[5] XXXI, 2, 17.

[6] XXII, 8, 27.

[7] On the Greuthungi-Ostrogoths, see Rosenfeld 1957b, 245-258.

the Danube,[8] and in still another one (following Ptolemy, *Geography* V, 9, 1) also east of the Don.[9]

Ammianus suffered from a sort of literary atavism, garbling the new reports with the old.[10] The chapter on the Alans in book XXXI includes a lengthy dissertation on the peoples whom the Alans "by repeated victories incorporated under their own national name."[11] Ammianus promises to straighten out the confused opinions of the geographers and to present the truth. Actually, he offers the queerest hodgepodge of quotations from Herodotus, Pliny, and Mela,[12] naming the Geloni, Agathyrsi, Melanchlaeni, Anthropophagi, Amazons, and Seres, as if all these peoples were still living in his time.

The Huns clashed with Alanic tribes in the Don area. This is all we can retain from Ammianus' account. If Ammianus had used the term *Tanaitae* as Ptolemy used it,[13] the "Don people" would have lived in European Sarmatia. But a river never formed a frontier between seminomadic herdsmen, and certainly not the "quietly flowing" Don. The archaeological evidence is unequivocal: In the fourth century Sarmatians grazed their flocks both east of the Don as far as the Volga and beyond it, and west of the river to the plains of Rumania. Exactly where the Huns attacked cannot be determined; like the later invaders, their main force probably operated on the lower course of the river.

Ammianus' account of an alliance between a group, or groups, of Alans and the Huns cannot be doubted. In the 370's and 380's Huns and Alans are so often named together, that some kind of cooperation of the two peoples would have to be assumed even without Ammianus' explicit statement:

> The Huns killed and plundered them [i.e., the Tanaitae] and joined the survivors to themselves in a treaty of alliance, [*reliquos sibi concordandi fide pacta iunxerunt*]; then in company with them they made more boldly a sudden inroad into the extensive and rich cantons of Ermenrichus.[14]

---

[8] XXXI, 2, 13.

[9] XXI, 8, 29.

[10] Thomson 1948, 352.

[11] XXXI, 2, 13-16.

[12] Malotet 1898, 15.

[13] Ptolemy, *Geog.* III, 5, 10. On the Tanaitae, see Kotsevalov 1959, 1524-1530; Boltunova 1962, 92-93.

[14] XXXI, 3, 1.

For a long time [*diu*],[15] the king of the Greuthungi "did his best to maintain a firm and continued stand, but as rumor gave wide currency to and exaggerated the horror of the impending danger," he killed himself. His successor Vithimiris

> resisted the Halani for a time [*aliquantisper*], relying on other Huns, whom he paid to take his side. But after many defeats which he sustained, he was overcome by force of arms and died in battle. In the name of his little son, Viderichus, the management of affairs was undertaken by Alatheus and Saphrax, experienced generals known for their courage; but since the stress of circumstances compelled them to abandon confidence in resistance, they cautiously retreated until they came to the river Danastius.[16]

Ammianus' account has been rejected by the Croatian scholar L. Hauptmann, who thought that either Ammianus made a bad blunder or that the text was corrupt.[17] Not *Hunis aliis fretus* Vithimir must have resisted the Alans but **Halanis aliis fretus*, the Huns. Hauptmann referred to Jordanes, in whose account the only enemies of the Ostrogoths are, indeed, the Huns. But Jordanes' compilation is tendentious from beginning to end. He not only retained the transfiguration of the early history of the Goths as he found it in Cassiodorus; he also changed what he read in Ammianus in favor of the Alans.[18] They were, wrote Ammianus, *Hunis per omnia suppares* (XXXI, 2, 21); Jordanes, *Getica* 126, changed this into *pugna pares*. According to Ammianus, the Alans were, in comparison with the Huns, *victu mitiores et cultu*; Jordanes replaced *mitiores* by *dissimiles*, and *cultu* by *humanitate*. He read in Ammianus that the Alans attacked the Ostrogoths after Ermanaric's death. But this did not fit the picture of the noble Alans, so he left it out.

The fights between the Alans and Goths also are attested by Bishop Ambrose of Milan (374-397 A.D.). In the *Expositio evangelii secundum Lucam*, probably written at the end of 378,[19] he summarized the events which led to the disaster of Adrianople: "The Huns threw themselves upon the Alans, the Alans upon the Goths, and the Goths upon the Taifali and Sarmatae; the Goths, exiled from their own country, made us exiles in Illyricum, and the end is not yet."[20]

---

[15] The war between the Huns and the Ostrogoths, usually dated in 375, is actually undatable ; cf. O. Seeck, *Hermes* 41, 1906, 526.

[16] XXXI, 3, 3.

[17] Hauptmann 1935, 18.

[18] On Jordanes' pro-Alanic prejudices, see Mommsen 1882, p. x.

[19] Rauschen 1897, 484; Dudden 1925, 681; Palanque 1935, 57-58, 499-500.

[20] X, 10, *CSEL* 34, 4, 458.

The information Ambrose received in Milan was not quite correct. Ermanaric's kingdom collapsed under the onslaught of the Huns. But the testimony of both Ammianus and Ambrose leaves no doubt that at one time in the apparently long struggle the main enemies of the Goths were, indeed, Alans. Were they only those Alans who had made an alliance with the Huns? This is possible. But the following strange story told by Jordanes might preserve a dim memory of an uprising of Alanic groups *within* the Ostrogothic kingdom:

> Now although Hermanaric, king of the Goths, was the conqueror of many tribes, as we have said above, yet while he was deliberating on this invasion of the Huns, the treacherous tribe of the Rosomoni [*Rosomonorum gens infida*], who at that time were among those who owed him homage, took this chance to catch him unawares. For when the king had given orders that a certain woman of the tribe I mentioned, Sunilda by name, should be bound to wild horses and torn apart by driving them in opposite directions (for he was roused to fury by her husband's treachery to him), her brothers Sarus and Ammius came to avenge their sister's death and plunged a sword in Hermanaric's side. Enfeebled by this blow, he dragged out a miserable existence in bodily weakness. Balamber, king of the Huns, took advantage of his ill health to move an army into the land of the Ostrogoths.[21]

Whereas Sunilda is unquestionably a Germanic name, the derivation of Sarus from Gothic *sarwa*, "weapon, armor," and of Ammius from Gothic *hama*, "to arm,"[22] is unconvincing. There is no satisfactory etymology of Rosomoni.[23] Sarus occurs later as the name of a Goth,[24] but this does

---

[21] *Getica* 129-130.

[22] Brady 1949, 18-19.

[23] The Germanic etymologies of Rosomoni are listed by Schönfeld 1911, 194-195, and G. Vetter 1938, 98-99. Brady thought that in oral tradition Roxolani could have been distorted into Rosomoni, but Müllenhoff (*Jordanes* 164) was probably right in rejecting such an explanation: *De Rhoxolanis in mythis fabulisque Gothorum cogitare absurdum est.* For the same reason it is unlikely that, as I thought for awhile, Rosomoni, *v. l.* Rosomani, *POΣOMANOI*, might go back to be misread *PO ΞOΛANOI.* Tretiakov's equation Rosomoni = Rus (Tretiakov 1953, 25) is as wild as the one suggested by Vernadsky (1959, 68) who takes -*moni* to be Ossetic *mojnae*, "man, husband"; the Rosomoni are "the Ros men."

Vernadsky finds pre-Ossetic "Ruxs-Alans" and Antes everywhere. The Acaragantes (*recte* Argaragantes) in Hungary, for instance, are supposed to be the "voiceless Antes," Ossetic *æqæræg*, their enemies, the Limigantes, the "weak Antes," Ossetic *læmaeg* (Vernadsky 1959, 70). Vernadsky overlooked the gigantes, corybantes, Garamantes, and the Ants in Christian Morgenstern's "Ant-ologie." His writings are full of such absurdities, based on *willkürliche Interpretation teilweise unbrauchbarer Quellen*

not necessarily make Sarus of the Rosomoni a Goth. The name can be compared with Sarosius or Saroes,[25] who in about 500 was king of the Alans in the Caucasus. Sarakos in an inscription from Tanais (early third century A.D.) probably is derived from the Sarmatian word that corresponds to Avestic *sara-*, Ossetic *sär-*, "head";[26] Sarus could mean "caput, captain." Saphrax (Safrax) and Lagarimanus, prominent leaders of the Goths, had Iranian names;[27] they might have been Alans. Although it cannot be proved that the Rosomoni were rebellious Alans, the *discessus* of an Alanic *gens* at a time when Alans attacked the Ostrogoths seems more likely than the treachery of Gothic noblemen.

It was almost certainly the *concordia* with large groups of Alans which enabled the Huns to move against Ermanaric. Ammianus does not say what the terms of the alliance were. When one considers that those Alans who in 418 subjugated themselves to the *patrocinium* of the Vandal king, retained their tribal organization until the end of the Vandal kingdom, it may be assumed that the Hunno-Alanic alliance guaranteed the Iranian partner a considerable degree of independence and a large share in the loot. It was certainly not the first time that other tribes joined the Huns, nor was it the last. In some cases the alliance seems to have resulted in a real symbiosis, in others the tribes united temporarily for raids and looting expeditions. The Hunno-Alanic alliance lasted three decades.

Ammianus' account on the Alanic attacks on the Goths is borne out by Ambrose, but there seems to be no other authority to confirm what it says about the Huns who sided with Vithimir. Why should Huns, even if they were paid by the Gothic king, fight for him at a time when his situation was so obviously hopeless? If they stayed with those hordes which not even the great Ermanaric could withstand, they could expect to loot at their hearts' desire; shortly afterward, the Huns who broke into the land of the Visigoths were quickly so loaded down with booty that they had to break off the attack.[28] Were the Huns siding with the Goths a

---

und haltlose Namenetymologien (F. Dölger, *BZ* 42, 1950, 133); cf. also W. B. Henning, *BSOAS* 21: 2, 1958, 315-318, D. M. Lang, *BSOAS* 22, 2, 1959, 371; and A. V. Soloviev, *BZ* 54, 1961, 135-138. In the following, I will refer no more to Vernadsky's etymologies.

[24] Olympiodorus 57a $_{11-12}$; his brother Singericus (60a $_{13}$) has a Germanic name.
[25] Menander, *EL* 4423, 453 $_{23,30}$; Theophanes Byz., fr. 4, *HGM* IV, 448$_{22}$ = *FHG* IV, 271.
[26] Zgusta 1955, sec. 199; cf. Abaev 1949, 180.
[27] Cf. Maenchen-Helfen 1957b, 281.
[28] Ammianus, XXXI, 3, 8.

part of the people who had crossed the Don? Or did Huns live west of the river, tribes which found themselves as threatened as the Goths and decided, when Vithimir appealed for their help, to make common cause with the Germans against the invaders?

A passage in the *Getica* of Jordanes, going back to the fifth-century historian Priscus, gives the answer. "Like a whirlwind of nations the Huns swept across the Alpidzuri, Alcildzuri, Itimari, Tuncarsi, and Boisci who bordered that part of Scythia."[29] As we shall see, the first two names stand for one, the Turkish name *Alp-il-čur*, which cannot be separated from the Hunnic names ending in -*čur*. The other names will occupy us later. In the present context this one name, *Alpilčur*, suffices to prove the existence of Turkish-speaking nomads [30] on or near the northeastern shore of the Black Sea before the Huns came. In the 430's the same peoples, listed in the same order and now under Hun domination, had their pastures along the Danube.[31] Whether they migrated or were settled there by their Hun lords is of minor importance. What matters is that their alliance withstood all the vicissitudes of those stormy decades. Because in both passages the *Alpilčur* are named first, they apparently were the leading tribe. Overrun by the Huns near the Maeotis, they were, sixty years later, still bitterly opposed to their masters; they made a treaty with the Romans. In a later chapter I shall come back to those "Huns before the Huns."

Ermanaric's Kingdom

It is often assumed that Attila ruled over all the peoples once under the king of the Ostrogoths, Ermanaric. Archaeologists perhaps would have hesitated to attribute graves in the forests of central Russia to the nomadic Huns had they not believed that at one time Ermanaric's Goths had ruled there. The assertion of the West Roman ambassadors at Attila's court that the Hun king was the lord over the islands in the ocean would not have been so widely accepted were it not for Jordanes' statement that the Aesti on the Baltic coast were Ermanaric's subjects. Lack of criticism and chauvinistic bias either enlarged the Gothic realm out of all proportions or practically denied its existence.[32]

---

[29] *Getica* 126.

[30] Although neither Priscus nor Jordanes says anything about their way of life, they must have been nomads. There were no Turkish farmers in South Russia before, almost a millennium later, the Tatars in the Crimea settled down to plough their fields and tend to their orchards.

[31] Priscus, *EL* $121_{4\text{-}5}$. Contrary to the text, προσοικοῦσι τὸν Ἴστρον, Thompson 1948, 71, locates them near the Azov Sea.

[32] The map in *Vorgeschichte der deutschen Stämme* III, 1185, published by the Reichsamt für Vorgeschichte in der Nationalsozialistischen Deutschen Arbeiterpartei

Jordanes' description of it is almost a hymn.[33] "Some of our ancestors," he wrote, "have justly compared Hermanaric to Alexander the Great." Obviously it was Jordanes' source Cassiodorus, not an illiterate Goth, who made this comparison and called Ermanaric "the ruler of all nations of Scythia and Germania." Jordanes listed thirteen peoples which the Amalung ruler Ermanaric conquered in the north: *Golthescytha*, *Thiudos*, *Inaunxis*, *Vasinabroncae*, *Merens*, *Mordens*, *Imniscaris*, *Rogas*, *Tadzans*, *Athaul*, *Navego*, *Bubegenes*, *Coldas*. The uncertain readings and the queer forms of these names make them an ideal hunting ground for name chasers. Tomaschek took Athaul for the name of a Hunnic tribe, Turkish *ataghul*, "archer."[34] Mullenhoff thought that *scytha* in *Golthescytha* was Latinized *chud*, the designation of Finnish tribes in the early Russian chronicles.[35] Marquart took *golthe* for another form of *Scoloti*, connected it with *thiudos*, dismissed *scytha* as a gloss, and arrived thus at "the Scolotic peoples."[36] He and Grienberger had no doubts that *thiudos* was Gothic, meaning "peoples," but Grienberger suspected in *golthe* Latin *gothice*, connected *scytha* and *thiudos*, and translated "in Gothic, the Scythian peoples."[37] To discuss these and equally fanciful etymologies would be a waste of time. The Mordens[38] are the Mordvins and the Merens the Mari.[39] Whether Ermanaric actually *domuerat* them is more doubtful. The ethnic names may merely reflect the extent of the geographical knowledge of Jordanes or his sources.

Ermanaric is also said to have subdued the Aesti on the Baltic coast "by his wisdom and might," which probably means no more than that there existed some trade relations between the Goths and the tribes in the amber countries, as they possibly existed in Hunnic times[40] and under the great Ostrogothic king Theoderic (Theodoric).[41]

---

on the eve of Hitler's invasion of the Soviet Union, turned eastern Europe to the Urals into Ermanaric's «Hoheitsgebiet.» Altheim 1951, 73, claimed even Dagestan in the eastern Caucasus for the Goths.

[33] *Getica* 116-120.

[34] *SB Wien* 117, 1889, 39.

[35] *Jordanes*, index 160.

[36] Marquart 1903, 378, n. 3.

[37] *ZfDA* 39, 1895, 158.

[38] Μορδία in Constantine Porphyrogenitus, *De admin. imp.*; Jenkins 1949, 168 [46].

[39] Matthews 1951, 29-30. To the literature listed there, add B. Munkacsi, *KCsA* 1, 1921, 62 ; A. Pogodin, *MSFOU* 67, 1933, 326-330 ; E. Lewy, *Transactions of the Philological Society* 1946, 133-136 ; J. V. Farkas, *Saeculum* 5, 1954, 331 ; Collinder 1962, 23-24.

[40] J. Werner, index, *s.v.* Bernstein, Bernsteinperle.

[41] Cassiodorus, *Variae* V, 2.

After the conquest of the northern peoples, Ermanaric "reduced to his sway" the Heruli near the Azov Sea, which is quite credible. Since the middle of the third century a tribe of the East Hermanic Heruli had dwelt on the shores of the Maeotis.[42]

Finally, Ermanaric attacked and subjugated the Venethi. Translated from the hymn into prose: "from time to time the Goths made raids into Slavic territory in the northwest." In the confused account of the years following Ermanaric's death, Jordanes speaks of a war between a section of the Ostrogoths and the Antes, led by King Boz.[43] After the victory over the Antes, the Goths were attacked by the Huns and defeated on the river Erac.[44]

The boundaries of the Ostrogothic "empire" cannot be defined because it had none. Around a more or less compactly settled Gothic area lay the sites of various tribes. Some of them may have paid regular tribute; others only bartered their goods, presumably mostly furs, for what the Goths got either from the Bosporan kingdom or the Danube provinces; still others occasionally may have joined the Ostrogoths in looting expeditions. The rapid collapse of Ermanaric's kingdom clearly indicates its lack of coherence.

To analyze once more Ammianus' account of the war between the Huns and the Visigoths, the southern neighbors of the Ostrogoths, is not our task. This has been done by all the historians of the Migration Period, most competently and succinctly, in my opinion, by Patsch.[45] The Visigoths under Athanaric expected the attack of the Huns on the right bank of the Dniester but could not hold it; they retreated behind the Sereth. The larger part of the people decided to seek a new home in the empire; Athanaric and his followers marched through Oltenia into *Caucalandis locus*. According to Patsch, Caucaland was the mountainous part of the Banat, between the rivers Maros, Theiss, and Danube.[46] The objections

---

[42] Rappaport 1899, 48.

[43] His identification with Buz in the Igor Song (cf. Shakhmatov 1919, 10 ; Perets 1926, 24) was called to question by A. Mazon (*Revue des études slaves* 19, 1939, 259-260) and has been conclusively refuted by N. Zupanič, *Situla* 4, 1961, 121-122. For the Slavic etymology, see S. Rospond, *Voprosy iazykoznaniia* 14: 3, 1965, 8. Boz might be an Iranian name, cf. *Bwzmyhr* (Frye 1952, 52 ; W. B. Henning, *BSOAS* 21: 2, 1958, 38, n. 41; *Burzmipuhr* in A 246, 1958, 353; D'iakonov and Lifshits 1960, 23). Bulgarian *Bezmer* is, in I. Dulchev's opinion, *Boz-Mihr* (*Archiv orientální* 21, 1953, 356).

[44] Either the Tiligul, N. Zupanič, *Ethnograf* 14, 1930, 113-121, or the lower Dnieper, E. Kh. Skrzhinskaia, *VV* 12, 1957, 25. This Erac had, of course, nothing to do with the Erax in Lazica (Constantine Porphyrogenitus, *De admin. imp.*, ch. 45).

[45] Patsch 1928, 2, 59-63.

[46] *Ibid.*, 64-65.

to his thesis[47] are based on doubtful equations of the name Cauca; they disregard the events in the late 370's, which definitely point to Visigoths in the eastern Banat. I, therefore, accept Patsch's location.[48]

From about 376 on, the Huns were the rulers of a large area in South Russia. They stood at the lower Danube. The picture that can be drawn from Ammianus is not wrong but onesided. He says nothing about the fate of the Bosporan kingdom, the life of the peoples whom the Huns overran, their economy, their social institutions, their interrelations. It would be unfair to blame Ammianus. He wrote a history of the Roman Empire, not one of the barbarians. Fortunately the cultures of the peoples west of the Don can, at least in their outlines, be reconstructed, mainly with the help of the archaeological material.

THE HUNS AT THE DANUBE

In the summer of 376, tens of thousands of Visigoths were encamped on the northern bank of the lower Danube around Durostorum (modern Silistra), anxiously waiting for permission to cross the river and settle in Thrace. They were the greater part of the proud nation which only a few years before had forced the Romans to deal with their leader Athanaric as an equal of the king of kings. Now, defeated by the Huns (see preceding section) and starving, they were deadly scared lest their enemies fall upon them again before they were admitted to a refuge in the empire.

Permission came in the fall. The Visigoths, shortly followed by Ostrogoths,[49] Taifali,[50] and other transdanubian barbarians,[51] crossed the Da-

---

[47] C. C. Giurescu, *Revista istorică romănă* 5-6, 1935-36, 564; K. K. Klein, *PBB* 79, 1957, 302-307; I. Nestor, *Ist. Rom.* 1, 1960, 697-699; R. Vulpe, *Dacia*, N. S. 5, 1961, 387, n. 110.

[48] The famous treasure of Pietroassa in the district Buzau has, therefore, nothing to do with Athanaric.

[49] Led by Vithericus, Alatheus, and Safrax (Ammianus XXXI, 4, 12; 5, 3).

[50] Ammianus speaks of them only once; in the late fall of 377, *autumno vergente in hiemem*, the Romans almost annihilated a horde of Taifali who shortly before, *nuper*, had crossed the Danube (XXXI, 9, 3-4). But Zosimus (IV, 25, 1) names them next to the Goths, and in the *Epit. de caes.* XLVII, 3, they take the second place among the invaders. The Taifali were apparently a numerous people. Before 370 they held Oltenia and the western part of Muntenia (Patsch 1925, 189, n. 2). How far to the east of the Aluta River their territory expanded could be determined only if the exact location of Athanaric's defense line, which "skirted the lands of Taifali" (Ammianus XXXI, 3, 7), were known; for recent attempts to localize it, see R. Vulpe, *Dacia* 4, 1960, 322. There is no proof for the constantly repeated assertion that the Taifali were Germans. It should be noted that in Gaul Taifali and Sarmatians were settled together (*Praelectus Sarmatarum et Taifalorum gentilium, Not. Dign.* [*occ.*] 42, 65); cf. Barkoczi 1959, 452.

[51] Multarum gentium bellicus furor (Ambrose, *Ep.* XV, 5); "other tribes that formerly dwelt with the Goths and Taifali" (Zosimus IV, 25, 1).

nube. The following struggle between the Visigoths[52] and the East Romans, which for years raged throughout Thrace, at times engulfing large tracts of Macedonia, has been thoroughly studied. This is understandable and legitimate. The Germanic invaders developed into great nations; in France and Spain they shaped the fate of the Western world. Except for the few years of Attila's reign, the Huns loomed on and beyond the periphery of the oecumene. Their history in the last decades of the fourth century seems to be bare of all interest. Even those scholars who made the Huns the special object of their studies paid no attention to it.[53]

It is true that our information about the Huns in that period is scanty, although not much scantier than for others. But this should be only a challenge to make the most of the few data. To extract from the annals, commentaries on the Bible, homilies, edicts, and poems the few passages dealing with the Huns and to determine what happened, when, and where, requires an inordinately large apparatus. But that cannot be helped if we want to learn how the Huns moved into central Europe.

Visigoths and Huns Cooperate

After the sanguinary battle Ad Salices in the northern Dobrogea between Visigoths and imperial troops (see Chapter XII) in the summer of 377, the Romans retreated behind the Haemus (Balkans). Their losses were not quite as heavy as those of the Visigoths. But even with the reinforcements being sent to him, the Roman commander could not risk another battle. The Visigoths were still far superior in numbers. Their strength was, however, at the same time their weakness. They were not an army, they were a whole people: women, children, sick people, old people, four or five times outnumbered the warriors. "Everything that could serve as food throughout the lands of Scythia and Moesia had been used up. All the necessities of life had been taken to the strong places, none of which the enemy even attempted to besiege because of their complete ignorance of these and other operations of the kind."[54]

The Romans hastily fortified the mountain passes. The Goths found themselves "crowded between the Hister [Danube] and the waste places." Their situation was rapidly getting desperate. Roman troops would easily have broken through the *aggeres celsi* or high ramparts of the Goths, obviously mere stockades: to the Goths they proved unconquerable. "Driv-

---

[52] "The greatest and most excellent of all the Scythian peoples" (Philostorgius XI, 8).

[53] Thompson (1948) gives the almost twenty years between the battle of Adrianople and the invasion of Asia in 395 half a page.

[54] Ammianus XXXI, 8, 1, 4.

en alike by ferocity and hunger," they attacked time and again, only to be driven back. Hemmed in by the sea to their left, the mountains to the right and in front of them, in their back the Danube, the Goths could not hold out much longer. "Compelled by dire necessity they gained an alliance with some of the Huns and Halani by holding out the hope of immense booty." As soon as the Roman commander heard of this, he evacuated his positions and retreated to the Thracian plain.

Ammianus Marcellinus gives a picturesque account of the events following. But instead of telling his readers what actually happened, he describes at great length and with gruesome details the horrors of the barbarian invasion. We hear much about the misery of women and free-born men driven along by cracking whips, but we do not learn why the Romans retreated. The Huns had as little experience in storming even improvised fortifications as the Visigoths. In the mountains their horsemen were as good as lost. The few who might have sneaked behind the Roman lines could be cut down easily. The Goths did not need more men; they had enough. Besides, Ammianus himself stresses that the number of the Huns and Alans was small, *Hunnorum et Halanorum aliquos.* Why, then, did the blockade break down? Looking at the map, Seeck found the answer: the Huns most probably crossed the Danube far to the *west.* Riding down the Morava valley to Naissus (modern Niš, Yugoslavia) and turning east, they threatened the rear of the Romans.[55] Saturninus, the Roman commander, had no choice. He left the passes. The Goths were saved.

A strategic move on such a scale required more than an agreement between the Visigoths and "some" Huns. It presupposed on the part of the Huns the capacity of throwing hundreds of horsemen into action. What the status of their leaders was we do not know. But whether they were "kings," or phylarchoi (tribal chieftains), or hetmans, whether their men followed them out of loyalty, or to gain military laurels, or simply in order to make, in the shortest time, as much booty as possible, is irrelevant compared with the fact that these horsemen *could* be assembled, that their leaders *did* come to an agreement with the Visigoths, that the Huns were kept together over hundreds of miles. The very first account of a Hun raid into the Balkan provinces refutes the view that for half a century after the invasion of South Russia Hun society consisted of a large number of tiny independent groups. But the problems of Hun society will occupy us in another context.

---

[55] Seeck, *Geschichte* 5, 109, 468-469.

It sometimes has been maintained that the Huns fought at Adrianople (see Chapter XII) side by side with the Goths.[56] Adrianople (378 A.D.) was a Gothic victory. "The Roman legions were massacred by the Goths" (*Romanae legiones usque ad internicionem caesae sunt a Gothis*), wrote Jerome one year after the catastrophe, and none of those who made use of his chronicle had in this respect anything to add from other sources. Ammianus' account of the battl eis far from being as precise as one would expect from an author of his military experience and grasp for essentials. Yet so much is certain: the decision fell with the arrival of the Ostrogoths. Fritigern's Visigoths could not withstand the fierce attack of the Roman cavalry. Driven back to their wagons, hard pressed by the advancing legions, they were rescued by Alatheus' and Safrax's Ostrogothic horsemen. The Visigothic leader avoided giving battle as long as he could, partly because he still hoped to come to an understanding with the emperor, but mostly because he did not dare to fight alone. The Romans had their Saracen horses; Fritigern needed desperately the Ostrogothic cavalry. Had they not rushed in just in time, the Visigoths in all probability would have been defeated, if not annihilated. The sudden Ostrogoth attack threw the Romans into confusion, then into panic, and what followed was a massacre.

Adrianople, one of the decisive battles of history, was won by *equitatus Gothorum*. It is true that there were a few men of other tribes with them, but these were not Huns. Ammianus speaks specifically of *Halanorum manus*.[57] Had the account been written by Jordanes, we might suspect that he did not want to give the Huns credit for a Gothic victory. Ammianus had no reason to prefer the Alans to the Goths. In his narrative the Huns reappear *after* the battle. When the Goths set up their camp at Perinthus at the Sea of Marmara, they were *Hunis Halanisque permixti*.[58] The Huns had stayed away from the fight. Their descendants, the "Massagetae" in the Roman army in Africa, did the same more than once. They waited to see who would win. The Huns were out for looting, and had no desire to spill their blood *pour le roi des Goths*.

In the following two years our sources repeatedly name Huns, Goths, and Alans together,[59] but whether the Huns looted and burned down the villages of the unfortunate population of Thrace alone or as the allies of the Goths is not known. Some contemporary authors saw in the Huns

---

[56] Thompson (1948, 25) is more cautious ("not impossible").

[57] XXXI, 12, 17.

[58] *Ibid.*, 16, 3.

[59] Themistius, *Or.* XV, K. W. Dindorf 1932, 252_{35}-253_1 ; Pacatus XIV, 4; *CM* I, 243; II, 60, 3792.

the worst villains. They were "more fierce than any kind of destruction" (*omni pernicie atrociores*).[60] Orosius names the Huns and Alans before the Goths.[61]

After 380, neither Huns nor Alans are mentioned among the barbarians in the Balkan provinces.[62] Goths served in the imperial armies by the thousands. The Roman commanders Botherich, Eriulf, Fravitta, Gainas, and Rumorid were Goths. But we do not hear of Hun contingents or Hun officers. The Huns returned beyond the Danube.

Although the Huns did not fight at Adrianople, indirectly they might have decided the outcome of the battle. The following chronological and geographical deliberations seem to lead away from the Huns. But without them the events in the barbaricum (the territories beyond the Roman frontiers) cannot be reconstructed.

The Huns Threaten Pannonia

In the beginning of June 378, Gratian's army, which was supposed to join as quickly as possible the Eastern Romans hard-pressed by the Visigoths, finally set out for Thrace. The young emperor's frivolous wish to present himself to Valens as the victor over mighty barbarians in the West delayed the march for at least a month.[63] But now Gratian hurried. He led his troops in long marches, *porrectis itineribus*, from Felix Arbor on Lake Constance to Lauriacum, the present Lorch in Upper Austria. There the army, which had marched 300 *milia*,[64] rested for a short time.[65] Gratian himself "sent on ahead by land all his baggage and packs, and

---

[60] *Epit. de caes.* XLVII, 3.

[61] *Hist. adv. Pagan.* VII, 34, 5.

[62] For the chronology of Theodosius' campaigns against the Goths in 380, see Ensslin 1948, 12-14. Gregory of Nazianzen (*De vita sua*, PG 37, 1098) has some additional information about Theodosius' headquarters.

[63] Gratian was "already on his way to the regions of the east," when he learned that the Alamannic Lentienses had suffered a crushing defeat at Argentaria near Colmar (Ammianus XXXI, 10, 11). The emperor left Trier after April 20 (Cod. Theodos. VIII, 5, 35), so the battle must have been fought at the end of April or early in May. "Filled with confidence at this happy success ... Gratian turned his line of march to the left and secretly crossed the Rhine," probably near Basel. Although the campaign in the Black Forest was carried out "with incredible energy and conspicuous rapidity" (Ammianus XXXI, 10, 18, perhaps following a panegyric ; cf. Seeck, *Hermes* 41, 1906, 484), Gratian could not have resumed his march east before the beginning of June at the earliest.

[64] *Itin. Anton.* CCXXXV, 1-237, 5.

[65] As shown by the great number of siliquiae and half-siliquiae coined in Trier, 364-378, which were found at Lorch; Elmer, "Geldverkehr in Lauriacum und Orilava," *Num. Zeitschr.* (Vienna) 67, 1934, 31-32.

descending the Danube. . . came to Bononia [in Pannonia superior; now Banostor] and entered Sirmium [in Pannonia inferior; now Sremska Mitrovica]. Having been delayed there four days, he went on over the same river to Castra Martis,[66] although attacked by intermittent fevers. In that region the Halani unexpectedly fell upon him, and he lost a few of his followers."[67] It was the first encounter with the enemy.

Gratian would not have dared to sail down the Danube with only "a band of light-armed troops," unless he could have been sure that the Quadi, Jazygi, and Sarmatae on the left bank of the river would keep the peace. They still suffered from the defeats which three years before Valentinian had inflicted on them. The Quadi were forced to provide recruits for the Roman army and the alliance with the Sarmatae Argaragantes in the Banat had been renewed. To prevent the recurrence of surprise attacks like those which in 374 and 375 carried the barbarians deep into Roman territory, the frontier fortifications were greatly strengthened.[68] Pannonian soldiers could be detailed for service in Britain.[69] In the spring of 378, Gratian's general Frigeridus with his Pannonian and transalpine auxiliaries joined the forces in Thrace.[70] Gratian had nothing to fear from the peoples east of the Danube. But only a few months later Valeria, the easternmost province of Pannonia, was overrun by Goths, Huns, and Alans.

Assuming that Gratian traveled as fast as Emperor Julian (A.D. 360-363) who, in the summer of 361, in exceptionally good weather, sailed with three thousand men from "the place where the river is navigable" to Sirmium in eleven days,[71] Gratian could have arrived in Bononia at the end of June or early in July. He probably was in Martis Castra not later than the middle of July. Whether he could have joined Valens before August 9 the day of the fateful battle, is a moot question. The letter he sent to Valens shows that he was determined to throw his cavalry into the struggle as fast as he could.[72] Yet a passage in Zosimus' New History, composed in the sixth century, seems to indicate that Gratian suddenly stopped, turned around, and rode back to Sirmium.

Victor, commander of the horse, one of the few high officers to survive the massacre at Adrianople, fought his way, with some of his horsemen, "through Macedonia and Thessaly to Moesia and Paiones to inform Gratian,

---

[66] The present Kula in Bulgaria. Patsch, *PW* 3, 1769.

[67] Ammianus XXXI, 11, 6.

[68] Patsch 1929, 31.

[69] J. W. E. Pearce, *Numismatic Chronicle* 1939, 128-142 ; N. H. Baynes, *BZ* 38, 1939, 582.

[70] Ammianus XXXI, 7, 3.

[71] Zosimus III, 10, 2-3; Ammianus XXI, 9, 2.

[72] Ammianus XXXI, 12, 4.

who was there, of what had happened."[73] Paiones stands here for the province of Pannonia secunda.[74] If Victor was indeed the first to report to Gratian the death of Valens and if he met him in Pannonia secunda, Gratian must have returned to Sirmium not, as is generally assumed, because he realized that after the annihilation of the Eastern army he alone was too weak to continue the fight with the Goths but *before* he learned about the catastrophe. Zosimus is not a very reliable author,[75] his τὸ συμβάν may only mean "all the details." The most important single news, that of Valens' death, Gratian may have received while he was still marching east.[76] If, however, he should have returned before, there could have been only one reason: his troops, although needed in Thrace, must have been needed even more urgently in Pannonia. Valens fought the Goths; Gratian had to fight the peoples driven into Pannonia by the Huns, and the Huns themselves.

Gratian had asked Bishop Ambrose, first in letters, later at their meeting in Sirmium,[77] to write for him a treatise on the orthodox faith. Ambrose

---

[73] Ἐπὶ Μυσοὺς καὶ Παίονας ἀναδραμών αὐτόθι διατρίβοντι τῷ Γρατιανῷ τὸ συμβὰν ἀπαγγέλλει (Zosimus IV, 24, 3).

[74] Zosimus used indiscriminately Paionia, Paioniai, and Paiones: Τὰ Μυσῶν τάγματα καὶ Παιόνων (I, 20, 2) = τὰ ἐν Μυσίᾳ καὶ Παιονίᾳ τάγματα (I, 21, 2) ; Παιονία = Παίονες (II, 46, 1). He knew that Pannonia consisted of a number of provinces, τὰ Παιόνων ἔθνη (I, 48), but he did not care to state in which of them this or that event took place. Cibalis, Sirmium, and Mursa were just "towns in Pannonia" (II, 18, 2, 5; 45, 3). In the combination "Paionia and Mysia" or "Mysia and Paionia" (I, 13, 1; 20, 2; II, 48, 3; III, 2, 2; IV, 16, 3, 4; 29, 3, 4), Paionia always means Pannonia secunda, and Mysia means Moesia superior. E. Polaschek's interpretation of Paionia in IV, 24, 3, as the Macedonian Paionia (*Wiener Prähistor. Zeitschr.* 18, 1931, 243, n. 19) is not acceptable.

[75] But Zosimus' addition to Eunapius (fr. 42, *EL* 597, 4-5) indicates that he had access to some sources which are now lost. According to Eunapius, Thrace, Macedonia, and Thessaly were ravaged by the Goths before the battle at Adrianople. Zosimus IV, 20, 7, copies Eunapius but adds "and Paionia."

[76] Neither the rescript of toleration which Gratian issued immediately after he learned of his uncle's death nor the edict of September 25, 378 (*Cod. Theodos.* X, 2, 1) gives any indication as to the date when the news reached the emperor. The edict was issued under the names of Valens, Gratian, and Valentinian, but this does not necessarily indicate that Valens was still believed to be alive; cf. Seeck 1919, 111-112. Acting on the rescript of toleration, the Macedonians met in synod in Antioch in Caria before the end of 378 (Duchesne 1924, 2, 343, n. 1). It is impossible to determine when exactly they learned of the rescript. Seeck, who dated it between August 18 and September 25 (1919, 250), did not state his reasons. As far as I can see, there are none.

[77] *De fide* III, 1. The council of Sirmium could not have been held during the four days Gratian spent in the city in July. This was most certainly not the time to discuss ecclesiastical affairs. If the council was held at all, which by now seems very likely (Dudden 1925, 189; Palanque 1933, 496-498 ; N. H. Baynes, *English Historical Review* 51, 1936, 303, 304), it must be dated in August.

composed the first two books *De fide* "hastily and summarily, and in rough rather than exact form."[78] He wrote them after he learned of the heretic Valens' death,[79] which did not particularly grieve him. He hailed the young orthodox emperor Gratian as "the ruler of the whole world" who would conquer the Goths.[80] In the midst of theological arguments and scriptural proofs for the consubstantiality of Father, Son, and Holy Ghost, there is a passage that calls for close attention: "Have we not heard," wrote Ambrose, "from all along the border, from Thrace and through Dacia ripensis, Moesia, and all of Valeria of the Pannonias [*omnemque Valeriam Pannoniarum*], a mingled tumult of blasphemers [*sc.* Arians] preaching and barbarians invading?"[81] Ambrose left out Pannonia secunda, where evidently Gratian's main force stood. That he stressed the invasion of Valeria, of *all* Valeria, is all the more significant.

In *De fide* the Goths were still the only enemy. Ambrose soon received more exact, and more alarming news. "The Huns," he wrote now, "threw themselves upon the Alans, the Alans upon the Goths, and the Goths upon the Taifali and Sarmatians; the Goths, exiled from their own country, made us exiles in Illyricum, and the end is not yet."[82] The blurred picture the Romans had of the happenings beyond the Danube became clearer: Athanaric's Visigoths, who had not joined Fritigern, threw themselves upon the Taifali in Oltenia and then upon the Sarmatians in Caucaland.[83] Throughout the barbaricum, "as far as the Marcomanni and Quadi,"[84] the peoples began to stir. We have no information about the resistance which the Sarmatians in Caucaland, the Banat, put up against the Goths. It must have been stubborn; the Argaragantes were known to be brave and resourceful.[85] But it was overcome, and an apparently large group of Sarmatians was forced to cross the Danube into Valeria. In December 378, the retired general Theodosius, hastily called from Spain, defeated the invaders.[86] Although the account of the battle by the church historian

---

[78] *De fide* II, 129.
[79] Dudden 1925, 189, n. 8.
[80] *De fide*, I, 3; II, 136-142.
[81] *Ibid.*, II, 16.
[82] *Ibid.*
[83] See Appendix.
[84] Ammianus XXXI, 4, 2.
[85] *Ibid.*, XXIX, 6, 14.

[86] Theodoret, *Hist. eccles.* V, 5; Themistius, *Or.* XIV, 182c, XV, 188c, 198a. Pacatus (X, 2-4) barely touches Theodosius' military activities before his elevation to the throne. Synesius (*De regno* III, *PG* 1061) seems to refer to Theodosius' victories in 374, not in 378. Theodoret's account has long been doubted. Tillemont 1738, 5, 715-716 (copied by G. Kaufmann, *Philologus* 31, 1872, 473-480) had to defend it against Baronius;

Theodoret is heavily embroidered, it is substantially true. One passage even sheds light on the composition of the invading hordes. "Many of the barbarians," wrote Theodoret, "were slain by their own countrymen." Evidently the Sarmatae Limigantes, the "slaves" of the Argaragantes,[87] turned against their lords and killed them with the weapons they were supposed to use against the Romans.

Theodosius' victory may have slightly eased the pressure on one sector of the front. But it was a mere episode in the gigantic struggle. In January 379, when Gratian proclaimed Theodosius emperor, the situation was almost hopeless. "The cities are devastated, myriads of people are killed, the earth is soaked with blood, and a foreign people [λαὸς ἀλλόγλωσσος] is running through the land as if it were theirs."[88] Gratian could no longer from his headquarters in Sirmium direct the operations on a front that reached from western Hungary to the Black Sea. Eastern Illyricum, comprising the dioceses of Dacia and Macedonia, was added to the praetorian prefecture Oriens, to be governed by Theodosius as Valens' successor.[89] The division of Illyricum into an eastern and a western portion was ne-

---

Wietersheim-Dahn II, 62-63, called it *ein albernes Märchen*; other historians who rejected it are quoted by Rauschen 1897, 39. The authenticity of the account is by now generally acknowledged; Seeck, *Geschichte* 5, 124-125; Stein 1959, 1, 295; Dudden 1925, 173. Theodoret erroneously located the battle in Thrace. It was fought at a considerable distance from Sirmium. The Sarmatians would not have dared to attack Gratian's forces in Pannonia secunda. Theodosius' friendship with Maiorian, whom he took with him as *magister utriusque militiae* when he assumed the command in the East (Sidnonius, *Paneg. on Maiorian* 107-115), dated from 378, when the general was commander of Aquincum. All this points to Valeria.

[87] Ammianus XVII, 13, 1; XIX, 11, 1.

[88] Gregory of Nazianzen, *Or.* XXII, 2, *PG* 35, 1140. On the date, see Gallay 1943, 252.

[89] The much discussed administrative history of Illyricum concerns us only insofar as it touches the military history of the years 379-395. Most earlier dissertations are by now superseded by Mazzarino 1942, 1-59. Cf. also Greenslade 1945; Demougeot 1947; Palanque 1951, 5-14; Grumel 1952, 5-46. With the removal of the Gothic danger, a separate Illyrian prefecture became superfluous. In the autumn of 380, Macedonia and Dacia fell back to the West and seemed to have remained Western until 387, the year in which Maximus drove Valentinian II from Italy. From then on, eastern Illyricum was neither Eastern nor Western but Theodosian. There are good reasons to assume that the actual control passed to Theodosius as early as 383; cf. Pearce 1938, 235-237. In 384, he handed the prefecture back to Valentinian II; Lot 1936, 334. It was merely a polite gesture. Whatever the administrative and ecclesiastical status of Illyricum from 383 to 395 may have been, it belonged for all practical purposes, and, first of all, militarily to the East. From the Drina to the Black Sea, the Huns faced the armies of Theodosius.

cessitated by purely military reasons. Gratian took over the fight against the invaders of Pannonia.

The ecclesiastical historians Socrates and Sozomen speak vaguely about the tribes from the banks of the Hister, or just barbarians.[90] The Roman orator Symmachus (ca. 340-402), too, refers to the victories of the two emperors without saying who the enemies were.[91] The poets are, fortunately, more specific. From Pacatus and Ausonius we learn that the peoples who had driven the Sarmatians against and west of the Danube were now attacking the *limes* themselves and piercing them at many points. Theodosius was still in Spain when the Goths, Huns, and Alans broke into Valeria. "Whatever the Goth wastes, the Huns plunders, the Alan carries off, Arcadius will later wish [to recapture]" (*Quidquid atterit Gothus, quidquid rapit Chunus, quidquid aufert Halanus, id olim desiderabit Arcadius*).[92] "Alas, I have lost the Pannonias" (*Perdidi infortunata Pannonias*) laments the *res publica*, imploring Theodosius to come to her rescue. Pacatus was exaggerating. Pannonia was not yet lost, but it was under heavy attack. At the end of 378, Ausonius, friend and teacher of Gratian, consul for 379, received in Trier good news:

All foes now vanquished (where the mixed Frankish and Suebian hordes vie in submission, seeking to serve in our Roman armies; and where the wandering bands of Huns had made alliance with the Sarmatians; and where the Getae with their Alan friends used to attack the Danube—for victory borne on swift wings me the news of this), lo now the Emperor comes to grace my dignity, and with his favor crowns the distinction which he would fain have shared.[93]

It perhaps would be wrong to attach too great importance to the differentiation between Sauromatae and Alani and the alleged alliance between the barbarians, though the Sarmatians, attacked by the Goths, actually might have turned to the Huns for help. The victories cannot have been as decisive as they looked from far-away Trier—for the war went on.

---

[90] Socrates V, 6, 572; Sozomen VII, 4.

[91] *Ep.* I, 95.

[92] Pacatus XI, 4.

[93] *Praecatio consulis designati pridie Kal. Ian. fascibus sumptis* 31-35. I follow the text and translation of H. G. E. White, *Loeb* I, 51-52. For another translation, see Jasinski 1935, 1, 35-37. The reading of v. 33 is not quite certain. Toll (1671, 345, n.14) suggested *Sauromatae . . . Chunus*; Schenkl, *MGH AA* V, 2, 18, note, *sua iunxerat agmina Chunis*. The meaning, however, is clear.

Gratian stayed in Sirmium throughout February and the first half of March. On April 5, he was in Tricciana,[94] the present Ságvár, a town on the road from Sopiana to Arrabona, about 10 miles south of the north-western shore of Lake Balaton.[95] What he did in northern Pannonia we again learn from a few passages in Ausonius. The Gallic rhetor may have somewhat exaggerated the emperor's exploits but he did not invent them, as the outcome of the fighting shows. In the thanksgiving for his con-sulship, addressed to Gratian at Trier at the end of 379,[96] Ausonius extols the young ruler for having "pacified in a single year the Danubian and the Rhenish frontiers."[97] He hails him as *Sarmaticus* "because he has conquered and forgiven [*vincendo et ignoscendo*] that people."[98] In an epigram Ausonius praises Gratian, who "midst arms and Huns ferocious and Sauromatae dangerous in stealth, whatever rest he had from hours of war, in camp he lavished it all on the Clarian muses."[99] In a nightmare Ausonius saw himself as a disarmed Alan prisoner of war dragged through the streets.[100]

By the middle of June the situation had so much improved that Gratian could hand over the command to one of his generals and leave for Italy.[101] Besides, the new uprising of the Alamanni in the West required his pre-sence on the Rhine.

Hunnic Pressure on the Lower Danube

We need not follow the struggle between the Visigoths and Theodosius' armies. If there were still Huns among the barbarians, they were at the most a few stragglers who had been separated from their hordes, or broken men. But the Hunnic danger was by no means over. In the winter 381/2, Sciri and Carpodacians, "mixed with Huns," crossed the Danube,

---

[94] Seeck 1919, 109, convincingly amended *Triv.* in the subscription of *Cod. Theodos.* XI, 36, 26, into *Tricc.*, i.e., *Tricciana*.

[95] A. Graf 1936, 122-123.

[96] Jouai 1938, 235-238, contra Rauschen 1897, 27, 44-45, who dated the poem, less probably, in September.

[97] *Gratiarum Actio ad Gratianum Imperatorem pro consulatu* II, 7-8.

[98] The Alans, whom Gratian "at an enormous price" won to his side (*Epit. de caes.* XLVII, 6; Zosimus IV, 35, 2), were probably among those whom he "forgave." Gratian was so fond of the Alans that he sometimes wore their dress. When he fled from Paris to Lyon, he had barely three hundred horsemen with him; the army almost to the last man had gone over to Maximus. The loyal horsemen were evidently the emperor's beloved Alans.

[99] *Epigr.* XXVI, 8-10, written 379 (Jouai 1938, 241).

[100] *Ephemeris* 7 (8), 17-18. On the date, end of 379 or 380, see Pichon 1906, 309-312.

[101] At the beginning of July, Gratian was in Aquileia (Seeck 1919, 250).

to be driven back after a few skirmishes.[102] The episode seems to be significant only insofar as it shows that the Huns were unable to prevent more active tribes north of the Danube from acting on their own. Yet Theodosius could not have failed to realize that the terrible horsemen who had made themselves masters, though as yet not absolute masters, of the teeming mass of barbarians in "Scythia" might someday prove to be a greater danger to his *pars* than the Goths. He made peace with the Visigoths in the fall of 382.

Weakened by epidemics,[103] their bands thinned out by desertions, deadly tired of incessantly moving from place to place, the Visigoths were more than willing to come to some agreement with the emperor. They wanted land to settle and, if they could get them, subsidies. Theodosius wanted soldiers. The peace treaty gave the Goths large tracts in Moesia inferior and eastern Dacia ripensis;[104] it gave the emperor troops to guard the Danube from Oescus (on the Danube near the confluence with the river Golem Iskr) to Durostorum. Themistius' New Year's address of January 1, 383, must not be taken literally. After his experiences with the barbarians Theodosius could not have expected that, like the Celts in Galatia,[105] the Goths would become good and law-abiding Roman cit-

---

[102] Zosimus IV, 34, 6, p. 190. The date is not quite certain. Zosimus places the short campaign between the submission of Athanaric and his retainers (Athanaric died shortly afterward, on January 25, 381) and Promotus' victory over the Greuthungi in 386. As a rule, the transdanubian barbarians timed their raids so that they crossed the river as soon as it was frozen in order to recross it with their booty before the thaw set in. In the second half of December and in January of the years 383, 384, and 385, Theodosius was in Constantinople. But he issued no laws between January 13 and February 20, 382, time enough to rush to the frontier and drive the robbers back, provided he actually took part in the action. In 381, the Huns on the lower Danube apparently kept quiet. Terentius, bishop of Tomis in Scythia minor, left his flock to take part in the council at Constantinople. Cf. N. Q. King, *TU* 63, 1937, 635-641, which indicates that at the time Scythia minor was comparatively safe.

The Sciri, probably the descendants of those named in the famous Protagenes inscription, cannot be localized. Carpodaci means Daci in the land of the Carpi; cf. U. Kahrstedt, *Prähist. Zeitschr.* 4, 1912, 83-87.

[103] "The Goths were perturbed and terrified not by groundless fear nor by unnecessary suspicion but because of a raging epidemic and an excessively hot and unhealthy climate. Lastly they then fled in order to escape; afterward they returned and asked for peace in order to live" (*Non enim inani metu, nec superflua suspicione, sed saeviente lue et ardenti pestilentia perturbati Gothi ac territi sunt. Denique tunc fugerunt, ut vaederent; regressi postea pacem rogaverunt, ut viverent*), (Ambrose, *Ep.* XV, *PL* 16, 989; written early in 383, Palanque 1933, 508-509.)

[104] Schmidt 1934, 185.

[105] *Or.* XVI (Themistius), 121c, d.

izens. But he certainly hoped they would serve him as a defense.[106] A year before, Athanaric's retainers were settled on the right bank of the river "to prevent any incursions being made against the Romans."[107] Zosimus, like Themistius, did not name the potential enemy. Eunapius of Sardes was explicit. The emperor, he wrote, gave the Goths cattle and land, expecting them to form "an unconquerable bulwark against the inroads of the Huns."[108] As federates the Visigoths were bound to serve whenever and wherever they were called, but their main and permanent assignment was to defend themselves. By fighting for their new home, they fought for Rome. As long as they held the watch on the Danube, the northern Balkan provinces, except easternmost Scythia minor, seemed to be safe. For a few, all too few years, the Roman population in the ravaged towns and villages enjoyed a modicum of peace. In 384 or 385 a barbarian horde crossed the frozen Danube near its mouth and took Halmyris.[109] But this was outside the Gothic territory. Shortly afterwards Hunnic hordes raided Scythia.[110]

In 386, again to the east and west of the Gothic watch on the Danube, barbarians struck, in some parts deeply, into Roman lands. An edict of July 29, 386, gives a strange picture of the situation in the Balkans: "Because the procurators of the mines within Macedonia, Dacia mediterranea, Moesia, and Dardania,[111] who are customarily appointed from the decurions and who exact the usual tax collections, have removed themselves from this compulsory public service by pretending fear of the enemy [*simulato hostili metu*], they shall be dragged back to the fulfillment of their duties."[112] The procurators were certainly willing to use any excuse for shirk-

---

[106] *Ibid.*, 212a.

[107] Zosimus IV, 34, 5.

[108] Fr. 43, *FHG* IV, 33. The fragment does not, as if often assumed, refer to 376 but to 382. In 376, the Goths were not given land and cattle. It was only in 382 that they went—for awhile, at least—behind the plough in Thrace; *Or.* XVII (Themistius), 212a, b.

[109] Philostorgius, *Hist. eccles.* X, 6, pp. 127-128. At the time of the raid Eunomius was in Halmyris, where he was exiled after the death of Gratian (X, 5), at the latest at the beginning of 385. He was sent to Caesarea in Cappadocia before the death of Flacilla (X, 7). Flacilla died before the winter of 386 (Seeck, *Geschichte* 5, 521). This raid has been strangely misdated and misplaced. Güldenpenning (1885) dated it in the winter, 381/2; Rauschen (1897, 198) confused it with the invasion of the Greuthungi in 386; Seeck, *Geschichte* 5, 519) thought the barbarians were the Sarmatians against whom Bauto fought, but that was in Hungary whereas Halmyris was in the Dobrogea.

[110] Callinicus LXI. Thompson 1948, 36, erroneously dated the raid in 395; he overlooked that it took place in Hypatius' twentieth year, i.e., 385 or 386.

[111] On the mines in the Balkan peninsula, cf. Cantacuzène 1928, 75ff.

[112] *Cod. Theodos.* I, 32, 5 = *Cod. Iust.* XI, 7, 4.

ing their most unpleasant duties, but they could not invent an enemy if there was none. The sequence in which the four provinces are named leaves no doubt that it was the Morava-Vardar Valley in which the enemy operated; that they could spread fear as far as Macedonia shows that the raiders were swift-riding horsemen. They may not have been many; still they were strong enough to overrun the Roman troops, probably by-passing fortified places, and returning unmolested with their booty from where they came. There was no other enemy then and there which could make such raids into the western Balkans but the transdanubian Huns.

The invaders in the East were Germans. In the summer of 386, Greuthungi, led by Odotheus, and their allies appeared on the left bank of the lower Danube and asked Promotus, master of the soldiers in Thrace, for permission to cross the river; they wanted land for settlement. When their request was rejected, they tried to force their way into the empire. Promotus inflicted a crushing defeat on them.[113]

Zosimus, following two sources, tells the same event twice. He gives a detailed account of the stratagem by which Promotus deceived the barbarians; the poet Claudian indulges in a gory description of the slaughter of the Greuthungi. But neither of these two authors, shows any interest in the antecedents of the short war: it was just another outbreak of the well-known "insanity" of the savages. Though unlikely, it is not impossible that Zosimus' sources contained more about the Greuthungi and the reasons why they trekked south. For it was a trek, the migration of a very large group of peoples in search of a new home. Zosimus stresses that they had their wives and children with them. How many they were we are not told. Claudian certainly exaggerates the number of boats manned by the flower of barbarian youth and sunk by the Romans. But even if their number was not three thousand, as he wrote, but only one thousand, with no more than three or four men in each, we would arrive at a figure of close to ten thousand arms-bearing men. A German army could number a quarter or a fifth of the population. However, even if the Greuthungi, together with all the tribes and fractions of tribes which joined them,[114] numbered not fifty but thirty or twenty thousand (both of Zosimus' sources call them "an immense horde"), the fact that such a great mass was able to defy their Hun lords and break through to the Danube is most significant.

---

[113] Claudian, *4th Cons. Hon.* 623-635; Zosimus IV, 35 and 38-39. The chroniclers (*CM* I, 386; II, 62) have only a few lines.

[114] From verses 22-28 in Claudian's *3rd Cons. Hon.*, nothing can be learned about the allies of the Greuthungi. Honorius, born September 9, 384, was still crawling when his father "came home victorius from his conquest over the tribes of the Danube" and

In 381, five years before, a few Huns had joined the Sciri and Carpodacians on a quick looting expedition. This time it was a whole people, led by an Ostrogothic prince,[115] that threw off the Hunnic yoke. No wonder that Cassiodorus-Jordanes ignores the trek of the Greuthungi: The other Ostrogoths, those who followed the Amalungs, Cassiodorus records, did not dare to rise against the Huns. Unfortunately, we know nothing about the circumstances under which the Greuthungi were able to escape the Huns. There might have been dissension among their masters; perhaps those Huns who ruled over the Greuthungi were engaged in a looting expedition in the north. But the fact remains that many thousand of the "human cattle" broke through the Hunnic fences. Hun power in the plains north of the lower Danube was still not firmly established.

Hunnic Horsemen Ride to Gaul

The situation at the borders of Pannonia and in the plain east of the Danube remained fluid also. Only a small part of the Sarmatians made peace with the Romans. The war with the others lasted throughout 383.[116] Whether the victory that Valentinian's troops[117] won over the elusive enemy in the spring of 384 was as decisive as it looked to the spectators in the Colosseum[118] in Rome is rather doubtful. The continuous attempts

---

brought him "Scythian bows, belts won from the Geloni, a Dacian spear, or Suebian bridle." The Scythians are evidently the Greuthungi; cf. *In Eutrop.* II, 180, where the Greuthungus Tarbigilus is called a Scythian. On the Geloni, see n. 165. The Dacians are named because they lived north of the river. The longhaired Suebus is, as in *4th Cons. Hon.* 655, the symbol of the unconquered Germans. Claudian transferred the Suebi from the West to the East, as he also did in *Bell. Gild.* 37. For the buckles and belt plaques studded with jewels, cf. *Cons. Stil.* II, 88; *Carm. min.* XXIX, 12; *Rapt. Pros.* II, 94 (*Parthica quae tantis variantur cingula gemmis*); they were not characteristic of any particular barbarian people.

[115] Odotheus = *Audatius (Schönfeld 1911).

[116] "Already before, the Roman people had explicitly agreed to the burial of the slain Sarmati" (*Dudum fando acceperat Romanus populus caesorum funera Sarmatarum*). (Symmachus, *Rel.* II, 47, *MGH AA* 6, 1, 315-316.) For the date, the summer of 384, see Seeck, *Geschichte* 5, 195, 512; cf. also McGeachy 1942, 102. In Symmachus, *dudum* means as a rule "for years"; cf. Hartke 1940, 89-90.

[117] Seeck, *Geschichte* 5, 208, suggested that they were under the command of Bauto. This is unlikely. As long as the tension between Maximus and the court in Milan lasted, the place of the generalissimo was in Italy, not at the Danube.

[118] "We have seen the host of the conquered nation led in chains and those so savage faces changed by a wretched pallor" (*Vidimus catenatum agmen victae gentis induci illosque tam truces vultus misero pallore*), (Symmachus, *Rel.* II, 47, *MGH AA* 6, 1, 315-316). The edict of January 30, 400 (*Cod. Theodos.* VII, 20, 12), provides for the drafting

of the Sarmatians to cross to the right bank of the Danube have their parallel in the migration of Odotheus' Greuthungi; they, too, seemed to have tried to shake off the Huns and find new pastures. Of the Huns themselves we get only a glimpse.

In the spring of 384, Hunnic horsemen rode through Noricum and Raetia towards Gaul, allies of the legitimate ruler, barbarians thrown against barbarians, called forth from their tents in the East as they were to be called so often afterward. The only source for the first appearance of the Huns in western Europe is a short passage in a letter of Bishop Ambrose to Valentinian II.[119] It is not easy to date. Ambrose alludes to events of which we know little or nothing. Yet in view of the absence of any other information about the Huns in those years, even the smallest bit of information is of value.

On his return from Trier to Milan in December 383,[120] Ambrose met in southern Gaul the troops of the usurper Maximus. They were on the march to occupy the passes over the Maritime Alps and the blocks along the Riviera. In Italy Ambrose saw the imperial army on its way in the opposite direction with the same destination. In the four months that had elapsed since Gratian was murdered, Maximus had made himself the undisputed master of Gaul; he could have invaded Italy anytime, and would not have hesitated could he have been sure that he had to fight there only the troops of Gratian's little brother Valentinian or, rather, of Bauto, his Frankish generalissimo.

Bauto was an experienced and resourceful soldier but his troops were few and, except for the Gothic mercenaries, not reliable. On the one side stood Maximus, a most orthodox man; on the other, the Arian empress-dowager Justina—the boy Valentinian did not count—and the pagan Bauto. When four years later Maximus marched into Italy, he met practically no resistance. Bauto's army would have fought better in 383 and 384, before Justina began to "persecute" the orthodox majority of her subjects, but it almost certainly would have been defeated had Maximus

---

of Laeti, Alamanni, Sarmatians, vagrants, sons of veterans, persons who "are subject to draft and ought to be enlisted in our most excellent legions." The Sarmatians were evidently those in Italy and Gaul under the command of special *praefecti* (*Not. Dign.* [*occ.*] XLII, 33-70). It is unlikely that nearly all those Sarmatian settlements were established long before Gratian, as Barkóczi (1959, 7:4, 444-446, 452-453) assumes ; quite a number of them must have included those Sarmatians who fought the Romans as late as the 380's.

[119] *Ep.* XXV-XXVIII, *PL* 16, 1081-1082.
[120] Palanque 1933, 510.

decided to march. It was only the fear of Theodosius, ruler of the East, that held Maximus back. It was only the hope for help from the East that kept Bauto up. Maximus knew that an attack on Italy meant war with Theodosius. Bauto displayed all his forces along the western frontier; their task was to hold out as well as they could until Theodosius' armies joined the battle.

Maximus *did* strike, but not at Italy. He instigated the Juthungi to reassume their raids into Raetia.[121] Still suffering from their defeats in 378 and 379, kept in check by the greatly strengthened garrisons along the *limes Raticus*,[122] the Juthungi did not move until the summer of 383. At that time, when a terrible famine hit a vast part of the Western empire, and particularly Italy,[123] "the second Raetia learned the danger of her own fertility. For being used to security from her own poverty, she drew an enemy on herself by her abundance."[124] The invaders were the Juthungi. Gratian was about to march against them when the greater danger in the West forced him to leave the defense of the province to the troops stationed there and throw the mobile army into Gaul to stop Maximus.[125]

In the first month of 384, the Juthungi were preparing a new attack. It is unlikely that Maximus concluded a formal alliance with the barbarians; all they needed was the consent, perhaps even only the tacit consent, of Maximus to the invasion of Raetia. If they pressed the attack, if they crossed the Alpine passes, Bauto was lost. Maximus could just walk into Italy, not as aggressor but as savior of the Roman world from the barbarians.

It was then that Bauto turned to the Huns and Alans.[126] From Ambrose's letter we learn nothing about the strength of the Hunnic and Alanic cavalry, the men who led them, the battles they fought. He speaks only

---

[121] Ambrose, *Ep.* XXV-XXVIII, *PL* 16, 1081-1082.

[122] *Cod. Theodos.* XI, 16, 15, of December 9, 382.

[123] Palanque 1931, 346-356.

[124] Ambrose, *Ep.* XVIII, XXIII, *PL* 16.

[125] According to Socrates (V, 11, 2), followed by Sozomen (VII, 13, 1), and John of Antioch (fr. 78, *EL* 116). Maximus "rebelled against the Roman Empire and attacked Gratian, who was wearied in a war with the Alamanni." This cannot be true. On June 16, Gratian was still in Verona. He was assassinated in Lyon on August 25. Gratian must have arrived in northern Gaul in the first week of August at the latest. This would leave about fifty days for the march from Verona across the Brenner Pass into Raetia, the war with the Juthungi, and the march from the Danube to Paris, an impossibility; cf. Rauschen 1897, 142.

[126] *Chuni atque Alani. . . Adversus Iuthungum Chunus accitus est.* The edition of the Benedictines of St. Maur, reprinted by Migne, has *Hunni* and *Hunnus.* The only work of Ambrose available in a critical edition in which the ethnic name occurs is *De Tobia.* There it is spelled *Chunus.* This was most probably also the spelling in the letter.

in passing about their triumphs. It seems that they crushed the Juthungi in one great sweep. Their task was fulfilled. The Juthungian danger was removed. The Huns could return to their country.

But they did not return. They kept riding west, "approaching Gaul" (*appropinquantes Galliae*). When the news reached Milan, Bauto must have been horrified. Athough Theodosius had decided to defend Italy, he was anything but willing to assist Bauto in an attack on Maximus. If the Huns, Bauto's allies, broke into Gaul, Maximus must take this as an open declaration of war. They had to be stopped, and they were. Bauto purchased the retreat of the federates with gold.[127] Again we are not told how much he paid them, but it may be assumed that they were richly compensated for the loss of booty they could have expected to make in Gaul. The Huns turned and rode home.[128]

In the history of the late Roman Empire all this would not deserve more than two lines; but for the study of the Huns the episode of 384 is of considerable importance. We can draw from it the following conclusions:

In one passage Ambrose names the Huns first, the Alans second, and in another one only the Huns, so the Huns were apparently not only the stronger but also the dominating group.

The Huns to whom Bauto turned for help cannot have lived deep in the barbaricum, far to the east. If their sites were not already west of the Danube, which is possible, they must have lived along or very close to the left bank of the river. As early as 384, large tracts of the Hungarian plain were held by the Huns and their Alanic allies.

The *ductus* of the Hun *primates* was not *tumultuarius*. As in 378, they made an agreement with a non-Hunnic power; they assembled the horse-

---

[127] *Tu [sc.* Maxime] *fecisti incursari Rhetia, Valentinianus suo tibi auro pacem redemit (Ep.* XXIV, 8, *PL* 16, 1081-1082). Ambrose knew, of course, that Valentinian bought peace for himself, not the murderer of his brother.

[128] The intervention of the Huns took place after Ambrose's first embassy to Trier in the last month of 383 and before the second embassy of which he gave an account in *Ep.* XXIV. The letter has been dated in the winter of 384/5 (Rauschen 1897, 487), 386 (Richterm Ihm, Förster, quoted in Rauschen 1897, 487; Palanque 1933, 516-518; Dudden 1925, 345), and 387 (Tillemont 1738). Stein (1959, 1, 312, n. 4) thought it impossible to determine whether Ambrose went on his second embassy before the middle of 384, or toward the end of the year, or early in 385. But at the end of *Ep.* XXIV, which Ambrose sent to Milan while he was still on his journey back, he implored Valentinian "to be on his guard against a man who concealed war under the cloak of peace." With the conclusion of a *foedus* between Theodosius and Maximus (Pacatus XXX) in August 384 (Seeck, *Geschichte* 5, 197, fn. pp. 513-514), the danger of an invasion of Italy was for the time being removed. It follows that Ambrose was in Trier in the spring or early summer of 384; cf. Seeck, *Geschichte* 5, 515; J. H. van Haeringen, *Mnemosyne* 1937, 233-239. In other words, the Huns were in Raetia in the early months of 384.

men, this time many more than in 378; they led them hundreds of miles through unknown lands. It would be absurd to suppose that Bauto's emissaries paid each Hun so and so many solidi. The gold was received by the Hun leaders. How they distributed it among their followers we do not know. But that they could keep their promise to ride back, although the temptation for a good number of the barbarians to take the money and continue looting must have been great, proves that the horsemen were firmly in their hands. These leaders, whatever their position, were men of authority.

Our information about the Huns, both west and east of the Carpathians, after 386 is even scantier than what we could extract from the very few sources so far. All we have are brief allusions in poetical works.

When in the summer of 387 Maximus offered to send a body of troops[129] from Gaul to Italy to assist Valentinian against the barbarians who were threatening Pannonia,[130] the situation along the middle Danube must have been very serious. Only the danger that the frontier defense might collapse completely and the barbarians pour into Italy itself could compel Valentinian, who had all the reasons to mistrust the unexpected readiness of his brother's murderer to help him, to accept the offer. Within a few weeks the "auxiliary" troops were, indeed, followed by Maximus' whole army, and Valentinian had to flee to Constantinople.

Zosimus, the only source for these events, wrote what his public expected from him. He did not say who the enemies were, where they attacked, and what the outcome of the fighting was. His readers were interested only incidentally in history; they wanted to hear court gossip and malicious anti-Christian anecdotes. Neither did the pious crowd which filled the cathedral in Milan care who were the savages against whom the soldiers of their emperor or, for that matter, those of the other one in Gaul were fighting. In his sermons at Whitsuntide 387, Ambrose called them simply *barbarus hostis*.[131] Fortunately, Pacatus is, though in a roundabout way, very explicit.

As is known, his *Panegyric on Theodosius* is the main source for the campaign against Maximus in 388. The army that the emperor assembled consisted almost wholly of barbarians. Theodosius made careful diplomatic and military preparations; the peace with Persia was renewed,[132]

---

[129] Seeck, *Geschichte* 5, 219, 519; Stein 1959, 1, 316.

[130] Zosimus IV, 42, 5. The Paiones were Pannonians (see fn. 74), not the inhabitants of Paionia in Macedonia as Mazzarino (1942, 43-44) asserts.

[131] *Apologia Prophetae David* XXVII, *PL* 14, 903; for the date, see Palanque 1933, 178-181 and 520-521; Dudden 1925, 1, 688, 713.

[132] In 387 or 388 (Güldenpenning 1885, 154; Rauschen 1897, 258-259).

the Saracens were appeased.[133] Theodosius "accepted the barbarian peoples who vowed to lend him their help as fellow combatants."[134] In concluding alliances with them, he not only removed the threat to the frontiers, he also increased the strength of his forces sufficiently to avoid the need to draft Roman citizens.

The barbarian horsemen fought magnificently. This was to be expected. But what surprised all who knew their barbarians was the exemplary discipline they held. "The army"—it is Christ who addresses the emperor[135]—"gathered from many unsubdued nations, I bade to keep faith, tranquillity, and concord as if of one nation." Pacatus has nothing but praise for the allies:

> O memorable thing: There marched under Roman leaders and banners as Romans those who before had been our enemies, following the signs against which they had stood, and as soldiers filled the cities of Pannonia which they had emptied with fiendish devastation. Goths and Huns and Alans answered the roll call, changed guards, and rarely feared to be reprimanded. There was no tumult, no confusion, no looting in the usual barbarian way.[136]

In another passage Pacatus refers to the allies as barbarians who came "from the threatening Caucasus and the iced Taurus and the Danube which hardens the gigantic bodies." The last ones are evidently the Goths. Causasus and Taurus are not the mountains from which the Huns and Alans descended to join Theodosius but their original homes "somewhere in the east."[137]

Theodosius marched from Thessalonica up the Vardar and Morava valleys to Singidunum (modern Belgrade) and from there westward along the Sava to Siscia (modern Sisak, Yugovlavia), where he inflicted the first defeat on Maximus' troops. The second battle took place near Poetovio (modern Ptuj, Yugoslavia). The road from Singidunum via Siscia to Poetovio leads through Pannonia secunda and Savia. The towns which the Goths, Huns, and Alans raided before 388 were in those two provinces.

---

[133] Pacatus XXXII, 2; cf. Galletier 1949, 98, n. 3.

[134] *Uti limiti manus suspecta decederet* (Pacatus XXXII, 2). This phrase alone proves that the barbarians, *omnes Scythicae nationes*, were not federates in Pannonia; they came from beyond the borders (Alföldi 1926, 68; L. Schmidt 1934, 261).

[135] Ambrose, *Ep.* XL, 22, *PL* 16, 1109.

[136] Pacatus XXXII, 4-5.

[137] Taurus and Caucasus form one big mountain range (Pliny, *HN* VI, 37; Solinus XXXVIII, 10-13; *Getica* 7). The Caucasus is a part of the Taurus (Orosius, *Hist. adv. Pagan.* I, 42, 36-37). The sources of the Tanais are in the Caucasus, which is the northermost part of the Taurus (Dionysius, *Perieg.* LXVI).

It is most unlikely that Valeria had been immune to their inroads. In 387, the barbarians must have penetrated deep into Pannonia prima. Ambrose would not have spoken about a few marauders at the Danube; they would not have prompted Valentinian to accept Maximus' help.

Pacatus' testimony bears out the conclusions drawn here from Ambrose's letter: Eastern Hungary was Hun land. It certainly was not one great pasture for the herds and flocks of the Huns alone; there were also Alans and Goths, allied or subject to the Huns, Jazygian Sarmatians, Germanic tribes, and the aboriginal Illyric population. But the Huns were the lords.

If in 388 Huns fought for the Romans, four years later Hunnic horsemen ravaged again the unfortunate Balkan provinces. From Claudian's *In Rufinum* and his *Panegyric on Stilicho's Consulship*, we learn that Huns crossed the Danube and joined the German enemies of the Romans. Claudian's poems, the one a vitriolic invective, the other a hyperbolic eulogy, are not exactly reliable sources for the dark period that followed Theodosius' victory over Maximus. Still, Claudian is a paragon of exactitude compared with Zosimus, whose anecdotic account permits the reconstruction of the events of those years barely in their broadest outlines.

A good number of barbarians, apparently mainly Visigoths, deserted the imperial standards on the eve of the campaign in 388 and turned robbers. For almost four years they terrorized Macedonia, pillaging farms, investing highways, swiftly rushing out from their hiding places in the swamps and forests and as swiftly disappearing "like ghosts."[138] Their ranks, swelled by more deserters after the end of the war in Italy, grew into large and well-organized bands, like the Vargi and Scamarae half a century later. In the summer of 391, the situation became so desperate that Theodosius granted civilians the right of using arms against the brigands,[139] a bold measure when one considers how easily the miners and other proletarians could have joined the bands as they had joined the Goths in 378.

In the fall the emperor himself took the field. Already the first encounters proved that the local forces were insufficient; after a severe defeat in which he almost lost his life, Theodosius called in reinforcements from the army in Thrace. The result was that large hordes of transdanubian barbarians broke through the *limes* and poured deep into the plain north of the Haemus (Balkans). What until then was a punitive expedition, though on a great scale, became a horrible war.[140] Jerome was not sure

---

[138] Zosimus IV, 48-50; cf. also Eunapius, fr. 58 and 60.

[139] *Cod. Theodos.* IX, 14, 2.

[140] In the standard histories, the war of 391-392 is barely mentioned. The leader of the Visigoths was possibly Alaric (Mazzarino 1942, 256; Demougeot, 1947, 115).

that in the end the Goths might not conquer.[141] John Chrysostom's letter to a young widow gives an idea of the magnitude of the catastrophe that befell Thrace. He consoled her by pointing out how much more miserable women like the empress were. Theodosius' wife

is ready to die of fear, and spends her time more miserably than criminals condemned to death because her husband ever since he assumed the crown up to the present day has been constantly engaged in warfare and fighting. . . . For that which has never taken place has now come to pass; the barbarians leaving their own country have overrun an infinite space of our territory, and that many times over, and having set fire to the land, and captured the towns, they are not minded to return home again, but after the manner of men who are keeping holiday rather than making war, they laugh us all to scorn. It is said that one of their kings declared that he was amazed at the impudence of our soldiers, who although slaughtered more easily than sheep still expect to conquer, and are not willing to quit their own country, for he said that he himself was satiated with the work of cutting them to pieces.[142]

Theodosius returned to Constantinople in 391, "so depressed at what he and his army had suffered from the barbarians in the marshes that he decided to renounce wars and battle, committing the management of those affairs to Promotus."[143] The experienced general had no better luck. Whether the enemy was actually as strong as Claudian indicates is not known. He never gives numbers in his poems; instead he heaps names upon names. In the invective against Rufinus Claudian lists Getae, Sarmatae, Daci, Massagetae, Alani, and Geloni,[144] in the *Panegyric on Stilicho*, written three years later, Visi, Bastarnae, Alani, *Huns*, Geloni,

---

[141] *Scio quendam Gog et Magog tam de praesenti quam de Ezechiel ad Gothorum nuper in terra nostra vagantium historiam retulisse; quod utrum verum sit, proelii ipsius fine monstrabitur* (Jerome, *Hebraicae quaestiones in libro geneseos* X, 21, CCSL LXII, 11). *Monstrabitur*, the reading in the Codex Monacensis 6299, formerly known as Frisingensis 99, saec. VIII-IX, is preferable to *monstratur* in the later codices. The war was still going on.

[142] *Ad viduam iunioram* IV, PG 48, 605. The date, between May and June 392, has been definitely established by G. Brunner, *Zeitschrift für katholische Theologie* 65, 1941, 32-35. Brunner's article escaped the attention of G. H. Ettlinger, who dates the treatise to 380-381 (*Traditio* 16, 1960, 374). The inscription on the equestrian statue of Theodosius, erected after the war, goes beyond the usual auxesis of the deeds of the hero; the emperor "destroyed the Scythians in Thrace" (*Revue des études grecques* 9, 1896, 43).

[143] Zosimus IV, 50, 1.

[144] *In Ruf.* I, 305-313.

Getae, and Sarmatae.[145] Promotus was killed in an encounter with the Bastarnae. Stilicho, his successor, is said to have scattered the Visigoths, and overthrown the Bastarnae;[146] he would have annihilated the barbarian hordes, penned in the limits of a small valley, "had not a traitor [Rufinus] by a perfidious trick abused the emperor's ear and caused him to withhold his hand; hence the sheathing of the sword, the raising of the siege, and the granting of treaties to the prisoners."[147]

Rufinus acted as did Stilicho three years later and again in 402 when he made a compact with the Visigoth king Alaric and allowed him to withdraw. What Claudian said in praise of Stilicho, he could have said about Rufinus: "Concern for thee, O Rome, constrained us to offer a way to escape to the beleaguered foe lest, with the fear of death before their eyes, their rage should grow the more terrible for being confined."[148] The "prisoners" with whom Rufinus, clearly with the consent of Theodosius if not at the emperor's direct instructions, concluded alliances were Goths and Huns.[149] What the conditions of the *foedera* were, Claudian does not say. But many of the Huns did not ride back to their tents across the Danube; they stayed, as we shall see, in Thrace.

In the summer of 394, Theodosius again led an army against an usurper in the West, Eugenius. It was at least as strong as the one with which he had taken the field in 388. "The fortunes of Rome stood at a razor's edge."[150] It was not, as six years earlier, a war between the legitimate ruler and an usurper; it was a war between Christ and Jupiter, the monks of the Thebais and Etruscan augurs, the God-loving East and the idol-worshippers of the West. Eugenius fought for the gods, and the gods fought for him. His soldiers carried on their standards the picture of Hercules Invictus[151] and on the height of the Julian Alps stood golden statues of

---

145 *Cons. Stil.* I, 94-96.

146 *In Ruf.* I, 317; Zosimus IV, 51.

147 *Cons. Stil.* I, 112-115.

148 *Bell. Goth.* 96-98.

149 *In Ruf.* I, 320-322, is a difficult passage: Rufinus *distulit instantes . . . pugnas/ Hunorum laturus opem, quos adfore bello/norat et invisis mox se coniungere castris.* Platnauer, *Loeb* I, 49, translates *Hunorum laturus opem* by "meaning to ally himself with the Huns," which is impossible. St. Axelson (*Studia Claudianea,* 23-24) assumes that *Hunorum laturus opem* is late Latin for *Hunis laturus opem*; this is entirely without foundation. At my request, Professor Harry L. Levy analyzed the passage in its context and rendered it by "postponed the impending battle, intending to give [to the Goths] the aid of the Huns, who he had ascertained would join the war and soon associate themselves with the camp [of the Goths] hated [by the Romans]." Approximately the same interpretation had been suggested by Gesner in his edition of Claudian (1749). It seems that the Goths and the Huns fought their own wars.

150 [*Reference missing in manuscript.—Ed.*]

151 Theodoret, *Hist. eccles.,* V, 24, 4, 17.

Jupiter,[152] ready to throw their thunderbolts at the Galilaeans should they dare to approach the sacred soil of Italy. In Rome, Nicomachus Flavianus, the leader of the turbulent pagan revival, read the coming victory of Eugenius in the entrails of the sacrificed bulls;[153] in Constantinople, Theodosius waited anxiously for an answer from the prophetic hermit John of Lycopolis as to whether he or the godless tyrant would win the war.[154] He prayed and fasted. "He was prepared for war not so much with the aid of arms and missiles as of fasts and prayers" (*Praeparatus ad bellum non tamen armorum talorumque quam ieiuniorum orationumque subsidiis*), said Rufinus,[155] and all Christian authors are agreed that it was the power of God which granted Theodosius the glorious victory over the pagans. Ambrose compared him with Moses, Joshua, Samuel, and David.[156] Yet when the emperor finally went to war he did not carry a sling; he marched at the head of a huge army.

Theodosius busied himself through the winter of 393/4 with elaborate military preparations.[157] His recruiting officers in the East enlisted Armenians, Caucasian mountaineers, and Arabs. The Visigothic allies were ordered to furnish as many troops as they could. Even if those did not number more than twenty thousand, as Jordanes asserts,[158] they must have formed a large contingent.[159] Alans came, led by Saul,[160] whom we shall meet soon again. And then came, to strengthen God's warriors, "many of the Huns of Thrace with their phylarchoi."[161]

The chronicler John of Antioch is the only one to mention the Huns. It is understandable that the church historians passed them over in silence; they were not interested in the composition of the auxiliaries.[162] That Jordanes spoke only of the Goths is in no way remarkable. But the absence of the Huns from the long list of peoples in Claudian requires an explanation.

---

[152] Augustine, *De civ. Dei* V, 26.
[153] Sozomenus VII, 22.
[154] Rufinus, *Hist. eccles.* XI, 33, *PL* 21, 539; Sozomenus, VII, 22.
[155] *Ibid.*
[156] *Ep.* LXII, 4, *PL* 16, 1239.
[157] Philostorgius, *Hist. eccles.* XI, 2.
[158] *Getica* 145.
[159] According to Crosius (*Hist. adv. Pagan* VII), thirty-five more than ten thousand Goths were killed in the battle on the Frigidus; the number is grossly exaggerated.
[160] Zosimus IV, 37; John of Antioch, fr. 187, *EI* 119.
[161] John of Antioch, fr. 187, *EI* 119.
[162] "Barbarian auxiliaries," Theodoret, *Hist. eccles.* V, 24, 3; "many barbarian auxiliaries from beyond the Ister," Socrates V, 25; "from the banks of the Ister," Sozomenus VII, 24.

The poet names Arabs, Armenians, Orientals from the Euphrates, Halys and Orontes, Colchi, Iberians, Medes from the Caspian Sea, Parthians from the Niphates, and even Sacae and Indians.[163] He mentions the Goths and, by a circumscription,[164] the Alans. But the Huns do not exist for him, although he must have known that they fought for Theodosius. He may barely allude to them by listing the Geloni among the auxiliaries.[165]

One could think that by ignoring the Huns Claudian expresses his abhorrence of those lowest of the barbarians, his reluctance to give them any credit for the victory of the good cause. But I believe the close relationship between the Huns and the hated Rufinus was the real, or at least, the stronger motive. It is true that Claudian depicts Rufinus in the blackest colors as the devoted friend of the Goths. But when Stilicho, at Rufinus' orders, had to give up the command of the Eastern troops, these were not, as one would expect, afraid that now the Goths would be their masters. They feared, rather, that Rufinus would make them "the slaves of the foul Hun or the restless Alan."[166] This is strange. The only explanation of which I could think would be Rufinus' decision to rely on the Huns and Alans to counterbalance the power of the Goths. It would have been not the most pleasant, but certainly the most efficient means. A few years later the anti-Gothic faction in Constantinople played, indeed, with the idea of allying itself with the Huns against the Goths,

---

[163] *Bell. Gild.* 243-245; *3rd Cons. Hon.* 68-72; *Cons. Stil.* I, 154-158.

[164] *Bell. Gild.* 245.

[165] It is doubtful that behind Claudian's Geloni a real people is hidden. Vegetius apparently took them for a poetic name of the Huns and Alans. He turned Claudian's *Parthis sagittas tendere doctior,/ eques Gelonis imperiosior* in *Fescennina de nuptiis Honorii Augusti* I, 2-3 into prose: *ad peritiam sagittandi, quam in serenitate tua Persa miratur, ad equitandi scientiam uel decorem, quae Hunorum Alanorumque natio uellit imitari (Epit. rei milit.* III, 26). This, by the way, is another proof that the emperor whom Vegetius addressed was Valentinian III (see *Cons. Stil.* I, 109-110); the Geloni are named *together* with the Alans, Huns, and Sarmatae. Claudius imitated Statius (*Achil.* II, 419) but to fit the hexameter he transposed the weapons: Statius' *falcemque Getes arcumque belonus* became *falce Gelonus. . . arcu Getae.* Claudian's Geloni are still tattooing their Todies (*In Ruf.* I, 313) because Virgil (*Georg.* II, 115) had mentioned *pictos Gelonos.* The epithet "fur-clad" (*4th Cons. Hon.* 486) was applicable to any northern barbarians. Indeed, the Geloni are just one of the various savage peoples somewhere in the north; cf. *Paneg. Prob.* 119; *Carm. min.* 52, 76-77 (*Gelonos sive Getas*); *In Eutrop.* II, 103. In *Epithal.* 221, the Geloni are coupled with the Armenians, again far to the north, opposed to Meroe, far to the south. In other words, they are what they were since Augustus' time, *ultimi Geloni* (Horace, *Carm.* II, 20, 19). The Geloni in Sidonius' *Paneg. on Avitus* 237, where they are still wearing the sickle sword, are a mere literary reminiscence.

[166] *In Ruf.* II, 270-271.

the wolf against the lion.[167] I suspect that Rufinus had the same intention. It cannot be a coincidence that in the autumn of 395 he had a Hunnic, not a Gothic, bodyguard; only after they were cut down to the last man could General Gainas' soldiers kill him.[168]

That he gave them land in Thrace points also to a most unusual and close relationship between Rufinus and the Huns. This is the only time that Huns were admitted into the empire. All other alliances with the Huns were concluded with tribes or tribal coalitions in the barbaricum. The Huns in Thrace must have numbered several thousand, for it is most unlikely that the Hun warriors, made Roman federates, should have been willing to live without their wives and children, herds of cattle, flocks of sheep, and their carts, which they obviously did not take with them when they broke into Thrace. They must have sent for them.

John of Antioch's explicit statement that the Huns lived under *phylarchoi* allows us also to draw some conclusions as to their political organization. In the usage of the Byzantine writers the term $\varphi\acute{v}\lambda\alpha\varrho\chi\sigma\varsigma$ is not sharply defined; it is interchangeable with $\mathring{\eta}\gamma\varepsilon\mu\acute{\omega}\nu$, $\mathring{\eta}\gamma\sigma\acute{v}\mu\varepsilon\nu\sigma\varsigma$, $\mathring{\alpha}\varrho\chi\omega\nu$, and even $\beta\alpha\sigma\iota\lambda\varepsilon\acute{v}\varsigma$. *Phylarchos* means the leader of any larger group; the *phyle* can be a tribe, comprising a number of clans, a multitude of tribes, or a whole people. If the Huns in Thrace had a king, a ruler over the *phylarchoi*, John could not have failed to say so. Their *phylarchoi* were almost certainly tribal leaders. But from this it does not necessarily follow that the Huns beyond the Danube were likewise divided into independent tribes without a common leader. It is conceivable that those Huns who allied themselves with the Romans did not want to submit to a ruler over them. In any case, there evidently was no Hun ruler in the 390's strong enough to enforce his will on all tribes, to prevent Hun groups from waging their own wars and making their own peace. Those in the Hungarian plain pillaged Pannonia, those in Rumania Thrace; they concluded alliances and broke them at their, not a king's, pleasure. This did not exclude the possibility of concerted action of groups of Huns on a large scale. Such was the great raid into Asia in 395.

THE INVASION OF ASIA

In the summer of 395, large hordes of Huns crossed the Don near its mouth, turned southeast, and broke through the Caucasus into Persia and the Roman provinces to the south and southwest of Armenia.

---

[167] The lions in Synesius' *Egyptian Tale* are the Goths, the wolves are the Huns; cf. Ch. Lacombrade, *RÉA* 48, 1946, 260-266.

[168] *CM* I, 650$_{34}$.

One group devasted the country south and west of the Anti-Taurus. When they crossed the Euphrates, the Romans attacked and destroyed them. Another group, led by Basich and Kursich, rode down the valleys of the Tigris and Euphrates as far as Ctesiphon. On the report that a Persian army was on the march against them, they turned back but were overtaken. One band was cut down; the other, leaving their prisoners behind, fled through Azerbaijan and returned over the Caspian Gates to the steppes. A third group ravaged eastern Asia Minor and Syria.

In the following year the East was trembling with fear that the Huns, this time as the allies of the Persians, would come back. But the danger passed, possibly because the Romans came to an agreement with the Persians. When in 397 a few Hun hordes broke once more into Roman Armenia, they were easily driven back.

The cause of the invasion in 395 is said to have been a famine in the country of the Huns. Indeed, they drove away as many herds of cattle as they could. But first of all they made thousands of prisoners. The raid became a gigantic slave hunt.

These are, in broad outlines, the events. Instead of referring to the texts in footnotes, which themselves would require more notes, I shall discuss the various topics and problems one by one, incorporating the material that ordinarily would go into annotations.

The Sources

The sources flow so copiously that there is no need to make use of works of doubtful value as, for example, *The Life of Peter the Iberian*.[169] Except Theodoret (see below), the Greek and Latin sources[170] are adduced by all standard works, but most of the information contained in Syriac literature has been disregarded. I refer to the legend of Euphemia and the Goth,[171] a *mamre* (poem) of Cyrillonas (fl. ca. 400),[172] John of Ephesus

---

[169] Cf. P.Peeters, *Analecta Bollandiana* 50, 1952-1959. According to the biography of St. Ephraem, attributed to Sem'on of Samosate, Edessa was besieged by the Huns while the saint was still alive; he died in 373. Such an important event should have taken a prominent place in the detailed report which Ammianus Marcellinus gives of the events in those years. He repeatedly mentions Edessa but says nothing about a siege by the Huns. The legendary biography evidently antedated the invasion of 394 by more than two decades. For the Armenian sources, see Appendix.

[170] Claudian, *In Ruf.* II, 26-35; Jerome, *Ep.* LX and LXXVII; Socrates VI, 1; Philostorgius XI, 8.

[171] Dobschütz 1911, 150-199 (Greek); Burkitt 1913 (Syriac). It is probable but not certain that the Syriac version is the original; cf. Peeters 1914, 69-70.

[172] On Cyrillonas (Qurilona), see Altaner 1960, 405.

ca. 507-586) ; [173] and the *Liber Chalifarum*.[174] In various respects they complement the Western sources. Some texts have been misunderstood and misinterpreted with the result that Hunnic history has been strangely distorted. Two examples will suffice.

The Arian historian Philostorgius (368 to after 433) begins his fairly detailed description of the Hunnic invasion of Asia in 395 with a brief summary of the earlier history of the people: "They first conquered and laid waste a large part of Scythia, then crossed the frozen Danube and, swarming over Thrace, devastated the whole of Europe."[175] These lines have been quoted as referring to a Hunnic invasion of Thrace in the same year.[176] Actually, Philostorgius telescoped three or more decades, from the Hunnic victory over the Goths to the repeated incursions into the Balkan provinces. The poet Claudian, too, is supposed to have described in the *Invective against Rufinus* an invasion of Europe by the Huns in 395. But the barbarians who devastated "all that tract of land lying between the stormy Euxine and the Adriatic" were Goths, *Geticae cavernae*.[177] Of the church historians, neither Socrates nor Sozomen[178] mentions a Hunnic invasion of Thrace or any other province of the Balkans in 395.[179] The Eastern sources, though mainly concerned with the events in the Orient, know nothing of Hun raids into Thrace, not to speak of the "devastation of the whole of Europe."

Another often misunderstood passage occurs in Priscus' account of the East Roman embassy to Attila's court, *Excerpta de legationibus Romanorum ad gentes* (cited as *EL*), 46. In a conversation between the envoys from Rome and Constantinople, the West Roman Romulus spoke about Attila's ambitious plans:

> He desires to go against the Persians to expand his territory to even greater size. One of us asked what route he could take against the Persians. Romulus answered that the land of the Medes was separated

---

[173] Nau 1897, 60, trans. and annot. by Markwart 1930, 97-99. According to Markwart, the passage on the Hun Invasion of 395 is taken from the second book of John of Amid or Ephesus.

[174] *CSCO* 4, third series, 106. A compilation of the eighth century based on two sixth-century chronicles.

[175] Philostorgius XI, 8.

[176] Seeck, *Geschichte* 5, 274; Stein 1959, 1, 228; Thompson 1948, 26.

[177] *In Ruf.* II, 36-38.

[178] *Hist. eccles.* VIII, 25, 1, cited by Seeck, whom Thompson follows, as referring to 395, actually deals with events in 404-405.

[179] Pseudo-Caesarius in *Dialogus* I (Sulpicius Severus), 68, speaks of the frequent crossings of the Danube by unnamed barbarians, not by the Huns in 395, as Seeck asserted, again followed by Thompson.

by no great distance from Scythia and that the Huns were not ignorant of this route. Long ago they had come upon it when a famine
was in their country and the Romans had not opposed them on account
of the war they were engaged in at that time. Basich and Kursich,
who later came to Rome to make an alliance, men of the Royal Scythians
and rulers of a vast horde, advanced into the land of the Medes. Those
who went across say that they traversed a desert country, crossed a
swamp which Romulus thought was the Maeotis, spent fifteen days
crossing mountains, and so descended into Media. A Persian host
came on them as they were plundering and overrunning the land and,
being on higher ground than they, filled the air with missiles, so that,
encompassed by danger, the Huns had to retreat and retire across
the mountains with little loot, for the greatest part was seized by the
Medes. Being watchful for the pursuit of the enemy, they took another
road, and, having marched . . . days[180] from the flame which rises from
the stone under the sea, they arrived home.

The scribes, who made the excerpts, shortened the text, as they, incidentally, also shortened the immediately following story of the discovery of Ares' sword, much better preserved in the *Getica*. It is unlikely
that Romulus merely said that the Romans did not oppose the Huns "because
of the war they were engaged in at that time." He must have been more
specific. And why should the Romans have opposed the Huns if their
goal was Media? Evidently, Romulus spoke also about the Hun incursions into Roman territory, but the scribes omitted everything that had
no immediate bearing on the invasion of Persian lands.

A comparison between Priscus and the *Liber Chalifarum* shows that
both sources deal with the same invasion.

Priscus: "When the Persians counterattacked, the Huns retreated.
The greater part of their loot was seized by the Medes."

Liber Chalifarum: "When the Huns learned that the Persians advanced
against them, they turned to flight. The Persians chased them and took
away all their loot."

Priscus is also in agreement with Jerome:

Priscus: "The Romans did not oppose them on account of war they
were engaged in at that time."

Jerome, speaking of the Hun invasion in 395: "At that time the Roman
army was away and held up by a civil war in Italy."

The war was the struggle between Stilicho and Rufinus in 395 (see
Chapter XII). The Huns broke into Asia while the greater part of the

---

[180] Lacuna in the codices B, M, P; "a few" in E, V, R.

Eastern army stood in Italy or was on the march to Illyricum; it did not return to Constantinople and Asia Minor until the end of November.

It is hard to understand how in spite of their preciseness the texts could have been so often and so strangely misunderstood. Bury identified the Huns with the Sabirs,[181] Demougeot with the Hephthalites.[182] Thompson dates the invasion of the Priscus account to 415-420;[183] Gordon, at least recognizing that the war in which the Romans were engaged had to be dated, decided on the one in the years 423-425.[184] That the leaders of the Huns who came to Rome to conclude an alliance were the same who rode to the Tigris proves that their sites were in Europe. The Hunnish federates of the Romans were not Huns in Dagestan or the Kuban region; Aetius' friends lived on the Danube.

Basich and Kursich may have come to Rome in 404 or 407. Emperor Honorius was in Rome from February to July 404; two years later Stilicho defeated Radagaisus with the help of Hunnic auxiliaries. Except for the month of February, Honorius was again in Rome throughout 407, where he stayed until May, 408.[185] In 409, Huns served in the Roman army.

The *Chronicle of Edessa* gives the most exact date: "In the year 706, the month tammuz (July 395), the Huns reached Osroene in northern Mesopotamia."[186] They waged a veritable Blitzkrieg, so they cannot have crossed the Caucasus much earlier. The years in the Syriac sources vary slightly,[187] but the texts agree in the main. "In the days of the emperors Honorius and Arcadius, the sons of Theodosius the Great, all Syria was delivered into their [*i.e.*, the Huns'] hands by the treachery of the prefect Rufinus and the supineness of the general Addai."[188] "But the Romans killed Rufinus, the hyparch of the emperor, while he was sitting at the feet of the emperor, for his tyranny was the cause of the coming of the Huns."[189]

They [*i.e.*, the Huns] took many captives and laid waste the country, and they came as far as Edessa. And Addai, the military governor

---

[181] Bury 1923, 1, 115, n. 1.

[182] Demougeot 1951, 190, n. 384.

[183] Thompson 1948, 31.

[184] Gordon 1960, 202. To deal with Altheim's views would be a waste of time. Reading the Priscus passage *à travers*, he dates Basich's and Kursich's visit to Rome *before* instead of *after* the invasion which he thinks took place in the third (*sic*) century (Altheim 1962, 1, 15; 4, 319).

[185] Seeck 1919.

[186] *TU* 89, 1, 1892, 104.

[187] The same month, without the year, in Michael the Syrian (Chabot 1904, 2, 3) and Bar Hebraeus (Wallis Budge 1932, 65), but in the year 708.

[188] Joshua Stylites, W. Wright 1882, 7-8; Pigulevskaia 1940, 131.

[189] Markwart 1930, 99.

[*stratelates*] at that time, did not give permission to the federates to go out against them because of treason in their midst.[190]

The rumor that Rufinus let the Huns into the empire was as current in the East as it was in the West. Rufinus was killed on November 27, 395. Addai (Addaeus), *comes et magister utriusque militiae per orientem*, is last named in an edict issued to him on October 3, 395.[191]

In 396, a new Hun invasion seemed to be imminent. "After a little while the Goths came again to Edessa with a certain general who had been sent by the emperor to his place to keep it from the enemies, the Persians, I mean, and the Huns, who had agreed to make war on this country."[192] Claudian, too, alluded to a threatening war with the Persians,[193] but did not mention the Huns as their allies. We learn more about the feelings of the Syrians from the moving *mamre* of Cyrillonas:

> Every day unrest, every day new reports of misfortunes, every day new blows, nothing but fights. The East has been carried into captivity, and nobody lives in the destroyed cities. The West is being punished, and in its cities live people who do not know Thee. Dead are the merchants, widowed the women, the sacrifices have ceased. . . the North is threatened and full of fight. If Thou, O Lord, doest not intervene, I will be destroyed again. If the Huns will conquer me, oh Lord, why have I taken refuge with the holy martyrs? If their swords kill my sons, why did I embrace Thine exalted cross? If Thou willst render to them my cities, where will be the glory of Thine holy church? Not a year has passed since they came and devastated me and took my children prisoners, and, lo, now they are threatening again to humiliate our land. The South is also being punished by the cruel hordes, the South full of miracles, Thine conception, birth and crucifixion, still fragrant from Thine footsteps, in whose river Thou wert baptized, in whose siloe Thou hast cured, in whose jars was Thine precious wine, and in whose laps Thine disciples lay at the table.[194]

There was no other invasion of Syria in 397 as Claudian, against his better knowledge, asserted.[195] He simply transferred the events of 395 to 397, equating the hated eunuch Eutropius with the equally hated Rufinus. No Greek or Syrian writer knows of a second coming of the Huns. Eu-

---

[190] Burkitt 1913, 130-131 (Syriac); Dobschütz 1911, 150 (Greek).
[191] *Cod. Theodos.* IV, 24, 6; Seeck 1919, 287.
[192] Burkitt 1913, 146 (Syriac); Dobschütz 1921, 186 (Greek).
[193] *In Eutrop.* II, 476-477.
[194] Landersdorfer 1913, 15-16.
[195] *In Eutrop.* I, 245-245; II, 114-115, 569-570.

tropius fought some barbarian hordes, among whom there may have been Huns, in the Caucasus.[196]

The Course of the War

If Claudian is to be believed, the Huns crossed the Caucasus over the *Caspia claustra*,[197] the Darial Pass; he adds: *inopino tramite*, "a pass where they were not expected,"[198] because the northern barbarians came, as a rule, over the pass of Darband.[199] It is difficult to determine how far the Huns penetrated into Asia Minor, Syria, and western Persia.

Socrates, Sozomen, and some Syriac sources describe the theater of the war in general terms: Armenia and other provinces of the East; Syria and Cappadocia; all Syria. In his commentary on Ezekiel 38:10-12,[200] probably written before 435,[201] Theodoret wants to prove that Gog and Magog, whom he identifies with the Scythian peoples, live not far from Palestine. He reminds his readers that "in our times the whole Orient was occupied by them." The Scythians are the Huns, as in Jerome. They made war on the Phrygians, Galatians, Iberians, and Ethiopians. The first three names stand for Θογαρμά, Γομέρ, and Θοβέλ in the Septuaginta as interpreted by Josephus.[202]

Philostorgius is more specific: The Huns broke through Greater Armenia into Melitene, reached from there Euphratesia, riding as far as Coelesyria.[203] Claudian speaks of Cappadocia, Mount Argos, the Halys River, Cilicia, Syria, and the Orontes. Jerome names the cities on the Halys, Cydnus, Orontes, and Euphrates.[204] The Huns came as far as Antioch and Edessa.[205]

Two Syriac sources give more details. There are, first, the excerpts from the *Ecclesiastical History* of John of Ephesus:

---

[196] *Ibid.*, II, praef. 55; II, 367. Fargues (1933, 44, 89) greatly overrated Eutropius' victories.

[197] *In Ruf.* II, 28.

[198] Cf. Claudian, 4 th *Cons. Hon.* 102: *Inopinus* [Theodosius] *utrumque* [Maximus and Eugenius] *perculit et clausos montes, ut plana, reliquit.*

[199] Lydus, *De magistratibus*, Wunsche 1898, 140. The Huns returned over it. The "flame which rises from the stone under the sea" (Priscus) points to the oil country of Baku; cf. Markwart 1901, 97.

[200] *PG* 81, 1204.

[201] Cf. M. Richard, *Revue des sciences philosophiques et théologiques* 84, 1935, 106.

[202] Jerome, *Comm. in Ezechielem* XI, *PL* 35, 356.

[203] Philostorgius XI, 8.

[204] *In Ruf.* II, 30-35; *In Eutrop.* I, 245-251; Jerome, *Ep.* LX, 16.

[205] *In Eutrop.* II, 30-35; Jerome, *Ep.* IX, 16 (obessa Antiochia); LXXVII, 8; Burkitt 1913, see n. 190.

In the same year the Huns invaded the country of the Romans and devastated all regions of Syria along the Cahjā mountains, namely Arzōn, Mīpherqēt, Āmid, Hanzīṭ, and Aršəmīšāt.[206] When they had crossed the Euphrates, the bridge was cut off and the troops of the Romans gathered from various sides against them and annihilated them, and no one of the Huns escaped.

"Syria" here means Mesopotamia; the cities named are on and to the north of the upper Tigris. The author continues to describe how the Huns, by cutting the aqueduct, forced the people who had taken refuge in the fortress of Zijāt to surrender; most of them were massacred, the rest led away into captivity.

The *Liber Chalifarum* gives the following account:

In this year the cursed people of the Huns came into the land of the Romans and ran through Sophene, Armenia, Mesopotamia, Syria, and Cappadocia as far as Galatia. They took many prisoners and withdrew to their country. But they descended to the banks of the Euphrates and Tigris in the territory of the Persians and came as far as the royal city of the Persians. They did no damage there but devastated many districts on the Euphrates and Tigris, killed many people and led many into captivity. But when they learned that the Persians advanced against them, they turned to flight. The Persians chased them and killed a band. They took away all their plunder and liberated eighteen thousand prisoners.

In the history of the Huns the invasion of Asia was an episode, though an important one. Three things can be learned from it. First, it shows what great distances the Huns were able to cover in one campaign, something often overlooked in the historical interpretation of isolated Hunnic finds. Second, the Huns carried many young people, "the youth of Syria,"[207] into captivity. Although this could have been surmised, the explicit testimony of the texts is definitely welcome. Third, there are a few lines in Theodoret which, as the whole text, have been ignored by all students of the Huns. According to Theodoret, many people in the regions overrun by the Huns joined them. Some were forced; we may assume that they had to do slave labor, collecting fuel, attending to the more unpleasant jobs in the households of the upper-class Huns, and so forth. But others ran over to the Huns and fought *voluntarily* in their ranks. Theodoret

---

[206] Arzōn is Arzanene; Mīpherqēt, Martyropolis; Aršəmīšāt, Arsamosata.
[207] Claudian, *In Eutrop.* I, 250.

did not paraphrase Ezekiel, nor did he interpret the words of the prophet; Ezekiel did not say that the Israelites would join the armies of Gog and Magog.

Theodoret's source is unknown. He was a small child when the Huns came dangerously close to Antioch, his birthplace.[208] What he says about the flight to the Huns he may have heard from older people. At any rate, it is most remarkable. I shall come back to it in another context.

ULDIN

After the shadowy Balamber,[209] Uldin is the first Hun mentioned by name. The literary evidence contains enough material for a picture, if not of the man, of his deeds. We know when and where he led his Huns into battle, and we even get a glimpse of the happenings in Hunnia.

In 400, Uldin was the ruler of the Huns in Muntenia, Rumania east of the Olt River. When Gainas, the rebellious former *magister militum praesentalis*, and his Gothic followers fled across the borders (see Chapter XII), Uldin "did not think it safe to allow a barbarian with an army of his own to take up dwellings across the Danube." He collected his forces and attacked the Goths. The short but sanguinary campaign ended with a Hunnic victory. Gainas was killed.[210] Because only eleven days later[211] his head was displayed in Constantinople,[212] the last fight probably took place near Novae, the place at the Danube nearest to the capital, connected with it by a first-rate road.[213]

Gainas wanted to join his countrymen; he fled "to his native land" (εἰς τὰ οἰκεῖα).[214] It follows that in Muntenia Goths lived under Hun rule. We do not know how far to the east and north Uldin's realm extended. In the west his power reached to the banks of the Danube in Hungary, which is evident from the alliance he concluded with the West Roman generalissimo Stilicho in 406.[215]

---

[208] Born about 393 (H. Opitz, *PW* 5a, 1791).

[209] *Getica* 248.

[210] Zosimus V, 22, 1-3.

[211] Seeck, *Geschichte* 5, 570 *ad* 325_25.

[212] Cf. Beshevliev 1960.

[213] It took Maximus' embassy thirteen days to cover the somewhat longer distance from Constantinople to Serdica (*EL* 123).

[214] Zosimus V, 21, 9.

[215] Referring to Zosimus (V, 22, 3), H. Vetters (1950, 39) maintains that in 400 Fravittas led a Roman army against Uldin in Thrace. He misunderstood the text. Fravittas fought fugitive slaves and deserters who *pretended* to be Huns.

At the end of 405,[216] Italy, barely recovering from the first Gothic war, again was invaded by Goths. Under their king Radagaisus the barbarians descended on Venetia and Lombardy,[217] overran Tuscany, and were nearing Rome when they were finally stopped. The regular Roman army was too weak to stem the Germanic flood. Stilicho turned to Uldin the Hun, and Sarus the Goth, for help. Near Faesulae the Hun auxiliaries encircled a large part of Radagaisus' hordes;[218] he tried to escape but was captured and executed (April 406). The survivors were sold as slaves.[219] What happened to those Goths who had not been with Radagaisus is not known. Some seem to have been enrolled in Stilicho's army,[220] others may have fought their way back to their transdanubian homes. The Gothic nation was "forever" extinguished. At least this was to be read on the triumphal arch erected in 406,[221] just four years before Alaric took Rome.

It has often been assumed that the Gothic invasion was a repetition of the events in the 370's. The Goths of Radagaisus are supposed to have

---

[216] Seeck, *Geschichte* 5, 375; Stein 1959, 1, 380; Mazzarino 1942, 75; Demougeot 1951, 354. N. H. Baynes' arguments for dating the invasion to 404 (*JRS* 12, 1922, 218-219, reprinted in *Byzantine Studies and Other Essays*, 339-340) are unconvincing.

[217] From Zosimus' statement (V, 26, 3) that Rhodogaisus, "having collected 400,000 of the Celtic and Germanic peoples which dwell beyond the Ister and the Rhine, made preparations for passing over to Italy," Seeck (*Geschichte* 5, 588) concluded that Radagaisus marched over the Brenner Pass. He identified the "Celtic peoples" with the Alamanni. But Zosimus' account of the Gothic invasion is a mixture of good information and nonsense. For the year 405-406 he was on his own. Eunapius, one of the authors he plagiarized, ended his history in 404, and Olympiodorus, the other, began his in 407. Zosimus apparently found in the latter a short retrospective of the events preceding Alaric's campaign in 408, enough to produce another galimatias. He maintained, for example, that Stilicho defeated Radagaisus beyond the Danube.

Demougeot (1951, 356-357) does not refer to Zosimus but she, too, assumes that Radagaisus came over the Brenner Pass. The road over the Julian Alps was, in her opinion, protected by Alaric and the fortress Ravenna. But Ravenna was by-passed by more than one invader, and Alaric stood at that time in Epirus.

Flavia Solvia, near Leibnitz an der Mur, was probably destroyed by Radagaisus' Goths; W. Schmidt, *Jahreshefte d. österr. archäolog. Inst.* 19-20, 191, Beiblatt 140.

[218] *Exercitum tertiae partis hostium circumactis Chunorum auxiliaribus Stilicho usque ad internecionem delevit* (*CM* I, 652₅₁).

[219] Orosius VII, 37, 16. According to Marcellinus Comes (*CM* II, 69), the prisoners were sold by Uldin and Sarus.

[220] Olympiodorus, fr. 9, has suffered in the epitomized form in which we read the passage in Photius: "The chief men [κεφαλαιῶται] of the Goths with Rhodogaisus, about 12,000 in number, called *optimati*, are defeated by Stilicho who enters an alliance with Rhodogaisus." In the original, the object of προσηταιρίσατο was of course not Rhodogaisus but the optimati; cf. Baynes 1955, 333, n. 11, and Mazzarino 1942, 302. Mazzarino (1942, 377, n. 4) tries in vain to make sense of those 12,000 optimati. It is just another of Olympiodorus' fantastic figures; see Appendix.

[221] *CIL* VI=Dessau 1916, 798.

fled from the Huns who themselves were pushed westward by other nomadic groups which, in turn, were set in motion by an upheaval in the Far East. It is the well-known billiard ball theory, the *primum movens* being hidden, "in the vast plains of Eurasia." Nothing in our authorities indicates that behind Radagaisus stood another barbarian leader whose people were pushed by still another one, and so on.[222] All we know is that the Goths came from the countries across the Danube.

If they actually were fleeing, it was not a headlong flight. Although the figures in Orosius and Zosimus are grossly exaggerated,[223] we may believe that Radagaisus led, indeed, a large army into Italy.[224] The Gothic warriors were not raiders; they were the armed part of a people on the trek to a new home. From the fact—if it is a fact—that Radagaisus was a pagan,[225] some scholars have concluded that his hordes were Ostrogoths, because by 400 all Visigoths are supposed to have been good Christians. But the Visigoth Fravittas, consul in 401, East Roman general, was a staunch pagan, and among the Visigoths beyond the Roman border there must have been many thousands not yet baptized.[226] Besides, a little-noticed entry in the Chronicle of 452 proves that there *were* Arian Christians among the Goths of Radagaisus.[227] Patsch might well have been right in assuming that a good part of them came from Caucaland.[228]

There is no reason to assume that Stilicho's Hunnic auxiliaries came from far away, or, specifically, from the Dobrogea.[229] Huns had camped in Hungary since 378. They are, as we saw, well attested there in the middle 380's. They certainly did not voluntarily give up the land, and no enemy was strong enough to drive them out. Stilicho concluded an alliance with the Huns in Hungary. Uldin was king of the Huns to the west *and* to the east of the Carpathian Mountains, in the Alföld as well as in Muntenia.

---

[222] Gibbon (3, 261) connected Radagaisus' march on Rome almost directly with the rise of the Hsien-pei power at "the eastern extremities of the continent of Asia."

[223] More than 200,000 Goths (Orosius VII, 37, 4).

[224] *Agmen ingens* (Augustine, *De civ. Dei* V, 23); *cum ingenti exercitu id* (*Sermo* CV, 10, 12, *PL* 38, 264).

[225] Orosius (VII, 37, 5) asserts that Radagaisus "had vowed the blood of the entire Roman race as an offering to his gods," but the barbarian invaders of Italy, from the Cimbri on, wanted land to settle, with the conquered working for them, not a graveyard. Augustine even "knew" the name of Radagaisus' chief god; it was Jupiter (*Sermo* CV, 10, 13), which is not the *interpretatio romana* but pure invention.

[226] Zosimus V, 20, 1; Philostorgius IX, 8, Bidez 1960, 139; Suidas, *s.v.* Φράβιθας, Adler 1938, III, 758-759.

[227] *Ex hoc Arriani, qui Romano procul fuerant orbi fugati, barbarorum nationum, ad quas se contulere, praesidio erigi coepere* (*CM* I, 652₅₁).

[228] Patsch 1925, 67.

[229] Baynes 1955, 337.

He was not the ruler of all Hun tribes; not even Attila at the height of his power was. But Uldin could throw his horsemen into Italy and Thrace. In the winter of 404/5 Uldin broke into the Balkan provinces. We read in Sozomen:

> About this time the dissensions by which the church was agitated were accompanied, as is frequently the case, by disturbances and commotions in the state. The Huns crossed the Ister and devastated Thrace. The robbers in Isauria, gathered in great strength, ravaged the towns and villages between Caria and Phoenicia.[230]

When Sozomen interrupts his narrative of the synods, elections of bishops, and the fights between the various cliques at the metropolitan sees to deal with secular events, he treats them, with rare exceptions, only as they have a bearing on the never-ending struggle between orthodoxy and heresy. The dates of the ecclesiastical history are given as precisely as possible; political events take place "about the same time." Still, I think Uldin's first invasion of Thrace can be dated fairly well.

The "dissensions" were the fights of the patriarch of Alexandria Theophilus (384-412) against John Chrysostom. Chapters 20 to 24 of Book VIII cover the period from the autumn of 403 to November 404.[231] In chapter 26 Sozomen gives the translation of the letters which in the fall of 404 Pope Innocent sent to John.[232] In chapter 27 he mentions the death of Empress Eudoxia (October 6, 404), the death of Arsacius (at the end of 405),[233] and the ordination of Allicus, his successor (late in 405, or in 406).[234] Therefore, the invasion of Thrace falls somewhere between 404 and 405. I believe it can be dated even more precisely. From John Chrysostom's letters we know that the Isaurians broke out of the valleys of Mount Taurus in the summer of 404, probably in June.[235] They were soundly defeated.[236]

---

230 *Hist. eccles.* VIII, 25, 1.

231 Ch. 20: autumn and winter 403; ch. 21: Easter 404; ch. 23: second exile of John Chrysostom, Sancta Sophia destroyed by fire, June 9, 404; ch. 23: persecution of the Joannites; ch. 24: death of Flavian, bishop of Antioch, September 26, 404; edict "Rectores provinciarum" (*Cod. Theodos.* XVI, 4, 6), November 18, 404.

232 Late in the fall of 404 (Baur 1930, 2, 289).

233 November 11, 405, according to Socrates VI, 20; the date is not certain (Baur 1930, 2, 305).

234 Baur 1930, 2, 291.

235 As a rule, the Isaurians did not come down from their mountains before Whitsunday; cf. John Chrysostom, *Ep.* XIV, 4, *PG* 52, 617. In 404, Whitsunday was on June 5.

236 Arbazacius defeated them while Empress Eudoxia was still alive. (Zosimus V, 25, 2-4.)

In the following year they repeated their raids, this time extending their ravages over nearly the whole of Asia Minor.[237] In 404, the Isaurians were unable to take walled towns,[238] so the conquests of both towns and villages, of which Sozomen speaks, must fall in the year 405. The transdanubian barbarians used to cross the river in winter, when the fleet was immobilized and they could recross while it was still frozen. All these considerations lead to the winter of 404/5 as the most probable date of the Hun invasion of Thrace.

Sozomen is the only early writer to mention it. The account of Nicephorus Callistus (1256-1311) is a paraphrase, but one with a notable exception: He gives the name of the Hun leader—Uldin.[239] Nicephorus' main source was probably a compilation of the tenth century, based on Philostorgius, Socrates, Sozomen, Theodoret, and Evagrius.[240] Which of these authors named Uldin cannot be determined. It may have been Philostorgius, of whose works we have only excerpts; it may have been Sozomen himself, because it is unlikely that the Sozomen text, as we have it, is word for word identical with the original. The possibility that Nicephorus himself supplied the name Uldin may be ruled out. He was too dependent on his sources to alter them; the best he could do was to dress up what others had written before him. Whatever Nicephorus' ultimate authority, there was one in which Uldin was named as leader of the Huns 404-405.

Sozomen mentions the invasion only in passing. It may have been a quick raid, or the Huns may have been looting the unfortunate provinces for weeks or months. Still, it was in importance far surpassed by the one which, a few years later, carried Uldin's horsemen deep into Thrace.

In the summer of 408, the Huns crossed the Danube.[241] As usual, well informed about the situation in the Balkans, they chose the right time to attack. In the spring of 408, Stilicho abandoned his plan to throw Alaric's Visigoths into Illyricum. Shortly afterward they were on the march to Italy.

With the danger of a Gothic invasion over, the greater part of the East Roman troops was moved to the Persian frontier where hostilities were expected to break out any day.[242] The government in Constanti-

---

[237] Baur 1930, 2, 312-313.

[238] Zosimus, V, 24, 2-4.

[239] *Hist. eccles.* XIII, 35, *PG* 146, 1040.

[240] Moravcsik, *BT* 1, 459.

[241] Güldenpenning 1885, 202-204; Seeck *Geschichte* 5, 408-409; Bury 1923, 1, 212-213; Stein 1959, 1.

[242] Sozomen IX, 4, 1. As the edict of March 23, 409 (*Cod. Iust.* IV, 63, 4) shows, the tension ended with the conclusion of a new commercial treaty.

nople was well aware that the transdanubian Huns might take advantage
of the weakening of the Balkan army to make inroads into the border
provinces. In April, 408, Herculius, praetorian prefect of Illyricum, was
instructed "to compel all persons, regardless of any privilege, to provide
for the construction of walls as well as for the purpose and transport of
supplies in kind for the needs of Illyricum."[243] If the Huns should by-pass
the strong places along the *limes*, they could, for awhile, plunder the helpless villages, but eventually they would be caught between the unconquered towns in the interior and the troops holding out in the fortifications
along the frontier, and forced back into the barbaricum. What the Romans
could not expect was that the Huns would take the strategically important fortress Castra Martis in Dacia ripensis by treachery.[244] Whether
other fortified places fell into the hands of the Huns is not known but is
possible.

Our main source for Uldin's second invasion is again Sozomen's *Ecclesiastical History*. The other one, Jerome's *Commentary on Isaiah*, has
been ignored by all students of the Huns. Commenting on 7:20-21, Jerome wrote:

> But now a large part of the Roman world resembles the Judaea of
> old. This, we believe, cannot have happened without God's will. He
> does by no means avenge contempt of him by Assyrians and Chal-
> daeans, rather by savage tribes whose face and language is terrifying,
> who display womanly and deeply cut faces, and who pierce the backs
> of bearded men as they flee.
>
> (*Ac nunc magna pars Romani orbis quondam Iudaeae similis est; quod
> absque ira Dei factum non putamus, qui nequaquam contemptum sui
> per Assyrios ulciscitur, et Chaldaeos: sed per feras gentes, et quondam
> nobis incognitas, quarum et vultus et sermo terribilis est, et femineas*

---

[243] *Cod. Theodos.* XI, 17, 4, dated "III Id. April. Constantinop. Basso et Philippo
conss." (*i.e.*, April 11, 408), is practically identical with the edict issued on April 9, 412
(*Cod. Theodos.* XV, 1, 9). Seeck (1919, 28-29) first presumed that both edicts should
be dated April 9, 407, when Alaric threatened to march into eastern Illyricum; later
(*Geschichte* 5, 68) he conceded that both edicts provided for the protection to the towns
exposed to Hun attacks. Stein (1959, 1, 376, n. 4), with some hesitations, referred XI,
17, 4 to the year 412. Thompson (1948, 29) dates both edicts to 412, Mazzarino (1942,
75, n. 2) to 407. However, there can be little doubt that the dates of the edicts as given
in the *Codex* are correct; cf. Güldenpenning 1885, 209, n. 74. The first refers to the critical months early in 408; the second is a repetition, a year later somewhat mitigated
by *Cod. Theodos.* XII, 1, 177, which, like the others, should be observed in *vastatum
Illyricum.*

[244] Sozomen, IX, 5, 2.

incisasque facies praeferentes virorum, et bene barbatorum fugientia terga confodiunt.)[245]

This was written in June or July 408.[246] That Jerome's *ferae gentes* were the Huns is evident from their description: They were formerly unknown and they cut their faces because they wanted to look like women rather than men with beards. As I have shown elsewhere,[247] Jerome followed Ammianus's description of the Huns. What matters here is the date of the passage in the commentary and in particular the phrase [*ferae gentes*] *bene barbatorum fugientia terga confodiunt.* If Jerome in faraway Jerusalem, as early as the summer of 408, received reports about the defeats of the Roman troops by the Huns, the losses must have been unusually heavy.

Even through Sozomen's edifying account one senses how serious the situation must have been. With his few troops the Roman commander in Thrace could not drive the Huns back. He made peace propositions to Uldin, who replied by pointing to the rising sun and declaring that it would be easy for him, if he so desired, to subjugate every region of the earth enlightened by that luminary. But while Uldin was uttering such menaces and ordering as large a tribute as he pleased, and that on condition peace could be established with the Romans or the war would continue, God gave proof of his favor toward the present reign; for shortly afterward Uldin's own people and captains, (οἰκεῖοι καὶ λοχαγοί) were discussing the Roman form of government, the philanthropy of the emperor, and the promptitude and liberality in rewarding the best men. Together with their troops, they seceded to the Romans, whose camps they joined. Finding himself thus abandoned, Uldin escaped with diffi-

---

[245] *PL* 24, 113.

[246] In the preface to Book XI, Jerome alluded to the execution of Stilicho in August 408, cf. Cavallera 1922, 1, 312. The exact day he received the news cannot be determined. He knew that his enemies, in particular "the scorpion" Rufinus, had attacked his work on the prophet Daniel in which he equated the Roman Empire with the last of the four kingdoms; he was rightly afraid that they would denounce him to the authorities, and that meant, most importantly, the all-powerful Stilicho, as subversively interpreting the scriptures; cf. Demougeot 1952. No doubt Jerome's Roman correspondents informed him as quickly as they could of the generalissimo's death. Jerome had excellent connections with his friends in the West; cf. Levy 1948, 62-68. We may assume that Jerome learned about Stilicho's death in September or at the latest in October.

The *breves praefatiunculae* to the commentary show with what incredible haste Jerome wrote it. He dictated the first book *celeri sermone. Dictamus haec*, he says in the preface to Book II, *non scribimus: currente notariorum namu currit oratio.* Book II, in which he speaks of the war with the "savage peoples," must have been dictated in June or July.

[247] *American Journal of Philology* 76, 4, 1955, 396-397.

culty to the opposite bank of the river. Many of his troops were lost, and among others the whole of the barbarian tribe called the Sciri. This tribe had been strong in numbers before falling into this misfortune. Some of them were killed, and others were taken prisoners and conveyed in chains to Constantinople. The authorities were of the opinion that, if allowed to remain together, they might revolt. Some of them were, therefore, sold at a low price, while others were given away as slaves for presents on the condition that they should never be permitted into Constantinople or anywhere in Europe, but be separated by the sea from the places familiar to them. Of these a number were left unsold, and they were ordered to settle in different places. Sozomen had seen many in Bithynia, near Mount Olympus, living apart from one another and cultivating the hills and valleys of that region.[248]

Sozomen does not say when the war came to an end, but from an edict of March 23, 409, it can be concluded that by that time the Huns had recrossed the Danube.[249]

Sozomen's account must not be taken literally, of course. The Sciri did not vanish from history.[250] But Uldin's boast sounds genuine, and Sozomen doubtless correctly reports the content of Uldin's demands. This is the first time our sources say something about the object of a Hun invasion. Uldin was not merely set on $\pi\varrho\alpha\iota\delta\varepsilon\dot{\upsilon}\varepsilon\iota\nu$,[251] "plundering," and taking prisoners who could be sold as slaves. He did not demand the cession of Roman territory either. There were no pastures large enough for all the Huns under Uldin. If, however, some groups stayed in the empire, like those around Oescus, they would have been separated from the other tribes, and this was counter to Uldin's interests. He rather demanded that the Romans pay him tribute, $\delta\alpha\sigma\mu\acute{o}\nu$, probably a fixed annual sum.

The Huns were mounted, the Sciri evidently mostly foot soldiers. The edict of April 12, 409,[252] provided only for the settlement of the Sciri. The Hun prisoners were either killed or drafted into the ranks of the auxiliaries. Who Uldin's "own people" were is not quite clear; the word may mean nothing more specific than the people who usually stayed with him. The members of Belisarius' $o\dot{\iota}\varkappa\acute{\iota}\alpha$, of which in the sixth century Procopius speaks so often, were not necessarily his kinsmen. Paulus, for instance,

---

[248] Sozomen IX, 5, 2-7.

[249] "We decree that when one of our provincials has acquired any booty that has been obtained from the plunder of the barbarians and from spoils which they have seized, he shall take it back to his home, etc." (*Cod. Theodos.* V, 6, 2).

[250] Cf. Tourxanthos' words to the same effect (Menander, *EL* 206[13-14]).

[251] Callinicus 61, LXI, 12; LXIV, 38; LXV, 1.

[252] *Cod. Theodos.* V, 6, 3.

who for a time was in charge of the οἰκία, was a Cilician;[253] Ataulf took over a man from Sarus' οἰκία.[254] The word *lochagos* is not well defined either. That some *lochagoi* went over to the Romans together with their troops seems to indicate that a close bond existed between them and their followers. Ammianus and Orosius speak of the *cunei* of the Huns. Although *cuneus*, as used by them, is a tactical unit, the word may still have preserved some of the meaning it had in Tacitus: "Their squadrons or battalions, instead of being formed by chance or by a fortuitous gathering, are composed of families and clans." (*Non casus nec fortuita conglobatio turnam aut cuneum facit sed familiae et propinquitates.*)[255]

The cohesion of Uldin's kingdom has been overrated,[256] but it should not be underrated either. Uldin was not the leader "of a mere fraction"[257] but of many tribes able to operate from the Rumanian plains to the Hungarian *puszta*. And yet, although the incipient royal power gradually was strengthened, it was by no means stabilized. How it weakened in Uldin's last years becomes clear when we return to the West.

Shortly before Uldin's Huns broke into the Balkan provinces, the Visigoths began the long trek which a century later ended in Spain. There is no need to recapitulate in detail the events preceding it; they have been thoroughly discussed by Santo Mazzarino in his masterful *Stilicone*. For our purposes a brief outline will suffice.

After the battle of Verona in the summer of 402,[258] Alaric led his hosts back to the Balkans. In the following three years he strictly kept his treaty with Stilicho. From the "barbarous region bordering on Dalmatia and Pannonia"[259] assigned to them, the Goths made occasional raids into eastern Illyricum,[260] but they were careful not to provoke a conflict with the West, partly because they had not yet recovered from their defeats, partly (and perhaps mainly) because they hoped to come to a closer and better agreement with Stilicho. In 405, he concluded, indeed, a *foedus* with Alaric, an alliance for the conquest of eastern Illyricum.[261] The Gothic king was promised the position of *magister militum per Illyricum*. He moved into Epirus where he stayed for three more years. First the invasion of Ra-

---

[253] Procopius VII, 36, 16.
[254] Olympiodorus, fr. 26.
[255] *Germania* 7.
[256] *E.g.*, by Kiessling, *PW* ·8, 2601.
[257] Thompson 1948, 60.
[258] The date has been definitely established by K. A. Müller 1938, 17-22.
[259] Sozomen VIII, 25, 1581; IX, 4, 1603.
[260] Late in 403 or early in 404; see Honorius' letter to Arcadius, written shortly after June 20, 404 (*Collectio Avellana* in *CSEL* 35, 85). Cf. Mazzarino 1942, 70-71.
[261] Mazzarino 1942, 73.

dagaisus, then the rebellion of Constantine in Britain forced Stilicho to postpone the Illyrian expedition, and finally the plan was dropped altogether.

Early in 408, Alaric turned against the West. By May[262] he had reached Noricum. Whether he encamped near Virunum, the present Maria Saal near Klagenfurt, or at Celeia[263] cannot be determined. What matters is that he passed through Emona (modern Ljubljana, Yugoslavia). The way from Epirus to Emona leads through Pannonia secunda and Savia.[264]

Of all the students of the Huns only Alföldi realized that their inactivity in the eventful years 408-410 calls for an explanation.[265] As we shall see presently, they did not keep so quiet. But it is true that in 408 Alaric could march westward as if there were no Huns, those Huns who, as Alföldi rightly stresses, were otherwise so eager to fish in troubled waters. Alföldi assumes that they did not join the Goths because they were allied with the Romans. According to him, Stilicho settled them in 406 as federates in the province Valeria, the same year in which, presumably, young Aetius went as hostage to the Huns.[266]

If this assumption were correct, the Huns should have done more than stay away from the fight. They should have *fought* the Goths, attacking

---

[262] Before the news of Arcadius' death (he died on May 1, 408) reached Rome.

[263] Jung 1887, 190, n. 1.

[264] Bury (1923, 1, 170) assumed that Alaric followed the road from Sirmium to Emona.

[265] Alföldi 1926, 87.

[266] It is usually assumed that the young Aetius went at that time as a hostage to the Huns. The date is not certain. "Aetius was for three years a hostage with Alaric, then with the Huns" ([Aetius] *tribus annis Alarici obsessus, deinde Chunorum*), an apparently shortened quotation from Renatus Frigeridus' lost work in Greg. Tur., *Hist. Franc.* II, 8, sounds more precise than it is. Bury (1923, 1, 180, n.3) surmised that Aetius was one of the hostages whom (in 409) Attalus gave to the Gothic king; but Alaric died the following year. Could Aetius be sent to Alaric in 405? This is the thesis of Seeck, *Geschichte* 6, 104-105; Stein 1959, 1, 380; Schmidt 1934, 441; Mazzarino 1942, 157 n. 2, and Demougeot 1951, 306. It is most unlikely. One has to read Merobaudes (*Paneg.* II, 123-130, and *Carmen* IV, 42-46) to convince oneself that the verses cannot refer to the years after the conclusion of the *foedus* in 405. Aetius, says Merobaudes, *intentas Latio faces removit ac mundi pretium fuit paventis*. Even with all the exaggerations granted to and expected from a panegyrist, Merobaudes could not say that Aetius "broke the rage of the enemy," that before he went to the Goths "the world was about to succumb to the Scythian swords and the nordic missiles assaulted the Tarpeian power," at a time when Stilicho concluded an alliance with Alaric who stayed in the Balkans. The verses describe aptly the situation immediately after the war in 402. I, therefore, accept Alföldi's date (1926, 78, n. 5): Aetius stayed as hostage with Alaric from 402 to 404 or 405. From *deinde Chunorum* it does not follow that Aetius, just returned from the Goths, was at once sent to the Huns. It may have been in 406, so Alföldi thinks, or later.

them in the right flank while Alaric's people, slowly traveling in their wagons, were on the move to Emona. But the Huns made neither common cause with the Goths nor did they fulfill their supposed obligations as allies of the Romans.

The reason for their inactivity is, in my opinion, much simpler. The Huns did not fight in Pannonia secunda and Savia because they fought under Uldin in Illyricum and Thrace. By dating Uldin's invasion to 409 instead of 408,[267] Alföldi had to find an explanation for something that does not need one.

This is not to say that the Huns had followed Uldin to the last horseman. There were Huns in the West Roman army under Stilicho, and Ravenna also had a Hun garrison after the execution of the great *ductor* in August 408.[268] Besides, many Huns must have stayed at home in order to prevent an uprising of their subjects while the "mobile" army was engaged in fighting south of the Danube. This was, I believe, an additional reason why they did not interfere in the war between Alaric and the Romans.

The Huns became active in the West only after Uldin's hordes had returned to their sites beyond the Danube. How the defeat he had suffered undermined his authority can be deduced from two passages in Zosimus, who copied them from Olympiodorus.

In the summer of 409, Honorius is said to have called ten thousand Huns to his assistance.[269] Most historians accept this figure as if it had come from an official document.[270] Actually, it is one of those exaggerations in which Olympiodorus indulged.[271] What did those ten thousand Huns achieve? Nothing. At the end of the year, Alaric stood again at the gates of Rome. In 410, he marched to Ariminium, into Aemilia, to Liguria, back to Ariminium. In August, he took Rome. We hear nothing about the gigantic Hun army. Evidently it was a small contingent, probably not more than a few hundred horsemen. Still, the fact that some Huns joined the Roman army while others fought against it indicates a weakening of the royal authority.

In the later part of 409, Visigoths in upper Pannonia—a part of Alaric's troops who for some reason had not marched with him all the way—rode

---

[267] Alföldi 1928, 87, n. 3.

[268] Zosimus V, 45, 6.

[269] *Ibid.*, 50, 1; *EL* 77$_{14}$.

[270] Wietersheim, Hodgkin, Seeck, Stein, Thompson 1948, 34, Demougeot 1951, 446. Only L. Schmidt (1934, 444) has some doubts. One codex of the *Excerpta de legationibus* seems to have εὔνους (*EL* 77$_{14}$).

[271] See Appendix.

into Italy. They were joined by Huns.[272] Their number may have been small. Yet they, too, acted on their own.

Still others, perhaps those who were still obeying Uldin, were engaged in fighting the Romans in Pannonia. In the summer or fall of 409,[273] Honorius "entrusted Generidus with the command of the forces in Dalmatia; he was already general of the troops in Upper Pannonia, Noricum, and Raetia, as far as the Alps."[274] This passage has been variously interpreted. Swoboda dismisses it as invention; there were, he maintains, no troops in Upper Pannonia after 395.[275] Alföldi thinks it supports his assumption that at that time Valeria already was ceded to the Huns.[276] Lot went a step further; from the fact that neither Valeria nor Pannonia secunda was under the command of Generidus, he concluded that both provinces were no longer held by the Romans.[277]

None of these assertions and assumptions is warranted by literary or archaeological evidence, direct or circumstantial. Even at the height of Attila's power a part of Pannonia prima was held by the Romans, and there was, in all probability, never a formal "cession" of Valeria.

Generidus held no well-defined title or rank; he was "one of those commanders of the field forces who were appointed during the reign of Honorius to meet the emergencies of the time."[278] From his position in the provinces named—Egger called it a *Generalkommando*[279]—it does not follow that there were no Roman troops in the provinces not named. True, we have no information about Roman forces in Valeria, but if it were not for the *Vita s. Severini*, we would have none about the garrisons in Noricum either.

In his pagan bias Zosimus probably exaggerated the achievements of his coreligionist Generidus, who is said to have drilled his troops, seen to it that the soldiers got their rations, and spent among them what he

---

[272] Zosimus V, 37, 1.

[273] After Olymmius was removed from office, spring or early summer of 409, and before Alaric's second march on Rome, end of 409. Bury (*JRS* 10, 1920, 144) dated Generidus' appointment in 408, but the pagan general accepted it only after the law of November 14, 408, which forbade "all enemies of the Catholic faith" to *militare* in the imperial palace, (*Cod. Theodos* XVI, 5, 42), had been repealed.

[274] Zosimus V, 46, 2.

[275] Swoboda 1958, 225-227. The people who built their houses in Carnuntum at the turn of the century were probably German and possibly also Alanic auxiliaries; cf. H. Vetters 1963, 157-163.

[276] Alföldi 1926, 86.

[277] Lot 1936, 314.

[278] Bury, *JRS* 10, 1920, 144; cf. E. Stein, *Röm.-germn. Kommission*, 18. Bericht, 1928, p. 96.

[279] *Jahrbuch des oberösterreichischen Musealvereins* 95, 1950, 144.

received from the treasury. "In this way he was terrible to the adjacent barbarians and gave security to the provinces which he was chosen to protect."[280]

There were no "adjacent barbarians" of importance but the Huns. The difference between 408 and 409 is striking. In 408, the Huns in the West did not move. In 409, the troops from Raetia to Dalmatia were put under the command of one man to repulse them.

The picture which emerges from the sources and their admittedly conjectural interpretation is blurred. Yet it seems that we can discern four groups of Huns in the early 400's. First, Uldin and his followers who, returning from the campaigns in Illyricum and Thrace, fought the troops of Generidus; second, Huns who in 408 formed a part of the Roman army in Italy; third, the Huns who joined it in 409; fourth, a group that rode with Athaulf's Visigoths against the Romans. The overall picture derived from the few bits of information is one of disintegration of the power of "the first king of the Huns," as Olympiodorus would have called Uldin.

In his time falls the dissolution of the Hunno-Alanic alliance. Until 338, Huns and Alans are constantly named together, the Huns mostly, though not always, in the first place. But in 394, only the transdanubian Alans, led by Saul,[281] joined Emperor Theodosius;[282] of the Huns only those in Thrace marched under the imperial dragons. Alans, but no Huns, served Stilicho in 398 and, still under Saul, in 402.[283] In 406, however, Stilicho's barbarian auxiliaries consisted of Huns and Goths; his bodyguard was formed by Huns.[284] Huns, but no Alans, served in the Roman army in 409.[285]

After 406, Western writers knew of Alans only in Gaul, Spain, and Africa. No author of the fifth century mentions Alans as allies of the Huns.[286] Jordanes knew of Sarmatians, not of Alans in Pannonia. The few Alans who after the fall of Attila's kingdom settled in Scythia minor and lower Moesia[287] evidently moved there from the Wallachian Plain. All this cannot be a coincidence, and we know, indeed, the reason: The Alans moved from their old sites to Gaul; together with the Vandals they crossed the Rhine on the last day of 406.[288]

---

[280] Zosimus V, 46, 5.

[281] The name is not biblical but Iranian; cf. Σαύλιος (Herodotus IV, 86).

[282] Claudian, 4th Cons. Hon. 486-487.

[283] Claudian, Bell. Goth., 580-587; 6th Cons. Hon. 218-225; Orosius VI, 37, 2;

[284] Zosimus V, 34, 1.

[285] Ibid., 45, 6.

[286] For a purely rhetorical passage in Jordanes-Cassiodorus, cf. Alföldi 1926, 97.

[287] Getica 265: certi Alanorum cum duce suo nomine Candac.

[288] Sarmatians, Gepids, and Roman coloni (Jerome, Ep. 123, PL 122, 1057) joined them in Hungary, and splinters of Germanic tribes while they were on the trek westward.

Why the Alans broke their alliance with the Huns is not known. There is a hint in Orosius that the relationship between the two peoples was already tense after 402. "I say nothing," he writes, "of the many internecine conflicts between the barbarians themselves, when two *cunei* of the Goths, and then the Alans and Huns, destroyed one another in mutual slaughter."[289] This passage has been strangely misunderstood. Most authors thought that Orosius referred to wars between Huns and Alans in their sites somewhere in the East.[290] But Orosius, who became jubilant whenever he could report how many barbarians in this or that battle were killed, most certainly would not have deplored the mutual slaughter of Rome's enemies. Orosius' *taceo* in VII, 37, refers to events unfortunate to the Romans: the escape of the defeated Alaric, and the "unhappy doings at Pollentia." The *cunei* of the Huns and Alans were Roman auxiliaries, and Orosius deplores that Stilicho could not prevent those savage clashes in his own army.[291] As Gothic troops also fought each other, national antagonism between Huns and Alans, if it existed at all, may have been only a contributing factor.

According to Procopius, the Vandals left Hungary because "they were pressed by hunger";[292] probably the people had outgrown the facilities for producing food.[293] The same may have been true for the Alans. Clashes with the Huns and the unwillingness to be forever the junior partners in an alliance which profited mainly the Huns may have been additional reasons for the Alans to seek new homes.

The Hunnic noblemen, Attila's relatives and retainers, have either Turkish or Germanic names. There evidently were few, if any, Alans among the leading group. As no people ever emigrated to the last man, some Alans presumably stayed in Hungary after 406, but they played a minor role. Most of their tribal and clan leaders had left.

The chroniclers name only the Vandals and Alans, so the number of other barbarians who joined them was apparently small. To Gepids in Gaul points perhaps an obscure entry in *Cont. Prosp.* ad. a. 455, *CM* I, 304: *at Gippidos Burgundiones intra Galliam diffusi.* Cf. Coville 1930, 120; Stevens 1933, 26, n. 8. The Sarmatians are named by Paulinus of Perigueux, *Epigr.* XVIII, *CSEL* 11, 504. For Jerome's *hostes Pannonii*, see Alföldi 1926, 70; Mazzarino 1942, 77, à. 1; L. Schmidt 1942, 15.

[289] VII, 37, 3.

[290] For instance, Thompson 1948, 28.

[291] Kulakovskiĭ 1899a, 34, came rather close to the the right interpretation.

[292] III, 3, 1.

[293] Courtois' conjecture (1955, 40-41) that the Vandals were driven out by the Roxolani has no support either in the literary or archaeological evidence.

CHARATON

No period in the political history of the Huns is darker than the 410's and 420's. The loss of Olympiodorus' *History* written in the second quarter of the fifth century, is, to quote Thompson, "a disaster for our knowledge of the nomads."[294] It is true that Olympiodorus lacked the capacity to present the obviously rich material at his disposal in a coherent narrative;[295] at times he was gullible;[296] his figures are fantastic.[297] Yet of all the writers of the fifth century only he and Priscus traveled to the country of the Huns. What would we give to have his account of the negotiations with King Charaton instead of the few lines to which Photius reduced it! I put the name of the Hun king at the head of this section more in conformity with the titles of the other sections than to indicate its content. All we have for the two dark decades are a few isolated facts. In some cases it is, paradoxically, the very absence of information about the Huns that sheds some dim light on the events.

A fragment of Olympiodorus runs as follows:

Donatus and the Huns, and the skillfulness of their kings in shooting with the bow. The author relates that he himself was sent on a mission to them and Donatus, and gives a tragic account of his wanderings and perils by the sea. How Donatus, being deceived by an oath, was unlawfully put to death. How Charaton, the first of the kings, being incensed by the murder, was appeased by presents from the emperor.[298]

The date is the end of 412 or the beginning of 413, after Sarus' death, referred to in the preceding fragment, and before Jovinian appointed his son Sebastian Caesar, reported in the following one. Altheim's assertion that Charaton and Uldin reigned together as late as 414[299] has no textual support, but he rightly rejected the assumption that Donatus was a Hunnic king.[300]

From these few lines of the Olympiodorus fragment several unwarranted conclusions have been drawn. Charaton is supposed to have been

---

[294] Thompson 1948, 8.

[295] He himself called the *History* a "forest."

[296] Photius at the beginning of fr. 13.

[297] See Appendix.

[298] Fr. 18.

[299] Altheim 1951, 98.

[300] Altheim 1962, 1, 363. Pritsak (1954b, 213) makes Donatus "the first of the kings" and offers a Turkish etymology: *donat*, "horse." A similar one was suggested by W. Bang, *SB Berlin* 37, 924-925. Both are unacceptable, see D. Sinor, *CAJ* 10, 1965, 311.

Donatus' successor.[301] The text contains nothing of that sort. Assuming that Olympiodorus was sent to the Huns by the East Roman government, most historians place the center of Hun power somewhere near the shores of the Black Sea. This is certainly incorrect. As Thompson noticed,[302] Olympiodorus' *History* deals exclusively with the Western empire. Haedicke assumed that Olympiodorus was in the civil service of the government of Ravenna.[303] Olympiodorus' knowledge of Latin, his use of Latin words, the Latin forms of barbarian names, leave, indeed, no reasonable doubt that Haedicke was right. Olympiodorus, sent to the Huns by Honorius, crossed not the Euxine but the Adriatic Sea.[304] The Huns he visited lived in Hungary. How long Charaton "reigned" is as unknown as the number of tribes who acknowledged his hegemony. If the Huns to the north of the lower Danube should have belonged to the confederacy headed by Charaton, a possibility which cannot be excluded, they certainly did not feel themselves bound by any agreement which he made with Honorius. "Their" Romans were those of the East.

New Raids into Thrace

At the same time that Honorius sent gifts to Charaton, the Huns in Muntenia began to stir again. Moesia inferior and Scythia were most exposed to barbarian inroads. The praetorian prefect Anthemius did what he could to strengthen the border defenses, in particular the Danube fleet.[305] In 413, the walls of Constantinople were rebuilt and enlarged.[306] In spite of the repeated orders which restricted trade with the barbarians, enterprising traders were still finding ways and means to buy from them and, more important, to sell them forbidden goods. The decree of September 18, 420, differs from similar previous ones in one respect: it prohibits the export of *merces inlicitae* in ships.[307] Could it have been aimed at the trade with the Huns on the shores and in the hinterland of the Black Sea? To answer this question we have to make a short digression.

---

[301] Thompson 1948, 34.

[302] *CQ* 39, 1944, 46.

[303] *PW*, 18:1, *s.v.* Olympiodorus of Thebes, Reihe 201.

[304] E. Kh. Skrzhinskaia (*VV* 8, 1956, 253) is, to my knowledge, the only author to consider such a possibility. Note that in 432 Aetius on his way to the Huns crossed the Adriatic Sea.

[305] *Cod. Theodos.* VII, 17, 1; cf. Güldenpenning 1885, 206, and Thompson 1948, 30.

[306] Seeck, *Geschichte* 6, 68, 401. Nicephorus Callistus (*Hist. eccles.* XIV, 1, *PG* 146, 1057) lumped together the work on the fortifications of Anthemius, Cyrus, and Constantinus.

[307] *Cod. Theodos.* VII, 16, 3.

In the third quarter of the third century, the Goths were the terror of Asia. They sailed from the Black Sea ports as far as Ionia; the Heruli took Lemnos and Skyros, the Borani pillaged Pityus and Trapezunt.[308] But the Huns never took to the sea.

The Goths were no sailors either. When, in the last years of Ostrogothic power in Italy, King Totila (541-552) decided to build a fleet to deny the Byzantines the hitherto undisputed command of the Italian waters, he could not find enough Goths to man the ships. The sea battle of Senigallia, in which the Romans sunk or captured thirty-six of the forty-seven enemy vessels, marked the end of the Gothic fleet.[309] Totila's ships were built by Romans. The boats which in the third century carried the barbarians across the Euxine were built in Panticapaeum and were sailed by Bosporan crews.[310] Unable to navigate the vessels themselves, the Goths and Borani forced the Bosporans to supply them with convoys for their expeditions to Pontus, Paphlagonia, and Bithynia. Why the Gothic naval actions ceased after 276, we do not know. But it is probably not a coincidence that Dacia was abandoned at about the same time. With the emigration of a large section of the Goths to the former Roman province, the tribes to the east of them could expand westward. As greedy as they were for the riches of the Roman cities, they wanted and needed, first of all, land to settle. This was not true for the Huns. Why, then, did they not turn into pirates like the Goths before and the Slavs after them? They tried, but they failed.

In 419, Asclepiades, bishop of Chersonese, petitioned the emperor to free from punishment "those persons who have betrayed to the barbarians the art of building ships, that was hitherto unknown to them." The petitions was granted. "But," concludes the edict, "we decree that capital punishment shall be inflicted both upon these men and any others if they should perpetrate anything similar in the future."[311]

Chersonese was the only place on the west coast of the Crimea still under Roman rule. The barbarians nearby were Goths and Huns. It is extremely unlikely that the Crimean Goths in their mountain homes should have wanted to build ships. This leaves the Huns. They probably needed ships both for piratical raids and for trade. They could not get them, and the government in Constantinople saw to it that no Roman ships sailed to Euxine Hunnia. If the Huns wanted *merces inlicitae*, they had to pillage the border provinces, which they did.

---

[308] Alföldi 1939b.

[309] Procopius VIII, 23, 29-39.

[310] N. H. Baynes, *Antiquarian Journal* 4, 1924, 218.

[311] *Cod. Theodos.* IX, 40, 24, addressed to Monaxius, praetorian prefect.

On March 3, 422, Theodosius II issued the following edict, which has not found the attention it deserves of students of the Huns:

Our most loyal soldiers returning from battle or setting out for war shall have for themselves the ground floor rooms of each tower of the New Wall of the sacred city. Landholders shall not be offended on the ground that the order which had been issued about public buildings has been violated. For even private homeowners customarily furnish one third of their space for this purpose.[312]

Nine years before, the landholders on whose properties the wall was built had been granted immunity from the law of compulsory quartering.[313] The upper part of the towers was set apart for military purposes; the lower part, however, could be used by the landlords without restrictions. When one considers what a heavy and hated burden the compulsory quartering of soldiers was, and how carefully the government refrained from extending it beyond the minimum just compatible with military necessities,[314] it becomes evident how tense the situation in and around Constantinople in the spring of 422 must have been to enforce the abolition of a regulation which was "to be observed in perpetuity." Translated from legal into military terms, the edict says that the garrison of the capital is to be held in constant readiness against an enemy nearby. A terse entry in the Latin chronicle of Marcellinus Comes, *s.a.* 422, furnishes the commentary: "The Huns devastate Thrace."

Nowhere in the history of the Huns is the one-sidedness of our sources more manifest. Hun bands skirmished with Roman soldiers almost at the gates of Constantinople. Yet no word about it appears in the detailed ecclesiastical histories, no allusion in the vast theological literature of the time. Theophanes registered that on September 7, 422, in Alexandria the *praefectus* Augustalis Callistus was killed by his slaves,[315] a fate he probably deserved. But neither Theophanes nor any other writer thought it worthwhile to mention the peasants killed in Thrace, to speak about the people thrown out of their homes in the towers, the drudgery of the soldiers. Unlike the "illustrious persons" and bishops, they were expendable.

The Huns Help Aetius and Lose Pannonia

We have no information about Hun raids in the West in the 420's. Among the troops which, in 424, Castinus, commander in chief of the

---

[312] *Ibid.*, VII, 8, 13.
[313] *Ibid.*, XV, 1, 51, of April 4, 413.
[314] See the edicts *De mentatis* (*Cod. Theodos.* VII, 8).
[315] A.M. 5914, C. de Boor 1883, 84.

usurper John (see Chapter XII), sent against Boniface in Africa were also Huns.[316] The date is of some importance. Because the expeditionary force left immediately after Castinus had gone over to John,[317] these Huns must have formed a part of the regular army. There was not enough time to turn to federates beyond the border; the Huns must have been stationed in Italy. This, in turn, points to friendly relations between the Western empire and at least some Huns at the time that Aetius was still holding the modest position of *cura palatii*. Sanoeces, one of the three *duces* in Africa,[318] might have been a Hun.

A year later, in 425, Aetius marched with a huge Hun army[319] into Italy, to help John in the war with the East Romans.

> John sent Aetius with a great sum of gold to the Huns, a people known to him since the time when he was their hostage and attached to him by a close friendship; he added the instructions that as soon as the enemy, that is, the army of the Eastern empire, entered Italy, Aetius should fall upon them from the rear while he himself would engage them at the front.[320]

The Huns came too late; three days before their arrival John had been executed. But Aetius, either unaware of what had happened or unwilling to believe the news, engaged the Eastern forces in a battle in which many were slain on both sides. The short campaign ended with the reconciliation of Aetius and Empress Mother Galla Placidia. The Huns received a sum of gold, returned hostages, exchanged oaths, and rode back to their country.[321]

Aetius, who probably spoke their language, was the best man John could find for his negotiations with the Huns. Of course, they sent their horsemen to Italy not out of friendship with Aetius but because they were paid "a great sum of gold." They received more for breaking off the fight, and it is almost certain that they were promised regular annual tributes. Had Aetius stayed in Ravenna, the alliance with the Huns might have lasted for years. But he was sent to Gaul, and, for reasons we cannot guess, in 427 the Romans attacked and conquered the Huns in Pannonia.

---

[316] *Non militem timebis, non Gothum, non Hunnum* (Pseudo-Augustine, addressing Boniface, *Ep.* IV, *PL* 33, 1095). The Goth is Sigisvult (*CM* I, 658₉₆₁, 470₁₂₆₈); cf. de Lepper 1941, 43.

[317] Stein 1959, 1, 427; W. Ensslin, *Klio* 24, 1931, 474-475.

[318] *CM* I, 471-472. On the date, see de Lepper 1941, 57-58. Cf. also R. Gentile, *Il mondo Classico* 5, 1935, 363-372.

[319] According to Philostorgius (XII, 14), it numbered sixty thousand men; probably it was not more than a tenth of this figure. Cf. Lot 1923, 53, and Thompson 1948, 49. Socrates (VII, 23, 789) has "several myriads."

[320] Renatus Frigeridus *apud* Greg. Tur. II, 8.

[321] Philostorgius XII, 14.

Under the year 427, the sixth-century chronicler Marcellinus Comes has the short entry, "The provinces of Pannonia, which for fifty years were being held by the Huns, were retaken by the Romans" (*Pannoniae quae per quinquaginta annos ab Hunnis retinebantur, a Romanis receptae sunt.*)

These two lines have been discussed by generations of historians;[322] they were dismissed as nonsense[323] and were made the basis for far-reaching conclusions; they were interpreted, and reinterpreted, translated and re-translated to fit all possible theories about the fate of the former Roman provinces in the Danube basin.

It has been maintained that Marcellinus' *Romani* must have been the Eastern Romans.[324] It is true that in the preface to his chronicle Marcellinus wrote that, in continuing Jerome's work, "I write of the Eastern empire only" (*orientale tantum secutus imperium*). On the whole he did. But before the entry *s.a.* 427 Marcellinus dealt with purely Western affairs no less than thirteen times.[325] Whether it was the Eastern or the Western Romans who took back Pannonia, Marcellinus could in either case use only one word, namely *Romani*.[326] Until 476, the two *partes* formed the one Roman Empire, *Romanum imperium* of the *Romanus populus* or *Romana gens*.[327]

If, taken by itself, the passage in Marcellinus permits an "Eastern" as well as a "Western" interpretation, the parallel in Jordanes, *Getica* 166, leaves no doubt about its meaning (see Chapter XII). Under the consulship of Hierius and Ardabures, we read there, "Almost fifty years after the invasion of Pannonia the Huns were expelled by Romans and Goths." (*Huni post pene quinquaginta annorum invasam Pannoniam a Romanis et Gothis expulsi sunt.*) Until recently it generally was assumed that Cassiodorus simply copied Marcellinus. That he smuggled the Goths into the text was in no way remarkable; he did that more than once.[328]

---

[322] See the survey A. Alföldi 1926, 94, n. 2; since then, Stein 1959, 1, 473-474; Lot 1936, 302-304; Solari 1938, 302. In *AA* 15, 1967, 159-186, T. Nagy deals with the relationship of the sources; on the events themselves he has nothing to say.

[323] Mazzarino 1942, 141, n. 1.

[324] Alföldi 1926, 94, n. 2.

[325] *S.a.* 398, 2, 4; 406, 2, 3; 408, 1; 410; 411, 2, 3; 412, 1; 413; 414, 2; 423, 5; 425, 2.

[326] *Romani* are (a) inhabitants of the city of Rome; (b) the people under the rule of a Roman emperor; (c) the Latin-speaking people, cf. "coins which the Romans call *Terentiani* and the Greeks, *follares*" (*nummi, quos Romani Terentianos vocant, Graeci follares*), *s.a.* 498.

[327] *S.a.* 382, 389, 476.

[328] It cannot be concluded from Theophanes (A.M. 5931, p. 94) that the Goths fought the Huns. As Alföldi (1926, 95) showed, the passage is a combination of Marcellinus and Procopius III, 2, 39-40.

The other differences between the *Getica* and Marcellinus were regarded as too minor to deserve attention. Ensslin made these differences between the *Romana*, *Getica*, and Marcellinus the object of an admirable study.[329] He proved that Cassiodorus and Jordanes as well as Marcellinus drew heavily on the lost *Historia Romana* of Symmachus († 525), great-grandson of the famous orator of the same name. It is practially certain that the two passages go back to it.[330] Bringing in the Goths, Cassiodorus had to change the colorless *receptae*—the Huns did not give up Pannonia, they were driven out. But he retained *pene quinquaginta* of the original.[331]

For the rest, the two passages need hardly a commentary. *Pannoniae* means the same as *Pannonia*.[332] *Retinebantur* is, perhaps, a little more emphatic than *tenebantur*.[333] *A Romanis receptae* means, of course, "were taken back, regained, recovered by the Romans." I mention this only because Lizerand translated *reçues des Romains*.[334] As he understood the entry in Marcellinus, *à une possession de fait succède en 427, pour les Huns, une possession de droit*, which is clearly incorrect.

The archaeological evidence does not bear out Symmachus. Nowhere in Pannonia prima or in Valeria exists a fortification, a military camp, or even a simple building that could be dated in the 420's. Yet Symmachus could not have simply invented the *reconquista*. He probably exaggerated the successes of the Romans. Perhaps they merely reoccupied a number of fortified places. It is likely that they drove back some Hun bands which had ventured too closely to Noricum. Possibly Roman horsemen dashed deep into long abandoned tracts; here and there they may even have reached the Danube. In any case, the Western Romans did go to war against

---

[329] Ensslin 1948.

[330] *Ibid.* 72.

[331] A comparison between Jordanes and Marcellinus shows that, as a rule, the latter was not interested in Symmachus' exact dates. In the following list, the words in italics are the dates in Jordanes left out in the corresponding passages in Marcellinus: Gildo *tunc Africae comis a Theodosio dudum ordinatus* (*Romana* 320; Marcellinus 398, 4); Constantinus *mox* (*Romana* 324) *non diu tenens regno praesumpto mox* (*Getica* 164; Marcellinus 411, 2); cuius nutu *mox* Maiorianus (*Romana* 335; Marcellinus 457, 1); qui [sc. Mariorianus] *tertio necdum anno expleto* (*Romana* 335; Marcellinus 461, 2); *anno vix expleto* (*Getica* 239; Marcellinus 472, 2); *mox initio regni sui* (*Getica* 243; Marcellinus 477); *sed non post multum* (*Romana* 349; Marcellinus 482, 1).

[332] Orosius used the two forms (Pannonia: I, 2, 44, 60; VI, 19, 2; VII, 15, 12; 28, 19; Pannoniae: VII, 22, 7; 32, 14) as indiscriminately as Ammianus before him (Pannonia: XXVIII, 1, 5; 3, 4; XXX, 7, 2; Pannoniae: XXX, 5, 3; XXXI, 10, 6) or Sidonius Apollinaris after him (Pannonia: *Paneg. on Maiorian* 107; Pannoniae: *Paneg. on Avitus* 590).

[333] Theoderic *pro tempore tenuit* river Dacis and Lower Moesia (*CM* II, 92).

[334] *Aetius*, 24, note.

the Huns, with whom only two years before they had concluded an alliance, and defeated them.

Güldenpenning rejected the "Western" interpretation of the passages under discussion on the ground that Placidia's government was so fully occupied in Gaul and elsewhere that it could not, at the same time, undertake an offensive against the Huns.[335] In a way, this is true. But now, because we know that in 427 Pannonia was, if not reconquered, at least partially made Roman again, Güldenpenning's argument must be turned around. The Romans, indeed, could not attack the Huns unless the latter were so weakened that even the limited forces along the "frontier" sufficed for a local offensive. The Romans had not much strength; the Huns must have had even less.

As so often in these studies, we are dealing with such scanty evidence that it might seem best to register the various fragments of information and leave it at that. The gaps are too wide, not to speak of the chronological and geographical uncertainties, to seek any trend or development. Still, seen as a whole and against the background of the events of Uldin's time, these dark decades seem to reveal at least two crises in the "body politic" of the Huns.

About 410, the Hun hordes acted as if there existed no ties, or only the loosest ones, to bind them together. It may, and it may not, be a coincidence that, shortly before, the Alans broke their alliance with the Huns. If, as we may assume, the mightiest Hunnic tribes were those which had forced the Alans to join them, the secession of the Alans must have sapped their strength.

Only a few years later, the Hun kings again acknowledged the leadership of one man. Charaton may have been only *primus inter pares*. However, even if he was not more, he probably owed his position not so much to his personal qualities, though they may have been of some importance, as to the preeminence of those Huns who followed him. The crisis was over. In 425, the tribal confederacy was again so well organized that the Huns could send several thousand horsemen to Italy, evidently more than what a single tribe was able to raise. The Huns whose help Aetius sought and got must have been under the leadership of a group in a position to coordinate the efforts of a number of tribes, perhaps even to enforce its will on others.

But then again, for reasons unknown, the confederacy lost much of its cohesion. Even if the successes of the Western Romans in Pannonia were relatively modest, the fact that the Huns west of the Danube had

---

[335] Güldenpenning 1885, 263ff.

to give up a part of what they had been holding indicates the inability of the Huns as a people to rally their forces for a common cause. When the Huns in Pannonia were attacked, they must have called on their countrymen in the East for help. They received none. Nor do we hear that in the following five years the Huns beyond the Danube made an effort to reconquer the lost territory.

OCTAR AND RUGA

Although the sources for the history of the Huns in the 430's flow comparatively copiously, it is not easy to reconstruct even the main events. In 432, Ruga was king of the Huns. This seems to be the only certain date. In what year he became king, over what territory he ruled, to what extent he expanded it, what wars he fought and when, who after 430 his coregent was (if he had one)—these are questions to which the most divergent answers have been given.[336] Under such circumstances the smallest bit of information has to be carefully scrutinized. We begin with a passage in the *Getica*:

> For this Attila was the son of Mundzucus, whose brothers were Octar and Ruas, who were supposed to have been kings before Attila, although not altogether of the same [territories] as he. After their death, he succeeded to the Hunnic kingdom together with his brother Bleda. (*Is namque Attila patre genitus Mundzuco, cuius fuere germani Octar et Roas, qui ante Attilam regnum tenuisse narrantur, quamvis non omnino cunctorum quorum ipse. Post quorum obitum cum Bleda germano Hunnorum successit in regno.*)[337]

Jordanes, or rather Cassiodorus, telescoped his source;[338] Octar died about 430, Ruga a few years later. But apart from this mistake, the statement is so precise that one can only wonder how it could have been misinterpreted. Yet both Bury and Thompson made Mundzuc the coregent of Octar and Ruga.[339] Jordanes' style is sloppy, but had he meant to say that the three brothers ruled the Huns, he would have written *Mundzuco, qui cum germanis Octar et Roa regnum tenuisse narratur.* No author mentions Mundzuc as king of the Huns. From Priscus we know that there was a fourth brother, Oebarsius, who was still alive in 448.[340] He did not

---

[336] The great Tillemont (1738, 6, 95, 606) even postulated the existence of two kings, Rugas and Ruas.

[337] *Getica* 180.

[338] *Roas* points to a Greek source, possibly Priscus.

[339] Bury 1923, 272, n. 1; Thompson 1948, 63, 119, 162, 208.

[340] *EL* 146$_{18-19}$.

share the rulership with Octar and Ruga either. Only these two were kings. Before discussing their alleged double kingship, I have to deal with Socrates' account of Octar's fight with the Burgundians.

In the first half of the tenth century the Magyars raided western Europe from the North Sea to the Mediterranean. Between 900 and 913, they devastated Silesia, Thuringia, Franconia, and Bavaria. In 912, they crossed the Rhine. In 915 they took Bremen. They ravaged Lorraine twice, in 917, and again in 919, when they turned south and raided northern Italy. In 924, they appeared in southern France; Verdun fell to them in 926. Magyar horsemen camped before Lyon in 937. In 951, they rode as far as Calabria.[341] Summoning all the forces of the empire, Otto I finally defeated them decisively in the battle on the Lechfeld in 955.

The Germanic neighbors of the Huns were split into tribes, none of them even approximately as strong as the weakest of the German principalities of the tenth century. Incapable of any concerted action for any length of time, divided by mutual mistrust, periodically at war with each other, they were incomparably less able to defend themselves against the Huns than five hundred years later the dukes of Bavaria or Thuringia against the Magyars. Even without the not-too-exact literary evidence we would have to assume that the Huns made raids into the territories of the Germanic tribes to the west as they raided the Balkan provinces to the south.

There exist, indeed, two accounts of such predatory expeditions. The first comes from Socrates. How he received the information is not known, except that Uptaros, the name of the Hun king in Socrates, Jordanes' Octar, points to informants who spoke Latin. Socrates wrote:

> There is a nation of barbarians dwelling beyond the Rhine, called Burgundians. They lead a peaceful life. Being almost all carpenters, they support themselves by their earnings from this craft. The Huns, by making continuous eruptions on this people, devastated their country, and often destroyed great numbers of them. In this perplexity, the Burgundians resolved to have recourse not to any human being, but to commit themselves to the protection of some god; and having seriously considered that the God of the Romans defended those who feared him, they all with common consent embraced the faith of Christ. Going therefore to one of the cities of Gaul, they requested the bishop to grant them Christian baptism; who ordering them to fast seven days, and having meanwhile instructed them in the principles of faith,

---

[341] Lüttich 1910; Fasoli 1945. D'Eszlary (1962, 63-78) discerns "higher political motives" in the raids of the supposedly amiable and cultured Magyars.

on the eighth day baptized and dismissed them. Accordingly becoming confident thenceforth, they marched against the tyrants;[342] nor were they disappointed in their hope. For the king of the Huns, Uptaros by name, having burst asunder in the night from surfeit, the Burgundians attacked that people then without a leader; and although few in numbers and their opponents many, they obtained a victory; for the Burgundians were but 3,000 men, and destroyed no less than 10,000 of the enemy. From that time on this nation became zealously attached to the Christian religion.[343]

Socrates' account of this Hun raid about 430[344] has been dismissed as devoid of any historical value.[345] No other author knows of a struggle between Huns and transrhenanian Burgundians. The traditional miracle motifs can be discounted. But there still remain such absurdities as the existence of a Germanic tribe of peaceful carpenters, their conversion within a week, and the victory of three thousand artisans over ten thousand of the most formidable warriors of the century. Besides, it has been asserted that the story is at variance with all we know about the history of the Burgundians. They crossed the Rhine shortly after 406. In 411, they helped Jovinus to the throne. In 413, they obtained *partem Galliae propinquam Rheno*.[346] Aetius' Hun auxiliaries slew King Gundahar, his whole family, and twenty thousand of the Burgundians.[347] If any Burgundians stayed behind on the right bank of the Rhine, they cannot have numbered more than a few hundred. These are strong arguments. And yet, Socrates' story contains a historical kernel.

In the *Panegyric on Avitus*, Sidonius lists Burgundians among the peoples who followed Attila on his march to Gaul.[348] His catalogue of

---

[342] κατὰ τῶν τυράννων, possibly to be emended to κατὰ τῶν Ὄυννων; but the *Historia tripartita* (XII, 4, 14, *CSEL* LXXII, 655₄₇) has also *contra tyrannos*.

[343] VII, 30.

[344] The chapter closes: "At about the same time, Barbas, bishop of the Arians, died on the twenty-fourth of June, under the thirteenth consulate of Theodosius and the third of Valentinian," which was in 430. A misplaced marginal note to *Marcianus regnavit annos VI* in an eleventh-century manuscript of Isidorus' *Chronica maiora* (*CM* II, 491) refers to the Burgundo-Hunnic war: *Burgundiones in Gallia baptisati revincunt fortier Hunnos et occident X milia ex eis*. This is merely an excerpt from the *Historia tripartita*.

[345] Wietersheim 1881, 2, 383; Schubert 1911, 13-18. Neither Bury nor Seeck mentions the story. Thompson (1948, 66) accepts it as authentic.

[346] Jerome, *Ep.* CXXIII; Orosius, *Hist. adv. Pagan.* VII, 38; Olympiodorus, fr. 17, *CM* I, 467₁₂₅₀.

[347] *CM* I, 475₁₃₂₂, 660₁₁₈; II, 22₁₁₀. Cf. Coville 1930, 105-108.

[348] *Pugnacem Rugum comitante Gelono / Gepida trux sequitur; Scirum Burgundio cogit; / Chunus, Bellonotus, Neurus, Bastarna, Toringus, / Bructerus, ulvosa vel quem Nicer alluit unda / prorumpit Francus* (vv. 321-325).

ethnic names has been denounced as untrustworthy,[349] and it must be admitted that it is a strange hodgepodge of names of real peoples and of those who had long ceased to exist or lived only in poetry.[350] Sidonius wrote the panegyric five years after the Hun war in 451.[351] Everyone in Gaul knew that Attila had neither Geloni nor Bellonoti among his troops, but no one would have objected to Sidonius naming them. It was different with the Burgundians. Avitus himself had fought them in Belgica prima.[352] In 443, after the catastrophic defeat by Aetius' Huns, they were settled in Sapaudia.[353] Eight years later they fought under Aetius and Avitus against Attila's Huns.[354] How could Sidonius, in an address delivered before Avitus and in the presence of the praetorian prefect,[355] have said that Attila had Burgundians among his hosts if he had none? The names of the Germanic tribes in his list shows how accurate Sidonius' list was (apart from the poetic names.) The Rugi, Sciri, and Gepidae marched indeed with the Huns to Gaul. No poet before Sidonius mentioned the Toringi,[356] no other source mentions them as having taken part in the war. All this makes it practically certain that transrhenanian Burgundians did join Attila.

Socrates' account of the conversion of the Burgundians to the orthodox faith is confirmed, though not in the details, by Orosius, according to whom the Burgundians "have by divine providence recently become Christians of the Catholic faith" (*providentia Dei Christiani omnes modo facti catholica fide*).[357] This statement, too, has been called a pious invention.[358] However, the thorough analysis of Orosius' text by Coville[359] leaves no doubt that the Burgundians before they became Arians, probably under Visigothic influence, had been Catholics.[360]

---

[349] Loyen 1942, 52.

[350] Sidonius owed some of the names to Valerius Flaccus and Claudian. The Geloni are coupled with the Huns in *In Ruf.* I, 310-322 and *Cons. Stil.* I, 110, where also the Bastarnae are named. In *4th Cons. Hon.* 446-453, the Bructeri are associated with the Bastarnae and Franks as in Sidonius' list. The Bellonoti are Valerius Flaccus' Ballonoti (*Argon.* VI, 161); Sidonius connected the name with Bellona. The Neuri had not been heard of since Herodotus except in poetry. Cf. Thompson 1948, 136, on the whole passage.

[351] He delivered it on January 1, 456.

[352] Sidonius, *Paneg. on Avitus*, 234-235.

[353] *CM* I, 660₁₂₈.

[354] *Leg. Burg.* 17, 1, de Salis, ed., 55.

[355] Priscus Valerianus; cf. Stevens 1933, 35, and Sundwall 1915, 23.

[356] They occur in Vegetius, *Mulomedicina* III, 6, 3.

[357] *Hist. adv. Pagan.* VII, 32.

[358] Schubert 1911, 3-18; K. D. Schmidt 1939, 404.

[359] Coville 1930, 139-152.

[360] Cf. also Neuss 1933, 75-76; F. Lot, *Le Moyen Age* 37, 1937, 224-225.

Werner considers it possible, even probable, that the Burgundians east of the Rhine were for some time the subjects of the Huns.[361] But the arguments he adduces indicate rather a symbiosis of Alans and Burgundians in Sapaudia. It seems best to take Socrates' story as it stands: The Huns raided the Main region as centuries later the Magyars raided Lorraine.

Seeck thought that Octar-Uptaros and Roas-Ruga might have been Uldin's sons.[362] Perhaps they were. They as well might have been relatives of Charaton. It is equally possible that their family came from a tribe which until then had played a minor role in the confederacy. We simply have no information about the forebears of Octar and Ruga, nor do we know how they acquired their positions of authority. If it were not for Jordanes, we would not even know that for some years they jointly ruled the Huns.

On the basis of the short passage in the *Getica* and some vague analogies it has been suggested that Hun kingship was a *Doppelkönigtum*. If this means that two kings jointly ruled a common territory, the suggestion should be dismissed because it is at variance with the texts.

Jordanes is quite explicit: "Bleda ruled over a large section of the Huns." (*Bleda magnae parti regnabat Hunnorum.*) After his death Attila "united the entire people under his rule" (*universum sibi populum adunavit*). The chronicler Prosper of Aquitaine says the same: "Attila, king of the Huns, killed Bleda, his brother and colleague in the royal office, and forced his peoples to obey him." (*Attila rex Hunnorum Bledam fratrem et consortem in regno suo perimit eiusque populos sibi parere compellit.*)[363] The sources do not indicate different functions for the two kings, for example, the one being the religious, the other the secular leader of his people. Against the thesis of dual kingship as an institution speaks also the fact that after Octar's death in 430 no one succeeded him; his brother became the sole ruler, like Attila after he had murdered Bleda. Dual kingship is supposedly characteristic for large groups of the Eurasian nomads. I doubt it. The Goths were not Turks or Mongols, but in the fourth century they had at one time two kings.[364] Among the Alamanni Chnodomarius and Serapio were *potestate excelsiores ante alios reges.*[365]

The distinction which Prosper made between Bleda's and Attila's peoples clearly points to a geographical division. That the "dual kingship"

---

[361] J. Werner 1956, 17.

[362] Seeck, *Geschichte* 6, 282.

[363] *Getica* 181; *CM* I, 480$_{1353}$.

[364] *Ibid.*, 112.

[365] Ammianus XVI, 12, 23. On the alleged dual kingship of the Vandals, cf. N. Wagner, *ZfDPh* 79, 1960, 239-241.

was indeed nothing but just that follows from two seemingly contradictory
entries in the Gallic chronicles. According to the Chronicle of 452, Bleda
succeeded Rugila;[366] the chronicler of 511 made Attila Rugila's successor.[367]
Considering that the Chronicle of 452 reflects in more than one passage
an Eastern source,[368] the contradiction becomes a plain statement: Bleda
ruled over the tribes in the east, Attila over those in the west. The same
division seems to have existed with their predecessors. Octar had nothing
to do with the East Romans, whose only enemy was Ruga.

It would be risky to make a rule of what very well may have been
caused by unique circumstances. After Attila's death his many sons "were
clamoring that the nations should be divided among them equally."[369]
That we hear later of only two kings, Dengizich and Ernach, does not
exclude the possibility that there were more before. Attila had his co-
regent killed, and Dengizich and Ernach may have killed their coregents too.
However, if the Huns, or rather their "eminent men," should have decided to have again two kings, they allotted to each a definite territory.
Dengizich and Ernach, though at times cooperating, ruled each over his
own lands. The possibility that such a geographical division was rooted
in cosmological or religious ideas cannot be ruled out, but there is no evidence for it. Perhaps it was dictated by purely practical reasons: Only
exceptionally able men could hold all the tribes together. The "dual kingship" may have been the result of the coalescence of two groups of tribes
which to a certain extent continued to preserve their identity. Finally,
it is even possible that the Huns divided their territories into two parts
to deal with the two *partes* of the Roman Empire.

Compared with Octar, Ruga is a more substantial figure. We do not
know how he, after his brother's death, became sole ruler of the Huns;
he was ruler at the latest in 432, when Aetius turned to him for help.

After the loss of his office, Aetius lived on his estate. When there some
of his enemies by an unexpected attack attempted to seize him, he
fled to Rome, and from there to Dalmatia. By way of Pannonia [*per
Pannonias*],[370] he reached the Huns. Through their friendship and help
he obtained peace with the rulers and was reinstated in his old office.[371]

---

[366] *CM* I, 116.

[367] *CM* I, 661₅₈₉; in Mommsen's edition the entry is erroneously printed in italics
as if it were taken from the Chronicle of 452.

[368] See Appendix.

[369] *Getica* 259. For analogies among the Germans, see Wenskus 1961, 321-322.

[370] A geographical, not an administrative, term.

[371] Prosper, *s.a.* 432, *CM* I, 660₁₂₂, dates Aetius' return in 433.

At that time "Ruga was ruler of the *gens Chunorum.*"[372]

The terseness of the few entries in the chronicles is a temptation to read more into them than they can yield. Whether the mere threat to march into Italy with a Hun army sufficed to make the Empress Placidia accept Aetius' terms, or whether he actually crossed the Julian Alps at the head of Hun horsemen is not known; still, most historians have decided for the latter view.[373] Prosper's *per Pannonias* has been taken as proof that in 432 the Romans were masters of all land west of the Danube,[374] although the two words only indicate that Ruga's residence was east of the river.[375] Still, these are at least interpretations of the sources. But the thesis that the cession of a large part of Pannonia was the price Aetius had to pay for the help of the Huns is not warranted by any text. Yet by now it has become almost an article of faith.

The alleged and actual cessions of Roman territory to the Huns take a prominent place in nearly all studies on the barbarians. I could have discussed Alföldi's view on the fate of the province of Valeria when I dealt with the events in 408, but it seemed preferable to approach the problem of the cessions as a whole and from a wider angle.

How should one imagine the abandonment of Valeria, which had no natural borders in the west and south? Neither to the Huns nor to any other barbarians on the frontiers of the empire did the delineations of the Roman provinces have any meaning. No Hun horseman would have stopped at the sight of a border mark—or turned around because only Valeria had been ceded to his chieftain. The lines that on the maps in the offices at Rome and Ravenna divided Valeria from Pannonia prima and secunda could not prevent a single Hun from driving his herds and flocks across them. Most students of the Huns are students of the later Roman Empire and cannot help thinking in Roman administrative terms. If the barbarians knew the borders of the provinces, they paid no attention to them. After the migration of the Ostrogoths to the Balkans, the Gepids held not only Sirmium but also the adjacent regions of Moesia prima.[376] By the treaty of 510, Pannonia secunda was divided: The far greater part of the province became Ostrogothic; only the territory of Bassiana remained Roman.[377] In 528, Justinian ceded to the Heruli a territory which

---

[372] Chronicle of 452; the Chronicle of 511 has *Rugila.*

[373] Cf., *e.g.,* Mommsen 1906, I, 537; Seeck, *Geschichte* 6, 117; Stein 1959, 1, 479.

[374] Wurm, 67.

[375] In 452, *Attila Italiam ingredi per Pannonias intendit* (Prosper, *CM* I, 482 [1367]); here, too, Pannoniae is a purely geographical term.

[376] Ennodius, *Paneg.,* 60; Procopius III, 2, 6.

[377] Cf. Stein 1925, 263, and 1959, 2, 156; L. Schmidt 1934, 350; Ennslin 1947, 155.

did not coincide with any of the old administrative units; it comprised tracts both on the right and left bank of the Sava.[378] Isidor of Seville gave the best definition of such a "cession." He did not enumerate the provinces which fell to the Vandals in 435; the barbarians, he wrote, received *partem Africae quam possederunt.*[379] When the Romans "ceded" land to the barbarians, they merely—with very few exception—recognized a de facto situation which the barbarians wanted legalized, to be acknowledged as federates (which meant the paying of tribute money) or to regulate trade relations.

The archaeological evidence cannot reveal the exact time when a province, or a part of a province, or a province and some regions of the adjacent one was abandoned. Again to take Valeria as an example: on archaeological grounds the evacuation of Aquincum (modern Budapest) has been dated in the last decades of the fourth century,[380] whereas the much smaller Intercisa is supposed to have stayed Roman beyond the beginning of the fifth century.[381] There is no proof for such dates and there can be none. The finds from Intercisa have been thoroughly studied. Many clay vessels are dated in the fourth century. But not even the most meticulous analysis of their shapes and decor can establish the decade, not to speak of the year, in which they were made. Was it 379? Perhaps. Or 390? Possible. 410? This, too, cannot be excluded. It is impossible to set a deadline after which these plain jugs or dishes could not have been made. The ethnic attribution of the finds with marked barbarian features is equally uncertain. After Klára Sz. Póczy assigned one type of vessel to the Visigoths, another to "an Ostrogothic, respectively Hunnic-Alanic people," whatever that means, she admits at the end of her study that it is hardly possible to differentiate between the pottery of the Goths, Huns, and Sarmatians. However, even if the exact dates when these vessels were made and the nationality of the makers could be established, we still would not know when and under what circumstances the garrisons were withdrawn. The dwellings in and around the squalid camps were occupied by barbarians, who probably included some Huns. Where these free Huns or, nominally, subjects of the emperor? We do not know. In Fenékpuszta in Pannonia prima, south of Balcum on Lake Balaton, Romans lived side by side with half-Sarmatized Germans.[382] Small Roman settle-

---

[378] Cf. Stein 1959, 2, 305.

[379] Isidor, *Hist. Wand.* 74, *MGH AA* XI, 297. See the map, Courtois 1955, 172.

[380] Cf. K. Sz. Póczy, *Budapest régiségei* 16, 1955, 41-87, known to me from the summary in *Bibliotheca classica orientalis* 2, 1957, 106-107; T. Nagy, quoted by A. Mócsy, *Eirene* 4, 1963, 138.

[381] Cf. L. Barkóczi, *AAH* 36, 1957, 543.

[382] Cf. T. Pekáry, *AÉ* 82, 1955, 19-29.

ments were holding out here and there. The Huns apparently found it to their advantage to spare them because they needed the artisans. Had they wanted, they almost certainly could have overrun Vindobona (modern Vienna) any time; they left the poor people there to live in peace.[383] It is quite probable that a strip of wasteland separated Hun land from Romania in the west, as it did for a number of years in the south. But wherever the borders were, if one can speak of borders, they were not those of the former provinces.

The assumption that Aetius ceded a part of Pannonia to Ruga rests on a misinterpretation of a passage in Priscus. In his account of the East Roman embassy to Attila, Priscus calls Orestes a Roman who "lived in the land of the Paeonians on the river Sava, which according to the treaty of Aetius, general of the Western Romans, belonged to the barbarian" (ᾤκει τὴν πρὸς τῷ Σάῳ ποταμῷ Παιόνων χώραν τ ῷ β α ρ β ά ρ ῷ κατὰ τὰς ᾿Αετίου στρατηγοῦ τῶν ἑσπερίων ῾Ρωμαίων συνθήκας ὑπακούουσαν).[384] The view that Aetius ceded Pannonian territory to Ruga is so firmly established that to my knowledge no one paid attention to the spaced words. Priscus could have written τῷ ῾Ρούᾳ or τοῖς βαρβάροις. But he wrote τῷ βαρβάρῳ. "The barbarian" occurs in the fragment in three more passages: (1) Attila ordered that neither Bigila nor the other East Romans must buy horses or anything else except the most necessary food.— "This was a shrewd plan of the barbarian";[385] (2) the West Romans sent an embassy "to the barbarian";[386] (3) "the barbarian" named the men whom he would accept as negotiators.[387] It follows that the barbarian to whom Aetius ceded the land along the Sava was Attila, not Ruga. Note also that not a province but a territory designated by the river was ceded.

Disregarding the precise statement of Priscus, historians of the Huns arbitrarily dated the "cession" of Pannonia prima[388] in 425,[389] 431,[390] or 433.[391] Another passage in the same fragment shows that not even in 448,

---

[383] Cf. Egger 1955, 76-81.

[384] *EL* 579₂₁₋₂₃.

[385] *Ibid.*, 130₃.

[386] *Ibid.*, 133₂₄.

[387] *Ibid.*, 143₄.

[388] H. Vetters (*Mitteilungen des Instituts für österreichische Geschichtsforschung* 60, 4, 1952, 422) asserts that Valeria also was ceded then.

[389] Gibbon 417.

[390] Seeck, VI *Geschicthe* 6, 115.

[391] Alföldi 1926, 90; Stein 1959, 1, 479 (Pannonia secunda and probably also Valeria); Thompson 1948, 64 (Pannonia prima). Alföldi's conjecture that Priscus confused the Drava with the Sava in based on his assumption that the territory was ceded in 433. R. Egger, (*Jahrbuch des oberösterreichischen Musealvereins* 95, 1950, 144) asserts

when Attila was at the height of his power, was the whole province Hun land. Constantiolus was a man "from the land of the Paionians that was ruled by Attila" (ἐκ τῆς Παιόνων χώρας τῆς ὑπὸ Ἀττήλα ταττομένης).[392] The specification makes sense only if a part of Pannonia was *not* under Attila's rule.

It is conceivable that Aetius paid for Ruga's help in land, which can only mean that he officially consented to the Huns' keeping, to vary Isidor's words, *partem Pannoniae quam possederunt*. It is equally possible that he paid for it in cash; he may have concluded an alliance with Ruga and promised to pay him subsidies. Or he may have done all that at the same time. But these are mere surmises. We should turn now to Ruga's relationships with the East Romans.

Our information comes from Socrates, Theodoret, Priscus, and the Chronicle of 452. The excerpt from Priscus[393] seems to be somewhat shortened, and in the second half there is a gap of a few words; still it is by far the most important and most reliable source for the history of these dark years.

When some tribes on the Danube fled into Roman territory and offered their services to Theodosius, Ruga demanded through his envoy Esla that these and all other fugitives be surrendered to him; a refusal he would regard as a breach of the peace. Shortly afterwards Ruga died, succeeded by Attila and Bleda. The new treaty they concluded at Margus (near the modern village of Dubravica east of Belgrade) with Plintha, the Roman plenipotentiary who was accompanied by the *quaestor* Epigenes, was entirely to the advantage of the Huns. It provided for the surrender of all fugitives from the Huns and of those Roman prisoners of the Huns who had returned to the empire without paying ransom; the latter had to be sent back, unless 8 solidi were paid for each of them. The Romans undertook not to form an alliance with a barbarian people with whom the Huns went to war. At the fairs Huns and Romans should have the same rights and the same security. The annual tribute was raised from 350 to 700 pounds of gold. Among the fugitives surrendered by the

---

that "the imperial government ceded the Vienna Basin and the Burgenland to the Huns"; needless to say, he gives no reason for changing Priscus' precise statement "along the Sava" into "east of Vienna," and referring it to 433. Demougeot (1951, 381, n. 153) goes even further. Aetius is supposed to have ceded to Ruga not only Pannonia prima but also Noricum ripense.

[392] *EL* 140$_{24-25}$.
[393] *Ibid.*, 121-122.

Romans were Mamas and Atakam, two young men of royal descent; they were handed over to the Huns at Carso[394] and crucified.

This Priscus fragment is in various respects most instructive. We learn from it of a previous war which the Huns had won. A tribute of 350 pounds of gold, 25,200 solidi, is not a very large sum, but the fact that the Romans paid it to Ruga indicates his eminent position. He must have been more than "the first of the kings," as Charaton was. He, and not the "kings" or *phylarchoi*, received the money. How he distributed the gold among the tribal leaders and other members of the Hun aristocracy cannot be ascertained. However, he obviously was able to enforce his decision: those who were dissatisfied could not rebel; they fled to the Romans. Ruga had his diplomats; Esla, says Priscus, was experienced in negotiating with the imperial government. It seems that Ruga played also, though indirectly, a role in the domestic struggle at the court, in Constantinople. Plintha urged him to negotiate with him and not with any other Roman, which makes sense only under the assumption that the ex-consul used his connections with the Huns as a weapon against his rivals, as Aetius did in Ravenna. Still, the power of the king was not yet unlimited. The Huns fought together, but, at the same time, each one fought for himself. The prisoners a Hun made were his, not Ruga's. Under Attila only men as prominent as Onegesius could keep their own prisoners;[395] all others were Attila's property. How far eastward Ruga's power reached cannot be decided. That he did not rule from Hungary to the Volga, as some scholars thought, follows from the treaty of Margus. The Romans could form alliances only with peoples who lived not far from their frontiers.

The chronology of Ruga's last years is not easy to establish. The Chronicle of 452 lists his death under 434: "Aetius is restored to favor. Rugila, king of the Huns, with whom peace was made, dies. Bleda succeeds him." (*Aetius in gratiam receptus. Rugila, rex Chunorum, cum quo pax firmata, moritur, cui Bleda succedit.*)[396] It is well known how unreliable the chronology of the Gallic chronicle is.[397] If it were our only authority, we could date Ruga's death as early as 431 or as late as 437. Seeck[398] thought that the date in the chronicle was confirmed by the edifying story about the ignominious death of the Hun king in Socrates.

---

[394] The present Harşova; cf. Patsch 1928, 49-50, and J. Bromberg, *Byzantion* 12, 1937, 459, n. 2.

[395] *EL*, 135_{32}-136_2.

[396] *CM* I, 660, 116.

[397] To give an example: Stilicho's victory over Radagaisus (406) and Arcadius' death (408) are listed under 405.

[398] *Geschichte* 6, 460, followed by Stein 1959, 1, 434, and Thompson 1948, 72.

The church historian relates[399] that Emperor Theodosius II (408-450), being informed that the barbarians were making preparations to ravage the Roman provinces,

> committed the management of the matter to God, and, continuing in earnest prayer, he speedily obtained what he sought. For the chief of the barbarians, whose name was Rugas, was struck dead by a thunderbolt. Then a plague followed which destroyed most of the men who were under him, and if this was not sufficient, fire came down from heaven, and consumed many of the survivors. On this occasion Proclus the bishop preached a sermon in the church in which he applied a prophecy of Ezekiel[400] to the deliverance effected by God in the late emergency, and was in consequence much admired.

Proclus succeeded Maximian as bishop of Constantinople in April 434. However, Socrates does not say that Proclus preached the sermon in the capital. The story forms part of a panegyric on Theodosius, who evidently was as devout and meek before 434. Ruga's death could have happened at a time when Proclus was still bishop of Cyzicus. And it did in the source from which Socrates drew. "It is because of this [*i.e.*, Theodosius'] meekness that God subdued his enemies without martial conflicts, as the capture of the usurper John [in 425] and the subsequent discomfiture of the barbarians[401] clearly demonstrate." Ruga's hordes were those whom John had called to his assistance against the Romans; they attacked "after the death of the usurper."[402]

The date in Socrates, not long after 425, is not only at variance with that in the Gallic chronicle; it is also irreconcilable with the one given by Theodoret, who tells exactly the same story both in his *Ecclesiastical History*[403] and the commentary on Psalm 22:14-15.[404] God helped Theodosius against the Huns because the emperor had proved his devotion to the true religion by issuing a law that ordered the complete destruction of all pagan temples. The victory over Ruga was "the abundant harvest that followed these good seeds." The edict was issued on November 14, 435,[405] so Ruga would have been killed after that date. That this was,

---

[399] Socrates VI, 42-43, *PG* 67, 832-833; John of Nikiu (Charles 1916, 100) copied Socrates.

[400] Socrates XXXVIII, 2 and 22.

[401] Ἡ ἐπιγενομένη μετὰ ταῦτα τῶν βαρβάρων ἀπώλεια.

[402] Μετὰ γὰρ τὴν τοῦ τυράννου ἀναίρεσιν, clearly immediately or very soon after his death.

[403] V, 37, 4, *GCS* 44 (19), 340.

[404] *PG* 80, 977.

[405] *Cod. Theodos.* XVI, 10, 25, given at Constantinople.

indeed, Theodoret's information is confirmed, if confirmation is needed, by the other victory which God granted Theodosius as a reward for his pious zeal. He smote the Persians[406] in 441.[407]

We have, thus, three dates for Ruga's death: shortly after 425, 434, and after November 435. Properly, none is correct, for Ruga died, as we know from Priscus, not in a campaign in Thrace[408] but in his own land. Still, Socrates' and Theodoret's accounts cannot be dismissed as valueless. The Romans *did* wage war against Ruga. The legend reflected and distorted its first phase. It has a close parallel in the homily of Isaac of Antioch. As the Huns in 447 had to retreat for a short time, incidentally also because of a plague, only to attack again and conquer, Ruga's hordes, too, apparently suffered a temporary reverse.

At the time of the negotiations which led to the treaty of Margus, the Huns were still holding Roman prisoners, so the peace seems to have been concluded not very long before.[409] This is also indicated by the Gallic chronicle: "Ruga, with whom peace was made, dies" (*Ruga, cum quo pax firmata, moritur*). Who made peace with Ruga? Not the West Romans, as it is usually assumed;[410] they had not been at war with the Huns. But the East Romans were. Furthermore, when we consider that the Gallic chronicle draws more than once on Eastern sources,[411] it is practically certain that the peace referred to is the one that brought the fighting in Thrace to an end.

The date in Socrates is unacceptable; the one in the Gallic chronicle uncertain. Theodoret's "after the end of 435" is in agreement with Priscus. Epigenes, Plintha's companion on the embassy to Ruga's successors, on November 15, 438, was still *magister memoriae*. Because Priscus describes him as *quaestor*, the embassy falls *after* that date.[412] Thompson thinks that Priscus made a slip, but his only argument is the date of Ruga's death which he, arbitrarily as we may say now, places in 434. Plintha's role in the negotiations with Ruga and, then, with Bleda and Attila, furnishes another argument for a late date. He was, says Priscus, *magister militum*. Anatolius, who in 447 concluded the peace treaty with Attila, was *magister militum praesentalis*. Plintha's position at the court, his apparently strained

---

[406] *Hist. eccles.* V, 37, 5, *PG* 80, 977.

[407] The second Persian war in Theodosius' reign; cf. M. Brock, *Revue d'histoire ecclésiastique* 44, 1949, 552-556.

[408] Theodoret, *Hist. eccles.* V, 37, 4.

[409] Stein 1959, 1, 435) dated it "about 430," which was a mere guess, and not a fortunate one.

[410] Most recently by Thompson 1948, 64.

[411] See Appendix.

[412] Cf. Ensslin 1927, 3; *PW* Supp. V, 665.

relationship with other high dignitaries, his interference in diplomatic affairs, all this leaves little doubt that he, too, had the rank of *m. m. praesentalis*. In 434, Saturninus, who was to take the place of Dorotheus, bishop of Marcianopolis, deposed by Maximian, came to the town *cum magnificentissimo et gloriosissimo magistro militae Plintha*.[413] At that time Plintha was still *magister militum per Thracias*. His promotion falls, thus, after 434.

To summarize, Ruga's war with the East Romans, his death, and the beginning of the reign of Bleda and Attila are to be dated in the second half of the 430's.

ATTILA

In the *Bazaar of Heracleides*, the ex-patriarch of Constantinople, Nestorius (428-431), since 436 exiled to Oasis in Egypt, with deadly monotony turned to the injustice done to him at the Council of Ephesus (June 431) and to the unspeakable evils that came from it. In its *rabies theologica* the book surpasses even the writings of the patriarch Cyril of Alexandria, Nestorius' enemy. Only occasionally does its author cast a quick glance at the world outside the conclaves where the enemies of God plotted his downfall. Yet this narrow-minded fanatic understood the causes of the rapid ascendancy of the Huns better than most of his contemporaries. Toward the end of the *Bazaar*, speaking of, or rather alluding to, the wars with the Huns in the last decade of the reign of Theodosius the Younger, Nestorius writes:

> The people of the Scythians were great and many, and formerly were divided into people and into kingdoms and were treated as robbers. They used not to do much wrong except through rapidity and through speed. Yet later they were established in a kingdom, they grew very strong, so that they surpassed in their greatness all the forces of the Romans.[414]

Though this is an oversimplification, basically Nestorius was right. Until the end of the 430's the Huns were a great nuisance, much worse than the Saracens or the Isaurians, but they were not a danger. Their inroads carried them at times deep into the Balkan provinces, but they were always either driven out or bought off.

At the end of the 440's, the barbarians were, in Nestorius' words, "the masters, and the Romans, slaves."[415] This, too, is an exaggeration, but not even the most abject flatterers of the Christ-loving Theodosius could

[413] *ACO* I:IV: 2, 88.
[414] Nestorius 366.
[415] *Ibid.*, 368.

have denied that within a few years the bands of "robbers" had grown into a military power of the first rank. They would have rejected Nestorius' explanation of the change, namely, that it was "the transgression against the true faith of God impassible" which made it possible for the Huns to unite under one ruler, and in their way, they would have been right. The Huns did not become mightier because the Romans grew weaker. The Eastern army was as strong in 447 as it was in 437, the fortifications along the *limes* were as well garrisoned, if not better, and there is no reason to assume that the Roman troops were led by incompetent generals. Besides, the great Hun victories fell in a time when the Eastern empire was at peace with Persia. The explanation of the radical change in the relative strength of the Huns and the Romans must be sought not in Romania but in Hunnia.

It has become the fashion to deny Attila practically any merit for the short-lived greatness of his people. He was, we are told, neither a military genius nor a diplomat of exceptional ability, but a bungler who would not have made such awful blunders had he had a professor of history as advisor. The purpose of the following pages is not to prove that Attila was another Alexander; if as a result of a new study of the years 441-447 the personality of Attila turns out to have been a decisive factor, I am far from maintaining that it was the only one. But before speculating about primary, secondary, and tertiary factors, about the direct and remote causes of this or that event, the events themselves must be established. The standard histories give, I believe, an erroneous picture of the Hun wars in the 440's and a distorted one of the relationship of the Huns with the West. A number of sources exist which have been either ignored or treated too cavalierly. None of them, taken by itself, is very revealing. Only by combining them all, and paying attention to the details, may we hope to reconstruct the happenings in this decisive decade of Hun history.

The Huns Threaten the West

Merobaudes' *Second Panegyric on Aetius*[416] is a mediocre poem (see Chapter XII). More than half of it is lost; many verses in the only extant manuscript are mutilated and can be restored with no more than a varying degree of probability. Like the other poems of Merobaudes, the panegyric takes a very modest place in late Latin literature. But its value as a historical document cannot be overrated. It sheds light on the relationships between the Huns and the Western empire in a period about which we know next to nothing from other sources.

---

[416] Merobaudes, 11-18.

It is not germane to my purpose to discuss the panegyric in all its historical aspects, but the parts dealing with the Huns can be set into the proper context only after the date has been established at which the poem was recited. Aetius was consul in 432, 437, and 446. Mommsen,[417] Seeck,[418] and Levison[419] assumed that Merobaudes addressed the consul of 437; Vollmer,[420] Bury,[421] Stein,[422] and Thompson[423] pleaded for 446. The obscure style of Merobaudes and his tendency to use circumlocutions instead of naming persons and places makes the interpretation often difficult. But taken as a whole the poem presents a clear picture of the events preceding the third consulship of the great *ductor*.

The year begins in peace (vv. 30-41). The clarions are silent, the arms at rest, Bellona has put down her helmet, her hair wreathed with olive, Mars stands by inactively while Aetius dons the consular toga. "The weapons and the chariot of the god are silent, and his idle steeds lay bare the pastures hidden under the Riphaean rime."[424] In Claudian, whom Merobaudes closely followed, Mars' steeds disport themselves in the pastures of the Eridanus.[425] The difference is significant. To Merobaudes the home of Mars is the far north. Aetius enters his consulship "with the northern regions subdued."[426]

But it is hard-won peace. To secure it, Aetius had to fight many wars.[427] In the prooemium the poet rapidly surveys the achievements of his hero. He does not follow a chronological order. Starting in the north, on the Danube, he proceeds westward to the Rhine and the *tractus Armoricanus* (modern Brittany), turns south to Gallia Narbonensis, and ends in Africa.

After a reference to Aetius' deeds at the Danube, which I shall discuss later, Merobaudes speaks of the Franks:

The Rhine has added an alliance serving the wintry world. The river is satisfied being bent by western chains and rejoices to see the Tiber [Rome] grow on its other bank.

---

[417] *Hermes* 46, 1901, n. 5.
[418] *Geschichte* 6, 418 *ad* p. 115. But in *Geschichte* 6, 471 *ad* p. 318, Seeck dates the panegyric in 446.
[419] Levison 1903, 139, n. 6.
[420] Vollmer in *Merobaudes*, p. iv; p. 10, note.
[421] Vollmer, 251, n.3.
[422] 1959, 1, 481, n. 4; 492, n. 3; 493, n. 1.
[423] *JRS* 46, 1956, 71, n. 34; *Analecta Bollandiana* 75, 1957, 137.
[424] Cf. Virgil, *Georg.* IV, 518.
[425] *4th Cons. Hon.* 15-16.
[426] *Scythici axe subacto cardinis* (vv. 33-34).
[427] *Hanc tot bella tibi requiem, Romane, dederunt* (v. 42).

(Addidit hiberni famulantia foedera Rhenus
orbis et Hesperiis flecti contentus habenis
gaudet ab alterna Thybrin sibi crescere ripa [vv. 5-7.])

These stilted verses are an example of Merobaudes' style. He means to say that Aetius forced the peoples on the Rhine to conclude an alliance with Rome: the territory east of the river has been made Roman again.[428]

Taken by itself, the passage could refer to the late 420's, the early 430's, or the 440's. Mommsen thought that Merobaudes alluded to Aetius' victory over the Franks in 428.[429] In 432, Aetius conquered the Franks again.[430] In a context which points to a time not long before 439, Jordanes speaks, somewhat vaguely, about the "crushing defeats" which Aetius inflicted on the proud Suevi and the barbarous Franks.[431] About 440, Cologne and a number of other cities in the Rhineland were a gain in the power of the Franks. A few years later—the exact date is unknown—they withdrew, to attack anew in 455. Because in 451 they fought against Attila as the allies of the Romans, the *foedus* between them and the empire, which means Aetius, must have been renewed after 440. Stein[432] was inclined to think that Merobaudes alluded to this last alliance. In other words, verses 5-7 are compatible with either date suggested for the panegyric. But the following verses 8-15, point unmistakably to 446.

The rosy picture which Merobaudes draws of the *tractus Armoricanus*, where the former Bacaudae (see Chapter XII), now law-abiding peasants, are peacefully tilling the long-neglected fields, was not true at any time in the first half of the fifth century. But even if all allowances are made for the exaggerations in which the panegyrist was expected to indulge,[433] Merobaudes could not have written those verses in 436. The Bacaudae, "an inexperienced and disorderly band of rustics" (*agrestium hominum*

---

[428] Vollmer in *Merobaudes*, p. 11.

[429] *Hermes* 46, 1901, 535, n. 4. He adduced Prosper, *CM* I, p. 472, *ad a.* 428: *Pars Galliarum propinqua Rheno, quem Franci possidendam occupaverant, Aetii armis recepta.* I fail to understand how Loyen (1942, 65, n. 1) can accept Mommsen's interpretation and still date the panegyric in 446 (p. 66. n. 3).

[430] Hydatius, *CM* II, 22₉₈.

[431] *Getica* 176.

[432] Stein 1959, 1, 492, with references to Salvian, Sidonius, *Hist. Franc.*, and other sources from which the events can be reconstructed with a fair amount of probability. Ch. Verlinden's article on Aetius and the Franks (*Bijdragen voor de Geschiedenis der Nederlanden* 1, 1946, 10 ff.) contains little that has not been said more briefly and better by Stein.

[433] Quinterios III, 7, 6.

imperita et confusa manus),[434] were no match for a regular army,[435] but to the motley hosts of federates, which were thrown against them by Aetius, they offered the toughest resistance. It took the Romans a long time to put down the uprising which began in 435.[436] Tibatto, the leader of the Bacaudae, was still fighting in 436 and 437. When Aetius entered his second consulship, Litorius and his Huns were fully occupied hunting down the elusive bands which, driven into the woods,[437] inaccessible to the horsemen, broke out again and again. It was only after most of their leaders were either killed or captured that the *commotio Bacaudarum* "came to a rest."[438]

Not only was the *tractus Armoricanus* not pacified in 437, war was also raging in southern Gaul. Narbonne, under siege by the Goths for months,[439] was at the point of surrender when Litorius relieved the city early in 437.[440] Merobaudes aptly describes Gallia Narbonensis, stressing the importance of the province as a link between Italy and Spain. Aetius drove the bandits out, the roads were open again, the people had returned to their towns.[441] Later in the poem (vv. 144-186), where he deals with the "warlike deeds" (πράξεις κατὰ πόλεμον) of his hero, Merobaudes draws a remarkable picture of the war in Gaul. The Goths were no longer the primitive savages whom Caesar had fought. They had learned the art of war, bravely holding out in fortified places, a people noble in deeds, if not noble in mind. In 439, the war ended with an alliance between the Goths and the Romans.[442]

Verses 24-29 refer to still later events. At a time when the Romans were still holding Carthage, Merobaudes could not have called Geiseric *insessor Libyae*, he could not have said that the Vandal king had torn down the throne of the Elissaean kingdom and that Nordic hordes filled the Tyrian towns.[443] Carthage fell on October 19, 439. Geiseric's eagerness to arrange a betrothal between one of his sons and a Roman princess,

---

[434] Orosius, *Hist. adv. Pagan.* VII, 25, 2. Cf. the Queriolus and Rutilius Namatianus, *De red. suo* I, 213ff.

[435] Cf. Aurelius Victor, *Caesar.* XXXIX, 19, on Herulius' brief campaign.

[436] *CM* II, 660₁₁₇.

[437] "To conceal in the forests the plunder gathered by savage crimes" (*Saevo crimine quaestias silvis celare rapinas*), Merobaudes, vv. 9-10.

[438] *CM* II, 660₁₁₉.

[439] Loyen 1942, 45.

[440] Coville 1930, 107.

[441] Merobaudes, vv. 19-23. *Belliger ultor* is an allusion to the battle at Toulouse in 439 in which the Romans were defeated and Litorius was killed.

[442] Sidonius, Carm. VIII, 308; *Getica* 177.

[443] L. Schmidt 1942, 76; Gitti 1953, 15.

to which Merobaudes alludes in verses 27-29, likewise presupposes that the war had come to an end. The peace concluded in 442[444] is the latest datable event named in the prooemium.

Now we can return to the beginning of the poem. The first verse is lost. It must have been a short praise of Aetius who

. . . *Danuvii cum pace redit Tanainque furore*
exuit et nigro candentes aethere terras
Marte suo caruisse iubet; dedit otia ferro
Caucasus et saevi condemnant proelia reges.

. . . comes back with peace on the Danube [or: from the banks of the Danube] and strips the Tanais of its furor, and orders the countries glistening under the black sky to be without their Mars. The Caucasus lets rest the iron, and the savage kings condemn the battles.

Mommsen's conjecture[445] that the four verses refer to Aetius' stay with the Huns after 409 (followed by Vollmer,[446] Bugiani,[447] and Thompson[448]) cannot be true. The $αὔξησις$ of the virtues of his hero was certainly the duty of the *rhetor*.[449] But there were limits. Not even the most servile sycophant could have said that the boy Aetius came back with peace on the Danube. He was sent to the Huns as hostage, to guarantee the observance of a treaty. He did not give orders, he received them.

---

[444] For the date, cf. Seeck, *Geschichte* 6, 121; Stein 1959, 1, 484; W. Ensslin, *BZ* 43, 1950, 43. It may seem strange that Merobaudes passes over the war with the Burgundians in 436-437. The senate erected a statue to Aetius (its base was excavated in 1937) *ob Italiae securitatem quam procul domitis gentibus peremptisque Burgundionibus et Gotis oppressis vincendo praestitit*; see Bartoli 1948, 267-273, and, with a better interpretation, Degrassi 1949, 33-44. That the Burgundians are named in the inscription but not in the panegyric may be because of the different dates of the two documents. After the Burgundians were settled in the Sapaudia (modern Savoie), they kept quiet. When the statue was set up, the memory of the war with them was still fresh. But in 446 the Burgundians were faithful allies who, indeed, a few years later fought at the side of the Romans against the Huns. The Goths, in contrast, maintained their hostility toward Aetius even after the treaty of 439; see Thompson 1948, 126. But Merobaudes probably had an additional reason for omitting the Burgundians. The "Roman" troops who destroyed the Burgundian kingdom were Huns, led by Litorius, in the service of Aetius. With the deterioration of Aetius' relationship with the Huns, and in particular such a short time after the actual threat of war with Bleda and Attila, Merobaudes may have considered it wiser to leave out the victory over the Burgundians, which was Aetius' only in name. N. H. Baynes (*JRS* XII, 1922, 221) rightly pointed out that the circumstances under which the Burgundian kingdom fell are obscure.

[445] Mommsen 1901, 518, n. 4.
[446] Merobaudes 11, note.
[447] Bugiani 1905, 43, n. 2.
[448] 1948, 34.
[449] Menander, Spengel 1956, 3, 368.

But it is not only the content of the verses which forbids taking them as an allusion to Aetius' youth, it is also the context in which they stand. Merobaudes puts the conclusion of the peace with the barbarians in the north at the head of the list of Aetius' achievements. All achievements— the reconquest of the left bank of the Rhine, the pacification of the Aremorica, the victory over the Goths, Geiseric's attempt at a rapprochement with the court at Ravenna—fall between 437 and 446. Aetius' dealings with "Caucasus" and "Tanais" must be dated in the same period.

Verses 50-97 refer again to the barbarians in the far north. A nefarious goddess complains that she is held in contempt everywhere. "We are beaten back from the waves and not admitted on land." Unwilling to bear this any longer, she is determined to call forth the distant peoples from the extreme north. Breaking the alliances of the kingdoms, *regnorum foedera*, she will plunge the world into misery. She drives to the Rhipaean Mountains where Enyo dwells. The goddess of war is depressed because peace has reigned for such a long time. The *diva nocens* exhorts Enyo to take heart and instigate the Scythian hordes of the Tanais to make war on the Romans.

These verses reflect Claudian's influence in thought as well as in words.[450] But it is the content that interests us. The speeches of the *diva nocens* cannot be the prelude to a description of the Gothic war as Vollmer suggested. Verses 52-53 indicate the date with all the precision one can expect from Merobaudes. "We are driven from the sea and are not allowed to rule on land" (*Depellimur undis nec terris regnare licet*). The only people to fight the Romans at sea were the Vandals. Prosper, Marcellinus Comes, and the *Chronicon Paschale* (see Chapter XII) record their piratical expeditions in 437, 438, and 439.[451] After the conquest of Carthage, "they created a fleet of light cruisers and attacked the empire by sea, as no other Teutonic people had done or was to do in the Mediterranean."[452] In 440, the Vandals landed in Sicily and ravaged Bruttium. It was only after 442, when Geiseric tried to get on better terms with the Romans, that the furies "were beaten back from the waves."[453] In a decade of the fiercest onslaughts on the empire, a period of three or four years of peace must have been regarded as a rather long one, *pax annosa*. The threat

---

[450] Cf. *In Ruf.* I, 25ff.; to the verbal imitations pointed out by Vollmer more could be added, e.g., vv. 57-59 = *In Ruf.* II, 17-18.

[451] L. Schmidt 1942, 66.

[452] Bury 1923, 257.

[453] In 445, the Vandals made a raid on Galicia (Hydatius, *CM* II, 24_{131}). But Galicia, under the Suebi, was no longer Roman territory.

of war, Enyo's appeal to the barbarians in the north, must be dated between 443 and 446.

The "savage Scythian hordes" were the Huns. By the middle of the fifth century no other people was strong enough to threaten Italy. Besides, Merobaudes characterizes the enemy so clearly that there can be no doubt whom he meant. The sites of the barbarians were near the Rhipaean Mountains, on the Tanais (the river Don),[454] and on the Phasis (the river Rion, east of the Black Sea): "Trembling Tiber will be attacked by his friend, the Phasis" (*Phasiacoque pavens innabitur hospite Thybris* (v. 56). The meaning of the bizarre metaphor is obvious: The people from the Phasis will break into Italy.

The Riphaean Mountains could be connected with any people in the north. The Tanais in poetic language is the river of the north, *kat' exochen*, as the Nile is that of the south.[455] Alaric's Goths were a people from the Tanais and the Hister.[456] Sidonius called even Geiseric a rebel from the Tanais.[457] But no Germanic tribe has ever been associated with the Phasis and the Caucasus. These were the regions from which the Huns came. The Hun auxiliaries in Theodosius' army poured forth from "the threatening Caucasus and the wild Taurus" (*minax Caucasus et rigens Taurus*).[458] In 395, the Huns broke into Asia "from the distant crags of the Caucasus."[459] They came from the land beyond the cold Phasis.[460] The Huns were not just barbarians far in the north. They were " a people from the farthest boundaries of Scythia, beyond the icy Don" (*genus extremos Scythiae vergentis in ortus/ trans gelidum Tanain.*)[461] And Merobaudes also so calls them: "tribes living in the farthest north" (*summo gentes aquilone repostas* [v. 55]). Caucasus, Tanais, Phasis, the extreme north—this is the country of the Huns, and only of the Huns.

---

[454] "He had driven away the Scythian quivers on the unknown shores of the Don" (*Scythicasque pharetras egerat ignotis Tanais bacchatus in oris*), vv. 75-76.

[455] Horace IV, 15, 24; Tibullus, *Paneg. Messallae* VII, 2; Seneca, *Hercules furens* 1323, *Herc. Oet.* 86; Claudian, *3rd Cons. Hon.* 44, *Bell. Goth.* 57, *Rapt. Pros.* II, 66. Tanais and Maeotis are the ends of the world (Florus II, 39, 6).

[456] Claudian, *Bell. Goth.* 603; Sidonius, *Paneg. on Avitus* 75 (*Tanais Getarum, i.e., Gothorum*).

[457] Sidonius XXIII, 257; cf. 479 (*Scythicae potor Tanaiticus undae*).

[458] Pacatus XXXIII, 10.

[459] Jerome, ep. LX, 16.

[460] "The mothers of Cappadocians are driven beyond the Phasis" (*Trans Phasin aguntur Cappadocum matres* [by the Huns]), Claudian, *In Eutrop.* I, 245; "neither Caucasus nor icy Phasis any longer sends the enemy against me" (*nec iam mihi mittit Caucasus hostes nec mittit gelidus Phasis* [as in 395]), *In Eutrop.* II, 574-575.

[461] Claudian, *In Ruf.* I, 323-324.

The study of Merobaudes' panegyric leaves no doubt that at one time between 437 and 446 the relationship between the Western empire and the Huns was extremely tense. The phrase "Caucasus granted leisure to the sword" (*dedit otia ferro Caucasus*) points to actual, though perhaps only limited war. Our interpretation is supported by the inscription on a (now lost) tombstone:[462]

Here the glory of Italy is buried, the hero Constantius,
who was the shield of his country, its walls and weapons.

Invincible in war, a lover of true peace,
though pierced with wounds, he was victorious everywhere.

He subdued the race that crossed the middle of the sea,
and likewise the land refused to give aid to the vanquished.

He was sober, mighty in battle, chaste, a powerful commander,
first in judgment, first in war.

He was as much burning in love and devotion to the Romans
as he was bringing terror to the Pannonian tribes.

In war he sought honors for himself and his sons,
to the nobles he gave as gifts the cut-off heads.

In the midst of his sons the father lies stabbed; the grievous mother
does not know whom to lament, overwhelmed by her sorrow.

Worse is the misfortune of Rome, robbed of so great a senator;
she has lost her ornament, she has lost her arms.

The saddened armies are standing still, after their great commander
has been taken away, with whom Rome was powerful, without whom
she is lying prostrate.

This tumulus, o great leader, has been erected for you by your wife,
who lies here, reunited with you.

> (*Hic decus Italiae tegitur Constantinus heros*
> *qui patriae tegmen, murus ac arma fuit.*
> *Invictus bello, non fictae pacis amator,*
> *confixus plagis, victor ubique fuit.*
> *Hic mare per medium gentem compressit euntem,*
> *et victis pariter terra negavit opem.*
> *Sobrius armipotens castus moderamine pollens*
> *primus in ingenio, primus in arma fuit.*
> *Romanis blando quantum flagravit amore,*
> *tantum Pannoniis gentibus horror erat.*
> *Iste sibi et natis bello marcavit honores,*
> *munera principibus colla secata dedit.*

---

[462] De Rossi, 1888, 1, 265 and 2, 284, n. 1; Fiebiger and Schmidt 1917, no. 34, 29-30.

Natorum medio fixus pater: anxia mater
  quem plangat nescit, stat stupefacta dolens.
Peius Roma gemit tanto spoliata senatu,
  perdidit ornatum, perdidit arma simul.
Tristes stant acies magno ductore remoto,
  cum quo Roma potens, quo sine pressa iacet.
Hunc tumulum, dux magne, tuum tibi condidit uxor,
  quae tecum rursus consociata iacet.)

Constantius, a man of modest origin, distinguished himself in the service of Rome. He fought a barbarian people at sea and on land; in an engagement with the Pannonian peoples he was killed.

Who was this Constantius, and when did he live? The name is extremely common; there must have been dozens of senators called Constantius. Mommsen[463] surmised that the verses glorify the emperor Constantius Chlorus (305-306). But they were written at a time when Pannonia, or at least the larger part of it, was no longer a Roman province.[464] That the sea-going people were the Vandals has been recognized by Seeck,[465] Sundwall,[466] and Fiebiger.[467] However, these scholars could not fit the deeds of Constantius into the history of the 430's or the 440's. I think we can. The only time that the West Romans fought a barbarian sea-going nation, first at sea and then on land, was between 437 and 440. *Tantum Pannoniis gentibus horror erat* points to fighting in and around Pannonia, to a commander of troops on the frontier, now repulsing raiding bands, now making inroads in the territory of the enemy, to constant clashes along the border: *munera principibus colla secata dedit.*

There exist two more documents which reflect the threat of war with a formidable enemy between the second and third consulship of Aetius. By the *novella* issued at Ravenna on July 14, 444,[468] a large group of officials lost with one stroke privileges they had enjoyed for more than thirty years. Not only had they been exempt from the duty of supplying recruits from among their tenants; they did not even have to make the money payments which most landowners made instead of furnishing the men.[469] The new law provided that the *illustres*, who were inactive, pay

---

[463] *Hermes* 28, 1893, 33.
[464] Cf. Fiebiger and Schmidt 1917, no. 34, 29-30.
[465] *PW* 4, 1102.
[466] P. 66, n. 110.
[467] 1917, no. 34, 29-30.
[468] *Nov. Val.* VI, 3; cf. Stein 1959, 1, 508.
[469] "To pay for the recruits in money" (*Tirones in adaeratione persolvere*), *Cod. Theodos.* XI, 18.

in money for three recruits each, the price of one recruit being assessed at 30 solidi; that the counts of the consistory and those of the first order, the tribunes and notaries and ex-provincial governors pay for one recruit each, and inactive tribunes, counts of the second and third class, and other *clarissimi* for one-third of a recruit. The government, aware what a storm of indignation would sweep through the middle and lower ranks of the bureaucracy, hastened to assure them that the decree was issued only for the present time. But the government had no choice: because of "the necessity of imminent expenses," the resources of the treasury did not suffice.

If Valentinian's ministers expected that the new tax would alleviate the frightful financial stress in some degree, *in aliqua parte*, they soon realized that more radical measures had to be taken. Whether, as the emperor said, the merchants and in particular the landowners were really unable to pay more taxes may be doubted. The other way out, a cut in the military expenses, was impossible. "Nothing is for the afflicted condition of the state as necessary as a numerous army." In the autumn of 444, the government devised a new tax, the *silignaticum*, a payment of 1 *siliqua* per solidus, that is a twenty-fourth, on all sales.[470] The government was barely able to feed and clothe the veteran army, and yet it issued the strictest orders to recruit more and still more soldiers. These were "difficult times"; an army as strong as possible was "the foundation of full security for all."[471]

The preparations for the war with the Huns—there is, as we now may confidently say, no other explanation of the laws—fall in the second half of 444. Aetius negotiated with the *saevi reges*, Bleda and Attila. If Bleda's death could be exactly dated, it would give the *terminus ante quem* for the renewal of the treaty between Huns and Romans. Our authorities give different dates. According to Prosper,[472] Attila put his brother to death in 444, possibly, as this is the last entry under this year, in the autumn or winter. Marcellinus Comes dates the murder early in 445,[473] the Chronicle of 452—notoriously inaccurate—in 446.[474] Theophanes, *Anno Mundi* 5943, is in his chronology hopelessly confused; Bleda was most certainly not killed in 441 as Theophanes seems to indicate.

That the tension was over in 445 can be concluded from the biography of the Greek renegade whom Priscus met at Attila's court. Made prisoner

---

[470] *Nov. Val.* XV, issued between September 11, 444, and January 18, 445.
[471] *Ibid.*, XV, 1.
[472] *CM* I, 480$_{1358}$.
[473] *CM* II, 81$_{445}$.
[474] *Ibid.*, I, 660$_{131}$.

in Viminacium (now Kostolatz, Yugoslavia) in 441, he fought under One-gesius first against the Romans, and then against the Acatiri, with such bravery that his lord made him a free man. He took a Hun wife who bore him children.[475] He told Priscus his story in 449. Therefore, his marriage falls in 446 at the latest. Because it is unlikely that the Roman prisoner immediately was put on a horse and sent against his countrymen, the campaign in which he fought was evidently the one in 442 or, more probably, 443. It preceded the war with the Acatiri, which, therefore, is to be dated in 443 at the earliest. Priscus says explicitly that Kuridach, the pro-Hunnic king of the Acatiri, appealed to *Attila* for help against the pro-Roman leaders of the people.[476] Therefore, the war falls after the death of Bleda. Attila led a large army against the Acatiri; he conquered them only after many battles. A hundred years later Jordanes still called them *gens fortissima*.[477] To fight the Romans and the Acatiri at the same time was beyond the power of the Huns. All this leads to 445 as the only year in which, all circumstances considered, the war with the Acatiri should be dated. And this, in turn, narrows the period in which "peace on the Danube" was concluded to the winter 444/5 or the following spring.[478] If follows, furthermore, that shortly afterward, that is, in 445, Attila murdered his brother Bleda.

Our information about the following years comes from three sources. Two of them have been ignored by students of the Huns, the third one has been misinterpreted. There is, first, the letter of Cassiodorus in which he describes his grandfather's[479] meeting with Attila:

> With Carpilio, the son of Aetius, he was sent on no vain embassy to Attila. He looked undaunted at the man before whom the Empire quailed. Calm in his conscious strength, he despised all those terrible wrathful faces that scowled around him. He did not hesitate to meet the full force of the invectives of the madman who fancied himself about to grasp the Empire of the world. He found the king insolent; he left him pacified; and so ably did he argue down all his slanderous pretexts for dispute that though the Hun's interest was to quarrel with the richest Empire in the world, he nevertheless condescended to seek its favor. The firmness of the orator roused the fainting courage of his countrymen, and men felt that Rome could not be pronounced defenseless while she was armed with such ambassadors. Thus did

---

[475] *EL* 135-136.
[476] *Ibid.*, 130.
[477] *Getica* 36.
[478] In July 445, Aetius was in Gaul (*Nov. Val.* XVII).
[479] Besselaar 1945, 9-10.

he bring back the peace which men had despaired of, and as earnestly as they had prayed for his success, so thankfully did they welcome his return.[480]

The grandfather of Cassiodorus dealt not with the *saevi reges* but with Attila alone. The characterization of the king as a man "who, driven by some fury, seems to strive for the domination of the world" (*qui furore nescio quo raptatus mundi dominatum videbatur expetere*) leaves no doubt that he had made himself the sole ruler of the Huns. The embassy must be dated after 445.[481] It would be of interest to know what Attila's *calumniosae allegationes* were. Perhaps he was complaining, as he did so often in his dealing with the East, that the Romans did not hand over all Hun fugitives. Or Aetius may not have paid the tribute as regularly as the king demanded. He may have tried to win to his side Germans over whom Attila claimed suzerainty. But all these are guesses. What we learn from the *Variae* is that the Huns renewed their threats to attack the West and that Aetius' ambassadors barely succeeded in preventing the savages from breaking into Italy or Gaul. It was, of course, not Cassiodorus' superior diplomatic skill that made Attila change his mind. Roman rhetorics never prevailed with Attila unless they were accompanied by the sound of Roman solidi.

The second source which sheds some light on the events in the second half of the 440's is a short passage in the work of Anonymus Valesianus, which contains, among other things, an account of King Theodoric the Ostrogoth (493-526): Orestes, the father of the last Western emperor Romulus Augustulus, joined with Attila at the time the king came to Italy, and was made his secretary.[482] In 449, Orestes had already a responsible position; he accompanied Edecon on his mission to Constantinople.[483]

---

[480] *Variae* I, 4, 11-13, *MGH AA* XI, 15. I follow the translation by Hodgkin 1886, 146.

[481] Seeck (*Geschichte* 6, 293) erroneously identified the older Cassiodorus with the East Roman ex-consul senator of Priscus, *EL* 122. Caspar (1933, 2, 556, n.4), who dated the embassy in 452, misunderstood Cassiodorus, who said nothing about a withdrawal of a Hun army from Italy. From the fact that Carpilio accompanied Cassiodorus, no conclusion as to the date can be drawn. We know from Priscus (*EL*, 128$_{22-23}$) that Carpilio served as hostage among the Huns before 449. Besselaar (1945) thinks that he joined Cassiodorus because he knew the Huns from the time he lived at Attila's court. But one could also assume, as Seeck (*Geschichte* 6, 293) did, that Carpilio went to the Huns to ensure the observance of the treaty which Cassiodorus concluded with them. Bury's date, 425, for the beginning of Carpilio's hostage (1923, 1, 241), is too early.

[482] *Orestes Pannonius, qui eo tempore, quando Attila ad Italiam venit, se illi iunxit et eius notarius fuit,* (Anon. Vales. 37, Cessi, ed, 13).

[483] Priscus, *EL* 579$_{20}$.

Considering Attila's mistrust of his Roman secretaries—he had one of them crucified[484]—it must have taken some time before he took Orestes in his confidence. But it is obviously impossible to date Attila's stay in Italy on such a shaky basis. Much more significant is the fact that the Hun king *did* go to Italy. In 449, in a tense situation, Attila notified the East Romans that he was willing to meet their ambassadors in Serdica (modern Sofia), provided they were men of the highest rank.[485] It was not Attila's custom to make pleasure trips to enemy country. We may assume that he met Aetius, or his plenipotentiaries, on Italian soil, probably not far from the frontier, because decisions of great importance had to be made.

The third source from which information can be drawn about the relations of the Hun king with Aetius is the short passage in Priscus discussed in the previous chapter. The Roman *ductor* ceded a large tract of Pannonia to Attila.

There can be no longer any reasonable doubt that Attila's journey to Italy, Cassiodorus' negotiations with him, and the cession of the land along the Sava belong together. It may have been on this occasion that Attila was nominated *magister militum*, naturally with the salary due him.[486]

Attila was appeased, but he did not become Aetius' friend, as nearly all modern authors maintain.[487] That Aetius sent him secretaries and gifts is of little importance. In 484, Eudoxius, leader of the Bacaudae, fled to the Huns.[488] Had he been extradited to the Romans, as Aetius undoubtedly requested, the chronicler who reported the flight would not have failed to say so. He did not. Eudoxius was certainly not the only rebel to whom Attila granted asylum. That the Huns did not raid Noricum and Raetia, as they raided the Balkan provinces, had nothing to do with their allegedly friendly feelings for Aetius; there was little to loot there. All treaties the Huns concluded with the East bound the government in Constantinople to pay them tribute. They doubtless demanded, and received, gold, and ever more gold, from the West as well. Aetius was no more Attila's friend than he was the friend of the other λῄσταρχοι from Africa to the Danube. The Hunnic invasion of Gaul in 451 was merely the continuation of politics by other means, if the word *politics* can be applied to systematic extortion.

---

[484] *EL*, 133_{10-12}.
[485] *Ibid.*, 579_{35}-580_1.
[486] *Ibid.*, 142_{8-10}.
[487] E. Barker, *CMH* 1, 414, Thompson 1948, 128, and others.
[488] *CM* I, 662_{448}.

The War in the Balkans

In the early summer of 440, the government in Ravenna learned that a large Vandalic fleet had left Carthage. Whether it was headed for Spain, Sardinia, Sicily, Egypt,[489] or even Rome or Constantinople, no one knew.[490] The treacherous capture of Carthage by Geiseric, in the year before, was a blow not only to the Western Romans. In possession of the best harbor west of Alexandria with its shipyards and experienced shipbuilders, Geiseric could be expected in a short time to have a fleet able to carry the Vandalic pirates anywhere in the Mediterranean. The walls of Rome were hastily repaired,[491] the shore and harbors of Constantinople were fortified.[492] In a proclamation to the Roman people, the emperor Valentinian III assured them that the army of "the most invincible Theodosius" soon would approach to take part in the fight against the Vandals.[493]

Geiseric landed in Sicily. The Vandals took Lilybaeum on the west coast of the island, pillaged the helpless towns and villages, persecuted the Catholic clergy, and even crossed the Strait of Messina.[494] Late in 440 or early in 441,[495] Geiseric broke off the campaign and sailed back to Carthage. The Eastern army under Areobindus as commander in chief, which was supposed to drive out the Vandals, arrived in Sicily after the evacuation of the island by the enemy.[496] Behaving not much better than the Vandals, the preponderantly Germanic troops[497] soon became "more of a burden to Sicily than a help to Africa."[498]

---

[489] In 467, "a report was spread [in Constantinople] that Genseric, king of the Vandals, intended to attack the city of Alexandria" (cf. 56 in Baynes and Dawes 1948, 39-40). It was certainly not the first such report.

[490] Satis incertum est, ad quam oram terrea possint naves hostium pervenire (Nov. Val. IX, of June 24, 440).

[491] Nov. Val. V, 3. For the fortification of Naples, cf. CIL X, 1485, quoted in Seeck, Geschichte 6, 119, 420.

[492] Chron. Pasch. ad a. 439 in CM II, 80.

[493] Nov. Val. IX.

[494] CM I, 478$_{1342}$; II, 23$_{120}$. Theophanes A.M. 5941; Cassiodorus, Variae I, 4, 14.

[495] The Vandals stayed in Sicily a considerable time; cf. the letter of Paschasinus, bishop of Lilybaeum, to Pope Leo I (PL 54, 606, 1270-1271). Like all Vandalic incursions, this too had only one goal: to carry off as much booty as possible. Cf. Giunta 1958.

[496] The edict Nov. Theodos. VII, 4, issued on March 6, 441, is addressed to Areobindus, who was to lead the expeditionary corps. At that time he was, thus, still in Constantinople.

[497] Four of the five generals had Germanic names: Areobindus, Ansila, Inobindus, and Arintheus, Theophanes A.M. 5941; CM I, 478$_{1344}$, cf. Schönfeld 1911, 27, 23, 26.

[498] CM I, 478$_{1344}$.

The Sicilian expedition was a failure. For one thing, it came too late. Valentinian's ministers may have been overly optimistic when they announced its coming as early as June 440. The difficulties and risks of such an enterprise were greater than the hard-pressed West was willing to concede. To assemble the transports, to provide the necessary supplies, to move the troops to the ports of embarkation—all this needed time.[499] Yet this alone does not quite account for the delay. The East could not come to the rescue of the West because it was itself threatened on two fronts, in the Balkans and in Armenia.[500]

About the short conflict with the Persians little is known.[501] They attacked the region of Theodosiopolis and Satala.[502] It seems that the Romans stayed entirely on the defense, eager to come to a quick agreement with the enemy. Theodoret's miracle stories[503] can be dismissed. But his source correctly connected the events in the East with those in the West:

At a time when the Romans were occupied against other enemies, the Persians violated the existing treaties and invaded the neighboring provinces, while the emperor, who had relied on the peace which had been concluded, had sent his generals and his troops to embark in other wars. Anatolius, *magister militum per orientem*, consented to all demands of the raging tyrant.[504]

By June, 441, the war in Armenia was over.[505]

But there was still another war raging in the western provinces. The Huns had broken into Illyricum. From Priscus[506] we learn that at the time of the annual fair, held at one of the *phrouria* north of the Danube, the Huns suddenly attacked the Romans and cut down many of them.

---

[499] *Cod. Iust.* XII, 8, 2; 50, 21, shows how carefully the expedition was prepared.

[500] Simeon the Stylite saw two rods in the sky, one pointing east, the other west; they announced attacks of the Persians and Scythians. See the epilogue to his vita in Theodoret, *Hist. relig.*, ch. 27, in Lietzmann 1908, 13-14. Lietzmann's conjecture that the epilogue was written by Theodoret himself has been convincingly refuted by Peeters 1950, 102-103.

[501] According to Eliše Vardapet (Langlois 1869, 2, 184), it began in the second year of Yazdgard's reign. Marcellinus Comes (*CM* II, 180) dates the war in 441. Procopius I, 2, 11-15, is more a romance than a historical account.

[502] *Nov. Theodos.* V, 1. Theodosiopolis is the modern Erzerum. For the strategic importance of Satala, the present Sadagh, see F. and E. Cumont, *Studia Pontica* II (Brussels, 1902), 343-344.

[503] *Hist. eccles.* V, 37, 5.

[504] *Ibid.*

[505] *Nov. Theodos.* V, 1, of June 26, 441: "The district of Armenia which has been exposed [*expositum fuisse*] at the present time to the invasions of the Persians. . ."

[506] *EL* 575-576.

When the government in Constantinople protested the breach of the treaty which provided that the fairs should be held with equal rights and with no danger to either side, the Huns maintained that they had only avenged grave injustices done to them. The bishop of Margus, they said, had crossed the river and robbed the royal tombs[507] of their treasures. Besides, contrary to the stipulations of the treaty, the Romans again had sheltered many Hun fugitives. Although the Romans denied these charges, the Huns were undoubtedly right.[508]

Crossing the Danube, the Huns took the important city of Viminacium in Moesia superior. The bishop of Margus, afraid that the Romans, to appease the barbarians, would give him up, treacherously handed the city over to the enemy, "and the power of the barbarians increased to an even greater extent."

For the following events our main source is Marcellinus Comes. Under 441, he has two entries dealing with the Huns. The first one is a telling example of the way in which Marcellinus thoughtlessly shortened what he found in his sources. "The Persians, Saracens, Tzanni, Isaurians, and. Huns came forth from their countries and ravaged the lands of the Romans. Anatolius and Aspar were sent against them and made peace for one year."[509]

Who was sent against whom? With which of the enemies was the armistice concluded? Not with the Persians, for the peace treaty which Anatolius signed was not limited to one year; in fact, there was no war between Rome and Persia for more than sixty years, from 441 to 502. The wild Tzanni and Saracens, not to speak of the Isaurian robbers, were not parties with which the imperial government concluded treaties. This leaves the Huns. Anatolius was in the east, commander in chief of the troops in the Orient since 438[510] at the latest. He held the same position

---

[507] θήκαι means most probably "tombs," not "treasure houses," as Hodgkin 1898, 2, 69, Seeck, *Geschichte* 6, 291, and H. Vetters 1950, 40, n. 37, think.

[508] Why should the bishop have felt scruples about robbing pagan tombs if not only lay people but also clergymen rifled Christian tombs? The *novella* of March 27, 347, is, in the first place, aimed at clerical *sepulcri violatores*. "Among all the other persons who are accused of this nefarious crime, the most vehement complaint pursues the clergy. . . . Equipped with iron tools, they harass the buried dead, and oblivious of the Divinity that rules over the heavens and the stars, they bring to the sacred altars of the Church hands that are polluted by the contagion of the ashes of the dead," (*Nov. Val.* XXIII, 1). They carried away marbles and stones, *pretiosa montium metalla*; the lay tomb robbers looked for jewels and precious garments. The sermons of John Chrysostom show how common these crimes were; he repeatedly condemned the violators of the tombs. See the references in Vance 1907, 59.

[509] *CM* II, 80₄₄₁.₁.

[510] *Nov. Theodos.* IV of February 25, 438.

in 441, 442[511] and still early in 443.[512] The truce with the Huns was arranged by Aspar, *comes, magister militum*, and ex-consul.[513]

That Areobindus, not Aspar, was made the commander of the army which finally was sent to Sicily illustrates the hesitations and doubts with which the expedition was undertaken. Aspar knew Africa. He had fought the Vandals in 431; he was in Carthage in 434.[514] He was the most distinguished general of the east. But he stayed in Illyricum, evidently because the situation, in spite of the truce, was too precarious to be handled by anyone else. In addition to his troubles with the Huns, Aspar was confronted with savage rivalries among his generals, which further reduced the fighting power of his army. "John, *magister militum*, a Vandal by race, was killed in Thrace by the treachery of Arnegisclus."[515]

Emperor Theodosius II began negotiations with Geiseric. The army in Sicily would possibly soon be needed at another front. It could not be brought back once it was engaged in fighting in Africa. Marcellinus Comes has as last entry under 441 the lines: "The kings of the Huns broke with many of their warriors into Illyricum; they lay waste Naissus, Singidunum, and other cities, and many towns in Illyricum." In 442, "the brothers Bleda and Attila, the kings of many peoples, ravaged Illyricum and Thrace."[516]

Ignoring the campaign in 441, Prosper has under 442: "Because the Huns ravaged Thrace and Illyricum with wild devastation, the army, which stayed in Sicily, returned to defend the eastern provinces."[517] In 442, Theodosius made peace with the Vandals.[518]

The first phase of the war can be reconstructed at least in its outlines, but its second phase is highly controversial. Since the publication of the sixth, posthumous volume of the great Tillemont's *Histoire des empereurs*, more than three hundred years have elapsed. Gibbon, Wietersheim, Gülden-

---

[511] *Chron. Edess. ad a.* 753, in *CSCO, Scr. Syri*, versio, seria tertia, t. IV, 7.

[512] Seeck 1919, 373. The year in which Anatolius built the Stoa in Edessa (Evagrius, *Hist. eccles.* I, 18, Bidez and Parmentier 1898, 27-28) cannot be determined. The letter which Theodoret wrote to him while he was commander in chief in the east (*PG* 83, 1221) is also undatable.

[513] Because Aspar did not take part in the Sicilian expedition, he could not have come from Sicily "ahead of the fleet," as Thompson (1948, 81) maintains.

[514] See the passages cited by Seeck, *Geschichte* 6, 417 *ad* 113-114.

[515] *CM* II, $80_{442 \cdot 2}$; John of Antioch, fr. 206, *FHG* IV, 616-617; *Chron. Pasch., CM* II, 80.

[516] *CM* II, $81_{442 \cdot 2}$. The *Chronicon Pasch. s.a.* 442 has only Illyricum (*CM* II, 81).

[517] *CM* I, 479_{1346} = Cassiodorus, *chron. ad a.* 442.

[518] Cf. Seeck *Geschichte* 6, 121; Stein 1959, 1, 484; W. Ensslin, *BZ* 43, 1950, 43; Courtois 1955, 173, 395.

penning, Kulakovskii, Bury, Seeck, Stein, and Thompson struggled with the chronological problems of the Hun wars in the 440's. Yet not a single date seems to be definitely established. When did the Huns take Philippopolis and Arcadiopolis? In 441-442, as Thompson assumes, or in 447, as Tillemont and Seeck maintained? When was the peace concluded of which Priscus speaks in fragment 5? Bury, Stein, and Thompson dated it in 443, Gibbon insisted on 446, Wietersheim and Kulakovskii favored 447, and Tillemont thought that the war did not end before 448. It would seem that the available evidence admits practically any date.

The crux is the long entry under A.M. 5942 in Theophanes' *Chronographia*. Its importance for the events in the 440's is obvious. That it cannot be accepted as it stands is, or should be, equally obvious. However, some historians were, and still are, making use of the passage as if it were written by Clio herself.[519] As a matter of fact, the long entry is a galimatias unusual even for Theophanes, who wrote in the ninth century. In A.M. 5942 the following events are said to have occurred:

1. Emperor Theodosius II, recognizing that he had been deceived by Chrysaphius, exiled the eunuch to an island.

If this were true,[520] it would lead to the first months of 450.

2. Empress Eudocia withdrew from the court and went to Jerusalem. This was in 443[521] or 444.[522]

3. On Theodosius' orders Presbyter Severus and Deacon John were executed.

This happened in 444.[523]

4. Pulcheria had Bishop Flavian's remains brought back to Constantinople and laid in the Church of the Apostles.

The translation took place in November, 450.[524]

5. Pulcheria converted a Jewish synagogue into a church, Θεοτόκος τῶν Χαλκοπρατείων.

---

[519] Neither Thompson (1948, 84) nor H. Vetters (1950, 40-42), to name only two authors who based their account of the war in 441-442 largely on Theophanes, analyzed his sources.

[520] Cf. Goubert 1951, 303-321. E. Honigmann (*Dumbarton Oaks Papers* 5, 1950, 239, n. 18) overlooked that Nicephorus Callistus, to whom he ascribed this passage, had it from Theophanes.

[521] Bury 1923, 230, n. 5.

[522] Ernest Schwartz 1939, 2, 363, n. 2.

[523] *CM* II, 81₄₄₄.

[524] Chadwick, *The Journal of Theological Studies* 6, 1955, 31, n. 4.

This might be true,[525] but it should be noted that in another passage[526] Theophanes gives Justin II credit for the pious deed.

6. "While the army was in Sicily, waiting for the arrival of Geiseric's ambassadors and the orders of the emperor, Attila, Mundius' son, the Scythian, overthrew Bdella, his older brother, made himself the sole ruler of the kingdom of the Scythians, who are also called Huns, and overran Thrace. Thereupon Theodosius made peace with Geiseric and recalled the army from Sicily. He sent Aspar with the forces under him, Areobindus, and Argagisclus against Attila who already had taken Ratiaria, Naissus, Philippopolis, Arcadiopolis, Constantia, and many other towns, making many prisoners and amassing an enormous booty. In a succession of battles the Roman generals suffered heavy defeats, and Attila reached the sea, both the Pontus and Propontis, at Callipolis and Sestus. He took every town and fortress except Adrianople and Heraclea, even the fortress Athyras. Theodosius saw himself forced to send ambassadors to Attila and grant him 6,000 pounds of gold for the retreat as well as an annual tribute of 1,000 pounds."

7. Theodosius II died (July 2, 450).

8. Pulcheria married Marcian, who was proclaimed emperor (August 24, 450).

The end of Theophanes' account of the war agrees, more or less, with the beginning of Priscus, fragment 5:[527] After the battle in the Chersonesus the Romans, through the ambassador Anatolius, concluded peace with the Huns. The fugitives were to be handed over, the arrears of tribute, 6,000 pounds of gold, to be paid at once. The annual tribute was fixed at 2,100 pounds of gold.

Theophanes squeezed within twelve months events which lay as much as eight years apart. The war with the Huns broke out (a) while the greater part of the army stood in Sicily, thus in 441-442; (b) after Bleda's death, thus 444 at the earliest; the war is (c) placed in A.M. 5942, which began on March 25, 450, and the forty-second year of Theodosius II, which was conventionally reckoned from September 1, 449, on. If (a) is right, (b) and (c) are wrong, and vice versa.

It could be argued that, since we know from other sources that the Huns did invade the Balkan provinces at the time of the Sicilian expedition, Theophanes had this first Hun war in mind, brought in Bleda's death by

[525] Janin 1953, 1:3, 246.
[526] A.M. 5942, C. de Boor 1883, I, 102.
[527] EL 576-577.

mistake, and in this way got mixed up in his chronology. This is, indeed, the opinion of most students of the late Roman Empire. They assume that the war which Theophanes mentions is the one that broke out in 441 and ended in 442 or 443. Consequently they date the events described in the Priscus fragment 5 in the same years.

The few dissenting interpretations have been practically ignored. Tillemont, who dated the war of A.M. 5942 in 447,[528] is almost forgotten. Kulakovskii held the same view, [529] but his excellent work, written in Russian, published in Kiev, remains unknown to Western scholars. It is true that Seeck came to the same conclusions.[530] However, like Tillemont and Kulakovskii, he merely opposed his chronology to the generally accepted one without stating his reasons.

The following considerations are not meant to establish the actual sequence of events for its own sake. *Sub specie aeternitatis* they are trivial. But the historian, a loyal citizen of the *civitas terrena*, cannot help going into details if he wants to determine Attila's place in the history of the Huns and the Roman Empire.

1. When did the Romans pay Attila 6,000 pounds of gold? The strain on the imperial treasury must have been heavy. Priscus may have exaggerated the hardships that befell the Romans, yet it is quite credible that many had to sell their furniture and the jewelry of their wives to raise the money the inexorable tax collectors demanded from them. A few are said to have committed suicide in their desperation.[531] Whether the tax load could have been more justly distributed need not be discussed. After paying 6,000 pounds at once and being forced to pay, year after year, 2,100 pounds of tribute, the government could not very well reform the tax system.

If the war that put such a heavy burden on the unfortunate East Romans was the one which ended in 442 or 443, one should think that the taxes in 444 were exceptionally high. The last thing one should expect would be a tax reduction. But the taxes *were* reduced in 444. "The exaction of delinquent taxes for the past time is remitted for the landed estates ... and in the future no such tax assessment shall be feared."[532] This edict was issued in Constantinople on November 29, 444. It alone would be sufficient proof that the great war, which ended with the financial catastrophe, took place *after* the issuance of the edict.

---

[528] Tillemont 1938, 6, 97-99, 108-111.

[529] Kulakovskiĭ 1913, 1, 276-281.

[530] *Geschichte* 6, 291-295.

[531] *EL* 577$_{9-22}$.

[532] *Nov. Theodos.* XXVI, 1.

2. In the late spring of 443, Theodosius made a journey through some provinces of Asia Minor. He stayed some time in Heraclea in Bithynia;[533] the emperor had a predilection for that province which, in tribute to his uncle, he renamed Honoria.[534] Turning south, he leisurely traveled to Caria. At the end of May, he was in Aphrodisias.[535] On August 27, he returned from the *expeditio Asiana* to Constantinople.[536] In the spring of 443, the war must have been over. Theodosius hardly could have left the capital while the fighting was still going on. But if he did, he would have crossed over to Chalcedon, as, for example, Leo did after the great fire of 465,[537] and stayed there. In the dedication of his *Church History* to Theodosius, Sozomen was flattering the emperor, but he could not have written about the journey the way he did[538] had Theodosius been on the flight from the Huns. Furthermore, there is good evidence that the war practically ended in 442. On January 11, 443, the Thermae Achilleae, τὸ δημόσιον λουτρὸν ὁ ᾿Αχιλλεύς, were solemnly opened.[539] The people of Constantinople were certainly pleasure-loving, but it is hard to imagine that they should have been in the mood to celebrate the opening of a new bath at a time when the Huns stood at the gates.

3. St. Hypatius, abbot of the monastery of Drys, a suburb of Chalcedon, died in June, 446.[540] Seven months later began the earthquakes which tumbled a large part of the great land wall of Constantinople. And *then* came the Huns. Callinicus, the biographer of Hypatius, was a conscientious chronicler. He not only recorded the many miracles his hero worked; he also kept a sharp eye on all secular events which affected his brethren. Callinicus would not have passed over a war in which the enemy came close to Constantinople. Indeed, he did not. But the only war of which he knew was the one in 447.

4. Evagrius mentions only "the famous war of Attila" in 447.[541]

5. Jordanes must have read in his sources that Bleda and Attila devastated Illyricum and Thrace in 441 and 442. But he mentions this first war neither in the *Romana* nor the *Getica*. As for Callinicus and Evagrius, for Jordanes there existed only *one* Hun war, the great war in 447.

---

[533] *Ibid.*, XXIII, 1, subscription.
[534] Malalas 365.
[535] May 22, *Nov. Theodos.* XXIII, subscription.
[536] Marcellinus Comes *s.a.* 443$_2$, *CM* II, 81; *Chron. Pasch. s.a.* 442, *CM* II, 81.
[537] *Vita s. Danielis Stylitae* in *Analecta Bollandiana* 32, 1913, 169.
[538] *Oratio* XIII, Bidez, ed., 3.
[539] See fn. 536.
[540] Callinicus 104; *AA SS*, June, IV, 281.
[541] *Hist. eccles.* I, 17.

6. Had the battle on the Chersonesus marked the end of the fighting in 442 or 443, the Romans would have had to negotiate the peace conditions with Attila and Bleda. In fragment 2, dealing with the first phase of the war in 441, Priscus speaks of the kings of the Huns. In fragment 5, which is supposed to conclude an account of the events in 443, Bleda's name does not occur. Anatolius has to deal with Attila, and only with him. Attila is *the* king of the Huns,[542] the Hun army is *his* army.[543]

7. During the first war Anatolius was not in Thrace but in Antioch, the headquarters of the *magister militum per orientem*. When he concluded peace with Attila he was *magister militum praesentalis*.[544]

All these data establish the date of the war in the Priscus fragment 5 beyond any reasonable doubt. It took place in 447.

We may now summarize: In 441, the Huns broke into the western Balkan provinces. After a short campaign, during which they took Viminacium, they agreed to a truce. In 442, the attacks were resumed. The Romans, led by Aspar,[545] suffered one defeat after another. After the fall of Margus, the key to the Morava Valley, the Huns pushed south and took Naissus.[546] Even if we did not know from Marcellinus Comes that Singidunum was lost in that year, we would have to assume that the defense system along the Danube and the Sava broke down. The road Sirmium-Singidunum-Margus-Viminacium-Naissus was for all practical purposes and, especially, for military purposes the only one that connected Pannonia secunda and Moesia superior with Thrace. With the fall of Naissus the fate of Singidunum was sealed. Everything west of Singidunum now was bound to fall to the Huns. They took Sirmium.[547] They broke into Thrace. Then something must have happened to the Hun armies. They may have been hit by epidemics as later in 447 and again in 452. There may have been an uprising in their rear that forced them to break off the campaign and turn against the rebels. Perhaps some of the peoples such as the "Sorosgi," with whom Attila and Bleda had waged wars before, used their chance and attacked the Hun heartland while the main strength of their enemy was engaged elsewhere.

---

[542] *EL* 578₂₈.

[543] *Ibid.*, 578₈.

[544] τῶν ἀμφὶ βασιλέα ἄρχοντα ταλῶν (*EL* 149₁₉₋₂₀).

[545] Suidas, *s.v. Ζέρκων.*

[546] Whether Priscus (fr. 1b, *HGM* 278-280) refers to 442 or 447 cannot be decided. Priscus' account is unreliable; cf. Thompson, 1945b, 92-94.

[547] Alföldi 1926, 96.

In preceding paragraphs, I adduced some arguments for the end of the war before the beginning of 443. The law of August 21, 442,[548] suggests that at least in most of the provinces it was over even earlier. The reference to the advocates, who resumed their practice in the Illyrian prefecture, presupposes that large parts of it were again firmly under Roman control In the fall of 443, the Danube flotilla was being strengthened, the camps along the river were repaired, the garrisons along the *limes* brought up to full strength.[549] In the same year or, perhaps, in 444, the Romans stopped the payments to the Huns.

In 447, Attila calculated the arrears of tribute at 6,000 pounds of gold.[550] This was apparently a lump sum, but it must have roughly corresponded to the actual arrears. In the treaty of Margus the annual tribute was fixed at 700 pounds.[551] From 447 on, the Huns received 2,100 pounds per annum, clearly a much higher sum than that agreed on in 442 or 443. Assuming that the latter was double the tribute of the treaty of Margus, say 1,400 pounds, the Romans must have refused to pay the Huns anything as early as 444 or perhaps even earlier, in 443. In any case, whatever the tribute was, it was not paid to the kings of the Huns for a number of years. After one or two payments, the government in Constantinople felt strong enough to repudiate its obligations, *and the Huns did nothing.* It was in those years that they tried to blackmail the West. The East was too strong for them.

From whatever angle we look at the war of 441-442, the picture is the same. All direct and indirect sources are in agreement. Favored by the absence of the Roman army from the western frontier, the Huns were able to inflict heavy defeats on the Romans. To get rid of the savages, Theodosius paid them off. Once they were back, Theodosius tore up the peace treaty. The Huns had proved to be a formidable enemy, but they were not yet a great power.

The contrast between the war in 441-442 and its results, and the war in 447 is so striking that it calls for an explanation. It cannot be a concatenation of coincidences, a mysterious weakening of the power of the Eastern *pars.* Between the two wars falls the ascendancy of Attila. Except for three fragments, and a few lines in the Gallic chronicle of 452, Priscus' account of the great war is lost. So is the chronicle of Eustathius of Epiphaneia who, in the main, followed Priscus.[552] Of the Western authors,

---

[548] *Cod. Iust.* II, 7, 9.

[549] Edict of September 12, 443 (*Nov. Theodos.* XXIV). Cf. Güldenpenning 1885, 349.

[550] Priscus, *EL* 576_{27-28}.

[551] *EL* 516_{28-29}.

[552] Moravcsik, *BT* 1, 483.

Quintus Aurelius Memmius Symmachus seems to have been the only one to write about the war in 447 but his work is also lost.[553] Prosper does not mention it. Under these circumstances the course of events can be reconstructed only in the broadest outlines.

The Priscus fragment 3 deals with the beginning of the war[554]: Attila, the king of the Huns, assembled his own army and sent letters to Theodosius, demanding the fugitives and the tribute which, under the pretext of that war, had not been paid. About the future tribute envoys should be sent to him. If the Romans should delay or prepare for war, not even he would be able to hold back the hordes. The advisors of the emperor read the letter and declared that the fugitives must not be surrendered; it would be better, together with them to wait for the outbreak of the war. However, envoys should be sent to settle the controversies. When Attila was notified about the decisions of the Romans, he got angry, devastated Roman territory, took some fortresses, and attacked the large and populous city of Ratiaria.[555]

Many historians date the events told in this fragment in 442.[556] This is certainly not correct. Attila is the sole ruler of the Huns, ὁ τῶν Οὔννων βασιλεύς. He sends letters to the emperor, he is ready to receive the Roman envoys, he demands the tribute money. There are no more "kings of the Huns." Bleda is dead. We are, at the earliest, in 445.

The phrase οὐδὲ αὐτὸν ἔτι ἐθέλοντα τὸ Σκυθικὸν ἐφέξειν πλῆθος has often been misunderstood. Thompson circumscribed it by "he would no longer hold back the Huns."[557] Actually, Attila warned the Romans that, unless his demands were granted, it would not be even in *his* power to prevent the Scythian mass from breaking loose.[558] The Romans did not pay the tribute προφάσει τοῦδε τοῦ πολέμου. What war? Not even Attila, with all his arrogance, could expect that Theodosius would send him the "subsidies," as if he were still an "ally," adhering to the stipulations of the *foedus*, while he was actually waging war with the Romans. Attila

---

[553] W. Ensslin, *BZ* 43, 1950, 73.

[554] *EL* 576$_{10-24}$.

[555] The present Arčar. The city was not utterly destroyed, as Thompson (1948, 83) thinks. Theophylactus Simocatta (I, 8, 10), writting under Heraclius, knows it as ʽΡατηρία.

[556] Ed. Bonn, 138, 138; *FHG*, 442; Seeck, *Geschichte* 6, 293; Bury 1923, 171; Stein 1959, 1, 437; Thompson 1948, 83.

[557] Thompson 1948, 83. Homeyer (1951, 73) translates it: *doch wolle er die skythischen Schwärme nicht länger zurückhalten*; Gordon (1960, 65): "he would not willingly hold back his Scythian horde."

[558] Doblhofer (1955) translates correctly: *so werde nicht einmal er selbst skythische Heerscharen zurückhalten können*: cf. also Seeck 1920, 293.

did not fight. He assembled his *own* army, τὸν οἰκεῖον στρατόν. The stress is on οἰκεῖον. There must have been other Huns, not those of Attila, who already were fighting the Romans while he was still negotiating with them. Attila declined any responsibility for "that war." But he let the Romans know that the Σκυθικὸν πλῆθος leaned toward those who already were raiding and looting Roman territory.

We can, I think, discern three groups of Huns. There was Attila with his army; there was "the Scythian mass," impatient, dissatisfied with their king, ready to go to war unless they got all the gold they thought they were entitled to; and there were Huns already waging war on the Romans.

This, and only this, is the context into which another Priscus fragment can be fitted. Theodosius sent the ex-consul Senator to Attila. But Senator, "although he had the name of an envoy, did not dare to go to the Huns by land; instead, he sailed up the Pontus to Odessus (modern Varna), where also the general Theodolos, sent there, stayed." In the *Excerpta de legationibus Romanorum ad gentes*, this fragment follows the one on the treaty of Margus and precedes the one that deals with the embassy of 449. Senator was consul in 436. But it does not follow that our fragment can refer to any time between 436 and 449.[559] Again it must be noted that Senator was sent to *Attila*, which narrows the date to the years 445-449. The men who negotiated with Attila in 447 were Anatolius and Theodolos, the latter as commander of the military forces in Thrace. Senator's voyage falls, therefore, in 445 or, more probably, 446.

Our fragment has either been ignored or misinterpreted by most students of the Huns. Thompson[560] thinks he can discover in it Priscus' contempt for the cowardly Senator. There is nothing of that sort in the text. The key to an understanding are the words "although he (Senator) had the name of an ambassador." They can mean only that he could not assume that the people in the area he had to pass through on his way to Attila would respect his status. And these could be no others than those Huns who, in defiance of Attila, were waging their own war with the Romans. Senator obviously returned to Constantinople without having achieved his purpose. Had he met Attila, we would read about the encounter in Priscus.

Marcellinus Comes has four entries under 447: In a tremendous war, greater than the first one, Attila ground almost the whole of Europe into the dust; the walls of Constantinople collapsed in an earthquake and were rebuilt in three months; Attila came as far as the Thermopylae; Arnegisclus,

---

[559] As Thompson (1948, 89) maintains.
[560] 1948, 187.

after bravely fighting and killing many enemies, fell in a battle against Attila near the river Utus in Dacia ripensis. The last battle occurs also in Jordanes, who adds that Arnegisclus was *magister militum Mysiae*, set out from Marcianople, and went on fighting even after his horse was killed beneath him.[561] The fall of Marcianople and the death of the brave general occurs also in the *Chronicon Paschale*.[562] All three references to Arnegisclus clearly go back to the same source. But where did Marcellinus read that Attila went to war before the earthquake? And could he actually have meant to say that the war began between January 1 and 27? Obviously not. It would seem that what is now the first entry under 447 was originally the last one under 446. From the Gallic chronicle of 452 nothing about the course of the war can be learned. Yet there are three sources which, in combination, throw some light on the sequence of the events.

We start best with the great earthquake. In 439, under the direction of Cyrus, *praefectus urbis*, the Anthemian wall, which protected the city only against attacks on land, from the west, was extended along the Golden Horn and the Sea of Marmora.[563] A part of it collapsed on Sunday, January 27, 447, in the second hour after midnight.[564] The whole district between the porticus Troadensis, near the Golden Gate, and the Tetrapylon, where now the Sahzade Mosque stands, was in ruins. When the morning came, ten thousand walked barefoot, the emperor at their head, to the campus of the Hebdomon where the patriarch held a special service.

Whether by that time the Huns already had opened hostilities or not, it was important that the walls were rebuilt as quickly as possible. They were. Flavius Constantinus, *praefectus praetorio orientis*,[565] mobilized the circus parties. He assigned to the Blues the tract from the Blachernae to the Porta Myriandri, and to the Greens the tract from there to the Sea of Marmora.[566] He had the moats cleared of rubble, "joined wall to wall,"[567]

---

561 Jordanes, *Romana* 331. T. Nagy's assertion that Jordanes' succinct account of the war in 447 is nothing but a paraphrase of Marcellinus Comes, sprinkled with some misunderstanding (*AA* 4, 1956, 251-256) is unconvincing. This sort of *Quellenkritik* is at the expense of the over-all picture.

562 Ed. Bonn, 586.

563 *Ibid.*, 583; Malalas 361; Theophanes A.M. 5937 (should be 5931). In Zonaras XIII, 22, and *Patria Constantinopolis* III:III (Preger 1907, 2, 252), Cyrus is confused with Flavius Constantinus; cf. Delehaye 1896, 219-221.

564 Marcellinus Comes *s.a.* 447, *CM* II, 82; Malalas 363; *Synaxarium Eccles. Const.*, 425.

565 Cf. A. M. Schneider in Meyer-Plath and Schneider 1943, 2, 132.

566 *Patria* II, 58, Preger 1907, 182.

567 ἐδείματο τείχει τεῖχος, in the inscription on the Mevlevhane kap, the old Myriandron. Cf. Van Millingen 1899, 47, 96; for the interpretation see A. M. Schneider in Meyer-Plath and Schneider 1943, 2, 132.

and built new towers and new gates. At the end of March the land wall stood as before, "even Pallas could not have built it quicker and better."[568]

In the *Bazaar of Heracleides* the ex-patriarch Nestorius could not pass over the earthquake, for it proved once more what happened to those "who denied that God the word was immortal and impassible." He wrote:

God shook the earth with earthquakes, the like of which there was none that remembered. . . . In Constantinople, the imperial city, the the towers of the wall collapsed and left the wall isolated. [This was at a time] when the barbarian again was stirred up against them, massacring and swarming over all the land of the Romans and overturning everything. And they had no means of escape nor refuge but were stricken with fear and had no hope. And he had closed them in and made them insufficient in everything they were doing for their salvation; and, because they understood not their former salvation, he had sent this man whom he had taken from pasturing sheep, who had protested against the privy purposes of the heart of the emperor. And already he had been stirred up by God, and he commanded to make a cross; and as though he, that is, the emperor, believed him not, he made it of wood with his own hands and sent it against the barbarians. But he planted another cross also within the palace and another in the forum of Constantinople in the midst of the city that it might be seen of every man, so that even the barbarians, when they saw it, fled and were discomfited. And the emperor himself, who was ready to flee, gained confidence to remain, and the nerves of the city which was enfeebled grew firm and all things happened thus. . . . The barbarians fled in discomfiture, while none was pursuing them, and the emperor was mightily heartened to engage in thought of his Empire. [But the barbarians returned, and this time the Romans became] the slaves of the barbarians and were subjected into slavery by the confession of written documents. The barbarians were masters and the Romans slaves. Thus the supremacy had changed over to the barbarians.[569]

The text is not very clear, possibly because of the awkwardness of the Syriac translator. Still one gets the impression that in his exile Nestorius had received some rather detailed information about the war in Thrace. What he wrote about the flight of the Huns is, indeed, confirmed by the *Homily on the Royal City* by Isaac of Antioch, another of those documents which have been ignored by the students of the Huns:

---

[568] Another inscription; see A. M. Schneider, *ibid.*, 133.
[569] Nestorius 363-368.

Again offer up praise to the power which delivered thee from the sword, again give thanks to the cross that it may again fence in the breaches. He [*i.e.*, God] did not wear away the strength in war, thou did not see the faces of the pursuer—by means of sickness he conquered the tyrant who was threatening to come and take thee away captive. Against the stone of sickness they stumbled and the steeds fell and their riders,— and the camp which was prepared for thy destruction was silenced.... With the feeble rod of sickness he smote mighty men and laid them low, and fierceness could not stand before the feebleness which struck at it. With a mean and weak staff he bound for thee the warlike forces, the swift ones sought their feet but sickness weighed them down. The horse came to nought, the horsemen came to nought, and the arms and the assault came to nought. . . . Through sickness he laid low the Huns who threatened thee. . . . By his fiat will he caused the sword to cease.... The Hun desired thy property and from desire he changed to wrath—his desire was transformed into anger and it roused him to war and sword. The greedy one mingled desire with wrath and dared to come against the city—for this is the character of plunderers that from desire they come to quarrel. The Hun in the midst of the field heard about thy majesty and envied thee, and thy riches kindled in him the desire to come for the plundering of thy treasures. He called and gathered together the beasts of the field, the host of the desert that he might bring the land into captivity. He hung the sword from his right hand and he had laid his hand on the bow and tested it with the arrow which he sent forth through it. But the sinners drew the bow and put their arrows on the string—and preparation had perfected itself and the host was on the point of coming quickly—then sickness blew through it and hurled the host into wilderness. . . . He whose heart was strong for battle waxed feeble through sickness. He who was skillful in shooting with the bow, sickness of the bowels overthrew him—the riders of the steeds slumbered and slept and the cruel army was silenced. The assembled army in which the Hun had boasted fell suddenly. Lo the tumult of the battles has died away. . . . The war with the foreigners has come to an end.[570]

C. Moss, the translator of the *Homily*, dates it to 441: "as it is obviously impossible that the author could have recorded the events of 447 without mentioning the great earthquake." This is not a convincing argument. An earthquake has no place in a homily on the royal, rich, flourishing

---

[570] Isaac of Antioch, "Homily on the Royal City," *Zeitschrift für Semitistik* 7, 1929, 295-306; 8, 1930, 61-72.

city. Besides, in 441 and 442, the Huns were not even close to Constantinople.

Two writers, independently of each other, describe the flight of the Huns: Nestorius conjuring up a God-inspired shepherd and the Syrian preacher, though with much flourish, ascribing it more soberly to "a sickness of the bowels." This has, incidentally, a parallel in the siege of Constantinople by the Arabs in 717: they, too, were hit by an epidemic, "and an innumerable number of them died."[571] The two pious writers with all possible exaggerations preserved to us a phase, or, at least, an episode in the war of 447. In April or May, after the walls had been rebuilt (that it was after the earthquake we learn from Nestorius), a group of Huns advanced to the Bosporus, and the walls collapsed. In 452, five years later, the Huns broke off the campaign in Italy when illness "hit them from heaven." In 447, they were more fortunate. The main army, under Attila as we may assume, apparently was not infected by the pestilence.

Callinicus certainly knew about the retreat of the advance group, but it paled into nothingness in comparison with the terrible fate that befell the poor people in Thrace:

> The barbarian people of the Huns, the ones in Thrace, became so strong that they captured more than a hundred cities and almost brought Constantinople into danger, and most men fled from it. Even the monks wanted to run away to Jerusalem. There was so much killing and blood-letting that no one could number the dead. They pillaged the churches and monasteries, and slew the monks and virgins. And they devastated the blessed Alexander and carried away the treasures and heirlooms, something that had never happened before, for although the Huns had often come close to the blessed Alexander, none of them dared to come near the martyr. They so devastated Thrace that it will never rise again and be as it was before.[572]

The "blessed Alexander" was the church of the martyr in Drizipera, the present Karishtiran, on the road from Heraclea (Perinthus) to Arcadianopolis.[573] From Priscus we learn that the Roman army was defeated in the Chersonesus, from Theophanes that the Huns reached the sea at Callipolis and Sestus, and that Athyras was occupied.

Theodosius begged for terms. Anatolius, who negotiated with Attila, was not in a position to reject anything the Hun king demanded. The arrears in tribute had to be paid at once; they amounted to 6,000 pounds

---

[571] Theophanes, A.M. 6209, C. de Boor 1883, 397_{27-28}.
[572] Callinicus 104.
[573] Cf. *Synaxarium Eccles. Const.*; C. Jirecek, *SB Wien* 136.

of gold. The annual tribute was set at 2,100 pounds.[574] This was harsh enough. But most dangerous for the future was the evacuation of a large territory south of the Danube, a belt "five days' journey wide," from Pannonia to Novae (modern Šistova).[575] Most towns within the march, and many to the south and east of it, had been laid waste. Naissus was deserted; when Priscus saw it in 449, the ground adjacent to the bank of the river was still covered with the bones of the men slain in the war; there were only a few people in the hostels.[576] Serdica was destroyed. But slowly, hesitatingly, timidly, the people who had fled would come back. In the march Attila would not even admit a Roman shepherd. He demanded again and again the strictest fulfillment of the treaty provisions.[577] Only the peasants, like peasants everywhere and at all times, tenaciously clung to their land. They fled when the Huns came, taking with them what they could carry, driving the cattle into the woods, and then filtered back when the storm had blown over. The emperor was as unable to drive the peasants out as the Huns were.

And yet, even though the march was not as devoid of any population as Attila wanted it to be, it served its purpose—it left the Romans defenseless. The Huns did not want, or need, the march for their herds and flocks; it was little suited to their extensive cattle and sheep breeding. Attila may have liked to go hunting there,[578] but there were other hunting grounds in his kingdom. The Huns aimed at one thing: at pushing the Romans back from the Danube, thereby removing the main obstacle that could prevent them from breaking into the empire. The Danube *limes* was not impenetrable. In the winter the riverboats were immobilized; the mostly barbarian garrisons in the forts were not entirely reliable, and even if they were, they could be overpowered. But it cost the Huns much blood to break through the frontier defenses. Despite its weaknesses, the defenses of the Balkan provinces along the Danube had been incomparably stronger than what the Romans now could hope to build up south of the new march. They were at Attila's mercy.

The war was over in the fall of 447.[579] It began, if my reading of the sources is right, with an incoordinated attack of Hun hosts; when it ended

---

[574] Priscus, *EL* 576_{27-29}.

[575] *EL* 579_{27-29}.

[576] 123_{15}. On the meaning of καταλύματα, cf. Thompson, 1947b, 63. Cf. Procopius, *De aedif.* V, 3, 20.

[577] Priscus, *EL* 579_{26-27}.

[578] *Ibid* 125_{5-6}.

[579] The land routes from Constantinople to Italy were again open. On October 1, 447, Theodosius sent to Valentinian the laws which he had promulgated after the issuance of the code in 438. In the edict of June 3, 448 (*Nov. Val.* XXVI), Valentinian wrote that the laws were "recently" dispatched to him.

with the greatest victory the Huns ever won, Attila was the ruler of a great power. Our texts tell us nothing about the apportionment of authority within the "Royal Scythians" after Bleda's death. When the big war broke out, Attila's authority, though great, was still not quite firmly established. The victory was *his* victory. From 447, Attila, king, commander in chief, supreme judge,[580] was unconditionally obeyed.

ATTILA'S KINGDOM

To determine the expansion of Hunnic power in the middle of the fifth century is a thankless task. A sober approach is bound to hurt feelings of pride and clash with long-cherished myths. Although no one in Hungary really believes any longer in the great Attila of the medieval chroniclers, his image has not lost its hold over the imagination. To be sure, the peasants, bearers of the national tradition, always named their boys István and Lájos, but in Budapest and Debrecen there still live not a few Attilas.[581] In the Germanic countries, Attila, *milte* and terrible at the same time, became at an early time a figure of superhuman greatness.[582] Even historians cannot free themselves from the idea that the Hunnic king was a forerunner of the great Mongol captains. Grousset subtitled his *L'Empire des steppes* "Attila, Gengiz-Khan, Tamerlane." Attila's kingdom, he wrote, *englobait et entraînait tous les Barbares sarmates, alains, ostrogoths, gépides, etc., répandus entre l'Oural et le Rhin*. Mommsen thought that the islands in the ocean over which Attila was said to rule were the British Isles,[583] Thompson thinks of Bornholm in the Baltic Sea,[584] Werner turns Bashkiria, 1,500 miles to the east of Attila's residence, into his province.[585]

The slight heuristic value of comparing Attila's kingdom with the great Inner Asiatic Mongol empires is, I am afraid, outweighed by the temptation to look for analogies where there are none. The Hun, whatever his ambition may have been, was not *regna or mundi*, but lord over a fairly well-defined territory. It was not much larger than the one held in the middle of the first century B.C. by the Dacian king Burebista, who in ten years expanded his rule form the mouth of the Danube to Slovakia and

---

[580] Priscus, *EL* 140$_{18-19}$.

[581] *Collectanea Friburgensia* N.S. IX, 1907, 38.

[582] H. de Boor 1932.

[583] Mommsen 1913, 4, 539, n. 5.

[584] Thompson 1948, 75-76. He refers to the fifth-century gold coins in the Baltic islands. They have nothing to do with the Huns, but are the payments and donative money brought back by Germanic mercenaries; cf. P. Grierson, *Transactions of the Royal Historical Society* 1959, 135.

[585] J. Werner 1956, 87.

subdued the greater part of the Balkan peninsula. Burebista's meteoric rise and the sudden collapse of his power were not due to the supposed latent possibilities and liabilities of nomadic societies. The Dacians were not mounted archers. Or, to take another example, to compare Attila with the Gothic *condottiere* Theoderic Strabo ("the Squinter") may to some sound sacrilegious. But with all the differences in magnitude the two have much in common. For a few years in the later half of the fifth century, the Squinter was the terror of the East Romans. He forced them to appoiot him *magister militum*, of course with the salary that went with it. He defeated one Roman army after the other. In 473, Emperor Leo pledged to pay him 2,000 pounds of gold yearly,[586] only 100 pounds less than what Attila received as annual tribute at the height of his power. Theoderic Strabo was not another Attila, but Attila was not another Genghiz Khan either. After the murder of Bleda, Attila was the sole ruler of the Huns, his "own people," τοῦ σφέτεϱου ἔθνους,[587] and lord of the Goths and Gepids, a mighty warrior, for a few years more than a nuisance to the Romans, though at no time a real danger.

Those romantic souls who still see in Attila Hegel's *Weltgeist zu Pferde*, should read the acts of the Council of Chalcedon. Among the voluminous documents there are a few letters with casual allusions to fights between Roman troops and Huns somewhere in Thrace. In the very detailed protocols of the meetings, the Huns are not mentioned. It is true the bishops were passionately involved in their dogmatic quarrels. Still, one could not understand their utter disregard for the deadly danger only a hundred miles away, threatening Christendom with extinction, had it really been so deadly.

In the West, Prosper has not one word about the invasion of Gaul in 451. He may have had a personal reason. In his hostility to Aetius, Prosper may not have wanted to give him credit for the victory. But he could not have passed over the invasion in silence unless he, and not only he, took it for just another of the constant barbarian raids into the empire, an episode as later the Magyar raids were episodes. As in the eighth and ninth centuries no one thought for a moment that the Magyars could make themselves masters of Europe, so the idea would have been absurd to the Romans that Attila could take Constantinople and hold it.

In the west, south of the Danube, Noricum remained a Roman province. In 449, the East Roman ambassadors met Promotus, governor of Noricum, at Attila's court.[588]

---

[586] Malchus fr. 2, *FHG* IV, 114.
[587] *EL* 128,7.
[588] *Ibid.* 132,20-21.

North of the Danube the Langobards successfully defended their independence from the Huns. With the help of the story of Agelmund, Lamissio, and the Vulgares, the disputes between the two peoples can be reconstructed in broad outline. The story is preserved in Paul the Deacon's *Historia Langobardorum*, who took it from the *Origo Gentis Langobardorum*, written about the middle of the seventh century. Not in spite of, but because of its gaps and inconsistencies,[589] the *Origo* is a historical document of the first order. To the living tradition of the Langobards it stands incomparably closer than Jordanes'-Cassiodorus' *History of the Goths* to the Gothic *cantus maiorum*. The story runs as follows:[590]

> The Langobards are said to have possessed for some years Anthaib and Banthaib, and in like manner, Vurgundaib. There they made Agelmund their king. He led them over a river, defended by Amazons. After passing it, the Langobards, when they came to the lands beyond, sojourned there for some time. Meanwhile, since they suspected nothing hostile, confidence prepared for them a disaster of no mean sort. At night, when all were resting, relaxed by negligence, the Vulgares, rushing upon them, slew many, wounded more, and so raged through their camp that they killed Agelmund, the king himself, and carried in captivity his only daughter.
>
> Nevertheless, the Langobards, having recovered their strength after these disasters, made Lamissio their king. And he turned his arms against the Vulgares. And presently, when the first battle began, the Langobards, turning their back to the enemy, fled to their camp. Then King Lamissio urged them to defend themselves. . . . by arms. Inflamed by the urging of their chief, they rushed upon the foe, fought fiercely, and overthrew the adversaries with great slaughter.

Lamissio was followed by Lethu, Hildeoc, and Gudeoc, at whose time Odovacar defeated the Rugi. "Then [under Gudeoc] the Langobards, having moved out of their territory, came to Rugiland and because it was fertile in soil they remained in it a number of years."[591]

After his victory over the Rugi in the winter 487/8, Odovacar broke their last resistance in 488. Rugiland is Lower Austria, north of the Danube, west of Korneuburg. It is the first identifiable geographical name in the *Historia Langobardorum*, and 488 the first identifiable date. Everything

---

[589] "It is hopeless to get any possible scheme of Lombard chronology out of the early chapters of Paulus," Hodgkin 1898, 5, 99.

[590] *Hist. Lang.* I, 16-17. Leaving out a few embroideries, I follow the translation in Foulke 1906.

[591] *Ibid.* I, 19.

before seems to be lost in impenetrable fog. Any interpretation seems to be as good as any other.

Kemp Malone dates the war between the Langobards and the Vulgares in the later half of the second century and places the story in the Baltic. He arrives at this astounding result by taking *Vulgares* for the Latinized form of Langobardic *Wulg(w)aras=wulg*, "she-wolf", and a Germanic plural suffix.[592] It would be difficult to find a more fanciful etymology, thought up in complete disregard of the text.

Convinced that the Langobards lived in Silesia before they moved to Rugiland, some scholars located the battle at the Oder.[593] Klebel is more specific. According to him, the Langobards defeated the Vulgares in the region of Glogau or still farther to the east.[594] He thinks the Vulgares are the Bulgars of South Russia; he even derives their name from that of the Volga.[595]

The question is not the etymology of Vulgares, but what the ethnic name meant in Paul's writings. In the *Historia* the Vulgares are (1) the enemies of the Langobards; (2) a people living among the Langobards in Pannonia, later in Italy;[596] (3) the followers of *dux* Alzeco, who left his country and joined the Langobards in the reign of Grimoald (662-671); settlers in former Samnium;[597] (4) the Vulgarians at the lower Danube.[598] The Bulgars of (3) and (4) are obviously not the Vulgares of our story. The Pannonian Bulgars (2), probably a tribe, or tribes, who stayed in Hungary after the collapse of Attila's kingdom, appear under this name only in the 480's, too late for the story.

As unreliable as the *Origo* and Paul are when they give the names of the stations of the Langobardic migration,[599] in listing the kings, they follow a tradition in which, like in that of the Goths and Burgundians, the names of the rulers and their succession are well preserved. Lamissio

---

[592] Malone 1959, 86-107.

[593] Most recently Mitscha-Märheim 1963, 112.

[594] Klebel 1957, 28.

[595] *Ibid.* 79.

[596] *Hist. Lang.* II, 26.

[597] *Ibid.* V, 29. To the literature quoted by Moravcsik, *BT* 2, 357, add Pochettino 1930, 118.

[598] *Hist. Lang.* VI, 31, 49 (*gens, quae super Danubium*).

[599] Their identifications with medieval or modern place names are without exception completely arbitrary. The "Bardengau" in the Lüneburg Heath, which is supposed to have preserved the ethnic name, is actually named after a Count Bardo who in the ninth century had estates there; see R. Dorgereit, *Deutsches Archiv für Erforschung des Mittelalters* 10, 1960, 601.

reigned forty years. How long his successor Lethu reigned is not known.[600] Allowing him a reign of only one and a half years, the shortest reign of a Langobardic king known from reliable sources, and assuming that Gudeoc led his people into Rugiland in the first year of his reign, the war with Vulgares would fall in the year 446. The average reign of the Langobardic rulers was nine years. Giving Hildeoc nine years, the victory would fall in the year 439. The computations are admittedly anything but conclusive. Still, both point to the first half of the fifth century. The powerful enemy of the Langobards must have been the Huns. This was conjectured long ago, and should never have been doubted. But why did Paul call the Huns Vulgares? Because had he spoken of the Huns, his readers might have thought he meant the Avars. In the *Historia Langobardorum* the Hunni are always the Avars, "who were first called Huns, but afterward from the name of their own king: Avars" (*qui primum Hunni, postea de regis proprii nomine Avares appellati sunt*).[601] Gregory of Tours, too, called the Avars Huns, and so did a century later the Langobard who wrote the *Origo*. In Byzantine historiography of the sixth, seventh, and eighth centuries, the use of Οὗννοι for Ἄβαροι is common.[602]

Until recently it would have been impossible to determine where the Langobards fought the Huns. Thanks to Werner's thorough study of the archaeological evidence,[603] we know by now that southern Moravia was held by the Langobards before they settled in Rugiland. Twenty-four findspots testify to their prolonged stay in this area.

[*It is possible that this section is incomplete. —Ed.*]

THE HUNS IN ITALY

The generally known sources for the Hunnic invasion of Gaul in 451 have been so thoroughly studied that their reexamination is unlikely to yield new relevant results.[604] But there are still a few which have been ignored. We learn, for instance, from the letters of Pope Leo (440-461) and only from them that in the early summer of 451 the West Romans expected Attila to march into Italy.

---

[600] The exact dates assigned to Agelmund and Lamissio in the Prosper edition of 1483 (*CM* I, 489-490) are without value. The interpolated passages referring to the Langobards are taken from Paul and fitted into Prosper's chronological framework.

[601] *Hist. Lang.* I, 27.

[602] Moravcsik, *BT* 2, 234.

[603] J. Werner 1962, 144-147.

[604] Because the Alamanni are not among Attila's Germanic allies, Wais (1940, 116-117) assumes that the Huns circumvented their territory in the north and marched to the Rhine through the valleys of the Tauber and Main; cf. also K. Weller, *ZfDA* 70, 1933, 59-60. Demougeot's "Attila et les Gaules" (1958, 7 ff.) contains nothing new.

In this letter of April 23 to Emperor Marcian (450-457), Leo expressed the conviction that by the concord of the two rulers of the empire "the errors of the heretics and the hostility of the barbarians" would be overcome.[605] This could have been said anytime; it is an ever-recurring commonplace. But when in May the emperor decided to convoke an ecumenical council in the East, in Nicaea, the Pope implored him to postpone it; because of the threat of war, the bishops of the most important provinces would be unable to leave their churches.[606] And when Marcian insisted on the convocation, Leo sent Paschasinus, bishop of Lilybaeum, as his delegate; Sicily was "the most secure province."[607]

Why Attila did not march into Italy but into Gaul is not known. He certainly did not undertake the campaign against the Visigoths because he was bribed by Geiseric, their enemy, as Jordanes asserts.[608] The idea that agents of the Vandal king, carrying bags of gold, sneaked through the empire, from North Africa to Hungary, is grotesque. The sixth-century chronicler Malalas' worthless account is still being given some credit. Malalas mixed everything up. He called Attila a Gepid, confused Theoderic and Alaric, and shifted the decisive battle from Gaul to the Danube. Attila is said to have sent ambassadors to Rome and to Constantinople who ordered the two emperors to make their palaces ready for him.[609] Gibbon, followed by Thompson,[610] thought he could recognize in the order "the original and genuine style of Attila." It is rather the style of the most stupid of the Byzantine chroniclers. I disregard the often told melodramatic story of the vicious Princess Honoria, her clandestine engagement to Attila, and what follows from it. It has all the earmarks of Byzantine court gossip.

After the battle at the *locus Mauriacus* in the first week of July 451,[611] Attila retreated to Hungary. About the situation in Gaul we again find some information in Pope Leo's letters. Leo was eager to communicate

---

[605] *Ep.* XXXIX (Leo I), *ACO* II: IV, 41.

[606] "The necessity of the present time by no means permits the clergy of all the provinces to assemble together, since those provinces from which especially they must be called are disturbed by war and do not allow them to leave their churches." (*Sacerdotes provinciarum omnium congregari praesentis temporis necessitas nulla ratione permittit, quoniam illae provinciae de quibus maxime sunt evocandi, inquietatae bello ab ecclesiis suis eos non patiunter abscedere.*) (*Ep.* XLI, *ACO* II: IV, 43.)

"The fear of hostilities details the bishops." (*Hostilitatis metus detinet episcopos.*) (*Ep.* XLVII, *ACO* II: IV, 48.)

[607] *Ep.* XLVI and L, *ACO* II: IV, 47, 49.

[608] *Getica* 184-185.

[609] Malalas XIV, ed. Bonn, 358.

[610] Thompson 1948, 138.

[611] Weber 1936, 162-166.

with the transalpine bishops, but it was only in January 452 that their spokesman, Ingenuus Ebredurensis, came to Rome.[612] Evidently the violent rivalry between the Visigothic princes after the death of King Theoderic made all travel impossible.

The acts of the Council of Chalcedon throw a little light on the Hunnic raids into the Balkans in 451. Emperor Marcian issued a summons to meet in Nicaea on September 1, 451. At that time he hoped to be able to be there, "unless some urgent affairs of state should detain him in the field."[613] He apparently expected trouble on the Danube frontier. It actually broke out in the summer. In August, Marcian asked the bishops assembled at Nicaea to pray for victory over the (unnamed) enemy.[614] He was then in Thrace;[615] fighting was still going on in parts of Illyricum. As no bishop from Moesia prima and Dacia ripensis attended the council when it was finally assembled in Chalcedon,[616] it may be assumed that the Huns were again ravaging the two unfortunate provinces. Scythia, too, was threatened: Alexander, bishop of Tomis, stayed with his flock.[617]

The archaeological evidence is of little help for the reconstruction of the campaign in Gaul. According to *Gesta Trevirorum*, Attila took Trier. This seems to be borne out by recent excavations: The Eucherius church was destroyed in the early 450's.[618] A few years ago a fragment of a Hunnic cauldron allegedly was found in northern France, allegedly near Troyes.[619] It gave new impetus to the search for the battlefield near the *locus Mauriacus*, a favorite hobby of local historians and retired colonels.[620]

All these additions do not change the over-all picture of the events in 451. Attila's campaign in Italy, however, calls for a reexamination. Nearly all modern historians, from Mommsen to Thompson, took it, first

---

[612] Leo's letter of January 27, 452, *ACO* II: IV, 55; cf. also M. Goemans in *Das Konzil von Chalcedon* 1, 256.

[613] *ACO* II: I: 1, 28, II: II: 2, 3_{20}.

[614] *ACO* II: I: 1, 28; II: II: 2, 4_4.

[615] Lector, fr. 4, *PG* 86, 168; *ACO* II; III: 1, 22-23.

[616] See the list of the bishops in Honigmann, *Byzantion* 16, 1944, 50-62.

[617] Laurent 1945. Valerius of Bassiana, who was at Chalcedon, was not bishop of Bassiana in Pannonia, as Eduard Schwartz (*ACO* II: VI, 51 and 66) thought, but of Bassiana in Africa; cf. Honigmann 1944, 58, n. 408.

[618] Ewig, *Trierer Zeitschrift* 21, 1948, 22, 48.

[619] Takáts 1955, 143-173.

[620] On the misnomer "Catalaunian fields" and its origin, see Alföldi 1928, 108-111. *In Campo Beluider*, in the Hungarian chronicle of Simon of Kéza (after 1282), possibly preserved a local tradition. Beluider is Beauvoir in the valley of the Aube, 25 miles east of Troyes. A. Eckhardt (*Revue des études hongroises* 6, 1928, 105-107) thinks Kéza could have heard the name in France or from a Frenchman or from a Teutonic knight who came to Hungary. In the thirteenth century Beauvoir was an important place, the main seat of the Teutonic knights in France.

of all, as an occasion to prove what an incompetent statesman and general Aetius was.[621] Some pious souls still regard the war in Italy as a duel between a blundering Roman leader and a bloodthirsty savage that ended happily with the intervention of Pope Leo as *pontifex ex machina*.[622] Aetius, whom his contemporaries called "the last Roman," is the *bête noire* of the moderns. It is not my intention to rehabilitate him. But I want to show, among other things, that Aetius did not make the dilettantic mistakes of which he has been accused.

The First Phase of the War

The losses of the Huns in 451 must have been very heavy. The mere fact that Attila began to move his army early in the summer shows how much time he required to recuperate from the disaster of the year before. He must have been aware of the dangers of a campaign in the hot season. Why did he attack at all? Attila was doubtless "furious about the unexpected defeat he had suffered in Gaul," to quote the Chronicle of 452,[623] the only source to establish some sort of connection between the two wars. He certainly hated Aetius. But why did he not wait another year to take his revenge? His relationship with the East Romans could not have been worse. When he marched into Gaul, in 451, ostensibly to fight the Visigoths, Emperor Marcian did not move. But Attila could not count on the neutrality of the eastern part of the empire if he invaded Italy. He may have hoped to crush Aetius' army before the East came to the help of the West. He may have thought that once his horsemen swarmed over the Po Valley Aetius would sue for peace. Perhaps he expected Valentinian to sacrifice Aetius in order to save his throne. We know nothing about the political situation in Italy; it may have been such that Attila had reason to expect a quick collapse of the enemy. But it also may have been the pressure of his own hordes, intent on looting and more looting, that forced the king prematurely to undertake another predatory war. There were times when the Huns in Upper Italy moved very slowly because their carts were loaded with so much loot.

When did the Huns cross the Julian Alps from present Yugoslavia into Italy? The chronicles do not give the date, and only a few years later, even the sequence of the major events was forgotten. Hydatius, otherwise so well informed, thought that Attila marched from Gaul straight into Italy;[624] according to the Chronicle of 511, the Huns took Aquileia (in the

---

[621] Only Freeman (1964) and Rubin (1960, 1) dissent from the common view.
[622] It is the basic topic of Homeyer 1951.
[623] *CM* II, 141.
[624] *Hunni cum rege Attila relictis Galliis post certamen Italiam petunt* (*CM* II, 26, 153.)

northeastern corners of the Adriatic Sea) on their retreat from Gaul to Pannonia.[625] Only Priscus seems to give a hint as to the date of Aquileia :

The siege of Aquileia was long and fierce, but of no avail, for the bravest of the soldiers of the Romans withstood him [sc. Attila] from within. At last his army was discontented and eager to withdraw. Attila chanced to be walking around the walls, considering whether to break camp or delay longer, and noticed that the white birds, namely the storks, who build their nests in the gables of houses, were bearing their young from the city and, contrary to their custom, were carrying them into the country. Being a very shrewd observer of events [sagacissimus inquisitor], he understood this and said to his soldiers: "You see the birds foresee the future. They are leaving the city sure to perish and are forsaking strongholds doomed to fall by reason of imminent peril. Do not think this a meaningless or uncertain sign; fear, arising from the things they foresee, has changed their custom." Why say more? He inflamed the hearts of the soldiers to attack Aquileia again.[626]

If Priscus' story should contain a kernel of truth, the fall of Aquileia would have to be dated at the end of August or the beginning of September. According to Pliny, the storks leave Italy after the Vulcanalia, August 23.[627] The siege is said to have lasted three months.[628] The Huns would, thus, have crossed the Julian Alps in May or June. But it is more than doubtful that the story of Attila and the storks permits such an interpretation. It rather seems to throw light on the superstitious awe with which his subjects, especially the Germans, looked up at the king.

The movements of birds were considered ominous by Greeks, Romans, and Germans. Like many heroes of Germanic tradition, Hermenegisclus, king of the Varni, understood the language of the birds.[629] The western Germans regarded the raven and the stork as prophetic birds.[630] One could, therefore, conjecture that Germans told Priscus the story; they may have spoken about Attila as in later times Swedes and Norwegians spoke about the dreaded Finnish and Lappish sorcerer. Priscus himself was possibly not above the superstition of the Greeks before and after him, to whom the "Scythians" were great sorcerers. The Hyperborean magician in Lucian's

---

[625] *Regrediens Attila Aquileiam frangit* (*CM* I, 663, 617).

[626] Priscus quoted by Jordanes, *Getica* 220-221; Paulus Diaconus, *Hist Rom.* XIV, 9; Procopius III, 4, 30-35.

[627] *HN* XVIII, 314.

[628] Paulus Diaconus' "three years" is evidently to be amended to read "three months." Cf. Graevius 1722, VI: 4, 133; Sigonoa, 1732, 498, n. 100.

[629] Procopius VIII, 20, 14.

[630] Cf. K. Helm 1937, 2: 1, 161.

Philopseudes[631] brings up supernatural beings, calls corpses back to life, makes Hecate appear, and pulls down the moon. In Empress Eudocia's *Discourse with the Martyr Cyprian* (Λόγοι εἰς μάρτυρα Κυπριανόν), Cyprian relates how the Scythians taught him the language of the birds, how he learned to understand the sounds of boards and stones, the creaking of doors and hinges, and the talk of the dead in their graves.[632] Geiseric, another "Scythian," and, like Attila, " a very sagacious man," interpreted correctly the flight of the eagle over the sleeping Marcian.[633] Thus, it is quite possible that the story was told by people disposed to believe it, but it is itself of more remote origin.

The legend of Attila and the storks of Aquileia is, in fact, a variant of a story which occurs in chapter 122 of the *Chin shu*, the biography of Lü Kuang who reconquered Turkistan for Fu Chien of the Former Chin. In February 384, he besieged Ch'iu-tz'u (Kuchā). "He once more advanced to attack the city. In the night he dreamed that a golden image flew over and beyond the city walls. Kuang said: 'This means the Buddha and the gods are deserting them. The Hu will surely perish.'"[634]

Folklorists presumably will be able to adduce other versions of this story, perhaps connecting them more closely with the proverbial rats which leave the sinking ship, a story widespread in the West. But stories like the ones told about Attila and Lü Kuang are unknown in Europe.[635] It must have been the Huns who brought them from the East.

Leaving the storks of Aquileia, we turn to the letters of Pope Leo; they provide a safer ground for dating the beginning of the Hunnic invasion. On May 22, 452, Leo wrote long letters to Marcian, Pulcheria, Anatolius, and Julian, bishop of Kios, in which he explained why he could not approve of the disciplinary canons passed by the Council of Chalcedon.[636] There is not one word in them that would indicate that Italy had become a theater of war. The same is true for the letter which the Pope sent to Theodor, bishop of Forum Julii,[637] on June 11. The decretal in which he defined the conditions that should govern the granting of absolution in the administration of penance could have been composed in any year of his pontificate.[638] It is unimaginable that the man who dictated it should have

---

[631] Ch. 13-14.

[632] II, 65-71, Ludwig 1897.

[633] Procopius III, 2, 2-6.

[634] Mather 1959, 33.

[635] As Professor Archer Taylor informs me.

[636] *ACO* II: IV, 55-62, *Ep.* LIV-LVII.

[637] The present Fréjus in Gallia Narbonnensis secunda, not Friuli, as assumed by Bugiani (1905, 184), followed by Solari (1938, 1, 329); cf. Caspar 1933, 1, 451, 452.

[638] *ACO* II: IV, 137-138, *Ep.* CV.

passed over the fate of the cities and towns in northern Italy had they been already under attack by the Huns. Aquileia had not yet fallen; probably it was not even besieged.

And then there is the *Novella Valentiniana* 36 of June 29, 452, on the duties of the swine, cattle, sheep, and goat collectors, a subject obviously of no interest to the students of the Huns, and, therefore, ignored by them. But the *Novella* is the only document of 452 which contains an allusion to the war. In the introduction the emperor praises Aetius, who even "among his warlike troubles and the blare of trumpets" finds time to think of the meat provision of the sacred city. The object of Aetius' *bellicae curae* at the end of June could be no other but the Hunnic invasion. Attila's hordes descended into the plains in the early summer of 452.[639]

If Prosper were to be believed, the invasion came to Aetius as a complete surprise. He wrote:

> After Attila had made up for the losses suffered in Gaul, he intended to attack Italy through Pannonia. Our general had not taken any provisions as he had done in the first war, so that not even the defenses of the Alps, where the enemy could have been stopped, were put to use. He thought the only thing he could hope for was to leave Italy together with the emperor. But this seemed so shameful and dangerous that the sense of honor conquered the fear.[640]

It is amazing that all modern historians believed Prosper. "The news of Attila's arrival in Italy," says Thompson, "must have struck the patrician with the violence of a thunderstroke."[641] Nothing could be further from the truth.

The passes over the Julian Alps, to begin with, can in no way be compared with the Gotthard or even the Brenner Pass. In the *Historia Langobardorum*, Paul the Deacon described the approaches to the peninsula:

> Italy is encompassed by the waves of the Tyrrhenian and Adriatic seas, yet from the west and north it is so shut in by the range of the Alps that there is no entrance to it except through narrow passes and over lofty summits of mountains. Yet from the eastern side by which it is joined to Pannonia it has an approach which lies open more broadly and is quite level.[642]

---

[639] Seeck, *Geschichte* 6, 311, thought that Attila, following Alaric's example, probably broke into Italy in mid-winter, when the passes were not defended. Most other historians date the invasion in the spring; none bothered to state his reasons.

[640] *CM* I, 482-483$_{1367}$.

[641] Thompson 1948, 145.

[642] *Hist. Lang.* II, 9.

Second, the *limes* on the Karst[643] consisted of light fortifications, or better roadblocks and watchtowers, garrisoned by forces which were unable to withstand a determined attack.[644] At the best they could delay the enemy; they could not stop them.

Third, and this is most important, Aetius acted exactly as other generals before and after him acted in the same situation. In the course of the fifth century Italy was invaded six times.[645] With the possible, though improbable exception of Radagaisus' hosts, each time the enemy descended into the plain from the east, each time he crossed the passes of the Julian Alps without having to overcome any resistance. This is true for Alaric in 401 and again in 408, the East Roman army under Aspar in 425, Attila in 452, and Theoderic's Ostrogoths in 489. Neither Stilicho, nor the usurper John, nor Odovacar defended Italy in the passes. It could be objected that they had not enough troops for both the passes, and, if those were broken through, the plain. But in 388, the rebel Maximus had a very strong army, and yet he made no attempt to stop Emperor Theodosius; the emperor "crossed the empty Alps" (*vacuas transmisit Alpes*).[646] In 394, the Alps again "lay open" to Theodosius' army.[647] The struggle for Italy began in the valley of the Isonzo or before the walls of Aquileia.

Attila could not by-pass the strong fortress; its garrison it seems, strengthened in anticipation of the siege.[648] Only after Attila used siege engines,[649] obviously built by Roman deserters or prisoners, were the walls of Aquileia breached and the city stormed. It was thoroughly plundered; those who could not flee in time were massacred or carried away into captivity.[650] The devastation was certainly cruel, but Jordanes' assertion that no trace of the former great city was left to be seen is one of those exaggerations of the Hunnic outrages which, enormous as they were, were later magnified out of all proportion. By the middle of the sixth century, Aquileia had long been rebuilt. It is true that the fortification had not been restored. The Ostrogoth Theoderic in 489 and the Byzantine general Narses

---

[643] *Not. Dign.* [*occ.*] 24.

[644] Cf. Saria 1939; Stuchi 1945, 355-356; J. Szilagyi, *AA* 2, 1952, 216, n. 296. The castellum *Ad pirum* had a very small garrison; cf. Brusin 1959, 39-45.

[645] Not counting the piratical expeditions of the Vandals.

[646] Orosius, *Hist. adv. Pagan.* VII, 35, 3; cf. also Zosimus IV, 46, 2.

[647] Claudian, *3rd Cons. Hon.* 89-90; cf. also Sozomen VII, 22-24.

[648] Cessi's assertion that Aquileia had the same small garrison as in peace time (1957, 1, 329) is unfounded. As always in troubled times, people from the surrounding districts fled to the city; cf. Panciera 1957, 8.

[649] *Getica* 222.

[650] Romantically embroidered by Paulus Diaconus, *Hist. Rom.* XIV, 8-9.

in 552 by-passed the city. But only a few years after the devastation by the Huns, Aquileia was again the seat of a bishop.[651] The Christian community was strengthened as more and more fugitives returned.[652] In the sixth century, a basilica with a splendid mosaic floor was built.[653] The metropolitan of Aquileia was in rank equal to the metropolitans of Milan and Ravenna.[654]

In the Po Valley

Jordanes, probably following Priscus, named three cities which fell to the Huns—Aquileia, Mediolanum (present Milan), and Ticinum (present Pavia)—speaking also vaguely about "the remaining towns of the Veneti" and "almost the whole of Italy."[655] Paul the Deacon copied Jordanes,[656] but as a native of Cividale he naturally was more interested in the towns of upper Italy than Jordanes. He first enumerated three places near Aquileia: Concordia, Altinum, and Patavium, and then "all the cities of Venetia," namely, hoc est, Vicetia, Verona, Brixia, and Pergamum.[657] It is quite possible that the Huns indeed took all those places, but Paul's hoc est makes the list somewhat suspicious.[658]

The Huns crossed the Po and devastated the province of Aemilia. to the south of the river. After his experiences before Aquileia, Attila could not hope to take the incomparably stronger fortress Ravenna. Like Alaric half a century earlier, he could have marched on Rome, where the emperor stayed.[659] However, the Huns did not cross the Apennines. Whether they tried and were repulsed, or were so heavily engaged by Aetius in the plain that Attila could not spare troops for an attack, is not known. Possibly the ranks of the Huns were already thinned out by sickness. Perhaps many horsemen had hastily been ordered back to Hungary. Our only source of information is a passage in Hydatius: "Auxiliaries were sent by the emperor Marcian, and under the commandership of Aetius they [i.e.

---

[651] Cf. Pope Leo's letter of March 21, 458, PL 54, 1136; Calderini 1930, 87.

[652] Brusin 1947, 11.

[653] Brusin 1948, 74-78.

[654] Ensslin 1947, 119.

[655] Getica 222.

[656] Crivelluci in his edition of the Hist. Rom., 1914, 196; Mommsen (1882, p. lviii) thought Paul followed an unknown author.

[657] Hist. Rom. XIV, 9-13.

[658] Cf. Bierbach 1906, 48.

[659] Valentinian did not flee from Ravenna to Rome, as it so often has been asserted. Cf. Gibbon 3, 472; Lizerand 1910, 109; Hutton 1926, 55; Romano and Somi 1940, 102. He was in Rome throughout 451 and 452. All the laws of these two years were issued in Rome. Marcian's portrait was sent to Rome, not to Ravenna (CM I, 490$_2$).

the Huns] were slain. Likewise they were subdued in their own seats, partly by plagues from heaven, partly by Marcian's army." (*Missis per Marcianum principem Aetio duce caeduntur auxiliis pariterque in sedibus suis et caelestibus plagis et per Marciani subiuguntur exercitum.*)[660]

This often has been misunderstood. It has been maintained[661] that the *dux* Aetius was an East Roman general, commander of the troops which attacked the Huns *in sedibus suis*, by coincidence bearing the same name as the West Roman generalissimo. But Hydatius makes a clear distinction between the *auxilia* sent by Marcian to Aetius and Marcian's *exercitus*. There is no reason whatever to postulate the existence of two generals, both named Aetius, both fighting the Huns.[662] The passage sheds some light on the preparations Aetius must have made when the first information about Attila's plans reached him. Because the East Roman *auxilia* could not march through Pannonia, they must have sailed from some eastern ports to Italy, probably Ravenna. To move the troops to the ports of embarkation, to assemble the ships, to provide food for the soldiers and fodder for the horses in the landing port, all this required considerable time. An expedition, if it were to be of real help to the West, could not be improvised. Aetius and the government in Constantinople must have worked out a plan of coordinated action against the Huns, should Attila invade Italy.

According to Paul the Deacon, the Huns took Mediolanum and Ticinum, but the two cities were not plundered nor the citizens massacred. As a sermon given after the Huns evacuated Milan shows,[663] Paul was misinformed. Many houses and churches were destroyed.[664] The basilica of St. Ambrose[665] was set on fire and collapsed.[666] The Huns killed not

---

[660] *CM* II, 27$_{154}$.

[661] Seeck, *Geschichte* 6, 312; Stein 1959, 1, 499; Thompson 1948, 148.

[662] Cf. San Lazzaro 1938, 336-339.

[663] *PL* 47, 469-472, reprinted in Paredi 1937, 169-170. In Bruni's edition of the sermons of Maximus of Turin, which Migne reprinted in *Patrologia latina*, it has number 94. Actually, its author is unknown; Almut Mutzenbecher did not include it in her new edition of Maximus' sermons (*CCSL* XXIII). On the date of the sermons which were supposed to refer to the Hun invasion of 452, see Maenchen-Helfen 1964, 114-115.

[664] "God almighty has given the abodes of the city into the hands of our enemies... What seemed to be our property was either looted by robbers or perished, consumed by fire and sword. ... And let us not lament that the houses have collapsed" (*Deus omnipotens hostium manibus habitacula tradidit civitatis . . . ea quae nostra videbantur aut praedo diripuit, aut igno ferroque consumpta perierunt . . . nec suspiremus collapsas esse domos*).

[665] It was the basilica nova intramurana; Cf. Captiani d'Arzagno 1952.

[666] "God did not decree his church, that which is in truth his church, to be consumed by fire, but because of our shortcomings he allowed the receptacle of the church

a few clerics and laymen.[667] Still many survived, not because the Huns were so mild, but because the Milanese ran away faster than the Huns could pursue them: heavily loaded with booty, the Hunnic carts were too slow, *ut velocissimi equites tarda atque onere gravata suo trepidantium plaustra fugerunt.*[668] It is quite possible, I believe, that Aetius abandoned the cities in northern Italy to slow down the savage hordes. Their loss may have been the price paid to save Rome. Attila took up residence in the imperial palace.[669] His horsemen looted and killed to their hearts' desire.

The Huns did not stay long in Milan;[670] they evacuated the city and retreated east. Food and fodder for the horses must have been hard to find among the charred ruins; besides, illness hit the Huns "from heaven."[671] This we learn only from Hydatius. Prosper certainly knew of the epidemic which raged among the Huns but, according to him, the merit of having rescued Italy from the savages belonged exclusively to the Holy Father.

Northern Italy became to the Huns what fifty years earlier it had been to Alaric's Visigoths, *regio funesta,*[672] a land of death, where "pestilence

---

to be burned out . . . the fury of the barbarians has levelled down this holy house" (*Deus . . . nec ecclesiam suam, quae vere est ecclesia, consumi iussit incendio, sed pro nostra correptione receptacula ecclesiae permisit exuri . . . furor barbarus sanctam hanc domum complanavit*). Cf. also the inscription in the newly built church, preserved in a copy: "The temples come to life again and are crowned with their former roofs. What the flames had burned returned to its shape. This he granted to the prayers of him, who rebuilt the temples of Christ. Because of Eusebius' merits the damaging fire perished" (*Prisca rediuiuis consurgunt culmina templis /In forman rediere suam quae flamma cremarat,/ Reddidit haec votis Christi qui templa novavit / Eusebii meritis noxia flamma perit*). De Rossi 1888, 2, 161; Forcella and Selotti 1897, 249; cf. Courcelle 1953, 23-37. On the author of the inscription, cf. Capitani d'Arzagno 1952, 31-32.

[667] "Some of the clerics and laymen lacked the chance or will to escape" (*Nonnulis de clerco, aut plebe evadendi aut possibilitas defuit, aut voluntas*).

[668] Paredi (1937, 169-170) misunderstood the passage. Cf Courcelle 1953, 33.

[669] A painting representing Scythians prostrate at the feet of the Roman emperors, presumably Theodosius and Valentinian, seated on golden thrones, roused Attila's anger. He ordered a painter to draw a picture of the Hun king and before him the emperors pouring out gold from bags at his feet; cf. *Suidas, s.v. Κόρυκος, Μεδιόλανον,* Adler 1938, 3, 161, 346. Barbarians bringing baskets with gold coins was a common motif; they are represented on the Arcadian column and the obelisk in Constantinople (Kollwitz 1941, Beilage 6, p. 35; Bruns 1935, figs, 37, 42, 43), the Barberini diptych, and elsewhere.

[670] The people of Milan began to rebuild the basilica before the Huns left Italy (Pseudo-Maximus, 471).

[671] *Divinitus partim fame, partim morbo quodam plagis caelestibus feriuntur (CM* II, 26$_{154}$).

[672] Claudian, *6th Cons. Hon.* 274.

raged, brought by foul food and aggravated by the season's heat."[673] The situation of Attila's army must have been almost the same as in 447 when he stood before Constantinople. Perhaps it can be best compared with the fate of the Frankish invaders in 540, who "were unable to obtain any provisions except cattle and the waters of the Po. Most of them were attacked by diarrhea and dysentery, which they were quite unable to shake off because of the lack of proper food. Indeed they say that one third of the Frankish army perished in this way."[674] The same fate befell another Frankish army in 553; it was almost wiped out.[675] It seems that the Goths, many of whom fought under Attila, were particularly susceptible to epidemic diseases.[676]

Retreat

In a few weeks, a month at the most, the Huns, under the threefold attack of Aetius' troops, Marcian's army, and sickness, would have been forced to ride back to Hungary. At that very moment the Romans decided to open negotiations with Attila. In Prosper's words:

In all the deliberations of the emperor, the senate, and the Roman people nothing better was found than to send an embassy to the terrible king and ask for peace. Relying on the help of God, who, he knew, never failed in works of piety, the most blessed Pope Leo undertook these negotiations together with the ex-consul Avienus and the ex-prefect Trygetius. Nor did it turn out otherwise than faith had expected. The king received the whole delegation courteously, and he was so flattered by the presence of the highest priest that he ordered his men to stop the hostilities and, promising peace, returned beyond the Danube.[677]

How should this passage be interpreted? Hydatius, a faithful son of the Church, knows nothing about such an embassy. It need not be proved that in the middle of the fifth century the "Roman people" had nothing to decide, and it is more than doubtful that Attila was so overwhelmed by the saintliness of the pontiff or, as he probably called him, the chief shaman of the Romans, that he meekly made peace. And yet, Prosper did not invent the meeting. Jordanes, too, knew about it and even named the place where Leo met Attila.[678] What, then, was Leo's mission? He

---

[673] *Ibid.*, 241-242.

[674] Procopius VI, 25, 17-18.

[675] Agathias II. 3, 69-71.

[676] Ambrose, *Ep.* XV, 7, *PL* 16, 998; Claudian, *4th Cons. Hon.* 466-467.

[677] *CM* I, 482$_{1367}$.

[678] *Getica* 223 ("in the Ambuleian district of the Veneti at the well-traveled ford of the river Mincius").

himself never mentioned it, not in his writings, nor letters, nor sermons. Legends embellished at an early time the encounter of the Pope who became a saint and the Hun king who became the "scourge of God."[679] Paul the Deacon knew of a venerable old man, who, standing at Leo's side, threatened the king with a drawn sword.[680] The man is the Christian counterpart of Achilles and Athena Promachos who protected Athens from Alaric.[681] Paul's warrior looks like a combination of Mars and Saint Peter, who "in all emergencies was close" to the Pope.[682] It is hopeless to search these stories for their historical content.

A fortunate coincidence has preserved a letter which the oriental bishops sent to Pope Symmachus in 512 or 513.[683] From it we learn that Leo negotiated with Attila about the release of the captives in the hands of the Huns, not only of the Christians, but also, "if that can be believed," of Jews and pagans.[684] How successful Leo was we do not know, but it is quite believable, even probable, that Attila released the more prominent prisoners, naturally for a substantial ransom.[685] The others, for whom no one was willing to pay, were dragged off to Hunnia. No chronicler was interested in their fate. What happened to them we shall learn presently.

Attila's campaign was worse than a failure. He could not force the Romans to conclude another treaty with him, to pay tribute again, or to reappoint him *magister militum*. The hated Aetius remained the factual ruler of the Western empire. The loot may have been considerable but it was bought at too high a price, too many Hunnic horsemen lay dead in the towns and fields of Italy. A year later Attila's kingdom collapsed.[686]

---

[679] Isidor of Seville, who is commonly regarded as the first to have applied Isaiah 14:5 to the Huns and Avars (*virga furoris dei sunt, Hist. Wand.* in *CM* II, 279, written between 624 and 636), probably repeated what he had read somewhere. The *flagella* in Pope Leo's letter of March 15, 453 (*ACO* II:IV, 65) undoubtedly refer to the Hun invasion of 452.

[680] *Hist. Rom.* XIV, 12.

[681] Zosimus V, 6. This has been pointed out by Caspar (1933, 1, 564, n. 2), who, however, mistakenly referred to the *Historia Miscella* as the earliest source for the legend.

[682] Leo's sermon 84, given in 455 (*PL* 54, 433-434).

[683] Caspar 1933, 2, 121-122.

[684] *PL* 52, 59-60.

[685] Leo's mission to Attila has a close parallel in the one of Epiphanius, bishop of Ticinum, the present Pavia, to the Burgundian king Gundobad in 495. The king was so impressed by the holy man that he released six thousand of the Italian prisoners, though only after he was paid a large sum for the others. See Cook 1942, 100-101. Paulus Diaconus (*Hist. Rom.* XV, 18) speaks of a "countless multitude."

[686] According to Altheim (1951, 146, repeated in 1962, 4, 333), the Huns, retreating through Noricum, pillaged Augsburg. The existence of a Roman city in Raetia prima (Augusta Vindelicorum was not in Noricum) in the middle of the fifth century comes as a surprise. Altheim refers to Ulrich-Nansa (1949, 226, n. 16), who, in turn, refers to a medieval Hungarian chronicler as his source.

Postscript

In March 458, Nicetas, bishop of Aquileia, asked Pope Leo for help and advice. His letter has not been preserved but its content can be reconstructed from Leo's answer.[687] In the beginning the Pope speaks of the wounds inflicted by the attacks of the enemy. Through the disasters of war and the grievous inroads of the enemy, families were broken up, the men were carried off in captivity and their wives remained forsaken. Now, through the Lord's help, things have turned to the better. Some of those who were thought to have perished have returned. Leo decided that the women who had remarried should go back to their former husbands. He let the bishop know what should be done with those who, while captives, were, by hunger and terror, compelled to eat sacrificial food, and those who were baptized by heretics. Leo concluded the letter with the request that its contents should be brought to the knowledge of the bishop's brethren and fellow bishops of the province.

Half a year later, Neon, bishop of Ravenna, had more questions to ask. Some of the returned prisoners craved the healing water of baptism; they went into captivity when they could have no knowledge of anything, and in the ignorance of infancy they could not remember whether they had been baptized or not. Should they be baptized, which could mean that perhaps they would be baptized twice?[688]

The theological and moral problems are of no interest to the present studies. What matters is the fact that men and children who a few years earlier had been dragged into captivity returned to the dioceses of Aquileia. The only enemy who had been there were the Huns. The circumstances under which the Huns let the prisoners go back will be discussed in a later chapter. When one considers how many must have died and how many still came back, one can imagine how large the number must have been of those for whom no one paid ransom. It should be noted that the Pope said nothing about women who came back. They apparently stayed in the harems of the Hunnic nobles and went with them, after the breakdown of the kingdom, to the northern Balkan provinces. The heretics who baptized the children must have been Arian Goths and, possibly, Gepids.[689]

---

[687] *Ep.* CLIX, dated March 21, 458, *PL* 54, 1135-1140. Cf. Jalland 1941, 101-103.

[688] Leo, *Ep.* CLXVI, dated October 24, 458, *PL* 54, 1191-1196.

[689] Two years later, Rusticus, bishop of Narbonne, submitted to Leo a list of questions similar to those which vexed Niceta and Neon. See Leo's letter, *PL* 54, 1199-1209; cf. Caspar 1933, 2, 451, n. 6, and Jalland 1941, 149-151. The captives came from Africa and Mauretania, apparently released by the Vandals; cf. Courtois 1955, 199-200.

COLLAPSE AND AFTERMATH

Attila spent the last months of his life preparing a campaign against the East. In the early fall of 452, his ambassadors threatened Emperor Marcian that their lord would "devastate the provinces because that which had been promised him by Theodosius was not paid; the fate of his enemies will be worse than usual."[690]

The Priscus text which Jordanes followed is partly preserved in fragment EL 9.[691] Attila sent the ambassadors after he returned from Italy and before the events referred to in fragment EL 11. The peace which Maximus concluded with the Blemmyes and Nobades provided that the barbarians were again admitted access to the Isis temple on the island of Philae. As a priest of the Blemmyes (a tribe living in the modern Sudan) dedicated an inscription to Osiris and Isis on Philae on December 19, 452,[692] the peace cannot have been concluded later than in October or November.[693] The emperor rejected the demands of the Hun even more firmly than in 450. At that time, Attila had been at the height of his power. Since then his glory had faded, the myth of his invincibility had been exploded, his armies defeated, his resources greatly diminished. Although the battle of the *locus Mauriacus* was in the strict sense undecided, for the Huns, a battle which cost them thousands of horsemen and in which they neither took prisoners nor could rob the dead was a lost battle. The invasion of Italy ended in failure. It now had been years since Attila had received tribute from either half of the empire. Although we have no evidence of unrest among his German subjects or among the ruling group of the Huns, we may safely assume that the former were more heavily exploited than ever and the latter grew increasingly dissatisfied with the king who failed to provide them with booty and gold. Nevertheless, Attila remained a formidable adversary. Marcian was "disquieted about his fierce foe."[694] Fortunately, Attila died in the beginning of 453.

The contemporary Prosper, whom Cassiodorus copied, the sixth-century chronicler Victor Tonnenensis, and the Gallic chronicle of 511[695] agree on the year. According to Hypatius, Attila died shortly after his retreat

---

[690] *Getica* 225. In the translation of *inhumanior solito suis hostibus appareret*, I follow Kalén 1934, 124.

[691] *EL* 583$_{11\text{-}14}$.

[692] Seeck 1919, 397. Cf. also Monneret de Villard 1938, 50.

[693] Maximus died late in 452 or early in 453; cf. Ensslin 1927, 7.

[694] *Getica* 255.

[695] *CM* I, 482-483$_{1370}$; II, 157$_{1258}$; II, 185$_{453,2}$; I, 663$_{662}$.

from Italy;[696] "454" in Marcellinus Comes[697] is certainly wrong. The circumstances of Attila's death were soon embroidered with all kinds of inventions.[698]

Except for a not very enlightening entry in Marcellinus Comes and a few insignificant lines in the *Vita s. Severini*,[699] Jordanes is the only source for the events after Attila's death. In the *Romana* he mentioned it in passing. For the *Getica* he drew on Cassiodorus and, either directly or through Cassiodorus, on Priscus, occasionally looking at a map;[700] in the main, he relied on oral tradition. The results are meager. The history of the transdanubian barbaricum after Attila's death can be reconstructed only in the broadest outlines:

Attila's sons were "clamoring that the *gentes* [*sc.* the Hunnic *gentes*] should be divided among them equally and that warlike kings with their *populi* should be apportioned to them like a family estate [*instar familiae*]." A coalition of Germanic tribes, led by Ardaric, king of the Gepids, revolted.[701] After a succession of battles they defeated the Huns in Pannonia at the Nedao River. Among the alleged thirty thousand slain Huns was Ellac, Attila's eldest son.

The Goths did not fight on the Nedao.[702] Some Goths may have joined the rebels; others probably remained loyal to the Huns. Goths trekked with Huns as late as 468. The great mass of the people remained neutral. On this point there is general agreement. There remain two questions: When was the battle at the Nedao fought, and where is the Nedao?

Revocatio Pannoniarum

According to Marcellinus Comes, the fight between the savage peoples was still raging in 453. Before the summer of 455, the Huns were defeated. This follows from Sidonius Apollinaris' *Panegyric on Emperor Avitus.* In the autumn of 455, Avitus "recovered the lost Pannonias after so many generations by a mere march."[703] These two verses puzzled histo-

---

[696] *CM* II, 27. [*Reference incomplete in manuscript.—Ed.*]

[697] *CM* II, 86₄₅₄,₁.

[698] Cf. Moravcsik 1932, 83-116.

[699] "At the time, when Attila, king of the Huns, had died, the two Pannonias and other districts bordering on the Danube were in a state of utter confusion" (I, 1).

[700] Mommsen 1882, p. xxxi.

[701] In his hatred of the Gepids, Paulus Diaconus (*Hist. Rom.* 15-16) distorted what he read in Jordanes, his only source for this period.

[702] Alföldi 1926, 97-99; L. Schmidt 1927, 459; Ennslin 1947, 11; Thompson 1948, 153. Altheim's arguments for the participation of the Goths in the battle on the Nedao (1962, 4, 340-346) are unconvincing.

[703] Vv. 589-590.

rians for more than two hundred years. *Je ne sçai pas quelle verité il peut y avoir dans ce que dit Saint Sidoine, qu'Avite avoit réuni les Pannoniens,* wrote Tillemont, and it would seem that we are not much wiser.

There is, first, the question of the date. Avitus was proclaimed emperor in Arles on July 9, 455; on September 21, he entered Italy.[704] On January 11, 456, he was in Rome where Sidonius delivered the panegyric.[705] When was he in Pannonia? Not between July and September, as Stevens thought.[706] Even if Avitus left Gaul immediately after he was raised to the throne, which is improbable, he could not have journeyed north, turned east, crossed Raetia and Noricum, received the submission of the barbarians in Pannonia, and still have been in Italy by September. He could not have gone later, either. To cross Italy from her western border—Avitus came from Gaul—to the Julian Alps and to proceed to Pannonia, to stay there, even only a few days, and to return in winter to Italy in order to be in Rome at the end of the year required incomparably more time than Avitus had in the last quarter of 455. Not Avitus, but one of his officers was in Pannonia. What he achieved there was, in the tradition of the βασιλικὸς λόγος, attributed to the emperor.[707]

Sidonius lavished the most extraordinary praises on Avitus. Like Claudian on such occasions before him, he set the whole divine machinery in motion to present to the assembled senators the new emperor as the savior of the world. Jupiter tells the gods and goddesses, even the fauns and satyrs, the exploits of the hero. Well informed by the poet who happened to be the emperor's son-in-law, the thunderer not only describes minutely all that Avitus had done for the beloved Gaul, he also invites the listeners to go back with him to the years when the future Augustus, still a boy, emulating Hercules, killed a she-wolf with a stone. He leaves out nothing; he spends forty hexameters on a duel between Avitus and a Hun. The panegyric contains 603 lines. But only at its very end, in one and a half verses, does Sidonius allude to what one should think was the most glorious deed of Avitus—the recovery of the Pannonian provinces, "whose march alone sufficed to recover the Pannonian provinces" (*Cuius solum amissas post saecula multa / Pannonias revocavit iter*). The discrepancy between Sidonius' words and the importance of the event is striking. The Western empire was losing one province after another to the barbarians. Only seven months before, the Vandals had looted Rome so thoroughly that we still speak of Vandalism. At such a time the recovery of the two

---

[704] Seeck 1920, 476 *ad* p. 328.
[705] Seeck 1919, 402.
[706] Stevens 1933, 30.
[707] See W. B. Anderson in his edition of Sidonius I, 168, n. 3.

long-lost Pannonias should have been hailed by Sidonius as the beginning of a new era. He should have compared Avitus to Alexander, Scipio, the divine Julius, and all the other great captains of the past. But instead of singing a paean, Sidonius whispers, as if not to forget, that the Pannonias were Roman again.

Seeck assumed that Avitus went to Pannonia to reconquer the country from the Huns and to wait there, closer to Constantinople, for recognition by Marcian before he presented himself to the senators in Rome,[708] to which Stein rightly objected that for Avitus to interfere in the Danube provinces would have been about the worst way of winning Marcian's favor; he thought Avitus' action actually forfeited his recognition by the Eastern court.[709]

The *revocatio Pannoniarum* is not mentioned in the chronicles. It is true, they are terse, but not so terse that they could have ignored such a momentous event. Neither the Western nor the Eastern sources contain as much as an allusion to the alleged reconquest of the provinces. However, the *Fasti Vindobonenses priores* have under 455 a curious entry: "and Sabaria has been destroyed by an earthquake seven days before the Ides of September on a Friday" (*et eversa est Sabaria a terrae motu VII idus Septembr. die Veneris*).[710]

As long as Pannonia prima was under Roman rule, Sabaria, the present Steinamanger (Szombathely), was the most important town of the province. The last indirect reference to it occurs in the *Notitia Dignitatum* of the early fifth century where (*occ.* VII, 82) the *lanciarii Sabarienses* are listed. Like the other Romans in Pannonia, the people of Sabaria must have lived a wretched life in the first half of the fifth century, but somehow they held out, possibly because they arrived at an agreement with Germanic settlers in the neighborhood who, as well as the Huns, needed the craftsmen of the town. When the power of the Huns broke down, there were still Romans in Sabaria. The entry in the chronicle, exact down to the day of the week when the earthquake struck, presupposes the resumption of relations with the West Romans. Pannonia did not become Roman again—otherwise Sidonius would have spoken in a different vein—but it was again, however loosely, in the orbit of the empire.

Sidonius contrasted *iter* to *bellis*. Avitus' officers did not fight in or for Pannonia, neither against the Huns nor any other barbarians. Avitus needed all the troops he had, his own and, hopefully, what the Visigoths might send him for the war against Geiseric's Vandals. Avitus will restore

---

[708] Seeck 1920, 328.

[709] Stein 1959, 1, 369. Both he and Seeck thought that Avitus went himself to Pannonia.

[710] *CM* I, 304₃₇₇.

Libya to Rome, exclaims Sidonius, immediately before he comes to the recovery of Pannonia. The only conceivable reason for Avitus' officers going to Pannonia must have been the same which Marcian had two years later, when he sent his officers to the Danube countries to recruit soldiers for the war against the Vandals. Avitus could not expect to succeed as long as Pannonia was under the Huns. And this, together with the report on the earthquake in Sabaria, presupposes that by that time the power of the Huns had collapsed. The battle at the Nedao was fought in the summer of 455 at the latest.

A passage by Sidonius in *Panegyric on Anthemius* points to a still earlier date. In 454, the future emperor, then a *comes*, "traversed the banks of the Danube and the whole length of the wide border, exhorting, arranging, examining, equipping."[711] The verses reflect the situation after the battle at the Nedao, when the defeated Huns, some of their Alanic allies, and splinters of the Germanic tribes which had fought on the side of the Huns crossed the Danube at a number of places and settled there. The battle was fought in 454.

The Nedao River

The name Nedao occurs only in Jordanes. This does not necessarily mean that the Nedao was an insignificant streamlet. The names of three more rivers in Pannonia[712] and two in Dacia[713] occur likewise only in Jordanes; he is the only author to call the Bug, certainly a major river, by the enigmatic name Vagasola.[714] On the other hand, it is conceivable that tradition preserved the name of a brook as small as the Katzbach where Blücher defeated Macdonald in the fall of 1813.

None of the various attempts to locate the Nedao has succeeded. It cannot be the Neutra, a left tributary of the Danube,[715] because the Neutra is not in Pannonia. Nato, mentioned once in Marcellinus Comes,[716] sounds vaguely similar to Nedao, but has nothing to do with it;[717] Nato was a fortress near Horreum Margi, a town not in Pannonia but in Moesia superior.[718] Netabio, according to the Anonymus of Ravenna a *civitas* in Pan-

---

[711] *Paneg. on Anthemius* 200-201.

[712] Bolia, Scarniunga, Aqua nigra (*Getica* 277, 268).

[713] Gilpil, Miliare (*Getica* 113).

[714] *Getica* 30; Mommsen 1882, index 166.

[715] Suggested by Wietersheim 1881, 271-272, and R. Huss, *Deutsch-ungarische Heimatblätter* 7, 1935, 41, quoted by Rosenfeld 1957, 252, n. 23.

[716] *CM* II, 96.

[717] As P. Vácsy suggested (*Attila*, 307).

[718] Sabianus, defeated by Mundo near Horreum Margi, fled to Nato (*CM* II, 96).

nonia,[719] was possibly named after the river;[720] unfortunately, Netabio cannot be located. Nedao might be the ablative of *Nedaus< *Nedavus,[721] a name that sounds Celtic. If it were, it would point to southern Pannonia, the old country of the Sordisci and Taurini; Neviodunum, Mursa, Sopiana, Taurunum, Cornacum, and Singidunum, all in southern Pannonia, were originally Celtic settlements.[722] Nedao might be Illyric.[723] The form of the name is of no help in locating the battle.

Nor can any conclusion be drawn from the singular Pannonia in *Getica* 260.[724] Jordanes uses both, Pannonia and Pannoniae, with a slight preference for the former.[725] Pannonia may be the name of the whole territory between Vindomina (Vindobona) and Sirmium;[726] or of one of the two provinces, Pannonia prima and secunda;[727] or of both. It may simply mean the former Roman land east of the Alps and north of Dalmatia.[728]

Linguistics and philology, thus, lead nowhere. There is, however, a passage in Jordanes' *Romana* which points to the region where the Nedao must be sought.

At the end of the *Romana*, Jordanes hastily added the latest news, the victory of the Langobards over the Gepids in 552.[729] More than sixty thousand fell on both sides. Such a battle, he added, has not been heard of "in those places in our times since the days of Attila, except that which had taken place before this battle under the magister militum Calluc, likewise with the Gepids, or the combat of Mundo with the Goths" (*in nostris temporibus a diebus Attilae in illis locis, praeter illa quae ante hanc contingerat sub Calluce mag. mil. idem cum Gepidis aut certe Mundonis cum Gothis*).

In 536, Justinian's general Mundo fought the Ostrogoths in "Dalmatia,"[730] which was "not far distant from the borders of Pannonia."[731] Three years

---

[719] *Itin. Anton.* 57.

[720] Diculescu 1922, 66.

[721] Cf. Saus<Savus, *Romana* 209, 243, 216; *Getica* 285.

[722] A. Graf 1936, 19, 47, 66, 113, n. 3, 117.

[723] N. Jokl, *Zeitschr. f. Ortsnamenforschung* 3, 1927, 240; H. Krahe, 1942, 208-218.

[724] "In Pannonia near the river called Nedao" (*In Pannonia, iuxta flumen, cui nomen est Nedao*).

[725] He changed, *e.g.*, Marcellinus' Pannoniae into Pannonia (*Getica* 166).

[726] *Getica* 264. The source is Cassiodorus; cf. Müllenhoff 3, 264.

[727] The Vandals receive Pannoniam (*Getica* 115); they live in *Pannonia utraque* (*Getica* 161). Valeria occurs in Jordanes only in quotations from Rufus, *Romana* 217, 218.

[728] *Getica* 140, 226.

[729] *Romana* 386-387. On the date of the battle, see Stein 1959, 2, 821; cf. also Wagner, 1967, 21-25.

[730] Procopius V, 7.

[731] *A Pannonios fines* (*Getica* 273). Jordanes uses the form *Pannonii* only once more, quoting Florus II, 24, in *Romana* 243.

later, in 539, the Gepids invaded the Roman provinces south of the Danube, in particular Dacia ripensis.[732] They set out from their newly won territory in Pannonia secunda. Calluc drove them back, but the Gepids rallied and the Romans suffered a crushing defeat.[733] The war in 551 began with an attack of the Langobards on the Gepids, with Sirmium as their aim.

The two campaigns were fought in "Dalmatia" and between the Morava and the Sava. Jordanes compares the great battles "in these regions" with the one fought there in the days of Attila. He must have thought of the battle on the Nedao; there was no other great battle in or near Pannonia in the middle of the fifth century. The Nedao was a river in *southern* Pannonia, probably a tributary of the Sava.

For the events after 454, Jordanes is again our main, though fortunately not our only source. There exists rich material in contemporary documents: poems, papal letters, ecclesiastical histories, the correspondence between Emperor Leo and the bishops of the Eastern empire, and of course, though indirectly, the Priscus fragments. Together with the *Getica* they permit a fairly accurate reconstruction of the last period of Hunnic history.

Jordanes writes: "When Ellac was slain, his remaining brothers were put to flight near the shore of the Sea of Pontus where we have said the Goths first [*prius*] settled."[734] The Gepids occupied Dacia, the territory of the Huns; the other nations, formerly subjects of Attila, received from Emperor Marcian the abodes allotted to them to dwell in. Then Jordanes turns to the Goths: "Now when the Goths saw the Gepids defending for themselves the territory of the Huns, and the people of the Huns dwelling again in their ancient abodes [*suis antiquis sedibus*], they preferred to ask for lands from the Roman Empire, rather than invade the lands of others with dangers to themselves. So they received Pannonia."

Macartney,[735] followed by Thompson,[736] thought that "the ancient abodes" were those of the Huns and located them in the Danube-Theiss Basin for two reasons. First, he said, Dacia was Transylvania; second, the Goths were in Pannonia. This leaves a geographical gap, for Dacia never extended west of the Theiss. The Huns had lived there before, and now, after a short flight to the east, they came back.

---

[732] Procopius VII, 33, 8; cf. Diculescu, 1923, 129.

[733] *CM* II, 106.

[734] *Getica* 263.

[735] Macartney 1934, 106-114. I want to stress that although I do not agree with Macartney's views, I found them stimulating and helpful.

[736] Thompson 1948, 153.

However, Jordanes' Dacia of the Gepids was *not* identical with Roman Dacia. In *Getica* 33 he stated expressly that the Theiss flowed *through*, *discurrit*, the land of the Gepids. It is true that a good deal of what Jordanes reports about the happenings in the following years makes no sense if the Huns should have lived in the Pontic region. In this respect, Macartney is right, but it does not entitle him to distort Jordanes' text. What Jordanes maintains is impossible, but what he means is clear; the Huns fled to the Pontus littoral, the ancient seat of the *Goths*. As we shall see presently, a large number of the Huns stayed for a long time in the northwestern Balkans.

Alföldi[737] and Schmidt[738] placed the Goths in South Russia before they "received" Pannonia. But how did they, not only the warriors, but the whole people, with their wagons, flocks, and herds, migrate from there to Hungary? Did they ask the Gepids for a *transit visum* through Transylvania? They were, Alföldi thought, ferreted out, *aufgescheucht*, by the Huns. But the Huns moved where the Goths *first* had settled, to the *ancient* seats of the people and not the ones held at the time of the breakdown of Attila's kingdom. These misunderstandings stem from the disregard for the other previously mentioned sources. Before we turn to them we have to listen again to Jordanes:

The. Sauromatae, whom we call Sarmatians, and the Cemandri and certain of the Huns dwelt in Castra Martis, a city given to them in the region of Illyricum.

By Sarmatae Jordanes obviously means those Sarmatian tribes which, like the Jazyges, had been in Hungary before the Huns. Jordanes continues:

Of this race [*ex quo genere*] was Blivila, duke of Pentapolis, and his brother, Froila, and also Bessa, a patrician in our time.

Blivila and Froila are Germanic names,[739] Bessa was "a Goth by birth, one of those who had dwelt in Thrace from the old and had not followed Theoderic when he led the Gothic nation thence into Italy."[740]

The Sciri, moreover, and the Sadagarii and certain of the Alani with their leader, Candac by name, received Scythia minor and Moesia inferior.

---

[737] Alföldi 1926, 100.
[738] L. Schmidt 1927, 459.
[739] Schönfeld 1911, 275-276; Holthausen 1934, 16 and 32.
[740] Procopius V, 16, 2.

On the Sadagarii, see p. 441. Braun emended *certi Alanorum*[741] into *ceteri Alanorum*, which would make the Sadagarii Alans, but *certi Alanorum* has a close parallel in the preceding *quidam ex Hunnis*:

The Rugi, however, and some other races asked that they might inhabit Bizye and Arcadiopolis.

Bizye is the present Vize, Arcadiopolis the present Lüleburgaz, 50 miles northwest of Constantinople.

Hernac, the younger son of Attila, with his followers, chose a home in the most distant part of Scythia minor. Emnetzur and Vltzindur, kinsmen of his, seized [*potiti sunt*] Oescus and Vtus and Almus in Dacia on the bank of the Danube, and many of the Huns, then swarming everywhere, betook themselves into Romania; descendants of them are to this day called Sacromontisi and Fossatisii.

In the *Getica*, *potiri* means "to seize by force" (cf. *Getica* 108, 138, 145, 250, 264, 288). Vtus, at the mouth of the river Vtus (Vit),[742] Oescus, near the present Gigen, at the mouth of the Isker,[743] and Almus, the present Lom,[744] were in Dacia ripensis.

In the fifth and sixth centuries, *fossatum*[745] meant "military camp." The *fossatisii* in the East correspond to the *castriciani* and *castellani* in the West.[746] Procopius lists four *fossata*: one in Moesia, the one of Longinus in the country of the Tzanni, the *fossatum* of Germanus in Armenia, and Gesila-*fossatum* in Haeminontus.[747] Gesila[748] is Gothic *Gaisila;[749] the camp was obviously garrisoned by Goths. *Fossatisii*, Latin with a Greek ending, points to Moesia, where the two languages met.[750] The Hunnic Fossatisii were probably those of the camp in Moesia. The Sacromontisi may have received their name from the "holy mountain" in Thrace.[751]

Although the greater part of the Huns preserved their tribal organizations, many were leaderless, broken men who had no choice but to surrender

---

[741] Braun 1899, 1, 124.

[742] *Not. Dign* [or.] XLII, 8, 21 (for *Lito* read *Vto*); *Itin. Anton.* 221 (Cuntz 1929, 32).

[743] Οἶσκος, Ἴσκος; cf. *Le Synekdemos d'Hieroclès* (Brussels, 1939), 20; Danoff in *PW* 17, 2, 2073ff.

[744] A castellum, *Not. Dign.* [or.] XLII, 10, 19; cf. Tomaschek in *PW* 1, 2, 1590.

[745] φόσσατον, φοσάτον, φουσάτον (V. Beshevliev, *Byzantion* 28, 1959, 267-268).

[746] Grosse 1920, 66.

[747] *De Aedif.* IV, 11; III, 4, 11; IV, 11.

[748] The name of an Ostrogoth (Cassiodorus, *Variae* IV, 14).

[749] Schönfeld 1911, 107.

[750] A. Alföldi, *AAH* 5, 1934, 106, n. 12.

[751] *Scholia Apoll. Rhod.* II, 1015, *FHG* IV, 453.

to the Romans. Jordanes contrasts Hernac, Emnetzur, and Ultzindur and their followers to the Huns who, "swarming everywhere, rushed into Romania." He also makes a distinction between the Hunnic leaders and the Alanic and Germanic fugitives—the Huns *seized* land, the others *received* it. Incidentally, the list of the Germanic refugees, Sciri, Rugi, and the Goths at Castra Martis, is rather instructive; had they fought against the Huns, they would not have fled across the Danube. Jordanes was so vague about the origin of Blivila, Froila, and Bessa because had he openly said they were Goths, he would have admitted that Goths did fight under Attila's sons.

After 455, there existed two Hunnic pockets within the empire: one under Hernac, in the Dobrogea, and the other one in Dacia ripensis. Of the former one we hear nothing before the second half of the 460's. The western Huns, however, having overcome the first shock, soon became active again. This we learn from Jordanes and the Nordic *Hervararsaga*.

THE FIRST GOTHO-HUNNIC WAR

The lines 119-122 of the Old English poem *Widsith*[752] allude briefly to a war between Huns and Goths:

Wulfhere I sought and Wyrmhere: there full oft war was not slack, what time the Hræde with sharp swords must defend their ancient seat from the people of Ætla by the Wistlawood.[753]

The Hraede are the Ostrogoths, Ætla is Attila, Wistlawood is Vistula Wood or the wood of the Vistula people.

Another, much later version of the same tradition is preserved in the "Lay of Angantyr," the oldest part of the Icelandic *Hervararsaga*. Heusler and Ranisch gave the "Lay" the first place in their edition of *Eddica minora*.[754] Some of its stanzas have such an archaic ring that Heusler and Genzmer dated the original (from which the "Lay" derives and of which it still contains so much) in the middle of the first millennium. Once it was imbedded in the *Hervararsaga*,[755] the Icelandic redactors tried to fit the "Lay" into the framework of the saga; a number of verses were dissolved into prose. But even in its diluted form the "Lay"[756] stands closer to the heroic epic of the Migration Period than any other Germanic poem.

---

[752] Composed in the second half of the seventh century.

[753] In R. W. Chambers' translation.

[754] Pp. 1-2.

[755] Malone 1925, 772-773, and H. Schneider 1934, 96-99, give an outline of the *Hervararsage*.

[756] See fn. 754 and Jonsson 1915, 2, 252-255. The translation is taken from Hollander 1936; for a German translation, see F. Genzmer in *Edda* 1 (Jena, 1920), 24-32.

Heithrek, king of the Goths, had two sons, Angantyr and, from a Hunnic wife, Hloth. Hloth was brought up by his maternal grandfather, Humli, king of the Huns. After Heitrek's death, Hloth claimed an equal share of the inheritance:

> The half will I have / of what Heithrek owned
> of awl and of edge, / of all the treasure,
> of cow and of calf, / of quern harsh-grinding,
> of thrall and of bond-maid, / and those born of them,
> the mighty forest / which is Myrkwith height,
> the hallowed grave / which in Gotland stands,
> the shining stone / which a stodum Danpar stands,
> half of the war-weeds / which Heithrek owned,
> of land and lieges / and of lustrous arm-rings.

Angantyr was willing to compromise, but his counsel Gizur, leader of the Grythings, objected that too much was offered to a bond-woman's son. Enraged, Hloth returned to the Huns. When spring came, King Humli and Hloth drew together so great a host that there was dearth of fighting men in Hunland. They rode through Myrkwith. As they came out of the forest, they saw a castle. There ruled Hervor, Angantyr's and Hloth's sister, and with her, Ormar, her foster father. In the ensuing battle Hervor was killed. Ormar escaped and made report to Angantyr; "From the South am I come / to say these tidings: / burned is the far-famed/ forest Myrkwith / all Gotland drenched/ with the gore of the fallen." Angantyr sent Gizur as herald to challenge the Huns to battle. The place should be

> at dylgiu and in the Dun-heath
> and all the Iassar mountains,

where the Goths so often had won victory. The battle lasted eight days. At last the Huns were forced to give way; Angantyr slew both Hloth and Humli. The Huns took to flight, and the Goths slew so many that the rivers were dammed up and overflowed their banks, and the valleys were filled with dead men and horses.

The *Widsith* and the "Lay of Angantyr" refer to the same struggle: (1) the Goths fight the Huns: (2) they defend their ancient seat, "the hallowed grave which in Gotland stands"; (3) there they had often won victories; (4) the Goths defeat the Huns; (5) Wyrmhere is Ormar.

One should think that these data, in combination with the personal and place names, would make it comparatively easy to determine when and where the battle was fought, provided, of course, that the "Lay" is not pure fiction. The vast literature shows the opposite. For awhile, Heinzel's interpretation was widely accepted—the kernel of the story was supposed to be the victory of the allied Visigoths and Romans over the Huns in Gaul in 451.[757] After this view was abandoned, the battlefield was located near the Waldai heights in Russia, in southern Silesia, somewhere in the Ukraine, and near the Marchfeld in Lower Austria. The dates suggested ranged from the first to the middle of the fifth century. There understandingly arose the question whether the problem could be solved at all. Was it not an equation with too many unknowns? The majority of the Germanic scholars seem now inclined to regard the Battle of the Huns *nicht als die dichterische Formung eines geschichtlichen Ereignisses, sondern einer geschichtlichen Zuständigkeit,*[758] whatever that means. But it was not so much the intricacy of the problem and the ambiguity of the poetic language that seemed to defy all attempts to date and place the battle as the wild guesses of the philologists. If the Dun of the Dun-heath is identified with the Don, the Iassar Mountains with Jasaníky (the stretch of hilly country which forms the broad gap between the Sudeten and the Carpathians), Gizur with the Vandal Geiseric, and Heithrek with the Gepid Ardaric, the Battle of the Huns becomes a geographic and historical monstrosity.[759]

Johannson[760] proved that the names Harwaða[761] and Grafá in the *Hervararsaga* have nothing to do with the original "Lay." Arnheimár, "river home," is not a real place name; anyway, it cannot be placed. Dylgia, v. 11, Dilgia and Dyngia, means "struggle, enmity."[762] Myrkwiðr, "murky wood," can be as little found on a map[763] as *der schwarze wald* in Stefan George's "Waffengefährten": *er zog mich heut aus manchen fesseln. Im schwarzen wald wo unheil haust war ich verstrickt in tiefen nesseln.* There

---

[757] Heinzel 1887.

[758] Schneider 1934, 114.

[759] These equations are by no means the most farfetched ones. N. Luckman (*Aarbøger for nordisk Oldkyndighed og Historie* 1946, 103-120) identified the Huns with the Greuthungi who in 386 Odotheus led across the Danube, and the Goths with the Romans who fought with the Greuthungi. The correspondences between the *Hervararsaga* and the war in 386 are exactly nil. Settegast's interpretation in *Quellenstudien zur gallo-romanischen Epik* is best passed over in silence.

[760] *Acta Phil. Scandin.* 7, 1932-33, 100-101.

[761] If this is the correct form; the MSS have also *Handa* and *Hanada*. The identification with the Carpathian Mountains is doubtful, cf. J. Mikkola, *Archiv f. slav. Philol.* 42, 1928, 87-88; G. Schütte *Acta Philol. Scandin.* 8, 1933, 256; W. Mohr, *Altgerman. Altertumskunde,* 56.

[762] R. Much, *ZfDA* 33, 1889, 5; C. C. Boer in *Aarbøger for nordisk Oldkyndighed og Historie* 1911, 59; H. Rosenfeld, *PBB,* 1955, 235.

[763] Heinzel (1887, 467) took it for the Sylvia Hercynia, Markwart (1903, 109) for the Erzgebirge.

remain Danpar, Dun, and Iassar. In spite of Heinzel's doubts,[764] partly repeated by Schramm,[765] Danpar is certainly the Dnieper. Duna is the Danube.[766] Iassar will be discussed later. Except for Grytingaliði, "leader of the Grytings=Greutingu," the personal names are obscure.

It seems, the only reasonable approach to the problem of the Battle of the Huns is to look for a historical event that fits the geographical setting of the "Lay." When and where did the Ostrogoths win a decisive victory over the Huns? Not in South Russia. There in the fourth century they were attacked, defeated, and, except those who succeeded in fleeing, remained loyal to their Hunnic lords to the very end. Nevertheless, Baesecke[767] and Altheim[768] indulge in wild speculations about the Iassar Mountains, which they connect with the Ossetes in the Caucasus. Baesecke, again followed by Altheim, brings together Dylgia and Kossa dolgjana, near Mariupol in the Ukraine. *Kosa dolgaya*—this is the correct form—is good Russian and means "a long narrow tongue of land."[769] The sandy Kosa dolgaya on the southeastern shore of the Azov Sea[770] is nowhere wider than 500 meters, as fit for a battle between horsemen as the top of the Matterhorn. Schramm's assumption that sometime before 375 the Goths clashed with nomads whom later tradition turned into Huns is sheer arbitrariness.[771] Malone, disregarding all other place names, makes the Vistula in the *Widsith* the basis of a peculiar hypothesis[772]—after overrunning the southern part of Ermanaric's Ostrogothic kingdom, the Huns are supposed to have tried to conquer the Ostrogoths in the Vistula Valley; the often renewed struggle has a happy ending. Needless to say, the Vistula woods were impenetrable to the Hunnic horsemen.

Jungandreas thinks the poet localized the battle on the Vistula because in Old English poetry the seats of the Goths were traditionally in the northeast.[773] Schramm assumes that the Vistula took the place of the Dnieper because no one in England in the eighth century had ever heard of the river in South Russia.[774] Linderski gives what I think to be the

---

[764] Heinzel 1887, 473.
[765] G. Schramm 1965, 4-5.
[766] H. Rosenfeld, *PBB*, 1955, 236; G. Schramm 1965, 15.
[767] *Vor- und Frühgeschichte des deutschen Schrifttums* 1, 177.
[768] Altheim 1951, 65.
[769] H. Rosenfeld, *PBB*, 1955, 236.
[770] *Bol'shaia Sovetskaia Entsiklopediia* 1, map opposite p. 532; 15, 12.
[771] G. Schramm 1965, 4.
[772] *Widsith* in *Anglistica* 13 (Copenhagen), 1962, 103.
[773] "Umlokalisierung in der Heldendichtung," *ZfDPh* 59, 1934, 236.
[774] G. Schramm 1965, 12.

best explanation of the alleged mistake:[775] King Alfred's Wislelond is taken from ancient maps; both in the *Divisio orbis terrarum* and the *Dimensuratio provinciarum*, "*Dacia finitur ab occidente flumine Vistula.*" *Wislelond* lies east of Moravia and west of Dacia. The Goths did not fight the Huns in Silesia but somewhere in the Carpathian Basin. It must be left to the philologists to decide how Vistula got into the *Widsith* or what it meant.

The Battle of the Huns reflects the wars which the Goths waged against the Huns *after* the collapse of Attila's kingdom.[776] We are well informed about them by Jordanes:

> Let us now return to the tribe with which we started, namely the Ostrogoths, who were dwelling in Pannonia under their king, Valamir, and his brothers Thiudimer and Vidimer. Although their territories were separate, yet their plans were one [*consilia tamen unita*]. For Valamir dwelt between the rivers Scarniunga and Aqua nigra, Thiudimer near Lake Pelso, and Vidimer between them both. Now it happened that the sons of Attila, regarding the Goths as deserters from their rule, came against them as though they were seeking fugitive slaves [*velut fugacia mancipia requirentes*] and attacked Valamir alone, when his brothers knew nothing of it. He sustained their attack, though he had but few with him, and after harassing them a long time, so utterly overwhelmed them that scarcely a portion of the enemy remained. The remnant turned in flight and sought the parts of Scythia which border on the stream of the river Danaber, which the Huns call in their own tongue the Var. Whereupon he sent a messenger of good tidings to his brother Thiudimer, and on the very day the messenger arrived he found even greater joy in the house of Thiudimer. For on that day Theoderic was born.[777]

The passage poses a number of difficult problems. Where, for instance, are the two rivers between which Valamir dwelt? Neither Scarniunga nor Aqua nigra is mentioned elsewhere. Alföldi identified Aqua nigra with Karasica, a tributary of the Drava, assuming that Karasica goes back to Karasu, in Turkish, "black water."[778] This has been rejected by

---

[775] "Alfred the Great and the Tradition of Ancient Geography," *Speculum* 39, 1964, 434-439.

[776] This has long been recognized by G. Schütte, *Arkiv. f. nord. filol.* 21, 1904, 30-44; H. Schück, *Uppsala Univers. Årsskrift* 3:2, 1918, 17-18; H. de Boor, *ZfDPh* 50, 1924, 192; A. Johannson, *Acta Phil. Scandin.* 7, 1932-1933, 111-112,

[777] *Getica* 268-269. Except for minor changes, I have followed Mierow's translation.

[778] Alföldi 1926, 103-104.

Moór.[779] There are so many Black Waters between Vienna and Belgrad that if the name of the river were the only thing to go by in localizing Valamir's territory, it might have been anywhere. It is true that Aqua nigra cannot be the Raab, as has been so long assumed and is now assumed again, but in northwestern Hungary alone there are the Schwarza, the Schwarzbach. the Schirnitzbach, and the Csörnöpatak, a now obsolete, originally Slavic name of the upper Herpenyö, a tributary of the Raab.[780] Other Black Waters can be found all over Pannonia secunda. Lake Pelso is Lake Balaton (in German, Plattensee). If Vidimer lived between Thiudimer at Lake Balaton, followed, evidently in the south, by Valamir, then Valamir must have lived near the Drava. Alföldi, though wrong in detail, was basically right.[781]

The Goths lived in Pannonia, but they did not occupy the two Pannonias from border to border. This follows not only from the previously quoted account—the Huns attacked Valamir "when his brothers knew nothing of it," which precludes a compact Gothic settlement—but also from the account of the second Hunnic attack: a part of inner Pannonia was held by the Sadagis. Two passages in the Vita s. Severini show that easternmost Noricum Mediterranense was Gothic.[782] The small Ostrogothic fibulae found in Slovakia north of the Danube[783] point to Ostrogoths, who did not follow the Amali princes.

When and under what circumstances the Goths settled in Pannonia either is not known. That they did not move there after Attila's death is by now almost generally agreed. Although Jordanes may have maintained that the Goths "received" Pannonia from Marcian merely in order to stress the bonds between them and the Eastern Romans, he probably was right. Avitus did try to make an agreement with them, but it evidently came to nothing. Whereas his finances were in such a bad state that he was forced to melt down the bronze statues of Rome and sell the metal in order to pay the soldiers, the rich East could afford to pay the Goths subsidies, not as much as to the Gepids, but enough to keep them quiet for a few years.

When did the Huns attack the Goths? Ensslin, who first dated the war in the winter of 456/7,[784] later took this overexact date back.[785] It would seem that the date of Theoderic's birth determines also the date

---

[779] UJb 6, 1927, 167.
[780] E. Moór, Acta Universitatis Szeged 10, 1936, 23.
[781] Cf. Egger 1962, 1, 117.
[782] Ibid., 118.
[783] J. Werner 1959, 428-429.
[784] Ensslin 1947, 12.
[785] Letter to me, February 17, 1956.

of the Gothic victory. Unfortunately, the historians cannot agree on the year. It might be 454, 455, and even 456.[786] Besides, the connection between the Gothic victory and Theoderic's birth could very well be due to the wish to let the heroic life of the great king start with a propitious event, auguring his later greatness. In any case, the battle on the Nedao cannot have been fought many years before the Huns attacked the Goths. The war is probably to be dated about 455.

Where did the Huns come from and where did they flee? The objections to the alleged trek of the Goths from the Pontus to Pannonia are equally valid for the march of a Hun army from the Black Sea to Hungary. How came the Huns to ride clean through the intervening nations, asks Macartney rightly.[787] He spoils his case by tampering with the text in the *Getica*. The Huns, he maintains, not only came from their center between the Danube and the Theiss, they also returned there after their defeat by the Goths, to the Danube, not the Dnieper.

The text in Jordanes translated previously runs as follows: *pars ostium . . . in fuga versa eas partes Scythiae peteret, quas Danabri amnis fluente praetermeant, quam lingua sua Hunni Var appellant.*

The *variae lectiones* of the name of the river are bewildering. For *danabri* in *H*, *PVO* have *danubri*, and *XYZ danapri; danubii* occurs only in the codex Ambrosianus, which teems with misspellings; *danubri* is obviously a cross between *danabri* and *danubii*. The scribes were not sure what to write. This is not so surprising. The names of the two rivers, Danubius and Danaper, sounded so similar that they easily could be confused, and actually often were. Jordanes himself wrote in *Getica* 54 Hister= Danubius where he should have written Danaper. Tanais and Danubius similarly were mixed up. In his account of Decius' campaign against the Goths in I, 23, Zosimus wrote three times Tanais instead of Danube= Hister. The seven mouths of the Danube are many times named in Greek and Latin literature, but Horace, *Troades* 8-9, has the seven mouths of the Tanais. In his commentary on Horace, Pseudo-Acro (fifth century?) stated explicitly that "a river of Scythia is called Tanais, which is the same as Danube" (*Tanais flumen Scythiae dicitur, qui et Danubius est*).

Still, Jordanes must have written Danabri, not Danubii. The river is in Scythia, not in Pannonia. *Var*, is, indeed, the Dnieper. The whole relative clause from *quam* to *appellant* cannot be a later addition either.

When the Huns attacked the Goths in Pannonia a second time, they again could not and did not ride all the way from the Danaber-Dnieper in the southern Ukraine to Hungary. There is only one explanation of

---

[786] See A. Nagl, *PW* 5a, 1746; and Skrzhinskaia 1960, 338, n. 679.

[787] Macartney 1935 [*1934? 1953?-Ed.*], 108.

the passage on the flight of the Huns after the first attack: Jordanes *proleptically* located the Huns of the later 450's where they were at his time. He displays the same cavalier treatment of geography in the account of the second Gothic war with the Huns. But before we deal with it, we have to look closer at the Huns in the northeastern Balkans. It was from there that they rode against Valamir.

Late in the year 457,[788] Emperor Leo sent a *sacra* to all metropolitan and many other bishops asking for their opinions on the validity of the consecration of Timothy Aelurus as bishop of Alexandria and on the point of upholding the Council of Chalcedon.[789] The list of the provinces to which the letter was sent as well as the answers to it[790] permit some conclusions about the situation in the Balkan peninsula in the first year of Leo's reign.

All provinces of the Thracian diocese were again firmly under Roman rule. Whereas none of the bishops of Moesia inferior had been present either at the Robber Synod of 449 or at the Council at Chalcedon in 451, now not only Marcianopolis, Nicopolis, and Odyssus, but also Novae, Abrittus, Appiaria, and Durostorum on the Danube[791] could freely communicate with Constantinople. Even the bishop of Tomis in the "Scythian region" received and answered the circular letter.[792]

It was different in eastern Illyricum. The bishops of Dyrrhachium, Scampa, Lychnidus, Bullis, Apollonia, and Aulona in Epirus nova assured the emperor of their unshakable orthodoxy.[793] A similar letter was sent from Dardania.[794] The answer of Zosimus, metropolitan of Dacia mediterranea, has not been preserved, but the fact that Leo wrote to him[795] shows that Serdica, which eight years ago was in ruins, had to some extent regained its former importance.[796] But the emperor did not send letters to the metropolitan bishops in Dacia ripensis, Moesia superior, and Praevalitana.[797] Evidently there were no bishops in those provinces to whom he could write.

---

[788] *ACO* II, 95: *maximam propter hiemis vehementiam.* Cf. G. Krüger, *Real-encyclopädie für protestantische Theologie und Kirche*, 13, 377-378.

[789] *ACO* II: V, 24-98. Cf. R. Haake in *Das Konzil von Chalcedon* 2, 109 f.

[790] Eduard Schwartz, *ACO* II: V, praef.

[791] *ACO* II: V, 32.

[792] *Ibid.*, 31. In the list p. 24, which, as Eduard Schwartz, praef. xiii, pointed out, *accurate secundum imperii dioceses dispositus est*, Tomi is not among the metropolitan sees of Thrace. This, and the term *Scythiae regio*, show that the former Scythia minor was no longer a province; it probably was joined to Moesia inferior.

[793] *Ibid.*, 95-96.

[794] Signed by the bishops of Scupi, Ulpiana (?), and Diocletiana (*ACO* II: V, 88).

[795] *ACO* II: V, 24, n. 62.

[796] Priscus, *EL* 123$_{15}$.

[797] C. Moeller in *Das Konzil von Chalcedon* 2, 668, note.

One could presume that communications with Ratiaria and Vimina-cium, or such an important place as Naissus, were interrupted because those bishoprics were in a war zone. But 457 had been a year of peace for the Balkan provinces. The "war-loving nation,"[798] "rebels,"[799] elusive bands "now so utterly crushed that not even their name could be found anymore,"[800] were probably Lazic marauders.[801] The letters from the bish-ops in Moesia inferior, Dardania, Epirus nova, and the "Scythian region" mention no military operations in their regions.[802] If anything bigger than occasional clashes with *latrunculi* had taken place, the bishops would have been likely to hint at it.

In 449, eight years before, there still existed Christian hostels in Naissus.[803] Shortly afterward the Huns evacuated the strip of territory south of the Danube they had occupied in 447.[804] One should, therefore, expect that since then the Roman population had come back, and with them the clergy. But if they did, they had fled again. They fled from the Huns who, after the collapse of their kingdom, seized not only the three places in Dacia ripensis which Jordanes names, but, to repeat his words, "swarming every-where betook themselves into Romania."[805] There is no other explanation of the breakdown of all ecclesiastical life in the northwestern Balkans.[806] If small Christian communities still existed, which is unlikely though not impossible, they were cut off from the churches farther east. They were not in Romania but in Hunnia.

This does not necessarily mean that the whole, rather large territory was held by the Huns only. Between the Timok and the Arčer lived Sar-matians, Cemandri, and some Huns. As late as the end of the 460's, Goths lived side by side with Huns. But the political power lay nevertheless with the Huns, the same who about 455 had tried to reconquer Panno-nia.

---

[798] *ACO* II: V, 29.

[799] *Ibid.*, 71.

[800] *Ibid.*, 581; cf. also p. 64 (in the beginning of Leo's reign).

[801] *Propterea siquidem alienigarum quidam populus, qui pridem nostram provinciam veluti suam invaserat, non magno labore subiectus est* (letter of the metropolitan of Pont Polemoniacus, *ACO* II: V, 79). The Lazi were defeated in 456 (Hydatius, *CM* II, 29$_{177}$): *orientalium naves Hisplaim venientes per Marciani exercitum caesos Lazas nuntiunt* (Priscus, *EL* 152$_{9-10}$).

[802] *Virtute tua cunctas regno vostro [deus] subdidit barbaras nationes* (*ACO* II: V, 88) in the letter of the bishop from Dardania is an empty phrase.

[803] Priscus, *EL* 124$_{13}$.

[804] *Ibid.*, 150$_8$.

[805] *Getica* 266.

[806] *Ces provinces étaient probablement désorganisées par les invasions barbares* (Bardy 1952, 282, n. 2).

By 456 at the latest, the government in Constantinople must have realized that it lacked the power to reconquer the Hunnic territories south of the Danube. It kept the peace, or, rather, the silent truce, and so did the Huns. In 457, Hunnia was still inaccessible to the Romans. The change came in 458.

Tuldila

The "very considerable" army which, early in 458,[807] the Western emperor Majorian (451-461) collected in preparation for the campaign against the Vandals consisted almost entirely of barbarians. In the panegyric which Sidonius Apollinaris addressed to the emperor in Lyon at the end of the year,[808] he named the tribes which followed the imperial standards:

> Thou dost carry off to the war the frozen army of the seven-mouthed Danube. All the multitude that the sluggish quarter of the north doth produce in the Sithonian region beneath the Parrhasian bear . . . Bastarna, Suebus, Pannonius, Neurus, Chunus, Geta, Dacus, Halanus, Bellonotus, Rugus, Burgundio, Vesus, Alites, Bisalta, Ostrogoths, Procrustes, Sarmata, Moschus . . . the whole Caucasus and the Tanaitic drinker of the Scythian water.[809]

This is one more of those lists of names in which Sidonius liked to indulge. Most names he borrowed from earlier poets,[810] others were obsolete,[811] adduced to impress the listener with his erudition. Among the names retained is Chunus, as the following verses show:

> Now thou wert moving thy camp and around thee thronged thousands under diverse standards. Only one race denied thee obedience, a race who had lately, in a mood even more savage than their wont, withdrawn their untamed host from the Danube because they had lost their lords in warfare, and Tuldila stirred in that unruly multitude a mad lust for fight which they must needs pay dear.[812]

---

[807] Seeck, *Geschichte* 6, 342; Stein 1959, 1, 558.

[808] On the date, see Coville 1930, 61, n. 2; Loyen 1942, 59, n. 1.

[809] Vv. 471-479.

[810] Bastarna, Neurus, Halanus, Bellonitus, Bisalta, Sarmata from Valerius Flaccus (*Argon.* VI, 42, 48, 96, 122, 161, 232, 507); Moschus from Lucian III, 270. *Scythicae potor Tanaiticus undae* is patterned on Claudian's *Alanus bibens Maeotim* (*In Ruf.* I, 312), which, in turn, goes back to Horace's *Rhodani potor* (*Carm.* II, 20, 20).

[811] Dacus, Pannonius; *Suebus* is used by Claudian as a vague term for northern barbarians. Procrustes seems to be Sidonius' own invention.

[812] Vv. 484-488.

The verses refer to the Huns.[813] They had lost Ellac and other *domini*; the battle on the Nedao was fought only a few years before, *nuper*; they had withdrawn from the Danube, and their sites had been occupied by their former Germanic subjects.

Although Sidonius did not say where Tuldila's Huns lived, it is clear that Majorian could not have recruited them in the Pontic littoral; Tuldila could not have come from the Dnieper. His Huns must have lived close to the borders of the Western empire. Priscus says, indeed, that Majorian "brought the peoples *near his domains* to his side, some by arms, some by words."[814] There were no Huns at the borders of Noricum; Pannonia was held by the Goths, the greater part of the regions east of the Danube by the Gepids. We are, thus, led to the same areas from which the Huns had moved against the Ostrogoths, that is, Moesia superior and Dacia ripensis. Whether Majorian had won the Huns "by words" or "by arms" we do not know.

Two pieces of information, so far not used by the students of the Huns, throw more light on the situation in 458. The year before, Moesia superior, Dacia ripensis, and Dacia mediterranea had been inaccessible to the messengers sent from Constantinople to the bishops in the Balkan provinces. But in the summer of 458, the body of Sancta Anastasia was transferred from Sirmium to Constantinople and buried ἐν τοῖς Δομνίνου ἐμβόλοις.[815] The routes from the capital to Pannonia secunda were open again. This presupposes the pacification of the northwestern Balkan provinces, the establishment of a modus vivendi with the barbarians there. The East gained from the peace the body of a martyr, the West auxiliaries and many women and young people who had been given up for lost. In the spring of 458 the first prisoners of war, carried off by the Huns in 452, came back to Aquileia. They were released by the Huns, the same, as we now may say with confidence, who joined Majorian's army and let the East Romans through their land to Sirmium.

THE SECOND GOTHO-HUNNIC WAR (463/4-466)

In the years following the pacification of the northwestern Balkans (before 458), the Huns were at peace with the East Romans but, as we

---

[813] Loyen's objections are unconvincing. Stevens (1933, 45) transforms the mutiny of the Huns into an invasion of the Huns.

[814] Priscus, *EL* 585$_{2-4}$.

[815] Theodor Lector, *Hist. eccles.* II, 65, *PG* 86, 1216 (= Theophanes A.M. 5951, C. de Boor 1883, 111). According to Theodor Lector, this happened under Patriarch Gennadius (458-471), thus at the earliest in the later part of 458; cf. Diekamp 1938, 55. Cedrenus (*PG* 121, 661) gives the first year of Emperor Leo, February 457-458, as the date of the translation. Diekamp (1938, 63-64) decides on the summer 458.

learn from Jordanes, and only from him, they once again, as in around 455, attacked the Goths in Pannonia.

Now after firm peace was established between Goths and Romans, the Goths found that what they received from the emperor was not sufficient for them. Furthermore, they were eager to display their wonted valor, and so began to plunder the neighboring peoples around them, first attacking the Sadagis, who held the interior of Pannonia. When Dintzic, king of the Huns, a son of Attila, learned this, he gathered to him the few who still seemed to have remained under his sway, namely, the Ultzinzures, the Angisciri, the Bittugures, and the Bardores. Coming to Bassiana, a city of Pannonia, he beleaguered it and began to plunder its territory. When the Goths learned this, they abandoned the expedition they had planned against the Sadagis and turned upon the Huns and drove them so ingloriously from their own land that those who remained have been in dread of the arms of the Goths from that time down to the present day.[816]

There follows the description of the war between the Goths and the Sciri.

What Jordanes' source was is difficult to decide, if it can be decided at all. Mommsen suggested that Jordanes followed Priscus.[817] The endings of the Hunnic tribal names point, indeed, to a Greek author, but why should Jordanes have changed Priscus' Dengizich into Dintzic? Priscus certainly did not praise "the wonted valor" of the Goths either. This sounds more like Cassiodorus. If Jordanes followed Cassiodorus, the strange sentence at the end of his account becomes understandable. In 551, the year he wrote the *Getica*, the Goths had been in Italy for more than seventy years and therefore could not be dreaded by the Huns "to the present day." By the middle of the sixth century there were no Huns even near Totila's kingdom. For a moment one might think of a passage in the letter which in 476 Apollinaris Sidonius wrote to his friend Lampridius, full of the most extravagant eulogies for Euric, king of the Visigoths in Gaul.[818] To him as the *arbiter mundi* came ambassadors from everywhere, even from Persia and the Ostrogoths who, with Euric's help, pressed hard on the Huns.[819]

---

[816] *Getica* 272-273.

[817] Mommsen 1882, p. xxxv, no. 65.

[818] *Istis Ostrogothus viget patronis | vicinosque premens subinde Chunos | his quod subditur, hinc superbit illis* (VIII, 91). Mommsen (1905, 136) thought it quite credible that the Ostrogoths sought the help of their racial relatives in the West; so does Stevens (1933, 165-166), but Dalton (1915, p. xlvi, n. 1) is, I believe rightly, sceptical.

[819] The Huns who in 474 crossed the Danube and devastated Thrace (Evagrius III, 2; Theophanes, A.M. 5966) may very well have clashed with the Goths.

From 475 on, Theoderic had his headquarters in Novae in Moesia secunda.[820] Sidonius' letter confirms our thesis about the prolonged stay of Huns in the Balkans, but neither Cassiodorus nor Jordanes could refer to the 470's as to "the present day." The phrase makes sense if the Huns were the Bulgars of 505, when Pitzia and his Goths defeated Sabinian's army, which consisted of ten thousand Bulgarian horsemen. Cassiodorus, writing his Gothic history in the 520's or early 530's, and Ennodius († 521) repeatedly calls the Bulgarians "Huns." It seems that Jordanes copied Cassiodorus without changing the text itself, a text which, with slight changes, was based on Priscus.

When did the Huns attack? The first two sentences in Jordanes' report give the answer.[821] In 459, the Goths, led by Valamir, took Dyrrhachium (Durazzo).[822] The Romans were under Anthemius, the future emperor.[823] In 461, Valamir concluded a *foedus* with the Romans and received a yearly subsidy of 300 pounds of gold.[824] It is unlikely that the Goths broke the treaty after only one year.

The war between the Huns and the Goths preceded the war between the Goths and the Sciri. Priscus dealt with its beginnings in *EL* 17. He wrote about the visit of Gobazes, king of the Lazi. In the preceding excerpt he described Gobazes' visit to Constantinople after the big fire. Emperor Leo, who had fled from the burning city,[825] met him in Chalcedon. The second Gotho-Hunnic war, therefore, falls between 463/4 and 466.

The Huns came from the south. The first fortified place which stood in their way was Bassiana, the *respublica coloniae Bassianorum* of the local inscriptions, between Sirmium (now Mitrovica) and Singidunum (now Belgrade). The tribal names lead likewise to the south of the Danube as the region from where the Huns marched against the Goths. The Ultzinzures lived between Utus (now Vit) and Almus (now Lom), both in Dacia ripensis, and the Bittugures joined the Ostrogoths on their trek from Moesia secunda to Italy in 488. The theater of both Gotho-Hunnic wars was Pannonia secunda. Of course, the Huns did not respect the borders of the former Roman provinces; the fighting certainly spread to the province of Savia, between the rivers Drava and Sava.

---

[820] Ensslin 1947, 135 (with references to the sources).

[821] *Getica* 270-271.

[822] *CM* II, 492.

[823] Sidonius, *Paneg. on Anthemius* 223-234.

[824] Priscus, *EL* 9. In the following excerpt he speaks about Geiseric's raids into Sicily after the death of Emperor Majorian on August 7, 461.

[825] Seeck 1919, 413; Malalas 372; "Life of Daniel the Stylite" in *Analecta Bollandiana* 32, 1913, 169-170.

And now we come back to the "Lay of Angantyr." Was southern Pannonia the ancient land of the Goths (as mentioned in *Widsith*), where the former kings lay in the hallowed grave? Were there mountains the name of which sounded like Jassar? Cassiodorus, inscriptions, and ancient geographers give the answer.

Theoderic, who in 504 had conquered Sirmium from the Gepids, sent there Colossaeus, *vir illustris* and *comes*. In the letter of appointment which Cassiodorus wrote and found so good that he included it in his *Variae*,[826] we read:

> You are sent with the dignity of the illustrious belt to Pannonia secunda, the former seat of the Goths [*quondam sedem Gothorum*]. Protect the province committed to you with arms, so that she can gladly receive her old defenders [*antiquos defensores*], as she used gladly to obey our fathers [*quae se nostris parentibus feliciter paruisse cognovit*].

Sirmium, says Ennodius, was in ancient times the border of Italy where *seniores domini* kept guard against the barbarians.[827]

The name Ias is well attested in the ancient land of the Goths.[828] North of the mountainous country between the Sava and the Drava, which might be the Myrkwiðr of the "Lay," lived the Iasi of Pliny. Iasi served in the Roman army. Aquae Iasae, the present Varazdinske Toplice, was a flourishing city as late as the fourth century. Constantine ordered a bath destroyed by fire to be rebuilt there. At the time the Goths moved into Pannonia the name Ias must still have been quite alive. It cannot be separated from the Iassar Mountains.

In the Germanic tradition the two wars were merged. That so much of the actual events and place names like the Danube heath and the Iassar Mountains has been preserved in it is truly remarkable.[829]

THE END

In 465 or, more probably, 466, Dengizich and his brother Hernach sent ambassadors to Constantinople. They wanted to make peace, pro-

---

[826] *Variae* III, 23; *MGH AA* XII, 91.

[827] *Paneg. on Theoderic* XII, Vogel 1885, 210.

[828] For the following, see A. Graf 1936, 16.

[829] The best on the Danpar shore has been said by Johannsen, *Acta Phil. Scandin.* 7, 1932-1933, 104: *Die Danparstadir fallen völlig aus dem Rahmen des Bildes, und ich kann mir des Auftauchen dieses Names hier nur durch die Annahme erklären, dass bei der dichterischen Behandlung des gotischen Sagenstoffes durch einen Nordmann, dem auch dunkle Kunde von den Schwarzmeer-Goten zugekommen war, dem aber schwerlich eine klare Vorstellung über Ort und Zeit vorgeschwebt hat, dieser in seiner Herzenseinfalt geographische und historische Verhältnisse verschiedener Jahrhunderte zu einem Bild gestaltet hat.*

vided that a market place be established at the Danube where "according to the ancient custom" Romans and Huns could exchange "what they needed." The emperor rejected their demands.[830]

After his last attempt to reconquer at least some land in Pannonia had failed, Dengizich had crossed into Wallachia. The Bittugures and apparently other tribes had left him and stayed south of the Danube. Under what circumstances Hernach gave up the Dobrogea is not known. In any case, the remnants of Attila's Huns were no longer anywhere in the border provinces; otherwise their demand for a market place on the Danube would not have made sense.[831]

When Hernach, engaged in disputes in his own country presumably with the Saraguri,[832] refused to join his brother, Dengizich moved his own hordes closer to the Danube, threatening to break into Thrace unless the emperor granted him and his people land and subsidies. Scorning the offers of Anagastes, "to whom the defense of the river was entrusted," to negotiate with him, Dengizich sent his envoys directly to the emperor. Leo "answered that he would readily do all these things if they would be obedient to him, for he rejoiced in men who came into alliance with him from his enemies."[833] At this point Priscus' text breaks off.

Gordon thinks that Constantinople's willingness to come to terms, contradicting her earlier attitude, may be accounted for by the necessity of protecting her northern frontiers in preparation for the approaching expedition against the Vandals in Africa.[834] He may be right. That the negotiations with the Huns eventually broke down had, I believe, another reason. The situation was, on a minor scale, a repetition of 376, though with the essential difference that the Huns, unlike the Goths, needed wide pastures for their flocks and herds, not land for the plough. To accommodate them in the empire would have necessitated the expulsion of the peasants from a large territory, including many of those Goths in the Thracian dioceses on whose support Aspar, for many years the nearly all-mighty major domus, brother-in-law of the Gothic leader Theoderic the Squinter, depended.

---

[830] Priscus, *EL*, p. 160, ll. 20 ff. [*This reference, and those in notes 833 and 836, were missing in the original manuscript and have been supplied from the edition by B. G. Niebuhr, Bonn, 1829. —Ed.*]

[831] "According to the ancient custom" is not the same as "at the same place as before," as suggested by Macartney (1935, 109), who built on this interpretation his queer theory of the sites of the post-Attilanic Huns in Hungary.

[832] Thompson (1948, 157) made him Master of the Soldiers in Thrace, a position held at that time by Basiliscus.

[833] Priscus, *EL*, p. 162, ll. 5ff.

[834] Gordon 1960, 135.

Dengizich crossed the frozen Danube. He evidently expected that the Huns still south of the river would join him. Some probably did. But large groups of barbarians acted on their own, using the chance to back their demands with arms:

Anagastes, Basiliscus, Ostryis, and other generals penned up and blockaded the Goths in a hollow place. The Scythians, hard pressed by starvation and lack of necessities, sent an embassy to the Romans. They said they were ready to surrender, if only they were given land. The Romans answered that they would forward their requests to the emperor. But the barbarians said that they must come to an agreement right away; they were starving and could no longer wait. The Roman generals took counsel and promised to supply food until the decision of the emperor came, provided the Scythians would split themselves into just as many groups as the Roman army was divided into. In this way the Roman generals could better care for them. The Scythians accepted the terms brought by their ambassadors and drew their forces up in as many sections as the Roman army. Chelchal, a man of Hunnic race, the lieutenant general of those in charge of Aspar's forces, came to the barbarian horde allotted to them. He summoned the prominent Goths [*logades*], who were more numerous than the others, and began a speech to the following effect: The emperor would give land, not for their own enjoyment but to the Huns among them. For these men did not care for tilling the soil and, like wolves, attacked and plundered the provisions of the Goths. They themselves, the Goths, were treated like slaves and forced to feed the Huns, although there never had been concluded a treaty between the two peoples, and the Goths had been pledged by their ancestors to escape from an alliance with the Huns. Thus, the Goths thought lightly of their ancestors' oaths and the loss of their own property. He, Chelchal, was a Hun and proud of it, but he was saying these things to the Goths from a desire of justice, so that they should know what must be done.

The Goths were greatly disturbed by this and, thinking that Chelchal had said these things with good will toward them, attacked the Huns in their midst and killed them. Then, as if at a signal, a mighty battle rose between the races. When Aspar[835] learned of this, he and the commanders of the other camps drew up their troops and killed the barbarians they came upon. When the Scythians preceived the intent of the trick and the treachery, they gathered together and turned against the Romans. Aspar's men anticipated them and killed the barbarian horde allotted to them to the last man. But the fight was not without

---

[835] Read Anagastes.

danger for the other generals, as the barbarians fought courageously. Those who survived broke through the Roman formations and escaped the blockade.[836]

The date is 467. Basiliscus, brother of Empress Verina, was still *magister militum per Thraciam*;[837] in the spring of 468 he was commander in chief of the African expedition. It throws an interesting light on the Byzantine armies of the late fifth century that Basiliscus was the only Greek among the commanders. Anagastes, *Anagasts, the son of Arnigisclus, and Ostrys were, as their names indicate, Goths.[838] Chelchal kept his Hunnish name; evidently he was not yet baptized. As his high rank shows, he had served a long time in the Roman army. Chelchal may have been one of those Huns who deserted to the Romans in Attila's time or joined them after 455.

The fact that Aspar sent a large contingent of his *buccellarii* against the barbarians shows their strength. Although the Romans had some successes,[839] the war dragged on for two more years. In 468, the greater part of the army was sent to Africa.

The end came only in 469. Marcellinus Comes has the short entry "The head of Dinzic, son of Attila, king of the Huns, was brought to Constantinople."[840] The *Chronicon Paschale* gives more details: "Dinzirichus, Attila's son, was killed by Anagastes, general in Thrace. His head was brought to Constantinople, carried in procession through the Middle Street, and fixed on a pole at the Wooden·Circus. The whole city turned out to look at it."[841]

The few Huns south of the Danube who did follow the Ostrogoths, like the Bittugur, gradually lost their ethnic identity or joined the Bulgarian raiders.

---

[836] Priscus, *EL*, p. 162, l. 18 to p. 164, l. 19.

[837] According to Theophanes, Basiliscus was appointed *mag. mil. per. Thraciam* in A.M. 5956, *i.e.*, between August 29, 463, and August 28, 464. The date might be right, although Theophanes placed the appointement of Zeno as commander of the troops in the Orient in the same year, which is wrong. Zeno was promoted when he married Ariadne, Leo's older daughter, Candidus (*HGM* IV, 136), presumably in 467/8 (Baynes and Dawes 1948, 81). He was *strategos* at the same time as Basiliscus (Zacharias of Mytilene V, 1; Ahrens-Krüger 59; Brooks, *CMH* 1, 145), thus before the fall of 468, when Basiliscus fell in disgrace; see also Ernest Schwartz, "Publizistische Aktenstücke zum Acacianischen Schisma," *Abh. München*, N.F. 10, 1934, 181. Fortunately it is not our task to straighten out the confused chronology of those years.

[838] 'Οστρύς (Theophanes, A.M. 5964, C. de Boor, 1883, 117$_{26}$; Malalas, *EI* 161$_5$) is the short form of a name which began with *Ostro-*. His loyalty to Aspar became proverbial.

[839] Theophanes, A.M. 5961.

[840] *CM* II, 90.

[841] Ed. Bonn, 598; *CM* II, 90.

III. Economy

THE WRITTEN sources contain little about the economy of the Huns before they made contact with the Roman world. It certainly changed in the eight or nine decades we can follow their history, though the change has been exaggerated. By the middle of the fifth century the great majority of the people lived almost the same nomadic life—with animal husbandry as the economic mainstay and hunting and fishing as subsidiary occupations—as their ancestors had lived.

Whether we realize it or not, when we speak of nomads, often Father Abraham, archetype of the Beduin sheikhs, comes to mind, pitching his tent one week here and the other there, constantly on the move from pasture to pasture. This is the way Ammianus described the Alans: "When they come to a place rich in grass they feed like wild beasts. As soon as the fodder is used up," they move to another place. It is the Chinese stereotype: "they follow water and grass." The mobility of the herders always has struck farmers—Greeks, Indians, and Chinese—as incomprehensible, uncanny, and inhuman. The archaeological evidence refutes Ammianus.

In the steppe and the wooded grassland from western Kazakhstan to the Carpathian Mountains many hundred kurgans have been excavated and thousands of graves of all Sarmatian periods opened. So far no traces of settlements have been found. One could think that the buildings, if the Sarmatians had any, were of perishable material, but then at least fireplaces and garbage pits should have been preserved. They were not. And yet two facts are incompatible with the idea of the restlessly wandering Sarmatians. First, the large grave fields. Sinitsyn was impressed by the many kurgans in the Sarmatian cemeteries on the Kolyshlei River; in some the burial mounds numbered fifty and more.[1] But they were in the

---

1 Sinitsyn 1932, 68.

wooded steppe, close to the forests, where the normal mobility of the sheep, horse, and cattle breeders was possibly restricted by natural obstacles. However, large kurgan grave fields also are known from the treeless steppe. In Berezhnovka II, on the left bank of the Volga, about two hundred kurgans were counted, and how many have been plowed over can no longer be determined. Sarmatians buried their dead there from the sixth century B.C. to the third or fourth century A.D. Of the burials excavated, 38 were Sauromatian, 29 Early, 18 Middle, and 17 Late Sarmatian.[2] In the two kurgan groups at Bykovo, in the same region, 20 burials were of the Sauromatian and 60 of the Early and Middle Sarmatian periods.[3] At Kalinovka, Shilov excavated 62 kurgans with 253 burials of which 5 were Sauromatian, 64 Early, 60 Middle, and 31 Late Sarmatian.[4] Those were not princes' graves, not sacred burial grounds as in the High Altai. Many graves contained very few goods or none at all. It was the same in the West. In the lower valley of the Molochnaya River there is one Sarmatian kurgan after another. Of the 369 burials excavated in 1950 and 1951, 54 were Sarmatian.[5] This points, as Vyazmitina rightly stressed,[6] to a semisedentary life.

Then there is the Sarmatian pottery. True nomads like the Beduins or the Mongols have leather and wooden not clay vessels. From the earliest to the latest period, the Sarmatians used clay pots, bowls, and dishes. This proves, as Arzyutov emphasized[7] (though other archaeologists did not see it), that the Sarmatians were shepherds. Even if all wheel-made clay vessels found in the graves were imported—a rather unlikely assumption— there are the many handmade flat-bottomed pots. People who frequently move from one place to another have, as a rule, round-bottomed vessels which can be put in the soft ground or carried on cords or in a net. The Sarmatians had vessels of both types, obviously used for different purposes. Still, that they did make vessels fit for a longer stay speaks, like the large cemeteries, for prolonged stays in one place.

The wanderings of the ancient, medieval, and modern nomads of central and eastern Asia may at times and depending on geographical factors have been very long,[8] but as a rule they always repeated themselves: from the same winter quarters to the same summer pastures, and back. There

---

[2] Sinitsyn 1960, 11, 155, 157, 159, 163.
[3] K. F. Smirnov 1960, 248-249, 253-257.
[4] Shilov 1959, 324.
[5] *APU* 8, 1960, 5.
[6] Viazmitina 1954, 243.
[7] Arziutov 1936, 88.
[8] [*Footnote missing.*—Ed.]

was a certain latitude in the choice of the summer pastures, but the winter quarters remained the same. "True" nomadism of the Beduin type was a rare exception; in central Asia only the Kazakhs and Turkmens of the Aral-Caspian steppes and half-deserts are or until recently were constantly moving from pasture to pasture.[9]

The seminomadism of a Hunnic tribe is attested by Jordanes: In the summer the Altziagiri put up their camps in the steppe near Cherson in the Crimea where their cattle found food pasturage, and in the winter they moved above the Pontic Sea,[10] presumably to Sivash, the *lacus putidus*, where the luscious reed provided good fodder for the animals.[11] Jordanes' statement, valuable as it is, must not be taken literally. There were and are no nomads who live exclusively on horned cattle. Compared with horses and sheep, cattle always and anywhere played a secondary role.

According to Ammianus, the Huns had all kinds of domesticated animals.[12] Whereas we are comparatively well informed about their horses, we hear very little about their cattle. In the version of the sacred-sword legend which Jordanes took from Priscus, we read of a herdsman and the heifer which stepped on the sword,[13] and Priscus mentions an ox which Attila sent to the Roman ambassador.[14] In the economy of the Eurasian nomads, goats take a small place. The skins of the *haedus* with which the Huns "protected their hairy legs"[15] were perhaps the skins of the ibex, a motif occurring quite frequently in the art of the Scythians and their relatives.[16]

No Greek or Roman author mentions sheep, without which the Huns could not have lived. The meat they boiled in the big cauldrons was mutton. Sheep provided milk and cheese. The tents were made of sheepskin or felt,[17] which was made out of sheep's wool. Like the shoes of the Sarmatians, those of the Huns were made of sheep's leather.[18] The curved caps of the Huns[19] were doubtless made of felt. Jerome corrected Ammianus' slightly vulgar term *galerus*.[20] He called the Huns' dress a tiara, which he describes

---

[9] [*Footnote missing.*—Ed.]

[10] Jordanes, *Getica* V, 37.

[11] [*Footnote missing.*—Ed.]

[12] Ammianus XXXI, 2, 3 (*semicruda cuius vis pecoris carne vescantur*).

[13] Jordanes, *Getica* XXXV, 183.

[14] Priscus, *EL* 126$_{31\text{-}32}$.

[15] Ammianus XXXI, 2, 6.

[16] Minns 1913, 193, fig. 85; 209, fig. 108; 211, fig. 110.

[17] [*Footnote missing.*—Ed.]

[18] [*Footnote missing. Ammianus XXXI, 2, 6, mentions the shoes but not the material.* —Ed.]

[19] Ammianus XXXI, 2, 6.

[20] Jerome, *Ep.* LXIV, 13; cf. Jordanes, *Getica* XI, 71-72.

as "a round cap, as we see it depicted in Odysseus, as if a ball were divided in the middle and one of the parts placed on the head. This the Greek and our people call τιάραν, some call it galerus" (*Rotundum pilleolum quale pictum in Ulixe conspicimus, quasi sphaera media sit divisa, et pars altera ponatur in capite. Hoc Graeci et nostri τιάραν, nonnulli galerum vocant*). But Ammianus' *galerus incurvus* was almost certainly not a round but a curved cap, pointed like the Phrygian cap, a type known from the Black Sea to the borders of China.

The Huns, maintains Thompson, could not weave because they had no time for it. How strange! The Sarmatians seem to have had plenty of leisure, for in their graves many hundred spin whorls have been found, made of stone, alabaster, and cut from the bottom of clay vessels. Burials on the Torgun and the right Ilovla yielded twilled wool fabrics. Like the Sarmatians, the Huns spun the wool of their sheep. They also made linen. Ammianus speaks of their linen dress; the canopies under which rows of girls met Attila when he entered his residence were of white linen, and in Queen Ereka's house linen cloth was embroidered. Did the Huns import linen? This is unlikely, for the Goths in south Russia also wore linen clothes, and pieces of linen were found in Late Sarmatian graves in the lower Volga region.

CAMELS

In the economy of the Huns in the Hungarian plain, camels were of little or no importance. Had Priscus seen any he could hardly have failed to mention them. On their retreat from Persia in 395, the Huns may have driven a few camels with them.[21] But on the Danube the beast could not have been more than an exotic curiosity. Farther to the east, however, in Rumania and particularly the Ukraine, the Huns, like the Sarmatians before them, may well have kept two-humped Bactrian camels.[22] In the last centuries before and the first centuries after the beginning of our era, the camel, long domesticated, served the barbarians from the Great Wall to the Crimea as pack and riding animal.

In an instructive article, Schafer marshalled the literary evidence for the presence of the camel among the Hsiung-nu, T'u-yü-hun, and T'o-pa, in Shan-shan, Kuchā, Karashahr, and K'ang-chü (Sogdiana).[23] The ar-

---

[21] A small number of camels from the regions south and southeast of Lake Urmia occur in the lists of booty drawn up for the Khaldian kings in the eighth and seventh centuries; cf. F. W. König, *Archiv für Völkerkunde* 9, 1954, 53-55, 62.

[22] The camels used in western Europe were one-humped dromedary. For Italy, see Ennodius, *Ep.* V, 13; for Merovingian Gaul, Greg. Tur., *Hist. Franc.* VII, 35.

[23] Schafer 1950, 177-181.

chaeological evidence is no less eloquent. A plate, representing two camels, was found in the Hsiung-nu cemetery at Hsi-ch'a-kou in the province Liao-ning;[24] camel bones were found in the Hsiung-nu settlement on the Ivolga near Ulan-Ude;[25] a bronze plaque with a camel rider[26] and another one with two standing camels[27] come from the Minusinsk area.[28] Among the rock pictures on the Pisannaya gora at Sulek in the old Kirgiz country are fighting camels.[29] A gold plaque in the Siberian collection of Peter the Great shows a tiger attacking a camel.[30]

Some objects showing representations of camels, found in Sarmatian territories, were of Western provenance. An open-work plaque from the Manych River showing a camel[31] can be dated to the first half of the second century B.C.; like the Greek cantharus in the same grave, the piece probably was imported. The same could be true for a finger ring with two kneeling camels found in a kurgan at Bolshaya Dmitrievka in the province Saratov.[32] In form, technique, and style, the ring is related to one showing a human head from Ust'-Labinskaya, datable to the first century A.D.[33] and another one showing goats of about the same date from stanitsa Tifliskaya.[34] But there also exist representations of camels which are of Sarmatian provenance. One is a bronze plaque showing two fighting camels from Pyatimary on the Ilek River[35] and another with a camel in low relief, a stray find from Aktyubinsk, farther to the east;[36] both are of the Sauromatian period (VII-IV B.C.). A buckle from Veselyi, east of Rostov on the Don, showing a lying camel,[37] is Early Sarmatian (IV-II B.C.).

---

[24] Sun Shou-tao 1960. Garutt and Iur'ev 1959, 81-83. [*In the manuscript there were two references numbered 24; they are combined here.*—Ed.]

[25] Petri 1928, 54, fig. 41.

[26] Teploukhov 1929, pl. 1:101.

[27] F.-R. Martin 1893, pl. 29:15.

[28] For a similar Ordos bronze, see Kiselev 1951, 235, pl. 21: 14.

[29] Appelgren-Kivalo 1931, fig. 88.

[30] Rudenko 1962b, pl. 5:2 (three identical plaques). A very realistic gold figure of a camel is only known from a plate in Witsen 1962, 9, fig. 1:16.

[31] M. I. Artamonov, *SA* 9, 1949, 321, fig. 18.

[32] Posta 1905, fig. 287:6-7; Spitsyn 1915, fig. 20; J. Werner 1956, pl. 65:3; E. K. Maksimov, *SA* 4, 1957, 159, fig. 3:2; 160, fig. 4. The grave goods include a Roman strainer of a well-known type; cf. *e.g.*, Curle 1923, 75-76. A similar strainer comes from the Kuban area; *OAK* 1902 (1904), 83, fig. 182.

[33] I. I. Veselovskiĭ, *Trudy XI AS*, 1, 1905, 361, fig. 53.

[34] *OAK* 1902 (1904), 81, fig. 176. This has been pointed out by E. K. Maksimov, *SA* 4, 1957, 160. Incidentally, these analogies speak against the assumption that the ring from Bolshaya Dmitrievka is of central Asiatic origin, as J. Werner (1956, 68) thinks.

[35] Smirnov and Petrenko 1963, pl. 21:6.

[36] Griaznov, *KS* 61, 1956, 14, fig. 14:4; Smirnov and Petrenko 1963, pl. 21:8.

[37] Moshkova 1963, pl. 25:16.

Camel bones were found in a settlement on the Yurgamysh River near Chelyabinsk,[38] at Zolotaya Balka on the lower Dnieper (not later than the second century A.D.),[39] and, in the fourth century, graves in the Necropolis at Panticapaeum.[40] There is, furthermore, the bashlyk made of camel hair in a burial near Phanagoria, datable to the third century A.D.[41] It is unlikely that such a simple hood should have been imported; it was made where it was found, in the Bosporan kingdom.

We may, therefore, assume that the Hunnic tribes in the Black Sea region, the conquerors and successors of the Sarmatians, had camels. Their herds were apparently small; no Byzantine writer mentions camels among the Pontic Huns.[42]

HUNNIC AGRICULTURE?

Our sources are unanimous in denying the Huns any knowledge of agriculture. "No one among them plows a field or touches a plow handle," wrote Ammianus. According to Claudian: "The chase supplies their food; bread they will not eat." Asterius of Amasea described the Huns at the Black Sea as a people "who have not learned to grow wheat and other grains"; they have no grapevines and do not till the soil. The Huns "despised" agriculture, said Chelchal, himself a Hun.[43] The same was said about the Alans. They, too "cared nothing for using the plowshare."[44] Literally taken, Ammianus was right. Neither the Huns nor the Alans, nor any other Sarmatians, plowed their fields. Nowhere between the Volga and the middle Danube has a plowshare been found that could be connected with the Huns or Alans. As late as 1925, when quite a number of kurgans had been excavated, Rykov could say that in the Sarmatian finds in the Volga region neither corn-grinders nor sickles occurred.[45] This is no longer true.

In 1936, Sinitsyn found in the mound over a Late Sarmatian grave at Tsagan-El'sin near Elista in the Kalmuk steppes the two parts of a primitive implement for crushing seeds of a cereal plant: a long, narrow,

---

[38] Sal'nikov 1948, 42.

[39] Viazmitina 1962, 117.

[40] Blavatskiĭ 1960, 184. For other finds of camel bones, see Tsalkin 1960, 101-104, 107.

[41] Kobylina 1956, 88.

[42] The later history of the camel in southern Russia is obscure. The Tatars of the Golden Horde had camels (Spuler 1943, 423). For the camels in Bessarabia and the Crimea, see Schafer 1950, 166.

[43] Ammianus XXXI, 2, 10; In Ruf. I, 327; PG 40, 381; EL 589$_{24-25}$. That the Huns were mere hunters before the doe led them across the Maeotis (Getica 123)—the source is Priscus—is pseudo-learned reconstruction.

[44] Ammianus XXXI, 2, 18.

[45] Rykov 1925, 48.

shallowly concave bedstone and a round grinding stone.[46] In Middle Sarmatian graves, millet had been found before and also occasionally charred wheat in the remnants of the funeral feast, but such finds were merely registered, and that was all.[47] The Sarmatian corn-grinder did not fit the picture of the shepherds who supposedly knew nothing of agriculture. Like P. D. Stepanov, author of a study on the history of agriculture in the lower Volga region,[48] Sinitsyn thought that the Volga Sarmatians got grain from the Kuban and Azov Sea areas;[49] they ground it—this could no longer be doubted—but they did not grow it. Why they imported it was not clear. Obviously only small amounts could be carried over such distances, so only two explanations were possible: either grain was used in religious ceremonies, or the chieftains cherished grain as a delicacy. Neither was exactly convincing. When later the fragments of another corn-grinder were found in a Middle Sarmatian grave at Berezhnovka,[50] they were not even recognized as such.

The find of an iron sickle in a Late Sarmatian grave at Kalinovka on the left bank of the Volga north of Volgograd[51] proves definitely that in the first centuries A.D. the Sarmatians did grow grain.

> The sickle, 16 cm. long, its point broken, lay at the feet of a man in the niche of a narrow rectangular pit; other finds were a wire fibula with a piece of cloth still on it; an iron buckle; bone strips from a bow; and bone arrowheads. The southwest orientation points to the early stage in the Late Sarmatian Period.[52]

> Agricultural implements are rarely found in graves. It is rather surprising that any were found in Sarmatian burials at all. The many hundred graves of the Gepidic peasant population in Hungary yielded *one* sickle.[53]

Whether the corn-grinders in some kurgans at Novo-Filippovka in the valley of the Molochnaya River, between the Dnieper rapids and the Azov Sea, are Middle or Late Sarmatian cannot be determined. They are only once mentioned in passing.[54] The graves in the cemetery are pre-

---

[46] Sinitsyn 1956b, 42, fig. 20.
[47] Only K. F. Smirnov (1950b, 111) recognized their importance for the economy of the Sarmatians.
[48] *Trudy Saratovskogo oblast'nogo muzeia kraevedeniia* 1, 1956, 105.
[49] Sinitsyn 1956b, 30.
[50] Sinitsyn 1960, 54, fig. 19:10.
[51] Shilov 1959, 492, fig. 60:11.
[52] *Ibid.*, 343.
[53] Csallány 1961, 285.
[54] M. I. Viazmitina, *Voprosy,* 243.

ponderantly Middle Sarmatian, but some seem to be as late as the third century A.D.[55]

In the 1920's, Rau found in a Middle Sarmatian grave on the Torgun River an iron implement which he called a lapped axe.[56] He did not comment on it, and for years nothing like it was found until Shilov opened a grave in kurgan 8 at Kalinovka, also of the Middle Sarmatian period. There lay what used to be called a celt.[57] It was an adz so well preserved that it was possible to determine its function: the weak socket, not even closed around, and in particular the bluntness of the edge leave no doubt that the material on which the adz was wrought was rough and loose, thus, earth.[58] On the walls of grave pits, the traces of narrow adzes, 3 centimeters, 4 centimeters, at the most 5 centimeters wide, are frequently visible.[59] Such adzes were used for digging pits as early as the fifth century B.C. It seems rather unlikely that the Sarmatians used the adzes for this purpose only.[60] These tools cannot have been lying around to be picked up when someone died. They must have been used for digging much more regularly. In other words, they were hoes, tools for tilling the soil in which seeds of cereal grasses were planted. The remnants of soft food found in pots were, as a rule, porridge of millet, *Panicum miliaceum*,[61] the fastest growing cereal grass, just right for shepherds.[62] Indeed, according to Pliny and Aelian,[63] millet was the food of the Sarmatians.

Future excavations undoubtedly will prove that in wide areas of Middle Asia agriculture played a greater role in the economy of the nomads and seminomads than we still are prepared to admit, certainly subordinated to sheep and cattle raising and yet of considerable importance. Kadyrbaev found corn-grinders in graves of nomads in central Kazakhstan, some to be dated as early as the fifth century B.C.,[64] Litvinsky in kurgans in the

---

[55] M. I. Viazmitina, *APU* 8, 1960, 20.

[56] Rau 1926, 37, fig. 52; cf. Sal'nikov 1940, 137.

[57] Shilov 1959, 344, 488, fig. 59:10.

[58] Cf. Flinders-Petrie 1917, 18.

[59] *E.g.*, Sinitsyn 1960, 26, fig. 7:11.

[60] This was supposedly the function of an adz found in a kurgan in Akchii-Karasu on the right bank of the Naryn river, datable between the fourth and second century B.C. (Kozhomberdiev 1960a, 119, fig. 5).

[61] Cf., *e.g.*, Sinitsyn 1947, 23.

[62] Therefore, K. F. Smirnov (*SA* 4, 1958, 271) and Shilov (1959, 488) assume that the Sarmatians grew mostly millet.

[63] Pliny, *HN* XVIII, 100; Aelian, *Var. Hist.* III, 39. In the Greek cities of Panticapeum, Myrmecium, and Tyritace only wheat, rye, and barley were found (I. I. Nikishin, *KS* 23, 1948, 84; I. B. Zeest, *KS* 33, 1950, 96-103).

[64] "Pamiatniki rannykh kochevnikov tsentral'nogo Kazakhstana," *Trudy Kazakh.* **7**, 1959, 192-193.

Kara-Mazar Mountains in Tadjikistan, datable to the second and third centuries A.D.[65] The long acquaintance with agriculture, though primitive and limited, made it comparatively easy for Sarmatians to give up their nomadic way of life. To give a few examples, in the small fortified settlements near the present Ivanovka and Tarsunov on the Kerch peninsula, Sarmatian soldiers of the Bosporan kingdom cultivated their fields like the *limitanei* in the West.[66] The Sarmatians of the settlement Kobyakovo at the mouth of the Don had become farmers.[67] In 442, to King Goar's Alans "land in farther Gaul was assigned by the patrician Aetius to be divided with the inhabitants. The Alans subdued those who resisted by force of arms, and, ejecting the owners, took possession of the land by force."[68] This is, so far as I know, the only case of resistance against barbarian *hospites*. Under the *hospitalitas* system the barbarians received a third of the land.[69] But apparently this was not enough for the Alans. They needed more land; they had come with their wives and children, tents and carts.[70] Though they could not have with them large herds and flocks, they probably wanted to live like their fathers in Hungary and their ancestors in South Russia. They wanted pastures, not just fields. Aetius made a mistake. But that he could think the Alans would be satisfied with what he gave them shows that he expected the Alans to cultivate the land.

As we now return to the writers who denied the Huns any knowledge of agriculture, we shall, perhaps, be less inclined to accept their statements. Claudian's characterization of the Huns as mere hunters is so much nonsense. Ammianus transferred to the Huns what Trogus had said about the Scythians. Nevertheless, he presumably was right for his time. In times of war and migration, the Huns lived on their sheep and cattle. Once they had made themselves masters of a peasant population, like the settled Sarmatians and Germanic tribes in Hungary, they found it simpler and more pleasant to rob their subjects than to work themselves. Only the poorest Huns may have been forced to supplement their meat, milk, and cheese diet with self-grown grain. But that was probably different in the past.

Finds in Kunya Uaz in Khwarezm and on the upper Ob indicate that in former times the Huns tilled the soil. The racially mixed population

---

[65] "Ob izuchenii v 1955 g. pogreben'nykh pamiatnikov kochevnikov v Kara-Mazarskikh gorakh," *Trudy Tadzh.* 63, 1956, 39.

[66] V. D. Blavatskiĭ in *Problemy istorii severnogo Prichernomor'ia*, 36-37.

[67] Kaposhina 1962.

[68] *CM* I, 660$_{442}$.

[69] Cf. F. Lot, *Revue belge de philologie et d'histoire* 8, 1928, 975-1011.

[70] See Paulinus of Pella in his *Eucharistos* on the Alans besieging Vasatae.

of Kunya Uaz, Europoids with a Mongolian admixture, people who practiced cranial deformation, cannot be separated from the Huns. They had
sickles.[71] It could be argued that by the third and fourth centuries the
Hunnoids in Kunya Uaz had been assimilated with the earlier local population; their sickles could have been taken over from the Khwarezmian
peasants. But the people on the upper Ob (likewise Europoids with a
Mongoloid admixture, likewise practicing cranial deformation, and at that
of the same circular type as in Kunya Uaz) met hunters and fishers when
they moved there in the second or third century. And yet, as Nerazik
noticed, their sickles resembled closely those of the Kunya Uaz people.[72] If
the Hunnoids on the Ob and east of the Aral Sea cut stalks of grain with
iron sickles, the conclusion that components of the great Hun horde, and
not only the Alans, did the same in the past seems inevitable.

HOUSING

"The Huns,"says Ammianus, "are never protected by any building,
but they avoid these like tombs, which are set apart from everyday use.
For not even a hut thatched with reed can be found among them. But
roaming at large amid the mountains and woods, they learn from the cradle[73]
to endure cold, hunger, and thirst. When away from home [*peregre*], they
never enter a house unless compelled by extreme necessity; for they think
they are not safe when staying under a roof."[74]

It would seem that the Huns had read Seneca, who praised the happy
age when men spent their lives under the branches of the trees, dwelling
according to nature in which it was a joy to live, fearing neither for the
dwelling itself nor for its safety.[75] Actually, Ammianus transferred again
on the Huns the primitive traits of the "Scythians," the "noble savages,"
so dear to the Stoic philosophers, only using them as evidence of the beastliness of the hated barbarians. In his time the northern peoples' fear of
houses had become a topos. He speaks of the Alamanni who avoided cities
"as if they were tombs, surrounded by nets."[76] The Goths are said to have
thought that people living in cities lived not like men but birds in a cage.[77]

---

[71] Nerazik 1958, 387, fig. 10:3.

[72] *Ibid.*, 390.

[73] *Per*—lacuna of seven or eight letters—*ab incunabilis*. I think Clark's *perferre*
is better than Pighi's *perperti iam*, or the *perferre ipsis* suggested by Brackman 1909,
20.

[74] Ammianus XXXI, 2, 4.

[75] *Ep. mor.* XL, 41-43.

[76] *Ipsa oppida ut circumdata retiis busta declinant* (XVI, 2, 12). Langen (1867, 19)
suggested *lustra* instead of *busta*, which is perhaps better.

[77] Petrus Patricius, see Boissevain 1910, *Dio* 3, 745.

Gainas fled Constantinople which looked to him like a crowded and sumptuous tomb.[78]

In South Russia, the Huns had no permanent dwellings but they certainly had shelters, tents of felt and sheepskin,[79] materials which probably most of them were still using after they had settled in the Hungarian plains. Priscus once mentions Attila's tent.[80] It probably was similar to the large tent of the Sarmatized Bosporan depicted on the wall of the catacomb of Anthesterius.[81] On the painting, the interior of the tent is blue, evidently representing a woolen carpet like the one in Queen Ereka's house.[82] Incidentally, as everyone who has lived in Mongolian felt yurts knows, they are quite comfortable, spacious, well aired, and easily kept clean. Living as a prisoner in the Chinese capital, Hsieh-li, kaghan of the Turks, refused to move into a house and put up his tent.[83] The crown prince Li Ch'eng-ch'ien preferred a Turkish tent to the palace,[84] but he was a noted and crazy Turkophile. Attila lay in state in a silk tent.[85] The one he used when he was not in one of his residences and some tents of high-ranking Huns may have been made of the same materials.

By the middle of the fifth century, the Hun nobles had houses in the villages which they owned,[86] better built than the modest huts of the native population,[87] probably similar to the wooden buildings in the king's residences, only on a smaller scale. The walls of the latter were made of well-planed planks and panels. Attila's "palace" consisted of a single square or rectangular room, furnished with seats and a bed or couch, $\varkappa\lambda\ell\nu\eta$, screened off at one end of the room by tapestries. Thompson rightly pointed out that the "palace," the other one-room houses, and the two stockades around the camp were not built by Huns but by either Romans or Goths.[88]

---

[78] Eunapius, fr. 79, *FHG* IV, 49; Suidas, Adler 1938, IV, 162.

[79] Asterius of Amasea, *Homily* XV, *PG* 40, 381.

[80] *EL* 125$_{20-21}$.

[81] *OAK* 1878-1879, pl. 1, fig. 1, and frontispiece; Minns 1913, 313, fig. 223; Rostovtsev 1914, atlas, pl. 51:2, text 182; Gaĭdukevich 1948, 400, fig. 71; Ivanova 1953, 152, fig. 54. Rostovtsev and Gaĭdukevich date the painting to the beginning of the first century A.D. The suggested by Ebert (1921, 332) is too early (second to first century B.C.); that by Minns, date too late.

[82] Priscus, *EL* 140$_{3-4}$.

[83] Liu 1958, 187.

[84] Maenchen-Helfen 1957a, 120.

[85] *Getica* 256.

[86] In a village the Roman ambassadors met a Hun princess (Priscus, *EL* 131-132). It was in summer, a season in which even those nomads and semi-nomads who, like the Volga Bolgars, dwelt in winter in wooden houses, lived in tents on the pastures; cf. Markwart 1927, 267. It is, therefore, to be assumed that the princess lived in a house.

[87] Párducz 1949, 90.

[88] See Thompson 1945a, 112-115.

Clemmensen adduced good arguments for the Germanic, which in our case means Gothic, technique of the wood construction.[89] In the second half of the fourth century there were Christian churches, monasteries, and convents in Gothia,[90] evidently wooden buildings.[91] Since the discovery of the Gothic long houses in the Chernyakhov settlements, the existence of Gothic wooden architecture need no longer be proved. The Sarmatian Jazyges had no houses in their old sites in South Russia, but after more than two centuries of close contact with the Germanic Quadi, they lived in thatched huts. Attila and his retainers most probably had their houses built in Gothic fashion by Gothic carpenters.[92]

INCOME IN GOLD

In the 440's, the East Romans paid the Huns about 13,000 pounds of gold, more than 900,000 solidi. This was, from whatever angle one may look at it, a great sum. In particular, the payment of 6,000 pounds of gold in 447 must have been a heavy blow to the imperial treasury. But did it really spell the complete financial ruin of the prosperous East, as Mommsen thought?[93] For a proper evaluation of the "subsidies" paid to the Hun "federates," a brief survey of comparable public and private expenditures in the fifth and sixth centuries may be helpful.

In 408, Alaric blackmailed the West Romans to pay him 4,000 pounds of gold;[94] in the same year, he blockaded Rome, and the senate bought him off with 5,000 pounds of gold, 30,000 pounds of silver, and other gifts in kind.[95] These figures, coming from Olympiodorus, may not be entirely trustworthy. But there is no reason to doubt Malchus' statement that in 473 Theoderic Strabo, leader of the Gothic federates, got an annual payment of 2,000 pounds of gold.[96] The sums offered or actually paid to the Goths varied considerably according to the circumstances. The subsidy paid to Valamir was only 300 pounds of gold per annum.[97] In 479, his nephew Theoderic, the later great king, was offered an annual subsidy of 10,000 solidi, that is about 140 pounds of gold, but immediate payment of 1,000 pounds of gold and 40,000 pounds of silver.[98] In 570,

---

[89] Clemmensen 1937, 1, 297. Vamos' arguments for the Iranian origin of the Hun buildings (1932, 131-148) are unconvincing.

[90] Thompson 1956, 1-11.

[91] They were burned down (Sozomen VI, 37, 13-14).

[92] Gothic timrja, "carpenter," is a Germanic word.

[93] Mommsen 1906, 1, 539, n. 4.

[94] Zosimus IV, 29; Olympiodorus, f. 4, Henry 1959, 168.

[95] Zosimus V, 41.

[96] Fr. 2, EL 570$_{21-22}$.

[97] Priscus, EL 152$_{24}$.

[98] Malchus, fr. 16, EL 574$_{11-12}$.

Emperor Tiberius offered the Lombards 3,000 pounds of gold if they would stop their raids in Italy.[99] This was the same year in which Bayan, the caganus of the Avars, was paid his annual subsidy of 80,000 solidi, or more than 1,000 pounds of gold.[100]

In 532, Emperor Justinian concluded the "endless peace" with Chosroes; one of its conditions was the payment of twenty annual contributions to the maintenance of the fortifications in the Caucasus for which the Romans were in arrears, amounting to 11,000 pounds of gold.[101] In 540, the Persians received again 5,000 pounds; in 545, 2,000 pounds; in 551, 2,600 pounds; and in 561, 3,000 pounds.[102] From 484 to 492, Zeno paid the gangs of robbers in the Isaurian highland a yearly subsidy of 1,400 pounds of gold.[103]

In order to put the tribute paid to the Huns in the proper perspective, it should not only be compared with the payments to the "allies." Measured by the expenditures made by high-ranking people on worthy and sometimes not so worthy causes, it was not so exorbitant. To give a few examples: Empress Eudocia contributed 200 pounds of gold to the restoration of the public baths in Antioch;[104] Empress Eudoxia gave the same sum for the building of a church in Gaza.[105] When Paul, ex-consul of 498, was in financial trouble, Emperor Anastasius helped him out with 2,000 pounds of gold.[106] In 514, Anastasius ransomed Hypatius from Vitalian for 5,000 pounds of gold.[107] In 526 and 527, Emperor Justin sent 4,500 pounds of gold to Antioch, which had been heavily damaged by an earthquake.[108] To celebrate his consulship in 521, Emperor Justinian spent 4,000 pounds of gold on the games and for distribution among the populace;[109] in 532, he gave 4,000 pounds of gold for the building of Saint Sophia.[110] The sums spent in the vicious ecclesiastical fights were enormous. In the 430's, Bishop Cyril of Alexandria bribed court officials with

---

[99] Menander, fr. 49, *EL* 469$_7$.

[100] Menander, fr. 63, *EL* 471$_{29\text{-}30}$.

[101] Stein 1959, 2, 295.

[102] *Ibid.*, 490, 502, 510, 519.

[103] John of Antioch, *EI* 142$_9$. Evagrius (*Hist. eccles.* II, 35) gives the figure 5,000.

[104] Evagrius I, 20.

[105] Marc le Diacre, Grégoire and Kugener 1930, 44; the *vita* is a sixth-century revision of the original. I pass over the incredible sums which Olympias is said to have given to the churches in Constantinople (*Vita Olympiadis*, ch, 7, *Analecta Bollandiana* 15, 1896, 415).

[106] Lydus III, 48.

[107] See Stein 1959, 2, 181, on the figures.

[108] Vasiliev 1950, 348-349.

[109] Marcellinus Comes, *s.a.* 521, *CM* II, 101-102.

[110] Lydus III, 76.

more than 2,000 pounds of gold.[111] Between 444 and 450, Nomus, *magister officiorum*, consul in 445, and *patricius*, extorted from Anastasius and Paul, Cyril's nephews, 1,400 pounds of gold.[112]

In the fifth century, the revenue of the Eastern empire has been estimated as being on the average 270,000 pounds of gold a year, of which approximately 45,000 were spent on the army.[113] The 6,000 pounds of gold paid to Attila in 447 were a little more than 2.2 percent of the money the treasury received in a year, and the highest annual tribute was about 4.7 percent of what the army required. Still, had this gone on for a number of years, it would have been a great, though still not an unbearable strain. But Attila was paid the tribute only in 448, 449, and, possibly, in 450. In the following three years he was at war with both the East and West and consequently received nothing.

A passage in John Lydus, which escaped Mommsen, shows how far from the alleged bankruptcy the East was. When Leo followed Marcian to the throne in 457, he found in the treasury more than 100,000 pounds of gold, "which Attila, the enemy of the world, had wanted to take."[114] Of all the Byzantine emperors after Marcian, only Anastasius left a larger reserve at his death.[115]

The tribute was not the only so-to-speak legitimate source of the gold income of the Huns. Before, and for some time while, they received annual subsidies, the Hun leaders were paid in gold for the auxiliaries they lent the Romans. Aetius, in particular, must have paid large sums for the contingents of horsemen he obtained in the 430's. Whether by the middle of the 440's Attila blackmailed the Western Romans into sending him gold for keeping the peace is not certain, but in 449 he drew a salary as Master of the Soldiers, which, as Priscus said, was a pretext for concealing the tribute.[116]

The Huns probably insisted that part of the tribute should be handed over to them in ingots. They must have known as well as the Romans

---

[111] *ACO* I: IV, 2, 222-225; Nestorius, Driver and Hodgson 1925, 350; Barhadbesabba Abbaia, *Hist. eccles.* XXV, *PO* 9, 5, 555. Cf. Battifol 1919, 154-179.

[112] Mansi VI, 1025-1028.

[113] A. Segré, *Byzantion* 16, 1944, 437.

[114] Μετὰ γοῦν Θεοδόσιον καὶ Μαρκιανὸν τὸ μέτριον ἐλθὼν ὁ Λέων καὶ τὸν πλοῦτον εὑρών, ὃν Ἀττίλας ὁ τῆς οἰκουμένης πολέμιος λαμβάνειν ἤμελλεν (ἦν δὲ ὑπὲρ τὰς χιλίας ἑκατοντάδας τοῦ χρυσίου λιτρῶν) (Lydus III, 43). Moravcsik (*BT* 1, 328) and L. Várády (*AAH* 14, 1962, 437) misunderstood the passage; Leo did not find "Attila's treasure."

[115] 320,000 pounds of gold (Procopius, *Anecd.* XIX, 7). Bury 1923, 446, and Stein 1959, 2, 193, accepted this figure as authentic.

[116] *EL* 142$_{3-12}$.

that many clipped, debased, and counterfeit solidi were in circulation. In 366, the taxgatherers were ordered to reduce the solidi "to a firm and solid mass of gold";[117] a year later, the edict was repeated: "Whenever solidi must be paid to the account of the sacred largesses, the actual solidi shall not be delivered, because adulterated coins are often substituted for such solidi. The solidi shall be reduced to a mass.... Whenever a definite sum of solidi is due under a title of any kind, and a mass of gold is transmitted, a pound of gold shall be credited for seventy-two solidi."[118] As the sixteen ingots found in 1887 at Krasna in Transylvania[119] show, the Visigoths were likewise on their guard against such attempts at deception. The Huns hardly put more trust in the honesty of the Romans. Besides, not all solidi were of the same weight, though the deviation from the standard was, as a rule, insignificant. It is, therefore, all the more remarkable that just in a barbarian hoard from Kireleny in the Moldavian SSR, hidden about 400 A.D., there was a solidus which, instead of the standard 4.54 grams, weighed only 3.90 grams.[120] The barbarian had been cheated. As the Huns had no mints,[121] they obviously demanded only that amount of gold in ingots which they intended to use for ornaments; for commercial transactions at the fairs, and otherwise, they needed coins.

The Persian kings often lifted the siege of a city as soon as the beleaguered raised the money demanded from them. In 540, Edessa, for example, paid Chosroes 200 pounds of gold and four years later 500 pounds.[122] There is no evidence that Attila or the kings before him made a town an offer to save it at a price. They obviously thought it more profitable to storm a place at the cost of a few hundred men, mostly expendable foot soldiers, to loot it, and to carry away the captives to be sold or ransomed.

After their victory at Adrianople, the Goths offered so many ten thousands of captives for sale; the Huns, temporarily allied with the Goths, certainly

---

[117] *Cod. Theodos.* IX, 22; XII, 7, 2.

[118] *Ibid.*, XII, 6, 12, 13.

[119] Babelon 1901, 1, 882-884; F. A. Marshall 1911, 376; *Sammlung Trau*, no. 4467; Horedt 1958, 31. The gold bars are stamped with the busts of three emperors and *DDD NNN*, probably Valentinian I, Valens, and Gratian. It seems that the payments to the Visigoths were not completely stopped in 369, as one could conclude from Themistius, *Or.* X, 135$_{c-t}$; some pro-Roman leaders were also later subsidized. On the date, see Alföldi, *Num. Közl.* 28-29, 1930, 10, n. 5.

[120] Kropotkin 1961, 95.

[121] Imitations of Roman gold coins of the fourth and fifth centuries, such as found in central Asia (Kropotkin 1961, nos. 1675-1678), are not known from Hungary.

[122] For Chosroes' levies on Syrian cities, see Priscus II, 6, 24; 7, 5-8; 8, 4; XI, 3, 24; XII, 2, 34; 27, 46.

had their share in the lucrative business. St. Ambrose did what he could to ransom the Christian prisoners. In *De officiis* he wrote:

The highest kind of liberality is to redeem captives, to save them from the hand of the enemies, to snatch men from death, and most of all, to restore children to their parents, parents to their children, and to give back a citizen to his country. This was recognized when Thrace and Illyria were so terribly devastated. How many captives were then for sale all over the world? Could one put them all together, their number would have surpassed that of a whole province.... It is then a special quality of liberality to redeem captives, especially from barbarian enemies, who are moved by no spark of human feeling to show mercy except so far as avarice has preserved it with a view of redemption. ... I once brought odium on myself because I broke up the sacred vessels to redeem captives, a fact that could displease the Arians. Who can be so hard, cruel, ironhearted, as to be displeased because a man is redeemed from death, or a woman from barbarian impurities, things that are worse than death, boys and girls and infants from the pollution of idols, where through fear of death they were defiled?[123]

In 395, the Huns took thousands of prisoners in the Asiatic provinces and the Caucasus. Far away from their homes, these unfortunates were not ransomed and most of them were sold at the slave markets on the Danube. Although the tribute was paid to the Hun kings, the prisoners were sold by the men who took them, who apparently received also the ransom for Roman soldiers who fell into their hands, 8 solidi a head before 435 and 12 thereafter. How much gold flowed into Hunnia in this way is difficult to say; it seems to have been rather considerable. The ransom for civilian captives could be quite high. When Attila wanted to show his generosity, he asked only 500 solidi for the widow of a wealthy citizen.[124] The ransom for Bigilas was 50 pounds of gold, that is, 3,600 solidi,[125] but this was a special case.

How much gold unminted and in coins the Huns brought back from their raids and looting expeditions cannot even be guessed. After their victory over the Ostrogoths they did not press the attack on the Visigoths "because they were loaded down with booty,"[126] certainly not cooking

---

[123] *De officiis ministrorum libri tres* II, 15, 70-71; 28, 136.
[124] Priscus, *EL* 146₇. Had he sold her to a slave merchant, he would have got 25 solidi at the most.
[125] *Ibid* 149₁₂, 150₁₁.
[126] Ammianus XXXI, 3, 8.

pots and wooden benches but gold, silver, and precious weapons. The same happened in upper Italy in 452.

In addition to the tribute, the Romans had to send "gifts" to the Huns. This was, in itself, nothing unusual. Even if the treaties between the Romans and the barbarian rulers provided only the payment of a certain sum, it was customary to give the latter presents,[127] among them objects of precious metal. The Huns did not expect gifts, they demanded them. When in 450 the Roman ambassadors whom Attila refused even to see would not hand over the gifts they had brought with them, the king threatened to kill them.[128]

On their departure from Constantinople, foreign envoys were given presents. It was an act of courtesy for distinguished guests. The sums involved could be huge. Procopius estimated the total lavished by Justinian on a Persian ambassador at 1,000 pounds of gold.[129] Attila made a lucrative business out of this custom. Under the flimsiest of pretexts he would send embassy after embassy to the imperial court. To keep the savage in good humor, they all were given rich presents for which, on their return, they had to give account to the king.[130]

Another, probably very considerable, source of income in gold was the sale of horses to the Romans. Besides slaves and, possibly, furs, there was not much else the Huns could offer the Roman traders. A passage in Vegetius' *Mulomedicina* shows that at times the export of horses from Hunnia was a flourishing business. It probably shrank in the later 440's, after the Huns in two sanguine wars lost not only many men but many horses.

A little-noticed passage in Priscus indicates that in Hunnia gold coins were, though probably only to a modest extent, in circulation as a medium of exchange. In 449, Attila forbade the Roman envoys "to buy any Roman prisoner or barbarian slave or horses or anything else except things necessary for food until the disputes between the Romans and the Huns had been resolved."[131] The king had a good reason for this prohibition; he wanted to catch Bigilas with the 50 pounds of gold to be paid to Edecon for killing his lord. When later Bigilas was led before Attila and asked why he was bringing so much gold, he was unable to explain away the 3,600 solidi he was carrying with him.[132] The passage shows that not only

---

[127] The Avars, for instance, received chains decorated with gold, silk raiments, and couches (Menander "Protector," fr. 5, 14, *EL* 442, 445).

[128] Priscus, *EL* 151$_{11-15}$.

[129] Procopius II, 28, 44.

[130] Priscus, *EL* 579$_{1-10}$.

[131] *Ibid.*, 129$_9$-130$_2$.

[132] *Ibid.*, 148$_{18}$-149$_1$.

at the frontier but also deep in Hunnia, slaves, horses, and food could be bought and sold for Roman gold coins. Whether in Attila's time the Huns used solidi as currency only in their contacts with the Romans or also among themselves we do not know. The latter possibility cannot be ruled out entirely.

TRADE

The long, costly, and indecisive war which Emperor Valens waged with the Visigoths ended in 369 with a treaty that reduced to a minimum the formerly fairly close contacts between the empire and the barbarians across the Danube. The Romans stopped paying the annual subsidies to which the Goths had been entitled as long as they were federates. The one-sided exchange of "gifts" between the emperor and his "friends" came to an end. Before the war, Romans and Goths had been bartering all along the river, and many officers of the frontier army were merchants and slave dealers rather than soldiers.[133] From 369 on, the trade between Romania and Gothia, which was now as independent as Persia, was restricted to two market places on the left bank of the Danube.[134] Even there, to judge from analogies, traders were permitted to bring their wares and transact business only at certain times of the year.

The imperial government saw strictly to it that the commercial relations between its subjects and the free barbarians were kept within the narrowest limits. There were only two market places for trading with the Quadi and Marcomanni.[135] To control the trade with the Jazygi, a *burgus* "Commercium" was built near Gran in 371;[136] the other *burgi* were obviously too engaged throughout the year to keep watch over the restless barbarians and to prevent "the furtive crossings of pillagers" (*clandestinos latrunculorum transitus*). A law of 368 forbade the export of wine and oil to the barbaricum.[137] A few years later, merchants who paid in gold for slaves or other goods were threatened with death.[138] The same punishment threatened those who sold weapons[139] and materials for making

---

[133] Themistius, *Or.* X, 136b; cf. Thompson 1961, 18.

[134] *Ibid.*, 135c.

[135] Cf. Alföldi, *AE* 1941, 41.

[136] Patsch 1929, 8.

[137] *Cod. Iust.* IV, 41, 1; on the date, see Seeck 1922, 124$_{23}$.

[138] *Pro mancipiis vel quibuscumque speciebus* (*Cod. Iust.* IV, 63, 2). On the date, see Seeck 1922, 126$_4$. Ebengreuth (1910, 9) dated the edict erroneously in the years 379-383, in which Werner (1935, 5) followed him.

[139] "Cuirasses, shields, bows, arrows, spathae, gladii, or any other weapons."

weapons to any and all barbarians.[140] Whether the trade treaties with the Persians stipulated what goods could be exported is not known, but we may be sure that the Romans did not sell arms to the King of Kings. On the Persian frontier, too, trading was restricted to a few places. In 409, "lest foreigners might find out secrets, which would be improper," the Romans permitted trade with the Persians at three places only: Nisibis, Artaxata, and Callinicum.[141]

What Priscus, our only authority on trade relations between the Eastern Romans and the Huns, has to say on the subject fits this picture. The fairs were held at fixed dates, once a year,[142] probably in late spring or early summer.[143] As long as the frontier ran along the Danube, the market was there, presumably on the northern bank. After 447, it was shifted to Naissus (Niš).[144] When Dengizich and Hernac, Attila's sons, asked for peace, they requested, among other things, that the market on the Danube be reopened "as in former times."[145] There apparently was only one place where Romans and Huns met for barter.

It does not follow that the trade with the Huns was negligible. In addition to the legal trade, Roman goods probably were smuggled into Hunnia, and Hunnic horses and slaves into Romania. Still, the volume of both legal and illegal trade was apparently modest. Thompson's assertion that the whole bourgeoisie of the Eastern empire was vitally interested in maintaining and expanding its commercial relations with the Huns[146] has no basis in either the literary or archaeological evidence. Undoubtedly, some people did good business. If at fairs within the empire profits of 50 percent could be made,[147] the trade with the barbarians was certainly even more lucrative, in particular because the traders had no pangs of conscience about cheating the Huns. Saint Ambrose thought it not a sin to lend barbarians money at usurious interest: "On him whom you cannot easily conquer in war, you can quickly take vengeance with

---

[140] *Alienigenis barbaris cuiuscumque gentis* (*Cod. Iust.* IV, 41, 2, given after August 1, 455; Cf. Seeck, 1922, 124₂₇). The prohibition was in force in the whole empire but first in Constantinople, where the barbarians came as ambassadors or "under any other pretext."

[141] *Cod. Iust.* IV, 63, 4; cf. Vasiliev 1950, 359.

[142] κατὰ τὸν τῆς πανηγύρεως καιρόν (Priscus, *EL* 575₁₀). Note the definite article. Cf. ἡ κατ᾽ ἔτος ἐγχωρίως γενομένη πανήγυρις, *Synaxarium Eccles. Const.*, 721-722.

[143] The campaign in 441, which began after the Hun attack on the Romans at the fair, lasted several months before the winter put a temporary end to it.

[144] Attila demanded that the market in Illyria should be held not on the Danube, as before, but in Naissus (Priscus, *EL* 579₂₉₋₃₁). Thompson (1948, 176) misunderstood the text. The market town could not be moved "from Illyria to Naissus" because Naissus *was* in Illyria.

[*Notes 145-147 are missing in the manuscript.—Ed.*]

the hundredth. From him exact usury whom it would not be a crime to kill. Therefore, where there is the right of war, there is also the right of usury."[148]

SILK

Like the barbarians on China's borders who valued silk more than any other product of their neighbor and enemy,[149] the barbarians in the West esteemed Roman silk very highly. In 408, Alaric demanded and received from the city of Rome four thousand silk tunics.[150] His successor, King Ataulf, gave fifty young men clad in silk as wedding present to Galla Placidia.[151] In the shiploads of clothes which the Eastern Romans for many years sent to the Visigoths[152] there were doubtless many silk tunics.

The Huns obtained silk in various ways. First, they brought it home from their raids. Like the Goths in Italy, the Huns, while they were still in Roman territory, bought silk from Roman dealers. *Unde pellito serica vestimenta?* asked Maximus of Turin.[153] Second, the Huns bought silk at the fairs; in the preceding centuries silk reached the barbarians in the steppe via the cities on the Euxine; silk was found near Kerch in the Crimea,[154] in a Late Sarmatian grave at Marienthal (now Sovetskoe) on the Big Karman River in the former German Volga Republic[155] and in a grave at Shipovo.[156] Finally, the emperor sent silk as gifts to the Hun nobles and Attila, as he later sent silk clothes to the Avar caganus.[157] Attila lay in state in a silk tent.[158] Edecon and Orestes may have looked strange in the Roman silk garments, but they evidently liked them.[159]

[*Note 148 is missing in the manuscript.—Ed.*]

[149] See the excellent study of the silks in the Hsiung-nu tombs at Noin-Ula by Lubo-Lesnichenko 1961.

[150] Zosimus V, 41, 4.

[151] Olympiodorus, fr. 24, Henry 1959, 175_{21-22}.

[152] Themistius, *Or.* X, 135b.

[153] *Homily* XVIII, 3, *PL* 57, 478; *CCSL* XXIII, 69. On the date, the end of 408, see Maenchen-Helfen 1964, 114-115.

[154] Toll 1927, 85-92; Lubo-Lesnichenko 1961, 29, pl. 9.

[155] Rau 1927, 68.

[156] Minaeva 1929, 199.

[157] Menander, fr. 5, *EL* $442_{31} = FHG$ IV, 203.

[158] *Getica* 256. Altheim (1962, 2, 83) translates *intra tenturia serica* by *unter chinesischer Seide* and concludes therefore that Attila got the silk from the Hephthalites, the alleged "mother people" of the Huns. But *sericum*, whatever its etymology may be, means just "silk." The silk most probably came from Constantinople where the silk factories were under the supervision of the *comes sacrarum largitonum* (*Cod. Theodos.* X, 20, 13, A.D. 406).

[159] Priscus, *EL* 123_{30}.

WINE

If Asterius of Amasea is to be believed, the Huns on the Black Sea did not drink wine,[160] probably not because they did not like it but because they could not get it. It was very different in Hungary. From Priscus we learn that at Attila's court wine was drunk in great quantities. Onegesius' wife offered Attila a goblet of wine. At the great banquet, before food was served, Attila toasted all the prominent guests, including the Roman ambassadors, with wine, and they in turn, toasted the king. After the first course again wine was drunk, and after the second, and when the Romans left, late at night, the Huns kept on drinking. At the dinner in Adamis' house each guest was given a beaker of wine from the others, and he had to reciprocate. As neither the Huns nor their subjects, with the possible exception of the few Romans, knew how to grow grapes and make wine, it is evident that wine was imported to Hunnia in great quantities. In the sixth century, the Massagetae—Huns in the Byzantine army—were the most intemperate drinkers,[161] even worse than the Goths.[162]

---

[160] *Homily* XV, *PG* 40, 381.
[161] Procopius III, 12, 8.
[162] *Bibunt ut Gothi* (Greg. Tur., *Dialogi* I, 9, quoted by Momigliano 1955, 207).

IV. Society

IN NO area of Hunnic studies is the discrepancy between the few facts and the theories built on them as striking as in the study of Hun society. The temptation to force the Huns into the favorite socioeconomic category of the student seems to be irresistible. Later Byzantine authors often transcribe the titles of the barbarians; they speak of the χαγάνος of the Avars, the βοιλᾶς of the Bulgars, and the τουδοῦνος of the Khazars. Priscus used only Greek words for the ranks and titles of the Huns. What word he rendered by βασιλεύς is not known. But some modern authors call Attila "kagan" as if they had been with Priscus at his court and, knowing Hunnish, understood how his subjects addressed the king. Others, lumping together all Eurasian nomads and seminomads, from the Scythians to the Kazakhs of the nineteenth century, construct what they call the nomadic society, throwing around supposedly technical terms like *il* and *ordu*. The worst sinner in this respect was T. Peisker, who still has his followers.[1] Thompson views the Huns as a howling mass of half-naked savages. In his tendency to push not only the Huns but also their allies way down the ladder of evolution, Thompson even mistranslates the texts. He refers to Sozomen IX, 5: "The ecclesiastical historian saw numbers of them [Sciri] scattered over the foothills and spurs of Mount Olympus in Bithynia, presumably acting as shepherds on Imperial estates."[2] Actually, Sozomen saw them tilling the soil, γεωργοῦντας. Soviet historians find for the Huns a place in the unilinear evolution of social functions drawn

---

[*The footnotes for this section were, in part, hand-written and sometimes difficult to interpret. They are to be used with caution.—Ed.*]

[1] Some of their writings on the Huns are quoted by Rafikov in *Voprosy istorii* 5, 1952, 126-131.

[2] Thompson 1948, 199.

up by Lewis Morgan and more or less faithfully followed by Engels. The Huns are said to have been in the last stage of "barbarism," when "gentile society" developed into "military democracy," which Engels characterized as follows:

> The military commander, the council, and the popular assembly formed the organs of military democracy, military because war and the organization of war were now the regular functions of life of the people. The wealth of their neighbors excited the greed of the peoples, who began to regard acquisition of wealth as one of the main purposes in life. They were barbarians: plunder appeared to them easier and even more honorable than productive work. War, once waged simply to avenge aggression or as a means of enlarging territory that had become inadequate, was now waged for the sake of plunder alone, and became a regular profession. ... The growth of slavery had already begun to brand working for a living as slavish and more ignominious than engaging in plunder.[3]

According to Engels, the Greeks in the heroic age were typical representatives of military democracy. The Soviet historians, untiringly repeating that the Huns had reached the same stage,[4] of course do not even try to prove it. Attila and Agamemnon shared the initial vowel in their names, but this is about all. If all peoples who under military leaders robbed their neighbors lived in a military democracy, Assyrians, cattle-raising Zulus, agricultural Aztecs, and the Viking pirates would belong together. After many attempts to define military democracy more precisely, it eventually has become an empty phrase. It is, we are now told, a type of political superstructure which does *not* reflect the processes going on in the economic base.[5]

The only Soviet student of the Huns who took Engels seriously was A. N. Bernshtam. Because the society that follows another is supposed to represent a higher stage in the development of mankind, the young military democracy of the Huns must in its time have played a progressive role. Bernshtam gave the concept of progress an original twist. He did not maintain that the Huns themselves were more developed than the peoples they conquered. Their contribution to progress was rather an indirect one: they helped to break down the "slave-holding" societies, including the Roman Empire, thereby clearing the way for more progres-

---

[3] Engels, *The Origin of the Family, Private Property and the State*, 268-269.
[4] *E.g.*, N. Ia. Merpert in *Ocherki istorii SSSR* 2, 153, and Pletneva, *SA* 3, 1964, 343.
[5] *VDI*, 1, 1952, 101-109; *Voprosy istorii* 5, 1952; *Bol'shevik* 11, 1952, 68-72.

sive feudalism. This was the thesis which Bernshtam presented in his *Ocherki po istorii gunnov* (*History of the Huns in Outline*).

He was furiously attacked.[6] It is true, Bernshtam committed some bad blunders;[7] instead of referring to the sources, he often quoted from hopelessly obsolete compilations. But his main sin was to put the Huns on the same level as the young barbarian peoples, the Slavic and—though this was merely whispered aside—the Germanic tribes. Like their successors, the Avars, Pechenegs, and Mongols, the Huns were the arch enemies of the peace-loving nations of eastern Europe. Bernshtam's book was taken out of circulation.

The obligation to stay within the Marxian framework leads to strange results. The Hungarian historian and philologist Harmatta published a number of stimulating articles on Hun society, with long quotations from the original Sanskrit, Akkadian, Pehlevi, and Sogdian.[8] After carefully weighing the pros and contras he came to the conclusion that Hun society became a state in 445 A.D., give or take one or two years. Yet the recalcitrant Huns refused to fit into one of the stages permitted by Engels. Hun society, Harmatta admitted, "had no definite character of its own."[9]

The meaning of the terms for the social institutions of the Huns has to be established by the context. $\Lambda o\gamma\acute{a}\delta\epsilon\varsigma$, say the dictionaries, means "picked men." Is this the meaning of the word in Priscus? Because students of the Huns read the early Byzantine texts as if they had been written by Thucydides, their works contain a number of misunderstandings. In the following I shall deal only with Thompson's and Harmatta's views of Hunnic society. They are the only authors who gave the subject some thought.

Priscus, the only writer to speak about the *logades* of the Huns, calls five of them by name:

1. Onegesius, "who held power second only to Attila among the Scythians." *EL* 134$_2$.

2. Scottas, Onegesius' brother. He boasted that he could "speak or act on equal terms with his brother before Attila." *EL* 127$_{18,23}$.

3. Edecon, a famous warrior of Hun descent. *EL* 124$_{6-7}$.

4. Berichus, lord of many villages. *EL* 147$_{10-11}$.

5. Orestes, a Roman from Pannonia, Attila's secretary. *EL* 125$_{22}$.

---

[6] Harmatta 1951, 139-142.

[7] For instance, he took Aetius and the Visigothic king Theoderic to be the same man.

[8] Harmatta 1951 and 1952.

[9] Harmatta 1952.

The word occurs also in eight additional passages:

6. Edecon and Orestes and Scottas "and the other *logades*." *EL* 125₂₂.

7. "The *logades* of the Scythians, after Attila, took the captives from the well-to-do because they sold for the most money." *EL* 135₃₂-136₂.

8. Onegesius took council "with the *logades*." *EL* 145₃₀.

9. The Roman ambassadors went to the house of Adamis "with some of the *logades* of the people." *EL* 146₉₋₁₀.

10. Attila ordered "all the *logades* around him" to show friendship to Maximinus. *EL* 147₂₆.

11. Chrysaphius inquired whether admission to Attila's presence was easy for Edecon, who answered that he was an intimate friend of Attila and entrusted with his bodyguard, "along with the *logades* chosen for this [duty]." *EL* 580₂₀₋₂₅.

12. Chelchal summoned the *logades* of the Goths. *EL* 589₂₀₋₂₁.

13. Kunchas, king of the Kidaritae, wishing to punish Peirozes for his falsehood, "pretended to have a war with his neighbors and to need men, not soldiers, suited for battle, for he had an infinite number of these, but men who would prosecute the wars as generals for him." Peirozes sent to him three hundred *logades*. *EL* 154₂₀₋₂₁.

In Thompson's opinion the *logades* were the hinge on which the whole administration of the Hunnic empire turned. He identified them with Attila's ἐπιτήδειοι and the οἰκεῖοι καὶ λοχαγοί of Uldin. They were supposed to have ruled over specific portions of the empire, kept order among the subject nations, and collected tribute and foodstuff from them. During a campaign they commanded not only specific squadrons of the Huns assigned to them, but also contingents of subject warriors provided by the districts they possessed. Thompson did not translate the word as if *logades* were a technical term; he even speaks of the time when the *logades* were "instituted."

Harmatta first stressed the fact that the *logades* mentioned by Priscus had not Hunnish but Germanic and Greek names; Attila was supposed to have liquidated the old tribal organization and to have ruled with the help of the *logades*. Later Harmatta rejected Thompson's equation of the *logades* with ἐπιτήδειοι, which, indeed, means nothing more specific than "friends," and also of Uldin's οἰκεῖοι καὶ λοχαγοί, his "kinsmen and officers." He dropped the dependency of the *logades* on Attila. Now they were supposed to have been the ruling class, comparable to the *vazurgān uδ āzāδān*, "the great and noble" of Sassanian Persia, or the *bäglär* of Turkish society in the sixth century. For the rest, Harmatta agreed with Thompson. His *logades* likewise ruled over their territories, collected taxes, and so forth.

Altheim takes the *logades* for "a new closed estate." They got their name, he says, because they were, literally, picked by Attila,[10] who employed them in his campaigns, on diplomatic missions, and for collecting taxes.

These scholars read too much into Priscus. He says nothing about the collection of taxes. He mentions that Berichus was lord over many villages, but it does not follow that all *logades*, even Attila's secretary, were large landowners. The wretched Goths who in the late 460's roved through the northern Balkans had their *logades*. As they had no land— they *asked* the Romans for land—their *logades* could not own large estates; nor did they have a king to "select" the *logades*. Fascinated by the word which they cannot find in the writings of Priscus' time, Thompson, Harmatta, and Altheim turn it into the designation of a well-defined social group.

Actually, since the third century, *logas* means just "prominent, outstanding, distinguished." In Περὶ ἐπιδεικτικῶν (ch. III, Menander), Rhetor speaks about the ἄνδρες λογάδες of Athens; they were not picked by anyone, owned neither land nor horses, but were full of wisdom and virtue, σοφίας καὶ ἀρετῆς τροφίμους.[11] Basil, the older brother of Gregory of Nyssa, was λογὰς ἀνὴρ καὶ ὀνομαστὸς κατὰ φιλοσοφίαν.[12] In his refutation of Julian's treatise *Against the Galileans*, Cyril of Alexandria, Priscus' contemporary, praises the *logades* of the Greeks, again neither landowners nor military leaders; the *logades* are Plato and Plutarch.[13] In the eighth century, Theophanes, probably quoting an earlier work, wrote of the *logades* in Antioch who followed Nestorius' doctrine.[14] I learn from Professor I. Ševčenko that in the Russian chronicles *logades* is rendered by *luchshie lyudi*, "the best people." In his translation of Anna Comnena's *Alexiad*, B. Leib translates *logades* by "elite."[15] This is also the meaning in modern Greek: οἱ τοῦ ἔθνους λογάδες are "the elite of the nation."[16]

There is no evidence that these prominent people of the Huns had anything in common except prominence. Had Priscus written Latin, he probably would have called them *optimates*. As used by Ammianus Marcellinus, *optimates* comes very close to *logades*. Ammianus was well informed about the ranks among the Alamanni against whom Julian fought.

---

[10] Altheim 1962, 4, 281-286. As so often, he misunderstood the Greek text.
[11] Spengel 1856, 3, 394.
[12] Gregory of Nyssa (d. 394) in the sermon against usury (*PG* 46, 433).
[13] *PG* 76, 908.
[14] A.M. 5925, *PG* 108, 241a.
[15] Leib 1945, *passim*.
[16] Pervonaoglu 1904, 465.

They were led by Chnodomarius and Serapio, *potestate excelsiores ante alios reges*; then came five kings, *potestate proximi*, then *regales*, a long train of *optimates*, and only then came the commoners (XVI, 12, 25-26). The Sarmatians in Hungary had *regales*, *subreguli*, and *optimates* (XVII, 12, 9, 12). It would seem that Ammianus' *optimates* stood just one step above the common people. But speaking about the *optimates* of the Armenians (XXVII, 12, 2) and Goths (XXXI, 4, 1), Ammianus evidently not only had the lower nobility in mind but all men who had something to say. Emperor Valens refused to talk to the people whom Fritigern sent to him as envoys because they were of low rank; he demanded that the Goths send *optimates*, prominent men (XXXI, 12, 13). Hortarius, one of the two Alamannic primates whom Valentinianus appointed to commands in his army, was in treacherous contact with King Macrianus and the barbarian *optimates* (XXIX, 4, 7); here again *optimates* means simply prominent people or, as we may now say, *logades*. To the Hunnic *logades* correspond the κορυφαῖοι of the Goths.[17]

Priscus was well aware that not all the prominent people at Attila's court had the same rank. He noticed that Onegesius sat at the right of the king, "the more honorable side," and others, like Berichus, at the left. Bigilas told him that the Hun Edecon was far superior to the Roman Orestes. But Priscus was not much interested in the finer differences among the prominent men. The Roman ambassadors had, first and last, to do with Attila, and besides him no one really counted. Only what Priscus says about the Akatir[18] gives us some information about the structure of Hun society.

The Akatir, a Hunnic people, ἔθνος, were divided into tribes and clans under numerous rulers, πολλῶν κατὰ φῦλα καὶ γένη ἀρχόντων. Kuridachus was the highest in power, πρεσβύτερον ἐν τῇ ἀρχῇ. The others were coregents, συμβασιλεύοντες.[19]

[*There is a break in the manuscript here.—Ed.*]

This is one of the rare cases in early Byzantine literature in which the context permits one to determine the meaning of the terms for the subdivisions of barbarian peoples and their leaders. The people, ἔθνος, consists of tribes, φῦλα, and clans, γένη. Kuridachus is (1) a βασιλεύς of the Akatir; (2) an ἄρχων; (3) as a leader of a φῦλον, a φύλαρχος.

Thompson maintains that Olympiodorus distinguished carefully between the military commander of a confederacy of barbarian tribes and the military leader of an individual tribe, calling the former φύλαρχος and the lat-

---

[17] *EL* 130₇₋₂₀.
[18] *Ibid.*, 130₇₋₁₀.
[19] *Ibid.*, 130₁₀₋₂₀.

ter ῥήξ.[20] He is mistaken. ῾Ρήξ is, of course, Latin *rex*, whatever its original relationship to Celtic *rigs* may be.[21] The Latin writers of the fourth and fifth centuries make no distinction between the *reges* beyond the frontiers. Ammianus Marcellinus calls the ruler of the Burgundians (XXVIII, 5, 10, 13, 14), Quadi (XVII, 12, 21), and wild Moorish tribes (XXIX, 5, 51) *reges* as well as the seven rulers of the Alamanni (XVI, 12, 25) and the great Shapur, partner of the Stars, brother of the Sun and Moon (XVII, 5, 3). The word, in the same meaning, was taken over by the Greeks. In a letter, written in 404, John Chrysostom speaks of the ῥήξ of the Goths in the Crimea.[22] At about the same time Olympiodorus, who was fond of Latin words, talks about the first among the ῥῆγες of the Huns; they were, in their way, great lords, and the translation "king" seems quite in place. But Olympiodorus calls also the condottiere Sarus, *dux* of a small group of Goths,[23] a ῥήξ.[24] In Malalas, Brennus is *rhex* of the Gauls, Odovacar of the barbarians, the Vandal rulers are *rheges* of Africa or the Africans, those of the Ostrogoths *rheges* of Italy; Styrax and Glones are *rheges* of the Huns, and Boa is a *rhegissa*.[25] One can, if one so wishes, translate *rhex* by "king," but it seems preferable to transcribe the word. In any case, *rhex* in Olympiodorus is no more the military leader of a tribe than the Gothic ruler who asked for a new bishop for his people.

βασιλεύς is another term with two meanings. In official documents as, for example, in diplomatic notes, it was used exclusively for the Roman emperor.[26] The West Romans were afraid that some day Attila would insist on being addressed *basileus* instead of *magister militum*, his (strictly nominal) title.[27] It would be of interest to know how the East Romans addressed the king. They could have used such neutral terms as *hegemon* or *hegoumenos* of the Huns. After Bleda's death *monarchos* would have been an appropriate title; Priscus called the Persian king *monarchos*,[28] and Menander did not feel he had to explain why he wrote about the *monarchos* of the Langobards.[29] Attila could have been addressed as κατάρχων τῶν Οὔννων, as Theoderic Strabo was κατάρχων τῶν Γότθων; the Squinter

---

[20] Thompson 1948, 58.
[21] *Contra* Harmatta 1952, 291.
[22] *PG* 52, 618.
[23] He had between two hundred and three hundred men.
[24] μοίρας Γοτθικῆς ῥήξ.
[25] Malalas 184, 372, 373, 383, 414, 459, 450, 460.
[26] R. Helm 1932, 383, n. 2.
[27] Priscus, *EL* 142$_{12-15}$.
[28] *Ibid.*, 152$_{13}$, 586$_{21}$, 587$_{6}$.
[29] *Ibid.*, 454$_{23}$.

was also ἀρχηγός, even αὐτοκράτωρ,[30] a title usually reserved for the imperator.[31]

Harmatta thought that Attila was the first barbarian ruler whom the East Romans granted the title *basileus* because his

social standing, power and absolute rule was similar to the position held by the Roman emperor; only once the term basileus became current in connection with Attila, *i.e.*, with a barbarian ruler, the earlier sharp distinction between the Byzantine monarch and the barbarian kings became gradually obliterated in linguistic usage. This explains in Harmatta's opinion why Priscus applied the term basileus on one occasion to the king of the Franks and on another to the chieftains of the Acatziri.[32]

This sounds quite plausible, but it is not true. Harmatta overlooked the way authors, when they wrote history, spoke about barbarian kings. Had Eunapius been sent as ambassador to a Visigothic leader, he most certainly would not have addressed him as *basileus*. But writing about Athanaric, he did not hesitate to call him *basileus*.[33] The ruler of the Chamavi, Julian's enemies, was a *basileus*.[34] Eunapius wrote many years before Attila. And Priscus himself was rather generous in bestowing the title *basileus* on Hunnic as well as on other barbarian rulers. Attila was not the first king of the Huns. Ruga was also βασιλεύων.[35] The βασιλεῖα[36] of the Huns devolved on Attila *and* Bleda;[37] they are the βασιλεῖς of the Huns.[38] Priscus speaks not only of the kings of the Franks and Akatir but also of the kingdom, βασιλεία, of the Lazi in the Caucasus.[39] In the writings of the sixth century we read about the kings of the Auxumitae[40] and Iberians.[41] Here again these kings were not acknowledged as such by the East Romans, but this was of no concern to historians.

A third ambiguous term, whose meaning Thompson and Harmatta defined much too narrowly, is φύλαρχος. According to Thompson, in Olympiodorus *phylarchos* means the military leader of a confederacy of

---

[30] Malchus, fr. 2, *FHG* IV, 114.

[31] Plutarch, *Galba* I; Olympiodorus, fr. 12.

[32] Harmatta 1952, 296-297.

[33] *EL* 594$_{14}$.

[34] *Ibid.*, 591$_9$.

[35] *Ibid.*, 121$_4$.

[36] *Ibid.*, 121$_{18}$.

[37] Suidas, *s.v.* Ζέρκων, Adler 1938.

[38] *EL* 576$_2$.

[39] *Ibid.*, 584$_{17, 19, 26}$.

[40] *FHG* IV, 179 (Nonnosus).

[41] *EL* 390$_{10-16}$. (Petrus Patricius).

tribes. The word occurs in Olympiodorus five times. Alarich and Valia are *phylarchoi* of the Visigoths, Gunthiarius is the *phylarchos* of the Burgundians, and the Blemmyes have *phylarchoi* and *prophetae*, the priests of Isis.[42] There is no reason whatever to assume that in the fifth century the Visigoths and Burgundians were confederacies of tribes.[43] And the Blemmyes did not consist of confederacies which in their turn consisted of so and so many tribes; their *phylarchois* were clearly tribal leaders. Even further from the truth is Harmatta's definition. "The word phylarchos," he says, "denotes an official title given by the East Roman or Byzantine emperors to the leaders of the allied barbaric peoples, at least since the end of the fourth century." But this is not enough. He continues: "These barbarian chieftains were given Roman auxilia, money, provisions, Roman advisers, and Roman dignities—in a word everything was done to stabilize their authority and power against the other members of their tribe."[44] Harmatta is mistaken; he refers to Olympiodorus. It is sufficient to read the first fragment on Alaric. Harmatta quotes only "Alarich, the phylarchus of the Goths." But in the following lines Olympiodorus narrates how this "ally" of the Romans takes Rome, sacks it ruthlessly, and carries Galla Placidia, the sister of the emperor, into captivity.

ARISTOCRACY

Above the common people, *qara budun*, as they are called in the Orkhon inscriptions, stood the noble families. Both Attila and his father were "well-born."[45] In 449, when Priscus met Attila, the king's beard was sprinkled with gray;[46] he cannot have been born later than about 400, his father about 370, or even earlier, which proves the existence of a hereditary aristocracy long before the Huns broke into the Ukraine.[47] How large it was, we have no means to determine. Priscus mentions noblemen only two times more. Berich, a prominent man, lord over many villages, was "well-born."[48] Somewhat more revealing is a passage preserved in Suidas: Bleda gave Zerco "from among the well-born women a wife who had been one of the attendants of the queen but who, on account of some misdemeanor, was no longer in her service."[49] The daughters of

---

[42] Olympiodorus, fr. 3, 17, 18, 31, 37.

[43] Thompson (1961), 20 ff. arbitrarily turns the council to which, according to Claudian *Bell. Goth.*, 479-480, Alaric summons *primos suorum* to a confederate council.

[44] Harmatta 1952, 292-293.

[45] Εὖ δε καὶ αὐτὸν φύντα καὶ τὸν πατέϱα Μουνδίουχον (EL $581_{23\text{-}24}$).

[46] *Raris barba, canis asperus* (*Getica* 182).

[47] *Contra* Thompson 1948, 162-163.

[48] EL 143_{25}.

[49] Suidas, *s.v.* Ζέϱκων, Adler 1938.

noblemen were, thus, also "well-born" but could be married to commoners, in this case the feeble-minded court jester, who was not even a Hun.

Provided that what Ennodius said about the Bulgars, whom he equated with the Huns, can be transferred to the latter, the distance between noblemen and commoners was apparently not great. In his *Panegyric on Theoderic*, Ennodius describes those Bulgars whom the Ostrogoths fought in Pannonia in 486 as a nation in which the man who killed the most enemies had the highest rank; their leaders were not born to nobility but became noblemen on the battle field.[50] This was, of course, seen through Gothic eyes. Theoderic was a scion of the half-divine Amalungs, the Goths had their great noble families, and the relative social mobility of the Bulgars must have struck them as sheer savagery.

SLAVES

Some of the captives whom the Huns led away from the Balkan provinces and Italy were ransomed by their relatives and friends. Others served under their masters in the Hun armies until they were able to buy their freedom with their share in the booty.[51] But most captives were sold to Roman slave dealers either at the annual fairs or, before these were held regularly, wherever the Huns had close contact with the Romans, even while the invaders were still in Roman territory. In 408, the Romans bought so many captives from Alaric's Visigoths that a law had to be issued to specify the conditions under which these unfortunates could regain their freedom.[52] According to a homily of Maximus of Turin, the barbarians sold country lads to Roman slave dealers not from distant districts but from villages near Turin.[53] It may be assumed that the same sordid transactions took place during the Hunnic raids south of the Danube.

The Huns sold most of their captives not merely because they "burned with an infinite thirst for gold."[54] They themselves had little use for them. In the economy of pastoral nomads only a small number of slaves can be usefully employed; besides, it is difficult to prevent their escape. This

---

[50] *Haec est natio, qui ante te [i.e., Theodericum] fuit omne quod voluit in qua titulos obtinuit qui emit aduersariorum sanguine dignitatem, apud quam campus uulgator [a pun] natalium nam cuius plus rubuerunt tela luctamine, ille putatus est sine ambage sublimior* (Vogel 1885, *MGH AA* 7, 205_{20}).

[51] Like the renegade who told Priscus how happy he was among the Huns (*EL* 135_{10}-138_{15}).

[52] *Const. Sirmond.* XVI, a fragment in *Cod. Theodos.* V, 7, 2. They had to restore their purchase price to the purchaser or "render recompense for the favor by their labor, subservience, or services during a period of five years."

[53] Cf. Maenchen-Helfen 1964, 114-115.

[54] Ammianus XXXI, 2, 11.

was true for the Mongols in Chinghiz Khan's times as well as for the Kazakhs of the eighteenth and nineteenth centuries.[55] It was also true for the Huns. They had domestic slaves. Priscus saw two slaves who had killed their masters and were caught;[56] the plural indicates that they were the only slaves of their masters. At Attila's court Priscus recognized the captives from their ragged clothes and the squalor of their heads.[57] Presumably they were held for eventual ransom. Once they became members of a Hunnic household they apparently were well treated. The captives from Aquileia took part in religious ceremonies; those kept by Christian subjects of the Huns were baptized.

---

[55] See Semeniuk's excellent article of 1958, 55-82.

[56] *EL* 147$_{17-20}$.

[57] *Ibid.*, 135$_{18-20}$.

V. Warfare

In the seventy years between the first clash of the marauders with Roman frontier troops and the battle at the *locus Mauriacus*, the warfare of the Huns remained essentially the same. Attila's horsemen were still the same mounted archers who in the 380's had ridden down the Vardar Valley and followed the standards of Theodosius. Their tactics were determined by the weapons they carried, and as these did not change, the Huns fought at Metz and Orléans as they had fought at Pollentia. It is true that in Attila's army there were men who could build and serve siege engines,[1] clearly not Huns but Roman prisoners or deserters. Unlike Alaric, who boasted that Thrace forged him spears, swords, and helmets,[2] Attila had no Roman *fabricae* work for him. But at least some Huns, like the Goths in 376, must have "plundered the dead bodies and armed themselves in Roman equipment,"[3] and others may have fought with Persian weapons. But all this has little significance. Had Priscus in the 470's described the weapons and tactics of the Huns, he would have written more or less as Ammianus Marcellinus wrote in 392:

When provoked they sometimes fight *singly but they enter the battle in tactical formation,[4] while their medley of voices makes

---

[1] Siege of Naissus, Priscus, *HGM* I, 279; siege of Aquileia, *Getica* 221.

[2] Claudian, *Bell. Goth.* 536-537.

[3] Ammianus XXXI, 6, 3, on the mutinous Goths in 376; after the battle at Marcianople, the Visigoths "put on the Romans' arms" (XXXI, 5, 9). In Conçesti a Roman officer's helmet was found (Matsulevich 1929, 125, pl. 49); in a Sarmatian grave at stanitsa Vozdvizhenskaya, Kuban, a Roman pilum (*OAK* 1899, 45).

[4] *Et pugnant non numquam lacessiti, sed ineuntes proelia cuneatim* in Pighi's edition makes no sense. Rolfe, omitting *sed*, translates, "They also sometimes fight when pro-

201

a savage noise. And as they are lightly equipped for swift motion, and unexpected in action, they purposely divide suddenly in scattered bands[5] and attack, rushing about in disorder here and there, dealing terrific slaughter; and because of their extraordinary rapidity of movement, they cannot be discerned when they break into a rampart or pillage an enemy's camp. And on this account you would not hesitate to call them the most terrible of all warriors, because they fight from a distance with missiles having sharp bone, instead of their usual points, joined to the shafts with wonderful skill; then they gallop over the intervening spaces[6] and fight hand to hand with swords regardless of their own lives; and while the enemy are guarding against wounds from sword-thrusts, they throw strips of cloth plaited into nooses over their opponents and so entangle them that they fetter their limbs and take from them the power of riding or walking.

The Goths from whom Ammianus gathered his information were even after so many years still deafened by the wild howls[7] of the Huns and dazed by the incredible speed of their attacks. About the social and political structure of the Huns the Goths knew next to nothing. They could not fail to notice that the Huns formed *cunei* but whether these consisted of the members of one clan or tribe,[8] or were formed *ad hoc*, they could not tell Ammianus. From a passage in Procopius it appears that in the initial phase of a battle hereditary privileges played some role with the later Huns.[9] The same may well have been true for their predecessors;

---

voked, and then they enter the battle drawn up in wedge-shaped masses." But the MS reading *lacessitis dineuntis* leaves no doubt that the librarian to whom we owe the Vatican codex Lat. 2969 rightly wrote *lacessiti sed ineuntes*. Entering the battle the Huns fought *cuneatim*, which means in tactical units. This requires in the first part of the sentence a word which characterizes the Hunnic way of fighting when "provoked." It must be the opposite of *cuneatim*. I suggest **singulatim*.

[5] Following Clark, Rolfe emended *iugescunt* to *incessunt*, which is better than Pighi's *vigescunt*.

[6] The lacuna of thirteen letters between *distint* and *comminus* is annoying but the meaning is clear. Brackman's *distantiis decursis* seems better than Pighi's *distinctis, corpora figunt*.

[7] For the howling of the Avars, cf. Suidas, *s.v.* ἐπιδουπῆσαι, λυκηθμός. The Magyars howled "like wolves", cf. I. Duĭchev, *BZ* 52, 1959, 91.

[8] The Langobards fought κατὰ φυλᾶς (Mauricius, *Strateg.* XI, 14).

[9] "Now there was a certain man among the Massagetae, well gifted with courage and strength of body, the leader of a few men. This man had the privilege handed down from his father and ancestors to be the first in all the Hunnic armies to attack the enemy. For it was not lawful to a man of the Massagetae to strike first in battle and capture one of the enemies until, indeed, someone from his house began the battle with the enemy" (III, 18, 13). Cf. Ammianus XIX, 2, 5, on the opening of the battle by the Chionite king Grumbates.

the *čur* probably handed down their rank for generations.[10] Strangely, Ammianus did not mention the feigned flight, a stratagem of the Huns as of all steppe warriors.[11] Still, incomplete as his description is, it shows that the tactics of the Huns was not markedly different from those of the other mounted bowmen of northern Eurasia. The volleys of arrows with which the enemy was showered were followed by hand-to-hand fighting.

I pass over the "war crimes" of which the Huns were so often accused. In an apocalypsis of the seventh century, a Syriac cleric let his fancy run a little too wild: the Huns (he probably meant the Hephthalites) roast pregnant women, cut out the fetus, put it in a dish, pour water over it, and dip their weapons into the brew; they eat the flesh of children and drink the blood of women.[12] Most Germans of the Folkwandering period behaved in no way more humanely than the Huns. In 406, the Germanic invaders of Gaul killed the hermits, burned the priests alive, raped the nuns, devastated the vineyards, and cut down the olive trees.[13]

HORSES

The Huns "are almost glued to their horses, which are hardy, it is true, but ugly, and sometimes they sit on them woman-fashion, and thus perform their ordinary tasks. And when deliberations are called for about weighty matters, they all consult for a common object in that fashion" (Ammianus, XXXI, 2, 6).

The Huns, indeed, carried on their negotiations with the Roman diplomats on horseback.[14] The Sarmatians in South Russia and the Lazi in the Caucasus often rode side saddle also.[15]

The characterization of the Hun horses as *deformes* is too vague to draw conclusions from it.[16] To a Roman most steppe horses must have looked as misshapen as the horses of the Scythians, with their short legs and big

---

[10] It may be assumed that the standard bearers—provided the Huns actually had them—were also of noble origin.

[11] Zosimus V, 20; Agathias I, 22. Cf. Darkó 1935, 443-469; T. Sulimirski, *Revue internationale d'histoire militaire* 3, 1952, 447-461.

[12] *S. Ephraem Syri Hymni et Sermones* 3, Lamy 1889, 194-200.

[13] *Carmen de divina providentia* 29, 38, 43-56, *PL* 51, 617-618, written about 415; cf. Courcelle 1948, 74-76. See also the letter of Bishop Maximus of Auranches to Theophilus, patriarch of Alexandria (S. Morin, *Revue Charlemagne* 2, 1912, 36).

[14] Priscus, *EL* 122₁.

[15] See the wall painting in a catacomb at Kerch (Minns 1913, 314, fig. 224), datable to the end of the first or the beginning of the second century. Gobazes, king of the Lazi, sat on his horse side saddle (Agathias III, 4, ed. Bonn, 144).

[16] Jerome, who contrasted the Hunnic *caballi* to the Roman *equi* (*Comm. in Isaiam*, *PL* 24, 113), merely paraphrased Ammianus; cf. Maenchen-Helfen 1955a, 393.

heads,[17] or those of the Sigynnae, shaggy and snub-nosed, allegedly too small to ride upon.[18]

The only author to give a good description of the Hun horse is Vegetius. For a long time, he complains in the prologue to the second book of his *Mulomedicina*, veterinary medicine has been steadily declining. Horse doctors are so poorly paid that no one devotes himself any longer to a proper study of veterinary medicine. Of late, however, following the example set by the Huns and other barbarians, people have altogether ceased to consult veterinarians. They leave the horses on the pasture the year round and give them no care whatever, not realizing what incalculable harm they thereby do themselves. These people overlook that the horses of the barbarians are quite different from Roman horses. Hardy creatures, accustomed to cold and frost, the horses of the barbarians need neither stables nor medical care. The Roman horse is of a much more delicate constitution; unless it has good shelter and a warm stable, it will catch one illness after another.[19] Although Vegetius stresses the superiority of the Roman horse, its intelligence, docility, and noble character, he concedes that the Hun horse has its good points. Like the Persian, Epirotic, and Sicilian horses it lives long.[20] In the classification of various breeds according to their fitness for war, Vegetius gives the Hun horse the first place because of its patience, perseverance, and its capacity to endure cold and hunger.[21] As his description shows, Vegetius, who probably kept a few Hun horses himself,[22] had ample opportunity to observe them. They have, he says, great hooked heads, protruding eyes, narrow nostrils, broad jaws, strong and stiff necks, manes hanging below the knees, overlarge ribs, curved backs, bushy tails, cannon bones of great strength, small pasterns, wide-spreading hooves, hollow loins; their bodies are angular, with no fat on the rump or the muscles of the back, their stature inclining to length rather than to height, the belly drawn, the bones huge. The very thinness of these horses is pleasing, and there is beauty even in their ugliness. Vegetius adds that they are quiet and sensible and bear wounds well.[23]

---

[17] See the realistic representation on the base from Chertomlyk, best reproduced in *Izv. RAIMK* 2, 1922, pl. 8.

[18] Strabo XI, 11, 8; Markwart 1932b, 2.

[19] Vegetius Renatus, Lommatzsch 1903, 95-96.

[20] *Ibid.*, III, 7, 1.

[21] *Ibid.*, III, 6, 2. Cf. Ennodius' praise of the *equus Huniscus: cana pruinosis mandentem gramina lustris* (*Carmen* II, 90, *MGH AA* 169).

[22] Vegetius IV, 6, Lommatzsch 1903.

[23] *Ibid.*, III, 6, 5. I follow J. K. Anderson's translation of 1961, 24. Thomas Blunderville's translation of 1580 is quoted by Ridgeway 1906, 319; German translations in Hauger 1921, 39-40, and Hörnschemeyer 1929, 46.

Although this description, in spite of its preciseness, does not permit a determination of the type of the Hun horse, it clearly precludes the Przewalsky horse, which has an upright mane and a turniplike tail with short hair, only the end part being longhaired.[24] A bronze plaque from the Ordos region (fig. 1) shows a warrior with a pointed cap and a small bow

FIG. 1. A horse with a "hooked" head and bushy tail represented on a bronze plaque from the Ordos region. From Egami 1948, pl. 4.

on a horse with a "hooked" head and a long bushy tail.[25] The man might be a Hsiung-nu. Another bronze from the river Yar in the former gubernie Tomsk, looks very much like the Ordos horse.[26] It seems, however,

---

The passage on the Hun horse furnishes additional proof of the correctness of Seeck's identification of Vegetius' *imperator invictus* in the *Epit. rei milit.* with Valentinian III (*Hermes* 2, 1876, 61-83). Had the *Epitome* and the *Mulomedicina* been written under Theodosius I, as recently again Mazzarino assumed (see Gianelli and Mazzarino 1956, 542-543), the pernicious example of the Huns could not have had its effect on so many Romans in barely fifteen years, unless the Romans began to trade with the Huns two years after Adrianople, which is most unlikely.

[24] My late friend Professor Franz Hančar obligingly called my attention to this difference.

[25] Egami 1948, pl. 4.

[26] *OAK* 1892 (1894), 72, fig. 39. The horse on a sacral bronze from Issyk (*KS* 59, 154, f. 6612) also has a big head and a strong neck.

that the Hsiung-nu had horses of various breeds,[27] among them one with an upright mane,[28] the opposite of the Hun horse with the mane "hanging below the knees." The "typical" Hun horse may have been not much different from some of the Hsiung-nu and the Scythian horses.

The Huns were superior horsemen. Sidonius compared them with centaurs: "Scarce had the infant learnt to stand without his mother's aid when a horse takes him on his back. You would think that the limbs of man and horse were born together, so firmly does the rider always stick to the horse; any other folk is carried on horseback, this folk lives there."[29] The horsemanship of the Huns and Alans was unsurpassed.[30]

As the Huns had no spurs, they had to urge the horses to a faster pace by using whips, handles of which were found in many graves.[31] So far no stirrups have been found which could be assigned to the Huns. If the Huns had them, they must have been of perishable material, wood or leather. A potent argument against the assumption that the Huns had stirrups is the fact that the Germanic horsemen rode without them for centuries after the fall of Attila's kingdom. Unlike the composite bow, leather or wooden stirrups could have been easily copied. But the specific factor that gave the Hun archers an advantage even over the best troops in the Roman armies *may* have been the stirrup. László rightly stresses the stability which stirrups give to the mounted bowmen.[32]

"The soldiers of Rome," wrote Jerome in the summer of 396, "conquerors and lords of the world, now are conquered by those, tremble and shrink in fear at the sight of those who cannot walk on foot and think themselves as good as dead if once they reach the ground."[33] Jerome's odd description of the Huns was not based on observation; he never had

---

[27] The horses kept in the Hsiung-nu settlement on the Ivolga were of the same height as those of the Buryats and northern Yakuts; Garutt and Iur'ev 1959, 81-82.

[28] Maenchen-Helfen 1957a, 95-97.

[29] *Paneg. on Anthemius* 262-266.

[30] Vegetius, *Epit. rei milit.* III, 26: The Huns and Alans try in vain to imitate the Emperor's dexterity in horsemanship. Vegetius may have been inspired by Claudian, who, in *Fesceninna de nuptiis Honorii Augusti* I, 3, praised Honorius who rode more daringly than the Geloni, and in *4th Cons. Hon.* 542-543, extolled Honorius' horsemanship as superior to that of the Massagetae, Thessalians, and centaurs.

[31] J. Werner 1956, 53-54. For Scythian whips, see Rostovtsev 1931, 335, 454, 472.

[32] *AAH* 27, 1943, 158. *Contra* L. White's interpretation (1962, 139, n. 4). Alföldi (1967, 17) again maintains that the Scythians and Parthians used leather stirrups; he refers to the vase from Chertomlyk and the gold and silver coins of Q. Labienus (1967, pl. 9:9, 10).

[33] *Ep.* LX, 17.

seen a Hun. Like Eunapius[34] who too maintained that the Huns could not "stand firmly on the ground," Jerome copied Ammianus, who wrote: "Their shoes are formed upon no last, and so prevent their walking with free steps. For this reason they are not adapted to battles on foot."[35]

Ammianus' explanation of the peculiar gait of the Hun horsemen when they dismounted and walked is naïve. All equestrian nomads who spend a great part of their lives on horseback walk clumsily.[36] And yet the Hun shoes must have struck Ammianus' Gothic informants as strange, very different from their own. Apparently these shoes were fitted to the specific needs of the horsemen. So were those of the Magyars in the tenth century. Their soles were soft and pliable, so that the shoes could be slipped into the nearly round wooden and iron stirrups and be held firmly on them.[37] The stirrups from the Korean tombs of the fifth and sixth centuries were likewise round. Some of them were of iron,[38] but the most sumptuous ones, overlaid with gold, were made of wood. The gold shoes in these tombs are evidently replicas of leather shoes.[39] Had Ammianus seen them, he probably would have called them *formulis nullis aptati*.

The problem of the origin of the metal stirrup is still unsolved.[40] If the stray finds of miniature metal stirrups in the Minusinsk area could indeed be dated to the Syr or Uibat period (first three centuries A.D.) or even to the Syr period (first and second centuries A.D.),[41] they would be the earliest stirrups so far known, but their date is controversial.[42] No riders with stirrups are found in the numerous representations of northern barbarians in Chinese art of the Han period; the horsemen on the gold plaques in the collection of Peter I are not using stirrups either.

---

[34] The source of Zosimus IV, 20, 4; cf. Maenchen-Helfen 1955a, 392-393. Suidas, *s.v.* ἀκροσφαλεῖς, Adler 1939, I, 93, might be a quotation from Eunapius: "He gave order to march against the Huns, whose way of walking was unsteady and shaky. For without their horses the Huns would not easily move on the ground" (῾Ο δὲ ἐκέλευσε χωρεῖν ἐπὶ τοὺς ἄποδας καὶ ἀκροσφαλεῖς Οὔννους. ἄνευ γὰρ ἵππων οὐ ῥαδίως ἂν Οὔννους τὴν γῆν πατήσειεν).

[35] XXXI, 6.

[36] Cf. Radlov 1893, 412, on the Kirgiz. "The cowboy was a superb rider although a bowlegged walker" (Morrison 1965, 757).

[37] Count Zichy *apud* László, *AAH* 27, 1943, 123, n. 4. On the wooden stirrups of the Magyars, see Diénes 1958, 125-142; on Mongolian wooden stirrups, Köhalmi Katalin 1958, 143-147.

[38] Kim 1948, pl. 39.

[39] J. Werner 1956, pl. 67:1.

[40] L. White 1962, 14-26.

[41] Kyzlasov 1960, 140.

[42] S. I. Vaĭnshteĭn, *SE* 1963, 64-65.

Saddles

After his defeat at the *locus Mauriacus*, Attila "shut himself and his companions within the barriers of the camp, which he fortified with wagons. But it was said that the king remained supremely brave even in this extremity and had heaped up a funeral pyre of horse saddles [*equinis sellis construxisse pyram*] so that if the enemy should attack him, he was determined to cast himself into the flames, that none might have the joy of wounding him."[43]

This passage in the *Getica* has often been adduced[44] as proof that the Huns had wooden saddles. But shabracks could have burned as well. The history of the saddle of the Eurasian nomads is anything but clear. In the third and fifth kurgans at Pazyryk and at Shibe in the High Altai rather primitive saddles were found. They consisted of two big leather pillows, stuffed with deer hair and covered with felt; small pillows at the front and back of the big ones were stiffened and strengthened with narrow wooden frames, the forerunners of the wooden saddle bows.[45] To judge from the representations,[46] the Scythian saddles were like those of the Altaians. The same is true for the saddles of two bronze horsemen from western Siberia, probably of the same date as the Pazyryk kurgans, and on an often reproduced later golden belt buckle in the Siberian Treasure of Peter the Great.[47]

On the other hand, what looks like the wooden front bow of a miniature saddle from the Uibat chaatas in the Minusinsk region,[48] datable to the beginning of our era, was possibly part of a true wooden saddle.[49] The fragments of a saddle of about the same date from the Karakol River, not far from Shibe, might also come from a saddle with a tree between the two bows.[50] In Kenkol, Bernshtam found a curved piece of wood which could be the bow of a saddle.[51]

The Chinese of the Han period had wooden saddles. Although most representations of the horsemen do not permit one to decide whether they

---

[43] *Getica* 213.

[44] Most recently by J. Werner 1956, 51.

[45] Rudenko 1953, figs. 101-103, and 1960, 226-229.

[46] Drawing on an ivory from Kul Oba, Minns 1913, fig. 103; Chertomlyk vase, *ibid.*, 160, fig. 47.

[47] Rudenko 1962b, pl. 7:1, 7.

[48] Kiselev 1951, 434, pl. 36:1.

[49] This is the opinion of Kyzlasov 1960, 130.

[50] Kiselev 1951, 346-347, pl. 32:12.

[51] Bernshtam 1940, pl. 26; J. Werner 1956, pl. 35:1. The Parthian horse on an aureus of Q. Labienus has a saddle cloth, that on a denarius a true saddle; cf. Alföldi 1967, pl. 9:9, 10.

rode on saddles, the riderless horses on some reliefs from Shantung un-doubtedly were saddled; the front and back bows and the saddle tree are clearly delineated.[52] It has become almost a dogma to derive every-thing in the equipment of the cavalry of the Chinese from their barbarian neighbors. One should, therefore, expect that the Hsiung-nu and other nomads on the Chinese frontiers not only had saddles, but that they had them before the Chinese. The archaeological evidence does not bear out such an assumption. The barbarian hunters on the stamped tiles from Loyang have only saddle pads.[53] In the Hsiung-nu graves at Noin Ula, wooden frames of the front and back pillows were found; they show that the Hsiung-nu at the beginning of our era had shabracks like the people in Pazyryk.[54] Whether later the Hsiung-nu rode on wooden saddles we do not know. The Koreans of the fifth century did. A number of front and back bridges exist, made of gilt bronze and even of iron.[55]

The literary evidence, one short passage in Jordanes, is ambiguous and the little we know from the earlier finds in the eastern steppes sheds only a dim light on the saddles of the Huns. However, the gold, silver, and bronze mountings of saddle bows in nomadic graves of the fourth and fifth centuries leave no doubt that the Hun saddle did consist of a wooden tree, with a straight vertical bow in front and a somewhat larger inclined bow in the back. Such mountings were found in the Hun heartland in Hungary, where they were unknown before the coming of the Huns, and in the steppes as far east as the Volga; silver sheet mountings from the front bow of a wooden saddle were found in the grave of a Germanic war-rior at Blučina near Brno in Moravia; one find was made in Borovoe in Kazakhstan.[56] Ten out of the thirteen mountings were decorated with a scale pattern, impressively showing that they belong to the same group. The Hun saddles were presumably similar to the wooden saddle from Bo-rodaevka (formerly Boaro), Marks, Saratov, on the right bank of the Big

---

[52] *Corpus des pierres sculptées Han* 1 (Peking, 1950), 276-279. However, there are also relief slabs with representations of horses with shabracks, *e.g.* Hsiao t'ang shan, *Corpus* 1, 10. The horses of the Hsiung-nu on the same slab have definitely only saddle pads.

[53] W. C. White 1939, 33, 37, pl. 49, 72.

[54] Umehara 1960, 86, fig. 58; Rudenko 1962b, pl. 14:3. Rudenko (49-50) thinks the wooden bows are from a packsaddle.

[55] Vorob'ev 1961, pl. 34:2. At Potchevash on the lower Ob River, clay figures of horsemen with saddles with high front and back bows were found (*MIA* 35, 1953, 210, pl. 12); unfortunately they are not even approximately datable.

[56] J. Werner 1956, 51-52. For the silver sheet mountings on the wooden saddle in a Germanic grave of the later half of the fifth century at Blučina near Brno in Moravia, see Tihelka 1963, 496, fig. 11:1-4. The warrior was buried with bone slips from a com-posite bow.

Karaman River.[57] It lay in a grave of a man with an artificially deformed head. The burial rite (a horse skull and four feet cut off above the hoofs) and the furniture are characteristic for the post-Hunnic burials in the Volga steppes, preserving many elements of late Sarmatian civilization, datable between the fifth and the seventh centuries.[58] The saddle from Borodaevka is similar to some Sasanian saddles.[59]

Horse Marks

Where horses, owned by several families, clans, or tribes, graze over a common pasture, they are marked, either by cuts in the ears or by burning the hindquarters or shoulders with a hot iron. The former, more primitive, method is attested as early as the fourth century B.C.; all horses in the first and fifth kurgans at Pazyryk in the High Altai were earmarked.[60] Until recently the Kirghiz on the Manyshlak peninsula in the east side of the Caspian Sea used to cut triangles in the ears of their sheep and to notch the ears of their horses.[61]

Marco Polo wrote about the Mongols:

> The land is so secure that each lord or the other men who have animals in plenty, have them marked with their seal stamped on the hair, that is, the horses and the mares and camels and oxen and cows and other large beasts; then he lets them go safely to graze anywhere over the plains and over the mountains without a watchman; and if on their return they are mixed the one with the other, each man who finds them recognizes the owner's mark and immediately takes pains to inquire for him and quickly gives back his own to him whose mark is found. And in this way each finds his own animals.[62]

Two horses of the K'itan on a painting by Hu Kuei have on their hind-quarters *tamgas*.[63] I use this Turkish word for "seal, property mark," because it was borrowed not only by the Mongols, but also by the Tadzhiks,

---

[57] Sinitsyn 1947, 130-131, pl. 9. Maksimov 1956b, 74 (with parallels), fig. 45.

[58] Maksimov 1956b, 84.

[59] The saddle of a Sasanian king on a silver plate in the collection Fouroughi has a high front bow; cf. R. Ghirshman, *Artibus Asiae* 22, 1959, 52, fig. 1. S. I. Vaĭnshteĭn's thesis (1966, 68-74) that the wooden saddle was invented by the Altai Turks does not take the early Chinese and the Hunnic saddles into account.

[60] Rudenko 1953, 147, fig. 86.

[61] Karutz 1911, 50. Paudler (1933, 267-277) has rich material on ear marks.

[62] Marco Polo, 175.

[63] *Three Hundred Masterpieces of Chinese Painting in the Palace Museum* 1, 30; cf. Wittfogel and Fêng 1949, 118, 130.

Persians, and even the Russians,[64] although the Persians branded their horses before they had any contact with Turks, and the Russians had their own, Slavic word for brandmark (*pyatna*). It may have been the technically superior form or application of the branding iron of the Turks that superseded the earlier methods of branding, and therefore the older word. The *T'ang hui yao*, chapter 72, contains a list of the tamgas of thirty-seven, mostly Turkish tribes;[65] the foreign, again preponderantly Turkish, horses in the great pastoral inspectorates in T'ang China were in addition branded on many parts of the body, to show ownership, age, type, quality, and condition.[66]

Turkish tribes marked their horses before[67] and after [68] the T'ang period. In Persia the brandmarks can be traced to the third century. A graffito in Dura-Europos shows an early Sasanian tamga.[69] The horse of Peroz at Taq-i-Bustan has a mark on the right hindquarter,[70] and the steeds of the Sasanian kings on a fabric in the Horyuji at Nara are branded on their flanks, but the Persian tamga has been changed into the Chinese character *chi*, "auspicious."[71]

Although the Sasanian tamga brings us closer to the Huns in time and space, the horse of a hunter on an often-reproduced mosaic from Borj Djedid, Carthage, now in the British Museum,[72] leads to a milieu intimately associated with the Huns. The man, to judge by his dress, could be a Roman, a Vandal, or an Alan.[73] The strange crosslike tamga on his horse has been taken for Roman.[74] But as Jänichen noticed, it has a striking resemblance to the tamga in a rock picture on the upper Yenisei,[75] datable to the middle of the first millennium A.D. It is an Asiatic tamga; the hunter must be an Alan.

---

[64] K. H. Menges, *Zeitschr. f. slav. Philologie* 31, 1, 1963, 22-42.

[65] Translated with good commentary by Zuev (1960b, 93-140).

[66] Schafer 1963, 66.

[67] The Kao-chü, *Pei shih* 98, the Ku-li-kan, and other tribes. The Chinese made a distinction between 記 -, *chi* "sign, mark," and 印, *yin*, "*seal*." The Kao-chü "chi-ed" their domestic animals.

[68] A tamga on a galloping horse on a wall painting at Khocho (Le Coq 1924, pl. 20). All later Turkish nomads brand their horses, cf. *e.g.*, for the Altai tribes and Kirgiz, Radlov 1893, 1, 279, 455; the Tuwans, Iakovlev 1900, 11, 87.

[69] Du Buison 1939, 163, fig. 112. On Sasanian horse marks, see J. G. Shepherd, *Bulletin of the Cleveland Museum of Arts*, April 1964, 77.

[70] Ghirshman 1962, 192, fig. 235.

[71] Simmons 1948, 12-14.

[72] Hinks 1933, pl. 57.

[73] Courtois 1955, 22, n. 4.

[74] Dölger 1932, 258.

[75] Jänichen 1956, pl. 30:1, 2.

Sarmatian tamgas of the second and third centuries are well attested. There is, first, a grave stela from Theodosia in the Crimea, of a type known from many places in the Bosporan kingdom. The stela has been set up by the religious society to which the deceased Atta, son of Tryphon, belonged. In spite of his Greek name, the man is dressed like a Sarmatian horseman; he carries a Sarmatian dagger with a ring handle and his horse is marked with one of those Sarmatian signs which occur on reliefs, mirrors, cauldrons, buckles, jewelry, and coins from the Bosporan kingdom and adjacent areas in the first three centuries A.D. (fig. 2).[76] There is, second, the fragment of a stela found at the khutor Malaya Kozyrka, north of Olbia, representing a hunting scene. The horse is marked on the flank; another Sarmatian

FIG. 2. Grave stela from Theodosia in the Crimea with the representation of the deceased mounted on a horse marked with a Sarmatian tamga, first to third centuries A.D. From Solomonik 1957, fig. 1.

---

[76] Solomonik 1957, 210, fig. 1.

tamga is between the front and hind legs.[77] There is, third, the clay figure of an ox, a toy, from Glinishche near Kerch-Panticapaeum, with a Sarmatian tamga branded on the shoulder.[78]

The Mongols, the K'i-tan, the Turks before and after the T'ang period, and the Kirghiz north of the Sayan Mountains branded their horses like the Sarmatians in the second and third centuries and the Alans in the fifth. The Huns had large herds of horses. In the campaign of 451, Attila's army is said to have numbered five hundred thousand men,[79] though actually it cannot have had more than a fifth of this figure, and probably even less. A good part of the army consisted of Germans, many of whom were foot soldiers. Still, counting the reserve horses and the draught horses, Attila must have had fifty or sixty thousand horses when he set out for Gaul. The long frontiers of the loosely knit kingdom had to be guarded while the mobile army was away, and a considerable force stayed at home to keep the conquered peoples in subjection. To these war horses the mares and foals have to be added. The Huns must have had *some* means of identifying the owners of their horses. It is, I believe, practically certain that they branded their horses with tamgas similar to those of the Sarmatians.[80]

Gelding

All frozen horses in the kurgans at Pazyryk were castrated:[81] The princes who were buried there rode only geldings. The same was true more than two millennia later: No well-off Altaian rode a stallion or a mare.[82] In the 1860's their herds consisted of 20 to 60 horses: 1 stallion, 8 to 25 mares, 5 to 15 one-year-old colts, 4 to 14 two- and three-year-old colts, and 5 to 10 geldings;[83] the stallion colts were castrated in their second year.[84] In the herds of the Kirghiz the relation between stallions and mares was one to nine.[85]

"The knowledge of castration," says Lattimore, "is essential to the technique of steppe pastoralism. Otherwise the unnecessary large number

---

[77] *Ibid.*, 212, fig. 3.

[78] *Ibid.*, 211, fig. 2; the same illustrations in Solomonik 1959, figs. 35, 36, 143.

[79] *Getica* 182.

[80] The unicorn on a deer horn, excavated at Pliska, Bulgaria, has a tamga on the shoulder; S. Mikhaĭlov, *Bulg. akad. naukite* 20, 1955, 68, fig. 20. As the physiologus was translated into Old Slavonic in the tenth century, and the letters engraved on the horn seem to be Cyrillic letters, the tamga could be either proto-Bulgarian or Slavic.

[81] Rudenko 1953, 148; Vitt 1952, 163-205; Hančar 1955, 365.

[82] Radlov 1893, 1, 282.

[83] *Ibid.*, 273.

[84] *Ibid.*, 281.

[85] *Ibid.*, 442.

of male animals, fighting each other and attempting to lead away bands of females, would make it impossible to keep stock in large, tractable herds on unfenced pasture."[86] The Scythians and Sarmatians in South Russia castrated their horses "to make them easy to manage; for although the horses are small, they are exceedingly quick and hard to manage."[87]

In spite of the absence of any literary evidence, there can be no doubt that the Huns, too, rode mostly geldings.[88]

Transportation

The literary evidence for the wagons of the Huns is scanty: a few lines in Ammianus, a sentence in Priscus, and a subordinate clause in the *Getica*.

According to Ammianus (XXX, 2, 10), "no one in their country ever plows a field or touches a plow-handle. They are all without fixed abode, without hearth, or law, or settled mode of life, and keep roaming from place to place, like fugitives, accompanied by the wagons [*cum carpentis*] in which they live." This is a paraphrase of the description of the Scythians in Trogus Pompeius.[89] Ammianus uses almost the same phrases when he speaks about the incessant wandering of the Alans (XXXI, 2, 18). In their wagons the Hunnic women cohabit with their husbands, bear children, and rear them to the age of puberty; in the wagons of the Alans the males have intercourse with the women, and in the wagons their babes are born and reared. If Ammianus were to be believed, the Hunnic women even wove their garments in the wagons. But he cannot be believed. He turned into the ordinary way of Hunnic life what his informants told him about a Hun horde on the move. Besides, he followed the Greeks who were so impressed by the wagons of the Scythians that they took the vehicles, mostly used for moving the tents, for the homes of the nomads. To the Greeks the Scythians were and remained "wagon dwellers" ($\dot{\alpha}\mu\alpha\xi\acute{o}\beta\iota o\iota$) and "men who carried their own houses with them" ($\varphi\varepsilon\varrho\acute{e}o\iota\kappa o\iota$),[90] epithets endlessly repeated and occasionally embroidered by Latin authors.[91]

---

[86] Lattimore 1940, 16.

[87] Strabo VII, 4, 8. On the Sarmatians in Hungary, see Ammianus Marcellinus XVII, 12, 2.

[88] So did the Mongols of the twelfth century (Vladimirtsov 1934, 39). It is, therefore, unlikely that Mongolian *axta*, "gelding," is a Persian loanword as Clauson (1962, 234, and *CAJ* 10, 1965, 162-163) maintains; cf. also Doerfer 1963, 1, 114-117. If, however, Clauson should be right, the Persian term would indicate that the Mongols took over a new and, presumably, better technique of gelding from the Persians.

[89] Justin, *Epit.* II, 2, 3-4. Ammianus was copied by Eunapius, whom Zosimus (IV, 20, 4) followed.

[90] The main passages are cited by Minns 1913, 50.

[91] *E. g.*, Horace, *Carm.* III, 24, 10.

Priscus mentions the wagons, ἄμαξαι, of the Huns, on which rafts or pontoons, σχεδίαι, for use in marshy places were carried.[92]

The third reference to the Hun wagons occurs in Jordanes' account of the battle at the *locus Mauriacus*. In the evening of the first day Attila retreated and "shut himself and his companions within the barriers of the camp, which he had fortified with wagons [*plaustris vallatum*]" (*Getica* 210).

Although Priscus says nothing about the number of the rafts put on a wagon, their size, and the material of which they were made—it could have been wood, wickerwork, or hides—the wagons were probably heavy four-wheeled vehicles. The Huns could not have encumbered their swift-moving cavalry with such carts. Those in Attila's army must have been light, probably two-wheeled wains. In the fourth and fifth centuries camps with a defensive barrier of wagons were nothing specifically Hunnic. "All the barbarians," wrote Vegetius, "arrange their carts around them in a circle and then pass their nights secure from surprise."[93] Like other Germans of their time and before it,[94] the Goths formed *carragines*[95] with great skill.

Although there is no archaeological evidence for the wagons of the Huns, we can form an approximate picture of them from the finds in the graves of other northern barbarians, who put the dismantled or broken funeral cart, or parts of it, into the pits or catacombs. Fragments of such carts were found in Scythian kurgans from the sixth to the third century B.C. in the Kuban, Taman, Dnieper, and Poltava groups,[96] in four of the five burial mounds at Pazyryk in the High Altai,[97] in Sarmatian graves from the fourth

---

[92] *EL* 131$_{10-11}$. The Huns crossed rivers in dugouts (*EL* 125$_{1-2}$, 131$_{8-9}$). The barbarian ferrymen who, in the summer of 449, rowed the Roman ambassadors across the Danube in monoxyli were probably Huns. Although the frontier ran at a considerable distance to the south, it was still the broad river that separated Hunnia from Romania. Once deserters reached the south bank of the Danube, they were safe. It seems, therefore, likely that the guard of the river, including the ferry service, was entrusted to Attila's own Huns. Fishermen and pirates used dugouts on the Danube long before the Huns; cf. Arrian, *Anabasis* I, 3, 6. In 376 the Visigoths and in 386 the Greuthungi rowed across the Danube in monoxyli (Ammianus Marcellinus XXXI, 4, 5; Zosimus IV, 38). The dugouts of the Germans (see Tacitus, *Ann.* II, 6) on the Batavi on the upper Rhine were sometimes of considerable size (Pliny, *HN* XVI, 203).

[93] Vegetius, *Epit. rei milit.* III, 10.

[94] Sadée 1938, 169-174; Rubin 1960, 1, 516, n. 1115.

[95] *Quas ita ipsi appellant* (Ammianus XXXI, 7, 7); καραγός in the Byzantine military writings. Cf. also Ammianus XXXI, 12, 11.

[96] Ebert 1921, 154-156; Rostovtsev 1931, index *s.v.* Leichenwagen.

[97] Rudenko 1953, 230-235.

to the first century B.C.,[98] and in the Hsiung-nu graves at Noin Ula.[99] Some Sarmatian carts were light vehicles with two or four wheels. The wheels in kurgan 12, grave 9, at Politotdel'skoe on the lower Volga measured 1.2 meters in diameter and had at least twenty spokes.[100] The wheels of the impressive four-wheeled cart in the fifth kurgan at Pazyryk, each with thirty-four spokes, had a diameter of about 1.5 meters; there was a raised seat for the driver, and a superstructure covered with black felt, decorated with stuffed felt swans.[101] The absence of metal parts indicates that the big cart was of local provenance, though possibly made in imitation of Chinese wagons. The Kao-chü tribes, the later Uigurs, had wagons with very high wheels; the Chinese named the people after them: *kao chü*

FIG. 3. Two-wheeled cart represented on a bronze plaque from the Wu-huan cemetery at Hsi-ch'a-kou. From *Sun Shou-tao* 1960, fig. 17.

---

[98] Early Sarmatians: Sinitsyn 1947, 76-77, 91, 95, figs. 49-50, 63, 67-68; Sinitsyn 1948, 81; K. F. Smirnov 1959, 268, 285-286, figs. 24:1a, 27:b; K. F. Smirnov 1960, 260. Middle Sarmatian: Rykov 1925, 54 (a detailed description by P. Stepanov on pp. 76-77); Rykov 1926, 99.

[99] Umehara 1960, 87-90, figs. 59, 60, pl. 78; Rudenko 1962a, 50-51, figs. 44, 45, pl. 24. The axle caps are Chinese.

[100] K. F. Smirnov 1959, 268, fig. 24:1a.

[101] Griaznov 1958, pl. 28.

means "high chariots." The various names under which the Kao-chü were known before, *ti-li*, *t'ê-lê*, *t'iê-lê*, and *ting-ling*,[102] are possibly variants of a Turkish word for wheel.[103]

There exist a few representations of carts of the eastern barbarians: a two-wheeled cart on a bronze plaque from the Wu-huan cemetery at Hsi-ch'a-kou (fig. 3),[104] another one on a Chinese incense burner of late Chou or early Han date in the Freer Gallery.[105] A bronze plaque from Sui-yüan shows a man in a long coat and wide trousers, holding a sword with a ring handle, in front of a car drawn by three horses (fig. 4).[106] The two heads on the cart are not the cut-off heads of enemies[107] but are meant to represent people in a small tent. The miniatures in the Radziwil manu-

FIG. 4. Bronze plaque from Sui-yüan with the representation of a man holding a sword with a ring handle before a cart drawn by three horses. From Rostovtsev 1929, pl. XI, 56.

---

[102] O. Maenchen-Helfen, *HJAS* 4, 1939, 83; Liu 1958, 2, 491-492.

[103] Hamilton 1962, 26.

[104] *Sun Shou-tao* 1960, fig. 17. As Tseng Fung (*Kaogu* 1961, 6, 332-334) proved, the people who buried their dead in this large cemetery were not, as Sun suggested, Hsiung-nu but Wu-huan. Among the rock pictures at Tebchi near Khobdo in Outer Mongolia, discovered in 1962, occurs a four-wheeled carriage drawn by four horses, supposedly of the Tagar period; see *Arkheologiia i etnografiia dal'nego vostoka* 161.

[105] Wenley 1949, 5, fig. 1.

[106] Rostovtsev 1929, pl. 11:56.

[107] As Rostovtsev 1929, 44, conjectured. In this instance the man would have carried the heads tied to the horse's harness like the warriors on a gold plaque in the collection of Peter I (Rudenko 1962b, fig. 29, pl. 22:18), or the horseman on the bottle from Nagy-szentmiklos (Sînicolaul Mare), (A. Alföldi, *Cahiers archéologiques* 5, 1951, 123-134).

script show the wagons of the Kumans with the same heads in the tents mounted on the vehicles (figs. 5A and 5B).[108]

Fig. 5A. Miniature painting from the Radziwil manuscript showing the wagons of the Kumans. From Pletneva 1958, fig. 25.

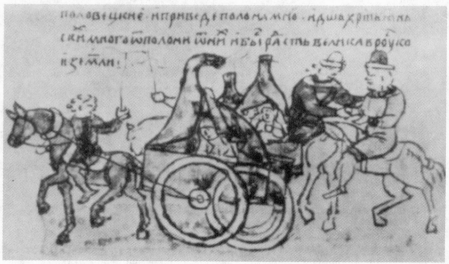

Fig. 5B. Miniature painting from the Radziwil manuscript showing human heads in tents mounted on carts. From Pletneva 1958, fig. 26.

---

[108] Pletneva 1958, 200-204, fig. 25.

Even without the specific statements in the cited passages it would have to be assumed that the Huns had wagons. They broke off the pursuit of the Goths because they were "loaded down with booty."[109] The Huns must have had wagons like those of Alaric's Visigoths in Italy which were loaded with precious stuff, such as mixing bowls from Argos and lifelike statues from Corinth.[110] On their migration to the Don and from the Don to the Danube, the Huns probably transported their old people, women, and children in wagons.[111] Toy wagons found in Kerch show what the wagons of the later Sarmatians looked like. Some of them have pyramidal towers, doubtless movable tents;[112] others are heavy four-wheeled vehicles (fig. 6).[113]

Fig. 6. Ceramic toy from Kerch showing a wagon of Late Sarmatian type. From *Narysy starodav'noĭ istorii Ukrains'koĭ RSR* 1957, 237.

---

[109] Ammianus XXXI, 3, 8.

[110] Claudian, *Bell. Goth.* 611-612.

[111] Like the Ostrogoths on their trek to Italy (*sumpta sunt plaustra vice tectorum*, Ennodius, *Paneg. CSEL* VI, 268).

[112] Minns 1913, 51, fig. 6; another view, *Ocherki* I, 511.

[113] *Narysy starodav'noĭ istorii Ukrains'koĭ RSR* 237.

The wagons of the Huns must have been similar to the toy wagons from Panticapaeum.

Horses played a prominent role in the economy of the Huns. Although our authorities do not mention that the Huns ate horse meat—perhaps because this went without saying[114]— they certainly did, like the Scythians,[115] Sarmatians,[116] and all other steppe peoples. The meat was boiled in large cauldrons[117] and fished out with iron hooks. The Scythians were ἱππημολγοί and γαλακτοφάγοι; the Alans "lived on an abundance of milk.[118] There can be no doubt that the Huns, too, drank mare's milk and made kumys and cheese.[119]

Claudian and Sidonius at times named the Geloni where we would expect the Huns. In addition to the reasons adduced in another context, Claudian and Sidonius may have thought of some epithets of the Geloni, like sagittiferi[120] or volucres,[121] which also fit the new barbarians whose hated name could, therefore, be exchanged for one almost consecrated by the great poets of the past. Sidonius may have had a verse of Virgil[122] in mind when he associated the equimulgae Geloni with the Sygambri and Alans of his time.[123] Like the Massagetae, the Geloni were said to have mixed milk and horse blood.[124] Perhaps by substituting Geloni for Huns, the poets[125] indicated that the Huns, too, drank the blood of their horses. When Ennodius ascribed this custom to the Bulgars,[126] he could have followed a topos. But neither Marco Polo[127] nor Hans Schiltberger[128] thought of Virgil when they described how the Mongols and the Tatars

---

[114] "Any kind of animal" (Ammianus XXXI, 2, 3).

[115] Minns 1913, 49.

[116] Jerome, Adv. Iovinian. II, 7. In Sarmatian graves of all periods horse bones were found: Rykov 1925, 69; Rau 1927, 31; Sinitsyn 1956b, 43, 46; 1959, 44, 59; Shilov 1959, 338, 359, 406; K. F. Smirnov 1959, 300. For unknown reasons the Sarmatian graves west of the Volga only rarely contain horse bones; for a diagonal burial at Ust'-Kamenka, see APU 9, 1960, 30.

[117] In the Middle Sarmatian grave Kalinovka 55/8 (Shilov 1959, 404), the bones were in a bronze cauldron, like in the Scythian kurgan at Chertomlyk (Minns 1913, 162).

[118] Ammianus XXXI, 2, 18.

[119] The ὀξύγαλα and ἱππάκη of the Scythians (Minns 1913, 49).

[120] Virgil, Aen. VIII, 725.

[121] Lucan III, 283.

[122] Virgil, Georg. III, 463.

[123] Ep. IV, 1, 4.

[124] Seneca, Oedipus 470; Periegesis 744-745, Avienus 921-922, Priscian 721. The costum is ascribed to still other peoples, e.g., the Concani (Horace, Carm. III, 4, 34).

[125] Thompson 1948, 39, n. 2, refers also to Prudentius.

[126] Paneg., CSEL VI, 267, 12-14.

[127] Marco Polo 173.

[128] Schiltberger 1885, 62.

of the Golden Horde bled their horses and boiled and ate the blood when they had nothing else to eat.

Bows and Arrows

"A wondrous thing," wrote Jordanes, "took place in connection with Attila's death. For in a dream some god stood at the side of Marcian, emperor of the East, while he was disquieted about his fierce foe, and showed him the bow of Attila broken in the same night, as if to intimate that this race owed much to that weapon [quasi quod gens ipsa eo telo multum praesumat]."[129]

The bow was *the* weapon of the Huns. In Ammianus' description of their armament, bow and arrow take the first place.[130] Olympiodorus praised the skill of the Hunnic leaders in shooting with the bow.[131] Aetius, who got his military education with the Huns, was "a very practiced horseman and skillful archer."[132] Shapely bows and arrows, said Sidonius Apollinaris, were the delight of the Huns; they were the best archers.[133] He found no higher praise for Avitus' bowmanship than by saying that he even surpassed the Huns.[134] In the battle on the Nedao the Huns fought with bows and arrows.[135]

A century later, after the East Romans had taken over so many of the weapons and tactics of the barbarians, they were "expert horsemen, and able without difficulty to direct their bows to either side while riding at full speed, and to shoot at opponents whether in pursuit or in flight."[136] And yet Belisars' Massagets,[137] that is, Huns, were still the best bowmen. Even dismounted and running at great speed, they "knew how to shoot with the greatest accuracy."[138]

Although Ammianus had the highest respect for the Hunnic bow, he was not well informed about it. The Huns could, he said, easily be called the fiercest of all warriors, because they fight from a distance with missiles having sharp bone points instead of the ordinary points, joined to

---

[129] *Getica* 255; the source is Priscus.

[130] XXXI, 2, 9.

[131] Fr. 18; *FHG* IV, 61.

[132] Greg. Tur., *Hist. Franc.* II, 8.

[133] *Paneg. on Anthemius* (Sidonius), 266.

[134] *Paneg. on Avitus* (Sidonius), 235-236, patterned on Claudian, *Cons. Stil.* I, 109-111. The *iacula*, like those of the Parthians in Claudian (*Rapt. Pros.* II, 200), are arrows, not javelins; cf. C. Mueller, *Dissertationes philologicae Vindobonenses* 4, 143.

[135] *Getica* 261.

[136] Procopius I, 1, 14.

[137] *Ibid.*, III, 18, 17; VI, 11, 11.

[138] *Ibid.*, VI, 1, 9-10.

shafts with wonderful skill. Why the bone points should have turned the Huns into such superior archers is by no means clear. From Ammianus' assertion that the Scythian and Parthian bows are the only ones that have a straight rounded grip[139] it would follow that the Hunnic bow was bent in a continuous curve, which is contradicted by the archaeological evidence. As so often, a single find tells us more than all the written sources.

As early as 1932, when only a few finds were known, Alföldi and Werner were able to reconstruct the Hunnic bow.[140] Their results are by now generally accepted, but in the past thirty years the material has grown immensely.[141] New problems have arisen. Unexpected finds reopen questions which seemed to be answered definitely. In a way, the history of Eurasia septentrionalis antiqua runs parallel to the history of the Hunnic bow.

It is a reflexed composite bow, 140-160 centimeters in length. Its wooden core is backed by sinews and bellied with horn. What distinguishes it from other composite bows are the seven bone plaques which stiffen the ears and the handle, a pair on each ear and three on the handle, two on its sides and one on its top. The string is permanently made fast to the end of the bow, which is stiffened for the greatest length; the nock is square, or almost square; in the finds it shows little evidence of rubbing. The nock in the ear of the shorter, more flexible arm is round; the string is looped into it when the bow is strung. In the finds it is much worn. This bow was spread from the British Isles to northern China. The earliest known bone strips come from graves of the fourth or third centuries B.C. The Russians used such bows as late as the twelfth century.[142]

Before attacking the specific problems which the Hunnic bow poses, some preliminary remarks and general considerations seem to be in order. The lack of a generally agreed on terminology in the study of the bow sometimes results in an annoying confusion.[143] I will use the following terms:

Self bow: the plain wooden bow in one piece.

Reflexed bow: a bow which, when unstrung, reverses its curve.

Compound bow: a bow built up by uniting two or more staves of similar material.

---

[139] Ammianus XXII, 8, 37, with Rolfe's note in the Loeb edition. Unlike later authors, Ammianus never calls the Huns Scythians. The Scythians in this passage are the ancient people.

[140] Alföldi 1932; J. Werner 1932.

[141] See the long list of findspots in Khazanov 1966. It is far from being complete. Khazanov knows practically nothing about the Far Eastern material.

[142] Cf. O. I. Davidan on the finds in Nizhnii Novgorod and Staraya Ladoga, *Arkheol. sbornik* 8, 1966, 110.

[143] Emeneau (1953, 78, n. 8) rightly blames Brown 1937 for using the term "compound" where most other authorities use "composite."

Reinforced bow: a bow with a layer of longitudinally disposed sinew applied to the back.[144]

Composite bow: a bow whose stave embodies a laminated construction involving more than one type of material, such as wood, sinew, and horn; as a rule the wooden core is backed by sinew and bellied by horn.[145]

Handle or grip: the space occupied by the hand in holding the bow.

Arms: the regions between the handle and the tip.

Nocks: the depressions or notches on the ear which serve to keep the string from slipping.

Ear: the part of the arm with the nock.

Back: the side of the bow away from the string; the concave side when the bow is strung.

Belly: the side of the bow next to the string; the convex side when the bow is strung.

Bracing: setting the string tight on the bow.

Length: the distance from tip to tip before the bow is strung.

Span: the distance from tip to tip when the bow is strung.

There are bows which do not fit these definitions. The English longbow, for example, is a self bow but also a variety of the compound bow. "In making a yew bow, the wood that is used is that which is nearest the outside of the log, consisting of practically all the light-colored sapwood immediately under the bark and only as much of the darker heartwood as may be needed. This combination of sap and heartwood in yew provides the two properties required, for the sapwood is resistant to stretch and therefore suitable for the back, and the heartwood resists compression and is therefore perfect for the belly."[146]

Representations

Representations of bows in paintings, reliefs, metalwork, and on coins are in general of limited value for determining their anatomy. Double-curved bows are not necessarily composite bows. Those in Attic Geometric

---

[144] The term is possibly a misnomer. The purpose of the sinew backing is supposed to increase the cast of the bow, but Pope's experiments seem to indicate that the sinew rather serve the purpose of allowing the wooden stave to be fully drawn without breaking; cf. Heizer in the preface to Pope 1962.

[145] Soviet archaeologists often distinguish between the composite bow, *sostavnoi luk*, and what they call *slozhnyi luk*, whose wooden core consists of several pieces of wood joined together, almost corresponding to the "split bow" in Western terminology. In archaeological studies this distinction is useless. The wooden core is practically never preserved, so it is impossible to determine what it was. This is, of course, also true of representations.

[146] Edwards and Heath 1962, 53-54.

art, for instance, their inward curve reaching almost to the string when they were strung, were self bows, made entirely of wood.[147] Brown's in some respects very valuable study[148] is in others misleading because he deals almost exclusively with representations. After having established the shape of a bone-stiffened bow at Yrzi in a necropolis on the Euphrates about 40 kilometers southeast of Dura-Europos, Brown looked for more bows like it. As could be expected, he found them nearly everywhere. The bows of the royal guard on the tile reliefs in Susa and on Chinese vases of the Han period looked to him like "Yrzi" bows, hence they *were* "Yrzi" bows. But Achaemenid findspots, in particular the arsenal at Persepolis where they should have been found by the hundreds, yielded not a single bone strip,[149] and the same is true for the Han graves. Emeneau collected an impressive number of representations in early Indian art;[150] so did Auboyer.[151] But whereas Auboyer, wisely in my opinion, merely classified them according to their curves,[152] Emeneau drew from the monuments conclusions as to the structure of the bows. In some cases they may be right, but there is no archaeological evidence to bear them out.

Had the bow which Stein found in the Tibetan T'ang fortress at Mazardagh[153] occurred in a wall painting, it easily could have been taken for a bone-stiffened bow. The gently curved ears with their notches look like those of bone-stiffened bows from the Chinese borderland. Khazanov included it in his list.[154] Evidently he did not read the text. In the dry desert bone strips would have been splendidly preserved. Stein found none. The ears, made of tamarisk wood, had no traces of glue on them. Bone plaques on the ears were sometimes painted or wrapped up in colored strings,[155] in which cases it is impossible to recognize them in paintings.

There are, however, representations of bows which can be of help in determining some of the anatomy of the bow. The strongly curled ends of the Scythian bow preclude the application of bone strips on the ears. There is, furthermore, a type of Sasanian bow with very long ears. They

---

147 Snodgrass 1964, 143.

148 Brown 1937.

149 This has been rightly stressed by Litvinskiĭ 1966, 65.

150 Emeneau 1953.

151 Auboyer 1956, 173-185.

152 Type *a* = self bow; *b* = *arc réflexe, dont les extrémités se retroussent plus ou moins, mais dont le corps présente une seule courbure; c* = *arc réflexe, dont le corps présente une double courbure, même quand il n'est pas bandé.*

153 *Serindia* 3, 1921, p. 1292; 4, pl. 51; Stein 1928, 1, 94; 3, pl. 6.

154 Khazanov 1966, 38.

155 Cf. Kibirov 1959b, 117.

must have been stiffened with bone plates, otherwise they could not have resisted the strain when the bow was drawn; ears of plain wood have been broken in pieces. Conversely, such very long bone strips in graves prove that the bow on which they were applied was of this Sasanian type.

Coexistence of Various Types

The bow of the Huns discussed on the following pages was a war bow, as presumably most bows in burials were; they lay in the graves of warriors. About the hunting bows of the Huns we have no information, but that they were different from the war bow is practically certain. The Huns could not have hunted ducks or foxes with their precious composite bows. War bows and hunting bows were often as different as rifles and shotguns. On a stela in already strongly Sarmatized Panticapaeum, a young man is drawing a long C-bow[156]; behind him stand his groom and his horse, which is neither bridled nor saddled; it is a peaceful scene.[157] The bow is a hunting bow. In the battle scenes in the Stassov catacomb in Panticapaeum[158] and the stelae with the likeness of the dead as warrior, the bows are short and double curved, of the Scythian type. Unless one keeps such differences in mind, one can easily draw wrong conclusions from one-sided evidence. On stamped tiles from Old Loyang, probably made from stamps designed in the third century B.C.,[159] occur hunters, Hsiung-nu or people closely related to them, chasing deer. The bows in these pictures tell us little about the war bows of the nomads.

The Skill Required

Composite war bows technically as perfect as those of the Huns could only be made by professional bowyers. They must have had workshops like those in the Roman fort at Carleon[160] and Parthian Merv.[161] The making of even such a simple bow as the English longbow required a good deal of craftmanship. It had to be tapered correctly, with patience and care, from the middle toward each end to bring it to an even curve when full drawn; all knots and irregularities in the grain had to be carefully watched and "raised" or followed skillfully to eliminate weak spots.[162] For a detailed description, the chapter on "Making the Bow" in Pope's classical *Hunting with Bow and Arrow*[163] should be read. "While the actual work

---

[156] I use this convenient term for the single-curved, and *M* for the double-curved bow.

[157] Kieséitzky and Watzinger 1909, 88, no. 501, pl. 35. For the inscription, see *CIRB*, no. 279.

[158] *CAH*, plates 5, 26a.

[*Footnotes 159-163 are missing.—Ed.*]

of making bows," he wrote, "takes about eight days, it requires months to get one adjusted so that it is good." Turkish manuals on archery contain the names of outstanding bowyers, and there exist long lists of Japanese bowyers, who wrote their names and the date on their bows. Elmer, one of the greatest experts on archery, wrote: "I know of only three men of our race who had been successful in making one or more composite bows, though none of them has produced a weapon which could vie in quality with the best products of the ancient Orient. All started with the slogan 'A white man can do anything a brown man can,' but none has seen his boast fulfilled."[164] Luschan estimated that the time required for making a good Turkish bow, including the intervals of drying and seasoning between operations, was from five to ten years.[165] These were, of course, particularly well made bows, mostly used for flight shooting. But the ordinary bows also required a high degree of skill and thorough familiarity with all details. In 1929 old men in the Barlyq-Alash-Aksu region in western Tuva told me that in their youth, in the seventies and eighties, there were only two men in their *khoshuns* who could make bows. To find the appropriate materials, to cut the wood, horn, and bone into the right shape, to mold the sinews for the back, to determine the best proportions between the weak and rigid parts of the bow, all this and much more presupposed long training. The idea that each Hunnic archer could make his own bow could have been conceived only by cabinet scholars who never held a composite bow in their hands.

Such bows were not easily replaced; once they were broken, they could not be repaired. This explains the character of the finds. Mere lists of findspots give a distorted picture. One has to go through the reports carefully to realize what the bows meant for their owners. Whenever a report is sufficiently detailed, it invariably turns out that the set of bone plaques is incomplete: one, two, or three instead of four from the ears, or only one plaque instead of three on the handle. The only complete set known to me, all the nine plaques of the bow of the latest Sarmatians found by Sinitsyn at Avilov's Farm, comes from a damaged bow.[166] Marmots dislocated the skull of the dead man; they damaged the quiver of birch bark. The bow lay *in situ*, and yet not a single bone plaque was intact. The more interesting cases are those in which the plaques do not belong together.

Werner mentions the plaques in the rich grave at Blučina in Moravia, where a Germanic nobleman was buried shortly after the collapse of Attila's kingdom; Khazanov refers to Werner, and Tihelka in his report gives them a few lines;[167] fortunately he also brings drawings, which allow

---

[Footnotes 164-167 are missing.—Ed.]

a closer study. The plaques do not fit one bow. Two fragments of end-pieces are of different width and have notches on the same side; they cannot have formed a pair. Two long strips cannot have come from one pair either; one is almost straight, the other markedly curved. The grave was not disturbed. The strange ensemble admits only one explanation: They are the broken part of two or, perhaps, three bows.

A find from Ak-Tobe in the Tashkent oasis throws more light on the reluctance to put an intact bow into the grave. In a burial dated to the end of the fourth century, the excavators found what they took to be a bow *in situ*. But the two long bone strips come from two bows. One has a round, the other one a triangluar notch; they are differently curved.[168] The people buried the dead warrior with a sham bow.

The difficulty of making a bow like that of the Huns is indirectly proved by the inability of the Germanic tribes to produce one.[169] The Gepids for many years had lived under and together with the Huns in Hungary. They buried their dead, even after their conversion to Christianity, with weapons. The graves contain swords, daggers, armor, helmets, umbones, arrow points, but not one bone strip.[170] Though the Goths had archers,[171] they never learned to shoot from horseback.[172] "Practically all the Romans and their allies, the Huns," Procopius wrote, "were good mounted bowmen, but not one among the Goths had any practice in this branch. Their bowmen entered battle on foot and under the cover of heavy-armed men."[173] The Goths in Italy were excellent riders[174] but unable to emulate the Huns because they had no bows like the Huns.[175]

As Alföldi recognized first,[176] the Hunnic bow had limbs of uneven length. It would not be worthwhile to mention it again if it were not for the insistence of some scholars on the inferiority of such a bow. I need not enumerate the peoples who had bows of this type. It will suffice to point to the Japanese. It is, to say the least, unlikely that they, who made the best swords in the world, should have been unable to make limbs of the same length.

Performance

Thanks to McLeod's careful analysis of the Greek and Latin sources, the range of the ancient composite bows has been definitely established: bowmen were quite accurate up to 50 to 60 meters, their effective range extended at least 160 to 175 meters, but not as far as 350 to 450 meters.[177]

[*Footnotes 168-176 are missing.—Ed.*]

[177] Wallace E. McLeod, "Egyptian Composite Bows in New York," *AJA* 66 (1962) 13-19.

According to a Moroccan archery manual of about 1500, "archers through-out the world agree that the limits beyond which no . . ."

[*The manuscript breaks off here in mid-sentence.—Ed.*]

The bone strips found in and near Roman camps from Scotland to Vindonissa and Egypt[178] show that Oriental *sagittarii*[179] used bows stiffened and reinforced like those of the Huns.[180] When one considers how strong Parthian influence on the armament of the Palmyreans[181] and other Syrians was and that bone lamellae began to appear only at the end of the first century B.C.,[182] the Parthian provenance of the bows of the Eastern archers seems highly probable. Possibly some bows, or rather fragments of bone strips, found along the *limes*[183] were actually Parthian; among the archers whom Severus Alexander sent from the Orient to Germania were Parthian deserters.[184] The archers who left bone strips in a late building in Carnun-tum[185] unfortunately cannot be identified. An ear piece was nailed to the wooden core[186] as in the camp of Bar Hill,[187] where a cohort of archers from Emesa in Phoenicia was stationed;[188] this could indicate that the troops in Carnuntum were Orientals, but this unusual way of attaching the strip occurs also in Avar and Hsiung-nu graves.[189] Alföldi is inclined to take the archers of Carnuntum for Huns.[190] The fragment of a Hunnic cauldron in Aquincum (Budapest) seems to support his suggestion, but near the cauldron fragment lay Oriental officers' helmets.

Sasanian Bows

Sasanian bows are known only from reproductions. The most common type, to be seen on numerous silver plates, has the long ears sharply set off the arms, exactly as on the wall paintings from Dura-Europos (figs. 7 and 8). The Sasanians took it over from the Parthians. Assuming that

---

[178] Balfour, *Journal of the Royal Anthropological Institute* 51 (1921), fig. 14. Found at Belmesa, now in the Pitt Rivers Museum.

[179] Cf. Weerd and Lambrechts 1938, 229-242.

[180] J. Werner 1932, 33-58; Alföldi 1932, 14-24, 90; Stade 1933, 110-114; Eckinger 1933, 289-290; J. Werner 1956, 47-48.

[181] Cf. Seyrig 1937.

[182] In the Augustean camp at Oberaden: Stade 1933, fig. 3. Date: 12-9 B.C. Cf. *Bonn. Jahrb.* 155/156, 1955/56, 108 (K. Kraft).

[183] Walke 1965, 55, pl. 105, 25-31.

[184] Herodian VI, 8, quoted by Weerd and Lambrechts 1938, 236.

[185] J. Werner 1932, 33-35, fig. 1.

[186] *Röm. Limes in Österreich* 2, 1901, 132, pl. 24:25.

[187] See Stade 1933, fig. 2.

[188] *Proceedings of the Society of Antiquaries of Scotland* 40, 1905-1906, 523ff.

[189] K. Cs. von Sebestyén, *Dolgozatok* 6 (Szeged, 1930), 178-220.

[190] Alföldi 1932, 21-22.

FIG. 7. Detail of a Sasanian-type silver plate from a private collection. Detail from Ghirshman 1962, fig. 314.

the handle is about 15 to 16 centimeters (the hand's width with one or two centimeters on each side), the length of the hunting bow, measured along the curve, varies from 70 to 110 or 115 centimeters. The latter figure is possibly an exaggeration: The great size of the bow corresponds

FIG. 8. Detail of a Sasanian silver plate from Sari, Archaeological Museum, Teheran. Detail from Ghirshman 1962, pl. 248.

to the superhuman height of the royal hunter. If the king is not on horse-back but stands in a boat, as on the reliefs at Taq-i-Bustan,[191] his bow is also extremely long.

On some plates the notch in the ear is clearly visible; on others the string just touches the bow, an indication of the craftsman's carelessness. As is known, not a few plates are copies of older originals, and not very exact ones. Occasionally the silversmith, who may never have held a bow in his hand, made even stranger blunders. On a plate from Kulagysh[192] the two heroes[193] carry bows with the strings fastened to loops on the belly. In most cases it cannot be decided whether the notch was cut in the wood or in the bone strip. There are, however, silver plates on which the bow has strings tied around the ear (fig. 7).[194] This would be superfluous had the nock been cut in the wood but makes sense as a means to hold the bone strips and the wood between them firmly together. From the fact that some bone strips from Carnuntum are roughened on the surface, Werner concluded that they were wrapped around with strings.[195] As in similar cases, the strings were probably colored. Incidentally, this shows that

---

[191] Ghirshman 1962, figs. 236, 237.

[192] In the Ural region, the former *uezd* Kungar. Ia. I. Smirnov 1909, pl. 23; Orbeli and Trever 1935, pl. 21; Pugachenkova 1965, pl. 122.

[193] Griaznov 1961, 9-10.

[194] Detail from the plate, Ghirshman 1962, fig. 314

[195] J. Werner 1932, 38.

the archer held the bow with the longer end up, the one to which the bow-string was permanently made fast.

The long ears are additional proof that the bows were stiffened with bone or horn. Unless the ears were encased in bone strips, they could not possibly be so rigid.[196] Sidonius Apollinaris had such bows in mind when, in the *Panegyric on Emperor Anthemius*, he wrote, "In boyhood it was his sport to handle eagerly arrows that had been seized from the foe, and on captive bows to force the resisting strings on to the curving horns."[197] Procopius, young Anthemius' father, fought against the Persians in 422.[198]

If the silver plates could be dated more exactly, it should be possible to follow the development of the Sasanian bow, or, better, bows, for it is unlikely that they were all of the same type, from Egypt to Afghanistan. The plate from Kulagysh is of Sogdian origin.[199] So is probably the often reproduced plate with the lion hunter, whose stirrups point to post-Sasanian times (fig. 9).[200] The Sogdians fought with weapons identical with or very similar to those of the Sasanian Persians. From the war bows on Sogdian plates we may conclude that the Sasanian war bows were the same, though possibly of slightly different size, as the bone-stiffened hunting bows.

There were others. On the plate from Akinovo the warriors defending the fortress carry M bows,[201] the same as the bow depicted on a vase from Merv, datable to the fifth century.[202] In a battle scene on a weave from Arsinoe in Egypt of about 600 A.D., both foot soldiers and horse-archers carry bows with strongly curled ends,[203] very similar to the Scythian and Scythian type bows of the Parthians.

The term Sasanian bow is, strictly, a misnomer, for the same type, the bow with the long ears set off at an angle, occurred also outside Sasanian

---

[196] The ear of the bow of the royal hunter on a plate from Sari, Ghirshman 1962, fig. 248 (our fig. 8) is as long as his arm from the shoulder to the wrist, thus about 35 centimeters.

[197] *Captosque per arcus/flexa reluctantes in cornua trudere nervos* (vv. 138-140).

[198] See Socrates VII, 20; Loyen 1942, 87.

[199] Pugachenkova 1965, 149.

[200] *SPA* 217, Orbeli and Trever 1935, pl. 3; see the thorough discussion by Zabelina and Rempel' 1948, and Pugachenkova 1965, 149-150. The style of writing of the Pehlevi inscription, misread by Herzfeld, is of a type which W. B. Henning, who corrected the reading, dated not prior to the seventh century; cf. Alföldi, *Dumbarton Oaks Papers* 11, 1957, 239, n. 19. For the reading suggested by V. A. Lifshits, see V. G. Lukonin, *Persia* 2 (Geneva, 1967).

[201] *SPA* 233b; Orbeli and Trever 1935, pl. 20; see the bibliography in Pugachenkova 1965, 404, n. 85.

[202] *VDI* 1, 1966, plate after p. 92.

[203] Ghirshman 1962, fig. 289.

Fig. 9. Silver plate from Kulagysh in the Hermitage Museum, Leningrad. From *SPA*, pl. 217.

Persia and before the Sasanids. Yet the term is so commonly used and so convenient that I will retain it, with the understanding that the "Sasanian" bow is not exclusively Sasanian but designates only a specific type. To deal with all "Sasanian" bows, from India[204] to southern Siberia[205] and Chinese Turkestan,[206] would lead us too far away from the Huns. Why, for instance, Virudhaka on a relief from the Silla kingdom in Korea holds a "Sasanian" bow[207] is a question for historians of Far Eastern art to answer.

[204] On the bows on Gupta coins, see Emeneau 1953, 86.

[205] On the rock pictures at Sulyek, Pisannaya Gora, see Appelgren-Kivalo 1931, figs. 78-79.

[206] In Bazalik (tenth century); see Andrews 1948, pl. 26.

[207] *Museum of Government General of Tyōsen* 1937, Museum Exhibits, vol. 4.

SWORDS

[*The section on swords is missing in the manuscript, except for the following fragments.—Ed.*]

The Sword of Altlussheim

The scabbard tip of the much-discussed sword from Altlussheim near Mainz* (fig. 10A)[208] was, as Werner proved, originally an attachable sword guard, comparable to the guards of the Chinese swords of the Han period. Because of its shape and material, Werner takes it to be of Sasanian or Hephthalite provenance (fig. 10B).[209]

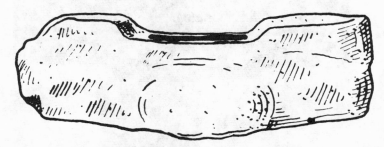

FIG. 10A. Scabbard tip of a sword from Altlussheim near Mainz. From J. Werner 1956, pl. 58:4.

He refers to the representation of a sword on a relief from Palmyra (fig. 11);[210] the lower edge of its guard has the same obtuse angle as that of the piece from Altlussheim. As so much in the armament of the Palmyreans, the sword is supposed to be either of Persian provenance or made in imitation of a Persian sword. The guard, so incongruously fixed to the shape of the sword from the Rhine, is cut from a piece of lapis lazuli. This semiprecious stone is said to be mined only in the Badakhshan Mountains in Afghanistan, an area which until the middle of the fifth century was a part of the Sasanian empire, later lost to the Hephthalites.

---

* *This sword was accidentally found by workmen in December 1932, as part of a princely grave, together with other objects. Pieces of the blade, the parrying bar decorated with almandites, and parts of the gold- and silver-decorated scabbard are extant. See F. Garscha in* Germania: Anzeiger der römisch-germanischen Kommision des Deutschen Archeologischen Instituts, *vol. 20, Berlin: 1936.—Ed.*

[208] J. Werner 1956, pls. 3, 58:4.

[209] *Ibid.*, 39.

[210] Ghirshman 1962, 79, fig. 91. J. Werner (pl. 58:10) gives a corrected version of the drawing in Seyrig 1937, 27, fig. 81.

FIG. 10B. Detail of the sword from Altlussheim. From J. Werner 1956, pl. 38 A.

Fig. 11. Stone relief from Palmyra, datable to the third century A.D. Ghirshman 1962, pl. 91.

Werner's argumentation is ingenious but inconclusive, for several reasons. First, the Palmyrean sword, if it should be of Persian origin, would go back not to a Sasanian but a Parthian prototype. Maqqai, on whose triclinium the sword is represented, died in 229, only one year after the collapse of the Parthian kingdom. Second, no sword guard of that type is known to have existed in Sasanian or, for that matter, in Parthian Persia. Third, if we apply the ratio between the guard and the neck or arm of the warrior in the Palmyrean relief to life proportions, the guard must have been, at least, 30 centimeters wide, that is, three times the width of the Altlussheim guard. It is almost certain that a guard of the size of the Palmyrean one could not have been detachable but must have formed a part of the sword, cast or forged together with the blade and the handle. Fourth, there is no indication of the saddle between the shoulders, which the lapis lazuli guard, though rather battered, shows quite clearly. Fifth, it is true that the source of lapis lazuli has long been the Kokcha Valley of Badakhshan, but it was not always the only one. Darius I got lapis lazuli for the building of the apadana at Susa from Sogdiana,[211] where the stone was still mined in Marco Polo's days.[212] Besides, lapis lazuli was worked by craftsmen from Egypt to China. The Chinese imported it via Kashgar and Khotan as early as the second century B.C.;[213] they may have obtained the sê-sê[214] either directly from Afghanistan or from Persia, where lapis lazuli was widely used by the Parthians.[215]

Although the piece of lapis lazuli from which the guard was cut may have come from an outlying province of the Sasanian kingdom, the guard itself shows Chinese workmanship. Such sword guards, with the characteristic saddle between the shoulders, cast of bronze,[216] carved out of jade, made of glass, or cast together with the handle and the blade, often inlaid with turquoise,[217] are among the most common objects found in Han tombs. Agate was another material used for the decoration of swords. The Chinese cut pommels of bluish and reddish agate[218] even before the Han period.[219] A sword guard of agate, of exactly the shape and size of the guard from the Rhine, was found in vault 1013 at Chersonese (fig. 12).[220] Its date is the same as that of the little rabbit of rock crystal found together with

[211] R. G. Kent, *JAOS* 53, 1933, 7.

[212] 1, 29, with Yule's note, third ed., 102.

[213] Fr. Hirty, quoted in Laufer 1913, 44, n. 1. See note.

[214] *Sê-sê* means, as a rule, lapis lazuli. Schafer 1963, 230-234.

[215] See the finds from Nisa, *Trudy iuzhno-turkmenistanskoi kompleksnoi ekspeditsii* 8 (Ashkhabad, 1958), 385-385.

[216] Loehr 1956, 206, pl. 39:103; Sekino Tadashi 1927, 4, 1, 361-363; 4, 2, 226, 228, 229, 236; Chou Wei, pl. 58:15 (a long sword found in Hsin-hsiang, Honan, now in the library at Chi-nan).

[217] Loehr 1956, pl. 38:98, 99.

[218] *Yamanaka Catalogue* (New York, 1943), no. 157.

[219] Chang Hung-shao, *Shih ya*, 30-36 on *ma-nao*.

[220] *Khersonesskii sbornik* 2, 138, fig. 21. Mr. E. Lubo-Lesnichenko was so kind to have it checked for me in the laboratory of the Hermitage.

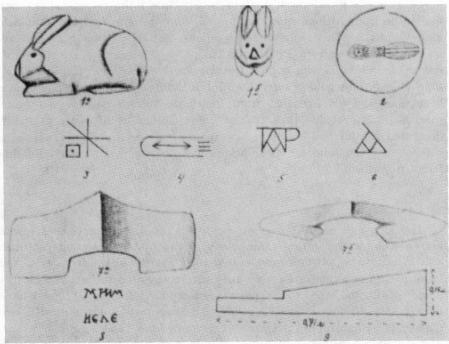

FIG. 12. Agate sword guard from Chersonese, third century A.D. From *Khersonesskiĭ sbornik*, 1927, fig. 21.

it: the third century A.D. As Chinese scabbard slides of jade and chalcedony have come to light from the Volga to Panticapaeum, and as far north as Perm,[221] the find of a Chinese sword guard of agate in Chersonese is in no way surprising. The piece from the Crimea is as Chinese as the sword guard from Altlussheim.

[*The following two paragraphs were found loose; since they discuss swords they are inserted here.—Ed.*]

Although Ostrogothic swords are not preserved or depicted or decribed, we know that they were heavy cutting weapons. In the battle Ad Salices in 376, the Ostrogothic cavalry "with mighty strength slashed at the heads and backs" of the fleeing Romans.[222] Even more instructive is John of Antioch (fr. 214a): Theoderic dealt Odovacar "a blow with his sword upon the collar-bone. The weapon pierced his body down to the hip. It is said that Theoderic exclaimed 'In truth, the wretch has no bones.'"[223]

---

[221] Maenchen-Helfen 1957a, 93.
[222] Ammianus Marcellinus XXXI, 7, 13.
[223] *FHG* V, 29.

There is no direct proof that in South Russia the Goths had swords like those from Altlussheim, Pouan, and from the grave of the Frankish king Childeric. These sumptuous weapons, glittering from gold and almandins, were made in Pontic workshops.[224] Two similar swords were, indeed, found at Taman and at Dmitrievka.[225] When one considers how fond of luxurious gold jewelry the Gothic nobles were—there must have been many hoards like that from Pietroasa, though perhaps not quite so rich—it is probable that at least some Gothic swords were as richly decorated as the just-mentioned weapons from South Russia. It is, I believe, not too bold an assumption that they were not markedly different from them.

LANCES

The long and heavy lances of the South Russian Sarmatians are well known from wall paintings and reliefs of the first and second centuries A.D. The artists at times exaggerated their length; in the frescoes of the tomb of Anthesterius in Kerch[226] they are represented to be 15 to 20 feet long.[227] Still, the lance on Tryphon's dedication from Tanais[228] must have been nearly 10 feet long; the galloping horseman is holding it with two hands. The Roxolani did the same, as we know from Tacitus, who, however, was not impressed by what he thought to be a clumsy weapon.[229] Other Romans thought differently. "Stretching out over the horse's head and shoulders," we read in Valerius Flaccus,[230] "the fir-wood shaft, firmly resting on their knees, casts a long shadow upon the enemy's field and forces its way with all the might of both warrior and steed." In the second century, Roman horsemen, heavily or light armored,[231] carrying long lances, $\kappa o\nu \tau o\acute{v}\varsigma$, attacked "in the manner of the Alans and Sauromatians."[232] The *hastae longiores* of the transdanubian Sarmatians[233] were probably javelins, whereas the *conti* of the Alans and Sarmatians, mentioned by Claudian,[234] were

---

[224] Their provenance was never seriously doubted.

[225] *Germania* 20, 1936, pl. 41:2, 3.

[226] Beginning of the first century A.D.

[227] *OAK* 1878-1879, pl. 1, fig. 1, and frontispiece; Minns 1913, 313, fig. 223; Rostovtsev 1914, atlas, pl. 51:2; text, 182.

[228] Minns 1913, 304, fig. 218. A lance found in a Sauromatian grave at Oktyabr'skoe on the right bank of the Aksai River in the lower Don region is 3.4 meters (more than 11 feet) long. *Arkheologicheskie otkrytiia 1965 goda* (Moscow, 1966), 87.

[229] *Hist.* I, 79. Cf. Walser 1951, 75-77.

[230] *Argon.* VI, 132-132.

[231] Arrian, *Tact.* IV, 9.

[232] *Ibid.*, 2.

[233] Ammianus XVII, 12, 2.

[234] *Cons. Stil.* I, 111; *Bell. Goth.* 586.

still the same thrust lances which the tribes in the East had carried since the sixth century B.C. They are attested for the Sauromatian,[235] Early,[236] and Middle Sarmatian periods, particularly for the latter (lance heads from stanitsa Kazanskaya and stanitsa Ust'-Labinskaya in the Kuban region,[237] Tarki in Dagestan,[238] Kalinovka[239] and Lyapichev[240] in the province Volgograd). The lance head in a woman's grave at Tri Brata near Elista in the Kalmuk steppe[241] is probably to be dated to the first century A.D., and the one from kurgan 28/2 at Kalinovka, 22 centimeters long,[242] cannot be much later. The lance head from the river burial at Pokrovsk-Voskhod[243] shows that the half-Alanized Huns on the Volga were armed like the Sarmatians in the preceding centuries.

It is a priori almost certain that the heavily armored Hunnic cavalry, like the Alanic and Roman cataphracts, carried long thrust lances. Avitus and the Hun wore the same equipment: the thorax and the lance. Among Narses' horsemen were Huns beyond the Danube; their weapons were σάρισσαι.[244]

In one of the graves at Hobersdorf in Lower Austria a 28-centimeter long lance head was found.[245] Werner and Mitscha-Märheim[246] date the graves to the first half of the fifth century which, I believe, is too early: in any case, the people buried there were Huns or closely related to them. The unsightly lance head from Pécs-Üszög[247] was probably the weapon of a Hun who rode in the king's "household" (comitatus, druzhina).

THE LASSO

"While the enemy are guarding against wounds from the sword-thrusts, the Huns throw strips of cloth plaited into nooses over their opponents and so entangle them that they fetter their limbs and take from them

---

[235] K. F. Smirnov 1961, 7-74; Smirnov and Petrenko 1963, pl. 74.

[236] Moshkova 1963, 35.

[237] OAK 1901, 77; Anfimov MIA 23, 1951, 182, fig. 12:1-6.

[238] K. F. Smirnov 1950a, 114; 1951b, 258-259.

[239] Shilov 1959, 462, fig. 50:1, 19.

[240] Arkheol. issled. 1934-1936, 186 (the lance seems to have been 2.5 meters long).

[241] Rykov 1936c, 119.

[242] Shilov 1959, 386, fig. 60:9.

[243] Sinitsyn 1936, 75, fig. 3.

[244] Agathias II, 8, ed. Bonn, 80.

[245] J. Werner 1956, pl. 11:1.

[246] Ibid., 110; Mitscha-Märheim 1963. It is regrettable that the apparently important finds are not properly published. One of the skulls is supposedly slightly artificially deformed; it should be measured.

[247] Alföldi 1932, pl. 2:3.

the power of riding or walking."[248] Ammianus' statement is confirmed by Sozomen:[249] A Hun "raised up his right hand in order to throw a rope [βρόχον] over Theotimus, bishop of Tomis, for the Hun intended to drag the bishop away to his own country; but in the attempt, the Hun's hand remained extended in the air, and the barbarian was not released from the terrible bonds until his companions implored Theotimus to intercede with God in his behalf."[250]

The Goths, the only Germans to use the lasso,[251] took it over either from the Huns or the Alans. The Alans almost caught King Tiridates with their throwing ropes;[252] in the fourth century, the lasso was their typical weapon.[253] The lasso was used throughout such a wide area[254] that it cannot be assigned to a specific cultural circle. It was known to the Scythians[255] and Sarmatians,[256] the Sargatians, a people "of Persian extraction and language,[257] the Thatae, Sirachi, Phicores, and Iaxamatae, peoples between Bosporus and the Don,[258] the Parthians,[259] and the Persians in Sasanian times.[260] In India the art of casting the lasso, pāśa, was one of the martial arts studied by princes.[261] It is the weapon of the Hindu gods.[262] In the fourth century, the Kuai Hu, west of Kuchā, used rawhide lariats which, whipping their horses, they threw at men.[263]

---

[248] Ammianus XXXI, 2, 9.

[249] VII, 26, 8, Bidez 1960, 342.

[250] A well-known miracle motive. The offender is often a barbarian: a Hun (John of Ephesus, *Lives of Eastern Saints, PO* 17, 20-21), a Hephthalite (Procopius I, 17, 8-9), a Frank (Greg. Tur., *Hist. Franc.* II, 27).

[251] Olympiodorus, fr. 17; Malalas 364 (Areobindus throws the lasso, σωκάρην, "in the Gothic fashion").

[252] Josephus, *BJ* VII, 249-250.

[253] *Laqueos iacere atque hostem innectere, ars Alanis bellandique mos est* (Hegesippus V, 50).

[254] Gy. Moravcsik, *KCsA* 1, 1921-1925, 276-280; Alföldi, *Folia Archaeologica* 1-2, 1939, 177-179.

[255] See the Scythian on a silver vase from Solokha (*Archäologischer Anzeiger* 1914, 270, fig. 19).

[256] Pausanias, *Descr. Graec.* I, 21, 5; cf. Valerius Flaccus, *Argon.* VI, 132.

[257] Herodotus VII, 85.

[258] Pomponius Mela I, 19, 17.

[259] Suidas, *s.v.* σειραῖς, probably from Arrian. According to Herzfeld (*Zoroaster and His World* 2, 787) *akavo* in Yasht 1, 18, means lasso.

[260] On a silver dish a king, possibly Shapur III, catches an onager with a lasso (*Jahrbuch d. Preuss. Kunstsammlungen* 57, 1936, fig. 6; *SPA* 4, pl. 209); on another one, found by Adler in 1942 in Krasnaya Polyana, Krasnodarskii krai, the king lassoes a bear (*Ars Orientalis* 2, 1957, pl. 5, after p. 62, and *Pamiatniki kul'tury sasanidskogo Irana*, pl. 3).

[261] Edgerton 1933, 344a.

[262] Zimmer 1947, 212, and 1956, 140.

[263] *Chin shu* 122, Mather 1959, 33.

Armor

Body Armor

To those historians who deny the Huns the capability of forging their swords,[264] the mere question of whether they made their own armor must sound strange. Besides, in his description of the Huns Ammianus Marcellinus says nothing about armor. No iron or bone lamellae, no scales, no plates from splint armor[265] have been found in Hun graves, or in association with what are doubtlessly Hunnic objects. The chain mail from Fedorovka in the former district Buzuluk, province Chelyabinsk,[266] and Pokrovsk-Voskhod[267] are suspect of being of Persian origin.[268]

However, to wear armor, and especially metal armor, was everywhere and at all times the privilege of a few. *Wegen des mühsamen, zeitraubenden und grosse Fertigkeit voraussetzenden Arbeitsgangs sind Kettenhemden zu allen Zeiten grosse Kostbarkeiten gewesen.*[269] Medvedev adduces telling testimonies for the esteem in which chain armor was held in late medieval Russia.[270] The much plainer scale armor also was apparently handed down from father to son and grandson rather than buried with the dead. A picture of Sarmatian civilization in Hungary, drawn from the finds, would not include scale armor. Yet we know from Ammianus that the cuirasses of the transdanubian Sarmatians were made of smooth and polished pieces of horn, fastened like scales to linen or leather shirts.[271]

There is good, though indirect archaeological evidence that the Hun nobles, and perhaps not they alone, long before their first engagement with armored Roman troops wore some covering to protect their bodies in battle.

Recent finds enlarge considerably the material on which Thordeman and Arwidsson[272] based their admirable studies on the history of armor.

---

[264] Thompson 1948, 5, 52.

[265] For the terminology, see E. H. Minns, *Antiquity*, no. 72, 1944, 197-200. It is often difficult to distinguish between scales and lamellae. Warriors of the same tribe, or of allied tribes, sometimes have both scale and lamellar armor; cf., *e.g.*, the often reproduced fifth-century wood sculpture from Egypt, *Die Kunst der Spätantike im Mittelmeerraum* 176, 63.

[266] Gol'msten 1928, 134. It is regrettable that this important find has been so inadequately published. The illustration in Gol'msten's article and Tallgren's short report (1929, 35) are poor. Sal'nikov (1952, 135) does not even mention the chain mail. It is nowhere reproduced.

[267] Sinitsyn 1936, 75.

[268] J. Werner 1956, 56.

[269] P. Post, *Zeitschr. f. hist. Waffen- und Kostümkunde* N. F. 7, 1943, 251.

[270] A. F. Medvedev, *SA* 2, 1959, 120.

[271] Ammianus XVII, 12, 2.

[272] See the bibliography in Arwidsson 1954, 141-144.

I realize that the following survey has many gaps and that in a few years it will be obsolete. Yet for our purpose I hope it will suffice.

Bone lamellae are known from a much wider area and from much older sites than had been assumed before. They were found in graves of the Glazkovo period (eighteenth to thirteenth century B.C.) at Ust'-Igla on the Lena River in Cis-Baikalia and at Perevoznaya near Krasnoyarsk.[273] Far to the west, on the lower Ob, bone lamellae and a technically and artistically marvelous breastplate of whalebone, found in settlements at Ust'-Polui near Salekhard, are datable between the fifth and third centuries B.C.[274] Bone lamellae of the late Ananino period (fourth to third century B.C.) are known from Bol'shoi Skorodum[275] and Konets-Gor[276] in the Kama Basin.

Bone and horn armor is not necessarily inferior to, nor always earlier than, metal armor. To judge by the other grave goods, the bronze scales in the cemetery on the Morkvashka near Kazan[277] are about two centuries earlier than the earliest bone scales found there. Pausanias greatly admired the Sarmatian corselets. The Sarmatians, he wrote,[278]

> collect the hoofs of their mares, clean them, and split them till they resemble the scales of a dragon. Anybody who has not seen a dragon has at least seen a green fir cone. Well, the fabric which they made out of the hoofs may not be inaptly likened to the clefts on a fir cone. In these pieces they bore holes, and having stitched them together with the sinews of horses and oxen, they use them as corselets, which are inferior to Greek breast-plates neither in elegance nor strength, for they are both sword-proof and arrow-proof.

The cuirasses of the horsemen in the Hellenistic armies were sometimes made of horn,[279] and if the author of the *Sylloge Tacticorum* does not copy earlier authors but describes the armament of the Byzantine army of his time, the *clibania* of the horsemen were, as late as the tenth century, either of iron or of horn.[280]

In the last centuries B.C. and the first centuries A.D., armor of one type or the other was widely used in northern Eurasia. I pass over the well-known

---

[273] Okhladnikov 1955, 248, fig. 118-120.

[274] Moshinskaia 1953, 99-101, pls. 11:18-19 and 15, and 1965, 34-34, p. 14, where she refers to the bone lamellae in the kurgans at Shadrinsk and near Omsk.

[275] O. N. Bader, *KS* 70, 1957, 51, fig. 15:11-15.

[276] Zbrueva 1952, 243, pl. 14:12.

[277] *Ibid.*, 310-319, figs. 56:a, 58:a, b, 62:b.

[278] Frazer 1965, I, 4.

[279] Arrian, *Tact.* IV, 1, Roos 1928, 132. Arrian apparently follows earlier authorities.

[280] *Sylloge Tacticorum* 31, 1, Dain 1938, 132.

and often discussed representations of armored warriors in Parthian[281] and Gandharan art,[282] but I would like to draw attention to two little-noticed metal figures from the Altai region and western Siberia.

A bronze pendant (fig. 12A),[283] said to have been found in a grave at Barnaul in the Altai region, shows a man wearing a scale armor and a conical helmet; his quiver has the hour-glass shape that occurs from China to the Caspian Sea. To draw any conclusion from the style of the pendant—provided the drawing is correct—would be risky. The earliest hour-glass quiver is datable to the fourth century A.D.[284]

FIG. 12A. Bronze pendant said to have been found in a grave at Barnaul, Altai region, showing a man in scale armor and conical hat with an hour-glass-shaped quiver, datable to the fourth century A.D. From Aspelin 1877, no. 327.

---

[281] For a gold plaque representing a Parthian in scale armor, see *Hesperia Art* 7:222 (New York, 1958). The Parthians on the relief at Tang-i-Sarvak (A. Stein, *Geographical Journal* 92, 1928, 323, fig. 8) seem to wear lamellar armor. In Nisa, iron plates from armor of various types were found (M. Masson, *VDI* 1, 1953, 154).

[282] The brassarts from Taxila (Sir J. Marshall 1951, pl 170:p, q)— the Han Chinese would have called them *han*, ô *Shuo wen*, *s.v.*—are without a parallel in Gandhara but similar to the pieces of plate armor from Chirikrabat in the ancient delta of the Syr Darya, datable to the fourth century B.C.; cf. S. P. Tolstov, *SE* 4, 1961, 137; *Irania antiqua* 1, 1961, 79; S. P. Tolstov 1962, 141. As the manufacture of this type of armor required a skill obviously far beyond that of the Hun metalworkers, it need not be discussed.

[283] Aspelin 1877, 1, 71, no. 327.

[284] A horseman, incised on a stone pillar at Tasheba near Minusinsk, carries this peculiar quiver (Appelgren-Kivalo 1931, 44, fig. 312). The pillar is part of a stone fence around a low barrow of a type characteristic for the fifth century A.D. (Teploukhov 1929, 54). The picture is upside down on the pillar, so it must have been on the stone when this was used for fencing the barrow.

Then there are the horsemen on two gold pendants from western Siberia (fig. 12B).[285] They also wear scale armor. Their similarity to the rider on the famous wall hanging in Pazyryk (fourth century B.C.)[286] indicates an early date. The short jacket, the boots, the horse trappings are the same here and there. The square tuft in the mane, clearly discernible on one plaque, corresponds to the crenelation of the mane in Pazyryk.[287]

FIG. 12B. Two horsemen in scale armor shown in gold pendants from western Siberia. From Kondakov and Tolstoĭ, 3, fig. 49.

The most common and probably the earliest type of armor in the steppes was scale armor. In spite of the strong influence the civilization of Urartu exerted on Scythian metal work, the Scythians did not take over Urartian lamellar armor.[288] Throughout the centuries that we can follow their history they wore scale armor.[289] The scales, sometimes gilded,[290] were of bone, bronze, or iron;[291] occasionally the two metals were combined.[292] As the finds from Kobylovka near Atkarsk west of Saratov, from Tonku-

[285] Radlov 1893, 123; Kondakov and Tolstoĭ 1889, 3, 47, fig. 49; Rudenko 1962b, 49, pl. 22:8, 9. Miller acquired the plaques in the northwestern Altai.

[286] Rudenko 1953, pl. 95.

[287] Maenchen-Helfen, 1957a, 125-126, 135-136.

[288] Piotrovskiĭ 1955, 3, 20-22, 30-35, figs. 21, 23, 24, pl. 14, and 1959, 166.

[289] Minns 1913, 73-74, 187, 224, fig. 45, 80, 134; Rostovtsev 1931, 283, 286, 298, 311-312, 316, 464, 472; Medvedev, *SA* 2, 1959, 120-122. The Maeotian tribes had scale armor as early as the fourth century B.C. (*MIA* 64, 1958, 305).

[290] Minns 1913, 14; Rostovtsev 1931, 316.

[291] Popovka: Bobrinskoĭ 1901, 3, 75, pl. 8:15-21; Losovaya: Rostovtsev 1931, 193; Volkovtsy: *RV* 8, 90. Cf. Blavatskiĭ 1954, 114. For the leather scale armor, see Chernenko 1964, 17, 144-152.

[292] Minns 1913, 206, 224, 229; L. Matsulevich, *Soobshcheniia Gos. Ermitazha* 4, 1947, 7, fig. 3.

shorovka (formerly Marienthal), and from the province Astrakhan show,[293] the Sarmatians of the Sauromatian period also had bronze scale and lamellar armor. Bronze lamellae of the Early Sarmatian period are rare.[294] Bronze, iron, and bone scales were found in Middle Sarmatian graves in the Trans-Ural steppes,[295] on the lower Volga (Kalinovka,[296] Pogromnoe,[297] Usatovo on the Eruslan[298]), in the Kuban Valley,[299] and in the southern Ukraine.[300] Scales in a grave at Vor'bi[301] indicate Sarmatian influence on the P'yany-bor civilization. Sarmatians and Sarmatized Bosporans,[302] horse and man covered with corselets of scale armor, are depicted on the wall paintings at Panticapaeum-Kerch.[303]

For the Late Sarmatian period (II-IV A.D.), we have the adduced testimony of Pausanias (about 175 A.D.). The Sarmatians of Emperor Galerius' bodyguard on the arch of Thessalonica[304] wear the same scale armor as the galloping horseman on a relief from Tanais,[305] datable to the third century (see also the figure of a member of the Roxolani tribe, fig. 12C), or the Bosporan kings Cotys II and Sauromates II on their coins.[306] There is, finally, a stone relief from Chester in the Grosvenor Museum.[307] It shows a Sarmatian, a cloaked horseman, with a tall conical helmet, holding

---

[293] K. F. Smirnov 1961, 75; Smirnov and Petrenko 1963, pl. 14:31, 32.

[294] Moshkova 1963, 35.

[295] Samarevskoe near Shadrinsk, province Kurgan (bone scales), Posta 1905, 361, fig. 214: 7-9. The date is not quite certain.

[296] Kurgan 55, burial 14 (more than 200 iron scales), Shilov 1959, 406, 462, fig. 50: 1, 8.

[297] Medvedev, *SA* 2, 1959, 122, n. 23.

[298] Sinitsyn 1947, 86.

[299] Rostovtsev 1931, 559, quoting Veselovskiĭ. The hauberk from Zubov's farm is in Minns 1913, 122, fig. 134, a mail shirt, in Blavatskiĭ 1954, 116, fig. 59.

[300] Dolina in the Molochnaya Valley (Furmans'ka 1960, 136); M. I. Viazmitina (*APU* 8, 1960, 20) dates the find to the beginning of our era.

[301] R. Urzhum, obl. Kirov (*MIA* 27, 1952, 21, no. 63; A. P. Smirnov 1952, 106; Oborin and Bader 1958, 133.

[302] There exists a large literature on the influence of Sarmatian warfare on the Bosporans. For a bibliography up to 1934, see M. I. Rostovtsev, *Yale Classical Studies* 5, 1935, 268; for more recent publications, see Blavatskiĭ 1954, 113-123, 138-150.

[303] Ashik's catacomb, Minns 1913, 314, fig. 224; Stassov's catacomb, best reproduction in Gaĭdukevich 1949, 419.

[304] *CAH*, plates 5, 150b.

[305] Minns 1913, 304, fig. 218 (drawing); Blavatskiĭ 1954, 143, fig. 66 (photograph).

[306] Minns 1913, pls. 8:4, 10.

[307] *The Roman Inscribed and Sculptured Stones in the Grosvenor Museum* (Chester, 1955), 51, no. 137; pl. 34:1; a good reproduction in Bacon 1963, 281. S. A. Richmond (*JRS* 35:1-2, 1945, 15-29) thinks the horsemen might be one of the numerus, later cuneus, Sarmatarum which in the third and fourth centuries garrisoned the fort at Chichester.

FIG. 12C. The representation of a Sarmatian member of the Roxolani tribe in a detail of the marble relief from Trajan's Column, in the Forum of Trajan, Rome. Datable to the second decade of the second century A.D. Photos courtesy Deutsches archäologisches Institut, Rome.

with both hands a dragon standard or pennon. The surface tooling on man and horse is much worn, but what remains suggests that both were shown clad in scale armor.

For the tribes on the eastern end of Eurasia we have in the main to rely on Chinese sources. We learn from them that the primitive, perhaps Tungus, Su-shên in Manchuria had leather and bone armor,[308] and we read about the armor of the Fu-yü[309] and Jo-chiang.[310] In the armies of the Hsiung-nu rode "cuirassed horsemen."[311] Their armor is called *chia* which, according to Laufer,[312] in Ssu-ma Ch'ien means "hide armor." But in 1956 Dorzhsuren found in one of the Hsiung-nu graves at Noin Ula an iron scale, with the fabric, to which it had been fastened, still on it.[313] Iron scales occur in Tuva in graves of the Shurmak period (second century B.C. to first century A.D.).[314] Like the Chinese of the Han period,[315] the Hsiung-nu probably also had bronze and leather scale armor.

Finds of metal lamellar armor in the steppes are rare. Those from Kutr-Tas, province Kustanai,[316] and Tomilovka on the Tobol River[317] are probably of Persian provenance. Gryaznov thinks an oblong iron plaque with perforations around the edges, found at Blizhnie Elbany north of Barnaul, is the lamella of an armor.[318]

---

[308] Ikeuchi (1930) quotes a number of passages dealing with the tribute sent by the Su-shên to the Chinese court. They mention no armor of leather or bone, except the report on the tribute in 262 (Ikeuchi 1930, 136), where "leather, bone, and iron armors" are named. Contrary to Laufer's assumption (1914, 266) that the Su-shên occasionally made iron armor, this entry in the annals is almost certainly not correct.

[309] Ikeuchi 1932, 38.

[310] *Ch'ien Han shu*, ch. 95; Bichurin 1950, 2, 172; de Groot 1926, 53.

[311] *Shih-chi* 110, 1b.

[312] Laufer 1914, 223, n. 3.

[313] *Mongol'skiĭ arkheologicheskiĭ sbornik*, 38. For iron scales in Sui-yüan, see Egami 1951, pl. 10:2.

[314] Kyzlasov 1958, 93.

[315] In the watch towers in the Edsen-Gol region in Inner Mongolia (Sommerström 1956, 1, 41, 94, 96; 2, 237, 245). Because the scales were lacquered, they must have been made in China. Egami (1951, 70-71) quotes a passage in *Lü shih ch'un ch'iu*, ch. 8, and another one in *Chan kuo ts'e*, which in his opinion prove that in the period of the Warring States the Chinese had metal armor, supposedly taken over from the Hsiung-nu. But neither *chia* 甲 nor *chia cha* 甲札 denotes specifically metal armor; cf. Laufer 1914, 210, n. 8. Besides, the barbarians who in the fourth century B.C. gave the Chinese new weapons and a technique of warfare were probably the Yüeh-chih; cf. Maenchen-Helfen 1945a, 25q.

[316] *Trudy Orenburgskoĭ uchenoĭ arkhivnoĭ komissii* 23, 191, 135. Medvedev (1959, 125) dates them not later than the third or fourth century A.D.

[317] Heikel 1894, 90, 92, 94. Talitskaia (1952, 282-283) dates them to the beginning of our era.

[318] Griaznov 1956, 104, pl. 41: 11.

At the beginning of our era, or, perhaps, even earlier, chain mail began to take its place next to scale armor among the Sarmatians in the Kuban Basin.[319] In the first century A.D., Valerius Flaccus[320] described the Sarmatian *catafractarii:* "Their armor is bristling with flexible chains and their horses have the same protective cover" (*riget his molli lorica catena, id quoque tegimen equis*). The chain mail in Karabudakhkent in Dagestan is certainly of Sarmatian provenance.[321] The same is probably true for the chain mail found in the basin of the Kama and its tributaries: Vichmar',[322] Atamonovy kosti,[323] Gainy,[324] and Pystain.[325]

The figure incised on a sheep astragal, found in Kobadian in Tadjikistan (third to second century B.C.),[326] seems to represent a warrior in a long coat, with what might be a helmet on his head; D'yakonov takes the crisscross lines on the coat for chain mail, but they could be just quilts. The same might be true for another figure of a warrior, incised on a bone, from the cemetery at Kuyu-Mazar near Tashkent (second to first century B.C.).[327] In the fourth century A.D., the armor of the Kuai Hu, west of Kuchā, was like "linked chain, impenetrable to bow and arrow."[328]

In view of the literary and archaeological evidence for the spread of body armor in the first centuries A.D. from the Ukraine to Manchuria, it is a priori unlikely that the warlike Hun tribes fought without protection of some sort of armor. In addition, we have the testimony of Greek and Latin sources.

The Huns, Alans, and Goths in the army which Theodosius led against Maximus in 388 were not Roman soldiers but free barbarians, enlisted for

---

[319] Rostovtsev 1931, 558. The Maeotic tribes had chain mail as early as the fourth century B.C.

[320] *Argon.* VI, 233-234.

[321] Cemetery 3, Ia. A. Fedorov 1960, 24, n. 42 (found together with swords with ring-handles).

[322] A. P. Smirnov 1952, 106; Talitskaia 1952, 22, no. 60.

[323] A. P. Smirnov 1952, 106; Talitskaia 1952, 19, no. 49.

[324] A. V. Schmidt 1927.

[325] Talitskaia 1952, 192, no. 1416 (dated VI-IX).

[326] I. M. D'iakonov, *MIA* 37, 1953, 268, fig. 21.

[327] Obel'chenko 1956, 223, fig. 20. I do not know what the figure on the horn plaque from Ak-Tam near the city of Ferghana (fourth to third century B.C.), N. G. Gorbunova, *KS* 80, 1960, 93, fig. 22, is meant to represent. That the fragment of an oval iron plaque in the same cemetery (Gamburg and Gorbunova 1957a, fig. 29:1) comes from an armor seems doubtful to me.

[328] *Chin shu* 122, 1b, in Mather 1959, 33. Mather (n. 74) refers to the murals at Kizil, Ming-Öi, depicting Kuchean horsemen and their armor. Laufer (1914, 247) asserted that the term *lien so chia* 連鑅甲 occurs for the first time in the Sung period; he overlooked the passage in *Chin shu.*

one campaign. They were not outfitted with weapons manufactured in the *armorum fabricae*; they brought their own equipment with them. It included heavy iron cuirasses.[329]

Fifty years later, some Huns under the command of Litorius in Gaul wore the same armor. They, too, were not *milites* but *auxiliatores* and *socii*.[330] Sidonius Apollinaris describes a duel between Avitus and a Hun in Litorius' contingent that reads like one taken from a medieval romance:

When the first bout, the second, the third have been fought, lo! the upraised spear comes and pierces the man of blood; his breast was transfixed and his corselet twice split, giving way even where it covered the back [*post et confinia dorsi cedit transfosso ruptus bis pectore thorax*] ; and as the blood came throbbing through the two gaps, the separate wounds took away the life that each of them might claim.[331]

The *thorax* was clearly not a mere breastplate but a piece of armor protecting the body on all sides, not a leather corselet but a metal shirt. It may have been of the same type as the one worn by the Hun Bochas, one of Belisarius' bodyguards:

He came to be surrounded by twelve of the enemy, who carried spears. And they all struck him at once with their spears. But his *thorax* withstood the other blows, which therefore did not hurt him much; but one of the Goths succeeded in hitting him from behind, at a place where his body was uncovered, above the right armpit, right close to the shoulder, and smote the youth, though not with a mortal blow.[332]

Pacatus in the fourth, Sidonius in the fifth, and Procopius in the sixth century testify that the Huns were "men with iron cuirasses" (ἄνδρες σιδέρῳ τεθωρακισμένοι).[333] There are three more sources which, to my knowledge, have not been utilized. The first is a homily on St. Phocas by Asterius of Amasea. The saint was venerated throughout the world. Even "the most ferocious Scythians who lived on the other side of the Euxine,

---

[329] *Loricis onustos inclusosqu ferro* (Pacatus XXXIII, 4). In passing, I may remark that where the texts mention armor without further qualification it is almost invariably iron armor. The Manchu-Tungus word for armor is derived from the word for iron (L. Ligeti, *AOH* 9, 1959, 261).

[330] Paulinus of Périgueux, *De vita s. Martini* VI, 219-220, *CSEL* 16, 147.

[331] *Paneg. on Avitus* 289-292. The only way an armed rider without stirrups can use the lance as a shock weapon is described by Heliodorus, *Aethiopica* IX, 15: The horseman's great lance "is thrust straight forward, and its forepart is lashed to the horse's neck; its butt is slung in a noose at the croupe" (quoted by Brown 1936, 445).

[332] Procopius VII, 2, 22.

[333] Grosse 1920, 325.

near the Maeotis and Tanais, and as far as the Phasis River," were deeply devoted to him. One of their rulers "took off his crown, sparkling with gold and jewels, and put off his war cuirass of precious metal (for the armor of the barbarians is ostentatious and sumptuous)" and sent them to St. Phocas' church in Sinope.[334] The homily[335] was written about 400,[336] at a time when the greater part of the territory described by Asterius was under Hun domination. The ἄρχων καὶ βασιλεύς[337] was most probably a Hun.

The other source is Merobaudes' panegyric on Aetius' third consulship. In verses 79-83,[338] the poet describes the equipment and weapons of the Huns:

> *fulgentes i]n tela ruunt: gravis ardeat auro
> *balteus, a]339 uratae circumdent tela pharetrae,
> *aurea cri]spatis insidat lamna lupatis:
> *incendant] gemmas chalybes ferroque micantes
> *cassidis340 a]uratis facibus lux induat enses.

Belts, quivers, horse bits, helmets, and the armor, studded with precious stones, were gilded. The hexameters cannot be dismissed as a mere imitation of what Merobaudes read in Claudian and Statius. They were obviously patterned on In Rufinum II, 352-377, and other passages dealing with the sumptuous equipment of the Roman elite cavalry. It is, furthermore, true that nearly all the golden or gilt weapons of the Huns have their Roman counterparts.[341] Some may actually have been of Roman

---

334 PG 40, 313.

335 One of the authentic works of Asterius; cf. Skard 1940, 86-132.

336 Bretz 1914, 3.

337 In his pious zeal Asterius was quite capable of promoting a simple chieftain to king.

338 I follow Vollmer's restoration of the hexameters. Because of the following ardeat, auratae, auratis, micantes, and lux, his *fulgentes is preferable to una omnes, suggested by Niebuhr. The verb in v. 82 must be *incendant; Niebuhr's *includant is too pale.

339 The heavy object blazing with gold could be the lance head, but none of the words of which one could think would fit the meter. Vollmer's *balteus is almost certainly correct. Cf. J. Werner 1956, 83-84, on the precious belt buckles of the Huns.

340 The light enveloping the flashing iron swords must be reflected by some piece of equipment. The armor has been named before, so it must be the helmet.

341 Belt: gladium bonum dices non cui auratus est balteus (Seneca, Ep. 76, 4); aurato religans ilia balto (Seneca, Hercules furens 553); a golden cingulus (Statius, Thebais VIII, 566-567).

Quiver: aurata pharetra (Claudian, Epithal. 134).

Armor: loricam induitur; ferro squama rudi permixtoque asperat auro (Silius Italicus, Punica V, 140-141); virides smaragdo loricas (Claudian, Cons. Stil. II, 789-790); Mars wears micantem loricam (Claudian, 4th Cons. Hon.).

Helmet: Fulget nobilis galea et corusca luce gemmarum divinam verticem monstrat (Nazarius, [word] Constantino dictus 29, 5). The references could easily be multiplied.

provenance;[342] a few Huns may have worn gilt Persian armor.[343] But all this does not detract from Merobaudes' description of the Hunnic arms. The poet could not have drawn such a picture had it not corresponded to reality. His public, and first of all Aetius, knew the Huns. By calling felt caps helmets and leather jackets armor, Merobaudes would have made himself ridiculous. Some Huns *did* wear costly armor.

There is, third, a short passage from Priscus, preserved in Suidas: Zercon, the Moorish jester, accompanied Bleda in his campaigns in full armor.[344]

Six authors, independently of one another, speak of the body armor of the Huns. This by no means proves that all Huns wore armor. Most of them were, as Ammianus said, lightly equipped, and remained so until the end of Attila's kingdom. But many Hun nobles were heavily armored, and their number was apparently growing as the Huns acquired riches from booty and tribute.

Helmets

The Huns in the army of Theodosius must have worn metal helmets. With their bodies protected by iron armor, they could not have fought bareheaded or worn soft leather or felt caps. As we know from Merobaudes, in the 440's the helmets of the Hun nobles were gilt. What such *cassides* looked like can be learned from Sidonius Apollinaris. In the *Panegyric on Avitus* (253-255), he describes how the heads of the Hun boys were flattened:

> The nostrils, while soft, are blunted by an encircling band, to prevent the two passages [*i.e.*, the nose] from growing outward between the cheekbones, that thus they make room for the helmets [*ut galeis cedant*]; for these children are born for battles, and a mother's love disfigures them, because the area of the cheeks stretches and expands when the nose does not interfere.

From these verses, stilted but clear in their meaning, Arendt rightly concluded that the Hunnic helmets had nosepieces.[345]

It is understandable that helmets do not occur in Hunnic graves. Like armor, helmets were so costly that they were handed down from generation to generation—the *Spangenhelm* from Gammertingen was more than a

---

[342] Alaric wore a Roman lorica (Claudian, *Bell. Goth.* 82). In the thirteenth century, the Mongols often armed themselves with captured weapons (Kantorowicz 1927, 2, 506).

[343] For the Achaemenian breastplates of golden scales, see Herodotus IX, 22. The scales of the Parthian armor reflected a glaring splendor (Ammianus XXIV, 6).

[344] Ἀναλαμβάνων ἐν ταῖς ἐξόδοις πανοπλίαν. Suidas, *s.v. Ζέρκων*.

[345] Arendt 1932b, 3.

hundred years old when it finally was deposited in the grave.[346] Perhaps the widespread belief that the dead were proof against attack also played a role.

The Hunnic helmet was possibly a Spangenhelm. If, as Post maintains, the Spangenhelme with a copper framework are to be strictly separated from those with an iron framework,[347] the Hunnic helmets cannot belong to the former group in which nosepieces occur in rudimentary form or not at all. They may, however, have resembled the iron Spangenhelm from Dêr-el-Medîneh in Egypt,[348] which Werner dates to the fifth century; he takes it for the helmet of a Roman officer.[349] The Sarmatian helmets on the Galerius arch in Thessalonica are provided with nasals, though whether they are Spangenhelme cannot be determined.[350]

Furthermore, there is the curious helmet, laced with leather thongs, from Kerch, uncovered by Kulakovskii in a catacomb.[351] It was found together with lamellae from mail shirts, a lance head, twenty arrowheads, pieces of gold-embroidered fabrics, golden plaques from a belt, and a coin of Emperor Leo (457-473). Because the coin was pierced, the find has been dated to the sixth century.[352] But the tomb was plundered at an early time, and the coin may have been lost, as Kulakovskii thought, by the tomb robbers. Grancsay dates the helmet to the fifth century and takes it for Avaric,[353] although in the fifth century the Avars were not even near the Crimea. If the man was buried in a catacomb built for him, he could have been a Hun. Such catacombs were not built after the fifth century. But the grave may be a secondary burial. *Non liquet.*

Lately it has become fashionable to give the Sasanians credit for every advance in military technique in late imperial times. The nasal of the Roman helmet is supposed to be of Eastern origin, but whether the Sasanians were the givers is at least doubtful. The few preserved Sasanian helmets have no nosepieces. The face of the horseman on the rock sculpture at Taq-i-Bustan is covered, except for the eyes, with a defense of mail, suspended from the rim of the helmet.[354] Around a Sasanian helmet

---

[346] J. Werner 1950, 182.

[347] Post 1953, 131-132.

[348] K. H. Dittmann, Germania 1940, 40, pl. 15.

[349] J. Werner, *Prähist. Zeitschr.* 34-35, 1945-1950.

[350] For an earlier Sarmatian helmet with a nosepiece, see E. E. Lents, *IAK* 4, 1902, 120ff.

[351] *IAK* 1891, 59-61; Arendt 1932a, 49-55.

[352] J. Werner 1935, 66.

[353] Grancsay 1949, 275.

[354] Best photograph in Porada 1963, 208.

in the Metropolitan Museum of Art in New York there are several perforations to which a similar defense of mail must have been attached.[355]

As for the mentioned conical helmets of the Sarmatians on the Galerius
arch, there existed more of this kind in the East. Among them are the iron
conical helmets found on the Vangai River between Tobolsk and Omsk
in western Siberia. One is gilt, the other has gilt inlays of dragon and
griffinlike figures.[356] In the hoard were also two Chinese mirrors of the
Han period[357] and a silver disk with the representation of Artemis (?),
probably made in Bactria in the first half of the second century B.C.[358]
It is evident that the helmets were not made where they were found, but
neither their construction nor their decoration gives an indication where
they came from. The incised figures of horsemen on the plaques found
together with the helmets[359] show that the tribes on the lower Ob wore
conical helmets with nosepieces about the beginning of our era.

It is possible that the Hun nobles wore helmets of various forms and
constructions, Spangenhelme, helmets like those of the Sarmatians on the
Galerius arch, helmets of the Vangai type, and still others.[360]

Shields

If the Hunnic shield had an *umbo*, the hollow boss of iron or bronze
covering the aperture of the Roman and common Germanic shield, one
should have been found in a Hunnic grave. Its absence indicates that the
shield of the Huns, like that of the Scythians,[361] the Persian infantry,[362] and
some of the Roman troops,[363] was of wickerwork, possibly covered with
leather.[364]

---

[355] *Bulletin of the Metropolitan Museum of Art*, April 1963, 260, fig. 13.

[356] Chernetsov 1953, 162-171, fig. i, 2; a color reproduction of the inlaid helmet
in *Po sledam* between pp. 176 and 177.

[357] Chernetsov 1953, pl. 19. They are coarsened versions of the *Ch'ing pai* mirrors.
In 1956, a similar mirror was found near Hsi-an; cf. *Shan hsi sheng ch'u t'u t'ung ching*
(Peking, 1958), 50, no. 40.

[358] Trever 1940, 61-64, pl. 12.

[359] Chernetsov 1953, pl. 20:2, 3.

[360] For instance, Roman helmets like the one found at Conçesti (Matsulevich 1929,
pl. 49).

[361] For the shields in Pazyryk, see Rudenko 1953, 262-263, pl. 87.

[362] *Persepolis* I, pl. 100-101; Xenophon, *Anab.* I, 8; Ammianus Marcellinus XXIV,
6, 8. Suidas, *s.v.* οἰσυΐανας. A bronze umbo with a Gorgo from Nisa (M. Masson, *VDI*
1, 1953, 154) is Greek.

[363] Vegetius, *Epit. rei milit.* I, 11.

[364] Aelian, *NA* II, 16, quoted in Minns 1913, 73.

Very little about the shields of the Sarmatians is known. According to Strabo, the Roxolani had shields of wickerwork.[365] The copper umbo in kurgan 10 of the Maeoto-Sarmatian cemetery at stanitsa Elizavetovskaya[366] seems to be of Greek provenance. Two umbones in the Sarmatian cemetery Malaaeshti in the Moldavian SSR[367] might have come from the Bosporan kingdom.[368] There remains the umbo in the Gepidic cemetery at Kiszombor in Hungary; it is in the shape of a high cone, different from the usual low or hemispherical umbo.[369] In Csongrád a similar umbo was found in a grave together with a trihedral arrowhead[370] which could be Hunnic or Sarmatian; Párducz takes the grave for Vandalic.[371] Another umbo of this type lay next to a sitting skeleton in a grave at Nyíregyháza,[372] possibly attributable to a Sarmatian. There is, as we see, very slight evidence that the western Sarmatians had wooden shields with umbones, and none that the Sarmatians in the East had them.

A passage in Sozomen tells us something about the shields of the Huns at the end of the fourth century. While talking to Theotimus, bishop of Tomis, a Hun leaned on his shield, "as was his custom when parleying with his enemies."[373] As the Hun was standing, his shield must have been at least as big as some of the Scythian oblong shields on the Kul Oba vase,[374] or those of the Sarmatized Bosporan foot soldiers on the wall paintings in Panticapaeum.[375] If we apply the ratio determined from the terra cotta figures of Sarmatians from Kerch, with their long shields,[376] to life proportions, the Hun, assuming that he was 5 feet, 5 or 6 inches, carried a shield 2 ½ and possibly 3 feet long. Such a large shield was not suitable for use on horseback. Narses' cavalry, which must have included many Huns, were armed with javelins, bows, long lances, and small shields, *peltai.*[377]

---

365 Strabo VII, 3, 7.

366 *IAK* 35, 104, fig. 9g.

367 G. B. Fedorov 1960b, 115; 326, pl. 19:5, 6.

368 On the Bosporan umbones, see Sokolskiĭ 1955.

369 Csallány 1961, 263, pl. 230:12.

370 M. Párducz, *Dolgozatok* 12, 1936, 54, pl. 41:7; Csallány 1961, pl. 207:5.

371 Párducz 1959, 371.

372 *Ibid.*, 326; Csallány 1961, 341.

373 Sozomen VII, 6, 8, Bidez 1960, 342.

374 Minns 1913, 200, fig. 93.

375 *Ibid.*, 317, fig. 227. Cf. the big oval shield on the stele of Gazurius, Chersonesus, *OAK* 1892, 26, fig. 23.

376 Minns 1913, 56, fig. 10; Blavatskiĭ 1954, 147, fig. 70. For an extraordinarily long shield, see Sokolskiĭ 1955, 10, fig. 2:2, the man is leaning on it like the Hun.

377 Agathias II, 8; ἡ γὰρ πέλτη σμικρότερον τῆς ἄσπιδος καὶ ἐλαφρότερον (Arrian, *Tact.* III, 4).

HUNS IN THE ROMAN ARMY

The *Notitia Dignitatum* lists Frankish, Alamanic, Gothic, Vandalic, Herulic, Marcomannic, Quadic, and Alanic *alae, vexillationes, cohortes, cunei,* and *auxilia*[378] but no Hunnic units. Those Huns who went over to the Romans were apparently distributed among the *numeri barbari* or the Theodosiani, Arcadiani, and Honoriani *equites, sagittarii,* and *armigeri.* Only under exceptional circumstances were Huns kept together. Such a formation was, I believe, the Unnigardae.

Of the units which in the first decade of the fifth century served in Libya Pentapolis, only the Balagritae were Africans; the cavalry consisted mostly of Thracians, the infantry of Dalmatians and Marcomanni.[379] The best troops were the Unnigardae. Synesius, bishop of Ptolemais, praised them as the savior of his beloved city. It was true, they sometimes got out of hand, "like young hounds," but their leader "would take them by the throat and call them in, even before they sated themselves with their charge and their wild-beast slaughter."[380] The Unnigardae[381] were a small corps of horsemen, excellent in lightning attacks and dashing raids, at their best as scouts and vanguards. "They are in need of a rearguard and an army drawn up in order of battle." From Synesius' letter to his friend Anysius in Constantinople,[382] we learn that the Unnigardae formed an independent troop, receiving their relays of horses, equipment, and pay directly from the emperor. Their status, tactics, and ferocity are comparable to those "Massagetae" who in the sixth century fought under Belisarius in Africa and Italy.

Unni is undoubtedly the ethnic name.[383] It must be left to Germanic scholars to decide whether *gardae* could reflect the Latin pronunciation of the Germanic word that gave Old Italian *guarda* and French *garde.*[384]

Another Hunnic formation was possibly stationed in Britain. One of the commanders *per lineam valli,* Hadrian's wall, was the *praefectus alae Sabinianae, Hunno.*[385] Could Hunnum be "the fort of the Huns"?

---

[378] Lot 1936, 319-320.

[379] Pando 1940, 129-130.

[380] *Catastasis, PG* 66, 1568.

[381] Οὐννίγαρδαι. Suidas has Ὀϊνγάρδαι · ὄνομα ἔθνους ; the lexicon of Zonaras, Οὐνίγαρδαι · ἐθνικόν. Cf. Moravcsik, *BT* 2, 236.

[382] *Ep.* LXXVIII, *PG* 66, 1443.

[383] Ch. Lacombrade (*RÉA* 48, 1946, 26-266) takes Unnigardae for another form of Hunuguri, which is most certainly wrong.

[384] Rattisti 1956, 633.

[385] *Not. Dign.* [*occ.*] XL, 37.

The ala Sabiniana, in Britain since the second century,[386] was of course not a Hunnic unit. But the *Notitia Dignitatum*, in the form it has come down to us, is a patchwork composed of "returns" of various times. The name *Hunno* might have been substituted for an older one. It would not be the only case where the compilers brought an obsolete "return" wholly or partly up to date.

Under Stilicho the defenders of the Wall were mostly native federates;[387] one or another of the more important forts was possibly held by auxiliaries. But it seems unlikely that Stilicho, who as we know did have Hun auxiliaries in his armies, would have used them for the defense of a half-abandoned province. If Huns were actually stationed at Hunnum, they could have been there in the last years of Gratian, who had Huns in his service.

There was a fort $Oὔννων$ near Oescus on the right bank of the Danube.[388] The place was named after the Hun garrison, as $Βαστέρνας$[389] after the Basternae and $Σαρμαθών$ in the Haemimons[390] after Sarmatians. However, Hunnum might be a Celtic word.[391]

The Unnigardae and the Huns in Britain—provided they were there —served far away from their homes. But there were also Huns in the garrisons of the Roman camps along the Danube in Pannonia and the Balkan provinces, both before and in Attila's time. Whether the bone strips of composite bows found in Carnuntum[392] point to Huns or Alans cannot be decided. The fragments of bronze cauldrons in Intercisa[393] and Sucidava[394] leave no doubt that at one time or another Huns lived there. Werner thinks that broken cauldrons and nomadic mirrors were left there by Huns and other barbarians who settled in the abandoned camps, where they also could find metal.[395] The find circumstances are not in favor of such an interpretation.

---

[386] Birely 1939, 213.

[387] Mazzarino 1942, 162; Stevens 1940, 148.

[388] Procopius, *De aedif.* III, 2, 130$_{35}$.

[389] *Ibid.*, 148$_{13}$.

[390] *De aedif.* 147$_{18}$.

[391] A. Holder 1896, 1, 2049. The Anonymus of Ravenna, *Itin. Anton.* 2, 107, has *Onno*. K. Jackson (*JRS* 38, 1946, 47) thinks it possible that *Onno* is the better form (the initial *h* cannot be Celtic), in which case the name could be derived from Celtic **onno*, "ash tree," Gallic *onno*, Welsh *onn*. S. A. Richmond and O. G. S. Crawford (*Archaeologia* 43, 1949, 143) offer another Celtic etymology; *onno* is supposed to mean "rock," Irish *ond*.

[392] J. Werner 1932. On the bone strips found at Carleon, see Alföldi 1932, 23, 90.

[393] P. Marton, *Prähist, Zeitschr.* 4, 1912, 185; Fettich 1931, 524; Alföldi 1932, 34-35; J. Werner 1956, 59.

[394] J. Werner 1956, 58.

[395] *Ibid.*, 92-93.

The fragment from Intercisa was found in a burned-down late Roman building; in another room lay the fragments of fifteen to twenty iron helmets. It is a priori unlikely that Huns, who disliked so intensely to live in houses, would have settled in the ruins of a Roman camp. It is even more improbable that the Huns, who were so desperately short of metal, should have overlooked the helmets in the other room. In Sucidava four fragments of Hunnic cauldrons were found in the layer of ashes which covered the whole area of the castellum. Two of the fragments lay near hearths, evidently to be melted for the fabrication of bronze objects. The *milites riparenses* were extremely poor. Neither gold nor silver coins were found. No wonder that every bit of bronze was to be used. The cauldrons were certainly not owned by Huns who settled in the former camp. There was nothing left of it. The barracks were burned down; of the amphorae in which the Danube flotilla brought oil even when both banks of the river were held by the barbarians only fragments were found; there were no human bones anywhere in the ashes. It is practically certain that the camp was hastily evacuated,[396] and it is quite possible that the garrison itself put the fortress on fire.[397] How did the Hun cauldrons get there? They could not have been booty; neither in the first nor the second Hun war in the 440's did the Romans defeat the Huns even in a single encounter. It is hard to imagine that at the annual fair on the Danube a Roman bought a Hunnic cauldron. There is only one explanation of the presence of the Hunnic vessels in Sucidava: They must have belonged to Huns serving in the Roman army.[398]

The archaeological evidence is supplemented by a few lines in Priscus. In his negotiations with the East Roman envoys in 449, Attila "would not allow his own servants to go to war against him, even though they were unable to help those who turned over to them the protection of their native land, for, said he, what city or what fortress he set out to capture would be saved by these refugees?"[399] Sucidava was one of those fortresses. There certainly were more of them along the lower Danube.

Like the Unnigardae, Aetius' Hunnic auxiliaries were excellent fighters, but their lack of discipline made them often more a terror to the provinces they were supposed to defend than to the enemy. Again and again they broke loose and "with raid and fire and sword and savagery and pillage

---

[396] In the asheş lay two boxes with 1,018 copper coins, ranging from Constantine to Theodosius II (Tudor 1948, 198-200).

[397] D. Tudor, *Ist. Rom.* 1, 660-661, and *Materiale* 6, 1961, 493.

[398] This is also the opinion of I. Nestor, *Ist. Rom.* 1, 1960, 703.

[399] *EL* 128$_{24-28}$.

destroyed all things nearby."[400] In Gaul the Romans had to keep garrisons in the cities to protect them from their own auxiliaries.[401] Years later the atrocities committed by the Huns were still vividly remembered. In his biography of St. Martin, Paulinus of Périgueux wrote, "Seized by sudden fear Gallia admits the Huns as auxiliaries. One can barely suffer as allies those who behave more cruel than the enemy, and in their savagery throw off the *foedus*."[402]

---

[400] Sidonius, *Paneg. on Avitus* 248-250.

[401] *Ibid.*, 255-256.

[402] *De vita s. Martini episcopi* VI, 218-228, *CSEL* 16, 147. The story Paulinus tells about the sacrilegious Hun occurs also in Greg. Tur., *De miraculis s. Martini* I, 2.

VI. Religion

THE HUNS, wrote Ammianus Marcellinus, were a people without religion. Like unreasoning beasts, they were utterly ignorant of the difference between right and wrong, deceitful and ambiguous in speech, faithless and unreliable in truce, *nullius religionis vel superstitionis reverentia aliquando districti* (XXXI, 2, 11).

There was hardly a barbarian people that did not lack the virtues in which the Romans excelled. The Parthians held their promises only as long as it was to their advantage.[1] The Heruli were not bound by any convention.[2] The Moors, like the Huns, "did not care for oaths," and for the same reason: "Among them was neither fear of God nor respect of men."[3] The Avars, successors of the Huns, were "the most faithless of all nomads."[4] The list could be continued.

Ammianus' statement about the irreligion of the Huns was not based on firsthand knowledge; it was the conclusion he drew from their behavior or, to be more exact, from what people who had unpleasant experiences with the Huns told him. Actually, he did learn about a religious custom of the savages from his informants, though he did not recognize it as such.

When they once put their neck into a faded tunic, it is not taken off or changed until by long wear and tear it has been reduced to rags and fallen from them bit by bit.[5]

Ammianus cannot be blamed for taking the aversion of the Huns to washing their clothes for just another mark of their beastliness. Ibn Fadlan,

---

[1] Justin XLI, 3, 10.
[2] Procopius VI, 14, 35, 41.
[3] *Ibid.*, IV, 8, 10.
[4] Theoph. Sim. I, 3, 1.
[5] Ammianus XXXI, 2, 5.

a keen observer and ever ready to ask questions, noticed the same unclean habit among the Oguz without suspecting that it might have religious significance.[6] The object of the Turkish and Mongol[7] custom was to avoid offense to the water spirits.[8] It probably was the same with the Huns, and it presumably corresponded happily with their natural inclinations. Priscus noticed as remarkable that Attila's dress was clean.[9] The "Massagetae"-Huns were as dirty as the Sclaveni.[10]

THE HUNS AND CHRISTIANITY

By the middle of the fourth century, the Roman and Romanized population of Pannonia was preponderantly Christian. Arianism was fairly strongly entrenched; the bishops of Mursa and Sirmium staunchly upheld the heretic tradition. In the 380's and 390's it took all the zeal of St. Ambrose, efficiently supported by the secular arm, to bring the Danube provinces back into the orthodox fold.[11] In Attila's time Pannonia, both the part which had been ceded to him and the ill-defined no man's land east of Noricum, was apparently solidly Catholic. In Pannonia secunda the Christian community of Sirmium survived the Huns,[12] Ostrogoths, and Gepids.[13] Sopianae in Valeria, from where Christianity had been carried north and west,[14] withstood all storms of the migration period.[15] In Pannonia prima urban life had almost ceased when the Huns came, but there too small Christian communities seem to have held out.[16]

Cut off from the churches in Romania, the Catholics in Pannonia offered no political problems to the Huns. The big landowners had fled, and the small people who stayed were utterly unable to organize any resistance against their lords. The danger that the Catholics might act as a fifth column for the Romans, at times so acute in Persia and a permanent threat to the Vandals in Africa, did not exist in Hunnia. Attila could

---

[6] Ibn Fadlan 1939, 29-30; 1956, 126; 1958, 68.

[7] Giovanni da Pian del Carpine, Dawson 1957, 17; Rockhill 1900, 75; Ibn Fadlan 1939, 131-132, 142-143; Spuler 1943, 461.

[8] Waley 1931, 115, n. 3.

[9] *EL* 144$_8$.

[10] Procopius VII, 14, 28.

[11] Dudden 1925, ch. 8.

[12] A few years after the battle on the Nedao, the relics of St. Anastasia were transferred to Constantinople.

[13] Alföldi 1938, 6-7.

[14] T. Nagy, *AÉ* 1949, 84.

[15] Alföldi 1938, 9-10; Gy. Gosztonyi, *AÉ* 1940, 56-61. For Triciana, see A. Radnóti, *AÉ* 1939, 268-276. On the churches in Pécs, see Gerke 1952, 115-122.

[16] Alföldi 1938, 12; Egger 1948, 58; Swoboda 1958, 177.

afford to be tolerant: He allowed his Catholic subjects to pray and fast as long as they meekly worked for him.

Most of the Christian Germans under Hun rule were Arians.[17] One may doubt whether Attila knew the difference between the Arian heresy and the orthodox creed. It is hard to imagine the Hun king listening to a discussion about the consubstantiality of the Father and the Son. But he must have been aware that his Germanic followers and subjects were not of the same religion as the emperors in Ravenna and Constantinople. The mere fact that the Arian clergy under the Huns were not persecuted for their faith as they were in the empire, both in the Western and Eastern part, ensured their loyalty to the Hun kings.

The Huns had Christian slaves. What Prosper said about the ways by which the gospel reached the pagans beyond the borders may also have been true, to a modest extent, for the Huns:

> Some sons of the church, made prisoners by the enemy, changed their masters into servants of the gospel, and by teaching them the faith they became the superiors of their own wartime lords. Again, some foreign pagans, while serving in the Roman armies, were able to learn the faith in our country, when in their own land they could not have known it; they returned to their homes instructed in the Christian religion.[18]

One or another Hun mercenary in the Roman army may have been baptized. A particularly zealous slave may have converted his master,[19] or, more likely, his master's wife. But it is improbable that men like Onegesius, Attila's prime minister, should have renounced the faith of their fathers because their bath attendants read the Bible to them.

Had their kingdom not so suddenly collapsed, the Huns would sooner or later have embraced Arian Christianity. The Arian Goths were much closer to them than the Romans. Compared with wretched Catholics in the dying towns of Pannonia, not to speak of the prisoners of war, the

---

[17] A small number of Goths belonged to the Audian sect: some were Catholics. Socrates' assertion (I, 8) that the Sarmatians east of the Danube after their defeat in 322 became Christians is definitely wrong; the archaeological material contains nothing Christian.

[18] *De vocatione omnium gentium* II, 33 *PL* 51, 717-718. I follow de Letter's translation (1952, 146).

[19] The Bulgar prince Enravota was converted by his Greek slave (Obolensky 1948, 65, n. 3). Two graves in a cemetery near the church in Sopianae, tentatively dated about 400, are supposed to indicate the early spread of Christianity among the Huns in Pannonia (T. Nagy, *Nouvelle revue d'Hongrie* 69, 1943, 503). But Christians were not buried with their horses as the people in Sopianae were.

Gothic chieftains were almost the equals of the Hun nobles. But two generations of slowly growing symbiosis of the upper strata of Hun and Germanic society were too short to bring the Huns over to the religion of the Goths.

Salvian, writing about 440,[20] classified the Huns among the heathen nations:

> I shall discuss the pagans first, since theirs is the older delusion: among these, the nation of the Saxons is savage, the Franks treacherous, the Gepids ruthless, the Huns lewd—so we see that the life of all the barbarians is full of vice. . . . Can you say that their vices imply the same guilt as ours, that the lewdness of the Huns is as sinful as ours, the treachery of the Franks as reprehensible as that of the Christians, the greed of the Alans as much to be condemned as that of a believer? If a Hun or Gepid is deceitful, what wonder is it in one who is utterly ignorant of the guilt involved in falsehood? Can it be said of the Huns: See what sort of men these are who are called Christians?[21]

The only Huns Salvian knew were those who served under the Romans in Gaul. But the Hun kings obviously did not draft only pagans into the auxiliary corps they lent to their Roman "friends." The Huns, as a people, were as pagan in the middle of the fifth century as they had been when they crossed the Don.

Salvian's statement is at variance with what Jerome and Orosius say. It seems, furthermore, contradicted by an often quoted passage in Theodoret about the successes of the priests whom John Chrysostom allegedly sent to the Huns. Niceta of Remesiana also is said to have carried his missionary activities beyond the Danube into the country of the Huns. A closer examination of the evidence reveals that it is either untrustworthy or has been misunderstood.

In 399, Jerome called the Huns "wild beasts."[22] But when shortly after, in his letter to Laeta, he described Christ's triumph over the demons, he wrote: "From India, from Persia, and from Ethiopia we welcomed crowds of monks every hour. The Armenians have laid aside their quivers, the Huns are learning the psalter, the frosts of Scythia are warmed by the fire of the faith."[23] At about the same time Jerome explained the

---

[20] Stein 1959, 1, 511, n. 1; after 439 and before 451 (Chadwick 1955, 165).

[21] *De gubernatione Dei* IV, 14; I quote from Sanford's translation (1930, 123, 127).

[22] *Avertat Iesus ab orbe Romano tales ultra bestias* (*Ep.* 77, 8).

[23] *Ep.* 107, 2; for the date, see Cavallera 1922, 2, 47. The same phrase occurs in Prudentius, *Apotheosis* 426-427: *laxavit Scythias verbo penetrante pruinas vox evangelica.*

psalter to two Goths, Sunnia and Fretela.[24] He may have lumped together the Huns and the Goths, both Scythian peoples, but it is more probable that he simply invented the psalm-singing Huns as he invented the crowds of monks from India.[25]

The Huns, wrote Orosius in 418, filled the churches of the West and the East.[26] This is the statement of a theologian. The early Christian belief in the imminent end of the world implied the certainty that the gospel was being preached to all nations.[27] What Tertullian and the apologists of the third century said about the spread of Christianity to the Scythians, Parthians, and Indians were merely the conclusions they drew from the scriptures. Had they known the Huns, they would have included them in the number of baptized barbarians. If the lists of converted peoples in Tertullian and Arnobius were the products of exegesis, those of the post-Nicaean fathers were pure rhetoric. Poets and theologians indulged in exotic names. The Scythians, Massagetae, Sauromatae, Tibareni, Hyrcanians, Caspians, Geloni, Moors, Indians, Ethiopians, Persians, Bactrians, Cimbri, even the Seres were now Christians.[28] Orosius was the pupil of St. Augustine, who rejoiced at the fact that "what as yet is closed to those who fight with iron is not closed to him who fights with the wood [cross]."[29] In a way Orosius was right: The Huns did fill the churches,[30] but only to ransack them. In the East, in Thrace, they killed the monks, raped the nuns, and put fire to the churches; first, of course, they carried the sacred vessels away. They did the same in the West, in Gaul.[31]

About the relationship between the Huns and the Christian priests in the border provinces only Sozomen has something to tell us:

---

[24] *Ep.* 106. B. Altaner (*Vigiliae Christianae* 4, 1950, 126-128) dates the letter in the years 404-410.

[25] The two Goths are perhaps fictitious figures, cf. D. de Bruyne, *Zeitschrift für neutestamentliche Wissenschaft* 28, 1929, 1-13; D. B. Botte, *Bulletin de théologie ancienne et moderne* 9, 1950, 29. J. Zeiller (1935, 238-250) pleads for their existence.

[26] *Hist. adv. Pagan.* VII, 41, 8.

[27] Mark 13:10; Matthew 24:14. *In omnem terram exivit sonus eorum et in fines orbis terrae verba eorum*, Psalm 18, was at an early time referred to the apostles.

[28] *Il faut bien convenir que ces premiers catalogues des nations chrétiennes ont un tour un peu trop oratoire pour inspirer plaine confiance* (P. Peeters, *Analecta Bollandiana* 50, 1932, 12). Prudentius (*Apotheosis* 420-424) ; and Theoderet (*Graec. Aff. Cur.*, ch. IX, J. Raeder, 223, 230) offer telling examples.

[29] *In psalm.* 95; cf. also *Ep.* 93, 7, 22.

[30] Callinicus 108. In Italy the "Massagetae" in Belisarius' army killed even those who sought asylum in churches (Procopius V, 10, 29).

[31] Paulinus of Périgueux, *Vita s. Martini* VI, 218-226, *CSEL* 16, 147; Greg. Tur., *De miraculis s. Martini* I, 2, *PL* 71, 915.

The church of Tomis, and indeed all the churches of Scythia [*i.e.*, Scythia minor], were at this time under the guidance of Theotimus, a Scythian. He had been brought up in the practice of philosophy, and his virtues had so won the admiration of the barbarian Huns, who dwelt on the banks of the Hister,[32] that they called him the god of the Romans, for they had experience of divine deeds wrought by him. It is said that one day, when traveling toward the country of the barbarians, he perceived some of them advancing toward Tomis. His attendants burst forth into lamentations, and gave themselves up for lost; but he merely descended from horseback, and prayed. The consequence was that the barbarians passed without seeing him, his attendants, or the horses from which they had dismounted.[33]

The passage, which refers to the last years of Theodosius I,[34] not only throws a sharp light on the inefficiency of the frontier defense, it also shows that Theotimus could not have had as much success with the Huns as has been claimed.[35] A missionary who has to make himself invisible when he meets those he is supposed to convert will not baptize many. Indeed, if Theotimus or his successors or any other bishop anywhere in the Eastern empire had won more than a few Huns to the faith, the Byzantine church historians are not likely to have failed to report their successes.[36]

Some scholars adduced the beautiful poem in which Paulinus of Nola praises the zeal of his friend Niceta of Remesiana[37] for spreading the gospel among the Scythae, Getae, and Daci[38] as another proof of the conversion of Hunnic tribes north of the Danube.[39] But Scythae, Getae, and Daci

---

[32] Nicephorus Callistus (*Hist. eccles.* XII, 45, *PG* 147, 908) has πάλαι οἰκοῦντες.

[33] Sozomen VII, 26, 6-8.

[34] Not specifically to 394, as Rauschen (1897, 429) has suggested. It is not known when Theotimus became bishop of Tomis. He was in 392 (Jerome mentions him in *De viris illustribus* 131, Herding 1879, 65). In 400, and again in 403, he was in Constantinople vigorously defending the orthodoxy of Origen against Epiphanius of Salamis. Theodimus died before 431 (Zeiler 1918, 353).

[35] The reason why the Huns called Theotimus "the god of the Romans" is anything but clear. He was a Scythian, which probably means Goth. Perhaps he was not called the god, Gothic *guþ*, but the priest, *gudja*, of the Romans. In the cemetery at Piata Frecătei in the Dobrogea, datable to the fourth and early fifth century, Goths were buried; cf. P. Aurelian, *Materiale* 8, 1962, 568-579.

[36] Cf. Thompson 1948, 38.

[37] Born about 330, still active in 414; see H. G. Opitz, *PW* 17, 179-180.

[38] *Carmen* XVIII, 245-264, *CSEL* 30, 2, 92-93.

[39] Zeiller 1918, 558; Alföldi 1938, 14; Amann 1931, 2, 477.

are only archaic names of the Bessi and other tribes in the mountain glens of Haemus and Rhodope.[40]

There remains Theodoret. John Chrysostom, bishop of Constantinople, says Theodoret in his *Church History*,[41] was informed that some nomadic Scythians, who pitched their tents along the banks of the Hister, thirsted for salvation but had no one to bring it to them. John sought men willing to imitate the labors of the apostles and sent them to these people. Theodoret himself saw the letter which John wrote to Leontius, bishop of Ancyra in Galatia, in which he informed Leontius about the conversion of the Scythians, asking him to send them men capable of guiding them.

The "nomadic Scythians" are supposed to be Huns.[42] It is true that in another passage Theodoret calls the Huns nomadic Scythians.[43] But it does not follow that all nomadic Scythians were Huns. Asterius of Amasea, John Chrysostom's contemporary, wrote about the nomadic Scythians on the Cimmerian Bosporus and near the Rhine.[44] In enumerating the nations to which the fame of Symeon Stylites spread, Theodoret named, besides the Persians, Indians, and Ethiopians, also the nomadic Scythians,[45] obviously a collective term without sharp ethnic or linguistic definition. In the *Vita Athonitae*, the Magyars were called nomadic Scythians.[46] In one of his orations[47] on John Chrysostom, Theodoret spoke once more about the Scythians whom the sainted bishop had converted. There he called them wagon dwellers, another of the stereotyped attributes of the Scythians carried over from one author to the other. In the *Church History* Theodoret wrote about the guidance which the Scythians still needed. In the oration they are already exemplary Christians: "The barbarian, dismounting from his horse, has learnt to bend his knees, and he, who was not moved by the tears of the prisoners, has learnt to cry over his sins." Theodoret was not satisfied with one nation converted by his hero. He let him bring the gospel also to the Persians, and they too worship Christ.

---

[40] Burn 1915, 24; D. M. M. Pipidi, *Revue historique du sud-est européen* 25, 1946, 99-117, and Pipidi 1958, 248-264.

[41] *Hist. eccles.* V, 31, *GCS* 19, 33-331.

[42] Zeiller 1918, 548; Alföldi 1918, 14; Thompson 1948; 1946, 74. Without stating her reasons, Demougeot (1951, 302, n. 400) maintains that they were Goths. Allwater (1959, 92) is noncommittal.

[43] V, 37, pointed out by Thompson 1946, 75.

[44] *Homily* XIV, PG 40, 381.

[45] *Hist. relig.* XXVI; *Das Leben des hl. Symeon Stylites*, Lietzmann 1908, *TU* 32, 4, 1. On the date, 442-444, see Peeters 1950, 101.

[46] "Zhitie propodobnago Athanasiia Athonskago," *Zapiski istoricheskago filologicheskago fakulteta S. Peterburgskago Universiteta* 25, 1895, 23$_{30}$.

[47] PG 84, 47.

Still, Theodoret's account cannot be dismissed as fiction. He embroidered the little he knew, but he had at least one reliable piece of information: John's letter to Leontius. Theodoret could not have invented it. Its content is too strange and its recipient too unfit for such an assumption. John wrote the letter in Constantinople, thus between February 398 and June 404, probably nearer the last date, for in the first years of his office he was fully occupied with reforms in the capital itself. Leontius played a leading role in the intrigues which resulted in the downfall of John. The hatred of the crafty scoundrel almost cost John his life on the journey to Cucusus.[48] It must, therefore, have been a very special reason that induced the bishop of Constantinople to ask the bishop of Galatia to send priests to the barbarians on the Danube. Why were people of this province in Asia Minor so much better equipped for such work than the priests of John's own diocesis?

There is, I believe, only one answer to this question. John must have thought that in the whole Eastern empire Galatians were the only ones who could preach the gospel to the "nomadic Scythians" in their own language. The missionaries whom John sent to the Goths were "talking the same language as those" (ὁμόγλωττοι ἐκείνοις).[49]

Besides Greek, not so few Galatians spoke their Celtic language as late as the end of the fourth century. Jerome recognized the close relationship of Galatian to the Celtic dialect he had heard spoken around Trier.[50] There was only one people on the Danube that spoke "Galatian," namely the Bastarnae. With the exception of Strabo, who had some doubts, all Greek authors regarded them as Celts. Plutarch spoke of the "Galatae on the Hister, who are also called Bastarnae."[51]

Only a few years before John wrote to Leontius, Bastarnae, Goths, and Alans crossed the Danube and ravaged Thrace.[52] After 400, the Bastarnae are not mentioned, but Βαστέρνας, the name of a fortress built by Justinian II in Moesia on the Danube,[53] shows that they lingered on in the northern Balkans, preserving their ethnic identity as late as the sixth century.[54]

---

[48] Baur 1930, 2, 239, 346.

[49] Theodoret, *Hist. eccles.* V, 30.

[50] *Galatas, excepto sermone graeco, quo omnis oriens loquitur, propriam linguam eandem paene habere quam Treviros* (*Comm. in Galatas* II, pref., *PL* 26, 357); cf. Sofer 1937, 148-158. Schneider's assertion (1954, 1, 581) that in Galatia sermons were not given in Celtic is not supported by any text.

[51] *Aemilius Paulus* IX, 4.

[52] Claudian, *In Ruf.* I, 305-313, 317, and *Cons. Stil.* II, 95; Zosimus IV, 51.

[53] Procopius, *De aedif.* IV, 11, 20.

[54] W. Tomaschek, *PW* 3, 313.

Later authors were puzzled by the "Celts" converted by John Chrysostom; they identified them with the Arian Goths,[55] although, of course, no author of the fifth century would have mixed up Goths and Celts. At the frontiers of the Eastern empire no other Celts existed except the "Galatian"-speaking "nomadic Scythians," the Bastarnae.[56]

The *Apocritus* of Macarius Magnes contains a list of the peoples to whom the gospel has not yet been preached: the seven races of the Indians who live in the desert in the southeast, the Ethiopians who are called Macrobians, the Maurusians, "and those who dwell beyond the great northern river Ister which shuts off the country of the Scythians, where twelve tribes of nomad barbarians live, of whose savage state Herodotus tells us, and their evil customs derived from their ancestors."[57]

SEERS AND SHAMANS

Litorius, one of Aetius' generals, was supposedly the last Roman general to perform the ancient pagan rites before battle.[58] In 439, under the walls of Toulouse, his army was destroyed by the Visigoths, he himself wounded, taken prisoner, and put to death. The Romans, maintained Prosper, were defeated because Litorius refused to listen to the advice of his officers; instead, "he trusted the responses of the haruspices and the monitions of the demons."[59] Can Prosper be believed?

It is, perhaps, not particularly significant that in his chronicle Hydatius said nothing about the soothsaying. He barely mentioned the war in 439;[60] besides, he may have thought it would cast a doubtful light on Aetius, whom he held in high esteem, if one of the *ductor*'s most trusted lieutenants was a pagan. Salvian's silence is more important. He lived in Gaul; he must have known Litorius. Ever ready to accuse his coun-

---

[55] For instance, Georgius Alexandrinus in the excerpts from his biography of John Chrysostom in Photius (Henry 1959, 2, 53). The original biography, published by Henry Savile in 1612, was not accessible to me.

[56] I do not want to be misunderstood. The letter of Leontius does not prove that the Bastarnae were Celts. But it does prove that John Chrysostom took them for Celts.

[57] *Apocritus* IV, 13, Crafer 1919, 125.

This could be valuable information if the date of the *Apocritus* were known. Altaner (1960, 388) thinks that the book was written about 400, but Crafer (1919, XIX) is inclined to date it a century earlier. Besides, the reference to Herodotus and the strange number of tribes make it doubtful whether Macarius, who probably lived in Syria, had any actual knowledge of the transdanubian peoples.

For later attempts to convert the Huns in the Caucasus, see Moravcsik 1946, 35, 38-39; Thompson 1946, 77-79.

[58] Stein 1959, 1, 481.

[59] *CM* II, 23$_{116}$.

[60] *Ibid.*

trymen of all possible sins, Salvian would not have passed over Litorius' "crime," had the unfortunate commander committed it. According to Salvian, the Romans lost the war because, unlike the Goths, they did not put their hope in God but relied on their Hunnic auxiliaries.[61]

That Litorius should have had professional Roman haruspices in his army is unlikely for another reason. In times of stress the Christian government was forced to tolerate the stubborn paganism of an exceptionally able general as, for instance, in 409 when an antipagan law was temporarily revoked in favor of Generidus. But since then one edict after another had been issued which threatened with capital punishment those who dared to indulge in the "insanity" of consulting haruspices. It is inconceivable that as late as 438 a Roman general could have the entrails of victims inspected before engaging the enemy.

And yet there must be a kernel of truth in Prosper's accusation. When we consider that the troops under Litorius' command were Huns,[62] the explanation becomes clear at once. Not Litorius but his Huns wanted to know the outcome of the battle they were about to enter. The *haruspicatio* was performed not by Roman but Hunnic diviners. Litorius' Huns did before Toulouse what twelve years later Attila, "a man who sought counsel of omens in all warfare," did on the eve of the battle at the *locus Mauriacus:* He "decided to inquire into the future through haruspices."[63] In the ninth century the Bulgars, before a battle, "used to practice enchantments and jests and charms and certain auguries" (*exercere incantationes et ioca et carmina et nonnulla auguria*)."[64]

The Hunnic diviners are also mentioned by Priscus. At the banquet at Attila's court he noticed that the king pinched Ernach's cheeks and looked on him with serene eyes. Priscus was surprised that Attila should take small account of his other sons but give attention to this one. He learned from a Latin-speaking Hun that the seers [οἱ μάντεις] had prophesied to Attila that his *genos* would fail but would be restored by this son.[65] We may assume that the seers were Prosper's and Jordanes' haruspices.

The Hunnic diviners may, at the same time, have been shamans. The shamans of the Turkish tribes in the Altai, informed by their guiding spi-

---

[61] *De gubernatione Dei* VII, 9, 39.

[62] Prosper and Hydatius, *CM* II, 23$_{116}$; Sidonius, *Paneg. on Avitus* 246-254.

[63] *Getica* 196.

[64] *Responsa Nicolai*, c. 35, p. 581, cf. Beshevliev 1939, 44-49. Zonaras (III, L. A. Dindorf 1875) speaks about the Bulgarian γοητεία; I. Duïchev (J. Dujčev), *BZ* 41, 1941, 2.

[65] *EL* 145$_{22-23}$.

rits, occasionally foretell the future;[66] they are also more experienced in
the interpretation of naturally occuring omina, but they have no mono-
poly on what Bawden calls "involuntary divination."[67] The same is true
for the Buryat shamans.[68] In the middle period the Mongols distinguished
between seers and shamans.[69] But as so often in these studies, we have
to resist the temptation to conclude from the customs and practices of
later steppe peoples what those of the Huns were or may have been. That
the Huns had shamans is certain. *Kam* in the names Atakam and Eskam
is *qam*, the common Turkish word for shaman.[70] To judge from the two
names of high-ranking Huns, the shamans seem to have belonged to
the upper stratum of Hun society. Malalas' ἱερεῖς were possibly shamans.

The Hunnic method of deliberate foreknowing was scapulimancy.[71]
Attila's haruspices "examined the entrails of cattle and certain streaks
in the bones that had been scraped."[72] From Eisenberger's excellent monograph[73] we have learned to distinguish between two forms of this method
of prognostication. In the "Asiatic" form the bones, mostly the shoulder
bones of sheep, after having been carefully scraped clean, are exposed to
fire: The fissures caused by the heat are then "read." In the "European,"
supposedly more primitive form, the bones are "read" as they are.

Because Jordanes does not state whether the bones were scorched
or not, Eisenberger does not dare to decide whether the Huns practiced
the "Asiatic" or "European" form of scapulimancy. The latter he traced
back to a Stone Age hunter culture. He may be right. In any case, the
"European" scapulimancy is attested only many centuries after Attila[74].
No ancient writer knows about it. It was unknown to the Alans.[75] Nothing

---

[66] Bawden 1958, 4.

[67] As, *e.g.*, the interpretations of the cries of birds.

[68] Nameraiev, a modern Buryat writer (quoted by Bawden 1958, 2) speaks about
"the terrible lot of seers and wisemen and quack doctors and such like lamas and shamans."

[69] Vladimirtsov 1934, 184, n. 6.

[70] In Chinese transcription *kan* 甘 , ancient *kam*, is equated with Chinese *wu* 巫
(*T'ang shu* 217b,.10b); cf. P. Pelliot and B. Laufer, *TP* 1916, 295; L. Ligeti, *AOH* 1, 1950,
150.

[71] Perhaps osteoscopy would be a better term. Besides shoulder blades, other bones,
even the breastbones of geese and chickens (E. Schneeweiss, *Revue internationale des études balkaniques* 1:2, 1935, 521) or tortoise shells, as in Shang and Chou China, were used.

[72] *Nunc fibras, nunc quasdam venas in abrasis ossibus intuentes* (*Getica* 196).

[73] Eisenberger 1938, 49-116.

[74] *Ibid.*, 57-58.

[75] "They have a remarkable way of divining the future, for they gather very straight
twigs of osier and sort them out at an appointed time with certain incantations and
then clearly learn what impends" (Ammianus XXXI, 2, 24).

in the earlier Sarmatian graves indicates that scapulimancy was ever practiced. Only in the Sarmatoid cemeteries at Vrevskiĭ, south-west of Tashkent,[76] and Lavyandak, near Bukhara,[77] both of them datable to the last centuries B.C., were shoulder blades of sheep, one of them scorched, found. If they had been used for divination, as Voronets and Obel'chenko think, they would point to an Eastern, non-Iranian element.

The Huns could not have borrowed scapulimancy from their neighbors and subjects in Hungary and the western steppes. In China it had been practiced since pre-Shang times.[78] The Turkish word for divination, $yrq <$ $yryq$, means originally "fissure, cracks"; the Mongolian $tülge$, "portent," goes back to $tüle$, $tüli$, "to burn."[79] There can be no reasonable doubt that the scapulimancy of the Huns was of Eastern origin.

DIVINE KINGSHIP?

At the dinner which the East Roman ambassador gave to Edecon and his entourage, the Huns lauded Attila and the Romans the emperor. Bigilas, the typical meddlesome Levantine dragoman, "remarked that it was not fair to compare a man and a god, meaning Attila by the man and Theodosius by the god. The Huns grew excited and hot at this remark."

This passage in Priscus' report[80] has been adduced as proof that the Huns regarded Attila as a god. But such an interpretation does not take into account the Roman meaning of "god" when applied to the emperor. As *dominus totius mundi* he was "God on earth" (*deus in terra*), not really god; *deus* was in the fifth century understood as *quasi* or *tamquam deus* "For when the emperor has accepted the name Augustus, sincere devotion must be offered to him as if he were God incarnate and present" (*Nam imperator cum Augusti nomen accepit, tamquam praesenti et corporali Deo fidelis est praestanda devotio*), wrote Vegetius.[81] Or to quote the sixth-century Agapetus: "Though an emperor in body is like all others, in power of office he is like God."[82] Pacatus could call the good Christian Theo-

---

[76] Voronets 1951, 48, 57.

[77] Obel'chenko 1961, 115, 161.

[78] Chêng Tê-k'un 1960, 2, 241.

[79] W. Bang and A. v. Gabain, *SB Berlin* 15, 1929, 4-5. For Mongol scalpulimancy, see Montell 1944, 380-381, and Bawden 1958 (with many parallels among other peoples in eastern Asia); cf. also Wittfogel and Fêng 1949, 216, 268, n. 139. For Sogdian scalpulimancy, see W. B. Henning, *BSOAS* 11, 1946, 729.

[80] Priscus, *EL* 123$_{22\text{-}26}$.

[81] *Epit. rei milit.* 2, 5.

[82] Quoted by I. Ševčenko, *Harvard Slavic Studies* 2, 1954, 147.

dosius a god,[83] and as late as the eleventh century the Byzantine emperor was "God on earth" ($\theta\varepsilon\delta\varsigma\ \dot\varepsilon\pi\iota\gamma\varepsilon\iota o\varsigma$).[84] The fugitive Athanaric, overwhelmed by the sight of Constantinople, conceded that the emperor was "truly God on earth," *deus terrenus*.[85] To acknowledge him as such meant acceptance of his claim to be the lord of the world, *domitor omnium gentium barbarorum*. It was this implication that aroused the ire of the Huns at Bigilas' remark.

The Roman ambassadors were not allowed to pitch their tents on higher ground than that on which Attila's tent stood.[86] G. Staunton's account of the first English embassy to Ch'ien Lung's court offers an instructive parallel:

> When a splendid chariot intended as a present to the Emperor was unpacked and put together, nothing could be more admired, but it was necessary to give instructions for taking off the box; for when the mandarins found out that so elevated a seat was destined for the coachman who was to drive the horses, they expressed their utmost astonishment that it should be proposed to place any man in a situation above the Emperor. So easily is the delicacy of this people shocked at whatever related to the person of their exalted sovereign.[87]

Ch'ien Lung was "the son of Heaven," but he was not a god. Neither was Attila. In his relationship with the Huns, Attila in no way behaved like a divine being. There was none of the elaborate ceremony which stressed the distance between the god-like *basileus* and his subjects, not to speak of the abyss that separated the Sasanian king of kings from ordinary mortals.[88] Attila wore neither a diadem nor a crown; his dress was plain; his sword, the clasps of his shoes, and the bridle of his horse were not, like those of the Hunnic nobles, adorned with gold and gems. He drank from a wooden goblet and ate from a wooden plate.[89] With only his bodyguard standing by, Attila, in front of his house, listened to the disputes of his Huns and arbitrated their quarrels.[90] The most Attila claimed for himself was that he was well-born.[91] In the dirge sung at his funeral the dead king was praised as a great conqueror, not worshipped as a god.

---

[83] *Deum dedit Hispania, quem vidimus* (Pacatus, *Paneg.* 4, 5). F. Taeger (*Charisma* 2, 1960, 654-655) calls this and similar phrases in the panegyric *unverbindliche Formeln, blosse Allegorien*.

[84] *Byzantion* 3, 1927, 97.

[85] *Getica* 143.

[86] Priscus, *EL* 123$_{19-21}$.

[87] 2 (London, 1797), 164-165.

[88] Christensen 1944, 401-402.

[89] Priscus, *EL* 144$_{13-21}$.

[90] *EL* 140$_{11-19}$.

[91] *Ibid.*, 581$_{23-24}$.

On the other hand, Kuridach, king of the Hunnic Acatziri, refused to come to Attila's court because, he said, it was difficult to face a god. "If it be impossible to look upon the orb of the sun, how could one behold the greatest of the gods [μέγιστον τῶν θεῶν] without injury?"[92] To be sure, Kuridach may have used this language merely because he feared a trap and hoped, by flattering the terrible king, to save himself. Still, this does not seem sufficient to explain his hyperbolic comparison of Attila with the sun.

In the late Roman Empire the ruler was often compared and even equated with the sun. The inscription on an equestrian statue of Theodosius I reads:

> You lept up from the East, another light-bearing Sun, O Theodosius, for mortals in the midst of heaven, O gentle-hearted one, with the ocean at your feet and the boundless earth.[93]

But the emperor was a mild, not a fierce and blinding sun. Kuridach's simile reminds one rather of Indian expressions. The great bowman Bhishma looked "like the all-consuming sun himself, incapable of being looked at like the sun when in his course he reaches the meridian and scorches everything underneath."[94] However, there is nothing else that could connect the Acatziri with India.

The titles and epithets of the Hsiung-nu kings and the rulers of the Orkhon Turks offer no parallels to Kuridach's word either. *Ch'eng li ku t'u*, the title of the Hsiung-nu king as given in the *Han shu*,[95] has been explained as *täŋri qut*, "heavenly majesty." *Ch'eng li - d'ʊng lji* is undoubtedly *täŋri*, "heaven, god." Pan Ku states expressly that this is the meaning of the word in the Hsiung-nu language. *Ku t'u*, he says, means "son."[96] Shiratori's etymology of *ku t'u*, which he took for a Tungus word for "son," may be unconvincing, but it is consistent with the text. F. W. K. Müller,[97] followed by A. von Gabain,[98] rejected Pan Ku's translation; convinced that the Hsiung-nu spoke a Turkish language, he

---

[92] *Ibid.*, 130₂₀₋₂₃.

[93] *Anthologia Palatina* XVI, 65, Dubner, ed., 2, 539; I follow the translation in King 1960, 15.

[94] *Mahābhārata*, Bhisma Parva 66, 107; Drona Parva 33, 18, Roy 1887, 4, 387; 5, 111. One of the five Pāndava wraps himself in his garment so as not to set the world on fire by his sight (Dumézil 1948, 4, 56).

[95] Groot 1921, 53-54.

[96] *JA* 202:1, 1923, 71-82.

[97] *Ostasiat. Zeitschr.* 8, 1919-1920, 316.

[98] Gabain 1955, 22.

maintained that *ku t'u* could be only Turkish *qut*. Müller was certainly wrong. Why should the Chinese have transcribed *qut* by two characters and not, as they did in T'ang times, by *ku<kuət*? If, however, the older form of *qut* was bisyllabic, it was probably **qawut*.[99] By adopting the Chinese title *t'ien tzŭ*, the shan-yü proclaimed himself the equal of the emperor.[100] There leads no way from "son of heaven" to Kuridach's "greatest of the gods."

In the Orkhon inscription the kagan is given his power by *Täŋri*; he fulfills the mandate of *Täŋri*. But he is not *Täŋri* himself, and he is never compared with the sun.[101] In the following centuries the epithet *täŋri* became quite common. In the eighth century a ruler of the eastern Turks,[102] in the ninth century an Uigur king[103] called themselves *täŋri qayan*. The *χatun* is *tänri qunčuy*, "the divine princess";[104] *täŋrim*, "my god," means "princess."[105] The Uigur king is *täŋri qan* or *täŋri ilig*, "divine king,"[106] but he can also call himself *täŋri* without any additions.[107] In the confessions of the lay sister Ütrat are named *taiχan χan*, *kümsä*, *χatun täŋrim*, *mišan*, *χan*, *čaiši wang bäg*," and the other *täŋri*."[108] In all these titles the meaning of *täŋri* fluctuates between "god" and "majesty," exactly like in *bayān* in Middle Persian.[109] However, Buddha is "the *täŋri* of the *täŋri*,"[110] and Mani "the greatest *täŋri*,"[111] which corresponds exactly to Kuridach's μέγιστος τῶν θεῶν. It seems that the Uigurs and also other Turks borrowed, though in an attenuated from, the concept of divine kingship from the Persians.[112]

Kuridach's words have a decidedly Persian ring. The deification of the Persian monarch began under the first Darius and persisted throughont the Parthian and Sasanian periods. Shapur I was θιός and "of divine descent"

---

[99] *Turfan-Texte* 1, 97.

[100] Unlike the Hsiung-nu shan-yü, no Turkish or Uigur ruler called himself *taŋri ury*, as *t'ien tzŭ* was rendered (*Uigurica* 2, 27, 49; cf. P. Pelliot, *TP* 26, 1928, 152).

[101] Roux 1959, 231-241.

[102] Liu 1958, 179, 180, 621-631.

[103] Hamilton 1955, 139.

[104] *Ibid.*, 91.

[105] *Uigurica* 1, 47, 49; 2, 13.

[106] *Uigurica* 1, 47; *Turfan-Texte* 1, 14, 27.

[107] *Turfan-Texte* 2, 6, 10.

[108] *Uigurica* 2, 80.

[109] W. B. Henning, *BSOAS* 21, 1958, 70. Referring to the Sogdian letters from Mount Mugh, Altheim (1962, 1, 214-215) suggests that μέγιστος τῶν θεῶν renders *bäglar bäg*. But Sogdian βγy means only "lord." Cf. W. B. Henning, *BSOAS* 23, 1960, 52, n. 5; V. A. Lifshits, *SE* 2, 1960, 99, and Lifshits 1962, 2, 41; Smirnova 1962, 396.

[110] *Uigurica* 1, 27, 28, 29; *Turfan-Texte* 4, 10, 12.

[111] *Turfan-Texte* 3, 20$_{166}$.

[112] W. Eilers, *ZDMG* 90, 1936, 166, note.

(ἐκ γένους θεῶν).[113] Bahram II was a god.[114] Chosroes called himself "the divinity who takes his form from the gods" (θεῖος ὅς ἐκ θεῶν χαρακτηρίζεται).[115] The Sasanian king, with his head crowned with rays, appears in the guise of the sun, *radiato capite solis in figura.*[116] When taking his seat on the royal throne the ruler had his face veiled. According to the New Persian court ceremonial, it was imperative when entering before the shah to cover one's face with one's hands, exclaiming at the same time, *"misuzam,* I am burning up!"[117]

Although to *his* Huns Attila was most certainly not a divine being,[118] the Acatziri, particularly after they had been forced to acknowledge him as their supreme lord, looked up to Attila as, in the same time, the Persians looked up to their king.

STRAVA

When Attila died, the Huns "as it is the custom of that race, cut off a part of their hair and disfigured their faces horribly with deep wounds, so that the gallant warrior should be mourned not with the lamentations and tears of women, but with the blood of men."[119] Sidonius had the Huns in mind when he wrote about the peoples "to whom wailing means self-wounding and tearing the cheeks with iron and gouging the red traces of scars on the threatening face."[120] A line in Kālidāsa's *Raghuvamśa* alludes to the same custom among the Huna on the Oxus: "The exploits of Raghu, whose valor expressed itself among the husbands of the Hūna women, became manifest in the scarlet color of their cheeks."[121]

Slashing or scratching the face as an expression of mourning was so widespread[122] that only a few parallels to the Hunnic custom need to be adduced: The Kutrigur cut their cheeks with daggers;[123] the Turks cut off their hair and slashed their ears and cheeks;[124] so did the Magyars[125]

---

[113] *Res gestae Saporis* 11.

[114] *Rex ille Persarum, numquam se ante dignatus hominem confiteri, fratro tuo* [*sc. Diocletiano*] *supplicat* (*Mamertini panegyricus Maximiano Augusto dictus* X, 6).

[115] Menander, *EL* 176₁₃, ₁₆.

[116] Petrus Chrysologus, quoted by L'Orange 1953, 41.

[117] G. Widengren in *La Regalità sacrà* (Leiden, 1959), 247.

[118] In his article of 1966, Czeglédy rightly ignored Attila.

[119] *Getica* 255. Ammianus (XXXI, 2, 2) misunderstood the custom.

[120] *Paneg. on Avitus* 238-240.

[121] Buddhaprakash 1957, 91, 118-119.

[122] Egami 1951, 144-157; he refers also to Claudian.

[123] Agathias.

[124] Menander "Protector," *EL* 207; the Memorial to Bilge qaghan, Malov 1959, 23; *Sui shu* 84, Liu 1958, 42.

[125] Liutprand, *Antapodosis* II, 3, F. A. Wright 1930, 70.

and Slavs;[126] on a wall painting in Pandzhikent, patterned on Parinirvāna scenes,[127] the mourners are shown cutting their cheeks with knives.[128] Until quite recently the custom was observed by Serbs and Albanians[129] and in some regions in Tadjikistan.[130] The lines on a gold mask found at the Shami Pass in the Chu Valley, datable to the fourth or fifth century, might represent scars.[131]

The *Getica* account of Attila's obsequies, going back to Priscus,[132] reads:

His body was placed in the midst of a plain and laid in state in a silken tent as a sight for men's admiration. The best horsemen of the entire tribe of the Huns rode around in circles, after the manner of circus games, in the place to which he had been brought and told of his deeds in a funeral dirge in the following manner:

Attila, the great king of the Huns,
the son of Mundzucus,
the ruler of the most courageous tribes;
enjoying such power as had been unheard of before him,
he possessed the Scythian and Germanic kingdoms alone
and also terrorized both empires of the Roman world
after conquering their cities, and
placated by their entreaties
that the rest might not be laid open to plunder
he accepted an annual tribute.
After he had achieved all this with great success
he died, not of an enemy's wound, not betrayed by friends,
in the midst of his unscathed people,
happy and gay,
without any feeling of pain.
Who therefore would think that this was death
which nobody considers to demand revenge?
(*Praecipuus Hunnorum rex Attila,*
patre genitus Mundzuco,
fortissimarum gentium dominus,

---

[126] Gaihānī, quoted in Markwart 1903, 112.

[127] Maenchen-Helfen 1957d, 306.

[128] D'iakonov and Iakubovskiĭ 1954, pl. 20. The custom is attested for the Sogdians by al-Beruni 1957, 1, 355.

[129] E. Schneeweiss, *Revue internationale des études balkaniques* 1, 1934, 176; M. S. Filipović, *ibid.*, 1936, 157-166.

[130] Rakhimov 1959, 118-119.

[131] Iamgerchinov 1963, 11, fig. 3a.

[132] Jordanes gave only an excerpt: *pauca de multis dicere non omittamus.*

qui inaudita ante se potentia
solus Scythica et Germanica regna possedit
nec non utraque Romani orbis imperia
captis civitatibus terruit, et
ne praedae reliqua subderentur,
placatus praecibus annuum vectigal accepit:
cumque haec omnia proventu felicitatis egerit,
non vulnere hostium, non fraude suorum,
sed gente incolumi
inter gaudia laetus
sine sensu doloris
occubuit.
quis ergo hunc exitum putet,
quem nullus aestimat vindicandum?)[133]

When they had mourned him with such lamentations, a *strava*, as they call it, was celebrated over his tomb with great reveling. They connected opposites and showed them, mixing grief over the dead with joy.[134] Then in the secrecy of night they buried the body in the earth. They bound his coffins, the first with gold, the second with silver, and the third with the strength of iron, showing by such means that these three things suited the mightiest of kings: iron because he subdued the nations, gold and silver because he received the honors of both empires. They also added the arms of foemen won in the fight, trappings of rare worth, sparkling with various gems, and ornaments of all sorts whereby princely state is maintained. And that so great riches might be kept from human curiosity, they slew those appointed to the work—a dreadful pay for their labor; and thus sudden death was the lot of those who buried him as well as of him who was buried.

Priscus' source is not known. If, as I am inclined to assume, *strava* is a Slavic word, his informant may have been an escaped prisoner of war, or one of those "Huns" who, after 453, took service in the East Roman army. Priscus may have heard the dirge from a Goth to whom it was translated from Hunnish and who rendered it into Greek. The song was translated at least once, probably twice, and possibly three times before Cassiodorus or Jordanes gave it in the present form. The "reconstructions"

---

[133] In the arrangement of the verses I follow Thompson 1948, 148-150.

[134] In the translation of *contraria invicem sibi copulantes luctu funereo mixto gaudio explicabant,* I follow Kalén 1934, 36. For another interpretation, see D. Norberg, *Eranos* 41, 1943, 39-40.

of the supposed Gothic text[135] from a version so far removed from the original are as fanciful as attempts to discover in it the *Weltanschauung* of the ancient Turks.

Mommsen praised the beauty of the song.[136] In the desert of Jordanes' prose it is certainly an oasis, but a small one. The Huns' boast that their king extorted so much money from the Romans might be genuine: It sounds, *mutatis mutandis*, like an epitaph for an American gangster of the prohibition era. The rest are banalities. Not a Hun poet but Cassiodorus-Jordanes called Attila king of kings, *rex omnium regum*;[137] one thinks, of course, of the title of the Persian kings, but as early as the first century B.C. Pharnaces, ruler of the Bosporus, called himself $\beta\alpha\sigma\iota\lambda\epsilon\dot{\nu}\varsigma$ $\beta\alpha\sigma\iota\lambda\dot{\epsilon}\omega\nu$.[138] Attila was "the lord of all Huns, and of the tribes of nearly all Scythia, he was the sole ruler in the world" (*Hunnorum omnium dominus et paene totius Scythiae gentium solus in mundo regnator*);[139] however, Ermanaric, a century before him, was also the ruler of "all the nations of Scythia and Germania."[140] *Non fraude suorum* almost sounds as if it were taken from Ammianus XXV, 3, 20, where Emperor Julian on his deathbed thanks the godhead that he does not die *clandestinis insidiis*. *Subdere* for *subicere*[141] and the spelling *Mundzuco* incidate that Jordanes made some changes in Cassiodorus' text. All in all, the song throws a very dim light on the poetry of the Huns.

The authenticity of Priscus' account of the funeral rites cannot be doubted, although in the shortened version of the *Getica* various themes seem to be telescoped. It is hard to imagine how the horsemen could ride around the tent and sing at the same time. *In modum circensium cursibus* may in the original have referred to horse races which so often and among the most different peoples are connected with burials.[142] Here and there a feature seems to have been misunderstood or misinterpreted. It is a little

---

[135] F. Kluge 1911, 451-455, and 1921, 157-159. Kluge's "reconstruction" went far beyond the assumption of earlier authors that there might be a Germanic original behind the text in Jordanes (Müllenhoff 1847; Kogel 1984, 1, 1, 47). *Contra* Kluge, see Fr. Riedl, *Egytemes Philologiai Közlöny* 25, 1911, 370-371; Schröder 1922, 240-244.

[136] *Jordanes*, p. xxxv.

[137] *Getica* 201.

[138] Gaĭdukevich 1949a, 586; *KS* 37, 1951, 226. Anthony appointed Cleopatra "Queen of the Queens," and her co-regent Caesarion "King of the Kings" (Dio XLIX, 41, 1).

[139] *Getica* 178.

[140] *Ibid.*, 120.

[141] *Jordanes*, index 198.

[142] The Kao-chü, P. Demiéville, *AOH* 15, 1962, 80, and T'u-chüeh, Liu 1958, 9, held horse races; so did the Huns in the Caucasus, Movsēs Dasxurançi 1961, 156. Rich material on the peoples in the Caucasus in Bleichsteiner 1946, 419-455. For Indo-European parallels, see Focke 1941, 47-53; for Turkish parallels, Harva 1938, 33.

strange that Attila's coffin should have been covered with gold, silver, and iron like the walls of the inner sanctum of the Serapaeum in Alexandria.[143] To kill the laborers who buried the king was an inefficient means to prevent the robbing of the tomb for thousands must have known of it. Besides, who killed the killers? The slaughter was probably a sacrificial act, comparable to the killing of prisoners after the death of Silzibulos.[144]

The Hunnic rites must have reminded Priscus of similar ones he knew from his Homer.[145] The Thracians, reported Herodotus (V, 8), "lay out the dead for three days, then, after killing all kinds of victims and first making lamentations, they feast; after that they make away with the body either by fire or else by burial in the earth, and when they have built a barrow they set on foot all kinds of contests." Priscus may have heard of the drinking bouts and horse races with which the Othtrysae honored the dead.[146] The association of burial and games is known from Greece to the Nicobar Islands, and from the Bedouins in the Sinai Peninsula to the Bashkirs on the Volga.[147]

There is nothing in the Hunnic rites to which analogies could not be found throughout Eurasia. The assertion that the Huns buried their dead like the Goths[148] is as unfounded as the opposite statement that no part of the rites at Attila's funeral can be claimed as Germanic. The mixture of grief with joy is well attested for both Germans[149] and non-Germans. The hunt for parallels is futile, and the assumption that the Huns buried their kings after Gothic, Sarmatian, Slavic, or any other but Hunnic fashion is untenable. Attila's shade, says Jordanes, was honored "by his tribe" (a sua gente), "as is the custom of that tribe" (ut gentis illius mos est). The strava, which the Huns celebrated over his tomb with great revelry, was a Hunnic custom.

THE SACRED SWORD

The Huns are said to have worshipped a sacred sword. At Attila's court the East Roman ambassadors were told the following story:

---

[143] Rufinus, Hist. eccles. II, 23.

[144] For the Hsiung-nu, cf. Groot 1921; the Yenisei Kirghiz and Danube Bulgars, Ibn Fadlan 1939, 237; the Mongols, Minns 1913, 88-89.

[145] Frazer 1915, 3, 93. A. S. Cook's assumption (Transactions of the Connecticut Academy of Arts and Sciences 25, 339ff.) cannot be taken seriously; cf. also Thompson 1948, 150.

[146] Xenophon, Hellenica III, 25.

[147] Frazer 1915, 4, 96-112; L. Malten, Mitteilungen des deutschen archäologischen Instituts, Römische Abteilung 38-39, 1923-1924, 333-337. For parallels among the early Turks in Central Asia, see P. Demiévile, AOH 15, 1962, 80-81.

[148] K. Helm 1937, 15.

[149] Grønbech 1931, 2, 184-185; Stumpfl 1936, 153-155.

When a certain shepherd beheld one heifer of his flock limping and could find no cause of this wound, he anxiously followed the trail of blood and at length came to a sword it had unwittingly trampled while nibbling the grass. He dug it up and took it straight to Attila. The king rejoiced at this gift, and, being ambitious, thought he had been appointed ruler of the whole world, and that through the sword of Mars supremacy in all wars was assured to him.[150]

Jordanes read this story in Cassiodorus, whose source was Priscus.[151] Cassiodorus shortened the passage but not as much as we have it now in the Constantinian excerpts. There it is compressed into a pale "discovered through the agency of an ox," but the sword itself is more exactly described than in the *Getica*. It was "sacred and honored among the Scythian kings, dedicated to the overseer of wars. It had vanished in ancient times."[152]

All this sounds like the combination of a folktale, transferred on Attila, and Herodotus IV, 62: "The Scythians worship Ares in the form of an *acinaces* [a scimitar-*Ed*.], set up on a platform of bundles of brushwood."[153] Herodotus' statement, with slight variations, has often been repeated. It occurs in Eudoxius of Cnidos,[154] Apollodorus,[155] Mela,[156] Lucian,[157] Solinus,[158] and, cited from secondhand sources, in the writings of Christian apologists.[159]

Occasionally newer tribes took the place of the Scythians. Hicesius ascribed the worship of the sacred sword to the Sauromatae,[160] Dionysius to the Maeotians,[161] and Ammianus, in a passage in which he is not above the suspicion of having followed the *styli veteres*, to the Alans (they "fix a naked sword in the ground and reverently worship it as Mars, the presiding deity of those lands over which they range").[162] If, however, Am-

---

[150] *Getica* 183.

[151] *Priscus istoricus refert.*

[152] *EL* 142$_{19-22}$. Jordanes has *sacer apud Scytharum reges* semper *habitus*. The comparison between the *Getica* and the Constantinian excerpts proves once more that in the excerpts the Priscus text has at times been radically shortened.

[153] Thompson (1948, 89) does not doubt the truth of the story, though he concedes that Priscus had the Herodotus passage in mind.

[154] Quoted by Clemens Alexandrinus, *Protrepticus* V, 64, 5, *GCS* 12, 49. Eudocius flourished about 365 B.C. (Rostovtsev 1930, 24, 26).

[155] *Quis ei* [sc. *Marti*] *a Scythis asinos immolari* [*dixit*]? *Non principaliter cum ceteris Apollodorus?* Arnobius, *Adv. Nat.* IV, 25, *CSEL* 4, 161.

[156] II, 1, 11.

[157] *Iov. Trag.* 42; *Toxaris* 38 (Scythians swear by the gods Wind and Acinaces).

[158] V, 1, 3, Mommsen, ed., 82 (repeats Mela).

[159] *E.g.*, Arnobius, *Adv. Nationes* VI, 11, *GCS* 4, 222.

[160] Cited Clemens Alexandrinus, *Protrepticus* V, 64, 5, *GCS* 12, 49.

[161] *Perieg.* 652-654.

[162] XXXI, 2, 23.

mianus should actually have referred to the Alans of his time, it could be argued that the Huns had taken over an old Iranian cult.

On the other hand, the Hsiung-nu of the Han period likewise worshipped a sword:[163] The *ching-lu* was both a sword, *tao*, and a god, *shen*, to whom prisoners of war were sacrificed in the same way as to the Scythian Ares-*acinaces*.[164] Besides, at least three more "Altaic" peoples held the sword so sacred that they swore by it. The Avar kagan took an oath after the manner of his people on his drawn sword,[165] the Bulgars swore on their swords,[166] and Suleiman the Great, undoubtedly following an old Turkish custom, took an oath on his sword.[167]

But there were more, neither Iranian nor Altaic, peoples for whom the worship of the sword is attested. The Quadi, "drawing their swords, which they venerate as gods, swore that they would remain loyal."[168] The Franks swore by their swords.[169] The warriors in ancient India worshipped their swords.[170]

In spite of the literary overtone, we may believe Priscus: Like so many peoples, from Mongolia to Gaul, the Huns worshipped the god of war in the form of a sword. The origin of the cult cannot be determined.

MASKS AND AMULETS

Like the Germans and the Celts in the West,[171] the nomads of the eastern steppes took a fancy to the frontal representations of heads, an old and

---

[163] Most of the previous studies on the Ching-lu shrines of the Hsiung-nu are superseded by Kao Chü-hsün's excellent article of 1960.

[164] *Ching lu,* 徑路, archaic *kieng-glak*, is more than a transcription; it is also an interpretation. *Ching lo,* 剄 駱 archaic *kieng-glak*, means "to cut the throat," *ching*, of a "white horse with a black mane," *lo.* Cf. *Han shu* 94b: "[Han] Ch'ang and [Chang] Meng, together with the shan-yü and his high officials, ascended the mountain east of the No River in the country of the Hsiung-nu. They killed a white horse. The shan-yü stirred the wine with a *ching-lu* knife." This makes the various attempts to equate *ching-lu* with similar sounding Turkish and Iranian words for "knife, sword" (cf. Pulleyblank 1963, 222-223) somewhat doubtful.

[165] Menander, *EL* 473$_{18}$.

[166] *Per spatham iuramentum agebatur* (*Responsa Nicolai* 67); cf. also the passages adduced by Runciman 1930, 74.

[167] *Orientalia periodica christiana* 15:3-4, 1949, 234.

[168] Ammianus XVII, 12, 21.

[169] *Sacramentum, ut eorum mos erat, super arma placata* (Fredegar, *PL* 71, 651-652). More on the Germanic peoples in Grundtvig 1870; Vordemfelder 1923, 41-44. On ecclesiastical prohibitions of swearing by the sword, some as late as the ninth century, see Amira and Schwerin 1943, 1, 75, 106.

[170] M. Scheftelowitz, *Archiv für Religionswissenschaft* 25, 1937, 357-358.

[171] A. Alföldi, *Num. Köz.* 28-29, 1930-1931, 20-24, and 40, 1932, 64, n. 142; H. Vetters, *Jahreshefte d. österr. archäolog. Inst.* 38, 1948, Beiblatt 40-55.

widespread motif in the higher civilizations to the south in direct or indirect contact with the barbarians.[172] Masklike heads occur on horse trappings, stamped silver and bronze sheets, in Hunnic burials as well as in those which in one way or another indicate a Hunnic milieu; in Szentes-Nagyhegy[173] and Pécs-Üszög[174] in Hungary, Novo-Grigor'evka in the southern

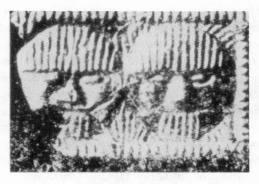

Fig. 13. Mask-like human heads stamped on gold sheet from a Hunnic burial at Pokrovsk-Voskhod. From Sinitsyn 1936, fig. 4.

Fig. 14. Mask-like human heads stamped on silver sheet on a bronze phalera from kurgan 17, Pokrovsk. From Minaeva 1927, pl. 2:11.

---

[172] To name a few examples: F. A. Marshall 1911, nos. 1103, 1108, 2097-2098; Reichel 1942, pl. 18:65, 22:79b; Siveo 1954, pls. 34-37; Becatti 1954, pl. 33:193, 38:215a-c, 70-71, 75, 92. In Greek art in the service of the Scythians and other barbarians in southeastern Europe, circular friezes of heads are quite common; cf. Bobrinskoĭ 1894, 1, 136, fig. 20, pls. 11, 12; Minns 1913, index *s.v.* Mask, decorative; Svoboda and Concev 1956, 144. Cf. also the masks on the Parthian palace at Hatra (Sarre 1922, pl. 60).

[173] Fettich 1953, pl. 58:2; *AAH* 7, 1956, pl. 17:13-15.

[174] Fettich 1953, 181,. pl. 58:9.

Ukraine,[175] and Pokrovsk-Voskhod (fig. 13)[176] and Pokrovsk kurgan 17 (fig. 14)[177] and 18[178] on the lower Volga.

The wooden and leather masks in the kurgans at Pazyryk in the High Altai, datable to the fourth century B.C., still reveal their foreign prototypes; some are derived from the head of Bes,[179] others betray in the palmette on top their origin in Greek art.[180] The gradual simplification of the heads, their progressive coarsening, whether they were Sileni, Negroes, Gorgoneia, the heads of Hercules or Dionysus,[181] led independently both in the East and West to similar results.[182] On early Celtic masks the hair is done in vertical strokes covering the forehead down to the eyebrows[183] as it is on the masks from Intercisa, Szentes-Nagyhegy, and Pokrovsk-Voskhod.[184] The masks may have been carriers of apotropaic powers, could (*pars pro toto*) have stood for god or demons, or may have been merely decorative. The juxtaposition and superimposition of the masks probably had no meaning: They seem to result from the technique of stamping thin metal sheets.[185]

Some of the Hunnic or probably Hunnic masks are of Iranian origin. The Huns, said Ammianus Marcellinus, looked like eunuchs. He exaggerated, as usual. But their thin beards also struck the observant Priscus.[186] The masks from Pécs-Üszög, Pokrovsk 17 (fig. 14), and Pokrovsk-Voskhod (fig. 13), with their luxuriant beards, cannot represent Huns, or their gods.

---

[175] Samokvasov 1908, pl. 9:15; Alföldi 1932, pl. 22:5.

[176] Sinitsyn 1936, 76, fig. 4; J. Werner 1956, pl. 40:12.

[177] Minaeva 1927, pl. 1:6, Alföldi 1932, pl. 6; J. Werner 1956, pl. 60:3.

[178] Minaeva 1927, pl. 2:11; Alföldi 1932, pl. 24:7; J. Werner 1956, pl. 60:3,

[179] Rudenko 1953, pl. 44. A statue of Bes was found in the Altai (A. Zakharov, *Tsaranion* 4, 227-229).

[180] Rudenko 1953, pl. 80:6. Cf. Azarpay 1959, 314-315; cf. also the head of Dionysus on a white kotyle in the Ny Carlsberg Glyptothek, *American Journal of Archaeology* 39, 1935, 479, fig. 4a.

[181] Fettich 1953, 180-181.

[182] The striking similarity of Celtic masks to a Carolingian stone relief, *De l'art des Gaules à l'art français* (Toulouse, 1956), pl. 13, of course does not prove the survival of Celtic traditions.

[183] Jacobsthal 1944, 14, pl. 21:20, 185:382.

[184] The publication of all Sarmatian objects with masks would be most desirable. Tikhanova (1956, 310, n. 1) mentions a mask from Kobelyak, province Poltava, and a mask-pendant from Inkerman in the Crimea, both unpublished. The faces on Sarmatian gold clasps from a catacomb cemetery at Bratskoe in the valley of the Terek River in Checheno-Ingushetia (*KS* 100, 1965, 48, fig. 17:2) have little to do with the masks; the eyes are rendered by inset blue stones, the mouth by a red stone.

[185] The same is true for weaves. The repetition of masks or heads is characteristic of Coptic tapestries of the fourth and fifth centuries (Weibel 1952, 76, n. 5).

[186] The source of *Getica* 182.

Fig. 15. The representation of the head of a Scythian in clay from Trans-caucasia. Photo courtesy State Historical Museum, Moscow.

Although most masks of the barbarians are mechanical and increasingly debased replicas of motifs unintelligible to their makers, occasionally one finds new and unexpected features in them, apparently attempts to make them more like the people who used them. The just-mentioned masks, with their shaved upper lip and the fan-shaped beard, render a fashion which at one time was current among Eurasian nomads. The head of a "Scythian" in the Historical Museum in Moscow (fig. 15), found in Transcaucasia,[187] makes it probable that originally it was the fashion of Iranian tribes.[188]

To Iranians point also the curious bronze mountings on a wooden casket from Intercisa on the Danube, south of Aquincum-Budapest (fig. 16).[189] They sometimes have been claimed for the Huns. Radnóti, on the other

Fig. 16. Bronze mountings from a wooden casket from Intercisa on the Danube. From Paulovics, *AÉ*, 1940.

---

[187] The piece, a stray find, is undatable. The face of a clay figure from a kurgan at the stanitsa Charvlennaya in Checheno-Ingushetia, datable to the sixth or fifth century, is quite similar. Cf. Vinogradov 1966a, 300.

[188] See the stone figure from the Terek, datable to about 500 B.C., in Vinogradov 1966b, 43.

[189] J. Paulovics, *AÉ*, 1940. Our figure is a reproduction from a plate in Paulovics' article; the mountings were lost in the last war.

hand, comparing the heads, or masks, of the figures with those on Germanic buckles, takes the mountings for Germanic; he dates them tentatively to the middle of the fifth century.[190] Now it is true that Germans settled, at one time or another, near Intercisa; however, the masks of the Ostrogothic buckles,[191] which, by the way, belong to the last third of the fifth century,[192] are quite different from those on the Intercisa casket. Apart from the higher relief, the mountings are technically identical with the many late Roman pieces found both on the Danube and the Rhine.[193] The man who made them must have been a Roman or a barbarian using Roman techniques. But this is of minor importance, for the figures on the mountings are as un-Roman as possible. The heads are distantly related to the mask-heads from Hunnic burials, but the impressive mustache occurs on none of them. It has some resemblance to the mustache of Turkish stone figures in Southern Siberia and Mongolia,[194] or on Sasanian silver phalerae.[195] But neither the Turkish nor the Persian heads have the luxuriant beards of the Intercisa figures, a feature which also rules out the Huns. This leaves only one possibility: The figures must be Sarmatian.

Their meaning is obscure. Still, perhaps we may make a guess. The two standing figures cannot be the images of mortal women. The finds in Sarmatian graves, from the earliest to the latest, prove that the Sarmatian women did not bare their breasts like the Intercisa figures; they wore shirts leaving only the neck free. Besides, the lozenges on the figures emphazise the genital region in the strangest way. In his *Aletheia*, Claudius Marius Victor of Marseille, who died about 425,[196] says that the Alans worshipped their ancestors.[197] I am inclined to assume that the women on the casket from Intercisa represent Sarmatian *matres*.

To Sarmatians lead likewise flat bronze amulets, angular figures of men and women, which Kruglikova took for Hunnic.[198] The women with marked breasts and the ithyphallic men (fig. 17) were evidently meant to avert evil. Such amulets were found in the Crimea (Chersonese, Panticapaeum, Tyritace), on the Kuban (stanitsa Pashkovskaya, cemetery 3)

---

[190] *AAH* 26, 1957, 279-280.

[191] *Vorgeschichte*, pl. 502:1, 3; 503:2; 521:2.

[192] On the "Maskenschnallen," cf. J. Werner 1959, 424.

[193] The style of the mask on the late Roman fibula from Fenekpuszta (*AÉ* 82, 1955, pl. 5:17) is quite different from the masks on the Intercisa mountings.

[194] Evtiukhova, *MIA* 24, 1952, figs. 2, 3, 14, 16, 18, 21, 24-26, 45, 57; Maenchen-Helfen 1931, 131.

[195] Alföldi, *Dumbarton Oaks Papers* 11, 1957, 238, fig. 1.

[196] Courcelle 1948, 221.

[197] *Aletheia* III, 192, *CSEL* 16, 349.

[198] Kruglikova 1957, 253-257.

FIG. 17. Flat bronze amulet in the shape of an ithyphallic human figure of Sarmatian type. (*Source not indicated in the manuscript.*—Ed.)

and in the northern Caucasus (Kumul'ta, Kamunta, Aibazovskoe).[199] The grave of a child at the Syuyur Tash on the Azov Sea, in which such an amulet was found, contained a fabric with a quotation from the New Testament and, written on it, the date: 602 of the Bosporan era=305 A.D.[200] It is, therefore, pre-Hunnic.[201]

Although from the masks little, if anything, can be learned about the religion of the Huns, some of them point to apparently early contacts between Huns and Iranian tribes, presumably Sarmatians.

EIDOLA

Between 452 and 458, some of the Roman prisoners of war in the country of the Huns "by hunger and terror" were forced to eat sacrificial food. Who forced them? The Goths. It is true that Athanaric, iudex of the Visigoths, ordered that the people who were suspect of being

---

[199] To the findspots listed by Kruglikova, add Gilyach on the Upper Kuban (Minaeva 1951, 296-297, fig. 14:4); Kyz-Aul, now Svetlachki, in the eastern Crimea (Gaĭdukevich 1959, 203-204); Chufut-Kala (*KS* 100, 1965, 111, fig. 44:6); Kamunta (V. A. Kuznetsov 1962, fig. 13:1-3; E. Chantre 1887, 3, pl. 17:5).

[200] Kruglikova 1957, 255.

[201] Gaĭdukevich (1958, 173) thinks that Alano-Sarmatians brought such amulets to Tyritace.

Christian worship a wooden figure[202] and make sacrifices to it.[203] But that was in the 370's. By the middle of the fifth century, most Visigoths and Ostrogoths were Christians, not always very devout ones, but definitely no longer fanatical pagans. The date of the conversion of the Gepids is controversial. Thompson thinks it improbable that they were baptized when they were still under Hunnic rule; he even suspects that their "most savage rites," of which Salvian wrote in the early 440's, may have been human sacrifices.[204] Schmidt's assumption that the Gepids embraced Christianity under King Ardarich[205] has no textual support. A Gepidic nobleman who died about 480 wore a finger ring with a cross on it but was buried with pagan rites. As late as 580, when the Langobards had long been Arian Christians, it could happen that forty Italian peasants who refused sacrificial meat were slaughtered.[206] However, after the battle on the Nedao, the Gepids, Christians and pagans, and the Huns no longer lived together.

This leaves the Alans and Huns. We seem to learn something about Hunnic sacrifices from a short passage in the *Getica* which probably goes back to Priscus: When the Huns first entered Scythia, they sacrificed to victory, *litavere victoriae*, as many as they captured.[207] This is the only time the Huns were accused of having sacrificed their prisoners. In Attila's time, and also before him, those captives who could not be sold or who were not ransomed were kept as domestic slaves. Priscus apparently transferred a Germanic custom, of which he knew from literature, to the Huns.[208] But the Huns may have sacrificed animals to their gods. Did they worship gods in human or animal form?

Throughout northern Eurasia, from Lapland to Korea, the figures of the shamanistic pantheon, in particular the shaman's "helpers," were represented in various ways: painted on drums; cut out of felt; cast in bronze and iron and attached to the shaman's coat; carved out of wood

---

[202] The sacred cult objects (Eunapius, fr. 25) which the Visigoths carried with them when they crossed the Danube in 376 were probably also of wood.

[203] On the persecutions, see Thompson 1961, 94-102.

[204] Thompson 1957a, 18.

[205] Schmidt 1934, 533.

[206] Gregory I, *Dialogi de vita et miraculis patrum Italicorum* III, 27, Moricca 1924, 539. The dialogues were written 593-594; the peasants were killed "almost fifteen years before."

[207] *Getica* 125.

[208] Before their conversion, the Goths worshipped Mars "with cruel rites, and captives were slain as his victims" (*Getica* 41); after the victory at Arausio, the Cimbri sacrificed the horses by drowning and the captives by hanging (Orosius, *Hist. adv. Pagan.* V, 6, 5-6); the Cherusci, Suevi, and Sugambri sacrificed twenty centuriones (Florus III, 19).

and put up in the tent or glued to the drum.[209] The shamanistic Huns, too, may have had eidola (I avoid the missionary term "idols"). There is, indeed, both literary and archaeological, though circumstantial, evidence of their existence.

According to Malalas, Gordas, prince of the Huns near Bosporus in the Crimea, was baptized in Constantinople in the first year of Justinian's reign, 527-528. After his return to his country, he ordered the ἀγάλματα, made of gold and electrum, to be melted down; the metal was exchanged for Byzantine money in Bosporus. Incensed at the sacrilege, the priests, in connivance with Muageris, Gordas' brother, put the prince to death.[210]

There is no reason to doubt Malalas' account. Besides, the statement that the figures were of gold and electrum, while the cliché would call for gold and silver, speaks in favor of the story. It does, of course, not prove that the Attilanic Huns, too, had figures of their gods made of precious metals. But the possibility cannot be ruled out, certainly not because of the low level of Hun metal work.[211] The impressive bronze horseman from Issyk in Kazakhstan, datable to the fifth or fourth century B.C.,[212] shows the skill of metalworkers in the early nomadic societies of Eurasia. The Hsiung-nu had their "metal men,"[213] and the silver figures at the court of the Turk Silzibulos greatly impressed the Byzantine ambassador.[214] The common Hunnic eidola—provided that they did exist—were probably much more like those of the Sarmatians, about which we are fairly well informed.

The earliest one is of sandstone, about one meter high, a pillar rectangular in cross section, except the upper part, which is rounded to represent the head (fig. 18); it was found in kurgan 16 at Tri Brata near Elista[215] in the Kalmuk steppe.[216] The arrowheads date the grave to the fifth century B.C.[217] Smirnov lists a similar stone figure from Berdinskaya Gora near Orenburg and two from the trans-Volga steppes which, however, stand closer to the well-known *kamennye baby,* "stone women." Two more

---

[209] For the cult objects of the shamanistic tribes in the Altai, see S. V. Ivanov's excellent monograph in *SMAE* 16, 1955, 165-264.

[210] Malalas 432; cf. Moravcsik 1946, 5, 38-39.

[211] The headless copper statue from Bántapuszta in western Hungary which Takáts published in *AOH* 9, 1959, 85-86, is, in his opinion, Hunnic; other Hungarian archaeologists take it for a part of a medieval aquamanile.

[212] Martynov, *KS* 59, 1958, 150-156; *BMFEA* 30, 1958, pl. 7:10.

[213] Cf. Kao Chü-hsün 1960, 221-222, on the *chin jen.*

[214] Menander, *EL* 194$_{16-18}$.

[215] The capital of the recently reconstituted Kalmuk ASSR.

[216] Sinitsyn 1956b, 32-34, fig. 11; K. F. Smirnov 1964, fig. 75:2.

[217] K. F. Smirnov 1961, 117.

Fig. 18. Sandstone pillar in the shape of a human head from kurgan 16 at Tri Brata near Elista in the Kalmuk steppe. (Height 1 m.) From Sinitsyn 1956b, fig. 11.

eidola from the lower Don, stone slabs showing human figures in silhouette, may be somewhat later.[218]

Smirnov assumed that these Sarmatian figures were put up on, or near, burial mounds as representations of local gods or deified ancestors. Their similarity to the silhouette stone slabs from the Bosporan kingdom, dating from Hellenistic to Roman times, speaks for the latter interpretation; the Bosporan figures, some of them with the name of the dead written on them,[219] are doubtless tombstones.

From the Early Sarmatian period two chalk eidola are known,[220] both about 13 centimeters high, too small to be erected on a kurgan or on the ground. The one from Bliznetsy, west of Ak-Bulak in the province Orenburg, is a human figure in the round, so crude that not even the sex can be determined; the other one from Zaplavnoe between Volgograd and Elista, one or two centuries earlier, is a slab with the merest indication of the head.

In the Middle Sarmatian period, eidola were made over a wide territory. In the grave of a young woman in kurgan 5/3, in the burial ground at By-

---

[218] K. F. Smirnov 1964, 172-173.
[219] Ivanova 1954, 242-244, figs. 4-7.
[220] Moskhova 1963, 46, fig. 15:1, 2.

kovo on the Volga, oblast Volgograd, a crude chalk figure was found, 8 centimeters high, head, shoulders, and legs barely indicated .[221] Four even cruder eidola from the Kuban area probably are to be dated to the early first century A.D.; one was found at Krasnodar, three at Elizavetskaya stanitsa.[222]

In a sacrificial pit at Neapolis near Simferopol in the Crimea lay unburnt clay figures: the head and neck of a ram, the fragment of a human torso, and two coarsely modeled heads;[223] the building near the pit was destroyed about 200 A.D., the beginning of the Late Sarmatian period when numerous elements of Sarmatian civilization began to appear in the late Scythian civilization of Neapolis. Of about the same time is the clay figure of a seated woman with a hollowed head, 7 centimeters high, found in the town site Zolotaya Balka on the lower Dnieper.[224] Clay figures of the Late Sarmatian period were found in small rural settlements on the periphery of the Bosporan kingdom: The terracottas from Semenovka represent women;[225] a female torso and a head were excavated at Mysovka,[226] and another head at Tasunovo.[227] A limestone figure, 9.5 centimeters high, 3.5. centimeters across the shoulders, comes from a kurgan at Perezdnaya in the uezd Bakhmut, gubernie Ekaterinoslav. It represents a woman with what looks like a vessel in her hands, the body apparently bare, the the head covered. Veselovsky took it for pre-Mycenean; Gorodtsov dated it rightly to the second or third century.[228]

Two chalk eidola have come to light from Alanic graves of the fifth century A.D. at Baital Chapkan in Cherkessia.[229] One is round in cross section, modeled on one side only, the shoulders being indicated by round projections (fig. 19); the other eidolon is merely a cone, somewhat wider in the upper part.

This list is incomplete. Many Sarmatian eidola mentioned in excavation reports are neither properly described nor properly illustrated. A few examples follow: a piece of wood with a human head in a kurgan at Susly in the former German Volga Republic;[230] two stone "stelae" in a cemetery

[221] K. F. Smirnov 1960, 181, fig. 6:10.

[222] V. A. Gorodtsov in Arkheologicheskie issledovaniia v RSFSR 1934-1936, 213, fig. 57:8, 9.

[223] Malikov 1961, 65-68, fig. 2-4, 6.

[224] Viazmitina 1962, 213, fig. 86: 11, 13. A similar stone figure is in the museum at Dnepropetrovsk (Viazmitina 1962, 213, n. 19).

[225] Kruglikova 1961, 76, fig. 30:2b.

[226] Kruglikova 1956, 254, fig. 11:6, 7.

[227] Blavatskiï and Shelov 1955, 111, fig. 45:4.

[228] Gorodtsov 1905, 252-255, fig. 59, and IAK 37, 1910, 9-91; N. I. Veselovskiï, IAK 35, 1910, 9-11, and IAK 37, 1910, 98-102.

[229] Minaeva 1956, 251-252, fig. 12.

[230] Rau 1926, 10.

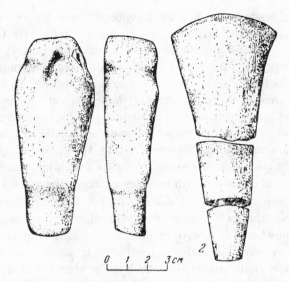

FIG. 19. Chalk eidola from an Alanic grave at Baital Chapkan in Cherkessia, fifth century A.D. From Minaeva 1956, fig. 12.

at Zemetnoe near Bakhchisarai in the Crimea;[231] wooden statues, 56 inches high, in a barrow in the former okrug Sal'sk, southeast of Rostov;[232] an anthropomorphic copper figure in a kurgan between Kapustin and Pogromnoe at the border of the oblasts Astrakhan and Volgograd.[233]

Some of the small terracotta, lead, and copper figures in Sarmatian graves in the Kuban area, excavated by Veselovsky, but never published,[234] may have been dolls. A small bronze figure in a Late Sarmatian grave at Ust'-Kamenka, district Apostolovo, oblast Dnepropetrovsk,[235] might also be a doll; its leather belt, with a bow at the back, is well preserved; the absence of a loop indicates that the statuette was not carried around the neck as an amulet. The silver figure of a mustachioed man in a short coat found in a grave in the cemetery at Novo-Turbasly near Ufa,[236] datable to the fourth or fifth century, had a loop at the back.

Minaeva compared the Alanic eidola from Cherkessia with the pieces of chalk in Late Sarmatian graves which for a long time have claimed the

[231] K. F. Smirnov 1950, 262.
[232] Gorodtsov 1905, 253.
[233] See the preliminary report on the Astrakhan expedition, SA 2, 1959, 285.
[234] Trudy XII AS 1, 1905, 345, 360, 367.
[235] Viazmitina 1962, 237, fig. 2; Makno 1960, 37, fig. 15:3.
[236] Mazhitov 1959, 130, fig. 4.

attention of Soviet archaeologists. Rykov[237] and Rau[238] attributed to them ritual significance without attempting to define it; Grakov[239] and K. F. Smirnov[240] think the white chalk symbolizes purity: the pieces of chalk meant to purify the corpse. This is an attractive suggestion which may be valid in some cases but does not account for all. In the Early Sarmatian cemeteries at Berezhnovka and Molchanovka, no pieces of chalk were found, but many of realgar. The same is true for the Don region.[241] The orange-red realgar cannot very well stand for purity. From most excavation reports, one gets the impression that the lumps of clay were just thrown into the grave pit. However, there are exceptions. In Susly, kurgan 35, in the grave of a woman with a deformed skull, the chalk lay in a small, round vessel with a hole in its side.[242] In the Late Sarmatian graves at Ust'-Labinskaya the pieces were carefully placed next to clay vessels; one was in a bowl and five were in pitchers, intentionally kept away from the corpses they were allegedly to purify.[243] It seems that it was rather the shape of the chalk pieces than their color that counted. Many seem to be merely irregularly shaped cones and pyramids, but others had been worked over. The piece in kurgan 8/3 in Susly looks like the cocoon of a silkworm.[244] In the Late Sarmatian grave of a woman, in Focşani in Rumania, lay a rather remarkable "piece of chalk" (fig. 20).[245] Almost 12 centimeters high, it represents a human being: the round line of the chin separates the head from the body; eyebrows, pupils, nose, and mouth are crudely but unmistakingly rendered.

So far, no sandstone or chalk eidola have been found in Hungary. In view of the very small number of Alanic graves in the Danube basin, this is not surprising. A curious find proves the identity of the religion of the Alans in Hunnic Hungary and Cherkessia. At Füzesbonyban, a cone-shaped cavity, lined with polished clay, contained a horse skull.[246] There was no cemetery nearby; nothing similar is known from Hungary. But in Cherkessia, in Baital Chapkan and Atsiyukh, three such small "graves" with only the skull and the fore- and hindlegs of a horse have

---

[237] Rykov 1925, 31.

[238] Rau 1926, 67.

[239] Grakov 1947, 109.

[240] K. F. Smirnov 1964, 94-95.

[241] Moshkova 1963, 24.

[242] Rykov 1925, 66.

[243] Anfimov 1951, 201-202.

[244] Rykov 1926, 103.

[245] Morintz 1959, 459, fig. 7.

[246] I. Meri, *Folia archaeologica* 3-5, 1941, 149, fig. 2.

FIG. 20. Chalk figure from a Late Sarmatian grave in Focşani, Rumania. (Height ca. 12 cm.) From Morintz 1959, fig. 7.

been found, again unconnected with other burials.[247] If the Alans in Cherkessia put eidola in their graves, those in Hungary almost certainly did the same.

The Alans in Hungary stayed as pagan until the end of the Hunnic kingdom as those who in the beginning of the fifth century moved to Gaul. About 440, Salvian of Marseilles spoke about the greedy pagan Alans.[248] In the sixth century a few Alans in Gaul were Christians. We hear of St. Goar from Aquitania whose parents, Georgius and Valeria, had already been baptized;[249] they apparently had left their compatriots and moved into a Roman milieu which, however, did not prevent them from giving their son the pagan Alanic name, Goar. In the second half of the sixth century, Venantius Fortunatus named the Alans among the peoples who worshipped the Virgin, but the list (Ethiopians, Thracians, Arabs, Dacians,

---

[247] Minaeva 1956, 259, fig. 14.
[248] *De gubernatione Dei* IV, 14.
[249] *MGH scr. rer. Merov.* IV, 411.

Alans, Persians, and Brittons)[250] is patterned on an old cliché and without value. In an inscription in Spain, St. Martin is praised for converting the Alans;[251] there, too, they are among the same exotic peoples as in Venantius Fortunatus. In any case, by the middle of the fifth century, the Alans in Gaul were still pagans. Their king, Goachar (Goar), *rex ferocissimus*, was *idolorum minister*.[252] If this is not a conventional phrase, Goachar's eidola were probably not different in shape from those in the Sarmatian graves in the East, though possibly bigger.

In his admirable study of the Sauromatian cult objects, K. F. Smirnov assumes that the small chalk eidola in the burials were replicas of large stone statues like the one in kurgan 16 at Tri Brata.[253] He lists more of its kind, unfortunately mostly undatable. Still, one needs only to compare the piece of chalk from Focşani with the stone figure from Tri Brata to see that the main, if not the only, difference between them is their size. The same is true for a stone figure found at khutor Karnaukhova near ancient Sarkel on the lower Don[254] and a small clay statue, a pyramid with a round head from Znamenka south of Nikopol on the lower Dnieper.[255] Both are Sarmatian. Had the eidola which Muageris melted down been of small size, he would not have received more than a few solidi when he exchanged the metal for Byzantine money. This speaks for the assumption that, in analogy with the Sarmatian custom, the Huns in the Crimea, and and not only there, also had small eidola. This seems to be borne out by two eidola from Altyn Asar in ancient Khwarezm.[256] They are of unburnt clay, the one 8 centimeters high and the other 4 centimeters high. The upper strata of the lower horizon in the "Big House" are datable to the third or fourth century.[257] The eidola belong to the same Hunnoid civilization as the bone lamellae and the clay cauldrons from Altyn-asar. The extremely crudely modeled eyes, nose, and mouth are barely indicated by dots and strokes. The small clay cauldrons from Altyn-asar are, as we saw, replicas of bigger copper cauldrons. Therefore, we may conjecture that the eidola from Altyn-asar stand likewise for bigger ones worshipped by the Hunnoid population in Khwarezm in the third or fourth century.

---

[250] *In laudem Mariae* 289, 291, *MGH AA* 4, 1, 378. Its authenticity is undisputed; cf. Blomgren 1934, 2.

[251] Vives 1922, 120.

[252] *Vita Germani* 28, *MGH scr. rer. Merov.* 7, 272.

[253] K. F. Smirnov 1964, 172.

[254] Liapushkin, *MIA* 62, 1958, 318, fig. 3.

[255] Pogrebova 1958, 140, fig. 14:1.

[256] S. P. Tolstov, *SA* 19, 1954, 260, fig. 16:8; the drawings in *Trudy Khor.* 1, 1958, 239, fig. 114:9, 10, are inexact; Levina 1966, 54.

[257] Levina 1966, 54.

In her analysis of the pottery from Altyn Asar, Levina found numerous parallels to the Late Sarmatian civilization on the lower Volga and to the west of the river, but neither she nor Tolstov noticed that one eidolon has a typically Sarmatian tamga cut into the clay. Exactly the same tamga is carved on the side of a stone slab at Zadzrost' near Ternopol' in former eastern Galicia (fig. 21).[258] On the front are more tamgas, likewise typi-

FIG. 21. Stone slab at Zadzrost', near Ternopol', former eastern Galicia, marked with a Sarmatian tamga. (Height 5.5 m.) From Drachuk, *SA* 2, 1967, fig. 1.

cally Sarmatian. The slab is no less than 5.5 meters high, and below 1.21, above 1 meter wide. How it got into the northwestern Ukraine, where Sarmatians never lived, is obscure. Some Polish archaeologists took it for a Gothic monument, others saw in it a Turkish *kamennaya baba* with Runic letters; Drachuk, who discussed it most recently, regards it as a symbol of Sarmatian power. Actually, it is an eidolon, the biggest known so far: the upper part, carefully cut and set off the carelessly cut lower part, represents the head and the neck of the figure. It is in large size what the clay eidolon from Bykovo is in a small size. Similar stone slabs,

<hr>

[258] Solomonik 1959, 70 (with bibliography); V. S. Drachuk, *SA* 2, 1967, 243-244, fig, 1.

also with tamgas on them, are known from the Crimea.[259] I do not dare to decide whether the eidola from Altyn Asar were those of Huns under Sarmatian influence or of Sarmatian under Hunnish influence. Because of the Hunnish cauldron and the bone lamellae, the former seems more likely.

The metal, stone, clay, and wooden anthropomorphic sculptures in ancient northern Eurasia must be left to scholars who have access to all museums in the Soviet Union, not just to those in Leningrad and Moscow. A first and promising attempt was made by Davidovich and Litvinskii.[260] The material presented in the foregoing makes it probable that the Attilanic Huns and their Alanic allies worshipped, next to the sacred sword, also eidola in human form.

---

[259] Solomonik 1959, 68-70.
[260] *Trudy Tadzh.* 35, 1955, 53.

VII. Art

Gold Diadems

About 400 A.D., a "leader and king of those most savage Scythians who hold the other side of the Euxine Sea, living on the Maeotis and the Tanais as well as the Bosporus and as far as the Phasis River," is said to have sent "his crown, covered with gold and set with stones," to the church of St. Phocas in Sinope.[1] The "Scythians" were Hunnic tribes, among them, on the Phasis, the Onogur,[2] and, probably, their Alanic allies. Asterius actually may have seen the crown; it is remarkable in any case that he spoke of a crown covered with, not made of gold, στέφανον. . . χρυσῷ περιλαμπόμενον. A number of such sumptuous headgears, usually, though not quite correctly, called diadems[3] have been known for some time. In his *Beiträge* Werner discussed them in a special chapter.[4] Recently three more and the fragment of a fourth, possibly a fifth one, have come to light, and a report on a sixth, now lost, has been published. Their study can now start from a fairly wide base; besides, the circumstances under which the diadems were found are now better known, which, as will be seen, is of some importance for their interpretation.

Before going into details, the two fragments of a gold plaque (fig. 22)[5] from Kargaly in the district Uzun-Agach, not far from Alma Ata in Ka-

---

[1] Asterius of Amasea, *Homily* X, *PG* 40, 313. The king was the same who sent the thorax to Sinope.

[2] Agathias.

[3] A diadem is a fillet of white stuff, often set with stones.

[4] J. Werner 1956, 61-68.

[5] Courtesy of the AN Kazakhskoĭ SSR; N. Nurmukhammedov, *Iskusstvo Kazakhstana* (Moscow, 1970) figs. 30-35.

FIG. 22. Fragment of a gold plaque from Kargaly, Uzun-Agach, near Alma Ata, Kazakhstan. (About 35 cm long.) Photo courtesy Akademiia Nauk Kazakhskoĭ SSR.

zakhstan, which Bernshtam published,[6] must be eliminated from the discussion. First, because they were not a part of a diadem. More than 35 centimeters long, straight, not curved, they could not have been worn around the head. Second, their decor has nothing to do with the Hunnic or Alanic diadems. Bernshtam, followed by Werner, admitted strong Chinese influence in the à jour relief but insisted that it still reflected the shamanistic reliefs of its barbarian owners. He thought he could recognize in the diadem a renaissance of Scythian art which had led a subterranean existence in a conservative shamanistic milieu, to come suddenly to the fore around the beginning of our era. Actually the design is purely Chinese. The horse standing on a column is a variety of the quadruped, its feet gathered together on a pole, known not only from Scythian graves in South Russia but also from Perm, Kazakhstan, the Altai, southern Siberia, and the Ordos region.[7] In China the motif occurs as early as the Chou period.[8] The winged horse is likewise a well-known Chinese motif which had a great appeal to the northern barbarians; the gold plaque from Noin Ula has often been reproduced;[9] gilt bronze plaques with winged horses were recently found in Inner Mongolia.[10] The long-haired genii, hsien jen, have hundreds of parallels on Han stone reliefs, metal work, tiles, lacquers, vases, and textiles. They represent no more the shamanistic gods of the T'ien-shan nomads than the Nereids on a Greek cylix found in South Russia represent the goddesses of the Scythians.[11]

I first list the diadems which were known to Werner.

1. CSORNA in western Hungary (fig. 23).[12] Found on the skull of a north-orientated skeleton. A gold sheet, broken in several pieces, 26.5[13]

---

[6] 1952, 130-132, fig. 65; 1954, pl. between pp. 280 and 281. I have not seen Bernshtam's article of 1950.

[7] Cf. Chlenova 1962, pl. 4:11, 12, 14, 15; Pazyryk: Griaznov 1958, pl. 29; Minusinsk: Kiselev 1951, pl. 20:3; F.-R. Martin 1893, p. 33; Borovka 1927, pl. 44:B, Perm: Aspelin 1877, fig. 306; Kazakhstan: Margulan et al. 1966, fig. 66: 77-79; Ordos: Salmony 1933, pl. 5:3, 6:1, 7:1. The closest parallel to the horse on the Kargaly plate is a gold horse on a pole from western Siberia, SA 2, 1965, 229.

[8] Karlgren 1952, 176, pl. 91.

[9] E.g., Rudenko 1962b, pl. 35:4.

[10] Li I-yu 1963, no. 59, 61.

[11] The other finds from Kargaly are described by L. K. Nifontova in Izv. Kazakh. 1, 1948, 116-117. For drawings of a finger ring with a camel and an earring with a mouse or rat and a kneeling man, see Rudenko 1962b, 38, fig. 43, 44; Rudenko dates the pieces to the fourth century B.C., long before the "diadem."

[12] Hampel 1905, 1, 345, fig. 893=2,13. Photographs in Alföldi 1932, pl. 8 and Archäologische Funde in Ungarn, 291.

[13] According to Archäologische Funde in Ungarn, 298; Hampel (1905, 2, 13) has carnelians, white glass paste, green glass, amber, and garnets, and J. Werner (1956, 62),

FIG. 23. Hunnic diadem of gold sheet, originally mounted on a bronze plaque, decorated with garnets and red glass, from Csorna, western Hungary. (Originally about 29 cm long, 4 cm wide.) From *Archäologische Funde in Ungarn*, 291.

(originally about 29) centimeters long, 4 centimeters wide; the edges had been bent around a bronze plaque which has disappeared. Traces of copper oxide on the skull indicate that the diadem was worn without stuffing or leather lining. Garnets and red glass in cloisons.

2. KERCH (figs. 24A, B, C).[14] Said to have been found on the Mithridates Mountain in a grave next to the skeleton of a man with an artificially deformed skull.[15] Gold sheet over bronze plaques. Except the two big round cells and the lozenge one on the top ornament, which enclose green glass pieces, the 257 cloisons contain flat almandines.[16]

3. SHIPOVO, west of Uralsk, northwestern Kazakhstan (fig. 25).[17] Found on the forehead of a north-orientated skeleton in a wide rectangular pit under a kurgan; 25.2 centimeters long, 3.6 centimeters wide.[18] Thin bronze sheets over bronze plaques, set with convex glass. The bronze plaques

---

"cabochons and flat almandines." Not having seen the diadem, I do not know which description is the correct one. Photos and drawings show a flat band; obviously the pieces were flattened, for a flat band 29 centimeters in length could not have been a diadem.

[14] Courtesy Rheinisches Museum, Bildarchiv.

[15] For the description of the skull, see J. Werner 1956, 104. The *marchand amateur* Mavrogordato, who sold Baron Diergardt the diadem and other ornaments allegedly found in the same grave (listed in *L'Art mérovingien*, 1954, 31-32), did not have the best reputation.

[16] For a detailed description, see G. Schramm 1965, 129.

[17] J. Werner 1956, pl. 6:8, after Minaeva 1929, 196, fig. 2.

[18] Minaeva 1929, 196-198.

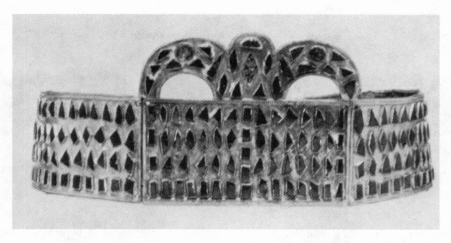

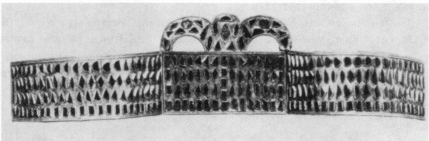

Figs. 24A-C. Hunnic diadem of gold sheet over bronze plaques decorated with green glass and flat almandines, from Kerch. Photos courtesy Rheinisches Museum, Bildarchiv, Cologne.

were originally lined with leather and, on it, thin silk; on the latter, small lozenges of gilt leather. The absence of weapons and a clay spin whorl indicate that the dead was a woman. Except for a crescent-shaped golden earring, the other metal objects in the grave were of bronze: buckles, a gold-covered necklace of twisted wire, and another earring. The bronze

FIG. 25. Hunnic diadem of thin bronze sheet over bronze plaques set with convex glass from Shipovo, west of Uralsk, northwestern Kazakhstan. From J. Werner 1956, pl. 6:8.

mirror with a long handle, preserved only in a fragment, is typical of the Middle Sarmatian period (I B.C.-I A.D).[19]

4. DEHLER on the Berezovka near Pokrovsk, lower Volga region (fig. 26).[20] The diadem was on the skull of the skeleton. Bronze plaques covered with gold sheets, which are set with convex almandines. Of the other grave goods, only big amber beads and a mirror were preserved. The mirror is of a type which in the Caucasus occurs from the fifth century A.D. on;[21]

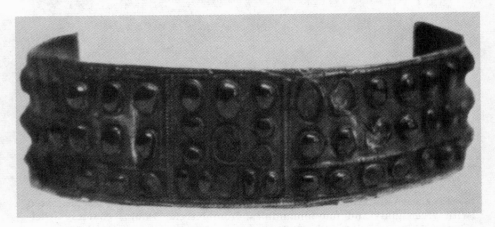

FIG. 26. Hunnic diadem of gold sheet over bronze plaques set with convex almandines from Dehler on the Berezovka, near Pokrovsk, lower Volga region. From Ebert, *RV* 13, "Südrussland," pl. *RV* 41:a.

---

[19] Khazanov 1960, group IV.
[20] Minaeva 1929, 206, fig. 32=M. Ebert, *RV* 13, "Südrussland," pl. 41a.
[21] Alekseeva 1955, 77.

in the West it made its appearance about the same time.[22] The diadem
was probably made about 400 A.D. or a little later.

5. TILIGUL (fig. 27).[23] Formerly in the Diergardt collection, now in
the Römisch-Germanisches Zentralmuseum, Mainz. Similar to the diadem
from Dehler but technically inferior. The bronze plaques are lost. On
the front part, convex almandines; flat triangular and rectangular ones
on the side parts. Allegedly none was found in the same grave "at Tiligul,"[24] which, however, is not the name of a place but a river between the
Prut and Dniester and the *liman* (lagoon) at its mouth.

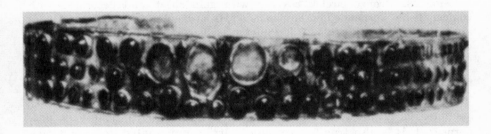

FIG. 27. Hunnic diadem of gold sheet over bronze plaques (now lost)
set with convex almandines, from Tiligul, in the Römisch-Germanisches
Zentralmuseum, Mainz. From J. Werner 1956, pl. 29:8.

6. KARA-AGACH, south of Akmolinsk in central Kazakhstan (fig. 28).[25]
Found near the skull of a skeleton in a stone cist under a kurgan. The
bronze circlet, 4 centimeters wide, 49 centimeters in circumference, is
covered with a sheet of very pale gold, decorated with stamped triangles
in imitation of granulation; fifteen conical "bells" (without clappers) hang
from bronze hooks. Among the other finds, there were two gold dragons
(fig. 29A),[26] the ends of a torque, richly decorated with garnets, amber,
and mother-of-pearl in cloisons and, in between, triangles in granulation.
Skalon published a very similar dragon found in a cemetery at Stavropol,
together with many ornaments typical of Sarmato-Alanic graves of the
fourth and fifth centuries in the North Caucasus.[27] The combination of
garnets and mother-of-pearl occurs in Conçesti[28] at the beginning of the

---

[22] J. Werner 1956, 22.

[23] *Ibid.*, pl. 29:8.

[24] *L'Art mérovingien*, 32.

[25] J. Werner 1956, pl. 31:2.

[26] *Ibid.*, pl. 31:5.

[27] Skalon 1962, 40-44.

[28] Matsulevich 1934, 101. This has been pointed out by J. Werner 1956, 78.

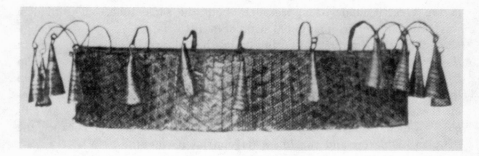

FIG. 28. Bronze circlet covered with gold sheet and decorated with conical "bells" suspended on bronze hooks, from Kara-Agach, south of Akmolinsk, central Kazakhstan. (Circumference 49 cm, width ca. 4 cm.) From J. Werner 1956, pl. 31:2.

fifth century. Emphazising the similarity, in many details amounting to identity, of the dragons from Stavropol and Kara-Agach, Skalon rightly assumes that they were made in the same workshops, probably in Bosporus.[29] This is also true for a type of earring represented in Kara Agach (fig. 29B).[30] Such earrings were worn over a very wide area. Their simplest, though not necessarily the original form, without the rings of granules

FIG. 29A. Terminal of a gold torque in the shape of a dragon, decorated with granulation and cloisonné garnets, amber, and mother-of-pearl. From Kara-Agach, south of Akmolinsk, central Kazakhstan. From *IAK* 16, 1905, p. 34, fig. 2.

---

[29] She dates the dragon from Stavropol to the fourth, that of Kara-Agach, because it is "dryer," to the fifth century. What she seems to mean is that the two pieces are a century apart.

[30] *IAK* 16, 1905, fig. 3:a-b.

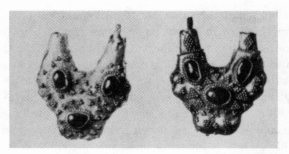

FIG. 29B. Gold earrings from Kara-Agach, central Kazakhstan. From *IAK* 16, 1905, fig. 3:a-b.

around the inlays, occurs as early as the second or third century; one, with inlays of glass, was found in a rich grave at Usatovo in the lower Volga region.[31] The earring from a grave at Kotovo (Mozhary), district Kamyshin, province Volgograd, of the same period or perhaps a little later, has the cloisons ringed with granulation.[32] A coarse version in silver comes from a kurgan at Pokrovsk (fig. 30).[33] Two such golden earrings

FIG. 30. Silver earring decorated with almandines and garnets from kurgan 36, SW group, near Pokrovsk. From Sinitsyn 1936, fig. 10.

FIG. 31. Gold earring from Kalagya, Caucasian Albania. From Trever 1959, 167, fig. 18.

---

[31] *Ibid.*, and Spitsyn 1905.
[32] *Ibid.*
[33] Sinitsyn 1936, fig. 10.

with an attached small tube and clusters of granules at the end were in a jug grave in Kalagya in Caucasian Albania (fig. 31).[34] Similar earrings are among the treasures in the Siberian collection of Peter the Great; they have gold balls and pyramids of granules attached.[35] Clasps of approximately the shape of the earrings from Kara-Agach, set with semiprecious stones clearly representing a face occur in Sarmatian graves in Checheno-Ingushetia in the northern Caucasus.[36] All these pieces of jewelry are by their form and technique so closely related that they must have been made by highly skilled goldsmiths who transmitted their craft from generation to generation in one and the same place.

The people who buried their dead in Kara-Agach in Kazakhstan were as unable to make the earrings and dragons as they were to make the glass beaker which . . . [*The manuscript breaks off here in mid-sentence.—Ed.*]

CAULDRONS

The Hunnic cauldrons have long claimed the attention of the archaeologists. In 1896, Reinecke separated a small group of cylindrical or bell-shaped bronze vessels, which until then had been classified as Scythian, from the hemispherical cauldrons of South Russia.[37] His assumption that they go back to Western prototypes, shared by Posta[38] and Ebert,[39] proved to be wrong, but he assigned them the right date. Because the bell-shaped cauldron from Jędrzychowice (formerly Höckricht) was found together with jewelry of the Folkwandering period, Reinecke dated it and, consequently, all similar cauldrons to the first centuries of our era. In 1913, Zoltán Takáts (Takács) published the first of a long series of articles[40] in which he argued for the Hunnic provenance of the cauldrons. Although Takáts at times indulged in wild speculations, in the main he was right, and his views prevailed: both the distribution of the vessels and the context in which they were found leave no doubt that they were cast by Huns for Huns.

Since Werner's discussion of the cauldrons in 1956,[41] so many more were found and so much new evidence on the cauldrons of the nomads in Central Asia and the Far East has accumulated that the problems which the Hunnic cauldrons pose call for a reexamination.

---

[34] Trever 1959, 167, fig. 18.
[35] Artamonov 1969, no. 98.
[36] M. Ebert, *RV*, *s.v.* Checheno-Ingushetia, northern Caucasus.
[37] *Zeitschrift für Ethnologie* 28, 1896, 12-13.
[38] Posta 1905, 523-524.
[39] *Prähistor. Zeitschr.* 4, 1912, 454.
[40] References to his earlier publications in Takáts 1955 end 1960.
[41] J. Werner 1956, 57-61.

Findspots

In the following list the numerous misspellings and distortions of the names of the findspots have been silently corrected. I did not aim at bibliographical completeness; to refer to the often poor illustrations in old Hungarian publications would serve no useful purpose; those in Japanese works[42] are taken from Western books and articles.

FIG. 32. Fragment of a bronze lug of a cauldron from Benešov, near Opava (Troppau), Czechoslovakia. (Height 29 cm, width 22 cm, thickness 1 cm.) From *Altschlesien* 9, 1940, pl. 14.

---

[42] Umehara 1938, 69-110; *Inner Mongolia*, 173-191; Egami 1948, 386-387.

CZECHOSLOVAKIA

1. Benešov (Bennisch) near Opava (Troppau). Fragment of a lug 29 centimeters high, 22 centimeters wide, up to 1 centimeter thick. Said to be found in a peat bog or on an old road running through a forest; the absence of patina typical of bronze objects found in bogs speaks for the latter. On the outside the cauldron had been exposed to strong fire. Fig. 32.

V. Karger, "Neues zu den Fund- und Erwerbsumständen des Bronze-kessels von Bennisch-Raase, Bezirk Troppau," *Altschlesien* 9, 1940, 112-114, pl. 14 (our figure 32). G. Raschke, "Zum Bronzekessel von Raase-Bennisch," *Altschlesien* 9, 1940, 114-119. Fettich 1953, 144, n. 47, took the vessel for a poor local imitation; he was certainly wrong.

POLAND

2. Jędrzychowice (Höckricht), district Oawa, Upper Silesia. Height, 55 centimeters. Fig. 33.

E. Krause, "Der Fund von Höckricht, Kreis Ohlau," *Schlesiens Vorzeit in Bild und Schrift*, N.F. 3, 1904, 47, fig. 12; Alföldi 1932, pl. 19:9; Werner 1956, pl. 27:10.

Fig. 33. Hunnic bronze cauldron from Jędrzychowice (Höckricht), Upper Silesia, Poland. (Height 55 cm.) From J. Werner 1956, pl. 27:10.

HUNGARY

3. Törtel, county Pest. Height, 89 centimeters, diameter, 50 centimeters. Found at the foot of a burial mound. Fig. 34.

Alföldi 1932, pl. 18: 2; Fettich 1940, pl. 10, and 1953, pl. 36: 1; *Archäologische Funde in Ungarn*, 293.

FIG. 34. Hunnic bronze cauldron found at the foot of a burial mound at Törtel, Hungary. (Height 89 cm, diam. 50 cm.) From *Archäologische Funde in Ungarn*, 293.

4. Kurdcsibrák, between Högyesz and Regöly in the valley of the Kapos River, county Tolna. Height, 52 centimeters; diameter, 33 centimeters; thickness of the wall, 0.8 centimeters; weight, 16 kilograms. Found in a peat bog. Fig. 35.

Fettich 1931, 523; Alföldi 1932, pl. 18:1; Fettich 1940, pl. 11; and 1953, pl. 36:2.

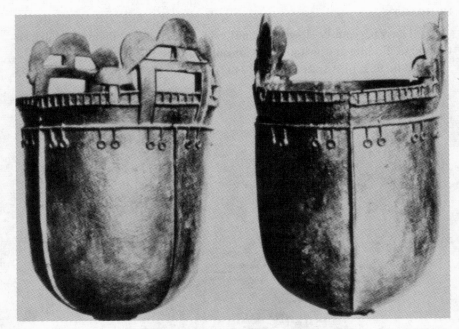

FIG. 35. Hunnic bronze cauldron found in a peat bog at Kurdcsibrák, in the Kapos River valley, Hungary. (Height 52 cm, diam. 33 cm, thickness of wall 0.8 cm, weight 16 kg.) From Fettich 1940, pl. 11.

5. Bántapuszta near Várpalota, county Veszprém. Said to have been found in a marsh. Dimensions not given. Fig. 36.

I understand that the cauldron is bigger than the one from Kurdcsibrák.

Z. Takáts, "Neuentdeckte Denkmäler der Hunnen in Ungarn," *Acta Orientalia* (Budapest) 9, 1959, 86, fig. 1.

6. Dunaújváros[43] (Intercisa), county Fehér. Fragment of a wall, found in a late Roman building; fragments of iron helmets were also found.[44] Fig. 37. Fettich 1931, 524; Alföldi 1932, 33, fig. 6.

RUMANIA

7. Desa, district Calafat, reg. Craiova, Oltenia. Height, 54.1 centimeters; diameter, 29.6 centimeters; maximal height of the lugs, 11.4 centimeters; height of the stand, 9.8 centimeters. Fished out from a lake between Ciuperceni and Ghidiciu. Fig. 38.

Nestor and Nicolăescu-Plopşor 1937, 178, pl. 3*a* and *b*; Fettich 1953, pl. 36:3, Takáts 1955, fig. 10; Werner 1956, 58, n. 10, pl. 28:3.

---

[43] Formerly Sztalinváros, originally Dunapentele.

[44] P. Marton (*Prähist. Zeitschr.* 4, 1912, 185) thought the helmets were those of Oriental troops.

FIG. 36. Hunnic bronze cauldron from Bántapuszta, near Várpalota, Hungary. From Takáts, *AOH*, 1959, fig. 1.

FIG. 37. Fragment of a bronze cauldron from Dunaújváros (Intercisa), Hungary. From Alföldi 1932, fig. 6.

FIG. 38. Hunnic bronze cauldron from a lake, Desa, Oltenia region, Rumania. (Height 54.1 cm, diam. 29.6 cm.) From Nestor and Nicolăescu-Plopşor 1937, pls. 3a-3b.

8. HOTĂRANI, district Vînju Mare (formerly Meheninţi), Craiova, Oltenia. Fragment of a lug, 16.2 centimeters high, 19.7 centimeters wide. Found in the mud of a lake. Fig. 39.

Nestor and Nicolăescu-Plopşor 1937, 178-179, pl. 39:1; Werner 1956, 58, n.8, pl. 28:1.

9. PROBABLY FROM WESTERN OLTENIA. Fragment of a lug, 84 centimeters high. Fig. 40.

Nestor and Nicolăescu-Plopşor 1937, 179-180, pl. 39:2; Takáts 1955, fig. 12; Werner 1956, 58, no. 11.

10. BOŞNEAGU, community Dorobanţu, district Calăraşi, reg. Bucureşti, Muntenia. Two fragments of lugs. The bigger one is 18 centimeters high, 12.7 centimeters wide, 1.3 centimeters thick. Found in 1958, 1.5 meters

Fig. 39. Fragment of a bronze lug from a lake, Hotărani, Oltenia region, Rumania. (Height 16.2 cm, width 19.7 cm.) From Nestor and Nicolăescu-Plopşor 1937, pl. 39:1.

Fig. 40. Fragment of a bronze lug probably from western Oltenia, Rumania. (Height 8.4 cm.) From Nestor and Nicolăescu-Plopşor 1937, pl. 39:2.

under the ground, at the border of the inundation area of the Danube, near the eastern shore of Lake Motiştea. Fig. 41.

Nestor 1960, 703; B. Mitrea and N. Anghelescu, "Fragmente de Cazan Hunic descoperite în sud-estul Munteniei," *SCIV* 11, 1960; Mitrea 1961, 549-558, figs. 1, 2 (our figure 41), 3, 4.

11. Celei (Sucidava), district Corabia, reg. Bucureşti, Muntenia. Four fragments of walls and a lug. Found in a layer of ashes in the Roman castellum. Fig. 42.

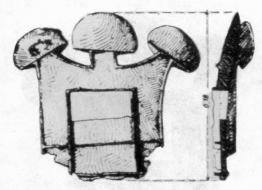

FIG. 41. Fragment of a bronze lug found near the eastern shore of Lake Motiştea, from Boşneagu, Rumania. (Height 18 cm.) From Mitrea 1961, figs. 1-2.

D. Tudor, *Dacia* 7-8, 1937-1940, 375, fig. 10c, and 11-12, 1945-1947, 189, fig. 35:1, 2, 7; Takáts 1955, 166, fig. 13:a-d; Tudor 1548, 161-162; Werner 1956, 58, n.8, pl. 64:18-21.

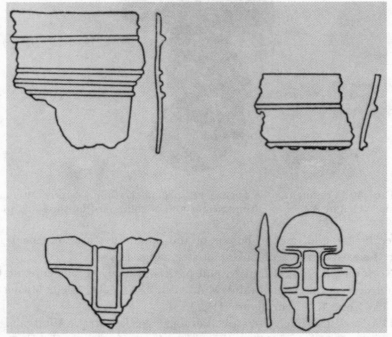

FIG. 42. Fragments of a lug and walls of a bronze cauldron from Celei, Muntenia, Rumania. From Takáts 1955, fig. 13:a-d.

SOVIET UNION

12. SHESTACHI, district Rezina, Moldavian SSR. Fig. 43.

L. L. Polevoĭ, *Istoriia Moldavskoĭ SSR*, 53; G. A. Nudel'man, *SA* 4, 1967, 306-308.

FIG. 43. Hunnic bronze cauldron from Shestachi, Moldavian SSR. From Polevoĭ, *Istoriia Moldavskoĭ SSR*, pl. 53.

13. District SOLIKAMSK, obl. Perm. Height 9 centimers. Fig. 44.

Alföldi 1932, 32, fig. 5 (after a sketch by Fettich); Fettich 1940, pl. 13:3 and 1953, pl. 26:11; Werner 1956, 58, n. 2. A poor photograph in *SA* 10, 1948, 201, fig. 15:5.

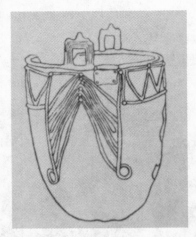

FIG. 44. Bronze cauldron from Solikamsk, Perm region, USSR. (Height 9 cm.) From Alföldi 1932, fig. 5.

14. Osoka, district Sengilei, obl. Ul'yanovsk (formerly Simbirsk).[45] Height, 53.2 centimeters; diameter, 31.2 centimeters; weight, 17.7 kilograms. Found in sand near the brook Osoka. Fig. 45.

V. Polivanova, "Zametka o proiskhozhdenii mednago sosuda iz Sengileevskago uezda, Simbirskoĭ gub.," *Trudy VII AS* (Yaroslavl) 1, 39, pl. 1; Werner 1956, pl. 27:11 (most of the other reproductions are poor drawings).

15. Verkhniĭ Konets, region of Syktyvkar, Komi ASSR (formerly Ust'sysol'sk). Fig. 46.

J. Hampel, "Skythische Denkmäler aus Ungarn," *Ethnologische Mittheilungen aus Ungarn* 1897, 14, fig. 1 after a drawing by Prince Paul Putyatin, repeated by all later authors.

16. Ivanovka, gubernie Ekaterinoslav.[46] Fig. 47.

Fettich 1940, pl. 8:10 (photo taken by A. Salmony in the museum in Novocherkassk), and 1953, pl. 36:4; a drawing in side view in Takáts 1955, 166, fig. 15.

17. Found near Lake Teletskoe in the High Altai. Height, 27 centimeters; diameter, 25-27 centimeters. Aspelin, who first published the cauldron, gave as its findspot Teletskoe,[47] which later authors changed

---

[45] Osoka, mostly misspelled Otoka or Otaka, is neither in the district Syrzan, misspelled Jizrani, as some authors maintain, nor near the Volga; it lies about 80 kilometers to the west of the nearest right bank of the river.

[46] Aspelin 1877, 70, fig. 318.

[47] I owe this information to Mrs. G. M. Levedeva, scientific secretary of the State Historical Museum in Moscow.

FIG. 45. Bronze cauldron found in the sand near the Osoka brook, Ul'ya-novsk region, USSR. (Height 53.2 cm, diam. 31.2 cm, weight 17.7 kg.) From Polivanova, *Trudy VII AS* 1, 39, pl. 1.

to Biisk; but Biisk, 100 miles northwest of the lake, was only the place where the cauldron was given to Grand Duke Vladimir Aleksandrovich, who donated it to the Historical Museum in Moscow. Fig. 48.[48]

[48] Courtesy of the State Historical Museum in Moscow.

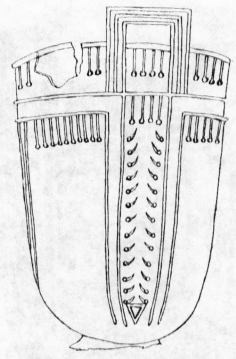

FIG. 46. Bronze cauldron from Verkhniĭ Konets, Komi ASSR. From Hampel, *Ethnologische Mittheilungen aus Ungarn* 1897, 14, fig. 1.

18. NARINDZHAN-BABA, district Turtkul, Kara-Kalpak ASSR. Fragment of a lug.[49] Fig. 49.

S. P. Tolstov, *Drevnyĭ Khorezm*, 130, fig. 74a.

19. Allegedly found on the "Catalaunian battlefield." Fragment of a lug 12 centimeters high, 18 centimeters wide. Fig. 50.

Takáts 1955, 143, figs. 1*a, b.* E. Salin, *Académie des inscriptions et belles-lettres. Comptes rendues des séances de l'année 1967*, 389, fig. 2.[50]

The cauldrons, from the plainest to the most ornate, have four features in common: Their cylindrical or bell-shaped bodies are supported on a stand in the shape of a truncated cone which is slightly curved inward; their rectangular lugs project vertically from the rim; they are cast; with the exception of one or two, they are technically inferior vessels.

---

[49] Like J. Werner, I suspect that the fragment was found somewhere in Russia or Bessarabia and brought to France.

[50] I disregard the cauldrons listed by J. Werner 1956, 58, nos. 5 and 6. They are not illustrated in the publications to which he refers and the descriptions do not fit the Hunnic cauldrons.

Fig. 47. Bronze cauldron from Ivanovka, gubernie Ekaterinoslav, USSR. From Fettich 1953, pl. 36:4.

Material

The cauldron from Törtel was cast in four,[51] those from Jędrzychowice, Kurdcsibrák, and Osoka in two molds, which is probably also true for the other vessels. Body and stand were cast separately, hooked, and soldered together. The stand, which broke off easily, is often missing.

The Huns were not good at casting the comparatively large vessels. The traces of the joints of the mold sections were rarely removed, the horizontal ribs running around the upper part of the body almost never meet where they should. Not even on the poorest Chinese ritual bronze would a dot like the one in the triangle of the cauldron from Teletskoe (fig. 48) have been left; apparently the casters had no tools to file it off.

---

[51] Fettich 1913, 512.

FIG. 48. Bronze cauldron found near Lake Teletskoe, in the High Altai, now in the State Historical Museum, Moscow. (Height 27 cm, diam. 25-27 cm.) Photo courtesy State Historical Museum, Moscow.

Fig. 49. Fragment of a bronze lug from Narindzhan-baba, Kara-Kalpak ASSR. From Tolstov 1948, fig. 74a.

It is regrettable that only one fragment from Boşneagu and another one from Sucidava have been analyzed;[52] the results might be of historical importance. As the chemical and spectrographical analysis of twenty cauldrons from the Semirech'e shows, the copper corresponds to the local copper ore, which makes it practically certain that the cauldrons were cast where they were found.[53] The metal of the Eurasian "bronze" cauldrons is actually copper, mixed with various impurities. The metal of the Scythian cauldron from Karagodeuakhsh is almost pure (99 percent) copper.[54] The alloy—if it can be called alloy— of the Semirech'e pieces consists of 95.4 to 99 percent copper. The two fragments from Rumania do not come from bronze but from copper cauldrons. The material of one is 75 percent copper, 25 percent red oxide of copper (ruby red, cuprite, Cu_2O), and a negligible amount of lead; that of the other one is 71 percent copper, 25 percent red oxide of copper, and 4 percent lead. The "bronze" of the cauldron from Desa is described as "reddish"; the material of the one from Benešov is "bronze with a strong content of copper." According to Polivanova, the metal of the Osoka cauldron is pure copper. In the cauldron from Jędrzychowice, "the ingredients are so unevenly mixed that in some places the copper appears almost pure; in others, tin is preponderant." The distribution of the metals in the alloy in the lug from Sucidava is "extremely irregular."

---

[52] E. Stoicovici in Mitrea 1961, 556-558.
[53] Spasskaia 1956, 160.
[54] *MAR* 13, 16, 21, 45.

FIG. 50. Fragment of a bronze lug, allegedly found "on the Catalaunian battlefield." (Height 12 cm, width 18 cm.) From Takáts 1955, fig. 1:a-b.

How the Huns got the copper is not known.[55] Its poor quality seems to indicate that the smiths themselves heated and reduced the ore with

---

[55] The Sarmatians on the lower Volga used copper from the southern Urals and Kazakhstan and lead from the western Altai; cf. I. Ia. Khanin, *Trudy Saratovskogo oblastnogo muzeia kraevedeniia* 3, 1960, 182.

charcoal or wood with the help of blast air in some form of furnace. Occasionally they may have pillaged graves. Had they melted Roman bronze vessels and recast the metal, the results would have been much better. The cauldrons are in every respect barbaric.

Yet with all their flaws and imperfections, the Hunnic cauldrons decisively refute the views of those historians who, like Thompson, deny the Huns the capacity of working metal. The Sarmatian cauldrons were cast by professional metalworkers;[56] so were those of the Huns.

Shapes

Like Alaric's Visigoths who drank from Greek mixing bowls,[57] if they did not cook in them, the Huns probably used all kinds of iron, bronze, copper, and silver vessels. Peoples on a trek and nomads cannot afford to insist on stylistic uniformity. Three of the four cauldrons in a hoard northeast of Minusinsk are of the common South Siberian type, but the fourth one is closely related to vessels best known from the Semirech'e.[58] In the hoard from Istyak in Kazakhstan, cauldrons with three legs occur side by side with cauldrons on conical stands.[59] The Hsiung-nu also had bronze vessels of various shapes.[60] Some they carried back from their raids into China or bartered for horses, but those cast for themselves also differed in shape and size; the one found in Noin Ula by the Kozlov expedition[61] and the high bronze vessels which Dorzhsuren excavated in 1954[62] have only the decoration in raised lines in common. The Germanic and Alanic chieftains of the fifth century likewise had metal vessels of various origin; I need only to refer to the silver jugs from Conçesti and Apahida. At Jędrzychowice a Hunnic cauldron was found together with a Roman bronze bowl. Looking around at a banquet in Attila's palace, a guest would have seen sacred Christian vessels like those which the bishop of Margus handed over to the Huns,[63] profane ones brought to Hungary from everywhere between the Loire and the Dardanelles, and Hunnic cauldrons.

---

[56] Maksimov 1966a.

[57] Claudian, *Bell. Goth.* 611.

[58] Levasheva and Rygdylon 1952, 132, fig. 44.

[59] *KS* 59, 1955, fig. 63.

[60] Fragments of two hu, Umehara 1960, 35, fig. 3-7; Rudenko 1962b, pl. 34:1, 2; another hu, Dorzhsuren 1962, 38, fig. 8:1.

[61] Rudenko 1962b, 36, fig. 29b.

[62] Dorzhsuren 1962, 39, fig. 8:3; another cauldron "with two vertical handles on the rim and an iron, conus-shaped stand" (*ibid.*, 43) is unfortunately not illustrated.

[63] Priscus, *EL* $133_{2\text{-}3}$.

Werner claims a footed bronze bowl from Münstermaifeld in the Eifel[64] for the Huns. In his opinion,[65] it is similar to a bronze cauldron from Brigetio-Oszony in Hungary[66] and another one from Borovoe in northern Kazakhstan (fig. 51).[67] Because he takes the other finds from Borovoe

Fig. 51. Bronze cauldron from Borovoe, northern Kazakhstan. From Bernshtam 1951a, fig. 12.

for Hunnic, he thinks that the bowl from the Eiffel must be Hunnic too. Actually, the three pieces belong to three different types.

The vessel from Brigetio is probably of late Scythian origin; in any case, the figures on its surface[68] set it widely apart from the two others. The finds from Borovoe play a prominent part in the speculations about the Huns in Central Asia. Werner thinks that they indicate the expansion of Attila's empire deep into Kazakhstan; only the other allegedly Hunnic findspot in Kara-Agach lies still farther east. To Bernshtam the finds are of even greater importance. They are supposed to prove the polychrome style of jewelry to be the product of the "creative" meeting of a local Central Asiatic culture and the political rise of the Huns. What bourgeois "falsificators" call Gothic art is actually the art of the Huns carried by them as far as Hungary.[69]

---

[64] J. Werner 1962a, pl. 134.
[65] J. Werner 1956, 57-58.
[66] Alföldi 1932, pl. 17:3.
[67] Bernshtam 1951a, 224, fig. 12; J. Werner 1956, pl. 51:5.
[68] Fettich 1931, 533.
[69] Bernshtam 1951a, 224, 228-229.

Borovoe[70] in the district Suchinsk, Kokchetav, lies in an archaeologically little known region. The grave has some unique features, for example, a granite slab on top of it 4.5 meters long, 1.5 meters wide, 0.7 meters thick, weighing 4,000 kilograms. Underneath there were two more slabs, each 0.12 meters thick and a layer of rubble and pebble in which the cauldron was found. Still deeper in the ground was the pit. Of the skeleton, only the skull was "more or less" preserved. It would be of interest to know what the original position of the skeleton was. Was it extended or flexed, lying in a niche or a catacomb at the end of a dromos? The very heavy stone slabs prove that the grave was not that of a Hun. Among neither the graves which Werner assigns to the Huns nor those which Bernshtam regards as Hunnic occurs anything similar to the construction of the grave in Borovoe.

The tomb furniture was a strange hodgepodge. The arrowheads were of three types, trihedral, three-flanged, and rhombic in cross section. Side by side with technically superb jewelry occur such primitive things as small blue-dyed bone beads, a copper buckle, and bronze wire earrings. As Werner noticed, a P-shaped sword mount is similar to one from the Taman Peninsula.[71] In the same direction, the Bosporan workshops, point also the gold objects with their combination of triangular clusters of granulation and cloisons filled with red stone. It is infinitely more probable that the pear-shaped cloison within a border of grains from Borovoe[72] comes from an East Roman workshop than that the almost identical one from Cyprus[73] was made by a Hun.

Some of the things found in Borovoe occur also in Hunnic finds. But this does not make the cauldron Hunnic. An almost identical one was found near Tashkent.[74]

There is little resemblance between the footed Münstermaifeld bowl and the cauldron from Borovoe. The former is an elegant vessel with two plain round handles, the latter a crude piece with four scalloped handles. The Münstermaifeld bowl contained the charred bones of a very young individual,[75] a form of burial foreign to the Huns. It may not be a coincidence that the bowl was found in a field next to which there were many traces of a Roman villa.[76] In the fourth century, Sarmatians were settled in the Moselle region.[77]

---

[70] Spasskaia (1956, 165) calls the findspot Barmashino.

[71] J. Werner 1956, 45, pl. 14:9, 22:1.

[72] Bernshtam 1951a, fig. 3; J. Werner 1956, pl. 14:11.

[73] F. A. Marshall 1911, no. 3134; cf. also no. 2679.

[74] Spasskaia 1956, 164.

[75] *Bonner Jahrbücher* 55-56, 1875, 226.

[76] *Ibid.*, 53-54, 1873, 309-310.

[77] *Arvaque Sauromatum nuper metato colonis* (Ausonius, *Mosella* 9).

Function

Compared with the big Scythian cauldrons as, for example, the one from Chertomlyk, which is 3 feet high,[78] or even those from Kazakhstan and Kirgizia, some of which could hold 140 liters,[79] the Hunnic cauldrons were, as a rule, of moderate size. They were cooking vessels. The solid conical stand was not quite as effective for the maximum utilization of fuel, always scarce in the steppes, as the tripod or the perforated stand,[80] but it helped. Like the Scythians and Sarmatians, the Huns used the cauldron for boiling meat; it was lifted out with a hook similar to those found in Verkhne-Kolyshlei and Khar'kovka. (Such hooks are still used by the Kazakhs and the Abkhaz in the Caucasus.)[81]

The usual assumption that nearly all Eurasian cauldrons were sacral vessels has rightly been doubted by Werner and Spasskaya. It is true that in the larger ones food for more than one person was prepared, but this does not prove that the meal was always sacrificial. The rock pictures from the Pisannaya Gora in the Minusinsk area (fig. 52)[82] have frequently

FIG. 52. The representation of a cauldron in a detail of a rock picture from Pisannaya Gora in the Minusinsk area. From Appelgren-Kivalo, fig. 85.

been interpreted as reproductions of religious ceremonies. Such big cauldrons, it was thought, cannot have been ordinary cooking vessels. However, their size in the drawings only betrays the artist's ineptitude.

---

[78] Minns 1913, 165.

[79] Spasskaia 1956, 163.

[80] Minns 1913, 80.

[81] Sinitsyn 1932, 63; B. N. Grakov, *MIA* 130, 1965, 219.

[82] Appelgren-Kivalo fig. 85; cf. also the drawings from Kizil Kaya, *ibid.*, fig. 219.

The ladle to scoop out the broth which the man to the left is holding is of the same gigantic proportions as the hook in the hand of the man to the right. There were cauldrons bigger than a man. On the Bol'shaya Boyarskaya pisanitsa, in the same region, twenty-one buildings and sixteen cauldrons are depicted. Evidently, such a small settlement could not have had so many sacrificial vessels; besides, they are of moderate size (fig. 53).[83]

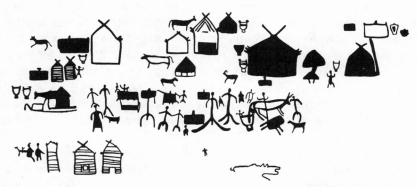

FIG. 53. Representation of cauldrons in a rock picture from Bol'shaya Boyarskaya pisanitsa, Minusinsk area. From Dévlet, *SA* 3, 1965, fig. 6.

Another argument in favor of the sacral character of the cauldrons from southern Siberia, Kazakhstan, and Kirgizia is the circumstances under which they were found. None of the numerous cauldrons from the Minusinsk area—I saw dozens in the museum in Minusinsk—and only two of thirty-three found in Kazakhstan and Kirgizia come from graves.[84] As they were not buried with the dead, they supposedly were not owned by one person but by a larger group and, therefore, clearly not used for preparing everyday meals. The findspots are probably the places where the sacrifices were performed.

With regard to the Hunnic cauldrons, we are confronted with a similar situation. Of the eighteen finds, only the cauldron from Jędrzychowice was allegedly found in a grave.

Alföldi and Werner agree that in Jędrzychowice a Hunnic nobleman was buried. The objects found were (1) the cauldron; (2) a Roman bronze bowl; (3) two iron buckles; (4) a gold buckle, its rectangular plate decorated with red stones in cloisons; (5) two gold strap ends; (6) six pieces

---

[83] M. A. Dévlet, *SA* 3, 1965, 128, fig. 3.
[84] Spasskaia 1956, 165.

of thin gold sheets with rectangular and triangular red stones encased in cloisons; (7) a gold chain.[85] Goetze recognized that the gold sheets were originally parts of a diadem which had been cut up to decorate a leather belt and a buckle. Straps and buckles are known, though not exclusively, from Hunnic graves. The cauldron is undoubtedly Hunnic. Jędrzychowice is supposed to be a Hunnic grave.

This, in my opinion, is open to doubt. In his article on the find, E. Krause reprinted the original report in the catalogue of 1838:[86] A peasant, ploughing a flat potato field, hit with his ploughshare the handle of the cauldron; the vessel lay [*3 feet deep?—Ed.*] in fine white sand and was filled with sand and dirt; in the same depth, about 2 feet to the west, was the bronze bowl; north of the cauldron was a strip of white sand, 12 to 16 inches wide, 5 to 6 feet long, and in it a dark brown band, about a hand's breadth and barely 1 inch high, in which lay scattered traces of bones, small wooden sticks of various shapes, mostly with silver mountings, the gold sheets, and the shoe buckle. At the end of the strip was a 3-inch square of dark brown dirt, and in it lay the gold chain.

As far as I know, only Takáts paid attention to this description.[87] He thought that the white sand was the bed of a small creek, but he drew no conclusions from this strange choice of a site for a grave. He only insisted that the *tiefernste* sacrificial vessel had nothing to do with the flimsy gold sheets from East Roman workshops.[88]

There is something else peculiar about the alleged grave. I asked Professor Paul Leser of the Hartford Seminary Foundation, the leading authority on early ploughs, what depth the plough of a Silesian peasant in 1830 could have reached. I quote from the letter he kindly sent me on August 28, 1964:

It would be quite impossible, in my opinion, that any plough used in Upper Silesia in the 1830's would have reached a depth of 3 feet. The average plough there at that time dug a depth of 4-10 inches (10-25 cm.) The deepest ploughing plough available in Central Europe in the first half of the nineteenth century scarcely ever ploughed as deep as 15 inches.

But this is not all that puts this "grave" in a peculiar light. Werner noticed that the gold platings of the strap ends and the gold sheets were

---

[85] Photographs in J. Werner 1956, pl. 27:1-10; a drawing of the chain in E. Krause 1904, 50, n. 1.

[86] E. Krause 1904.

[87] Takáts 1960, 121.

[88] Takáts 1955, 153.

fastened to the leather in such a sloppy way, with one or two tiny rivets, that the belt and the straps could never actually have been used. The sheets must have been cut out from the diadem and fastened to the belt of the *dead* man; the gold platings were specially made for shoes to be put into the grave. Werner's observations are correct. What follows from them? Did the horseman carry with him the gold platings for his shoes and straps and the diadem, whole or already cut to pieces, for his belt in case he died far away from home? Was he accompanied by a goldsmith who made the gold rivets on the spot? Or did the survivors send a man from Silesia to Hungary to fetch the gold things for the burial? One explanation is more farfetched than the other. They are all to be rejected, for, unless the report on the finds is utterly unreliable, the "grave" contained no skeleton. At least the skull should have been preserved. The few bones probably were in the cauldron and fell out when it was overturned.

From whatever angle one looks at this curious ensemble in the bed of a creek, this "grave" without a pit, less than a foot under the ground, it remains puzzling. One could think of a hoard, consisting of objects of various provenance, partly loot (the cauldron, the bowl, the gold chain), partly from a pillaged grave, but the bronze buckles were hardly objects worthy to be hoarded.

On the other hand, the parallel with the find from Osoka is striking. There, too, the cauldron was found in the sand near a creek. This could be a coincidence, if not a third find, still farther to the east, would not make it probable that the two cauldrons were intentionally deposited where they were found. A cauldron with round handles, the surface decorated with raised lines in the same pattern as on one from Noin Ula and many from the Ordos region, was found in the bed of the Kiran River in northern Mongolia.[89] Although the connection of the cauldron from Jędryzchowice with the other objects in the find remains obscure, it lay, like the other cauldrons, in or near running water. To the same, though somewhat looser connection with water, point, as Nestor and Takáts noted,[90] our numbers 4 (bog), 5 (marsh), 7 (lake), and 10 (near a lake), to which we now can add number 17 (near a lake).

Such a location was not limited to the Huns and Hsiung-nu. The Hsiung-nu were never in the Cis-Baikal forests, yet a large cauldron was found on the bank of the river Kutullaki in the former district Kiren, gubernie Irkutsk, and a similar, only smaller one, on the island Shchukin in the Angara River, about 13 kilometers north of Irkutsk.[91] Three-legged caul-

[89] Sosnovskiĭ 1947, 39, fig. 28.
[90] Nestor and Nicolăescu-Plopşor 1937, 182; Takáts 1959, 86-89.
[91] Rygdylon and Khoroshikh 1959, 255.

drons, typical for the Semirech'e long before the Huns, came to light on the shores of the Issyk-kul.[92] In the Minusinsk area cauldrons were found on the left and right bank of the Yenisei and on the bank of the river Shush.[93]

In his discussion of the cauldrons from Kazakhstan and Kirgizia, Spasskaya offers an attractive explanation of their location.[94] She thinks that the nomads performed some rites on watercourses in the spring, stored the vessels near the water when they moved to the higher summer pastures, and used them again when they came down in the fall. This assumption seems to be supported by the association of cauldrons, sometimes more than one, with other bronze objects in sacrificial rites. If thereby the cauldron itself should have acquired a sacred character, one would understand a find like the one from Boşneagu, where a lug was buried 1. 5 meters under ground; it must not be profaned. One may conjecture that the particularly sacred part of the more sumptuous Hunnic cauldrons was the handles with the "mushrooms"; following other considerations, Werner arrived at similar conclusions.[95] Although there were no high summer pastures in the Hungarian and Rumanian plains, in depositing cauldrons near creeks, lakes, or marshes the Huns might have preserved an old custom under changed circumstances. In any case, the location of a number of cauldrons near water strongly points to their use in some ceremonies.[96] On the other hand, there is no reason why other cauldrons could not have been just everyday cooking vessels like those found in Late Sarmatian graves.

Development

This or that feature of our cauldrons occasionally appears in pre-Hunnic times, which is in no way surprising. Their function bound all cauldrons togethers; they all must have a round body and handles. A Sauromatian cauldron from the Orenburg area, for example, has an almost cylindrical body, but its handles are round with a knob on the top.[97] On the whole, however, the differences between the Scythian, Sarmatian, Semirech'e, and Far Eastern cauldrons are sharply marked.[98] Werner

---

[92] Bernshtam 1926, 40-42.

[93] Levasheva and Rydgylon 1952, 134.

[94] Spasskaia 1956, 166-167.

[95] J. Werner 1956, 59.

[96] The sacrificial meat which the Roman prisoners were forced to eat was probably cooked in copper cauldrons.

[97] K. F. Smirnov 1963, 129, fig. 70a: 3; for a similar cauldron from the northern Kazakhstan, see Spasskaia 1956, 158, n. 2, pl. 1:25.

[98] For the main characteristics of the Eurasian cauldrons, see Levasheva and Rygdylon 1952, 134- 135, fig. 45. By "Hunnic" the authors mean not our cauldrons but those from the northern borders of China.

derived the "mushrooms" of the Hunnic cauldrons from the three knobs on the handles of late Sarmatian cauldrons.[99] Taken by itself, this seems to be quite plausible. But the Sarmatian egg-shaped cauldrons had no stand; and by the beginning of the third century they went out of existence.[100] The round, low, flat-bottomed imported Roman kettles mainly known from the lower Volga region,[101] have nothing to do with ours.

The Huns did not create their cauldrons out of nothing. Their affinity for those of the first centuries A.D. from northern China, Mongolia, and the Ordos region long has been recognized by Japanese[102] and Western scholars.[103] It is true that the cauldrons from the Hsiung-nu graves at Noin Ula and the Kiran River (fig. 54)[104] have their almost hemispherical

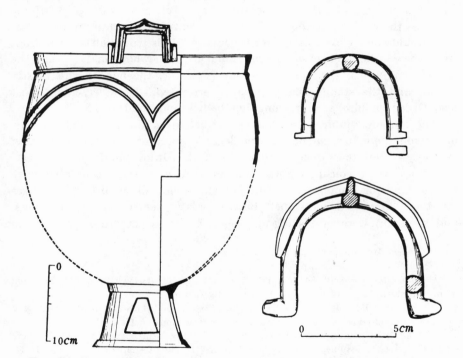

FIG. 54. Bronze cauldron of a type associated with Hsiung-nu graves at Noin Ula and the Kiran River. From Umehara 1960, p. 37.

---

[99] J. Werner 1956, 59.

[100] Maksimov, 1966a.

[101] Cf. Berkhin 1961, 150. Add. Sinitsyn and Erdniev 1963, 24, fig. 25:8.

[102] See no. 6.

[103] First by Takáts, who for a long time stood alone.

[104] Umehara 1960, 37, fig. 21; Rudenko 1962a, 36, fig. 29.

bodies decorated with raised lines in wide waving curves which have no parallels in the Hunnic cauldrons. The handles, round or rectangular with a scalloped upper rim, do not occur in our cauldrons either. However, plain rectangular handles, comparable with those on the cauldrons from Jędrzychowice and Osoka, are also known from Ordos cauldrons.[105] On a footless vessel with an elongated body, found in 1950 in a rich Hsiung-nu grave of the later Han period in Inner Mongolia near Erh-lan-hu-kou, one handle was round and the other rectangular.[106] It seems that the rectangular handle with a scalloped upper rim is merely a variant of the plain rectangular handle. There exist, indeed, a number of handles with scallops so shallow that the upper rim looks almost straight.[107]

Takáts was, I believe, right in comparing the scalloped rim from Noin Ula with the rim of the cauldron from Lake Teletskoe (fig. 48).[108] If one imagines the rounded triangles of the cauldron from the Altai put on stalks, they would come close to the "mushrooms."[109] It is true that the cauldrons from the borderlands of northern China are somewhat smaller than the Hunnic cauldrons; they are, as a rule, squatter, the handles are mostly round, and the stands nearly always perforated. However, there exist also Ordos cauldrons with elongated bodies and solid stands.[110]

The Hunnic cauldrons cannot be derived from the Scythian and Sarmatian ones, not to speak of the three-legged cauldrons from the Semirech'e. If they are not the direct descendants of the Ordos cauldrons, they certainly are their cousins. Some, probably many, Ordos cauldrons were cast by and for Hsiung-nu.[111] But not all, as not all small Ordos bronzes (all those knives, daggers, belt buckles, discs, pendants, horse-frontlets, and so forth) were of Hsiung-nu origin.[112] Ordos cauldrons were bound

---

[105] *Inner Mongolia*, pl. 26=fig. 113:6.

[106] Li I -yu 1963, no. 52, pl. 33.

[107] *Inner Mongolia*, pl. 34=fig. 113:3; p. 180, fig. 106: 1 (excavated at Ching-yang in northeastern Kansu)=Umehara 1960, 37, fig. 22.

[108] Takáts 1955, 150; 1960, 122. As so often, Takáts spoiled his arguments by bringing in matter unrelated with the cauldrons as, *e.g.*, the scallops on Han mirrors.

[109] This is of course just a conjecture but, I think, still better than what others suggested. László assumes that the "mushrooms" represent shaman crowns (*AAH* 34, 1955, 89, 249-252). Karger thought they were stylized horses (Karger, *Altschlesien* 9, 1940, 113); Fettich derived them from the half-round headplates of the tibulae (1953, 142).

[110] I. H. Anderson, *BMFEA* 4, 1932, pl. 19; *Inner Mongolia*, pls. 23, 24, etc.

[111] The alloy of the Noin Ula cauldron, 90 percent copper, 7 percent tin, and 2 percent lead, is similar to the alloy of the Chinese mirror found in the same kurgan. The cauldron was probably cast by a Chinese in the service of the Hsiung-nu.

[112] In a vast cemetery near Lo-shan hsiang, Hsi-feng hsien, Liao-ning Province, many Ordos bronzes were found, some of them identical with those from the Buryat Republic, Inner and Outer Mongolia. See *WWTK* 1, 1957, 53-56; *WW* August-September 1960, 125-132. The findspot is more than 700 miles east of Sui-yüan.

together with small Ordos ornaments.[113] But in Inner Mongolia Ordos cauldrons were found in graves which the Chinese excavators, probably rightly, date to the Northern Wei period (424-534 A.D.).[114]

The farther to the west the cauldrons were cast, the more they differ from their prototypes. It looks as if they fell under the influence of basically related but more richty decorated bronze and copper vessels. On the cauldrons from Lake Teletskoe (no. 16) and Solikamsk (no. 15), two raised lines or ribbons, starting below the handles, run down the body, sharply curving outward at the lower ends. This pattern, foreign to the Ordos bronzes, occurs on Scythian cauldrons from the Don region as early as the fourth century B.C.[115] and on the Kuban as late as the first century A.D.[116] The same two Hunnic cauldrons have, along the rim, square compartments formed by raised lines, with one or two lines between the opposite corners. This pattern, likewise foreign to the Ordos, seems to be related to the one on the cauldron from Chertomlyk.[117]

The origin of the "pendants" on the cauldrons from Törtel, Desa, Shestachi, Osoka, and Verkhniĭ Konets is obscure. Takáts noted that similar "pendants" occur on Chinese pots from the Neolithic period, and derived the former from the latter.[118] In view of the two or more millennia which separate the clay from the copper "pendants," such a connection is out of the question. But the parallel may give a hint to the origin of the Hunnic "pendants": They might be replicas of cords or fringes. In the early art of the barbarians at China's border as well as in China proper the rendition of cords on bronzes was quite common. The cords probably served also a practical purpose. The Korean vessel from the Gold Bell Tomb at Kyongju in Korea (fig. 55)[119] shows how the nomads transported the cauldrons over long distances.

To arrange all Hunnic cauldrons in a typological series does not seem possible. The upper edge and the sides of the handle of the Ivanovka cauldron (fig. 47) are curved as on the fragment from Boşneagu (fig. 41), which seems to indicate that the two vessels were cast at approximately the same time. Fragment no. 19 (fig. 50) shares with the cauldron from Shestachi (fig. 43) the circles on the "mushrooms." It seems reasonable to assume that the cauldrons with the plain handles are earlier than those with the "mushrooms." But the Huns may very well have cast plain and

---

[113] *KKTH* 1956, 2, pl. 15; Li I-yu 1963, no. 53-58, pl. 34-36.

[114] Li I-yu 1963, no. 103, pl. 65.

[115] Liberov 1965, pl. 27.

[116] P. D. Liberov, *SA* 9, 1942, 19, fig. 8. See also the Sarmatian cauldron from Zubov's farm (Minns 1913, 230, fig. 133).

[117] Minns 1913, 162, fig. 50.

[118] Takáts 1955, 147.

[119] *Government General Museum of Chosen 1933, Museum Exhibits Illustrated*, vol. V.

FIG. 55. Ceramic vessel from the Gold Bell Tomb at Kyongju, Korea, showing the manner in which cauldrons were transported by nomads. From *Government General Museum of Chosen 1933, Museum Exhibits Illustrated* V.

elaborately decorated cauldrons, perhaps for different purposes, at the same time. If someday it should be possible to date the cauldrons more exactly, they still would give the context in which they were found only a *terminus post quem*, for they were used for generations. Many were repaired. "A man's life span is fifty years, a cauldron can be used for a hundred," says a Kazakh proverb.[120]

Scattered from the borders of China to eastern Europe, the cauldrons of course can not indicate the way over which they spread to the West. They are absent from Tuva and the Minusinsk area,[121] have so far not turned up in Kazakhstan, but are known from Khwarezm.

---

[120] Spasskaia 1956, 163, n. 3.

[121] A cauldron from the Barabinsk steppe (Kyzlasov 1960, 70, fig. 26:1) and one from the cemetery Kokel in Tuva (Vaĭnshteĭn and D'iakonova 1966, 194, fig. 9) have the bell-shaped body and the solid stand of the Hunnic cauldrons but their handles are half round. A cauldron with a rectangular handle and an elongated body in the museum in Minusinsk comes from a local findspot (Levasheva and Rygdylon 1952,

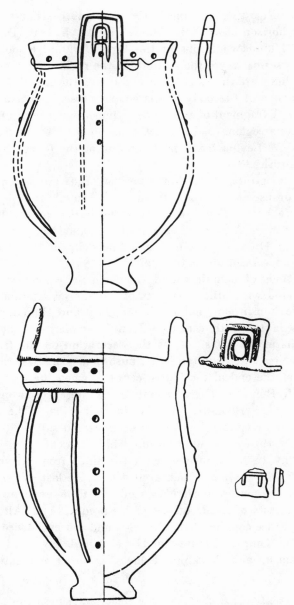

Fig. 56. Clay copy of a Hunnic cauldron of the Verkhniĭ Konets type (see above, fig. 46), from the "Big House," Altyn Asar, Kazakhstan. (Height 40 cm.) From Levina 1966, fig. 7:37-38.

135); it seems to have been brought there from the East, for none of the numerous miniature bronze cauldrons and the imitations in pottery has such handles; theirs are half round, with or without knobs. See the literature referred to by Levina 1966, 57, n. 47.

A number of clay vessels (fig. 56),[122] about 40 centimeters high, found in the upper horizon of the "Big House" at Altyn Asar (Dzheti Asar 3), are copies of Hunnic cauldrons of the type Verkhniĭ Konets. They not only show the seams where the sections of the mold met; the handles with their parallel lines are the same here and there; the rings of the pendants on the upper zone of the body of the copper vessel appear as dots on the pottery copy. A fragment of a lug with a "mushroom" comes from approximately the same region. Tolstov dates the upper horizon from the third to the seventh,[123] Levina from the beginning of the fourth to the seventh or eighth centuries.[124]

In the upper strata of the lower horizon, thus not much earlier than the clay cauldrons, and in the kurgans near Dzheti Asar lay bone strips from composite bows. Some of the persons buried in the kurgans were Europeoids with a Mongoloid admixture; some had deformed heads. The Hunnic (or Hunnoid) population in the delta of the Syr Darya had cauldrons of the Verkhniĭ Konets type.

The imitations of Hunnic metal cauldrons in Khwarezm are just as closely connected with other elements of Hunnic civilization as the cauldrons with the "mushroom" handles in Hungary and Rumania, areas ruled by the Huns in the fifth century. Hunnic soldiers in Sucidava broke their cauldrons in the 440's. If, as the decoration on the fragment from Intercisa indicates, the cauldron had "mushroom" handles, the type must have existed at the end of the fourth century, when the camp on the Danube was still Roman. There remain three more cauldrons with such handles: Ivanovka, Benešov, and Narindzhan-baba. The vessel from Ivanovka has "no passport," as the Russians would say. How it got into the museum in Rostov is not known. The fragment from Narindzhan-baba is possibly to be connected with the finds from Altyn Asar. But what about Benešov? It has been argued that the last owner of the cauldron as well as the man who carried a cauldron to Jędrzychowice in Silesia were Huns, subjects of Attila or one of his predecessors. Alföldi, Werner, and Sulimirski[125] are convinced that Benešov and Jędrzychowice were Hunnic camps. By the same reasoning the Huns should have had garrisons in Osoka, Solikamsk, and Verkhniĭ Konets. Werner evidently feels that

---

[122] Levina 1966, 56, fig.7: 37-39. Tolstov (1952, 21, and 1962, 191) mentions only one clay cauldron, but there were fragments of several. The illustration in Tolstov 1952, fig. 11:b is slightly deceptive; it shows the restored cauldron. For an illustration of the fragments, see *Trudy Kazakh.* 7, 1959, 231, pl. 4:6.

[123] Tolstov 1962, 190.

[124] Levina 1966, 69.

[125] Alföldi 1932, 35-36; J. Werner 1956, 88; Sulimirski 1964, 49, and the map p. 43, with the "graves of Hunnic governors."

would expand the Hunnic "empire" too far and consequently speaks somewhat vaguely about the *Fundmilieu östlicher Reiterkrieger*.[126]

A glance at the map is sufficient to exclude the possibility that Huns or any other "Eastern mounted warriors" could push even close to Solikamsk or Verkhniĭ Konets, across the forests and swamps into the land of the Komi (Zyryans). Verkhniĭ Konets is at the latitude of Helsinki. The cauldron from Solikamsk is no more proof of the presence of Huns in the northern parts of the oblast' Perm than the Roman,[127] Sasanian,[128] and Byzantine[129] bronze and silver vessels prove the existence of foreign troops in northeastern Russia; the primitive hunters on the Vyshegd were not the subjects of the *basileus* in Constantinople or the king of kings in Ctesiphon. They never had heard of Attila. As the Sasanian and Byzantine luxury vessels and coins [130] testify to fur trade, over many middlemen, between the Permian lands and the higher civilizations in the south,[131] the Hunnic cauldrons probably point to similar relations between the northern tribes and the ancestors of the Huns. I say *ancestors* because a considerable time must have passed before the cauldrons from Lake Teletskoe, Solikamsk, Osoka, and Verkhniĭ Konets changed into the vessels of the fourth and fifth centuries.

It is to be assumed that future excavations will close the many gaps between the Kerulen River and the Danube. Still, even now there can be no doubt that the Hunnic cauldrons originated on China's northern and northwestern borders. The crude, often truly barbaric copper cauldrons link the Huns with the area of the Hsiung-nu confederacy.

Mirrors

Objects of Central Asiatic origin have been found at various places in eastern Europe: Bactrian silver phalerae of the second century B.C. at Novouzensk in the oblast' Kuibyshev;[132] a Bactrian tetradrachm in Chersonese;[133] Kushan coins in the Volga region[134] and in Kiev.[135] They

---

[126] J. Werner 1956, 60.

[127] A. P. Smirnov 1952, 51-52, 108; *Ocherki* 1, 533.

[128] One has a Khwarezmian inscription (Henning 1958, 58).

[129] L. A. Matsulevich, *MIA* 1, 1940, 139.

[130] The Sasanian coins are listed under the findspots by Talitskaia, *MIA* 27, 1952. In 1950, at Bartym 264, Byzantine coins were found; cf. Bader and A. P. Smirnov 1952, 6.

[131] Three of the presumably Greco-Bactrian silver dishes in the Hermitage come from the oblast' Perm; cf. Trever 1940, pls. 22-27.

[132] Trever 1940, 49, pl. 3-5.

[133] *Materialy z arkheolohii pivnichnoho Prychornomor'ia* 3 (Odessa, 1960), 250-252.

[134] *Numismatika i epigrafika* 3, 1962, 145.

[135] *APU* 1, 1955, 180, fig. 3; *Arkheologiia* 7, 1952, 157. In the Dnieper near the rapids, a barbarian imitation of a coin of Eutydemus was found; see Kropotkin 1961,

are oddities, though not quite as odd as the Shang bronze fished up at Anzio, the Late Chou bronzes unearthed at Rome and Canterbury, and the Chinese coins of the third century B.C. dug up in southern France.[136] Chinese objects found in eastern Europe belong to a different category. They were actually used by the barbarians. The jade scabbard slides in Sarmatian graves, for instance, came from China; the nomads had no access to the gemstone, and the dragons carved on some slides are unmistakably Chinese. The Sarmatians fitted them on their scabbards in the same way they used their wooden slides.[137] Pieces of Chinese silk from dresses were found in a Late Sarmatian grave at Marienthal (now Sovetskoe), on the Big Karman River in the former German Volga Republic,[138] and in a grave at Shipovo.[139] The Han mirror in kurgan *E* 26, burial 19, on the Torgun River in the lower Volga region (fig. 57)[140] may have been cherished for its magical power, but it was also a toilet implement.

Fig. 57. Chinese mirror of the Han period found in burial 19, on the Torgun River, lower Volga region. From Ebert, *R V,* « Südrussland, » pl. 40: c:b.

1961, 58, no. 437. From the same region come two typically Central Asiatic flasks, one from Zhuravka (Symonovich 1964a, 25, fig. 2:14), the other one from Volosskoe (Braĭchevskaia 1960, 189, pl. 4:2).

[136] Bussagli 1959, 151, 152, n. 22.

[137] Maenchen-Helfen 1957a, 85-94.

[138] Rau, *Ausgrabungen*, 68.

[139] Minaeva 1929, 199. The Sarmatians probably imported silk also from the Bosporan kingdom (N. Toll 1927, 88-92).

[140] *R V* 13, Südrussland, pl. 40c:b, Sinitsyn 1946, 92, fig. 26.

As there existed no direct trade relations between the Chinese and the Sarmatians on the Volga, the Chinese objects reached the east European steppes via Central Asia. The striking similarity of Sarmatian gold and clay vessels with animal handles to a Chinese ritual bronze with a tiger handle in the British Museum finds its explanation in the origin of the motif in Central Asia, possibly Fergana, from where it spread both east and west.[141] The westward spread of Chinese mirrors through Central Asia and their gradual transformation can be fairly well traced.[142]

The earliest Chinese mirrors found outside of China are two Huai mirrors in the Hermitage. The one from Tomsk[143] is identical with a mirror in the Lagrelius collection which Karlgren dates to the fifth century B.C.;[144] the other one, from the sixth kurgan in Pazyryk in the High Altai,[145] is about a century later.[146] In the past forty years no more Huai mirrors have turned up in southern and western Siberia, and it is unlikely that many more will be found in the future. Han mirrors, however, have come and are constantly coming to light in northern Eurasia, from Outer Mongolia to the Ob River and the lower Volga.

Some of those found near the frontier as, for instance, in the tombs of the Hsiung-nu princes at Noin Ula, were probably gifts of the emperors; others testify to trade relations with China. In the barbaricum Chinese mirrors were bartered from tribe to tribe. Even fragments were highly appreciated. The edges of a broken Han mirror in the Izykh chaatas in the Minusinsk[147] region were smooth, not sharp as they would have been had the mirror, as so often, been intentionally broken before it was put in the grave. This proves that the fragments had been held in many hands.

To draw up a list of the Han mirrors found in the barbaricum must be left to scholars who have access to the museums in Inner and Outer Mongolia and the Soviet Union. Only a small fraction has been published; many more are merely listed as "ancient Chinese mirrors." Still, even the little that is known is impressive.

As was to be expected, Han mirrors were found in the barbarian graves beyond the northern and northeastern frontiers of China: in the Hsiung-

---

[141] Maenchen-Helfen 1941, 43, C16, pl. 11.
[142] The map in Egami 1948, 288, is by now obsolete.
[143] Umehara 1931, fig. 7:1, and *Shina kodo seikwa* 4, pl. 14a, and 1938, pl. 17.
[144] *BMFEA* 13, 1941, 43, C16, pl. 11.
[145] Rudenko 1953, 144, fig. 85.
[146] Azarpay 1959, 339.
[147] Kyzlasov 1950, 85, fig. 30:1.

nu graves at Noin Ula,[148] Il'mova Pad',[149] and Burdun,[150] and in the large, presumably Wu-huan, cemetery at Lo-shan-hsiang in Manchuria.[151] Of the numerous stray finds in the Minusinsk area only a few have been published. One is of the *i t'i tzu* ("quaint script") type, five are "TLV" mirrors.[152] In the Kenkol cemetery in the Talas Valley a *chang i tzu sun*[153] and a "hundred nipples" mirror[154] were found. With the exception of a TLV mirror in Kairagach,[155] the mirrors from Fergana were *chang i tzu sun* mirrors: three from Tura-tash,[156] one from Kara Bulak,[157] one and a fragment from the kurgans in the Isfara Valley.[158] Of the same type was a fragment from the northwestern part of the oblast' Leninabad[159] and a mirror from Vrevskiĭ southwest of Tashkent.[160]

Like most of the objects in the Istyatsk hoard on the Vangai River between Tobolsk and Omsk in western Siberia, the *chang i tzu sun* mirror[161] must have been brought from the south. The same is true for a Han mirror in a kurgan near Tobolsk.[162] In a kurgan at Zarevshchina in the former gubernie Astrakhan, a "four *S* spirals" mirror was found together with a Turkish stirrup.[163] How the Turkish nomads got the mirror can only be guessed. They were not averse to occasional grave robbings; a Sarmatian kurgan at Politotdel'skoe in the lower Volga region for example, was ransacked in the time of the Golden Horde.[164] Mirrors were often used for a long time before they accompanied the dead to the other world. To give just one example, in a kurgan at Naindi sume on the Tola River, about 120 kilometers southwest of Ulan Bator, a Han mirror was found

---

[148] (1) Trever 1932, pl. 26:3; Umehara 1960, pl. 71; Rudenko 1962a, fig. 65:g; (2) Dorzhsuren 1966, 39, fig. 7:7.

[149] (1) Rudenko 1962a, fig. 65:v; (2) Sosnovskiĭ 1946, 62, fig. 12.

[150] Talko-Hryncewicz, *Trudy Troitsko-Kiakhtinskago otdeleniia Russkago geograficheskago obshchestva* 4:2 (1902), 50, pl. 2.

[151] Sun Shou-tao 1960, fig. 19-21.

[152] Umehara 1938, pl. 15:2; Kyzlasov 1960, 85, fig. 20:1; 86, n. 2. [*Mirrors showing a pattern resembling the letters TLV.—Ed.*]

[153] Kozhomberdiev 1960b, 72, fig. 14.

[154] Kozhomberdiev 1963, 40, fig. 6:2.

[155] Zadneprovskiĭ 1960, 100-101, fig. 59:1.

[156] Baruzdin and Brykina 1962, 15, 23, 28, fig. 15:4-6.

[157] Baruzdin 1957, 27, fig. 5:1-3, and 1961, 65, fig. 14.

[158] Davidovich and Litvinskiĭ 1955, 64-65, fig. 31. Litvinskiĭ 1961, 76, fig. 12.

[159] Litvinskiĭ 1959, 116, fig. 4.

[160] Voronets 1951, 52-54, fig. 5.

[161] Chernetsov 1953, 166, pl. 19:1.

[162] Moshinskaia 1953a, 218.

[163] Posta 1905, 237, fig. 148:4.

[164] K. F. Smirnov 1959, 301.

together with a piece of Chinese silk which the Sasanian pattern dates to the sixth or seventh century.[165]

From Middle Sarmatian graves in the lower Volga region two Han mirrors are known: a fragment of what seems to be a "four nipples" mirror from a diagonal burial at Berezhnovka II, kurgan 3,[166] and the above-mentioned mirror from the Torgun.[167] The westernmost Han mirror with a long inscription,[168] unfortunately without a date, comes from the Kuban region in the Caucasus.[169]

The list, incomplete as it is, shows how popular Han mirrors were among the peoples and tribes west of the Great Wall. The absence of mirrors of the Six Dynasties period finds its explanation in the breakdown of Chinese power in the western regions; Chinese mirrors reappeared in Central Asia only in the T'ang period.

When the supply from the big state factories dried up in the latter half of the second century, but occasionally also before, the barbarians tried to cast their own mirrors in the shape and with the designs of the admired Chinese bronze disks. In many cases the so-called imitation mirrors, the *hō sei kyō* of the Japanese archaeologists,[170] can be easily recognized, though not all coarsened versions of the standard types are necessarily imitations. There exist a large number of small mirrors of the later Han period[171] and the Three Kingdoms of such poor casting and such crude décor that they were rarely collected and, except in recent publications, hardly ever illustrated. Being very cheap, they must have been eagerly sought by the barbarians. I listed a mirror from Kenkol as a *chang i tzu sun* mirror, although it has small circles between the leaves of the quatrifoil instead of the four characters *chang i tzu sun*. It could be argued that the barbarians, having no use for them, transformed the characters into ornaments. But identical mirrors are known from undoubtedly Chinese graves.[172]

The imitations of Han mirrors vary greatly in quality. In Japan they are, as a rule, well cast; their decoration, deviating from the original sometimes

[165] Borovka, 1927, 2, 74, pl. 4:1, pl. 5.

[166] Sinitsyn 1960, 46, fig. 17:7.

[167] The inscription is a wish, quite common on such mirrors: "May you see the sun, the world is very bright."

[168] Similar to the one in Karlgren 1934, 23, no. 72.

[169] Umehara 1931, pl. 21, and 1938, pl. 17.

[170] They have been discussed by Umehara, Egami, and others.

[171] See, *e.g.*, Liang Shang-ch'un 1942, 3, 47; *Lo-yang ching* 1959, 82; *Shen-hsi ching* 1959, 30.

[172] See, *e.g.*, *Hu-san ching* 1960, 70; *Shen-hsi ching* 1953, 39; *Szu-ch'uan ching* 1960, 34.

slightly, sometimes drastically, often foreshadows the future breakthrough of the native genius. In Korea the earlier imitations can barely be distinguished from Chinese mirrors, but they soon became cruder and thicker; their decoration has less and less in common with the prototypes. The least changed imitations come from the oasis cities in Hsin-chiang; only the simplification of the decoration gives them away. Whereas these three groups, in particular the Japanese one, have often been studied, very little about the imitation mirrors found farther to the west is known. Possibly some of the above-listed mirrors look genuinely Chinese only in the inadequate reproductions. Sometimes the excavator did not recognize the imitation. A mirror from the kurgan cemetery Kok-el in Tuva[173] is, as the odd decoration shows, most probably a *hō sei kyō*.

In the second and third centuries Chinese mirror decorations were transferred to Sarmatian so-called pendant-mirrors, widely spread through the steppes between the Volga and the lower Danube from the first century B.C. to the fourth century A.D. The small bronze disks, occasionally silvered on the smooth side, sometimes with a high content of tin, were worn around the neck on a cord which ran through a perforated square or rectangle on the edge (fig. 58);[174] some mirrors have instead of a rectangle a short flat tang (fig. 59),[175] to be fitted into a wooden, bone, or horn handle. The designs in raised lines are the same in both variants.

FIG. 58. A Sarmatian bronze disc in the shape of a pendant-mirror, of a type found in the steppes between Volga and lower Danube, from the first century B.C. to the fourth century A.D. From Sinitsyn 1960, fig. 18:1.

The origin of the pendant-mirror is controversial. Rau thought it reached the steppes from the Caucasus,[176] but it appeared in both areas at about the same time.[177] Khazanov traces the pendant-mirrors back to Siberia; however, the mirrors to which he refers[178] have handles in the shape of

173 Vaĭnshteĭn 1964, 53.
174 Sinitsyn 1960, 49, fig. 18:1.
175 Gushchina 1962, 208, fig. 2:5.
176 Rau 1926, 90-95.
177 Khazanov 1963, 65.
178 Kiselev 1951, 281.

FIG. 59. Bronze mirror of a type similar to that shown on fig. 58, but provided with a tang that was presumably fitted into a handle. From Gushchina, *SA*, 2, 1962, fig. 2:5.

animals.[179] The earliest undecorated pendant-mirrors were found in Wusun graves of the third or second century B.C.[180] But we are less interested in the origin of the pendant-mirrors than in their decorations, particularly in a group from the lower Volga region and the northwestern Caucasus. The findspots are

1, 2. The cemetery at Susly in the former German Volga Republic (figs. 60,[181] 61).[182]

3. Alt-Weimar (now Staraya Ivantsovka), kurgan D 12 (fig. 62).[183]

4. Kurgan 40 in Berezhnovka in the lower Eruslan, a left tributary of the Volga (fig. 63).[184]

5. Kurgan 23 in the cemetery "Tri Brata" near Elista in the autonomous Kalmuk SSR (fig. 64).[185]

6. Lower Volga region (fig. 65).[186]

7. A catacomb burial at Alkhaste in Checheno-Ingushetia in the northeastern Caucasus (fig. 66).[187]

---

[179] Khazanov refers also to the Ordos mirror in Salmony 1935, pl. 14:4. Its Hsi-Hsia inscription dates it a millennium later than the Sarmatian mirrors.

[180] Akishev and Kushaev 1963, pl. 1:13, 14, pl. 11:23, 37. *Ocherki* I, 257, fig. 6.

[181] Rau 1926, 9, fig. 1a.

[182] Rykov 1925, 63; Khazanov 1963, 66, fig. 4:7.

[183] Rau, 1927, 30, fig. 22b.

[184] Khazanov 1963, 66, fig. 4:9. The drawing in Sinitsyn 1960, 49, fig. 18:6, is too schematic.

[185] Rykov 1936a, 152; Khazanov 1963, 66, fig. 4:8.

[186] Khazanov 1963, fig. 4:6. According to Khazanov, the mirror was found in Blumenfeld (now Tsvetnoe), k. B 6. Rau, who excavated the kurgan and described the grave goods in his usual meticulous way (1926, 37-38), has nothing about such a mirror. Probably it was wrongly labeled in the museum in Saratov, but there is no doubt that it comes from the same region as the ones listed above.

[187] Vinogradov 1963, fig. 27.

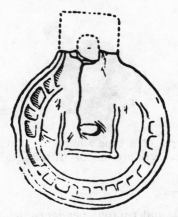

FIG. 60. Bronze pendant-mirror from the cemetery at Susly, former German Volga Republic. From Rau, *Hügelgräber*, 9, fig. 1a.

FIG. 61. Bronze pendant-mirror from the cemetery at Susly, former German Volga Republic. From Rykov 1925, 68.

FIG. 62. Bronze pendant-mirror from Alt-Weimar, kurgan D12. From Rau, *Ausgrabungen*, 30, fig. 22b.

FIG. 63. Bronze pendant-mirror from kurgan 40 in Berezhnovka, lower Eruslan, left tributary of the Volga. From Khazanov 1963, fig. 4:9.

FIG. 64. Bronze pendant-mirror from kurgan 23, in the "Tri Brata" cemetery, near Elista, Kalmuk ASSR. From Khazanov 1963, fig. 4:8.

FIG. 65. Bronze pendant-mirror from the lower Volga region. From Khazanov 1963, fig. 4:6.

FIG. 66. Bronze pendant-mirror from a catacomb burial at Alkhaste, northwestern Caucasus. From Vinogradov 1963, fig. 27.

It is, first of all, the border, a band filled with radiating lines, which sets this group of mirrors apart. Rau derived the motif from the Caucasus, where it occurs on an antimony medallion of the Early Iron Age, and traced it back to Mycenean times. Such a simple motif can originate everywhere and at all times, and it might be a mere coincidence that it is found on small Sarmatian bronze mirrors and small Chinese bronze mirrors of about the same date. Such bands, encircling the central field, are known from Chinese mirrors before, in, and after the Han period. It is, however, remarkable that there exist imitation mirrors whose whole décor consists of two bands, one with radial lines and the other with dog-tooth ornaments.[188] The mirror from Berezhnovka has *two* concentric bands. This, too, would not be particularly remarkable if the strokes in the outer one were not slanting, something alien to all other Sarmatian mirrors. Not the technique of casting a mirror, nor its shape, nor any other conceivable reason accounts for the combination of a square in the center field and a striated band around it as on these Sarmatian mirrors. The chances that this identity with the squares and the same borders on hundreds of Chinese TLV mirrors is still coincidental are very small. They become zero when we see the Sarmatian craftsman put a small knob in the center of the square. It has no function. It has no aesthetic value. It is the imitation of the perforated knob on the Han mirrors.

TLV mirrors were imitated in Japan, Korea, and the western regions of China. On a mirror from Lou-lan (fig. 67),[189] only the cross stroke of

FIG. 67. An imitation of a Chinese TLV mirror from Lou-lan. From Umehara, *Ō bei*, 39, fig. 7.

the *T* is left; *L* and *V* have disappeared. On some Japanese imitation mirrors the TLV's have been entirely discarded. The Japanese craftsmen to whom inscriptions on the Chinese mirrors meant nothing changed them into fancy lines, but kept the dog-tooth, zig-zag, and radial lines of the border. The Sarmatian coarsened the Chinese patterns much more radically but still not beyond recognition. It would be unfair to place one of the Sarmatian mirrors next to a fine Chinese TLV mirror. They should rather be compared with the small Chinese mirrors in which the decoration has also been radically simplified as, for example, two mirrors recently found at Lo-yang, both lost the central square and the *L*'s and *V*'s (fig. 68, 69).[190]

---

[188] Umehara 1938, pl. 18:2.
[189] Umehara 1931, 39, fig. 7.
[190] *Lo-yang ching* 1959, 80, 82.

In one of them the *T*'s consist only of strokes, and the hundred and more radial lines of the border on good TLV mirrors are so widely spaced that they approximate those on the Sarmatian mirrors.

FIG. 68. Small bronze mirror with simplified decoration from Lo-yang. From *Lo-yang ching* 1959, 80.

FIG. 69. Small bronze mirror with simplified decoration from Lo-yang. From *Lo-yang ching* 1959, 82.

The Sarmatians not only transferred Chinese designs to the pendant-mirrors, they also cast mirrors in direct imitation of bronze mirrors of the Han period. Werner was the first to recognize the importance of what he called the *östliche Nomadenspiegel* for the study of the Huns.[191] They are disks of whitish bronze with a loop or perforated knob on the back for attaching the cord which served to hold them. The decoration consists of various patterns in raised lines. With few exceptions and in contrast to the manifold and often gracious ornaments on the pendant-mirrors, the décor is monotonous: two or more concentric circles, divided by lines radiating from the center, occasionally with dots in the compartments

---

[191] J. Werner 1956, 19-24; eighty findspots on the list 114-119. Their number is steadily growing. Kovrig (1959, 221) lists nine mirrors of the Chmi-Brigetio type from the middle Danube which were not yet known to Werner. Three from the Kama region were published by Sadykova (1962b, 259-260). One was found in Alsace in 1964 (Hatt 1966, 263, fig. 7).

thus formed; in later mirrors a zig-zag line runs between the circles. Rau called the group "Sibero-Chinese,"[192] Khazanov lists it as Group X of the Sarmatian mirrors.[193] For brevity's sake, I shall call them loop-mirrors.

Werner distinguishes four types of decoration. The earliest one is supposedly found on four mirrors from Mozhary, Susly, Atkarsk, and Tanais.[194] Actually the group "Mozhary" consists only of two mirrors. The one from Atkarsk belongs to another type, and the mirror from Susly does not exist. Neither Rykov, who excavated the cemetery, nor Pater Beratz, who dug three kurgans in it, knew of such a mirror. The drawing in Merpert's article[195] is the Mozhary mirror; Merpert mixed up his notes. In 1963, Khazanov published more mirrors of the Mozhary type, but the best and most important of the group remains the mirror from Mozhary (diameter, 7.4 centimeters), often reproduced[196] and dated between the first and fourth centuries (fig. 70).[197] It was found by peasants who did

FIG. 70. Bronze mirror from Mozhary, Volgograd region, now in the Hermitage Museum, Leningrad, datable to about A.D. 200. (Diam. 7.4 cm.) From Umehara 1938, 55.

a little grave robbing in a kurgan on the mountain Mozhary near the settlement Kotova in the district Kamyshin, gubernie Saratov, later oblast' Stalingrad, now Volgograd. Only after I. I. Berkhin published the whole find[198]—it is in the Hermitage—could it properly be evaluated. One may

---

[192] Rau 1926, 90, 94-95.

[193] Khazanov 1963, 67-68.

[194] J. Werner 1956, 114.

[195] N. Merpert 1951, 24, fig. 2:13.

[196] *OAK* 1898 (1901), 78, fig. 142; Rau 1926, 92, fig. 90b; Mizuno and Egami 1935, 169, fig. 99:3; Egami 1948, 382, pl. 31:5; J. Werner 1956, pl. 44:8; Berkhin 1961, 146, fig. 2:1; Khazanov 1963, 68, fig. 5:6.

[197] Rostovtsev 1931, 602 ("Makhary" is a misprint), dated it to the first century; Borovka (oral communication to Umehara 1938, 55) to the third; J. Werner (1956, 19) to the fourth century.

[198] Berkhin 1961, 141-148.

disagree with Berkhin on minor points, but the date at which he arrived after a thorough study cannot longer be in doubt: it is the beginning of the third century.[199] As the mirror was evidently used for a considerable time, it cannot have been cast much later than about 200 A.D.

Werner rejected the possibility that the patterns on the loop-mirrors could have anything to do with the "artistic ornaments" of the Chinese mirrors; Khazanov would not exclude it entirely. As Rau before them, the two archaeologists think that the patterns on the loop-mirrors had been taken over from the pendant-mirrors. In some cases this might be true; as a whole, however, the two groups have very little in common. No loop-mirror has a tamga or a swastika or any of the ingenious combinations of patterns of the pendant-mirrors.

Berkhin and Solomonik tried to interpret the design on the Mozhary mirror. Berkhin took the "trees" on the square for a possible reflection of the cult of the Tree of Life, which is not exactly convincing.[200] Solomonik spoke of "birds' claws,"[201] by the quotation marks indicating that this is meant to be a purely descriptive term. She referred to a mirror from Krasnodar and another one from Kosino in Slovakia (fig. 71).[202] In the Krasnodar mirror she saw a combination of a swastika with "birds' claws"; the same on pendant-mirrors from the Dnieper and the Volga

FIG. 71. Bronze mirror from Kosino in Slovakia. From Eisner, *Slovensko v pravěku* 1933, fig. 2:7.

(fig. 72, line II, last on the right). The similarity between the "birds' claws" on the mirror from Kosino and the "trees" on the Mozhary mirror cannot be denied. However, the differences between the Slovakian and the Kuban mirrors on the one side and the mirror from Mozhary on the other outweigh

---

[199] The date was accepted by Ambroz 1966, 42.
[200] Berkhin 1961.
[201] Solomonik 1959, 145.
[202] Hampel 1897, 3, pl. 44:4; Eisner 1933, 237, fig. 21:7.

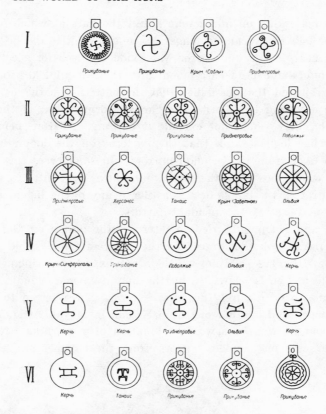

FIG. 72. Bronze pendant-mirrors from the Dnieper and Volga regions. From Solomonik 1959, fig. 6.

by far the similarities. The first two mirrors have neither a rim with radial lines nor a square in the center field.[203]

The design on the Mozhary mirror remains a riddle to Western archaeologists. Japanese archaeologists riddled it long ago. As early as 1925, Umehara wrote, "Anyone who looks at the design must certainly conclude that it is an extremely crude imitation of the popular TLV mirror."[204] Mizuno and Egami and a few years later Egami again listed the Mozhary mirror among the imitation mirrors of the West. The Sarmatian craftsman possibly transformed the lines on mirrors like the one from Lo-yang (fig. 69) into "birds' claws," but for the rest he copied the Chinese design as well as he could.

---

[203] The design on a pendant-mirror from Mitoc in Rumania (Rikman 1967, fig. 8:14) is so similar to that on the Mozhary loop-mirror that the one must be derived from the other. I assume that the loop-mirror served as model for the pendant-mirror on which the border with the radial lines is missing.

[204] Umehara 1938, 55; chapter 3 in 1938 is the reprint of an article published in 1925.

Even more simplified imitation mirrors of this type, without the "tree," have been found at Blumenfeld and Khar'kovka in the lower Volga region.[205] In mirrors from Norka (fig. 73)[206] and Kalinovka[207] only the rim with the radial lines is left.

FIG. 73. Sarmatian imitation of a Chinese mirror (cf. the example from Lo-yang, above, fig. 69), from Norka, lower Volga region. From Berkhin 1961, fig. 2:2.

The influence of Chinese mirror designs on non-Chinese mirrors before and after the period in which we are interested would deserve a special study. The scallops on a mirror with a long side handle from Tyukova near Tobolsk,[208] for example, are doubtlessly copied from Western Han mirrors, Karlgren's type k.[209] Even designs on other metal objects occasionally betray their origin from Chinese mirrors. A stamped bronze plaque in the grave of later nomads at Akkermen[210] looks almost like a "hundred nipples" mirror.

Although the present studies are not concerned with the origin of the Scythian and Sarmatian loop-mirror, I may remark that in my opinion they ultimately go back to Chinese mirrors. The earliest Chinese loop-mirrors precede those of the Scythians by at least half a millennium.[211] It is hardly a coincidence that the earliest datable Sarmatian loop-mirror, the Mozhary mirror, is an imitation mirror. Unadorned loop-mirrors, which might be the forerunners of the Sarmatian loop-mirrors, have been

---

[205] Khazanov 1963, 68, fig. 5:3.4. Dots instead of radial lines as on the mirror from Blumenfeld occur also in China; see Liang Shang-ch'un 1942, 2, 95, 103.

[206] Berkhin 1961, 146, fig. 2:2.

[207] Shilov 1959, 495, fig. 62:16. Kurgan 15 is a typical Late Sarmatian burial: narrow pit, orientation NNW.

[208] Moshinskaia 1953a, 219, pl. 17:1. A loop-mirror with a scalloped border from northern Kazakhstan (Kadyrbaev 1962, 75, pl. 1:4), seems to be an early imitation mirror.

[209] Maenchen-Helfen 1941, 111-113. See Bulling 1960, pls. 13-16, 26-27.

[210] APU 8, 1960, 94, fig. 74:3.

[211] This has been rightly stressed by Watson 1962, 81-82.

unearthed in Central Asia. Werner refers to one excavated in the T'ien Shan by A. N. Bernshtam, who dated the grave between the fourth and third century B.C.[212] Others were found in the upper Irtysh Valley,[213] the Chu Valley in Kirgizstan,[214] and in western Siberia.[215] Dated in the sixth or between the sixth and fourth century, they may very well be later, though not much. But there exist also plain pre-Han Chinese mirrors, but they are little known; collectors, interested in beautiful decorations and inscriptions, paid no attention to them. In recent years such mirrors were unearthed in Ch'ang-sha,[216] Hsi-an,[217] and Ch'eng-tu;[218] those from Hu-nan have tentatively been dated between the seventh and fourth century. Their relationship with the plain mirrors of the Western barbarians needs further investigation.

The preceding survey has shown once more how strong the influence of the civilizations of Central Asia, themselves in contact with China, was on the Sarmatians. Mirrors of the Mozhary type were fairly common in the lower Volga region in the Late Sarmatian period. They represent the earliest phase in the development of the loop-mirrors of the Sarmatians, forerunners of the type which Werner after the easternmost and westernmost findplace, Chmi in the Caucasus and Brigetio on the Danube, calls the Chmi-Brigetio type; its décor consists of a circle in the center and radial lines between it and the rim. The type Berezovka-Carnuntum is typologically more developed, but on the whole contemporaneous with Chmi-Brigetio. Still later, but again not much later, is the type Karpovka-St. Sulpice.

On the basis of the rich evidence, collected from often rather remote publications, Werner shows that the loop-mirrors of all three types spread from the east westward as the Huns did. None of the mirrors is, in his opinion, earlier than about 400 A.D. Their bearers were supposedly the Huns, from whom their Germanic subjects took over the mirrors.

More recent finds are incompatible with Werner's thesis. Chmi-Brigetio mirrors occur in Sarmatian graves as early as the third century. One was found in a grave at the stanitsa Vorozhenskaya in the Kuban area which by its furniture, among other things an amphora, must be dated

---

[212] Bernshtam 1952, 40.

[213] Zhol-Kudul, *oblast'* Pavlodar (Ageeva and Maksimova 1958, 41).

[214] *Oblast'* Frunze (Kibirov and Kozhemiako 1956, 39-40, fig. 5).

[215] Ancient cemetery at Tomsk (Komarova 1952, 31, 37, 43, fig. 17:4; 17, 21, fig. 21; 15, fig. 25:1-7).

[216] *Hu-nan ching* 1960, 25, no. 2, 27, no. 1.

[217] *Shen-hsi ching* 1959, 14, no. 4.

[218] *Szu-ch'uan ching* 1960, 8-9, no. 4.

to the third century.[219] The Sarmatians in the necropoles of Phanagoria and Tanais were buried together with their Chmi-Brigetio and plain loop[220] mirrors before the 370's. The Huns wiped out the Chernyakhov civilization, so the Chmi-Brigetio mirror in the Chernyakhov cemetery at Vorokhtanskaya Ol'shanka southwest of Kiev[221] was cast before the Hun storm. A "flat," that is, unadorned mirror of 7.5 centimeters' diameter, which originally had a loop on the back, was found in a building at Toprakkala in Khwarezm,[222] datable to the middle of the third century at the latest.[223] Werner is right: The loop mirrors came to the West together with the Huns. But they were not Hunnic mirrors. They were the mirrors of Sarmatians, who had them long before the Huns. We can be even more specific: They were the mirrors of eastern Sarmatians, those whom the Huns forced to join them east of the Don and those with whom they made an alliance on the Don.

These small bronze mirrors permit an answer to a question rarely asked. Where did the Huns cross the Carpathian Mountains into Hungary? Some hordes may have ridden through the passes over the southern Carpathians into Transylvania and from there into the Hungarian plain, but this would have been difficult for horsemen accompanied, as they most probably were, by their wagons. In the course of her history Hungary was repeatedly invaded from the northeast, through the valley of the upper Theiss: Kolomyya-Yablonsky (Tatar) Pass→ Sighet (Sziget)→ Khust (Huszt). The Huns and their Alanic allies took this route.

Studying the distribution of the Chmi-Brigetio and the Berezovka-Carnuntum mirrors south and west of the Carpathians, Ilona Kovrig noted that it almost coincided with the distribution of artificially deformed skulls.[224] Loop-mirrors were found in several graves with deformed skulls. One group of mirrors, associated with silver fibulae, is rather dense in the Upper Theiss Valley, another one stretches north of the Danube from the bend at Waitzen to Vienna. Compared with these two groups, the number of loop-mirrors in the Danube Valley and the great Hungarian plain is insignificant. From this distribution Kovrig drew the conclusion that the greater part of the ethnic groups which brought the mirrors to Hungary came—probably in several waves—through the passes of the

---

[219] Anfimov 1952, 213, fig. 3.

[220] (1) Marchenko 1956, 126, fig. 5:12; (2) Shelov 1966, 94, fig. 34:5. For a Chmi-Brigetio mirror from Inkerman in the southwestern Crimea, see Gushchina 1967, 49, fig. 4:3.

[221] *SA* 10, 1948, 61, fig. 6:23.

[222] S. A. Trudnovskaia, *Trudy Khor.* 1, 1952, 120.

[223] W. B. Henning, *Asia Major*, N.S. 11, 1965, 169-170.

[224] Kovrig 1959, 222-223.

northeastern Carpathians. This argument is strengthened by the absence of pendant-mirrors in Hungary. They are, on the other hand, characteristic of the Late Sarmatian graves in Rumania where loop-mirrors do not occur. Had the Huns and their allies and subjects come from the southeast, Sarmatians in the Rumanian plains, forced or voluntarily, would have joined them. But not a single grave of the fifth century in Hungary contains a pendant-mirror.

Now we can take a step further. In the third century the loop-mirrors were Sarmatian. In Hungary they still were almost absent from the Hunnic heartland east of the Danube. In other words, even at a time when the Huns and Alans lived closely together, the Huns did not take over the Sarmatian mirrors. This, of course, does not mean that only Sarmatians had them. It is unlikely that all Hunnic women, out of national pride, refused to look into a loop-mirror. The one found in Strazhe in Slovakia[225] comes from a grave in which a racially mixed Europoid-Mongoloid individual was buried. Many fifth-century graves with loop-mirrors were Germanic. If Goths and Gepids in Hungary followed the Sarmatian custom, the Huns could not reject it forever.[226] Still, chances are that the graves with loop-mirrors are not Hunnic. We have gained another criterion for separating Hunnic and non-Hunnic finds.

The observation that many loop-mirrors were intentionally broken when they were put in the grave led archaeologists to all kinds of speculations.[227] The plethora of ethnographical parallels and the lack of at least relatively constant association of the custom with other features in the archaeological material account for the futility of such often ingenious and erudite essays.

PERSONAL ORNAMENTS

Gold Plaques on Garments

In Attila's time and long before it, the custom of sewing small stamped gold plaques on garments was widespread in the barbaricum. To trace it back to its origin is not our task, nor need we investigate who the givers and takers in each case were. The Vandals in Slovakia[228] may have adopted the fashion from the Jazygi[229] and carried it to Africa,[230] although some

---

[225] J. Werner 1956, 116.
[226] So far no loop-mirror has been found in Ostrogothic Italy; in Gepidic Hungary they are fairly common (Csallány 1961, 394).
[227] See, for instance, J. Werner 1956, 22; Khazanov 1964, Litvinskiĭ 1964, 97-104.
[228] Beninger 1931a, pl. 7.
[229] Alföldi 1932, 59, pl. 35.
[230] Rostovtsev 1922, figs. 23, 24.

plaques found there could have been Alanic. The Kushans who had rosettes and ringlets sewn on their coats possibly imitated the Parthians;[231] the small plaques on the coats of nobles in Parthian costume in Hatra[232] are doubtless of gold, and in Sirkap small gold rosettes were found in a Parthian stratum.[233] But both Kushans and Parthians independently may have followed an older Central Asian fashion. In a grave at Kyzyl-kyr in the Bukhara oasis, datable between the third and second centuries B.C., ninety small hemispherical gold plaques lay on the chest of a woman.[234]

The custom is well attested for the Sarmatians as early as the Sauromatian period,[235] for the Scythians (see for example, the plaques in the Chastye kurgan),[236] and in Khwarezm.[237] In the Middle Sarmatian period, garments were decorated with gold plaques from the Volga (Kalinovka,[238] Berezovka)[239] to the Ukraine (Svatova Luchka and Selimovka).[240] The garment of a woman in a Late Sarmatian grave at Wiesenmüller (Lugovoe) on the Eruslan was richly decorated with gold and silver plaques.[241] Such plaques are also known from the possibly Hunnic burials at Shipovo[242] and Novo-Grigor'evka.[243]

In the unquestionably Hunnic find from Szeged-Nagyszeksos occur twenty-six electron plaques and seventeen fragments.[244] They are square; a beaded frame encloses four triangular faces meeting at a point; the corners are pierced. The Hunnic plaques are identical with those from Pusztabakod and from Carthage.[245] As the similarity, at times amounting to identity, of the gold plaques in the fourth and fifth centuries from one end of the barbaricum to the other proves, they were the products of Roman workshops using the same technique and the same patterns. Among the plaques on the dress of the Germanic or Alanic lady from Airan in Normandy[246]

---

[231] L. Bachhofer, *JAOS* 61, 1941, 249.

[232] Ghirshman 1962, figs. 100, 105, 110.

[233] Wheeler 1951, 2, 637, nos. 179-198; 3, pl. 191:r.

[234] Nil'sen 1959, 76-77.

[235] K. F. Smirnov 1964, 139-140.

[236] S. N. Zamiatin, *SA* 8, 1946, fig. 10:23, 32, 33.

[237] *Khor. Mat.* 4, 1960, 27, fig. 18:5-7.

[238] Hundreds of plaques in a woman's grave (Shilov 1959, 402-404, 462).

[239] Sinitsyn 1960, 57, fig. 21:3.

[240] On the sleeves (Rostovtsev 1931, 581-582).

[241] Rykov 1926, 113.

[242] Minaeva 1929, 199, figs. 13, 15.

[243] Alföldi 1932, pl. 22:11,18.

[244] *Ibid.*, 59, pl. 15; Fettich 1953, pl. 3:21-63.

[245] Alföldi 1932, 59, pl. 15.

[246] Salin and France-Lanord 1949, 119-135, pl. 13-15. Unfortunately, nothing is known about the grave in which the woman was buried with the splendid gold and silver

are some exactly like plaques from Novo-Grigor'evka;[247] others have counterparts in Papkezsi in Hungary[248] and Panticapaeum.[249] In other words, the Huns of the fifth century followed an "international" fashion.[250]

Embroidery

"In the house of Queen Ereka, maidservants, sitting on the floor in front of her, were embroidering with color fine white linen to be placed as ornaments on the barbarian clothes."[251] Spherical, cylindrical, and flat embroidery glass beads are known from most Middle and Late Sarmatian women's graves, even the poorest ones. They were all imported. They were sewn on the shoes, the lower part of the trousers, the sleeves, the collar of the tunic.[252] In grave F16 at the khutor Schulz (now sovkhoz Krasnyi Oktyabr') on the Torgun, almost seven hundred, mostly green and blue ones, lay near the feet of the woman;[253] they were in the same position in grave 3 in the second- or third-century cemetery Bel'bek II in the Crimea.[254] In some cases the shoe soles could have been embroidered as in Pazyryk;[255] the woman sat crosslegged on the floor.

Huns and Sarmatians shared their love for multicolored articles of dress with many northern barbarians. On the silk cloths in the Hsiung-nu graves at Derestui, beads of carnelian, jasper, gilded glass, limestone, and paste were sewn.[256] In Noin Ula, very small perforated pyrite crystals were found, originally fastened to cloth or leather.[257]

---

pieces. None of them was of local origin. The assumption that the dead was the wife of a Visigothic chieftain is unwarranted. The Visigoths never came even near Normandy. The woman may well have been married to one of those Alans who invaded Gaul in 406; cf. Courtois 1955, 47, n. 1.

[247] Alföldi 1932, pl. 22:11.

[248] *Ibid.*, 59, fig. 18.

[249] Michon, *Bulletin de la Société des antiquaires de France* 1920, 257-263; Rostovtsev 1922, 115, fig. 10.

[250] For a good survey of the gold plaques in South Russia, see Piatysheva 1956, 20-23. The number of gold plaques in Sarmatian and Hunnic graves is small compared with that in some graves in the Caucasus. In the tomb of a woman at Mtskheta (second to third century A.D.), 5,130 small, flat, and hemispherical plaques were found; *Mtskheta* 1 (Tiflis, 1958), 107, fig. 52:2, 3.

[251] Priscus, *EL* 140$_{6-7}$.

[252] The borders of a knitted bag in a Late Sarmatian grave at Alt-Weimar were embroidered with small beads (Rau, *Hügelgräber*, 28).

[253] Sinitsyn 1947, 53, fig. 28:11-13.

[254] Mosberg 1946, 116.

[255] Rudenko 1953, pl. 25.

[256] Sosnovskiĭ 1931, 1-2, 170.

[257] Rudenko 1962b, 47.

Beads

Like their Sarmatian sisters, the Hunnic women wore necklaces and bracelets, perhaps also anklets, of beads of all sorts of material: coral, carnelian, mother-of-pearl, quartz, pyrite, lapis lazuli, Egyptian paste, amber, lignite, but also stone and clay.[258] Only the latter were homemade; the others came from all parts of the Roman Empire, Persia,[259] Khwarezm,[260] India,[261] and also the barbaricum itself. By the fifth century a good part of the amber, worked into beads or used for inlays, came from the banks of the Dnieper and other places in the Ukraine.[262] Lignite[263] seems to have been imported from the Caucasus where lignite beads are quite common. Bracelets and necklaces formed by amber, glass, and semiprecious stones were worn throughout the northern steppes, as far east as Tuva and Outer Mongolia.[264]

---

[258] On Late Sarmatian beads, see Shilov 1950, 499-500.
[259] E. Schmidt, *Persepolis* 1 (Chicago), 76-77.
[260] I. V. Ptashnikova, *Trudy Khor.* 1, 1-5-11.
[261] Wheeler 1951, 2, 729-750.
[262] Fersman 1922, 2, 362-367.
[263] In Russian *geshir*, absent from most dictionaries.
[264] Rudenko 1962b, pl. 71:1, 2; Umehara 1960, 42, fig. 254.

VIII. Race

THE FOLLOWING investigation is largely based on paleoanthropological evidence.[1] To the reader who has been exposed to so much that was merely a reasonable guess, exact measurements must come as a relief. The date of a battle may be controversial, but the naso-malar angle and simotic height of a skull are never in doubt. And yet the many hundred pages and the tens of thousands of figures with which the paleoanthropologists overwhelm us are of little value for historical studies unless they are supplemented by literary and archaeological evidence. Even if, for instance, the number of skulls from the thirteenth-century graves between the Kerulen and the Volga were twenty times greater than it is now, they would be useless in retracing the campaigns of Genghiz Khan, Batu, and Subotai. Mongoloid skulls of the paleo-Siberian type in the Avar graves in Hungary prove that one group of the multiracial hordes came from northeastern Asia, but they cannot tell us when these Mongoloid Avars left their pastures and over which routes they reached the middle Danube. These are limitations which are almost self-evident, but the historian faces other difficulties which he is well advised to recognize in order not to set unrealistic hopes in paleoanthropological studies.

Paleoanthropology is a relatively new science, and its terminology is still fluid. At times this can be rather bewildering. To give examples which refer directly to our problems, Nemeskéri regards the "Ural-Altaic" or "Sub-Uralic" type as Mongoloid;[2] other anthropologists assign it to an intermediate position between Mongoloids and Europoids (or Europeids

---

[1] Following the usage of the Russians to whose works I so often refer, I mean by anthropology what in the English-speaking countries is called physical anthropology.

[2] Nemeskéri 1952.

or Europids; there is not even general agreement on what the adjective should be). Debets' distinction between the paleo-Siberian and Baikal type[3] is ignored by others. "South Siberian" and "Turanian" mean the same, but there is no equivalent to the "Tungid" type of the Hungarian anthropologists in Soviet taxonomy, although its "short-faced" Mongoloid type seems to be the same; Debets' suggestion to call it the Katanga type has not been generally accepted.[4]

In the present studies mainly the paleoanthropological material from the Soviet Union will be discussed, so I adhere to the terminology used in *Osnovy Antropologii* by Roginskii and Levin, and *Ethnic Origins of the Peoples of Northeastern Asia* by Levin.

"Great race" designates the three basic racial divisions of mankind, the Negroid, Europoid, and Mongoloid; "race," the large subdivisions within the great races. Thus the Mongoloid great race comprises, among others, the North Asiatic, Arctic, and Far Eastern (Sinid) races. Within the races "types" are distinguished, for example, within the North Asiatic race, the Baikal and Central Asiatic types.[5]

The paleoanthropological findings permit only a partial reconstruction of the physical appearance of the people. They remain silent about so much one would like to know; the color of the skin, eyes, and hair; the shape of the lips and eyelids; the patterning of the subcutaneous fat, to mention some of the characteristics by which, without measuring the skull, we can tell between, say, a Russian from Vologda and a Madrileño.

For reasons I do not quite understand the Soviet paleoanthropologists are exclusively, or almost exclusively, interested in skulls. This is all the more regrettable as stature is often of considerable importance for the racial diagnosis. To give an example, the burials in the kurgan cemetery at Shipovo take a prominent place in Hunnic studies. The furniture in kurgans 2 and 3 has been minutely described by Minaeva.[6] Maslovski carefully measured the skull from kurgan 3.[7] But only Rykov gave the length of the skeletons. The woman in kurgan 2 was 176 centimeters, the man in kurgan 3 was 170 centimeters tall; the man in kurgan 2 had the imposing height of 185 centimeters.[8] These people could not be Huns, who were *exigui forma*, of small stature, as Jordanes said.[9]

---

[3] Debets 1948, 311-312.

[4] M. G. Levin used it; cf. *TDPMKV* 3, 1963, 396.

[5] The Russians distinguish between Middle Asia and Central Asia, Haute Asie of the French, *i.e.*, Mongolia and Tibet.

[6] Minaeva 1929.

[7] *ESA* 4, 1929, 209-210.

[8] Rykov.

[9] See footnote 21.

In the evaluation of the paleoanthropological evidence one must, further-more, not lose sight of the fact that the reconstruction of the racial history of the Eurasian steppes rests on a narrow base. According to the *Han shu*, the Wu-sun numbered 630,000,[10] which is of course too exact; who could have counted them? Still, the figure probably was in the neighborhood of half a million. In the five centuries we can follow the history of the people, there lived several million Wu-sun. But to date not even two hundred of their skulls have been found. In 71 B.C., the Wu-sun took 39,000 Hsiung-nu prisoners.[11] Where are their skulls? About 150 B.C., the Chinese princess Hsi-chün for political reasons had to marry a Wu-sun king.[12] She came to his tents with several hundred servants and eunuchs.[13] It was sheer luck that in the Wu-sun graves at least one Chinese skull was found.

Finally, it must not be overlooked that the graves can very rarely be dated as exactly as the historian would wish. The skull in kurgan 12 at Kurgak in the Alai Valley is artificially deformed.[14] Bernshtam dated the grave to the third century B.C., which puzzled Ginzburg, for cranial deformation was supposed to make its appearance with the coming of the Huns in the first century B.C. So he called this premature occurrence an echo, *otgolosok*, of the connections of the Kurgak people with the Huns,[15] although the echo does not precede the sound. Later Bernshtam changed his mind and dated the kurgan to the beginning of our era.[16] Perhaps he was right this time, perhaps not. I do not want to be misunderstood. The paleoanthropological contributions to the study of the Huns cannot be overrated, but the uncertainties inherent in them must not be overlooked either. They can be somewhat reduced if the written sources come to our help. We now turn to them.

There exist four descriptions of the appearance of the Huns. The first and earliest one, written by Ammianus Marcellinus[17] in the winter of 392/3, was paraphrased by Jerome[18] and Claudian.[19] The second was the Gaulish writer Sidonius Apollinaris; although some of his expressions were taken

---

[10] Groot 1928, 122.

[11] Groot 1921, 197.

[12] For the best translation of the famous poem in which she laments her lot, see Waley 1946, 43.

[13] Groot 1926, 185.

[14] Ginzburg 1954, 364. [*The text has two footnote numbers 14.—Ed.*]

[15] *Ibid.*, 359

[16] *Ibid.*, 373, n. 2.

[17] XXXI, 2, Pighi 1948, 68-71.

[18] Cf. Maenchen-Helfen 1955a, 386-399.

[19] *In Ruf.* I, 323-331; II, 270.

over from Claudian, his description of the Huns is based on autopsy.[20] The third picture of the people was drawn by Jordanes,[21] who must have seen Huns in the East Roman army. His portrait of Attila,[22] however, goes, through Cassiodorus, back to Priscus, our fourth source. As the king "showed the evidence of his origin," we may take what Priscus said of him to be racial characteristics of the Huns.[23]

Ammianus' description begins with a strange misunderstanding: "Since the cheeks of the children are deeply furrowed with the steel from their very birth, in order that the growth of hair, when it appears at the proper time may be checked by the wrinkled scars, they grow old without beards and without beauty, like eunuchs." This was repeated by Claudian and Sidonius and reinterpreted by Cassiodorus. Ammianus' explanation of the thin beards of the Huns is wrong. Like so many other people, the Huns "inflicted wounds on their live flesh as a sign of grief when their kinsmen were dying."

Ammianus not only misinterpreted the Hunnic custom; his description of the Huns as beardless is at variance with Priscus. Ammianus may have seen an occasional Hunnic mercenary; in the main he had to rely on his Gothic informers. Priscus, in contrast, was personally acquainted with Attila, his sons, his uncles, and many Hunnic dignitaries. Attila, Priscus wrote, had a thin beard, *rarus barba*. To a Roman of the fifth century, a time when the beard was valued as a sign of manhood, *indicium virilitatis*, as Jerome said,[24] the beards of the Huns may have looked sparse. But Attila did not look like a eunuch. His thin beard was not necessarily a racial characteristic, a Mongoloid feature as has been maintained, any more than the sparse beard of Mynheer Pepperkorn in Thomas Mann's *Magic Mountain*. The definitely Europoid Scythians were often depicted with thin beards.[25] Besides, Ammianus speaks of the hairy legs, *hirsuta crura*, of the Huns.

That in the eyes of the Romans and Germans the Huns were an ugly crowd[26] does not mean much, and when Ammianus compares them to

---

[20] *Paneg. on Anthemius* 2, 43-269. I am not convinced that Jordanes followed Sidonius as Dalton (1915, 1, 143, n. 5) and M. Schuster (*Wiener Studien* 57, 1940, 119-130) maintain.

[21] *Getica* 127-128.

[22] *Ibid.*, 182.

[23] [*Incorporated into the text.—Ed.*]

[24] Jerome, *Comm. in Isaiam* VII, *PL* 24, 112. Cf. *Barba significat fortes* (Augustine, *In Psalm.* 132, 7, *PL* 37, 1733).

[25] H. Schoppa 1933, 21-22.

[26] The codices of Ammianus have *formes & pandi*. Clark's emendation, *deformes et pandi*, accepted by Pighi, is preferable to *formae et pavendae*, which was suggested by Gardthausen 1869, 43.

"the stumps, rough-hewn images, that are used in putting sides to bridges," he evidently wants to emphasize the coarse features of the Huns. Only reluctantly he has also two good words for the hated savages: They have compact, strong limbs and, like Ammianus' beloved emperor Julian,[27] strong necks.

The wide shoulders and the broad chest, *scapulis latis* (Jordanes), *lato pectore* (Priscus), *insignes umeri, pectora vasta* (Sidonius) are for the racial diagnosis as irrelevant as the narrow waist, *succincta sub ilibus alvus* (Sidonius). The great sitting height might be of more importance: "The figure of the foot soldiers is of medium height, but it is elongated if you look at the horsemen. Thus they often are considered tall when they are sitting" (*Forma quidem pediti media est, procera sed extat, si cernas equites; sic longi seape putantur, si sedeant*, Sidonius). Like the Huns, the Bashkirs, with their considerable Mongoloid admixture, are long-bodied, well muscled, and robust, with wide shoulders.[28] But the Belgian Flemings and Walloons also are described as "moderately thick-set in bodily build; their shoulders are broad, and their relative sitting height great."[29]

Jordanes stressed the small stature, *exigui forma*, and the swarthy complexion of the Huns, *species pavenda nigridinis*; Priscus described Attila as swarthy, *teter color*, and of short stature, *forma brevis*. Althias, commander of the Hunnic auxiliaries in Belisarius' army, was "lean and not tall of body."[30] Asterius of Amasea called the Huns nimble and slender.[31] But Emperor Arcadius was also of short stature and dark complexion.[32] Ammianus called the Persians *subnigri*;[33] Emperor Valens was *nigri coloris*;[34] so was the Egyptian philosopher Pamprepius,[35] whom Hodgkin[36] took for a Negro.[37] Whereas their height and the color of their skin did not markedly set the Huns apart from many Romans, the difference between them and their Germanic and Alanic white-skinned and tall subjects and allies must have been striking. The Alans were a tall, blond people.[38] In the Middle and Late Sarmatian graves in the Volga region lay men as tall as 182, 185, 187, and 189 centimeters.[39]

---

[27] Ammianus XXV, 13, 13.
[28] Coon 1930, 578.
[29] *Ibid.*, 527.
[30] Procopius IV, 4, 22.
[31] *PG* 40, 381.
[32] Philostorgius XII, 3, Bidez 1960, 134.
[33] XXIII, 6, 75. Constantius was also *subniger* (XXI, 16, 19).
[34] Ammianus, XXXI, 4, 7.
[35] Suidas, *s.v.* Pamprepius.
[36] Hodgkin 1898, 3, 53.
[37] On μέλας, *niger*, see Tarn 1952, 267, n. 5; 452.
[38] Ammianus XXXI, 2, 21.
[39] Rykov 1925, 66, and 1926, 103, 117, 123.

Only the statements about the heads and the physiognomy of the Huns are really revealing. The heads were round and shapeless (*informis offa*, Jordanes), "a round mass rises into a narrow head" (*consurgit in artum* [or *arcum*] *massa rotunda caput*, Sidonius); the eyes small and deepset: "tiny eyes, perforations rather than lights" (*minutis oculis, havens magis puncta quam lumina*, Jordanes), "their sight is there in two hollows beneath the forehead; while the eyes are not visible, the light that enters the dome of the skull can hardly reach the receding eyeballs" (*geminis sub fronte cavernis visus adest, oculis absentibus acta cerebri in cameram vix ad refugos pervenit orbes*, Sidonius). The nose was flat; this follows from Sidonius' description of the way the skulls of the children were deformed, and Jordanes, quoting Priscus, says expressly that Attila had a flat nose, *semo nasu*.

The weakly accentuated profile, together with the small eyes, point to a Mongoloid strain in the Huns. How strong it was cannot be determined from the few words in our sources. The more pronounced racial features in a mixed population always attract the most attention. Movsēs Dasxuran̄çi ignored the Europoids among the Khazars and described the whole people as "an ugly, broad-faced, eyelashless mob".[40] The women in the Kiptchak horde, wrote William of Rubruk, were exceedingly fat "and the smaller their noses, the fairer they were esteemed";[41] he was so impressed by the flat Mongol faces that he had no eyes for the non-Mongols who constituted the majority of the population.[42] One must also not forget that Ammianus and Jordanes hated the Huns with such an intensity that, however the savages may have looked, they had to be depicted as subhuman monsters. A comparison between Ammianus' and Jordanes' descriptions of the Huns and what Western chroniclers wrote about the Magyars is instructive. To the Germans and Italians the Magyars were "a monstrous nation, a horrid tribe, a tribe more cruel than any wild beast" (*mostrifera natio, horrenda gens, gens omni belua crudelior*). Crossing Hungary on his voyage to the Holy Land, Otto of Freising admired God's patience in giving so beautiful a country not to human beings but such monsters.[43] But Gardīzī, a disinterested observer, called the Magyars handsome and pleasant-looking.[44]

Ammianus and Jordanes may be forgiven, but what excuse have modern authors who ascribe to the Huns swollen lips, beady eyes, and bandy legs?[45]

---

[40] Movsēs Dasxuran̄çi 1961, 83. According to Iṣṭakrī, quoted by Minorsky (1937, 45), the Khazars were of two types, one very dark, the other fair-haired and handsome.
[41] *Sinica Franciscana* 1, 1929, 183, 190.
[42] Spuler 1943, 281.
[43] Dümmler 1888, 3, 448; Fasoli 1945, 164.
[44] Quoted by Marquardt 1903, 144.
[45] Dudden 1925, 1, 1; Coon 1930, 229.

Eickstedt's mistranslation of the Latin texts is fantastic; Attila had *auseinanderstehende Zähne*, which pretends to be the translation of canis aspersus, "sprinkled with gray," said of his beard.[46]

The descriptions give a somewhat distorted picture of the Huns. What is known about other steppe peoples of northern Eurasia in the first millennium A.D. makes it unlikely that the Huns were as Mongoloid as, say, the Yakut or Tunguz of our times. Many Huns were halfbreeds. Balamber married a Gothic princess,[47] Attila's last wife had the Germanic name Ildico,[48] the Gepid Mundo was of Attilanic descent.[49] Though we do not hear of Alano-Hunnic marriages, the Mongoloid strain in the Alans of Sapaudia shows that such marriages were fairly common. The leader of Stilicho's Alanic auxiliaries was a small man;[50] among his ancestors were probably Huns.

Most large cemeteries of the post-Hunnic centuries in the steppes reveal a mixture of races. The Gepidic cemetery at Kiszombor shows *ein Rassenkonglomerat, das sich aus den Elementen der nordischen, mediterranen, osteuropiden, turamiden, mongoliden und paläoasiatischen Rasse zusammensetzt.*[51] In their Scandinavian home the Gepids may not have been pure Nordics, but there were no Mongoloids among them; in Hungary they mixed with the Huns. In the Avar cemeteries; next to Europoids, at least four Mongoloid types are represented: Sinid, Baikal, Tungid, Yenisei.[52] In the cemetery at Kyukyal'dy in the valley of Kzyl-Alai, datable to the sixth and seventh centuries, Mongoloids with both wide and narrow faces were buried side by side with Europoids of the Andronovo and proto-Mediterranean type with varying degrees of Mongoloid admixture, testifying to the complex composition of some groups in the western Turkish kaganate.[53]

The paleoanthropological evidence indicates that the Huns were likewise racially mixed. In 1939, when Bartucz published his fundamental study on the races in Hungary, he did not know "of a single skull which could, beyond any doubt, be regarded as Hunnic."[54] This is still true.

---

[46] *Historia Mundi* 1, 150.

[47] *Getica*, 249.

[48] *Getica*, 254.

[49] *Getica*, 301. Cf. Theophanes, A.M. 6031, Malalas, 450. The genealogy suggested by Diculescu 1922 is not convincing.

[50] *Cui natura breves animis ingentibus artus finxerat* (Claudian, *Bell. Goth.*, 584-585).

[51] Bartucz 1940, 289.

[52] Lipták 1959, 251-279. On the other hand, of the skulls from the Avar necropolis at Alattyán, county Szolnok, only two in the earlier group are Mongoloid of the Baikal type and even they show Europoid admixture; cf. P. Lipták, *AAH* 40, 1963, 246.

[53] Ginzburg 1954, 374-378.

[54] Bartucz 1940, 303.

The chances that someday a tombstone will be found with the inscription *Hic iacet . . . genere Hunus* and a well-preserved skeleton beneath it are slim. Yet the situation is not as bad as it looks. The following list of non-Europoid skulls in graves of the Hunnic period is probably not complete,[55] but it suffices for our purposes:

Vienna-Simmering: Skull of a mature man. *"Alles deutet darauf hin, dass wir einen Mongolen oder Mongoliden vor uns haben."*[56]

Strazhe I near Piešt'any, Slovakia: woman. E(uropoid)+M(ongoloid).[57]

Bešeňov V, district Šurany, Slovakia: man. E+M.[58]

Adony, Hungary: One artificially deformed skull of a child which "seems to belong to the Europid type." Of the twenty-one skulls not deformed, "ten are dolichocranic, six mesocranic, and four brachycranic. In one case it was impossible to determine the index. As to the distribution of varieties, the Europoid type is represented by the Northern, the Mediterranean, and the East-Europid varieties. In the case of four skulls, we have to do with the so-called dolimorphic Ural-Altaic or Sub-Uralic varieties of the Mongolid type. The skulls belonging to this type are characterized by a long and moderately wide cranium cerebrale (mesocrany); by a low cranium viscerale, by a moderately vaulted forehead, and pronounced browridges."[59]

Györ, Széchenyi Square, Hungary: Twenty-three skulls from a cemetery in and outside of a Roman camp. One artificially deformed skull of a child. "The skulls belong to the Europid and Mongolid types, represented by six skulls each. No clear assignation to types was possible in the rest of the cases. The Mongolid varieties show a predominance of Tungid characteristics. Special importance attaches to the skulls found in graves nos. 9 and 21: these skulls belong to the dolichocranic Mongolid type. The closest parallel is the classical type found in the Avar cemetery at Mosonszentjános."[60]

Dulceanca, rayon Roșiori in Muntenia, Rumania: Deformed skull of a man of about fifty years. E+M.[61]

---

[55] Some publications of provincial museums were not accessible to me.

[56] Geyer 1932. Geyer's "Mongole" means what is usually called Mongoloid, belonging to the Mongoloid division of mankind; his "Mongolid" means the presence of some Mongoloid features.

[57] Vlček 1957, 403, 405, 432-424.

[58] *Ibid.*, 410-411.

[59] Nemeskéri 1952, 225-226.

[60] *Ibid.*, 226-227.

[61] Nicolăescu-Plopșor 1961, 543-547.

Although none of these finds can be dated exactly, they cannot be earlier than the last quarter of the fourth century. No Mongoloids lived between Vienna and Dulceanca before the coming of the Huns. On the other hand, the locations and the grave goods preclude the possibility of dating the skulls later than the fifth century. They are those of Huns or people who came with the Huns.

The descriptions and racial diagnoses which have been quoted verbatim require some comment. There are first the skulls that show both Europoid and Mongoloid features. Some anthropologists refuse to go beyond the statement that in a given skull characteristics of the two major races can be discerned. The artificial, and in particular the circular, deformation affects nearly all cranial indices to such a degree that it is often impossible to determine even the major races.[62] If, in addition, a deformed skull shows, or seems to show, features of both major races, the diagnosis of the types becomes an extremely difficult task. Most Soviet anthropologists are content with classifying such skulls as Europoid-Mongoloid.

In the list of skulls of the Hunnic period, I did not include the deformed skulls from Szekszárd, Mohács, Gyöngyösapáti, and Szirmabesenyö. Neméskeri thought he could detect Mongoloid features in them. Werner accepted his diagnoses and drew from them far-reaching conclusions.[63] But the diagnoses seem to be wrong. Lipták measured the skulls again, and his results were quite different from those of Nemeskéri. According to Lipták, none of the skulls shows any Mongoloid admixture.[64] Of those from Strazhe and Bešeňov which Vlček took for Mongoloid,[65] Lipták accepted only two as E+M.[66]

The historian finds himself in a quandary. Whose judgment should he believe? The Soviet anthropologists whom I asked were inclined to take Lipták's side. Fortunately, the situation is not hopeless. For even after the elimination of the controversial skulls, there remain a number of Mongoloid and E+M skulls datable to the Hunnic period. To be sure, the possibility that one or another of the supposedly Mongoloid skulls may turn out to be E+M or even Europoid cannot be ruled out. However, it is unlikely that *all* diagnoses were wrong. Nemeskéri could not have been mistaken when he found the closest parallels between two skulls

---

[62] Debets (*Antropologicheskiĭ zhurnal* 1, 1936) excluded all deformed skulls from racial diagnosis; K. F. Sokolova (in A. P. Smirnov 1958, 63) disregards the artificially deformed skulls from Chufut-Kala.

[63] J. Werner 1956, 108-109.

[64] Lipták 1961, 231-246.

[65] Vlček 1957, 403, 406, 410-414.

[66] Letter to me, June 1959.

from Györ and the Avar skulls from Mosonszentjános. It is by now generally agreed that the latter are of the Baikal type.[67]

The material from Hungary, Slovakia, and Rumania is by far too small to determine the numerical relationship of the various races in the Hunnish hordes. Besides, most of the skulls come from the graves of poor people. The prominent Huns, or, to be more cautious, some of them, cremated their dead. Some E+M skulls might also be Alanic. There were individuals of the South Siberian type among the Sarmatians at Kalinovka in the Volga region. The skulls in the graves at Saint Prex, canton Vaud, with their considerable Mongoloid admixture, were in all probability the skulls of Alans or descendants of Alans. Such a halfbreed was also the man in whose grave at Vienna-Simmering objects were found[68] that could be Hunnic. The man himself was 180 centimeters tall,[69] thus clearly not a Hun.

The Hsiung-nu

Until the 1940's, the identity of the European Huns with the Hsiung-nu on China's borders was rarely questioned. As no one doubted that the Hsiung-nu were Mongoloids, the Huns must have been Mongoloids too. Are there paleoanthropological finds to reconstruct the routes over which they migrated into eastern Europe?

The answer given by A. N. Bernshtam in 1926 was for a while widely accepted: In the last century B.C., Hsiung-nu were supposed to have moved to eastern Middle Asia and from there spread westward. Bernshtam's thesis centered on a catacomb in the cemetery on the Kenkol River in the Upper Talas Valley. Bernshtam excavated kurgan 10. "In the catacomb," he wrote, "lay two Mongoloid skeletons with deformed skulls; the skeletons in the dromos were Europoids, apparently slaves from the local population of the Pamiro-Fergana race."[70]

Bernshtam was an excellent and indefatigable excavator who went on digging when he hardly could walk any more; he died from cancer at the age of forty-six. Bernshtam was also a courageous man. He defended the views of the eminent but often mad linguist N. Marr at a time when so many Soviet scholars who had praised Marr to heaven were kicking the dead lion after Stalin had branded him an anti-Marxist. But Bernshtam

---

[67] Lipták 1959, 255-259; T. A. Tóth, *Voprosy antropologii* 12, 1962, 137. Debets (1918, 132) concluded from the identity of the skulls from Mosonszentjános, which he erroneously took for Hun skulls, and the Hsiung-nu skulls that the Huns were Hsiung-nu; so did L. M. Gulimev (*VD* 4, 1964, 124, n. 23).

[68] Beninger 1931, 72-76.

[69] Geyer, see footnote 57.

[70] Bernshtam 1940, 30-31.

wrote in too great haste, reconstructing whole periods of world history on the narrowest foundations. His interpretation of the Kenkol finds is a telling example. The two Mongoloids became in no time Turkish-speaking Hsiung-nu, and the Europoids in the dromos Wu-sun slaves. Because the Mongoloids were buried in catacombs, all catacomb burials in Middle Asia were declared Hsiung-nu burials. The shepherds from Kenkol were the missing link between the Hsiung-nu in Mongolia and the Huns in Hungary.

Zhirov doubted Bernshtam's interpretation as early as 1940.[71] But it won, as I said, wide acceptance both in the Soviet Union and in the West. By now it is practically abandoned. A closer study of the Chinese annals led S. S. Sorokin[72] and N. Negmatov[73] to doubt that the Mongoloids in the Talas Valley had anything to do with the Hsiung-nu of Chih-chih's short-lived robber state as Bernshtam thought. The date of the finds suggested by Bernshtam became questionable. Gryaznov proved that the "slaves" in the dromos belong to a secondary burial.[74] Finally, the alleged difference between the "lords" and the "slaves" turned out to be nonexistent. Debets measured the horizontal profiles of the couple in the catacomb and the two men in the dromos.[75] They are as follows:

	Naso-malar angle	Zygo-maxillary angle	Dacryal height	Simotic height
Catacomb, man	141	129	13.3	4.4.
Catacomb, woman	133	132	13.9	4.0
Dromos, man	140	139	12.3	2.8
Dromos, man	140	132	11.1	3.2

The angle of nasal prominence of the skulls in the catacombs is 26, of those in the dromos, 26 and 25. In other words, there are no real differences between the "lords" and the "slaves" in the degree of the horizontal profile of the face. The ones are not more Mongoloid than the others. All four skulls are Europoids with some Mongoloid admixture.

Debets' almost indignant refutation of Bernshtam's thesis of course does not solve the problem of the Kenkol finds. Where did the Mongoloid admixture come from? The wider question still remained whether the Mongoloids in the graves in Hungary had anything to do with the Mongoloid Hsiung-nu.

---

71 Zhirov 1940, 85.
72 Sorokin 1956a, 7, n. 1.
73 Negmatov 1957, 56.
74 Griaznov, *KS* 11, 1945, 148.
75 Debets 1962, 135-136.

The number of Hsiung-nu skulls is still small but large enough to draw from them rather important conclusions. Debets measured sixteen from the kurgans in the Selenga Valley near Ust'-Kiakhta, between 1897 and 1903 excavated by the Polish anthropologist Talko-Hryncevics (in Russian transcription, Tal'ko-Gryntsevich), and a female cranium from Noin Ula, found by the Kozlov expedition in 1925.[76] The skull of a man, found by the Hungaro-Mongolian expedition in Noin Ula in 1961, has been measured and described by T. Tóth.[77] He found in it the features of the Baikal (paleo-Siberian) type: dolichocephalic, low skull, high and orthognathous face, very slight horizontal profile, that is, a very flat face and a broad, flat nose, sloping forehead, strong browridges. The other skull from Noin Ula is of the same type; so are the skulls from the Selenga Valley, although among them one has somewhat attenuated Mongoloid features (as, possibly, the whole series).[78] The skull from the Ivolginskoe gorodishche which Gokhman studied is likewise of the Baikal type.[79]

The earliest Baikal skull was excavated in 1952 in a cave near the Shilka River; Okladnikov dates it to the Glazkovo period (about 1700-1300 B.C.), though it might be later.[80] The skulls from the slab graves in Transbaikalia of the beginning of the Iron Age (fourth to second century B.C.) are of greater importance to us. They are the low-faced skulls of the pre-Hsiung-nu population of the area.[81] When the Hsiung-nu came, the low-faced skulls gave way to the high-faced ones of the Hsiung-nu. In the early and the beginning of the later Han period a great part of the Hsiung-nu confederacy, perhaps we may say its nucleus, consisted of Mongoloids of the Baikal type. This does not make all Mongoloids of the Baikal type into Hsiung-nu. Nor does it prove that all members of the confederacy were of the Baikal type. Besides, what was true for the last two centuries B.C. and the beginning of our era was not necessarily true for the third and fourth centuries. We turn to the written sources and the archaeological monuments.

EUROPOIDS IN EAST ASIA

A stone horse at a tomb in the valley of the Wei River in Shensi is trampling a barbarian under its hoof.[82] The tomb has been identified

---

[76] Debets 1948, 120-122; Appendix 2.

[77] Tóth 1962.

[78] Debets 1948, 350-351.

[79] Gokhman 1960, quoted by Tóth 1962, 251-253.

[80] Levin 1962, 148, 188-189.

[81] Gokhman 1958, 18, 441-443.

[82] First published in Segalen, de Voisins and Lartigue 1924, 33-34. See also Bishop 1929, 1, fig. 1.

as that of Ho Ch'ü-ping, who died in 117 B.C., the great general famous
for his victories over the Hsiung-nu. Although the exact date of the sculpture is not quite certain,[83] it is doubtless of the Han period.[84] The general
buried under the earth mound was perhaps not Ho Ch'ü-ping, but he must
have been an outstanding man, and the enemy was definitely a Hsiung-nu.
He has a flat face and prominent cheekbones, but a luxuriant beard which
is quite un-Mongoloid.[85] In this respect he closely resembles the horseman
on a small bronze plaque found by P. S. Mikhno near Troitskovavsk in
Transbaikalia (fig. 74).[86] A bronze in the British Museum, from the Ordos
region, which was for a long time held by the Hsiung-nu, represents a
Europoid; note the thick moustache and the wide open eyes (fig. 75).

FIG. 74. Small bronze plaque showing a horseman with prominent cheekbones and full beard, from Troitskovavsk in Transbaikalia. From Petri,
Dalekoe proshloe Pribaĭkal'ia 1928, fig. 39.

The Mongoloid elements in the Hsiung-nu were considerably strengthened
by the many Chinese renegades[87] and prisoners of war. Of the Hsiung-nu's
Ch'iang, Ta Hu, and Ting-ling slaves in the third century,[88] the Ch'iang
were almost certainly Mongoloids. But from their raids into the oasis

[83] Ferguson 1929, 228-232.

[84] Sickman in Sickman and Soper 1956, 291.

[85] Bishop 1929, 37; Sickman and Soper 1956, 25. Z. Takáts published in *Dissertationes in honorem Dr. Eduard Mahler* (Budapest, 1937) drawings of the head he made
from the original in which the moustache and beard are rather sparse, but Takáts seems
to have looked at the withered sculpture with some prejudices.

[86] Petri 1928, 52, fig. 39.

[87] The Han sources are full of reports on soldiers and "rabble" on the borders who
went over to the Hsiung-nu.

[88] *San-kuo-chih*, ch. 30.

FIG. 75. Bronze plaque from the Ordos region, showing a man of Europoid stock with wide open eyes and moustache. British Museum. Photo G. Azarpay.

cities of Hsin-chiang,[89] the Hsiung-nu must have brought back quite a number of Europoids. A double burial in the desert region north of Min-feng hsien is instructive. The polychrome silk, jackets, trousers, stockings,

[89] Kuchā, Kao-ch'ang, and other towns in the northern Tarim basin.

and shoes are the same as in Noin Ula. But on a fabric a man is represented whose features are distinctly Europoid. The couple in the grave was also Europoid.[90]

We are not concerned here with the first appearance of the Europoids on the borders of China. Two references will suffice to indicate the problem. Karlgren pointed out that the bronze figure of a kneeling man from one of the Chin Ts'un graves, datable between about 450 and 230 B.C., does not represent a Mongoloid;[91] I would rather say that the flat face is Mongoloid, but the wide open eyes are Europoid. The hunter on an often reproduced gold plaque in the Siberian collection of Peter the Great[92] is undoubtedly Europoid. The plaque has been dated between the third and first century B.C., if not earlier.[93]

As the account of the massacre of the Hsiung-nu Chieh in Chao in 349 A.D. shows, the great majority of that people were Europoids. When Jan Min made himself lord of Chao in northern Honan, which until then had been ruled by the Chieh, he ordered the extermination of all Chieh. In and around Yeh more than two hundred thousand were slain. The Chieh soldiers were recognized by their high noses and full beards.[94]

Uchida Gimpū[95] and I,[96] independently of each other, adduced this characterization of the Chieh as proof of the existence of a Europoid group among the Hsiung-nu in the fourth century.[97] This was rejected by Tsunoda Bumie, who maintained that the Chieh were not of Hsiung-nu origin,[98] and again by S. G. Klyashtornyi with reference to Yao Wei-yüan, who tried to prove that the Chieh were originally Yüeh-chih.[99] Taking one step farther, Pulleyblank declared the Chieh to be Tokharians.[100]

It is entirely possible that the Chieh were ethnically different from other Hsiung-nu; but this does not change the fact that they *were* one of the nineteen tribes of the Hsiung-nu. When they joined the Hsiung-

---

[90] Li Yü-chun, *WW*, June 1960, 9-12; the reproduction of the fabric is too poor to be re-reproduced.

[91] Karlgren 1952, 211.

[92] Most recently reproduced by Rudenko 1962b, pl. 4.

[93] Griaznov 1961, 21.

[94] *Chin shu* 107, 8a.

[95] *Gakugei* 36, 28-32, and *Yūboku minzoku no shakai to bunka*, see Gimpū 1953.

[96] Maenchen-Helfen 1945b, 235-236.

[97] A. Soper (*Artibus Asiae* 23, 1960, 78) objects that the text has *Hu jen*, not Hsiung-nu. But in the context *Hu jen* means Hsiung-nu.

[98] 1954, 197-200.

[99] Kliashtornyĭ 1964, 107, n. 74.

[100] Pulleyblank 1963, 247-248. His reasoning is somewhat involved. In his opinion the Hsiung-nu spoke a language related to Yenisseian. He compares *chieh* 羯 Old Chinese *kat, with Yenisseian *khes, kit,* "stone." *Chieh* would, thus, have been the Hsiung-nu

nu confederacy is not known. At any rate, by the middle of the fourth century there *were* Europoids among the Hsiung-nu.

Liu Yüan, the Hsiung-nu conqueror of Lo-yang in 311, was 184 centimeters tall; there were red strains in his long beard.[101] The Hsiung-nu Ho-lien Po-po, founder of the short-lived Hsia dynasty, a contemporary of Attila, was 195 centimeters.[102] Some T'u-yü-hun princes were also very tall.[103] The Mu-jung T'u-yü-hun were a branch of the Hsien-pei. An anecdote in the *Shih-shuo hsin-yü*, compiled by Liu Yi-ch'ing in the first half of the fifth century, shows that the Hsien-pei, who are supposed to have spoken a Mongolian language, were racially anything but Mongoloid. When in 324 Emperor Ming, whose mother, née Hsün, came from the Hsien-pei kingdom of Yen, heard about the rebellion of Wang Tun, he rode into the camp of the rebels to find out their strength. He rode in full gallop through the camp. His puzzled enemies thought he was a Hsien-pei

---

name of the "Stone" people. Shih Lo, the founder of the Later Chao, was a Chieh; his ancestors came from the separate Hsiung-nu tribe Ch'iang-ch'u. Chinese 石 *shih* means "stone"; 羌渠 *ch'iang-ch'ü*, Middle Chinese khiaŋ-gio could be Tokharian A dialect *kānka-*, "stone." This Tokharian word was once transcribed and twice translated, first into Hsiung-nu-Yenisseian, then into Chinese.

It is a little bold to compare the Old Chinese transcription of an ethnic name of unknown meaning with a word in the language spoken by small tribes of fishermen in Siberia in the eighteenth century. How did *kit*—or was it *khes*?—sound at the time when *chieh* was **kat*? Because the Chinese transcriptions so often imply the meaning of the foreign word, one should expect a similarly sounding word that means "stone," for instance, the homonym 碣 *chieh*, "rock, stone pillar," instead of *chieh*, "wether." But the main objection to Pulleyblank's thesis is that *chieh* is a shortening of *li* 力 *-chieh*; cf. Yao Wei-yüan 1958, 356.

[101] *Wei shu* 45.

[102] *Ibid.*, 95.

[103] In *Das Toba-Reich Nordchinas*, 78-83, Eberhard, listing seventy-eight persons of above-average height in the San kuo, Chin, and Wei periods, finds no difference between the various ethnic elements of the population. I am afraid that such statistics, as much one has to admire the effort that went into them, are of limited value. To make them meaningful, the author should have listed not only all persons whose height the analysts give but also all the analysts did not give, presumably because their height was average. (If the analysts did not mention their height because they did not know it, the statistics would of course, lose all meaning.) Eberhard emphasizes the fact that the seventeen tall Hsien-pi, Hsiung-nu, and Tibetans in the list of thirty-two tall persons in the Chin period were rulers or chieftains who, he thinks, were so tall because they grew up under better living conditions. However, most prominent Chinese were members of the gentry who in their childhood and adolescence were not starved either. The disproportionately large number of tall barbarians indicates a racial difference between them and the Chinese.

because of his yellow beard.[104] One would like to know from what tribe Sakanoke no Tamuramaro's "Chinese" ancestor Achi no Omi came; he had a reddish face and a yellow beard.[105]

The T'ang period falls outside the framework of the present studies. I mention only in passing the Europoid "Tokharians," depicted with their red hair and green eyes on the wall paintings in northern Hsin-chiang. K. I. Petrov thinks the Chinese misinterpreted the ethnic name (which, according to him, means "the red ones," after the red color of the earth), and ascribed to the people red hair![106] The barbarian horsemen from Yu-chou in a poem by Li Po, probably Turks, had green eyes. Even later the Chinese knew of Mongol Huang t'ou Shih-wei, "Shih-wei with the yellow heads," and Gengiz Khan and his descendants had blond or reddish hair and deep-blue eyes.[107]

One could think that the Europoid Hsiung-nu were originally members of subjugated tribes, prisoners of war, or slaves. Some probably were. But Chin-jih-ti, 191 centimeters tall, a contemporary of Ho Ch'ü-ping, was crown prince of the Hsiu-t'u, a royal branch of the Hsiung-nu.[108] After the conquest of present Tuva by the Hsiung-nu in the second century B.C., the population, which had been racially mixed with a preponderance of Europoid features,[109] became not less but more Europoid.[110]

Yen Shih-ku's often quoted descriptions of the Wu-sun, neighbors and hereditary enemies of the Hsiung-nu, seems to prove that at one time the Wu-sun were preponderantly Europoid: "Of all the Jung of the western lands the Wu-sun look the most peculiar. Those of the present Hu who have cerulean eyes and red beards and look like Mi monkeys[111] are their descendants."[112] Yen Shih-ku (579-645) evidently relied on an earlier source. But is the earlier source reliable?

Already at a time when only a small number of skulls from the territory held by the Wu-sun were known, they were recognized as Europoid.[113] Debets admitted a slight Mongoloid admixture. The Wu-sun were not

---

[104] Quoted by G. Schreiber, *Monumenta Serica* 14, 1949-1944, 389.

[105] Wedemeyer 1930, 114, n. 244.

[106] In *Ocherk proiskhozhdeniia kirgizskogo naroda*, 38.

[107] *Yüeh fu shih chi*, ch. 25.

[108] Groot 1921, 132.

[109] V. A. Alekseev, *Trudy Tuv.* 1, 1960, 148, 295.

[110] V. A. Alekseev 1956.

[111] According to some dictionaries a monkey with a long tail; according to others, the short-tailed macaque.

[112] Groot, 1926, 123. The Chinese belief that the Russians were the descendants of the Wu-sun, first attested in the Yüan period, was based on Yen Shih-ku's statement; cf. Kiuner 1961, 68.

[113] Oshanin 1954, 21.

as purely Europoid as the preceding Saka, who looked like Afghans or North
Indians, but "physiologically the Wu-sun resembled the present day clan-
less Uzbeks or Fergana Tadjiks, that is, the Europeoid features were still
decidedly prominent."[114] As the material accumulated, local differences
turned out to be more prominent than it was first thought. The development
also did not go in the same direction. As late as the third century some
Wu-sun were almost purely Europoid, whereas others were of the South
Siberian type, that is, with a marked Mongoloid admixture.[115] Still, there
was nothing in the material that would have confirmed Yen Shih-ku's
statement until the young Kazakh anthropologist, O. Ismagulov, published
the results of his studies. Of eighty-seven skulls from graves in the Semirech'e, six, datable around the beginning of our era, were either of the
European type or close to it.[116] These Wu-sun did not resemble Uzbeks
or Tadjiks; they were people with "cerulean eyes and red beards."

The paleoanthropological work in Hsin-chiang has barely begun. It
is, therefore, all the more remarkable that some of the skulls collected
by the Sino-Swedish Expedition in 1928 and 1934 and studied by C. H.
Hjörtsjö and A. Walander point to Europoids of the northern type in
the ancient population. Of the three skulls from Mirān, datable between
the last century B.C. and the third century A.D., one is probably Chinese,
one probably Tibetan with a strong Nordic admixture, one preponderantly
Nordic, possibly with some Indoid or Mongoloid features. In the third
century Mirān was a Tibetan fortress, so the Mongoloids were possibly
soldiers of the garrison. The presence of Indoid features could be expected;
the men on the third-century wall painting are Indians, the inscriptions
are in Karoṣṭhi.[117] But the Nordic features come as a surprise. A skull
from Charchan, unfortunately undatable, is predominantly Nordic, with
Indoid and Mongoloid admixture. One of the earlier crania from the
Lopnor region, presumably datable to the first three centuries A.D.,
is Mongoloid with some Nordic features. From the mass cemetery in the
same region, which only approximately can be dated after 200 A.D., comes
the skull of a Mongoloid with some Nordic features and another one which
is Indoid with Nordic and weak Mongoloid admixture.[118] Around the
beginning of our era, Europoids of the Nordic type lived, thus, both in
the Semirech'e and Hsin-chiang.

---

[114] Debets 1962, 141.

[115] Cemetery at Baty (Chernikov 1951a, 76-77). Cf. also on the Wu-sun in the Ili
Valley Akishev and Kushaev 1963, 188: E+M in the last century B.C.; Europoids in
the third century A.D. (153, 155, 211, 212).

[116] 1962, 72, 73, 76, 86.

[117] Bussagli 1963, 18-25; Andrews 1948, 21.

[118] Hjörtsjö and Walander 1947, 74, 76, 77, 86.

IX. Language

SPECULATIONS ABOUT THE LANGUAGE OF THE HUNS

The Germans in Attila's kingdom apparently did not use the script which Wulfila had invented to translate the Bible into Gothic; they scratched their runes on swords, lance heads, brooches, and buckles as their ancestors had done. The Huns, "barbarous even in the eyes of the barbarian peoples around them,"[1] had no script. Attila's scribes were not Huns but Romans: the Gaul Constantius,[2] an Italian by the same name,[3] the Pannonian Orestes,[4] and Rusticus from Upper Moesia.[5] In the middle of the sixth century Procopius described the Huns west of the Maeotis as "absolutely unacquainted with writing and unskilled in it to the present day. They have neither writing masters nor do the children among them toil over the letters at all as they grow up."[6]

All we know of the language of the Huns are names. Our sources do not give the meaning of any of them. These names have been studied for more than a century and a half.[7] Some were assigned to this, others to that group of languages, from Slavic to proto-Chuvash and Old Khvartelian.[8] The task of the historian with some linguistic training or the phil-

---

[1] Sidonius, *Paneg. on Anthemius* 240.

[2] Priscus, *EL* 132_{12}.

[3] 127_9

[4] *Anon. Vales.* 37, Cessi 1913, 13.

[5] Priscus, *EL* 145_{32-34}.

[6] Procopius VIII, 19, 8.

[7] B. F. Bergmann (1804) was the first to etymologize Hunnic names; he took them for Mongolian.

[8] For a survey until 1926, see Inostrantsev 1926. Recently E. Moór (*Beiträge zur Namenkunde* 14, 1963, 63-104) suggested that the Huns spoke a North Caucasian language. His arguments are based on a misunderstanding of the Greek and Latin

ologist with a knowledge of history cannot consist of singling out this name or that and comparing it with what he happens to know. It should consist, rather, of studying the entire material in all its complexity. This has been done only once. Vámbéry listed not merely the names he thought he could explain but all he could find.[9] His list is incomplete, and many of his etymologies strike us as fantastic. Yet methodologically Vámbéry was on the right track.

Although the present studies deal with the Attilanic Huns (to use the perhaps not quite correct but convenient term coined by B. von Arnim[10]), the lists on the following pages also include names of other Huns. It has often been maintained, and I have said so myself, that the Byzantines spoke of Huns as loosely as they spoke of Scythians. This is true for later writers, but in the fifth and sixth centuries Byzantine authors definitely distinguished the Huns from other northern barbarians.

Priscus, who was interested in foreign languages, set Hunnish apart from other languages spoken at Attila's court. During his stay with the Huns, and perhaps also before, he learned enough Hunnish and Gothic to be able to distinguish between them at least by their sound. He described how Zerco, the Moorish jester, threw the guests at the king's banquet "into fits of unquenchable laughter by his appearance, his dress, his voice, and the promiscuous jumble of words, Latin mixed with Hunnish and Gothic."[11] By calling Edecon a Hun,[12] Priscus implied that the man's tongue was Hunnish.[13]

Although Procopius' definition of an ethnic group would not satisfy modern anthropologists, it is not as vague as it is sometimes presented. He wrote:

There were many Gothic peoples in earlier times, just as also at the present, but the greatest and most important of all are the Goths, Vandals, Visigoths, and Gepids. All these, while they are distinguished from one another by their names, do not differ in anything at all. For they all have white bodies and fair hair, and are tall and handsome

---

transcriptions of the Hunnic names; cf. O. Maenchen-Helfen, *Beiträge zur Namenkunde* 14, 1963, 273-278.

[9] Vámbéry 1882, 40-50.

[10] Arnim 1936, 100.

[11] *Τῇ γὰρ Ἀυσονίων τὴν τῶν Οὔννων καὶ τὴν τῶν Γότθων παρμίγνυ γλῶτταν* (for the reading *παρεμίγνυ* instead of C. de Boor's *παραμιγνύς*, see G. A. Papabasileios, *Ἀθηνᾶ* 1896, 74), EL 145$_{12\text{-}13}$.

[12] Priscus, EL 122$_{6\text{-}7}$.

[13] Cf. Thompson 1948, 10-11.

to look upon, and they use the same laws and practice a common religion. For they are all of the Arian faith, and have one language called
Gothic; and, as it seems to me, they all came originally from one tribe,
and were distinguished later by the names of those who led each group.[14]

Procopius applied to the Huns two of the four criteria of what con-
stitutes a people in his view. Like the Goths, the Οὐννικὰ ἔθνη were characterized by their racial type—they were ugly and their bodies were
dark; and by their manner of life—they were nomads.[15] That Procopius
passed over their religion is understandable: unlike the antagonism between
Arianism and orthodoxy, it played no role in the relationship with the
Romans. Nor had Procopius any reason to pay attention to the language
of the Huns. As Belisarius' *consiliarius* he had the opportunity to pick
up some Gothic and possibly Vandalic; these were the languages of great
kings and warriors. But it was not worthwhile to learn the gibberish
which the uncouth Massagetic bodyguards spoke. To Procopius' ear
it must have sounded, to use a Chinese simile, like "the croaking of a
shrike." Yet he spoke of Hunnic peoples as he spoke of Gothic peoples. If
the latter had one language, the same must be true for the former. In
one instance we are explicitly told that the Kutrigur and Utigur, called
Huns by Procopius,[16] Agathias,[17] and Menander,[18] were of the same stock,
dressed in the same way, and had the same language.[19] "Same" does
not necessarily mean identical. Vandalic was certainly close to Gothic
but not the same. There may have been marked dialectical differences
in the speech of the various Hunnic peoples and tribes, yet they apparently understood one another.[20]

A little-noticed passage in John of Antioch sheds more light on the
early Byzantine concept of the ethnic name "Hun." In 513 Hypatius,
the nephew of Emperor Anastasius, was made prisoner by Vitalian's Hunnic
federates. Polychronius and Martyrius "whose office it was to deal with
the envoys of the Huns" (τάς τῶν Οὔννων πρεσβείας ἐπιτετραμένοι),

---

[14] Procopius III, 2, 2-5. Part of the passage may go back to Priscus.

[15] I, 3, 4-5.

[16] VIII, 4, 13; 5, 23; 18, 18.

[17] V. 11, Keydell 1967, 177.

[18] *EL* 196, 458.

[19] 170₂₇.

[20] The Hephthalites seem to be the only exception. The Byzantines had no direct
contact with them, and it seems doubtful that they knew anything about their language.
It was probably the similarity of their ethnic name to that of the Huns which earned
them the name "White Huns" (Maenchen-Helfen 1959, 227-228). In all other respects
the Hephthalites were, as Procopius I, 3, 25, stresses, totally different from the Huns.

were sent to the Huns with 1,100 pounds of gold to ransom Hypatius.[21] This shows that among the *interpretes diversarum gentium*[22] under the *magister officiorum* some were in charge of dealing with the envoys of the Huns. Not with this or that tribe, but with the Huns who evidently spoke *one* language.

The present investigation could not have been undertaken without Gyula Moravcsik's invaluable *Byzantinoturcica*. They lead to the sources. Only by a careful study of the literary context in which the names appear can we hope to bring the problem of the Hunnish language closer to its solution. It is of little help to know the alleged Byzantine rules for transcribing foreign names. They change from author to author and from century to century. Before the twelfth century β could render both foreign *b* and *v*. Sozomen has $Bαρδησάνης$[23]=Bar-Daisan, and $Βίκτωρ$,[24] Priscus $Ἀρδαβούριος$[25]=Ardabures in the Latin sources, and $Βαλάμερος$[26]=Valamer. $Mπ$ for initial *b* appears for the first time in the twelfth century;[27] the traditional transcription $Βούλγαροι$ was retained much longer. Only by lumping all transcriptions together, from the earliest to the latest, and regardless of the language of the author, ranging from classical pure Greek to vulgar colloquial, can one say that *a* stands for *a, o, u, e, ä, i*, and *ï*, in Turkish names.[28] What matters is the specific idiom of the writer, his dependence on earlier works, the manuscript tradition, and a number of other factors, to be discussed presently, which account for the form of a name in a text.

TRANSCRIPTIONS

They were Tatos and Chales and Sesthlabos
and Satzas (for I must give the names of
the highest-born of these, although the
elegant appearance of my history is spoiled by
them).[29]

---

[21] John of Antioch, *EL* 145₃₄₋₃₅. Mommsen (*Hermes* 6, 1872, 355, n. 2) drew attention to the passage but no student of the Huns realized its importance. It is not listed by Moravcsik.

[22] *Not. dign.* [*occ.*] XI, 35.

[23] *Hist. eccles.* III, 16, 5, Bidez 1960, 128.

[24] *Ibid.*, VII, 19, 1, Bidez 1960, 330.

[25] *EL* 583₁₅.

[26] *Ibid.*, 152₂₁.

[27] In Ioannes Kinnamos' *Epitome*.

[28] Moravcsik, *BT* 2, 31.

[29] Anna Commena, *Alexiad* 6, 14 (Dawes 1928; Leib 1945).

It is a priori certain that the phonetic system of the Hunnish language, whatever it may have been, was different from that of Greek and Latin. Even if an author wanted to render a Hunnish name faithfully, the mere fact that he had to use the letters of his own alphabet forced him to distort it. A few names may have passed the process of transcription relatively unscathed; others must have suffered badly. What name is hidden behind Ἀδαμις? The name of Queen Erekan's steward occurs only in Priscus, and in the dative case at that: Ἀδαμει.[30] -ις is not the Greek ending tacked on to the name. Priscus may not have been a good Christian but he must have heard of the protoplast. If the Hun's name had been Adam, Priscus would have written Ἀδάμ. The Greek, having no letters for supradental ṣ and palatal ś, transcribed these consonants by sigma. Ἀδαμις could be Adamis or Adamiš (ṣ, ś). But because in the transcription of Germanic names the ending iþ is sometimes rendered by -ις, Ἀδαμις could also be Adamiþ.[31]

Foreign names were not only adapted to Greek and Latin phonetics but also to the morphology of the writer's language. The Byzantines often treated names ending in -an or -in as if they were in the accusative. If we had only the forms Οὔλδης and Οὔλδις,[32] it would be impossible to determine whether the name of the Hun king was Uldis or Uldin. Fortunately Orosius mentions it in the nominative: It was Uldin.[33] In some transcriptions the Greek and Latin endings can be relatively easily distinguished, but in others it is impossible to decide where the barbarian name ends. Procopius admired Belisarius so much that he even described the horse of his hero. "Its body was dark grey, except that the face from the head to the nostrils was of the purest white. Such a horse is in Greek called φαλιός, the barbarians call it βάλαν."[34] Was it Balas, or Balan, or Bal? Balas is a Germanic word, OHG balas, equus maculosus, English blaze, German Bless.[35] The word can be recognized because it occurs in a group of well-known languages. But what if the meaning of a name is as unknown as the language? The Hunnic names in the Latin and Greek sources can be reconstructed within limits, but these limits are rather wide. Ἧσλας could be the transcription of Esl, Esla, Eslas, Ešl, Ešla, Ešlas, Eslaš, Ešlaš,

---

[30] EL 146₈; Moravcsik, BT 2, 56.

[31] Schönfeld 1911, 69.

[32] Zosimus and Sozomenus, Moravcsik, BT 2, 230.

[33] Hist adv. Pagan. V, 37-2<Huldin, Marcellinus Comes, CM II, 69>Jordanes, Romana 321.

[34] Procopius VI, 18, 61.

[35] Ph. Thielmann, Archiv f. latein. Lexicographie 4, 1887, 601; E. Schröder, ZfDA 35, 1891, 237; E. Schwyzer, ZfDA 66, 1929, 94-100 and Schwyzer 1914.

Eslan, and Ešlan. Was the stress on the first or the second syllable? Was the š—if it was an š—palatal or supradental? We do not know.

Besides the orthography of the writer and the possibility of morphological change, three more factors must be considered when we try to "retranscribe" Hunnish names. It is, first, not certain that all the names in our sources are those by which the Huns called themselves. Before the East Romans had any contact with the Huns, they heard about them from the Goths. They must have heard many names as they were pronounced by Goths and other non-Huns. *Octar*, the name of Attila's paternal uncle, is a good example of the modification which a Hun name underwent in the course of transmission from Hunnish through Latin into Greek. Jordanes has Octar,[36] Socrates Οὔπταρος[37]. These forms have a parallel in Accila and Optila. Eastern writers call the Ostrogoth, who killed Valentinian III, Accila or Occila; Marcellinus Comes, Jordanes, and John of Antioch call him Optila.[38] The transition from -ct- to -pt- is characteristic of Balkan Latin.[39] It was probably there that Octar became Optar-Uptar.

The second factor to keep in mind is the tendency of late Roman and Byzantine writers to alter foreign names until they sounded like Latin or Greek ones. In this way Bagrat became Pankratios.[40] The name of the Langobard Droctulft appears in his Latin epitaph as Drocton.[41] At times names were translated: Ammianus Marcellinus mentions an Iberian prince by the strange name of Ultra;[42] the prince's name was Pîrān; so Ammianus made it into πέραν and then translated it into Latin.[43]

The third reason for treating transcribed Hunnish names with utmost caution lies in the circumstances under which they have come down to us. Proper names are particularly liable to corruption in the manuscript tradition. The Procopius manuscripts have Οὐρβιβέντος for Urbs Vetus and Οὐρβισαλία for Urbs Salia.[44] It seems unlikely that Procopius is responsible for such forms.[45] Most of the Priscus fragments are in the collection of excerpts made by Constantinus Porphyrogenitus in the tenth century.

---

[36] *Getica* 105.

[37] *Hist. eccles.* VII, 30, *PG* 67, 805c; Moravcsik, *BT* 2, 237.

[38] Schönfeld 1911, 178; add *Occila*, Greg. Tur. *Hist. Franc.* II, 7 (8).

[39] The change from Octar to Uptar may have been facilitated by the existence of the Gothic name Ὄπταρις (Schönfeld 1911, 173).

[40] Justi 1895, 67.

[41] Paulus Diaconus, *Hist. Lang.* III, 19.

[42] XXVIII, 12, 26.

[43] Peeters 1932, 39, n. 3.

[44] Procopius VII, 11, 11; 16, 24.

[45] For other distorted names, see Schwyzer 1914, 312-313.

All existing codices, none older than 1500, are copied from the one burned in the fire which destroyed the greater part of the library in the Escorial in 1671. Six Hun names in Priscus are hapax legomena: Adamis, Basich, Eskam, Mamas, Kursich, and Oebarsius. The last one appears in all manuscripts as ὠηβάρσιον.[46] In a Priscus fragment dealing with the siege of Naissus by the Huns, preserved in a single manuscript of the tenth century, the city is said to be situated ἐπὶ Δάνουβα.[47] Naissus was not an obscure village but an important town, the junction of several roads. Priscus could not have called the river "Danube." Δάνουβα is evidently a scribal error. But what *was* the name of the river? As a rule, if a name occurs in a single passage in the writings of a single author in a single manuscript, it has to be taken as it is. But identical forms in all codices are not necessarily the correct ones. If Persian were as unknown as Hunnish, Ἀρταβίδης in Theophanes Simocatta III, 18, 9, could never have been recognized as a clerical mistake for * Ἀργαβίδης = Arghabad.[48]

Different transcriptions of the same name are of help, though not always. The name of the commander of the troops in Thrace in 447 appears in Priscus as Ὀρνιγίσκλος,[49] in Theophanes as Ἀγάρσκισλος,[50] and in the *Chronicon Paschale* as Ἀνάργισκος.[51] Which of these forms is the correct one? None, for they are all distorted from Arnigisclus,[52] Arnegisclus,[53] and Ἀρνήγισκλος,[54] Germanic *Arnegisl.[55]

ETYMOLOGIES

Many languages were spoken in Attila's kingdom. His "Scythian" subjects were "swept together from many nations."[56] They spoke, wrote Priscus, "besides their own barbarian tongues, either Hunnish, or Gothic, or, as many have dealings with the Western Romans, Latin; but not one of them easily speaks Greek, except captives from the Thracian or Illyrian frontier regions."[57] We must be prepared to meet among the names borne by Huns Germanic, Latin, and (as a result of the long and close contact

---

[46] Moravcsik, *BT* 2, 350.

[47] Thompson 1947b, 62.

[48] Christensen 1944, 107.

[49] *EL* 588$_{26}$.

[50] C. de Boor, 120$_{20}$.

[51] *CM* II, 82, 82, ed. Bonn, 586b.

[52] Marcellinus Comes, *CM* II, 80$_{28}$, 82$_{30}$.

[53] Jordanes, *Romana* 42$_{25}$.

[54] John of Antioch, *EI* 130$_2$.

[55] Schönfeld 1911, 30.

[56] ξύγκλυδες γὰρ ὄντες, *EL* 135$_{14}$. On the derogatory meaning of the term, see Wais 1942, 16ff.

[57] πάραλυς is *ripa*, not "sea coast," as Bury (1923, 283) translated.

with the Alans) also Iranian names. Attempts to force all Hunnic names into one linguistic group are a priori doomed to failure.

"Let no one," warned Jordanes, "who is ignorant cavil at the fact that the tribes of men use many names, the Sarmatians from the Germans and the Goths frequently from the Huns."[58] Tutizar was a Goth[59] and Ragnaris a Hun,[60] but Tutizar is not a Gothic name and Ragnaris is Germanic.[61] The Byzantine generals who in 493 fought against the Isaurians were Apsikal, a Goth, and Sigizan and Zolban, commanders of the Hun auxiliaries.[62] Apsikal is not a Gothic but a Hunnic name; Sigizan might be Germanic.[63] Mundius, a man of Attilanic descent,[64] had a son by the name of Mauricius;[65] his grandson Theudimundus bore a Germanic name.[66] Patricius, Ardabur, and Herminiricus were not a Roman, an Alan, and a German as the names would indicate, but brothers, the sons of Aspar and his Gothic wife.[67] There are many such cases in the fifth and sixth centuries. Sometimes a man is known under two names, belonging to two different tongues.[68] Or he has a name compounded of elements of two languages.[69] There are instances of what seem to be double names; actually one is the personal name, the other a title.[70] Among the Hun names, some might well be designations of rank.[71] It is, I believe, generally agreed that the titles of the steppe peoples do not reflect the nationality of their bearers.[72] A kan, kagan, or bagatur may be a Mongol, a Turk, a Bulgar; he may be practically anything.

---

[58] *Getica* 58.

[59] Cassiodorus, *Variae* VII, 27; Theoderic's letter *saioni Tutizar*.

[60] Agathias II, 13, 3, Keydell 1967, 57$_{19}$.

[62] Schönfeld 1911, 184, 244.

[61] John of Antioch, *EI* 142$_{21\text{-}22}$.

[63] Cf. $\Sigma\iota\gamma\iota\tau\zeta\alpha\varsigma$ ($\Sigma\iota\gamma\eta\tau\zeta\alpha\varsigma$), a Gothic martyr (Loewe 1923, 416).

[64] *Getica* 301.

[65] Procopius VII, 1, 36.

[66] Schönfeld 1911, 234. Lal Bahadur (Mongol) Shastri, the Indian prime minister, named his son Kennedy, which after the assassination of the President was changed to Kenny.

[67] O. Seeck, *PW* 2, 606-610.

[68] The Ostrogoth Gundulf was also called Indulf (Procopius VIII, 23, 1). In what language could Germanic Gundulf become Indulf?

[69] Asperulfus is compounded of Alanic *Aspar* and Germanic *wulf* (R. Loewe, *Indogermanische Forschungen* 14, 1903, 18, n. 1).

[70] $'E\nu\varrho\alpha\beta\omega\tau\tilde{\alpha}\varsigma$, $\ddot{o}\varsigma$ $\varkappa\alpha\grave{\iota}$ $Bo\ddot{\iota}\nu o\varsigma$ $\dot{\epsilon}\pi\omega\nu o\mu\acute{\alpha}\zeta\epsilon\tau o$ (Theophylactus of Achrida, *PG* 126, 193c). *Enravota* is Slavic, *Boinos* is Baian (Moravcsik, *BT* 2, 125).

[71] See p. 407 on Ellac.

[72] Tarqan, later so common among Turkish tribes, occurs in the first century A.D. in an entirely non-Turkish milieu. T'a-kan-ch'eng 它 (他) 乾 城 near Kuchā, Pan Ch'ao's residence in A.D. 191 (Chavannes 1906, 233-234), is undoubtedly "the Tarqan town."

The names of the Danube Bulgars offer an illustration of the pitfalls into which scholars are likely to stumble when they approach the complex problems of the migration period with their eyes fixed on etymologies. In spite of the labor spent on the explanation of Bulgarian names since the thirties of the past century, there is hardly one whose etymology has been definitely established. The name *Bulgar* itself is an example.[73] What does it mean? Are the Bulgars "the Mixed ones" or "the Rebels?" Pelliot was inclined to the latter interpretation but thought it possible that *bulgar* meant *les trouveurs*.[74] The Turkish etymology was challenged by Detschev; he assumed that *Bulgar* was the name given to the descendants of the Attilanic Huns by the Gepids and Ostrogoths and took it for Germanic, meaning *homo pugnax*.[75] Still another non-Turkish etymology has been suggested by Keramopoulos.[76] He takes *Bulgarii* to be *burgaroi*, Roman mercenaries garrisoned in the *burgi* along the *limes*. Without accepting this etymology, I would like to point out that in the second half of the sixth century a group of Huns who had found refuge in the empire were known as *fossatisii*.[77] *Fossatum* is the military camp.

In addition to the objective difficulties, subjective ones bedevil some scholars. Turkologists are likely to find Turks everywhere; Germanic scholars discover Germans in unlikely places. Convinced that all proto-Bulgarians spoke Turkish, Németh offered an attractive Turkish etymology of Asparuch; other Turkologists explained the name in a different, perhaps less convincing way.[78] Now it has turned out that Asparuch is an Iranian name.[79] Validi Togan, a scholar of profound erudition but sometimes biased by pan-Turkism, derived *shogun*, Sino-Japanese for *chiang chün*, "general," from the Qarluq title *sagun*.[80] Pro-Germanic bias led Schönfeld to maintain, in disregard of all chronology, that the Moors took over Vandalic names.[81]

---

[73] "Türk" is perhaps an even better one. In 1949, Kononov listed twelve etymologies and added one of his own ("Opyt analiza termina Türk," *SE* 1, 1949, 40-47). Clauson (1962, 87) denies any connection between the ethnic name which, according to him, is *Türkü* and *türk*, meaning "ripeness, maturity."

[74] Pelliot 1950, 224-230.

[75] "Der germanische Ursprung des bulgarischen Volksnamens," *Zeitschr. f. Ortsnamenforschung* 2, 1927, 199-216.

[76] Βλάχοι in Keramopoulos 1953, 334-336.

[77] *Getica* 266.

[78] Moravcsik, *BT* 2, 75-76.

[79] ’Ασπαυρουκις was *pitiaxš* in Iberia in the second century A.D. See the intaglio in *Mtskheta* 1 (Tiflis, 1958), 29, fig. 4; Abaev 1949, 157, 177; Duǐchev, *Archiv Orientální* 21, 1953, 353-356, and *Bulg. akad. naukite* 19, 1955, 335; V. Beshevliev, *ibid.*, 24, 1961, 5.

[80] Ibn Fadlan 1939, 293.

[81] The Moor Gildo, whose name Schönfeld (1911, 276) compared with Germanic Alalgildus, died in 397, almost thirty years before the Vandals landed in Africa. Numidic *gildo* means "king" (Friedrich 1954, 101).

In view of the difficulties concerning the study of Hun names—the inexactness inherent in transcriptions, the morphological changes which many names must have undergone, the ever present possibility that the names were Gothicized, the wide margin of error in the manuscript tradition——in view of all these one cannot help marveling at the boldness with which the problem of the Hunnish language has been and still is being attacked.[82]

---

[82] The etymologies suggested until 1957 are listed in Moravcsik, *BT* 2. To deal all of them would serve no useful purpose.

Although to historians familiar with the works of Franz Altheim the following lines may seem superfluous, I would like to state why I chose to refrain from discussing the etymologies of Hun names which he has offered in dozens of books and articles.

Altheim thought he found in Parthian and Pehlevi ostraca from Dura-Europos five Turkish, *a potiori* Hunnish names. In 1953 he published his discovery in a special book, *Das erste Auftreten der Hunnen*, as a chapter in another book, and in Hungarian and Argentine periodicals. W. B. Henning (*Gnomon* 26, 1954, 476-480) showed that these Hunnish names owe their existence solely to Altheim's ignorance of the script and languages he attempted to decipher. The wonderful Hunnish names *Ärk Qapxan*, *Quwratyl* or *Kirtül*, *Silil*, *Tarqānbäg*, and *Topčak* are actually *Wrwd msynk*, "Orodes the elder," *kpškly*, "shoemaker," *swlkly*, "bootmaker," *tlkčyny*, "trapper," and *sgp'n*, "master of the hounds."

In *Geschichte der Hunnen* 1, fig. 16, Altheim reproduced an inscribed pebble, said to be found in the Kuban region, and dedicated to it a whole chapter. Discerning in the inscription a Greek sentence, an Alanic adjective, and a Turkish word, he drew from it far-reaching conclusions for the history of the alphabet in the kingdom of the Kidaritae and the early spread of Christianity among the Huns. Actually the "inscription" is a galimatias like other "inscriptions" on the forgeries which a man in Sebastopol turned out in the early years of this century. Being ignorant of the language, he copied—always with some distortions—Greek sentences or Homeric verses from some elementary textbooks; cf. Kurz 1962, 553-554.

Whereas the Greek sources and the Slavic translation of Malalas render the name of a Hun in the Caucasus as Στύραξ, *Sturaks* (Moravcsik, *BT* 2, 292-293), the chronicle of John of Nikiu has *ěstērā*. It is well known how in the course of repeated translations from one language into another the names in the chronicle were cruelly distorted; see the literature referred by G. Graf 1944, 1, 471-472. Altheim (*Geschichte der Hunnen* 5, 253) chose the distorted form and etymologized *ěstērā* as Turkish **öz-tura, der selbst ein Setzschild ist*. One should think that he would reject Styrax, but he retains it and explains it as Turkish **öz-turač*. For kappa as a possible transcription of *č* he refers to Moravcsik, *BT* 2, 3, who lists κελεπῆς for *čelebi* and κιαούσης for *čauš* in chronicles of the fifteenth and sixteenth centuries. This is held sufficient to justify the transcription of *č* by kappa is a name attested for the sixth century. For the suffix *č* Altheim refers to Gabain 1950a, 59, § 22 (read 44), without stating that this *č* is a diminutive and affectionate suffix. Gabain gives two examples: *ögüčüm, mein Mütterchen*, and *atačïm, mein Väterchen*. Στύραζ, **öz-turač, der selbst ein Setzschirmchen ist* is not exactly an appropriate name for a Hun. These examples will I hope suffice.

GERMANIZED AND GERMANIC NAMES

Attila

The name[83] seems to offers neither phonetic nor semantic difficulties. Attila is formed from Gothic or Gepidic *atta*, "father," by means of the diminutive suffix *-ila*. It has often been compared to *batyushka*, the diminituve of *batya*, "father," as the Russian peasants used to call the tsar. In 1962 the Özbek poet Kāmil Nughman Yäsin addressed Nikita Khrushchev as "the dear father of the Özbek people."[84]

Attila is not a rare name. Venantius Fortunatus mentions a *regulus aulae domesticus* by that name.[85] Ætla, bishop of Dorchester,[86] was certainly not named after the Hun king.[87] Ætla seems to be concealed in some English place names (Attleford, Attlefield, Attleborough, Attlebridge).[88] Attila occurred as a monk's name in Switzerland as late as the twelfth century.[89]

Some scholars, impressed by the similarity of Attila to Ätil, the Turkish name of the Volga, equated the two names without caring for their phonetic and semantic relationship.[90] Rásonyi was slightly troubled by the final *-a* in Attila, but he thought that he could dispose of it by going back to what he took to be the earliest from. He regarded *-ας* in Priscus' Ἀττήλας as the Greek ending and *-a* in Kézai's *Ethela* as the old Magyar diminutive. In this way he arrived at Atil = Ätil, Volga or perhaps just "big water."[91] However, the thesis that Kézai, who dedicated his *Gesta Hungarorum* to Ladislaus IV (1272-1290), preserved genuine Magyar traditions about the Huns has long been refuted. Eighty years ago Hodgkin wrote: "The Hungarian traditions no more fully illustrate the history of Attila than the *Book of Mormon* illustrates the history of the Jews."[92] Rásonyi's explanation of the name in Priscus is unconvincing. As Latin *Attila* shows,

---

[83] To the forms listed by Moravcsik, *BT* 2, 79-80, add Nordic *Alli* and Old English *Ætla, Etla*. See F. Kluge, *Englische Studien* 21, 1895; A. Heusler, *ZfDA* 52, 1910, 104; Malone 1962, 128.

[84] *CAJ* 7:2, 1962, 148.

[85] *Vita s. Germani* in *MGH AA* IV:II, 23, 25.

[86] Beda, *Hist. eccles.* IV, 23.

[87] For other examples, see Radin 1919, 147.

[88] Ström 1939, 62, n. 1.

[89] *Das Necrologium des Cistercienser Priorates Münchenweiler* in *Collectanea Friburgensia*, N.F. 10, 1909, 60, 61.

[90] Moravcsik, *BT* 2, 80. The first was Bergmann, quoted by Inostrantsev 1926, 20.

[91] Rásonyi 1953, 349.

[92] Hodgkin 1898, 20. For a masterful analysis of the *Gesta Hungarorum*, see Macartney 1951, and 1953, 89-109.

the name ends in *-a*, not in *-l*; compare Ἀνσίλας = Ansila, Οὐνίλας = Hunila, Τωτίλας = Totila, Οὐλφίλας = Vulfila, and so forth.

Pritsak[93] offered an etymology of both the name of the king and that of the river. In his opinion *Atil*, *Adil*, and so forth, *meant* the same as Attila. He argues as follows:

1. In the Byzantine sources the name of the Volga appears as Ἀττίλαν[(acc)], Τίλ, Ἀστήλ, and Ἀτήλ.

2. These forms show that the Altaic name of the Volga is compounded of two words: ας and τιλ, τηλ, τελ. The second word could have the enlarged form τιλ + α.

3. There are two rivers called *Tal*; one flows into Lake Balkhash and the other one is in the region of the Syr-Darya.

4. Common Turkish *a/ä* changed in Chuvash into *i/ï* in very early times,

5. Chuvash *as*, preserved only in suffixed forms, means "great, big."

6. In Hunnish, which developed into Bulgar-Chuvash, *äs-tïl*, *äs-tïl-a* must have meant *grosse Wassermenge*, *grosser Fluss*, *grosses Meer*.

7. On analogy with *Čingis qa'an* and *dalai-in qa'an*, "oceanic = universal ruler," the Uigur title *köl bilgä qan*, which is said to mean "the qan whose mind is like a lake," and *Dalai lama*, "oceanic = universal religious lord," Attila, *ättïla* < *äs-tïla* means "oceanic > all embracing > universal (ruler)."

This is an ingenious but for many reasons unacceptable etymology. To begin with the arguments based on Chuvash words and forms, according to Benzing (the leading authority on Chuvash), Turkish *a/ä* changed to Chuvash *i/ï* not before the eleventh or twelfth century.[94] Even if there existed a Chuvash word *as*, "big, great, large," how can we know that in the language of the Huns in the fifth century the same word existed with the same meaning? [*At this point, one or two manuscript pages are missing.—Ed.*]

Bleda

Attila's older brother. The Greek sources have Βλήδας and Βλίδας, the Latin *Bleda*.[95] The Arian bishop whom Marcian sent as his ambassador

---

[93] Pritsak 1956, 404-419. His article takes some liberties with Priscus' text. In order to weaken the thesis of the Gothic origin of the name Attila, Pritsak maintains that Priscus negotiated with the king through the Roman Rusticius. But Maximianus, not Priscus, negotiated with Attila, and the interpreter was not Rusticius but Bigila who, as his names indicates, was most probably a Goth.

[94] *Fundamenta* I, 705; *ZDMG* 98, 1944, 24-27.

[95] Moravcsik *BT* 2, 91; Schönfeld 1911, 51.

to Geiseric,[96] and one of Totila's generals[97] had the same name. It is generally agreed that Bleda is Germanic, the short form of a name like OHG *Bladardus, Blatgildus, Blatgisus*.[98] Bleda of Marcellinus Comes (*s.a.* 442) appears in Bede's *Chronicle* in the strange form Blædla.[99] The English scribes "corrected" the name; they knew it as Blædla from oral tradition where the name was adapted to Ætla.[100]

'Εδέκων

One of Attila's counselors,[101] by birth a Hun.[102] Edekon is Grecized *Edika*;[103] the hypocoristic form applied to a person whose true name began with *Ed-*, such as Edivulf.[104]

Laudaricus

Killed in the battle at the *locus Mauriacus*. The Gallic chronicle of 511 calls him *cognatus Attilae*.[105] Laudaricus is Germanic *Laudareiks*.[106]

'Ονηγήσιος

Attila's prime minister.[107] Onegesius is evidently not Greek[108] but the Grecized form of a barbarian name. Hodgkin[109] boldly Hunnicized it into Onegesh. *Oneges* seems to be Hunigis,[110] as a spatharius of Theoderic the Great was called.[111] *-gis* appears in Greek transcriptions as γις and γης,[112] *huni-* is rendered by οὐνι- and ὀνω-.[113] *Hun-* in East Germanic

---

[96] Priscus, *EL* 151$_{26}$, 152$_1$ (Βλήδας).

[97] Procopius VII, 5, 1 (Βλέδας).

[98] Schönfeld 1911, 51.

[99] *CM* III, 303.

[100] E. Schröder, *ZfDA* 41, 1897, 28.

[101] Moravcsik, *BT* 2, 121.

[102] Priscus, *EL* 124$_7$.

[103] Cf. Stilika, Stilikon.

[104] There is no more reason to identify the Hun Edekon with Idikon or Edico, Odovacar's father (cf. Maenchen-Helfen 1947, 836-841) than with Edica, primas of the Sciri (*Getica* 277). The latter has nothing to do with Odovacar's father, as O. Vaĭnshteĭn (*Istorik marksist* 6, 143-146) convincingly demonstrated. According to Klebel (1957, 70, 118), the Bavarian name Etich, attested for the tenth century, is a later form of Edica.

[105] *CM* I, 66$_{615}$.

[106] Schönfeld 1911, 277.

[107] Moravcsik *BT* 2, 218.

[108] B. Krusch (*MGH, Scr. rer. Merov.* 7, 286) derived the name from 'Ονηγήσιος.

[109] 1898, 2, 74, n. 1.

[110] First suggested by K. V. Müllenhoff, *ZfDA* 10, 1855, 159.

[111] Cassiodorus, *Variae* III, 42.

[112] Schönfeld 1911, 145, 183, 269.

[113] Honoriopolis, Hunuricopolis, Unuricopolis, the former Hadrimetum, was named after Humeric. Cf. L. Schmidt 1942, 41, n. 2; Courtois 1955, 243, n. 6.

names is most probably the same as *hun* in OHG, OE, and ON names, namely either ON *húnn*, "cub of a bear, young man," or proto-Germanic *hūn*, "high."[114] Hunila, a Gothic bishop of about 400,[115] was born and named before the Huns crossed the Don.

I think Thompson is right in identifying Onegesius with Hunigasius, Attila's interpreter and spokesman in the *Vita s. Lupi*.[116] Rásonyi, taking *-sios* for the Greek ending, suggests a Turkish etymology: *oneki*, "twelve."[117] However, among the hundreds of transcriptions of foreign names listed by Moravcsik there is not one ending in *-esios*. Oneki would have been transcribed *Onekios*. Onegesius is spelled like Ὀνήσιμος, Ὀνησικράτης, and so forth.

Ῥάγναρις

Leader of the Ostrogoths in the last campaign against the East Romans in 552-554.[118] He was not ὁμόφυλος with them but a Hun from the Βίττορες.[119] Ragnaris is a Germanic name.[120]

Ruga

The Eastern sources call Attila's uncle Ῥούγας, Ῥοῦνας, and Ῥωίλας,[121] the Western Ruga,[122] Roas,[123] and Rugila.[124] These forms lead to Ruga > Rua and, with the suffix *-ila*, to Rugila > Ruila. Compare Rugemirus, Rugolf, and similar names.[125] The connection with Turkish *uruq*, favored by Markwart,[126] is phonetically unsound.

With the possible exception of Laudaricus and Ragnaris, these names were not the true names of the Hun princes and lords. What we have are Hunnic names in Germanic dress, modified to fit the Gothic tongue, or popular Gothic etymologies, or both. Mikkola thought Attila might go back to Turkish *atlïγ*, "famous";[127] Poucha finds in it Tokharian *atär*,

---

[114] See Maenchen-Helfen 1955b, 106.

[115] John Chrysostom, *Ep.* 14, *PG* 72, 618.

[116] Thompson 1948, 223. This is also the opinion of Malone, who, however, denies that the name is Germanic (1959, 106).

[117] Rásonyi 1961, 64.

[118] Procopius VIII, 25, 4; Agathias II, 13-14.

[119] So Agathias; Procopius calls him a Goth.

[120] Schönfeld 1911, 184; the name is not listed by Moravcsik.

[121] Moravcsik, *BT* 2, 260.

[122] *CM* I, 659$_{587}$, 661$_{589}$.

[123] *Getica* 105$_4$ (*roac* in *YZ*). The ending points to a Greek source, possibly Priscus.

[124] *CM* I, 658$_{112}$, 660$_{116}$.

[125] Schönfeld 1911, 279.

[126] *TP* 11, 1910, 664.

[127] *JSFOU* 30, 1933, 24.

"hero."[128] The first etymology is too farfetched to be taken seriously, the second is nonsense.

IRANIAN NAMES

Αἰσχμάνος

"Massaget," doryphorus in the Byzantine army about 540.[129] -manos is Iranian -mani- or -manah-, which is also transcribed manus, manes, and menes.[130] No satisfactory etymology has been offered for the first element.

Ἀμβαζούκης

A Hun chieftain in the Caucasus about 500.[131] "Having arms with power," Old Iranian *ama-bāzuka.[132]

Βάλας

Together with Sinnion, commander of six hundred Massaget auxiliaries, all mounted archers, in Belisarius' army in 533.[133] Balas, transcribed Βάλας, Οὐαλᾶς, Βλάσης, and Βλάσος, is a common Persian name.[134]

Hormidac

Leader of the preponderantly Hunnic hordes which in the winter 465/6 devastated Dacia ripensis and mediterranea. When one considers that poets often slightly changed foreign names to fit them in the meter— Valerius Flaccus, Argonautica VI, 96, has Batarna instead of Bastarna; in Dionysius, Periegesis 302, Σαρμάται became Σαμάται—it seems quite probable that Hormidac is Hormizdak, a common Middle Persian name in Sasanian times.

Χορσομάνος

"Massaget," bodyguard of Belisarius.[135] According to Abaev, Ossetic xorz-aman, "(having) good intentions."[136]

---

[128] CAJ 1, 1955, 291.

[129] Moravcsik, BT 2, 58.

[130] Justi 1895, 345-346. Lagarimanus, a Visigothic optimas (Ammianus XXXI, 3, 5), has an Iranian name with the same element.

[131] Moravcsik, BT 2, 65.

[132] I owe this etymology to my late friend Professor W. B. Henning.

[133] Procopius V, 16, 1.

[134] Justi 1895, 345-346; Abh. Göttingen, N.F. 15, 1, 1917, 27 (Balas, 449 A.D.).

[135] Procopius V, 16, 1.

[136] Abaev 1949, 169, 172. Herzfeld (1924, 186) compared the name with Khvarasman, lord of Mokan, in the Paikuli inscription.

Χορσομάντις

"Massaget," bodyguard of Belisarius.[137] Abaev takes it to be Ossetic *xors-amond*, "(having) good luck."[138]

Στύραξ and Γλώνης

The only source for the war between the Sabir and the Caucasian Huns, led by Styrax and Glones, is the *Chronography of Malalas*, preserved in a single manuscript, the codex Baroccianus,[139] which bristles with corrupt readings.[140] Some of them can be emended with the help of quotations in later works. Theophanes, in particular, often has the correct forms, confirmed by the Slavic translation of Malalas and, though to a very moderate degree, by John of Nikiu. In the codex Baroccianus the names of the two Huns are Τύραγξ and Γλώμ. Theophanes has Στύραξ and Γλώνης; the Slavic translation, *Sturaks* and *Eglon*; John of Nikiu, *Astêrâ* and *'Aglânôs*.[141] These forms show that the original Malalas text had *Styrax* and *Glones*.

Glones is the Grecized form of a Persian name. The general Γλώνης, commander of the garrison of Amida in 503, was "a Persian man."[142] Γλωνάζης was the *mōbadhan mōbadh* who "refuted" the Mazdakites in the great religious discussion which marked the beginning of the end of the heresy.[143] Although *les formes iraniennes des noms de Glonazes and Boazanes* [bishop of the Persian Christians] *ne se distinguent pas avec certitude*,"[144] there can be no doubt that the name of the highest Zoroastrian priest was Persian.

As Professor W. B. Henning informed me, Glones may be compared with Gołon-Mihran, a Persian commander in Armenia mentioned by Sebeos; there is a variant in other Armenian sources—Włon-Mihran. Henning took Włon-Gołon-Γλών for a late form of Vṛthraghna (*Varhrān, Bahrām*, and so forth.)

Styrax is a common Greek name.[145] Malalas altered the barbarian name of the Hun into one which was familiar to him and sounded better to his ear. Styrax is, I believe, the same as Στύρακος in an inscription

---

137 Procopius VI, 1, 21, 32-34.

138 Abaev 1949, 172.

139 Moravcsik, *BT* 1, 329-330.

140 For the best evaluation of Malalas, see Stein 1959, 2, 702-704 (*vulgaire au plus degré et sous tous les rapports*).

141 Moravcsik, *BT* 2, 114, 292.

142 Procopius I, 7, 33; I, 9, 4-19, 21, 23.

143 Theophanes, A.M. 6016, C. de Boor 1883, 170$_{12}$.

144 Christensen 1944, 360, n. 4.

145 Moravcsik, *BT* 2, 293; Preisigke 1922, 397.

from Gorgippia, a transcription of *sturak, which V. Miller connected with Orgor stur-, "big."[146]

Ζαβέργαν

Leader of the Kutrigur Huns about 550-560.[147] Justi compared the name with Ζάβαργος in two inscriptions from Tanais, assuming that -an was the patronymic -ana, -an.[148] Zabergan is a Persian name. In the inscription of Shapur I, 261, A.D., it occurs as Pahlavi zplk'n, Parthian zbrkn, and Greek Ζαβρίγαν.[149] Although Ζαβέργαν, the general who in 586 defended the fortress Chlomaron against the Romans,[150] might have been the commander of barbarian auxiliaries and, therefore, a barbarian himself, Ζαβεργάνης, a minister of Chosroes I,[151] was certainly a Persian.[152]

Ζαρτήρ

"Massaget" in the Byzantine army about 549.[153] The etymology has been found by Professor Henning.[154] The second half is the Persian divinity Tīr.[155] Zar-tīr is a twin brother of Zar-mihr, a name of the same period. Ζαρτής stands to Zarmihr in the same relationship as Τηριδάτης to Μιθριδάτης

TURKISH NAMES

In the Turkish "runic" inscriptions occur many names with the apposition čur (or čor),[156] for example,

Alči čur kuč bars;[157] Qan čur;[158] Tadïqïn čur;[159] Köl čur of the Tar-

---

[146] V. Miller, IAK 47, 1913, 89. Zgusta 1955, § 1148, referring to the Greek name Στύραξ, prefers a Greek etymology. He does not know the two Hun names.

[147] Moravcsik, BT 2, 128. Menander has τὸν Ζαβέρταν (EL 170$_{14,20}$) and τῷ Ζαβέργᾳ (170$_{24}$); he would, thus, have written Ζαβέργας.

[148] Justi 1895, 377, 523; Zgusta 1955, 109.

[149] Honigmann and Maricq 1953, 59.

[150] Theoph. Sim. II, 8, 7. For Ζαβέρτας, read Ζαβέργας, cf. M. de Saint Martin in Lebeau 1820, 10, 242.

[151] Procopius I, 23, 25-26; II, 8, 30; 26, 16-19; Anecd. II, 32.

[152] Mutafčiev (1932, 67) maintains that Zabergan was a Hephthalite. He does not state his reasons; there are none.

[153] Moravcsik, BT 2, 129.

[154] I retract the etymology I suggested in Oriens 10, 1957, 281.

[155] Ancient Tīrī; cf. W. B. Henning in a note to A. D. H. Bivar, "A Rosette Phialē Inscribed in Aramaic," BSOAS 24, 1961, 191.

[156] In the Runic script the word can be read čur or čor. The spelling in Tokharian and Tibetan texts indicates čor. The Byzantines transcribe the word by τζουρ or ζουρ.

[157] Radlov 1893, 319-320; Malov 1952, 37, Orkun 1941, 117 (he reads elic). Alči, "envoy," occurs also as a personal name (Malov 1951, 21).

[158] In a badly preserved inscription from Tuva (Kiselev, VDI 3 (8), 1939, 133).

[159] Thomsen 1924, 151; Malov 1951, 24, 31, 40.

duš;[160] Unagan čur;[161] Yigän čur;[162] Isbara tamγan čur;[163] Sabra tamγan čur;[164] . . . t čur;[165] Bäg čur.[166]

It has long been recognized that *čur* is a title or rank;[167] its meaning, however, has not been ascertained so far. Though all the men called *čur* were members of the aristocracy, their status was not the same. The *čur* who represented the Kirghiz qaghan at Köl Tegin's obsequies,[168] and Išbara bilgä köl (i) čur of the monument at Ikhe-khushotu[169] were high dignitaries; Bögü čur, to judge by the simple slab used for his epitaph,[170] held a modest position. The various *čur* named in Arabic sources[171]—all Turks as it seems—were great lords, but whether *čur* designated a rank in the military or administrative organization, was hereditary or not, higher or lower than *bäg* or *tarqan*, is anything but clear. The same is true for the *chari* and *chara* = *čur* in the Khotanese documents.[172] *Čor* (*ḫjor*) in the Tibetan names Drugu čor, 'Bug čhur, and Khri-skugs-ḫjor in the old Shan-shan kingdom and western Kansu[173] are Turkish *čur*,[174] but what it means is not known.

---

[160] Radlov 1893, 261; Malov 1959, 47; Giraud 1960, 80.

[161] Thomsen 1912, 186, 188.

[162] Samoïlovitch in Kotwicz and Samoïlovitch 1926, 21; Malov 1959, 28.

[163] Radlov 1893, 322; Malov 1952, 40.

[164] Malov 1959, 10.

[165] Radlov 1893, 322; Malov 1952, 40.

[166] Malov 1959, 61-62.

[167] Radlov 1893, 372; F. W. K. Müller 1915, 34; Thomsen 1924, 172; Németh 1939, 27 and *in JA* 1951, 70.

[168] Malov 1951, 27, 33, 42. Ïnanču occurs both as a title and personal name (Orkun 1941, 4, 157).

[169] Samoïlovitch in Kotwicz and Samoïlovitch 1926, 2-24.

[170] Iu. L. Aranchyn, *Epigrafika vostoka* 5, 1951, 77.

[171] Two governors of Damascus (Zambaur 1927, 28, 29); conqueror of Damascus (Zambaur 1927, 29); governor of Azerbaijan (Zambaur 1927, 177); Spuler 1952, 66); governor of Cairo (Zambaur 1927, 27); ambassador of the prince of Fergana (Barthold in *Encyclopedia of Islam*, 201); ruler of Wakhsh and Halaward (Barthold in *Encyclopedia of Islam*, 74, n. 6; Zambaur 1927, 204); lord of Üzgänd (Barthold in *Encyclopedia of Islam*, 157); founder of a family of governors of Khorasan (Justi 1895, 301; Barthold, *Encyclopedia of Islam* 1, 77; Zambaur 1927, 29). The list could be easily multiplied.

[172] *ttrūki chāri* (Bailey 1939, 9); *Maṃgali chārā ttāttānä=Mängli čur tutuq* (Bailey 1949, 48); *Saikarä ttrūkā chārä=Syqyr turk čur* (ibid., 50); *Yaṃgai chārä=Yangy čur* (Bailey in *Togan's armagan*, 202).

[173] Bacot 1940, 45; Thomas 1951, 2, 175, 203, 230, 236, 276. On *Bug-čor*, cf. J. Bacot, *JA* 244, 1956, 145; Clauson, *JA* 244, 1956, 245, and *JA* 255, 1957, 12; Macdonald, *JA* 250, 1962, 541; in an annotation to Bacot's article, Pelliot identified *Bug-čhor* as *Mo-cho* (see n. 177).

[174] It would not be the only Turkish rank or title known to and taken over by the Tibetans. A Tibetan princess had the title *ko-t'un, qatun* (*Chiu T'ang shu* 196a, 6a).

The Chinese sources are of no help either. In the dynastic annals a considerable number of *čur* among Turkish-speaking groups are named. As in the inscriptions, *ch'o*[175] (=*čur*) is often added to another title: for instance, in A ch'o,[176] Mo ch'o,[177] P'ei-lo ch'o,[178] or Shih-chien ch'o.[179] It frequently occurs in the names of qaghans and other persons of high rank,[180] sometimes preceded *and* followed by more titles, as in the monstrous Hsieh to teng-li ku ch'o mi-shih ho chü-lu ying yi chien li pi-ch'ieh k'o-han = El töbär täŋri qut čur toɣmïs alp chü-lu ying yi chien li bilgä qaɣan.[181] But none of the chroniclers stated exactly what *čur* meant.[182]

The closer one studies the titles of the steppe peoples in the Chinese annals, the more perplexing are the constant contradictions. They are only partly due to misunderstandings on the part of the recorders, although the Chinese, bewildered by the complexities of social and political systems

---

[175] Ancient *tś'įwät*; cf. *T'ang shu shih yin* 22, 3b. *č'war*; cf. Chavannes and Pelliot 1913, 249, n. 1.

[176] For *A-po ch'o*, Apa čur, Kirghiz ruler (790-795), see Hamilton 1955, 140.

[177] Died in 716 (Chavannes 1903, 346). P. Pelliot, *TP* 26, 1929, 151; R. N. Frye, *HJAS* 1951, 120; Hamilton 1955, 147. In 698, the Chinese changed his title into *chan-ch'o*, "decapitate the *ch'o*" (Liu 1958, 163, 217, 652).

[178] Turkish *Boila cur* (Hirth 1899, 105).

[179] A high rank with the Tongra (*T'ang shu* 217b, 7a); cf. Chavannes 1903, 321.

[180] For instance,

A-shih-na chu-po ch'o, about 682 (Chavannes 1903, 315, 339). *Chu-po* seems to be a title;

A-shih-na ch'ü ch'o chung chieh, a western Turk, about 700 (Chavannes 1903, 315);

Chü pi shih ch'o su-lu, a western Turk, about 777 (Chavannes 1903, Errata supplémentaires *ad* p. 81).

Mo-yen ch'o, Bayan cur, Uyghur ruler (747-759) (Hamilton 1955, 189);

Ni-shu ch'o, a western Turk about 640 (Chavannes 1903, 349); cf. the names Ni-shu, Ni-shu baɣa šad, Ni-shu ärkän (*ibid*);

Pi-ch'ia ye-hu tun a-po i-chien ch'o, Bilgä yabɣä to n a apa irkän čur, ruler of the three Qarluq tribes in 746 (Chavannes, *TP* 5, 1904, 76). *Tun* is the Turkish title *toŋa* (Malov 1951, 432), *ttäṃga* in Khotanese (Bailey 1939, 87), *tuñā* in Tocharian (W. Krause, *ZDMG* 1955, p. *69*). It often occurs in Chinese transcriptions, *e.g.*, Tun a-po (Chavannes 1903, 369); Tun pi-ch'ia (*ibid.*); Tun baɣa tarqan (Hamilton 1955, 140). Tun chien ch'eng (Chavannes 1903, 10) is "the town of the Tun (i) chien"; cf. *Tunkāth*, chief town of Ïläq (Barthold, *Enc. of Islam*, 172);

T'u huo hsien ku ch'o, leader of the Türgäš, about 740 (Chavannes 1903, 371);

Wu li ch'o, western Turk, about 640 (Chavannes 1903, 350);

Wu mo choo, about 626 (Liu 1958, 139, 198);

Ch'u mu k'un chih mi ch'o of the Pa hsi mi, about 716 (Liu 1958, 225);

Mei lu ch'o, about 730 (Liu 1958, 793).

[181] Uyghur ruler (*T'ang shu* 217a, 5b). *Mi-shi* could also transcribe *yarutmïš* (Hamilton 1955, 160).

[182] In a gloss to the *T'ung chien kang mu* (Hirth 1899, 6, n. 1), *čur* is defined as *ta ch'en*, "minister," evidently a guess, and not a good one.

so unlike their own, must often have been tempted to twist titles and ranks until they somehow fitted their ideas of a state, be it ever so barbaric. The nomadic societies, especially those nearer to China and therefore more exposed to her influence, were not unchangeable entities. As testified by the numerous Chinese titles in the Turkish inscriptions, the barbarians saw themselves forced to take over a number of institutions from the hated and admired empire. This meant more than the addition of a set of Chinese titles; it meant a marked change in the political structure. The old titles themselves, as far back as they can be traced, were by no means uniform. Some of them seem to be rooted in the shamanistic oligarchy of an early period, becoming unstable as the functions to which they belonged were withering away; others were closely connected with the ascendancy of the qaghanate. If the pictures the Chinese drew of a given nomadic society differ from one another, at times in the same chapter of the annals, the cause has to be sought primarily in the continuous, now slow, now accelerated shift of importance and power from one group to another. Confronted with reports which contradicted one another because they referred to different periods—not necessarily far apart—the chroniclers often saw no way out but to tuck together what they found in their material and leave it to the reader to make sense out of it. One of the titles which must have puzzled the Chinese was *čur*.

About 635, Sha-po-lo tieh-li-shih qaɣan divided the western Turks in ten tribes. The five Tu-lu tribes, forming the left division, were under the five "great *čur*," the Nu-shih-pi tribes of the right division under the five "great *ch'i-chin*."[183] The titles of the chiefs were as follows:

Tu-lu	Nu-shih-pi
Lü čur[184] (tribe Ch'u-mu-k'un)	Ch'üeh ch'i-chin[186] (A-hsi-chieh)
Ch'üeh[185] čur (Hu-lu-wu)	Ch'üeh ch'i-chin (Ko-shu)

---

[183] *Chiu T'ang shu* 194a, 3b-4a; *T'ang shu* 225b, 6a.

[184] *Lü=ch'ü-lü*. In the transcriptions of names and titles *ch'ü-lü*, *ch'ü-li*, and *ch'üeh-lü* are often interchanged. Whether in a given case they render *köl*, *küli*, or *külüg* (Pelliot 1926, 210, note; Hamilton 1955, 96, n. 8; Clauson 1962, 89) cannot be determined unless the man so named is also mentioned in Arabic texts. As Marquart (1898b, 181-182) recognized, Baɣa tarqan, Ch'üeh-lü of the Ch'u-mu, who in 738 killed the Türgäš Su-lu, is Ṭabarī's *kūrṣul*, misspelled for *kūlṣur = köl čur*; for Arabic *s=* Turkish *c*. Cf. Pelliot 1950, 72. On *kol*, "lake", cf. L. Bazin, *Revue de l'histoire des religions* 149, 1956; Hamilton 1962, 52, n. 10.

[185] See the preceding note. For the weak enunciation of the final *t* in *ch'iuet*, see Boodberg 1951, 2-3.

[186] For *ch'i-chin*, see Hamilton 1955, 98, n. 1.

T'un[187] čur (She-she-t'i)   T'un sha-po[189] (Pa-sai-kan)
Ho-lo-shih čur (Tu-ch'i-shih)   Ni-shu ch'i-chin (A-hsi-chieh)
Ch'u-pan čur[188] (Shu-ni-shih)   Ch'u-pan ch'i-chin (Ku-shu)

The "great čur" obviously have the same rank as the "great ch'i-chin."
But we have lists of high dignitaries of the western Turks in which the ranks
are quite differently arranged: yi-chin, ch'ü-li čur, yen-hung-ta, hsieh-li-fa,
t'u-t'un, ch'i-chin,[190] The ch'u-lu čur is also the second in a list of high
dignitaries of the Turks in T'ang Shu,[191] but he again heads the list of the
officials of the Northern Turks.[192] Both lists end with ch'i-chin.

It seems that Sha-po-lo promoted the ch'i-chin from a lower rank to
that of the čur. The whole system was an innovation, and not a stable
one. According to it, there should be no čur in the right division. But
the two ch'üeh čur whom Mi-she, leader of the Tu-lü, killed in 659 were
Nu-shih-pi chieftains.[193] The Kirghiz seemed not to have been divided
into a left and right division. Yet they had their külüg čur's, as, for example,
Külüg čur Baina Saŋun, who was buried by the Barluk River in Tuva.[194]

One gets the impression that čur was a rather general term, whose
specific meaning was determined by the preceding adjective: the great
čur, the minor čur, the wise čur, the loyal čur and so forth. Still, the čur
of the western and northern Turks were all men of considerable importance.[195] This was not so with the Uyghurs in the eighth century.

The Mahrnāmag[196] lists eleven Manichaean auditores whose names end
in čur. None of them was a high official. The princes are called tegin.
The "rulers" have either Chinese titles[197] or are addressed as tiräk and
il ügäsi. Then follow officials with the title ügä. Of the following "lords"

---

[187] T'un stands for t'u-t'un, Turkish Tudun; cf. T'u-t'un ch'o, an Eastern
Turk (Chiu T'ang shu 194a, 9a). T'un ch'o was also the title of an Uyghur dignitary
(T'ang shu 217a, 3a).

[188] Turkish čopan, an Iranian loanword (Markwart 1929, 85).

[189] Sha-po or sha-po-lo is Turkish išbara (Pelliot 1926, 211); Mehmed Fuad Köprülü,
KsCA 1, Erg. Band 4, 1938, 341-343.

[190] Chiu T'ang shu 194b, 1a; Chavannes 1903, 21.

[191] 215a, 36.

[192] Ch'ü-lü ch'o, a-po, hsieh-li-fa, t'u-t'un, ch'i-chin (Chiu T'ang shu 194a, 1a; Wu
tai shih chi 74, 6a; Hamilton 1955, 96-97).

[193] Chavannes 1903, 72; cf. also page 35. The five čur f the Tu-lu and the five
chi'-chin of the Nu-shih-pi are still mentioned in 715 (Liu 1958, 170, 258).

[194] Radlov 1893, 309, Malov 1952, 22-23.

[195] In the Bilgaγqa, an epitaph of 735, the Köl čur are the leaders among the Tarduš
bäg (Orkun 1941, 1, 70; Gabain 1950a, 136; N. Poppe, HJAS 1951, 648).

[196] F. W. K. Müller 1912.

[197] Tutuq, čigši.

of towns only two are *čur*. The other *čur* are a physician, a scribe, and various lower officials. The last one is the long list is *kül čur*.

The names of the Uyghur *čur* are as follows:[198]

kwrtl' čwr = *körtlä*, "beautiful," *čur*.
bgr'k čwr = *bägräk*, "princely," *čur*.
yδδwγ čwr = *yduq*, "holy," *čur*.
lywl'ng xwm'r čwr. *Liu-lang* is evidently Chinese. Benveniste takes *xwm'r* to be Buddhist Sogdian *γwm'r*, **humār*, "consolation, encouragement."[199]
xr'kwl l" čwr. Whether this is one name or two is not clear. *xr'kwl* = *qara qul*.[200] *L" might* be Chinese.
'wn čwr. Perhaps *on*, "ten."[201]
by'mnwrz čwr. A Sogdian name.
twnk whmn čwr. Another Sogdian name.
sp'r xr' čwr = *išbara qara čur*.
'lp cwr = *alp*, "hero," *čur*.
qwyl čwr = *köl čur*.

In the *Mahrnāmag*, *čur* is not the designation of a function. If it was an inherited title, it amounted at best to a honorific adjunct to a name. We know too little about Uyghur society to determine the causes of this devaluation of *čur*. Life at the court of the Manichaean qaghan was not the same as in the steppe. The change, the disintegration of the old order which made *čur* an empty title, was possibly the result of the strong impact of Sogdian civilization. Together with the new religion, new arts and crafts, new techniques, a new division of labor came into the life of the herdsmen. The *Mahrnāmag* mirrors an urban civilization. Those Uyghurs who returned to their more primitive life after the collapse of their kingdom kept *čur* as a title as, for example, Na hsie ch'o t'e-le = Nahid

---

[198] With Prof. W. B. Henning's help I have transcribed the names in the usual way.

[199] *Ḥumār-tegin* and *Ḥumār-bäg* (Pelliot 1950, 211; Zambaur 1927, 102).

[200] *Qul* in *qaraqul* has not necessarily always had the meaning "slave". Originally *qul* was "the outsider, foreigner," living within the tribe but outside the connubium (Bernshtam 1946, 125). The man whom Kulug Togan (Malov 1952, no. 44) addresses as his "white *qul*," was certainly not his slave, nor was the high-ranking officer Qul Apa Uruγu (in a military document from Miran, Thomsen 1912, 189) a slave; cf. also Qul Bort in a Talas inscription (Orkun 2, 137). Until recently the T'ien shan Kirghiz gave a child born after all the children in the family had died a name ending in *qul*; in this case *qul* actually meant "slave" (S. M. Abramzon, *SMAE* 12, 1949, 107).

[201] Rásonyi 1961, 63.

("Venus") čur tägin.[202] The latest datable Uyghur name of the type *x-čur* is Ïnal čur; [203] it occurs in an inscription of the tenth century.[204]

The meaning of *čur*, like that of any other title, was bound to change in time. A closer study of the titles of the Turks and non-Turks in the post-T'ang period may reveal more instances of the restricted or modified use of *čur*. But it is doubtful whether much more can be learned from Chinese sources. They certainly cannot tell us what the archaic meaning of *čur* was.

Pelliot was inclined to assume that *čur* was an Avar word; he even thought it might ultimately be of Indo-European origin.[205] But no such Avar word exists. I know of no word in the vocabulary of the Hsiung-nu, T'o-pa, or any supposedly Altaic people that might be regarded as an older form of, or related to, *čur*.[206] We know practically nothing of

---

[202] Chavannes and Pelliot 1913, 249.

[203] F. W. K. Müller 1915, 23, 34; Pelliot 1950, 182, n. 3.

[204] Hamilton (1955, 143) dates it in 947. The Turkish name čk'yn čwr bylk' č. čur bilgä occurs also in the Sogdian documents from Mt. Murg (Lifshits 1962, 47, 51).

[205] *TP* 28, 1931, 449. Russian *čur*, "go away," of obscure origin, has of course nothing to do with our *čur*.

[206] Since Gabain 1950a (Nachtrag zum Glossar) has pointed out that in Tokharian texts our title is written *cor*, some historians as, e.g., Altheim (*Geschichte* 1, 8), and phi-lologists as, e.g., J. Németh (*Voprosy iazykoznaniia* 12, 6, 1963, 128), take the word for Tokharian, borrowed by the Turks; Németh calls it even an Iranian (sic) loanword. Had these scholars looked up von Gabain's source (Sieg, Siegling, and Schultze 1931, 50 and 63), they would have seen that the authors themselves regard *cor* as a Turkish title. Poucha (1955, 101) has "appelatic Turcica?" At my request, Professor W. Winter checked the passage. He wrote to me:

"Das Wort ist insgesamt zweimal belegt: einmal auf einem winzigen Fetzen der Avadānasammlung A 399-404 in der Form des Akk. Sg; einmal in A 382 a 3 auf dem Rest eines isolierten Blattes, der eine metrische Widmung enthält, in dem sich eine Reihe nichttocharischer Wörter findet, die wohl die Stifter des in a 2 erwähnten Buddhabildes sind. Unglücklicherweise ist an dieser Stifterliste beinahe alles unklar. Wir haben// alle Brüder; bhek uri helkis āpruts lpik kokuntāṃ hkhonāñc kārā cor lpi ·o//. In *bhek* und *kārā* möchte man natürlich turkisch *bäg* und *qara* sehen, aber wie steht es dann um den Rest? . . . Das Einzige, was sich wirklich vertreten lässt, ist die Behauptung, *cor* im A-Text sei aller Wahrscheinlichkeit nach ein fremdes Wort, und zwar entweder ein Titel oder ein Name eines Mannes. Da sehr viel dafür spricht, dass die Stifter der A-Handschriften Türken waren, kann man wohl einen Schritt weiter gehen und vermuten, dass der Träger dieses Namens oder Titels ein Türke war. Das macht aber natürlich *cor* noch nicht zu einem türkischen Wort oder besser einem echttürkischen Wort. Entleh-nung aus dem Tocharischen ins Türkische ist grundsätzlich als möglich anzusehen, es gibt aber nichts, was die Möglichkeit zur Wahrscheinlichkeit macht: eine tocharische Etymologie kann ich nicht angeben. Zum Vokalismus ist lediglich zu bemerken, dass eine wirkliche Sicherheit über die Vorform von *cor* kaum zu erzielen ist; allerdings deutet

the Indo-European languages spoken at the borders of China in early times. Yet there are some documents which lead further back and are more revealing than those discussed so far.

The date of the Turkish inscriptions from the Talas Valley and the shores of the Issyk-kul is the sixth and seventh centuries.[207] They were the epitaphs of warriors who stood culturally much lower than the Turks in the Orkhon region, not to speak of the Uyghurs. The letters do not have the more or less standardized forms they have on the Orkhon, and the lines are so irregularly arranged that it is often difficult to read them. We may hope to learn from the Talas inscriptions, if not the original, at least the more primitive meaning of čur.

There is, first, an inscription found by Kallaur in the district Aulie Ata. It has been translated three times,[208] and although a few words are still obscure, the content is clear: A man named čur says farewell to his thirty oγlan, his loyal men, and to the pleasures and blessings of the world; he leaves behind his widow and oγlan čur.

There is, second, a much longer inscription from the same region with a similar content, known since the 1890's, but translated only in 1926 by Németh. He had to use a squeeze published by Heikel, the same text which Malov translated some years later.[209] In the fall of 1961 the inscribed stone was rediscovered in situ, photographed and edited by Ch. Dzhumagulov.[210] It turned out that Heikel's squeeze was imperfect; both Németh's and Malov's translations are therefore obsolete. Dzhumagulov's new translation probably is not final either; the sequence of the lines is still not quite certain and some letters are unreadable. Nevertheless, further study will not change what matters to us: A man bearing the "heroic" name

---

das erhaltene -u- in hkhatuṃ (wenn = qatun) und in hkutteṃ (wenn = qutïn) wohl darauf hin, dass eher mit -o-Vokalismus ausserhalb von Tocharisch A zu rechnen ist."

Ramstedt 1951, 77, derived čur from Avestan śura, "strong, heroic." This is one of those etymologies which nothing recommends but a vague assonance and an unrestrained imagination.

In his letter to me of April 10, 1967, Professor O. Pritsak maintained that čor "cannot be of Turkic origin because of č which never occurs in original Turkic words." But in Handbuch der Orientalistik, Altaistik, Turkologie, p. 33, published in 1963, Pritsak included č- in the "alttürkische" initial consonants. G. Doerfer (UJb 59, 1-2, 1967) includes č- in the list of initial consonants common to all Altaic languages.

[207] A. v. Gabain, Anthropos 48, 3-4, 1953, 539; Kliashtornyĭ 1964, 53.

[208] (1) Melioranskiĭ (1899, 271-272, after an imperfect rubbing); (2) Németh 1926, 140-141, with the reproduction of pl. 12 in Heikel 1918; (3) S. E. Malov, 1929, 799-802 (with commentary not repeated in Malov 1951, 74-75). Orkun 2, 134, follows Malov.

[209] Németh 1926, 137-138; Orkun 1941, 3, 134-135; Malov 1959, 60-61.

[210] Nakhodki v Kirgizii 1962, 23-27, 39, see also 7-10; Epigrafika Kirgizii 1, 18-21.

Qara Čur leaves behind his loyal (or close) friends, the thirty *oγlan*, and his son *Qara Čur*.

Thirty *oγlan* occur in a third, recently found inscription. Again a man is separated from them. His name is Aguš, he is *sü čur*.[211] The phrase *otuz oγlan* occurs once more in a fourth, newly found, very mutilated inscription.[212]

In the Yenisei inscriptions *oγlan* means "boy, son, warrior"; in those on the Orkhon, "son of someone, hidalgo, prince."[213] Malov thinks the thirty *oγlan* were the sons of the deceased and their comrades,[214] which obviously cannot be true for all four inscriptions. But why then the recurrent thirty? When one considers that the armies of nearly all Turkic peoples were divided into units of tens and multiples of tens, it seems much more likely that the thirty *oγlan* were a military unit. It could be a coincidence that a document from the Tun-huang, written in runes, mentions thirty "men of rank and distinction" under the command of a higher officer.[215] But the men in another inscription who, led by a nobleman, rode nine times around the tomb of their lord, likewise numbered thirty.[216]

In the inscriptions the thirty *oγlan* are under a *čur*, whose son is also a *čur*. With the western Turks under Išbara qaghan the title and rank of "eminent *čur*" were handed down from father to son. The same must have been true for the more primitive tribes in the Semirech'e.

The Talas inscriptions permit, I believe, only one interpretation of *čur*: It must mean "commander, leader, captain." Compared to the great Tarduš köl čur, the Čur and Qara čur of our inscriptions were minor figures. They had thirty men under their command; the Tardus officer must have led thousands. But both he and they were "commanders, captains." Our interpretation is also borne out by the rank of Aguš in the third Talas inscription. He was *su čur*, "*čur* of the troops." This corresponds to *sü baši*, "captain of the troops," in the Toňukuk inscription and in the Vienna manuscript of the Qutaδγu Bilig.[217]

---

[211] *Nakhodki v Kirgizii* 1962, 18-19; *Epigrafika*, 28-29.

[212] *Nakhodki v Kirgizii* 1962, 15-16; *Epigrafika*, 24-25.

[213] *Oγlan* and *oγul* were apparently not as interchangeable as in later usage. Where the context permits to distinguish between "child(ren)" and "boy(s), son(s)," *oγlan* has the latter meaning. *Oγlan toγdïm* (Orkun 1941, 3 105; Malov 1952, 57) can only mean "I was born a boy." A man leaves behind his wife, his only daughter, and two *oγlan* (Radlov 1895, 320; Orkun 1941, 3, 134; Malov 1952, 38). "Seventy thousand *oγlan*" (Radlov 1895, 330; Orkun 1941, 3, 134; Malov 1952, 49) are evidently "seventy thousand warriors." Cf. Pokrovskaia 1961, 15-17; Hamilton 1962, 32.

[214] Malov 1951, 403.

[215] Thomsen 1912, 219.

[216] Malov 1952, 63.

[217] *Ibid.*, 369, 423.

Κουαρτζιτζούρ (for short *Τζούρ*), one of the eight tribes, *γεννεαί*, or units of the military administration, *θέματα*, of the Pechenegs in the tenth century,[218] were **küärči čur*, "the *čur* with the pigeon-blue horse-tail flag."[219] The Pecheneg *čur* had nothing to do with the fire of the hearth or the drum, they were neither shamans nor judges, but horsemen and leaders of horsemen. In the language of the Pechenegs *čur* must have meant "commander, leader." Among the Kirghiz the word has preserved its military connotations to the present day. It is true, it does not amount to much but it shares this fate with many feudal-military terms. As John Smith, Esq. < *scutarius* no longer bears a shield, so the Kirghiz *čoro* no longer rides into battle at the head of his *oylans*. In everyday language *čoro* means "boy, lad" in the household of a nobleman.[220] In the epic, however, *čoro* is still "the warrior, companion in arms, one of the troop [*druzhennik*]."[221] Now we can turn to the Huns.

In his account of the war in Lazica in 556,[222] Agathias[223] mentions among the Byzantine officers of barbarian origin a Hun by the name of *'Ελμίγγειρος*; he was *lochagos*, commander of a *lochos*, a regiment. Agathias also mentions the name and the nationality of Elmingeiros' superior: He was the *taxiarchos* Dabragezas of the people of the Antes. In order to overcome the difficulties of transmitting orders, a formidable task in mercenary armies of as many different nationalities as the armies of Justinian and his successors, barbarians of the same regions were kept together in the same units. Dabragezas[224] must have come from those Antes who, according to Procopius, together with Huns and Sclaveni, "lived across the Danube or not far from it."[225] Elmingeiros was probably from the same region. The battle in which he distinguished himself took place in the spring of 556.

In the summer of the same year Justin, commander of the army in Phasis, sent one of the *taxiarchoi*, a Hun by the name of *'Ελμινζούρ*, with

---

[218] Constantine Porphyrogenitus, Moravcsik 1949, $166_{17, 21}$' 168_{35}.

[219] G. Györffy (*AOH* 18, 1965, 77), J. Németh ("Zur Kenntnis der Petschenegen," *KCsA* 1, 1921-25, 220-221, and 1930, 3), and Menges (1945, 267) assume that the color of the horses was meant. On *čur* as a family name among the Pechenegs settled in Hungary, see G. Györffy, *KCsA*, Ergänzungsband 6, 1939, 440.

[220] K. K. Iudakhin, *Kirgizsko-russkiĭ slovar'*, 133; in the Turkish edition, *Kirgiz sözlügü* 1, 281.

[221] *Manas* 368. The *druzhina* of Manas consists of forty *čoro* (Abramzon 1946, 125, 127). Cf. K. K. Iudakhin, *Kirgizsko-russkiĭ slovar'*, 868. A warrior in the legend of the origin of the Sayaq is called Qara *čoro* (Vinnikov 1956, 148).

[222] For the date, see Stein 1959, 2, 813.

[223] III, 21, ed. Bonn, 186.

[224] The name may contain Slavic *dobry*, "good."

[225] Procopius V, 27, 2.

two thousand horsemen to occupy the fortress Rhodopolis.[226] In the index
of his edition of Agathias, Niebuhr listed Elminzur with the note, *fortasse
idem cum praecedente*, i.e., *Elmingeiro.*"[227] Stein identified Elmingeir and
Elminzur.[228] It would be a strange coincidence indeed if in the same army
and in the same months, there had been two Hun officers bearing names
as similar as Elmingeir and Elminzur.

It is not necessary to know the exact foreign sounds represented by
the Greek letters,[229] nor what the names mean, to recognize that the first
is compounded of *elmin* and *geir*, the second of *elmin* and *zur*. If Elmingeir
and Elminzur were actually two names of the same man, the change from
-geir to *-zur* could correspond to his promotion from *lochagos* to *taxiarchos*,
or, to use the Latin terms, from *tribunus* to *dux*.[230] This would support
our assumption that *čur* means "captain, leader."

There are three more Hunnish names ending in *-zur*:

1. After the collapse of Attila's kingdom, his kinsmen Emnetzur and
Ultzindur occupied Oescus, Utum, and Almus on the right bank of the
Danube.[231] On the analogy with Elminzur, Emnetzur must be Emne-tzur.

2. Another name of this type is Ultzinzures, Οὐλτίνζουροι.[232] Together with other Hunnic tribes they followed Dengizich in the second
war with the Goths.

3. Priscus' Ἀμίλζουροι, Ἰτίμαροι, Τούνσουρες, and Βοῖσκοι appear in Jordanes as Alpidzuri, Alcildzuri, Itimari, Tuncarsi, and Boisci.[233]
The explanation of the difference between Priscus and Jordanes was found
by Krasheninnikov:[234] The archetype of the Jordanes manuscripts had
alpidzuros, with the emendation *alcildzuros* written over it, which leads
to **alpildzuros*. Only this form is compatible with the name in Priscus
which, therefore, must be emended to read **ΑΛΠΙΛΖΟΥΡΟΙ > ΑΜΙΛ-
ΖΟΥΡΟΙ*.

In the Chinese annals, the titles of tribal leaders are sometimes used
for the tribes themselves. In Han times the Chinese spoke of the Sai wang,

---

[226] Agathias LV, 15, ed. Bonn, 236.

[227] Ed. Bonn, 403.

[228] Stein 1959, 2, 815.

[229] Agathias took great care in transcribing foreign names as faithfully as the Greek
alphabet permitted. His Ναχοργάν (III, 2, 17) is closer to the Persian word (Christensen
1944, 21, n. 3) than Menander's Ναχόεργαν, his Χλωθάριος preferable to Procopius'
Κλοαθάριος; cf. Schönfeld 1911, 140.

[230] On ταξίαρχος = *dux*, see Stein 1959, 2, 814-815.

[231] *Getica* 266.

[232] *Ibid.*, 128₂₂; Agathias V, 11, ed. Bonn, 300; Moravcsik *BT* 2, 230.

[233] *Getica* 90₁₀₋₁₁. To v. 11, add *Alpizuros*, *Lizuros* which Jiménez de Rada read
in his copy of the *Getica*; cf. Alarcos 1935, 18.

[234] Krasheninnikov 1915, 42, n. 1.

the "Saka kings," under the T'ang of the Hu-lu-wu chüeh, She-she-t'i tun, and Shu-ni-shi ch'u-pan.[235] This was not a misunderstanding on the part of the Chinese, as some scholars thought.[236] To the Tibetans the kingdom of the second dynasty of the northern Turks was known as Bug-čor = Mo ch'o.[237] Did they make the same mistake as the Chinese? Should we assume that Constantine Porphyrogenitus was also misinformed when he spoke of the *küärčičur? And before him Priscus about the *alpildzuri, or, as we now may say, the *alpilčur? This is most unlikely. Even today Kirghiz tribes, subtribes, and clans exist which call themselves čoro and x-čoro: Qara-coro (tribe), Čoro, Zol-čoro (subtribes), Boro-čoro, Ono-čoro (clans). The Kazakh have the clans Zhan-čura, Bai-čura, and Qara-čura.[238]

In an epitaph from Uibat in Tuva the deceased glories that he exerted himself for the people il čur.[239] Whatever the origin of čur may be, in the inscription from Uibat il čur is as Turkish as il qan and il baši. Hunnish *Alpilčur cannot be anything else but alp-il-čur, "hero-people-čur."[240]

The thesis that the Huns spoke a Turkish language has a long history behind it. Its earlier phase is no longer of interest. The later is still with us. Taking the identity of the Huns and the Hsiung-nu for granted, some scholars have no doubt and need no proof that the Huns spoke the same language as the "eastern" Huns, which they take to be Turkish. By the same reasoning the Norman conquerors of England should have spoken Old Norse.

That the Huns included Turkish-speaking tribes can be regarded as established only if a number of personal and tribal names of the Huns are undoubtedly as Turkish as orfèvre is French, goldsmith English, and Goldschmied German. One such name is *alp-il-čur.

The formal analysis of Turkish-sounding Hunnic names requires utmost caution. If English were as unknown as the language of the Huns, one could conjecture that fe- in female is a prefix and -dict in maledict a suffix to the root male.

-gir, like čur, occurs in both a Hunnic personal name (Elmingir) and the name of a tribe of the Pontic Huns, named twice in Jordanes, Getica 37. In the first passage, page 63_{11}, all codices, except the inferior ones of the secundus ordo, have altziagiri or altziagri. In the next line, page

---

[235] T'ang shu 225b, 8b.

[236] The coexistence of Sai and Sai wang puzzled G. Haloun, ZDMG 1927, 252.

[237] See footnote 173.

[238] Abramzon 1946, 125, 127, 128, and 1960, 5, 31, 42, 45, 108, 111, 115, 126; Vinnikov 1956, 148, figs. 3, 6.

[239] Radlov 340; Orkun 1941, 3, 144; Malov 1952, 62-63.

[240] Tucked in an article on the Scythian name of the Maeotis, this etymology was suggested by J. Markwart as early as 1910 (Keleti Szemle 11, 1910, 13) and 1932, 108.

63_{12}, the forms are: primus ordo *altziagiri* (*H*), *ultziagiri, uultziagiri, autziagiri;* secundos ordo *alugiagiri, aulziagri;* tertius ordo *ultziagri, altziagri* (*Y*). Mommsen put *Altziagiri* in both passages in his text. Closs in his edition of the *Getica*, page 29, preferred *Ultziagiri*. He was right, in my opinion. In the second passage the name began with *u*. Three codices still have it; *au* obviously was *u* with superscribed *a*; the forms in *H* and *Y* were adapted to *altziagiri* in the first passage. We have, thus, *altziagiri* and *ultziagiri*. Although *Altziagiri* has no parallel in Hun tribal names, *Ultziagiri* can be compared with *Ultzinzures*, Ὀυλτίνζουροι. When we think of the personal name *Uldin*, and in particular of *Elming(e)ir* and *Elminzur*, the conclusion that * ΟΥΛΤΙΑΓΙΡ is but a slightly blundered *ΟΥΛΤΙΓΓΙΡ, *Ultingir, seems inescapable. *Gir*, like *čur*, must be a rank or title. It seems to occur in κυριγήρ, a Bulgarian *genos*,[241] and Yazghyr and Ürägir, two Oghuz tribes named by Kashghari.[242]

Five Hun names end in ιχ: Ἀψίχ, Βασίχ, Βεριχος, Δεγγιζίχ, and Κουρσίχ. Standard pronunciation treated χ as aspirant in Byzantine Greek until the ninth century.[243] In the Greek transcription of Germanic names χ corresponds to *c* in Latin forms. The same is true for Hunnic names. Δεγγιζίχ and Διυζίχ appear in Latin sources as Denzic and Dintzic. Priscus wrote Ἡρνάχ, Jordanes *Hernac*. There is no evidence that in fifth-century Greek transcription of foreign names χ can reflect *g* or γ.[244] Therefore, etymologies based on the equation ιχ = ig, ιγ or αχ = ag,αγ are inadmissible.

The name of an Utigur prince about 550-560 occurs in two forms. Agathias and Menander call him Σάνδιλχος; in Procopius his name is Σανδίλ.[245] Sandilchos is Sandilk, Sandil-k.

Κουρσίχ is[246] the name of a Hun leader in 395. It could be Kurs-ik or Kur-sik. Κούρς, the name of a barbarian officer in the Byzantine army about 578,[247] seems to indicate that Kursik is Kurs-ik.

---

[241] Beshevliev 1959, 289.

[242] Brockelmann 1928, 244, 251; for Ürakir read Ürägir (Pelliot 1950, 190). The origin and the meaning of -*gir* in Tungus tribal names is obscure, cf. Kotwicz 1939, 185; Pelliot 1950, 229; Menges 1951a, 87; N. Poppe, *UJb* 24, 1952, 75. Whether it has anything to do with -*gir* in the adduced names is doubtful.

[243] Sturtevant 1940, 85.

[244] Of the five cases adduced by Moravcsik, *BT* 2, 36, four are of the tenth century and later. The spelling Τζαχατάϊδες for Čagatai in Laonicus Chalcocondyles, who flourished about 1485, has no bearing on the phonetic value of γ in the writings of authors who lived a millennium before him.

[245] Moravcsik, *BT* 2, 266.

[246] Priscus, *EL* 141_{13}; Moravcsik, *BT* 2, 169.

[247] Moravcsik, *ibid.*, Evagrius calls him a Scythian.

Τουλδίχ was the qaghan of the western Turks about 580,[248] Tuldila a Hun leader in Majorian's army in 458.[249] -*ila* is evidently the same as -*ila* in Attila and Rugila, namely the Germanic diminutive suffix. It corresponds to the Turkish diminutive suffix +°q, +°k.[250] *Tuldiq* would be in Turkish what *Tuldila* is in Germanic: "little Tuld." This *tuld* can be compared with *Ult*inzur, *Uld*in, and *Uld*ach, names which seem to be compounded of *uld* or *ult* and *in/ach* = *in/aq*.

To maintain that all Hun and Turkish names ending in *ιχ* are diminutives would probably be wrong, but some of them apparently are. Take, for instance, *Βασίχ*.[251] Basich and Kursich are named together. If Kursich is Kurs-ich, *Kurs-iq, then Basich is probably Bas-ich, *Bas-iq, which can hardly be anything else but *bašiq*, "little captain."

It is almost generally agreed that *Δεγγιζίχ* contains Turkish *däŋiz*. Dengizich cannot be Dengir-siq[252] because if it were, Priscus would have written *Δεγγιρσίχ*,[253] nor can it be Dengis-siγ (see above). *Δεγγιζίχ* is a perfectly normal transcription of *däŋiz-iq*, "little lake."

Another formant in Hun names is +l. *Ἀψικάλ*, the name of a barbarian exarch,[254] stands in the same relation to *Ἀψίχ*[255] as *Σάνδιλχος* to *Σανδίλ*. It evidently is *Apsik-al*.

The number of Hun names which are certainly or most probably Turkish is small. But in view of the wild speculations and irresponsible etymologies still being expounded, to lay a narrow but firm basis for studying all the names seems preferable to dreamily wandering through dictionaries. Some of the names in the following list have been etymologized before; instead of repeating the arguments brought forward, in particular the many parallels, I refer to Moravcsik, *BT* 2, where the literature is carefully listed.

Ἀλθίας

Leader of Hun auxiliaries in the Byzantine army about 530.[256] *Altï*, "six." In his study of names formed by numerals, Rásonyi (1961, 55-58) listed the Kazakh patronymic Altyev and a large number of personal and clan names having *altï* as the first element: Altybai, Altyortak, Altyate, and so forth. Compare also Alty bars (Sauvaget 38).

---

[248] Theoph. Sim. 259$_{23}$; Moravcsik, *BT* 2, 318.

[249] Sidonius, *Paneg. on Maiorian* 488.

[250] Gabain 1950a, § 57.

[251] Priscus, *EL* 141$_{13}$; Moravcsik, *BT* 2, 87.

[252] As Pritsak 1956, 418, assumes.

[253] He wrote *Ὠηβάρσιος*.

[254] Moravcsik *BT* 2, 82. Malalas has *Ἀψκάλ*.

[255] Theoph. Sim. 67$_2$, 73$_{13}$; Moravcsik, *BT* 2, 83.

[256] Moravcsik, *BT* 2, 62 (for 430, read 530).

'Ατακάμ

A Hun of noble birth, about 433.[257] The name could be compared with Iranian 'Αρτακάμας.[258] In an Iranian dialect spoken in South Russia the change from -rt- to -t- can be followed in the inscriptions: 'Αταχαῖος[259] cannot be separated from 'Αρταχαίης.[260] Some names beginning with ata are Iranian, for example, 'Αταμάζες and 'Ατταμάζας[261] (*maza, "greatness")[262] or 'Ατακούας[263] There exist dozens of Iranian names ending in kam, "wish," from Μασκάμης[264] to Xudkām and Šadkām.[265] However, Eskam, another name ending in kam, has no similarity to any Iranian name and a most plausible Turkish etymology. Therefore, I accept Vámbéry's etymology: ata, "father," and qam, "shaman."[266] Similar Turkish names, for example, Atabag, are[267] fairly common.[268]

Βασίχ

Hun leader about 395. Basich is probably Bašīq.

Βέριχος

Lord of many villages,[269] Berik, "strong."[270] The king under whom the Goths are said to have left Scandinavia had a similar name: Berig, Berg, Berigh, Berich, Berice, Berige; see Getica 25₉₄. Although the Goths took over Hunnic names, they certainly did not rename one of their half-mythical rulers. Berig is probably *Bairika, the hypocoristic form of a name beginning with Bere-, like Beremod.[271]

---

[257] Priscus, EL 122₁₈; Moravcsik, BT 2, 76.

[258] Xenophon, Cyrop. VIII, 6, 7; Anab. VII, 8, 25.

[259] IOSPE 4, 423, 2; not later than the fourth century B.C.

[260] Herodotus VII, 22, 117; 63, 8.

[261] Mostly from Gorgippia (Vasmer 1923, 34, Zgusta 1955, § 596). Add 'Αταμάζας (Numismatika i epigrafika 1, 1960, 200).

[262] Miller 1886, 257; he compared these names to Atakam.

[263] Zgusta 1955, § 596; cf. Φαρναχύας (Ctesias, Pers. 45, Justi 1895, 93).

[264] Herodotus VII, 105; Justi 1895, 199, 498.

[265] Justi 1895, 177, 271, 377, 498.

[266] Vámbéry 1882, 40.

[267] Moravcsik, BT 2, 77.

[268] D. Pais, MNy 28, 1932, 275.

[269] Priscus, EL 143₂₅, 147₁₀,₂₁,₂₈, 148₁,₈; Moravcsik, BT 2, 89-90.

[270] L. Rásonyi, MNy 23, 1927, 280, and Archivum Europae Centro-Orientalis 1, 1935, 228. On bärk <bärig, cf. W. Bang. UJb 4, 1924, 17.

[271] Müllenhoff in Jordanes, index 147; Schönfeld 1911, 50. One should expect Berica, but Berichus is also possible.

Δεγγιζίχ

A son of Attila. *Däŋiziq, "little lake."[272] Dengizich, as Priscus heard the name pronounced at Attila's court,[273] is the only authentic form. Denzic,[274] Dintzic,[275] apparently renders the Germanic pronunciation *Denitsik, with the frequent dropping of g. Δινζίριχος is assimilated to names like Γενζέριχος.[276]

The fact that täŋiz, däɣiz is not attested before the eleventh century is of little importance.[277] It occurs in all Turkish languages; besides, there is no language known from which the Turks could have borrowed the word. Mongol Tängiz is a Turkish loanword.

″Ellac

Attila's oldest son.[278] The scribes who made the excerpts from Priscus left the name out. It should be in EL 130₃₆ and 183₂₈. Jordanes' Ellac presupposes *Ηλλαχ in Priscus; compare ″Ηρναχ = Hernac. Ellac seems to be älik (ilik), "ruler, king."[279] To be sure, in Priscus' transcriptions of Germanic personal and Latin place names alpha always renders a, never i.[280] But a in the second syllable occurs also in Armenian, alphilaq > alp ilig.[281] Apparently Ellac was not the name but the title of the prince who was governor of the Acatziri. Latin and Greek authors often mistook foreign titles for names.[282]

’Ελμίγγειρος

*Elmingir. Tunguz elmin, "young horse," also the name of a Manchu tribe,[283] is probably a coincidental homophone; it would be the only Tun-

---

[272] To the names adduced by L. Rásonyi, MNy 28, 1932, 102, add Sauvaget 1950, 45, nos. 78, 79. Markwart (1929, 83) recognized the diminutive suffix; he thought that dengi- might be the older form of yaŋi.

[273] Priscus, EL 588₆,₂₄,₂₈; Moravcsik, BT 2, 117.

[274] Marcellinus Comes, CM II, 90₇.

[275] Getica 120₂₁.

[276] Chron. Pasch. (besides δινζίχ and δινζίχος).

[277] It would be of interest to know at what time the Ossetes borrowed dengiz (Abaev 1958, 362) from the Turks. Incidentally, Tängiz, the youngest of the six sons of Oɣuz Qaɣan, is not the "oceanic" prince but Prince Ocean; his brothers are Sun, Moon, Star, Sky, and Mountain (W. Bang and G. Rachmati, SB Berlin 1932, 689, 691, 703; Abul Ghazi, Rodoslovnaia Turkmen, trans. by Kononov 1958 48, 50-52).

[278] Getica 125₂₆.

[279] For the etymology, see W. Bang, UJb 10, 1936, 23.

[280] ’Αναγαστου, ’Αρδαβούριος, ’Αρεοβίνδος, Βιμινάκιον, Παταβίωνος, and many more.

[281] Pritsak 1953, 19, n.10, quoting Mehmed Fuad Koprülü.

[282] Cf., e.g., Christensen 1944, 21, n. 3, on Ammianus' Nohodares.

[283] Pritsak 1955, 68.

gus word in the language of the Huns. *El* seems to be *el*, *al*, *il*,[284] "realm"; *-min-* can be compared with *-min* in Bumin, Chinese T'u-men and Ch'i-men.[285]

᾽Ελμινζοῦρ

*Elminčur, see p. 401.

Emnetzur

*Emnečur, see p. 402.

῾Ηρέκαν

Priscus mentions Attila's wife, Ellac's mother, in two passages. In the first, EL 139$_{22}$, all codices have κρέκα; in the second, EL 146$_7$, M and P have ἠρέκα B and E ἠρέκαν, C has ἠρέκαν. The copyists repeatedly dropped ν at the end of personal names, but they never added it where it did not belong.[286] The name ended in *-αν*. To choose between κρεκαν and ηρεκαν would be impossible were it not for the Germanic names of Attila's wife: Herche, Helche, Hrekja, and Erka.[287] They prove that Priscus wrote ηρεκαν. Bang's etymology is convincing: ηρεκαν is **arī(γ)-qan*, "the pure princess."[288] *Aruvkhan* (*aruv*, "pure") is a Qaraqalpak girl's name.[289],[290]

῎Εσκάμ

Eskam's daughter was one of Attila's many wives.[291] Eskam is most probably **as qam*, *as*, "friend, companion", and *qam*, "shaman."[292] The

---

[284] Rásonyi 1953, 333-336, listed numerous Turkish names and titles with *el* in the first syllable. For the Chinese transcription of *el*, see Pelliot, *TP* 1929, 226-228, and 1950, 182-183; Hamilton 1955, 151. Cf. also S. V. Kiselev 1948.

[285] Chavannes 1903, 336. Cf. also *Mo-yo-men*, the name of two ambassadors from Maimargh and Samarkand (*ibid.*, 135, n. 6, 145, n. 1).

[286] For αττηλαν all codices have αττηλα in EL 142$_7$; C has three times the accusative αττηλα, EL 125$_{34}$, 142$_7$, 149$_{18}$. βιγιλαν appears four times as βιγιλα, EL 124$_4$, 129$_{30}$, 130$_3$.

[287] Markwart 1929, 9, n. 1.

[288] Bang 1916, 112, n. 2, accepted by Arnim 1936, 100, and Németh 1940, 223. On *qan* and *arīγ* in names of women, see L. Rásonyi, *UJb* 34: 3-4, 1962, 233.

[289] Bashakov 1951, 176, 403.

[290] W. Tomaschek (*SB Wien* 117, 1889, 65) surmised in Kreka the ethnic name *Qyrqyz*; he had to work with the Bonn edition which had only *Kreka*. Why Haussig (1954, 361) still takes Kreka for the correct form is hard to understand; he maintains that the name is Gothic and means "the Greek woman." P. Poucha (*CAJ* 1, 1955, 291) takes *Kreka* or Hreka (*sic*) for Mongol *gargai*, "wife;" he repeats this etymology in 1956, 37, n. 39.

[291] Priscus, *EL* 131$_2$; Moravcsik, *BT* 2, 126.

[292] Vámbéry 1882, 43.

non-Tokharain name *Yarkom* in a Tokharian document[293] might be a hybrid name with the same meaning (Persian *yar*, "friend").

Ἰλιγερ

A Sabir, about 555.[294] Probably *Ilig-är*.[295]

Κούτιλζις

A Sabir, about 555.[296] When one thinks of the many Turkish names with *qut*, "majesty," it seams very likely that the name was *qut-il-či* or *qut-elči*.

Mundzuc

The name of Attila's father occurs as Μουνδίουχος in Priscus, *Mundzuco*[abl] in Jordanes, and Μουνδίου[gen] in Theophanes.[297] The last one is so corrupt that it can be disregarded.[298] Cassiodorus undoubtedly wrote *Mundiucus*, which Jordanes changed to Mundzucus as he changed Scandia to Scandza[299] and Burgundiones to Burgunzones.[300] In vulgar Latin *d* before *i* and *e*, followed by a vowel, became *dz*.[301] Jordanes pronounced *Mundiucus* as *Mundzucus*, and consequently wrote *Mundzucus*. But this does not necessarily prove that the Hunnic name was *Mundiuk*. If Priscus should have heard a Pannonian Roman or a Latin-speaking Goth say "Mundzuk," he still could have written Μουνδίουχος on the assumption that his informant mispronounced the name in the same way he said *dzaconus* for *diaconus*.[302]

---

[293] W. Krause 1954, 327.

[294] Agathias III, 17, ed. Bonn, 177₅.

[295] Moravcsik, *BT* 2, 138, following Németh and Rásonyi.

[296] Agathias III, 17, ed. Bonn, 177; Moravcsik, *BT* 2, 170.

[297] Moravcsik, *BT* 2, 194.

[298] Codex B has Ἀττίλα ὁ τοῦ Μουνδίου παῖς. Although it is better than the codices which have μνουδίου und μνοδίου (C. de Boor, *EL* II, 516), it is still not good. The name was distorted at an early time; Anastasius in his Latin version left it out (C. de Boor, *EL* II, 107₂₄); Nicephorus Callistus (*PG* 146, 1269c) has the monstrous Νουμιδίου. Note that in the same passage and in all codices occurs Βδέλλας, corrupt for Βλέδας.

Mundo (Moravcsik, *BT* 2, 194), the name of a Gepid of Attilanic descent (*Getica* 311), could be a variant of Theophanes' *Mundios*, provided that such a name existed. It has also been connected with *Mundzucus*; to the references in Moravcsik, *BT* 2, 194, add Pritsak 1955, 66. But Mundo's father Γίεσμος (Theophanes 218₂₂), has a name with a Germanic ring (Diculescu 1922, 58) and Mundo itself may be Germanic; cf. Munderichus and Mundila (Schönfeld 1911, 169); for *-o*, see Schönfeld 1911, 52. *Non liquet*.

[299] *Getica* 55₁₉, 58₂,₆,₁₄.

[300] *Jordanes*, index 158. Cassiodorus has of course Burgundiones (*Variae* 503).

[301] Kent 1940, 46.

[302] *Zaconus* in an inscription of 358 from Salona (Dessau 8254); *zie* for *die* (Detschev 1952, 1, 23.)

Németh and Rásonyi[303] take Μουνδιουχος, Mundzucus, to be the transcription of Turkish *munǰuq, bunčuq, Perle, Glasperle, Kügelchen oder Perlen, die man am Halse des Pferdes befestigt* (Radlov). "Pearl" would indeed be an appropriate name for a prince.[304] I prefer Vámbéry's etymology which took the name to mean *Fahne, eigentlich Fahnenknauf, Koralle, die apfelartige Rundung, in welcher der Rossschweif, die primitive Fahne des Türkenvolkes befestigt wurde, und nach welcher das ganze militärische Abzeichen später den Namen erhielt.*[305]

In his review of Moravcsik's *Byzantinoturcica*, Ligeti doubted the correctness of Németh's etymology.[306] At my request to state his reasons, he was so kind to write to me: *L'exposé des raisons de ma réserve vis-à-vis de cette étymologie depasserait les cadres de cette lettre. Je me contenterai de vous indiquer qu'il m'est impossible de concilier cette etymologie avec ce que nous savons de l'histoire des langues turques. Ainsi, le j̱ est caractéristique des langues oghouz, en face du č offert par les autres langues turques. En même temps l'initiale m̱ caractérise les langues offrant un č, en face de l'initiale ḇ qu'on attend dans les langues oghouz.*[307]

To these objections of the eminent Hungarian scholar one could perhaps answer that to a Greek, in whose language j̱ and č did not occur, the two must have sounded very much alike. More important is the known fact that *b* interchanges with *m within* a number of Turkish languages: *bän* in Osmanli in the eastern and *man* in the western Crimea,[308] *mindi* and *bindi* in Nogai; *börü* in the southern and *mörü* in the northern group of Altai Turkish.[309] One cannot even say that the Oghuz languages have the initial *b*, for although Osmanli, its Rumelian dialects, and Azerbaijan Turkish have it, the East Anatolian dialects have *m*.[310] Except the *Auslaut*, in the Osmanli dialect of Kars our word has the allegedly impossible form *munǧuχ*.[311]

"Flag" as title or rank of the flagbearer occurs in many languages. *Ensign*, for instance, is both the insignium and the one who bears it: "hee is call's aunchient Pistoll," *Henry* V (*aunchient*, corrupt for ensign). It

---

[303] Moravcsik, *BT* 2, 194; cf. Brockelmann, Kāšγarī: "a precious stone, lion's claw, or amulet hung on a horse's neck."

[304] "Pearl" was the title of the highest official of the Tibetans in the T'ang period (Demiéville 1952, 285).

[305] Vámbéry 1882, 46. In Russian, Ukrainian, and Polish borrowed from the Tatars in the Crimea (M. Vasmer 1955, 1, 145).

[306] *AOH* 10, 1960, 303.

[307] Letter of September 10, 1962.

[308] G. Doerfer, *Fundamenta* I, 379.

[309] O. Pritsak, *Fundamenta* I, 579.

[310] L. Bazin, *Fundamenta* I, 311.

[311] A. Caferoğlu, *Fundamenta* I, 251.

is the same in the East. *Tuγ*,[312] "standard with a horse or yak tail," occurs by itself or with a suffix in early Turkish and Uyghur names: *Tuγ Ašuq*, *Tuγluγ*, "he who was the *tuγ*," *Tuγič*, "*Tuγ* bearer."[313] *Munǰuq* probably means the same. Qïzïl Mončuq, the name of a Mongol commander in Afghanistan about 1223[314] means "Red Flag" rather than "Red Pearl."

In the eighth century the leaders of the ten arrows (tribes) of the Türgäš bore the standards.[315] The *cauda equi* was the *signum militare* of the proto-Bulgars.[316] It may have been that of the Huns, too.

The Germanic etymology of Mundzucus[317] is to be rejected. It is not only phonetically unsound. About 370, when Mundzucus was born, no Hun could have been given a Germanic name.[318]

---

[312] Gabain (1955, 23) is inclined to derive Chinese 纛 *tu < duok*, "standard with a yak tail or pheasant feathers," listed in the *Erh ya*, from Turkish *tuγ*. It seems to me that *tuγ* is rather a Chinese loanword. *Tu < duok < d'ok* or *tao < d'âu < d'og* (GS 1016) is undoubtedly the same as 翿 *tao < d'âu < d'ôg*, "staff with feathers" (GS 1090z) and 斿 *yu < iâu < diôg*, "pendants of a banner" (GS 1080a, *yu* 游 ; ancient *diôg*, "pennon" (GS 1080f), words which occur in the *Book of Odes* and the *Tso-chuan*, centuries before the first appearance of the Hsiung-nu, from whose allegedly Turkish language the Chinese are supposed to have borrowed *duok*.

[313] Pelliot 1950, 69; Hamilton 1955, 157, 158. Proto-Bulgarian *ΤΟΥΚΟΣ* means probably "the flag bearer", cf. Menges 1951a, 113.

[314] J. A. Boyle, *Islamic Studies* 2:2 (Karachi, 1963), 241. The Mongols believed that Chinghiz Khan's soul went into his flag, *tuǧ-sülde*, which became the patron saint of his clan and the whole Mongol people. Cf. Banzarov 1891, 24; Vladimirtsov 1934, 145.

[315] Markwart 1920, 290-291.

[316] *Responsa Nicolai, Carm.* XXXIII, p. 580. For the Kirghiz on the upper Yenisei, see Appelgren-Kivalo 1931, n. 93 (their flags are mentioned in *T'ang shu*, ch. 217b); for the Kurdykan, Okladnikov and Zaporozhskaia 1959, 121, 57; on the jug from Nagy Szen Miklos, see A. Alföldi, *Cahiers archéologiques* 1950, 132-133. On the flag of the Seljuk, see V. A. Gordlevskiĭ, *Izbrannye sochineniia* 1, 1960, 179; on Yak tail banners of Mongols in the time of Genghiz Khan, see Poucha 1956, 137-139.

[317] Schönfeld 1911, 278.

[318] This has been rightly stressed by G. Schramm 1960, 129-155. As an entirely tentative surmise, Schramm would derive Gundiok, the name of a Burgundian king, from Mundiuch, as he reconstructs the name of the prince. To judge the linguistic side of this derivation must be left to Germanic scholars. What we know about the relations of the Burgundians with the Huns in the 420's and 430's is not in its favor.

Whether *Τζειουκ* in an undatable epitaph from the northern Dobrogea (Moravcsik, *BT* 2, 311) has anything to do with Mundzuc is doubtful. 'Αταλα, Tzeiuk's son, served in the corps of the Sagittarii. Cf. Diculescu 1923, 52; V. Parvan (*Rendiconti della Pontifica Academia Romana di archeologia* 2, 1924, 131) and Fiebiger (1939, 31-32) took Tzeiuk and Atala for Germanic, V. Beshevliev, *Godishnik na Bulgarskiia Narodniia Muzeĭ* 7 (1942), 1943, 232-234, and I. Stoian, *Tomitana* (Bucharest, 1962) 54, for proto-Bulgarian names.

Σάνδιλ, Σάνδιλχος

Ruler of the Utigur, about 555.[319] *Sandil* cannot be separated from the Mamluk name *Sandal*, "boat."[320]

Ζόλβων

Commander of Hun auxiliaries in the Byzantine army, 491 A.D.[321] *Zolbon* is "the star of the shepherd," the planet Venus, *colban*, *colbon*, *solbon*, and so forth.[322] *Colpan* is a Mamluk name.[323]

NAMES OF UNDETERMINED ORIGIN

The following names, taken by themselves, might be Germanic, Iranian, Turkish or even Latin, or they defy any attempt to connect them with any known language group.

Ἀδάμις

Steward in Queen Erekan's household. See p. 380.

Ἀϊγάν

"Massaget," cavalry commander in Belisarius' army, first in the Persian, then in the African campaign.[324] Without stating his reasons, Justi listed the name as Iranian, but left it out in the enumeration of names ending in *-an* or *-gan*.[325] Ἀϊγάν might be Turkish *aï-χan*, "prince moon," as one of the six sons of Oyuz-χan was called.[326] Compare Aï-bak,[327] Aï-tekin,[328] Aï-taš, and Aï-kün.[329] Incidentally, the Manichaean terms *aï täŋg* and *kün aï täŋgri* in the *Chuastanift*[330] and other Manichaean writings have nothing to do with these Turkish names. Mas'ūdi's Aiγan in Gilgit were probably Tibetans; see Markwart 1938, 101, 110.

---

[319] Moravcsik, *BT* 2, 266.

[320] Sauvaget 1950, 49, no. 120.

[321] John of Antioch, *EI* 142$_{22}$; Moravcsik, *BT* 2, 131.

[322] Menges 1944, 264; Cf. Joki 1952, 294.

[323] Sauvaget 1950, 47, no. 91. K. H. Menges (*CAJ* 8, 1, 1963, 56) surmises that *Č'orpan* in the Khazarian name *Č'orpan T'arxan* is *colman*.

[324] Named together with Sunikas, Procopius I, 14, 44; Moravsik, *BT* 2, 57.

[325] Justi 1895, 11, 522-523.

[326] Rashid-ad-Din, *Sbornik letopisel* 1 (Moscow and Leningrad, 1952), 76, 86; Pelliot 1950, 27, n. 1.

[327] Rashid-ad-Din, *Sbornik letopisel* 1, 195; 2, 140; Mayer 1933, 148 ; Zambaur 1927, 30, 31, 97, 103; Sauvaget 1950, 39.

[328] Zambaur 1927, 222, 285; Sauvaget 1950, 40.

[329] Sauvaget 1950, 39.

[330] Malov 1951, 117, 119.

'Ακούμ

Magister militum per Illyricum in 538.[331] Malalas calls him "the Hun." Not even the correct form of the name can be established,[332] so speculations about its etymology are futile.[333]

'Ανάγαιος

Ruler of the Utigur about 576.[334] Anagai has been equated with A-na-kuai,[335] the name of the Juan-juan ruler whom the Turks defeated in 552.[336] Could Anagai be the Turkish name of a bird? According to E. Frankle (1948, 54), "the suffix -qaj, -kaj, -γaj, -gaj, embraces the function of forming designations for bird and the like." She adduces Osmanli *daraγai*, "black bird," *durγaj*, "lark," and similar names of birds. Durγaj, Turγaj, and Torγaj are both Turkish and Mongol names.[337] One is also reminded of Mongol names like Piano Carpini's Eldegai, or Taqau, Taγai.[338]

'Αργήκ

Hun doryphorus who distinguished himself in the defense of Edessa in 544.[339]

'Ασκάν

The Massagetae Simmas and Askan were commanders of a corps of six hundred horsemen in Belisarius' army in the Persian war about 530.[340] Justi regarded Askan as an Iranian name.[341] It might be Turkish *as-qan*, "the qan of the As (Az)," although the leader of such a small troop would hardly have been called qan. Besides, it is anything but clear who the As or Az were.[342]

---

[331] Moravcsik, *BT* 2, 59. On the campaign, see Stein 1959, 2, 306-307.

[332] Malalas has 'Ασκούμ, Theophanes 'Ακούμ.

[333] Vámbéry 1882, 40, suggested *aq-qum*, "white sand," or *aqyn*, "raid."

[334] Menander, *EL* 204$_{18}$, 208$_2$.

[335] First by Hirth 1899, 110, n. 1.

[336] Chavannes 1903, 221, 240.

[337] Sauvaget 1950, 50; Hambis 90, n. 1.

[338] Pelliot 1950, 91, note.

[339] Moravcsik, *BT* 2, 71.

[340] Procopius I, 13, 21; 14, 44; 18, 38, 41; Moravcsik, *BT* 2, 75.

[341] Cf. Aškan, the legendary ancestor of the Parthian kings (Wolff, 1935, 63 and Justi 1895, 43).

[342] See the discussion in Giraud 1960, 193-196. It has often been assumed that the Assan (Assantsy, Asantsy, Azantsy; cf. Dolgikh 1934, 26), a small tribe encountered by Russian travelers in the eighteenth century near Krasnoyarsk, were the descendants of the Az named in the Orkhon inscriptions. In the beginning of the nineteenth century,

Balamber

Rex Hunnorum about 370.[343] *Nomen nemo nisi imperitus pro germanico vendet,* said Müllenhoff more than eighty years ago.[344] The name of the king who is said to have married a Gothic princess[345] was apparently assimilated to Gothic Valamer. It was Balimber.

Βαλάχ

Leader of the Sabir, husband of Boarex, about 520.[346] *Balaq is possibly *malaq,* "calf."[347]

Βωαρήξ

Queen of the Sabir. The bewildering variety of the readings[348] makes any attempt to etymologize the name a hopeless task. Sinor sees in ϱηξ Germanic *reiks,*[349] which for historical and geographical reasons is unacceptable.

Βόχας

Massaget, one of Belisarius' doryphori in the Gothic war about 536.[350] I do not know why Justi (1895, 72) listed the name as Iranian; perhaps he thought of Beuca, mentioned in *Getica* 277 as king of the Sarmatians in southern Pannonia about 470. Bochas could be *Bochan, Βώχανος.[351]

---

the Assan were already "Turkized" but the few words of their former language preserved in J. E. Fischer 1803, 213, show that it was closely related to that of the Ket. It is perhaps not a coincidence that *az* and *qïrqïz* are named together in the incriptions. A clan Yas lived side by side with the Kirghiz clans Adzhu-khurman, Dzhup-par, and Khudai-bery among the Khoton in northwest Mongolia; cf. Grum-Grzhimaǐlo 3:1, 276. On Asan-Kot, see Alekseenko 1967, 30, n. 19.

[343] *Getica* 91₁₉, 121₂₃, 122₅.

[344] *Jordanes,* index 147. This did not prevent some scholars from taking the name for Gothic; see Schönfeld 1911, 275.

[345] *Getica* 249.

[346] Moravcsik, *BT* 2, 85-86.

[347] Németh and Rásonyi, quoted by Sinor 1948, 25. Βαλμάχ in Agathias III, 17, 5, Keydell 1967, 106₁₂ (another Sabir, ca. 555) is possibly a scribal error for Βαλάχ.

[348] Moravcsik, *BT* 2, 107-108.

[349] Sinor 1948, 25-29. Altheim and, more recently, R. Werner (1967, 491, n. 18) "etymologized" Wārāks in the *Chronicle of John of Nikiu,* although Wārāks is just a distortion of Βωαρήξ.

[350] Moravcsik, *BT* 2, 108, v. l. Βούχας.

[351] A Turk, 576 (Menander, *EL* 208₁).

Either by itself or with some addition, *buqa* (*buγa*), "bull," occurs as a name since very early times among nearly all Turks.[352]

Ἠρνάχ

Attila's favorite son.[353] Ernak is supposed to be Turkish *er*, *är*, *ir*, "man," with the suffix *-näk*, *-nik*. Professor O. Pritsak informs me that *-näk*, *-nik* as diminutive suffix occurs only in the Altai dialects and in Tuva. He regards *-nik* as a combination of *-n* and *-k*, suffixes which are sometimes used to express not a diminution but an augmentation: *är-än* means "he-man, hero." In his opinion Ernak could be **är-än-äk > *är-näk*, "great hero." Ernak has often been identified with ирникъ in the Bulgarian Princes' List.

On the other hand, it is noteworthy that the Armenian Arnak lived at the same time as Ernak (see Justi 1895, 27). Compare also Ἀρνάκης in an inscription of the second century from Tanais (Vasmer 1923, 33, Zgusta 1955, § 543).

Ἦσλας

A Hun of high rank, first in Rugila's, then in Attila's service.[354] Harmatta (1951, 145) suggested a Germanic etymology; he thought the name might be **aisila > *esla* and connected it with **ais*, "to be respectful, to honor." But the name might be Turkish: *aš*, *eš*, "comrade," + *-la*.[355]

Γορδᾶς

Hunnic ruler near the Maeotis.[356] Γρώδ in Malalas is almost certainly misspelled. The Turkish etymologies listed by Moravcsik are not particularly convincing.

Γουβουλγουδοῦ

Doryphorus of Valerian in 538.[357] Although the best codices have γουβουλγουδοῦ, Comparetti and Moravcsik prefer the reading βουλγουδοῦ. There can be little doubt that the longer form is the correct one. To some scribes the accumulation of the barbaric syllables, with their *u-u-u-u*, in addition preceded by another word ending in *u*, Βαλεριανοῦ proved

---

[352] *Buγa* in a Yenisei inscription (Malov 1952, 98); *Solda Buqa* and *Qara Buqa* in Uigur documents from Turfan (Malov 1951, 210, 213). Of the 209 Mameluk names listed by Sauvaget (1950), no fewer than sixteen contain *boγa*.

[353] Priscus, *EL* 588$_8$ (145$_{17}$: Ἠρνάς). *Getica* 127$_1$: Hernac.

[354] Moravcsik, *BT* 2, 133, v. ll.

[355] On the Turkish adjectival suffix *-la*, see Gabain 1950a, section 76; Clauson 1962, 145.

[356] Moravcsik, *BT* 2, 114.

[357] *Ibid.*, 106.

too much. They decapitated the monster. *Gubul* occurs as a Jazygian name in a Hungarian document of the fourteenth century.[358]

Χαλαζάϱ

Doryphorus in the Byzantine army about 545.[359] Chalazar brings Tutizar to mind.

Χαϱάτων

"The first of the kings of the Huns," about 412.[360] Olympiodorus, the only author to mention the name, took great liberties with foreign names. His Βελλεϱίδος,[361] possibly taken from a Latin source, seems to be a capricious rendering of *Valariþ. Instead of Ἀλάβιχος,[362] Olympiodorus wrote Ἀλλόβιχος,[363] as if to indicate that the man was ἀλλογενής. -*on* in Charaton may be the Greek ending. If we had only Μοϱτάγων, Μουϱτάγων, and Μοντϱάγων,[364] it would be impossible to decide whether -*on* belongs to the name of the Bulgarian ruler. As the inscriptions with Ομουϱταγ[365] show, it does not. -*on* might also stand for -*a*. Note that Olympiodorus, like all Greek authors, wrote Στελίχων for Stilika.[366] As so often in the endings of foreign names, -*on* could be -*o*. Finally, -*ton* may stand for -*tom*. Nearly all Greek writers had a marked aversion to -*m* at the end of a word. Propocius wrote κέντον (I, 22, 4), πόντην (*De aedif.* VI, 6, 16), πάκεν (*De aedif.* VI, 3, 11), and σέπτον (III, 1, 6). In other words, the name transcribed Χαϱάτων may have ended in -*tom*, -*ton*, -*to*, -*ta*, and -*t*.

Vámbéry (1882, 45) took Charaton for Turkish *qara ton*, "black mantle." This is phonetically sound. But can we be sure that *ton* was a Turkish word as early as the fifth century? Uigur *ton* is borrowed from Khotanese or a related dialect: *thauna*, later *thaum*, *thau*, "piece of cloth, silk."[367]

---

[358] Gombocz 1924, 110; J. Németh, *Abh. Ak. Wiss.* 4, 1958, 26. The dropping of the initial *gu-* has an amusing parallel in the name Bulawayo in Rhodesia, which originally was Gubulawayo, "place of execution"; see P. J. Nienaber in *Proceedings of the Eighth International Congress of Onomastic Sciences* (The Hague, 1966), 345.

[359] Moravcsik, *BT* 2, 337.

[360] *Ibid.*, 341.

[361] Henry 1959, 58a$_{32}$.

[362] Sozomen IX, 12.

[363] Henry 1959, 58a$_{11,17}$.

[364] Moravcsik, *BT* 2, 217-218.

[365] Beshevliev 1963, 337.

[366] Schönfeld 1911, 209-210.

[367] Bailey, *Transactions, Philological Society* 1945, 26, and Bailey 1961, 53. G. Doerfer (*UJb* 39, 1-2, 1967, 65) postulates "Urtürkisch" **tom* because Turkish *tön*, Chuvash *tum*, would speak for the existence of *n* > *m*, which runs against his views.

If *-ton* in Charaton were the Iranian word, *chara-* might be the same as in the Parthian name Χαράσπης[368] "having a dark (*hara, xara*) horse (*aspa*)".[369] Charaton, furthermore, is reminiscent of Sardonius, *Sardon, the name of a Scythian, that is, Rhoxolanic leader whom Trajan defeated,[370] and the Ossetian Nart name Syrdon.[371]

If Charaton should actually mean "black mantle," μελάγχλαινος, it could be the name of the clan or tribe to which the man belonged. There is the Kirghiz tribe *Bozton*, "Gray Coats," and the Kirghiz clans "White Coats," "Yellow Caps," and "High Caps" have analogous names.[372] However, it must be stressed that both the Turkish and Iranian etymologies presuppose that the name ended in *-ton*.

Χελχάλ

Hun general in the East Roman army, about 467.[373] If Chelchal were Chel-chal, one could think of Chalazar. If *-al* were the formans *-al*, one could think of Chelch, Κολχ, an Ogur tribe.[374] *Kolk* might be *kölül, kölök*, "(pack) animal," Kirghiz *külük*, "race horse."[375] But this threatens to degenerate into the well-known play with assonances.

Χινιαλών

Leader of the Kutrigur, about 550.[376]

Κουρίδαχος

See page 437.

Μάμας

A "royal Scythian," who fled to the Romans.[377] Hammer-Purgstall and Vámbéry compared the name with Mamai, emir of the Golden Horde.[378]

---

[368] Justi 1895, 170, 486.

[369] Cf. Bailey 1954 on *xara*, "dark"; on *xara*, "ass," see E. Schwentner in *Zeitschrift für vergleichende Sprachforschung* 72, 1955, 197.

[370] Aurelius Victor, *Caesar*. 13, 3.

[371] V. I. Abaev in *Iazyk i myshlenie* 5, 1935, 71.

[372] Abramzon 1946, 128.

[373] Moravcsik, *BT* 2, 344.

[374] Theoph. Sim. 259$_{12}$. On the interpretation of the passage, see Moravcsik, *BT* 2, 162-163. I wonder whether the tribal name could be Külüg, "famous"; cf. Malov 1952, 44-45, and L. P. Kyzlasov, *SE* 1965, 105.

[375] Malov 1951, 395; Shcherbak 1959, 123. The name of the Roman general Calluc, who fought against the Gepids (Jordanes, *Romana* 387), is possibly the same.

[376] Moravcsik, *BT* 2, 344.

[377] Priscus, *EL* 122$_8$.

[378] Quoted Moravcsik, *BT* 2, 180.

But Mamas, bishop of Anaea,[379] the presbyter Mamas, Eusebius' coadjutor at the council of Constantinople in 448,[380] and Mamas, *cubicularius*, later *propositus* under Anastasius,[381] were not Turks or Mongols. They were named after St. Mamas, the great martyr of Cappadocia.[382] The fugitive Hun was perhaps baptized. The Arria Mama of *CIL* III, 7830,[383] lived long before Attila. Mama is in all probability one of those *Lallnamen* which occur in any language.

Μονάγερις

Hunnic prince near the Azov Sea, about 527.[384] The name has been discussed by Hungarian philologists for decades.[385]

'Οδολγάν

Hun commander of the Roman garrison of Perugia in 547.[386] The readings 'Ολδογάνδων and 'Ολδογάδων lead possibly to *oldogan*, which brings the common Turkish name *toγan*, *doγan* "falcon" to mind; compare Äl toγan tutuq.[387]

'Ωηβάρσιος

Attila's paternal uncle.[388] The similarity of Oebarsios to Oebasius in Valerius Flaccus is striking. In *Argonautica* VI, 245-247, we read, *Oebasus Phalcen | evasisse ratus laevum per lumina orbem | transfigitur* (Oebasus. . . thinks he has evaded Phalces, when he is hit in the left eye). Could Valerius have dropped -*r*- in Oebarsius as he dropped -*s*- in Bastarna, and for the same reasons? Could Oebasius be the name of a Hun? The question seems absurd. Valerius wrote the *Argonautica* during the siege of Jerusalem or shortly after the fall of the city in 70 A.D. Yet Agathias reports that the place in Colchis where in his time (the latter half of the sixth century) the fortress Saint Stephen stood, was formerly called 'Ονόγουρις.[389]

---

[379] *ACO* II: 6, 43.

[380] Ernest Schwartz, *SB München* 1929, 15, 17, 19.

[381] *Vita Theodori*, *TU* 49, 2, 240.

[382] *AA SS* August III, 423-446; Delehaye 1933, 174-175. In 383, Mamas' compatriot Gregory of Nazianzen made a speech in his honor (Gallay 1943, 255).

[383] Alföldi 1944b, 15.

[384] Moravcsik, *BT* 2, 192-193.

[385] The common view that Muageris is Mod'eri, "Magyar," has been rejected by D. Sinor, *Cahiers d'histoire mondiale* 4, 3, 1958, 527; Boodberg (1939, 238) takes *Mog'er* to be an Altaic word for "horn."

[386] Moravcsik, *BT* 2, 214.

[387] In an inscription from the Uyuk-Tarlak, a tributary of the Ulug-kem in Tuva (Malov 1952, 11).

[388] Priscus, *EL* 146$_{18}$.

[389] Agathias III, 4, 6, Keydell 1967, 89$_{9-13}$.

In past times the Hunnic Onoguri had fought with the Colchians and been defeated; in memory of their victory and as a trophy the Colchians called the place Onoguris. The Anonymus of Ravenna, writing about 700 A.D., places the *patria quae dicitur Onogoria* near the Sea of Azov and the lower Kuban.[390] That in the poem Oebasius is a Colchian and not an Onogur might be a misunderstanding. Onogur, "ten Ogur," is Turkish, which, however, does not exclude the possibility that one of their leaders had an Iranian name.

My late friend Henning[391] thought Oebarsios, if Iranian in origin, could represent Middle Persian *Weh-barz*, "of good stature," compounded of *weh*, "good, better," and *barz*, "height, figure"; it would be closely related to the earlier name *Wahub(a)rz*, Ὄβορζος, which belonged to a king of the Persis.[392] But Henning thought that these names need not be connected with Valerius Flaccus' Oebasus, which was probably identical with the Persian name Οἰόβαζος of Achaemenian times; Herodotus mentions three bearers of it.[393]

It is, indeed, unlikely that Oebadus of the *Argonautica* is *Oebarsus. There exists neither literary nor archaeological evidence that Huns were on the Kuban as early as the first century. Agathias' "past times" can very well refer to the middle or latter half of the fourth century when Hunnic tribes, moving east, were on or near the Kuban.

Henning's etymology of Oebarsios is philologically sound. But the same is true for the usual Turkish explanation of the name.[394] *Bars*, "tiger, leopard, lynx,"[395] is one of the most common words in Turkish names. ωη is probably not *oi*, as Vámbéry, Bang, and Melich thought; *oi* is used only for the color of a horse.[396] Gombocz and Németh suggested *aï*, "moon"; there are, indeed, quite a number of Turkish names beginning with *aï*.

Sanoeces

One of the three *duces* of the Gothic and Hunnic troops sent to Africa in 424. Sanoeces is possibly to be emended to *Sandeces; compare *Sondoke* in a list of Bulgarians in the evangeliary of Cividale (eighth or ninth century), *Sundice*[dat] in a letter of Pope John VIII to a Bulgarian nobleman, 879 A.D., and *Nesundicus* (*Sundicus*) *uagatur*, the name of a

---

[390] *Cosmographia*, Pinder-Parthey 1848, 170₁₅-171₂.

[391] Oral communication.

[392] Justi 1895, 231, 341.

[393] *Ibid.*, 232.

[394] Moravcsik, *BT* 2.

[395] Maygar *borz*, "badger," is a loanword from Chuvash; cf. Z. Gombocz, *MSFOU* 30, 52.

[396] Laute-Cirtautas 1961, 107, 110.

Bulgarian who attended the eighth ecumenical council in Constantinople in 869-870.[397]

Σιγίζαν

Hun officer in the Byzantine army, about 491.[398] If the name is not misspelled,[399] it might be Germanic.

Σίμμας

"Massaget" in the Byzantine army, about 530.[400]

Σιννίων

He shared with Balas the command over six hundred "Massagetae" in Belisarius' army in 530; later he became ruler of the Kutrigur.[401] Theophanes' description of the Byzantine forces in Africa, A. M. 6026, is taken from Procopius III, 11. Of the twenty-one names of his source, Theophanes selected the twelve more important ones. The biblical, Greek, Latin, and two barbarian names, Pharas and Balas, are in Theophanes the same as in Procopius, but where Procopius has Ἀλθίας and Σιννίων, Theophanes has Ἀλφίας and Σισίννιος. There can be no doubt that Ἀλθίας is the correct reading; it occurs four times without any varia lectio. Σιννίων was assimilated to Σισίννιος, a Byzantine name of probably Persian origin (see Justi 1895, 303-304).

Σκόττας

Brother of Onegesius.[402] The double consonant of the beginning seems to preclude a Turkish origin. Harmatta (1951, 148) thought Skottas might be Germanic *Skutta; he compared the name with OHG scuzzo, OE scytta, ON skyti, "shot, Schütze." If Szemerényi's analysis of Skolotoi (Herodotus IV, 6)[403] should be correct, there existed an Iranian word *skuda, "shot," which, however, was doubted by W. Brandenstein.[404] I think it quite possible that Priscus himself assimilated the Hunnish name to Skythes, either by dropping a vowel at the beginning (*Es-kota?) or between s and k (*S-kota?); it may have ended in -an.

---

[397] See Moravcsik 1933, 8-23; Moravcsik, BT 2, 355-357.

[398] John of Antioch, EI 142₂₂; Moravcsik, BT 2, 274.

[399] Cf. the Kuman name Συτζιγάν (Moravcsik, BT 2, 294).

[400] Moravcsik, BT 2, 276. Justi (1895, 301) lists two Turks named Sīmā.

[401] Moravcsik, BT 2, 276-277.

[402] Priscus, EL 125₂₂, 127₁₁,₂,₆₃₄; Moravcsik, BT 2, 279.

[403] ZDMG 1951, 216.

[404] WZKM 1953, 199.

Σουνίκας

A "Massaget" by birth, later baptized.[405] Tomaschek proposed a Turkish,[406] Justi an Iranian etymology.[407] *Sunika could be the hypocoristic form of Suniericus, Sunhivadus, and similar Germanic names.[408] It could also stand for *Sunikan.

Ταρράχ

After the collapse of Vitalian's second revolt in the fall of 515, Tarrach, "the fiercest of the Huns" in the service of the "tyrant," was captured, tortured, and burned at the stake in Chalcedon.[409] In Vitalian's army were mercenaries from "various tribes,"[410] Bulgars, Goths, and "Scythians,"[411] but the Huns were apparently the strongest group.[412] Like Vitalian himself, who is sometimes called a Goth, sometimes a Scythian, but also a Thracian,[413] Tarrach may have been of mixed origin. If he was baptized, which is possible, his pagan name probably was assimilated to Tarachus, one of the three famous martyrs from Cappadocia. Tarachus and Probus had churches in Constantinople before the end of the sixth century.[414] As Professor A. Tietze informs me,[415] Tarrach is not a Turkish name.[416]

Τουργοῦν

A Hun in Vitalian's army.[417] Rásonyi takes the name for Turkish.[418] It might be an "Iranian" title.[419]

---

405 Moravcsik, *BT* 2, 289. Cf. Zacharias Rhetor, Brooks II, *CSCO*, 64.

406 *Zeitschr. f. d. österr. Gymnasien* 1877, 685, quoted by Moravcsik, *BT* 2, 289.

407 He referred to Avar *suni*, Armenian *sun*, "dog."

408 Schönfeld 1911, 218.

409 John of Antioch, *EI* 147$_9$: Moravcsik, *BT* 2, 300.

410 "Many savage people" (Zacharias Rhetor, Brooks II, *CSCO*, 185); *cum valida manu barbarorum* (Victor Tonnennensis, *CM* II, 195).

411 Malalas 404-405.

412 *Hypatius ab Hunnis auxiliaribus capitur* (Jordanes, *Romana* 358).

413 See Stein 1959, 2, 179, on the contradictory statements.

414 Delehaye 1902, 165, 241.

415 Letter of December 13, 1962.

416 In the present studies the many etymologies of Hunnish names suggested by Haussig 1954, 275-462, have been disregarded. One example will suffice: He writes (p. 354), *Die* (sic) *Tarraq* (*Ταρράχ*) *werden in dem Werk des Johannes von Antiochia als zu den Hun* (*Qun* [sic]) *gehörig erwähnt.*

417 John of Antioch, *EL* 147$_{10}$.

418 Quoted by Moravcsik, *BT* 2, 319.

419 *Twryn, trywn, try'n* (A. A. Freiman, *Trudy instituta vostokovedeniia* 17, 1936, 164; *Zapiski inst. vostokoved.* 7, 1939, 30 ; *Sovetskoe vostokovedenie* 3, 1958, 130-131).

Uldin

Hun king about 400.

Οὐλδάχ

Hun general in the Byzantine army, about 550.[420]

Ultzindur

Consanguineus Attilae.[421] On analogy with Tuldich, Tuldila, the first element in these three names must be *uld-, ult-*.

Ζιλγίβις

Hun princes in the Caucasus, about 520.[422]

HYBRID NAMES

Αψίχ

Hun officer in the Byzantine army, about 580.[423] Apsik could be *Apsïq, Alanic *apsa, "horse,"[424] and Turkish -ᵒk, -ᵒq, "little horse."

Ἀψικάλ

A Byzantine general of Gothic origin;[425] if he was actually a Goth, he must have been one of those who "borrowed their names from the Huns" (*Getica* 58). Apsikal is *Aps-ik-al*.

Κουρσίχ

Hunnic leader, about 395. If Kursich is, as I believe, *Kurs-ik*, Kurs can be compared with Churs, prince of Gardman in northeastern Armenia,[426] and the Ias personal name Hurz,[427] Ossetic *xorz*.[428]

Tuldila

See above and p. 405. *Tuld-* has nothing to do with τοῦλδος, "train", in the Byzantine military language; the word is of Latin origin.[429]

---

[420] Agathias 181₆, 182₇. *Οὐλδάχ* seems preferable to Moravcsik's *Οὐλδαχ*.

[421] *Getica* 127₂.

[422] Moravcsik, *BT* 2, 131, with many different readings.

[423] Theoph. Sim. 67₂; 73₁₇. An Avar general had the same name (Moravcsik, *BT* 2, 82).

[424] Cf. Ἄψαγος, Ἀψώγας, Βωράψαζος (Zgusta 1955, §73, 281, 90). Ossetic *digor æfsæ*, "mare."

[425] John of Antioch, *EL* 142₂₂.

[426] Koriun 1927, 219; *Gardmanorum princeps nomine Chors* (P. Peeters, *Analecta Bollandiana* 51, 1933, 28).

[427] Gombocz, *MSFOU* 30, 109.

[428] For Turkish *k*, *q* < Iranian, cf. *qormusta* < *xwrmzd*.

[429] A. Dain, *Annuaire de l'institut de philologie et d'histoire orientales et slaves* 10, 1950, 161-169.

There remain a small number of supposedly Hunnic names and words which have not been included in the preceding lists. The connection of the bearers of the names with the Huns was loose, if it existed at all. Some of these names and words, provided they were Hunnish, were possibly borrowed from other languages.

῎Αλαθαρ

Byzantine captain, about 515. Bury (1923, 449) and Stein (1959, 2, 180) called him a Hun. John of Antioch (*EI* 144₃₁), the only Greek writer to mention the man, says that he was of Scythian origin. In *Romana* 46₂₂ he appears as *mag. mil. Alathor* or *Alathort*, which might be Germanic (see Schönfeld 1911, 11).

Δονάτος

Altheim (*Geschichte* 1, 363) rightly rejects the often repeated assertion[430] that Donatus was a Hun king. Donatus may not even have been a Hun but a Roman who fled to the Huns as did later the physician Eudoxius.[431] The Latin name Donatus was extremely common in the fourth and fifth centuries.[432]

Μοδάρης

General of the East Roman army in 378, "of royal Scythian lineage" (ἐκ τοῦ βασιλείου τῶν Σκυθῶν γένους, Zosimus IV, 25, 2). Modares was not a Hun, as some authors thought. No Hun could have held such a high position in 378. Modares was possibly a Visigoth. Zosimus (IV, 3, 4, 3) calls Athanaric the leader τοῦ βασιλείου τῶν Σκυδῶν γένους. The name seems to be the short form of a Germanic name beginning with *Moda-*; see Schönfeld 1911, 118.

Σηγγιλάχος

Priscus, *EL* 121₁₆. Moravcsik (*BT* 2, 274) erroneously calls him an envoy of Ruga. He was a client of the East Roman official Plinta.

Ουάλιψ

Leader of mutinous Rugians in the northern Dobrogea who between 434 and 441 took, and for awhile held, Noviodunum.[433] *Val* might be

---

[430] *E.g.*, Thompson 1948, 58; Moravcsik, *BT* 2, 119.

[431] *CM* I, 662₄₄₈.

[432] Pritsak's Turkish etymology (1955, 43-44) is ingenious but unconvincing.

[433] Priscus, *HGM* I, 278₄. Noviodunum is the present Isaccea, not Neviodunum-Dernovo near Gurkfeld in Carinthia, as H. Mitscha-Märheim (*Mitteil. d. anthropolog. Ges. in Wien* 80, 1950, 224) and Ernest Schwarz (*Forschungen und Fortschritte* 28, 1944, 369) maintain. Valips rebelled against the *East* Romans.

Germanic, the ending is obscure. But this is no reason to call Valips a Hun.[434]

Ζέρκων

The name of the feeble-minded jester[435] has nothing to do with proto-Bulgarian *ičirgü*, in Latin transcription *zerco* or *zergo*. The *ičirgü boila* had a high rank; he was perhaps minister of foreign affairs.[436] There lay a world between him and the repulsive creature at whom Attila would not even look. Zerkon is probably a "Maurusian" name.

Var

Var, the Hunnish name of the Dnieper,[437] is the same as *bor-* in Borysthenes, the Iranian name of the river. It means "broad, wide," Avestan *varu-*, Ossetic *üäräx, urux*.[438] Ptolemy's Οὐαρδάνης,[439] the Kuban or one of its tributaries, is **var-dan*, "the broad river," Urux, a left tributary of the Terek, "the broad one." The Huns and after them the Pechenegs took over the ancient Iranian name.[440]

It is hard to understand why Pritsak[441] disregarded these river names. The involved Chuvash etymology[442] he offered has rightly been rejected by B. A. Serebrennikov.[443]

Κάμος and μέδος

"In the villages," wrote Priscus (*EL* 131[11-15]), "we were supplied with food—millet instead of corn—and *medos* as the natives call it. The attendants who followed us received millet and a drink of barley, which the barbarians call κάμον."

---

[434] As Polaschek (*PW* 17, 1194) and Moravcsik (*BT* 2, 223) do. Cf. Thompson 1948, 217-218.

[435] Priscus, *EL* 145[4], *HGM* 324[22], 325[20].

[436] Beshevliev 169-170.

[437] *Danabri amnis fluenta. . . quam lingua sua Hunni Var appellant* (Getica 127[19-20].) Pritsak's assertion (1954b) that all scholars agree that the passage goes back to Priscus is wrong; neither Moravcsik nor Markwart, to whom he refers, says anything of this sort. The context points to Jordanes as the author.

[438] Vasmer 1923, 65-66, and 1955, 1, 355; Abaev 1949, 183.

[439] Ptolemy V, 8, 5; *Waldanis* in Armenian (Markwart 1896, 88).

[440] Markwart 1903, 33; cf. E. Dickmann, *Beiträge zur Namenkunde* 6, 1955, 273.

[441] Pritsak 1954b.

[442] It rests on the assumption that the Chuvash *v*-prothesis is of a very early date. Magyar *ökör*, "ox," Turkish *öküz*, Chuvash *vᵊGᵊr*, and *or*, *oru*, "thief," Chuvash *vᵊrᵊ*, were borrowed at a time when in Chuvash the *v*-prothesis had not yet developed. Cf. M. K. Palló, *AOH* 12, 1961, 42-43.

[443] *AOH* 19, 1966, 59.

As is known from Julius Africanus' *Embroideries* and Diocletian's *Edictum de Pretiis*,[444] the Pannonians drank *kamos* (*kamum*) long before Attila. The word is Indo-European.[445] Vámbéry's Turkish etymology *kamos = qymyz*, followed by Dieterich,[446] Parker,[447] and, for a while, Altheim,[448] is to be rejected. *-os* is the Greek ending, *kam-* is not *qymyz*, and *qymyz* is a drink made of milk, not of barley. *Medos*, too, is Indo-European, either Germanic[449] or Illyric.[450]

STRAVA

"When the Huns had mourned him [Attila] with such lamentations, a *strava*, as they call it, was celebrated over his tomb with great revelling" (*Getica* 258).

Jacob Grimm[451] drew attention to Lactantius Placidus' scholion on Statius: "Pile of hostile spoils: from the spoils of enemies was heaped up the pyre for dead kings. This rite of burial is said to be observed even today by the barbarians, who call the piles 'strabae' in their own language" (*exuviarum hostilium moles: Exuviis enim hostium exstruebatur regibus mortuis pyra, quem ritum sepulturae hodieque barbari servare dicuntur, quae strabas dicunt lingua sua*), (Thebais XII, 64). The passage would be of great importance if it actually were written in the fourth century, the date of the scholion. However, *quae strabas dicunt lingua sua* is a marginal note which slipped into the text, penned by a man who knew his Jordanes.[452]

The initial consonant cluster precludes the Turkish etymology offered by B. von Arnim.[453] Grimm reconstructed from Gothic *straujan*, "to strew," *stravida, das auf dem Hügel errichtete, aufgestellte gerüste, eine streu, wenn man will ein bette* (*lectisternium*). Since then this etymology has been

---

[444] *Thesaurus linguae latinae s.v.* camum; *Bulletin Du Cange* 11, 1937, 39.

[445] Holder, 1896, 1, 728; Ernest Schwarz, *Mitteilungen des österreichischen Instituts für Geschichtsforschung* 43, 1929, 210; J. Harmatta, *AAH* 2, 1952, 343.

[446] *Byzantinische Quellen zur Länder und Völkerkunde* 2 (Leipzig, 1912), 139.

[447] *A Thousand Years of the Tartars* (London, 1924) 136.

[448] 1951, 209, n. 20 (and Altheim and Stiehl 1953, 85 f.), vigorously rejected my objections to this etymology. In *Geschichte* 4, 59, Altheim dropped it.

[449] M. Vasmer, *Zeitschr. f. slav. Philologie* 2, 1925, 540.

[450] Cf. B. Zástěrová in *Vznik počatku slovanů* 5 (Prague, 1966), 40. The Turkish word for *liquor ex milio et aqua* was *boza*, J. Németh, *Abh. Ak. Wiss.* 1958, 4; 1959, 17.

[451] *Kleine Schriften* 3, 135.

[452] Cf. R. Landi, "Strava," *Bulletin Du Cange* 5, 1950, 50-51; Woestijne 1950, 149-169.

[453] Arnim 1936, 100-109. H. Jacobsohn (*Anz. f. DA* 42, 1923, 88) thought *strava* might be Scythian.

repeated[454] so often that to doubt it is by now almost a sacrilege. How exactly "to strew" acquired the meaning "funeral feast"—for that is the meaning of *strava*, not *Streu* or *Bett*—remained obscure. Starting with "to strew" some authors arrived at "funeral feast" via "to heap > pyre >" to make a bed for the dead"; others associated strewing with strewing sacrificial gifts for the dead > honoring the dead> funeral. They would have found a way to connect *straujan* with *strava* even if it should have meant coffin, tombstone, or quarreling heirs. Actually, no Germanic language exists in which a word derived from "to strew" means *cena funeraria*.

There remains the Slavic etymology. *Le festin qui suivait la tryzna*[455] *s'appellait piru ̆ ou strava. Strava est slave; le mot est employé de nos jours encore au sens de "nourriture," et on le trouve dans les documents vieux-tchèques et vieux-polonais de XIVᵉ et XVᵉ siècles avec la signification spécial de "banquet funèbre."*[456] Vasmer and Schwarz[457] objected to this etymology in that in Jordanes' time the word for "food" must have been *sᵘtrava* and therefore could not have been rendered as *Strava*. This cannot be taken seriously. Should Priscus have written $\sigma^o \tau\rho\alpha\beta\alpha$? Besides, Popović proved,[458] to my mind convincingly, that the form *strava* could have existed side by side with *sᵘtrava*.[459] Occasionally and under special circumstances foreign words were borrowed for an old, native burial custom.[460] But it is most unlikely that the Huns turned to Slavs for a term to designate what was doubtless a Hunnic custom. One of Priscus' or Jordanes' informants seems to have been a Slav. Knowing neither Hunnic nor Slavic, Priscus or Jordanes could have taken *strava* for a Hunnic word.[461]

---

[454] *E.g.*, Leicher 1927, 10-19; E. Roth, "Gotisch Strawa, Gerüst, Paradebett," *Annales Acad. Scient. Fennicae*, ser. B, 84, 1954, 37-52; W. Pfeifer, "Germanisch Straujan," *PBB* 82, 1960, 132-145.

[455] *La tryzna n'était pas un simple festin, mais une fête de caractère dramatique, dont un combat formait l'épisode principale.*

[456] Niederle 1926, 53.

[457] M. Vasmer, *Zeitschr. f. slav. Philologie* 2, 1925, 540; Ernest Schwarz 1929, 210.

[458] *Sbornik Radova vizantoloshkog instituta* 7, 1961, 197-226.

[459] The Slavic etymology, first suggested by Kotliarevskiĭ (1863, 37-42), has been accepted by Nehring (1917, 17) and Trautmann (1944, 23). Later scholars turned Mommsen's conjecture (*Jordanes*, index p. 198) that the Slavs borrowed *strava* from the Goths, into a proved fact. See, *e.g.*, A. Walde-Hoffmann, *Lateinisches etymologisches Wörterbuch* (Heidelberg, 1952), *s.v.* strava.

[460] Ossetic *dug̃*, *dog̃* (Markwart 1929, 81; Abaev 1958, 373) is Turkish *doy* ("in their [i.e., the Turks'] language the funeral customs are called $\delta\acute{o}\chi\iota\alpha$," Menander, *EL* 207).

[461] Contrary to Altheim's emphatic statement (Altheim and Stiehl 1953, 48), *strava* has nothing to do with the Bulgarian $\sigma\tau\acute{a}\beta\iota\tau\zeta\alpha$ in a Byzantine compilation of the tenth century (*BNJb* 5, 1926, 15, 370). On Slavic *zdravica* meaning "to your health", see I. Duĭchev, *Byzantinoslavica* 12, 1951, 92, n. 76. In Marco Polo, it occurs as *stravitsa*.

CUCURUN

Hubschmid takes Middle Greek κούκουρον, Middle Latin *cucurum*, and Old English *cocer*, "quiver," to be a loanword from Hunnish.[462] He adduces numerous similar sounding Mongolian and Turkish words for leather bottle, bow, and container, though none which means "quiver." Hubschmid finds this in no way surprising for, as he asserts, after the beginning of the nineteenth century quivers were no longer used. He is mistaken. Not only is *sadaq* still the common Turkish word for quiver, as it has been for centuries, the Kirghiz shot whith bows and arrows until the 1870's and in the Altai guns displaced the bow only about 1890, in some remote valleys even later. In 1929, I saw Tuvans carry bows and quivers full of arrows at ceremonial shooting contests. If *cocer* and so forth were of Altaic origin, it would be Avaric rather than Hunnish.

TRIBAL NAMES

Akatir

The literature about the name of the Hunnic people, which in Priscus occurs as Ἀκάτιροι and Ἀκάτζιροι, and in Jordanes as Acatziri, is extensive. Tomaschek was the first to suggest a Turkish etymology, which has won wide acceptance; he thought Acatziri was *aɣac-ari*, "forest men."[463] This etymology seems to be supported by *Aɣaj-eri* in the Turko-Arabic dictionary of 1245[464] and in Rashid-'d Din, who refers to the Mongol synonym *hoi-in-irgan*.[465] Sinor[466] called attention to *yis-kisi*, as some Turks in the Altai are named; it, too, means "people of the wood." The names of the Russian Drevlyane and the Gothic Tervingi in the Ukraine have often been adduced as parallels to *aɣac-ari*. The Drevlyane are said to have received their name "because they lived in the woods,"[467] and Tervingi is supposed to have the same meaning:—"forest man."[468]

The Turkish etymology was rejected by F. W. K. Müller, Henning, and Hamilton. Müller[469] maintained that *aɣac* means "tree," not "wood,

---

[462] *Essais de philologie moderne* (Paris, 1951), 189-199; *Schläuche und Fässer* (Bern, 1955), 113-125. Dutch *koker* became kokor in Russian (*Slovar' sovremmennogo russkogo literaturnogo iazyka* 5, 1132).

[463] *Zeitschr. f. d. österreich. Gymnasien* 23, 1872, 142.

[464] Houtsma 1894, 23, 49.

[465] Quoted by Pelliot 1950, 210.

[466] Sinor 1948, 3.

[467] "Zane sedosha v lesekh," *Povest' vremennykh let* 1.

[468] Schönfeld 1911, 222.

[469] F. W. K. Müller 1915, 3, 34.

forest." Henning[470] regards the usual derivation of the name as "scarcely better than a popular etymology." Hamilton[471] finds Aɣaj-eri as strange a name as Qum-eri, "man of sand," Turuk-eri, "Turk," or Rum-eri, "man of Rum," also listed in the Turko-Arabic dictionary. He maintains that no such names exist except in the contemporary Rashid-'d Din. Pelliot,[472] although he eventually accepted the usual etymology, confessed to some doubts. He pointed out that aɣac occurs only in the Altai and some western dialects; the Turfan texts have iɣac, Kas ari has yiɣac and yiɣac, and Turki ɣaɣac: *Ainsi, au cas où* Ἀχάτζιϱοι *serait bien* Aɣac-eri, *nous devons admettre que, dès le milieu du* Vᵉ *siècle, les principales caractéristiques qui séparent les divers dialects turcs s'étaient déjà partiellement établies.*

Unless one is convinced that in the fifth century all Turks, or even all "Altaians," as some scholars believe, spoke the same language, Pelliot's doubts carry little weight. Hamilton's suspicion that Aɣaj-eri of the Mongol period was a book word is not justified either. Aɣac-eri, named together with the five Uigur, occur in the Čagatai version of the Oguz-name;[473] there were Aɣac-eri in Anatolia,[474] and there still are Aɣac-eri in Khuzistan.[475]

These names, undeniably, have some resemblance to Acatziri. But whether there is more to it, whether the Acatziri actually lived in woods as their name supposedly indicates, is a question which neither dictionaries nor analogies but only the texts can answer. The interpretation of Drevlyane and Tervingi is anything but certain. Tretyakov thinks that Drevlyane is a distortion of an unknown name, an attempt to give it a meaning.[476] According to Hermann, *ter-* in Tervingi does not mean "tree" but "resin, resinous wood" and, possibly, a kind of pine.[477] The Greutungi, those Goths who allegedly were named after the "sandy" steppes in the Ukraine, bore this name when they were still living in Scandinavia.[478] It is strange how scholars on the hunt for etymologies of *Wörter* are apt to forget the *Sachen*; Ammianus Marcellinus called the "sandy" land of the Greutungi Ermanaric's "fertile country," *uberes pages.*[479]

---

[470] 1952, 14/3, 506.

[471] 1962, 58.

[472] 1950, 213.

[473] Ibn Fadlan 1939, 147-148.

[474] Pelliot 1950, 212, n. 1.

[475] Barthold, *Encyclopedia of Islam* 2, 838; W. B. Henning 1952, 506, n. 8.

[476] *Vostochnoslavianskie plemena*, 249.

[477] *Abh. Göttingen* 3:8, N.F., Fachgruppe 4, 1914, 271-281. Cf. also the controversy between H. Rosenfeld and F. Altheim in *Beiträge zur Namenkunde* 7, 1956, 81-83, 195-206, 241-246; 8, 1957, 36-42.

[478] Cf. W. Krause 1955, 12; Rosenfeld 1957b, 246. Cf. also Ernest Schwarz 1951, 34.

[479] XXXI, 3, 1.

And now to the texts:

Jordanes speaks of the sites of the Acatziri and their way of life in the much-discussed chapter V of the *Getica*. To take up the complex problem of the chapter's composition is not germane to my purpose.[480] It is evident that Jordanes did not simply copy Cassiodorus' *Gothic History*. He is indebted to Cassiodorus for a good part of the description of Scythia,[481] but he adapted his source to his own work. He wrote, as Cassiodorus could not have written: *In Scythia medium est locus; indomiti nationes*, and so forth. A number of passages are undoubtedly his own. He speaks of the Bulgars *supra mare Ponticum, quos notissimos peccatorum nostrorum mala fecerunt*. *Peccata* is a specifically East Roman word, meaning "neglect, failure" (on the part of the emperors, generals, and so forth).[482] Not Italy but the Balkan provinces were raided and devastated by the Bulgars who crossed the Danube almost every year. It is unlikely that Cassiodorus in Ravenna was even aware of the existence of Noviodunum in Scythia minor, not to speak of the Lake Mursianus,[483] the lagoon of Razelm which the Moesian Jordanes must have known very well.

Although it is impossible to distinguish in each case between Jordanes' text and the shorter or longer borrowings from Cassiodorus, the passage in which we are interested can be assigned to its authors with a fair degree of probability:

Introrsus illis [sc. *fluminibus*] *Dacia est, ad coronae speciem arduis Alpibus emunita iuxta quorum sinistrum latus, qui in aquilone vergit, ab ortu Vistulae fluminis per immensa spatia Venetharum natio populosa consedit* (Getica 34). (Within these [rivers] is Dacia, fortified with steep Alps in the form of a crown, next whose left side, which inclines northward, from the source of the Vistula through immense distances, dwells the populous nation of the Venethae.)

The passage has a strong Cassiodorian ring.[484] The following may also go back to the *Gothic History*:

Quorum nomina licet nunc per varias familias et loca mutentur, principaliter tamen Sclaveni et Antes nominantur. (Whose names, though

---

480 For *Getica* 30-35, see L. Hauptmann, *Byzantion* 4, 1927-1928, 138-139.

481 Cf. Cipolla 1892, 23.

482 Cf. J. Friedrich, "Über einige kontroverse Fragen im Leben des gotischen Geschichtsschreibers Jordanes," *SB München* 1907, 405-407.

483 On this name, see F. J. Mikkola, *Symbolae grammaticae in honorüm Ioannis Rozwadowski* 2 (Cracow, 1928), 533; G. Nandris, *The Slavonic and East European Review* 18, 1939, 144; H. Łowniański, *Opusculum C. Tymienicki* (Poznan, 1959), 211-224. Another name of the lagoon is Ἄλισχος (*Analecta Bollandiana* 31, 1926, 216).

484 Cipolla 1892, 23.

perhaps now changed through different families and places, are chiefly called Sclaveni and Antes.)

But now the tone changes:

Sclaveni a civitate Novietunense *et laco qui appellatur* Mursiano *usque ad Danastrum et in boream* Viscla *tenus commorantur.* (The Sclaveni dwell from the city of Novietunum and the lake which is called Mursian as far as the Dniester and northward as far as the Viscla.)

Both the words in Roman type and the content give the passage to Jordanes. Note in particular the switch from Vistula to Viscla.

Proceeding eastward, the author describes the sites of the other group of the Venethae:

Antes vero, qui sunt eorum fortissimi, qua Ponticum mare curvatur, a Danastro extenduntur usque ad Danaprum, quae flumina multis mansionibus ad invicem *absunt.* (The Antes, indeed, who are the strongest of them, extend from the Dniester to the Dnieper, where the Pontic sea is curved. These rivers are many days' journey apart from each other.)

The words in Roman type point definitely to Jordanes. Suddenly we listen again to Cassiodorus, evidently carefully copied:

Ad litus autem Oceani, ubi tribus faucibus fluenta Vistulae fluminis ebibuntur, Vidivarii resident, ex diversis nationibus adgregati; post quos ripam Oceani item Aesti tenent, pacatum hominum genus omnino. (But on the shore of the ocean, where the streams of the River Vistula are discharged by three mouths, dwell the Vidivarii, compounded of several nations, after whom again the Aesti hold the shore of the ocean, a race of men wholly pacified.)

The allusion to Tacitus, *Germania* 45, 3,[485] and the change from Viscla back to Vistula points to Cassiodorus. And now the crucial passage:

quibus in austrum adsidet gens Acatzirorum fortissima, frugem ignara, quae pecoribus et venationibus victitat. (To the south of them [quibus] resides the most mighty race of the Acatziri, ignorant of agriculture, which lives upon its herds and upon hunting.)

Mommsen listed *victitare* as typical for Jordanes.[486] To what does the relative pronoun refer—to the Antes or the Aesti? *Getica* 23-24 is in this respect rather instructive:

---

[485] As in *Variae* V, 2, first pointed out by Schirren 1846, 49-50.
[486] In his edition of *Jordanes*, index 199.

The Suetidi are of this stock and excel the rest in stature. However, the Dani, who trace their origin to the same stock, drove from their homes the Heruli who claim preeminence among all nations of Scandza for their tallness.

Sunt quamquam et horum positura Granii, Augandzi, Eunixi, Taetel, Rugi, Arochi, Ranii. quibus non ante multos annos Roduulf rex fuit, qui contempto proprio regno ad Theodorici Gothorum regis gremio convolavit, et, ut desideravit, invenit. (However, there are in the place of these people the Granii, Augandzi, Eunixi, Taetel, Rugi, Aprochi, Ranii. Over these, not many years ago, Rudolf was king, who, spurning his own kingdom, fled to the bosom of Theodoric king of the Goths and found the refuge he desired.)

As the text stands, *quibus* refers to the seven peoples named just before. Yet Rodvulf was not their king but king of the Heruli.[487] After the short digression Jordanes returns to the nation of which he had spoken before. He was, thus, quite capable of referring by *quibus* not to the Aesti in the quotation from Cassiodorus but to his own Antes. That *quibus* must, indeed, be understood in this way is shown by the following part of the *catalogus gentium:*

Ultra quos [sc. Acatziros] *distendunt supra mare Ponticum Bulgarum sedes, quos notissimos peccatorum nostrorum mala fecerunt. hinc iam Hunni quasi fortissimorum gentium cespes bifariam populorum rabiem pullularunt. nam alli Altziagiri, alii Saviri nuncupantur, qui tamen sedes habent divisas: iuxta Chersonam Altziagiri, quo Asiae bona mercator importat, qui aestate campos pervagant effusas sedes, prout armentorum invitaverint pabula. hieme supra mare Ponticum se referentes. Hunuguri autem hinc noti sunt, quia ab ipsis pellium murinarum venit commercium: quos tantorum virorum formidavit audacia.*

(Beyond them [the Acatziri] extend above the Pontic sea the territories of the Bulgars, whom the punishments of our sins have made notorious. After these the Huns, like a cluster of mighty races, have spawned twofold frenzied peoples. One people are called the Altziagiri, the other the Saviri. These hold separate territories; near the Chersonese the Altziagiri, where the merchant imports the goods of Asia. These in summer wander through the plains, scattered territories, as far as the pasture of the flocks invites them. In winter they withdraw again to the coast of the Pontic sea. After these are the Hunugiri, well known because from them comes the trade in ermine. Before them the courage of many brave men has quailed.)

---

[487] Mommsen 1882, 154.

Even if one or the other flosculus should go back to Cassiodorus,[488] the passage as a whole must be attributed to Jordanes. The Bulgars have their sites *ultra*, that is, east of the Acatziri, and *supra*, that is, north[489] of the Black Sea; from there the "Huns sprouted out into two savage hordes." As Schirren recognized more than a century ago, Jordanes' Bulgars and Huns in this chapter of the *Getica* are but two names of the same people[490] Schirren thought that Jordanes simply followed Cassiodorus, who in *Varia* VIII, 10, 4, likewise identified the Bulgars with the Huns. But in the sixth century this equation was quite common. Ennodius, for example, called a horse captured from the Bulgars *equum Huniscum*.[491] To Jordanes' Bulgars, Antes, and Sclavini (*Romana* 388) correspond Procopius' Οὖννοί τε καὶ ῎Ανται καὶ Σκλαβηνοί (VII, 14, 2) and Οὖννοί τε καὶ Σκλαβηνοί καὶ ῎Ανται (*Anecdota* 18, ed. Comparetti, 122).

Saviri and Hunuguri, too, denote in Jordanes one, and only one, people. After describing the sites and economy of the Altziagiri, he turns to the other of the *bifaria rabies*. One expects that he would deal with the Saviri. Instead the speaks of the fur trade of the Hunuguri.[492] Jordanes' identification of the two peoples is quite understandable. Although Priscus, Agathias, Menander, and Theophylactus Simocatta clearly differentiate between them, their accounts show that from the 460's to the end of the seventh century the Onogurs (Hunuguri) were the closest neighbors of the Sabirs. They lived north of the Caucasus, on the eastern shores of the Black Sea, in the Kuban area.[493] In the list of nations in the appendix to the chronicle attributed to Zacharias of Mitylene, written in 555,[494] the Onogur are named first, the Sabir third.

---

[488] For *pullullare* Mommsen (1882, 63, n. 2) referred to *Variae* III, 6. But, as Cipolla (1892, 23) rightly remarked, *la fraseologia non può dare sufficente guarentigia di sicura attribuzione, perchè tra scrittori più o meno contemporanei è cosa agevole trovare riscontri di sifatte specie.*

[489] For *ultra* and *supra* in geographical descriptions, see H. Sturenberg 1932, 199ff.

[490] Schirren 1846, 50.

[491] *MGH AA* VII, 169.

[492] *Pellium murinarum commercium. Mus* means any of the numerous species of small rodents, from ermine and marten to squirrel and mole; cf. Stein, *PW* 14, 2398. The "mice" of the Hunuguri were apparently the "wild mice" of whose skins, according to Hesychius, the Parthians used to make their coats; in the Parthian language they were called σίμωρ, *i.e.*, *samōr*, "sable." Cf. E. Schwentner, "Ai. samura-ṣ, samuru-ṣ und die pontischen Mäuse," *Zeitschrift für vergleichende Sprachforschung* 71, 1953, 90-94. Turkish *samur*, "sable," is an Iranian loanword.

[493] Moravcsik 1930.

[494] To the translations listed in Moravcsik *BT* 2, 219, add F. W. K. Müller, *Ostasiat. Zeitschr.* 8, 1919-1920, 312, and Pigulevskaia, *VDI* 1 (6), 1939, 107-117. The story about the Hun Honagur in Movsēs Dasxurançi (1961, 63-65) is as confused as its chronology; its historical value is nil.

The Bulgars—nomads, mounted archers, entirely dependent on their horses—lived, of course, in the steppe. Although no one ever doubted that, no one seems to have drawn from it the necessary conclusions as to the sites of the Acatziri. The discussion about them centered almost exclusively on their supposed proximity to the Aesti.[495] Because the Altziagiri, the western branch of the Bulgars, "were near Cherson" in the western Crimea and "in the winter betook themselves north [supra] the Black Sea," they must have roamed over the plain east of the Dnieper. To a region not far from the Roman frontier point also the frequent raids of the Bulgars across the Danube. This, in turn, permits an approximate localization of the Acatziri. West of the Bulgars, south of the Antes, leads to the lower course of the Bug and Dniester, perhaps as far west as the Pruth.

The southern border of the forest steppe in the Ukraine runs from the northern edge of the Beltsk steppe in Bessarabia to Ananyev, the upper course of the Ingul, Kremenchug on the Dnieper, Poltava, Valuiki, Borisoglebsk, to the Volga north of Saratov.[496] "It was believed," wrote the eminent Soviet geographer Berg, "that at one time the steppe was covered with forests which were destroyed by the nomads. This view is mistaken."[497] Of Herodotus' Hylaea, Minns rightly said that it hardly required many trees to attract attention in the bare steppe land.[498]

The sites of the Acatziri were *south* of the just indicated line, in the level, woodless steppe. Priscus is in agreement with Jordanes. He too places the Acatziri "in Scythia *on* the Pontic Sea."[499] The Acatziri were a people of the steppe, not "forest men," not *aγac-eri*.

Being aware of the risks involved in the analysis of a text as patched up as the *Getica*, I·do not delude myself about the fragility of some of my suggestions. But I trust that in the main point, the localization of the Acatziri in the steppe, I am not mistaken.

Now we can return to the name itself. I leave aside the question whether *aγac* means tree or forest; in the fifth century it may have meant both. It is conceivable, though unlikely, that at the time we hear of the Acatziri they had moved from the forests in the north to the steppe, and their neighbors called them "forest men" because they came from there. Their name alone would not make them Turks; the Nez Percés in Idaho did

---

[495] W. B. Henning (1952, 503) at least considers the possibility of locating the Acatziri with the help of the data on the Bulgars, but in his opinion it is "by no means clear where precisely one is to imagine their seats."

[496] Berg 1950, 68.

[497] *Ibid.*, 108.

[498] Minns 1913, 15.

[499] τὴν πρὸς τῷ Πόντῳ Σκυθικήν.

not speak French nor the Black Feet in Montana English. But all this is beside the point. If Acatziri had been Aɣac-eri, Priscus would have written *'Aγάτζιϱοι. He never rendered a foreign *g* by kappa. He wrote *x* not *γ*; his 'Ρεκίμεϱ is Recimer, Ricimer, Ricimerius, not Regimer; 'Εδήχων is Edecon, Edica, 'Ανηγίσχλος Anegisclus. He wrote Βιμινάκιον for Viminacium and Σεϱδιχή for Serdica but Μάϱγος for Margus.

After the elimination of the equation *Acat(z)iri = Aɣac-eri*, geographically untenable and phonetically unsound,[500] there remain two more attempts to explain the ethnic name. The one suggested by L. N. Gumilev need not detain us; he takes Acatziri for Turkish *aka*, "older," and *carig*, "army,"[501] which is nonsense. The other explanation has been offered by a number of scholars, most recently by Henning and Hamilton. They assume that the Acatziri were the "white Khazars," *aqxazar*. Before turning to Henning, we have briefly to deal with Hamilton's excursion into Chinese. He thinks he found the name Xazir in a list of the T'ieh-le tribes in the north, preserved in *Sui shu*, chapter 84: "North of the kingdom of K'ang on the river A-te are *ho tieh ho chieh po hu pi ch'ien chu hai ho pi hsi ho yang su pa yeh woi k'o ta* and others, with more than thirty thousand soldiers."[502] To Hamilton's ear A-te, ancient *a-tək*, sounds very much like Atil, the Turkish name of the Volga. *Ho tieh*, ancient *xa-d'iet*, is, he believes, a transcription of Adil, again the Volga, and *ho chieh*, ancient *at-dziet*, seems to transcribe Xazir.[503] In this way Hamilton arrives at "on the Atil are the Adil Xazir." Xazir and Xazar are, in his opinion, the same: *L'altérance a/i dans le suffix aoriste- était en turc ancien des plus banales.* He refers to Armenian Xazirk. The Chinese name and the Armenian support in his view the equation *Akatzir = *Aq-Qazir* or *Aq-Xazir*.

Hamilton's equations are unconvincing. *Ho tieh* is clearly the name of a tribe, not of a river. *Atil* cannot in one short passage be transcribed in two different ways. And the Volga does not flow north of K'ang = Samarkand.

In identifying the Acatziri with the Khazars, Henning follows another line of reasoning. Like Hamilton, he refers to Armenian *Xazir = Khazar*, which, however, he does not take for a variant of the name but of its original form. He stresses that no nation was as close to the Khazars as the

---

500 The spelling Agazari (*Chazaros . . . Iordanis Agaziros vocat*) in the anonymous geographer of Ravenna IV, 1 (Cuntz 1940, 2, 44) is of no consequence; cf. J. Schnetz, *SB München* 6, 1942, 34.

501 In M. I. Artamonov, *SA* 9, 1949, 56.

502 Hamilton 1962, 26-27. The same list in *Pei Shih*, ch. 99, has some different scriptions. In most cases it is impossible to decide whether the names are binoms or trinoms.

503 Hamilton 1962, 53, n. 14; 57, n. 47.

Armenians. This is certainly true, but Pelliot nevertheless called Xazir *peu concluant*[504] for the reconstruction of an original with *i* instead of *a* as in all other scriptions of the name. Henning thinks Xazir is supported by Χάζαροι, a name he found in Moravcsik. Χάζαροι undoubtedly stands for Khazar. But the writings in which this name occurs (the *Notitia Episcopatum* and the glosses of an unknown scholiast) abound with corruptions. In the discussion of the names Acatziri and Khazar, Χάζαροι can be disregarded.

The link between Acatziri and Khazar is, in Henning's opinion, *KSR* in the mentioned list of nations north of the Caucasus.[505] *KSR* can be Xasar and Xasir; in Khazarian *Xacir may have become Xazir and later Xazar. Whether such a development in the practically unknown language of the Kasars was possible or not has little interest to us, for Ἀκάτζιροι—Acatziri was definitely not *Aq-Xacir.

The ethnic name occurs in Priscus six times: (1) *EL* 130$_8$: ἀκατζίρων (Cantabrigiensis, Bruxellensis, Escorialensis) and ἀκατζόραν (Monacensis, Palatinus); (2) *EL* 130$_{26}$: κατζίρων (all codices); (3) *EL* 136$_3$: ἀκατήρων (all codices); (4) *EL* 139$_{23}$: ἀκατήρων (the same); (5) *EL* 586$_{12}$: Ἀκατίροις (the same); (6) *EL* 588$_{10}$: Ἀκατίροις (the same).

Of all the scholars who struggled with the problem of the Acatziri only Markwart realized the importance of the textual tradition. He discussed it in a work where one should not expect it, the posthumously published *Entstehung der armenischen Bistümer*.[506] Markwart showed that Priscus in all probability wrote Ἀκάτιροι, which later scribes "emended" to Ἀκάτζιροι. They did it the first two times only. Later they let the name stand as it was, perhaps expecting that the reader would now correct it himself. Suidas, quoting Priscus, has Ἀκατίροις.[507]

It is unlikely that τζ in Priscus was meant to render -*ts*- or -*c*-, as Markwart thought. Since he wrote Ἀμιλζύροις (*EL* 121$_4$), what could have prevented him from writing Ἀκάζιροι for Akacir or Akatsir? There are three possibilities, as far as I can see, to account for the difference between Ἀκάτιροι and Jordanes' Acatziri. The first could be the change from *ti* to *tsi* in vulgar Latin. Second, the same change may have occurred in the language of the Acatiri in the eighty years which separate Priscus from Jordanes. And, third, one could think that Priscus "reconstructed" the name; he might have heard Akatsir and still have written Ἀκάτιροι.

The last possibility seems somewhat far-fetched. Against the second one, in itself not exactly likely, speaks the spelling Οὐλτίζουροι in Agathias

---

[504] 1950, 207, n. 3.
[505] For a new view of the list, see K. Czeglédy, *AOH* 13, 1961, 240-251.
[506] *Orientalia christiana* 27 (Rome) 1932, 208-209.
[507] A. Adler, ed., I, 4$_{13}$, 77$_{13,14}$.

versus Ultzinzures in Jordanes; Agathias wrote his history *after* the *Getica*. Only the first possibility remains: Jordanes changed Ἀκάτιροι to Acatziri as he changed Scandia to Scandza or Burgundiones to Burgundzones. In my opinion, the "emended" forms in Priscus go back to the spelling in Jordanes. All manuscripts of the *Excerpta de legationibus* are copied from one codex. The apographs were made by Andreas Damarius and other scholars in the later part of the sixteenth century, at which time already three printed editions of the *Getica* existed.[508] It seems more probable to me that the sixteenth-century scholars, following Jordanes, "corrected" the Priscus text rather than Greek scribes of the sixth century as Markwart thought.

Henning's historical arguments for the identification of the Acatiri with the *KSR* are based on Priscus, fragments 30 and 37. In about 463, the Saraguri subdued the Acatiri after many battles; they themselves had been driven out of their country by the Sabirs who had been set in motion by the Avars, and the Avars in their turn by peoples which fled from maneating griffins coming from the ocean (fr. 30). In 466 the Saraguri, after their attack on the Acatiri and other peoples, Ἀκατίροις καὶ ἄλλοις ἔθνεσιν ἐπιθέμενοι, marched against the Persians, crossed the Caucasus, ravaged Iberia, and overran Armenia (fr. 37). Combined with Priscus' statement about the sites of the Acatiri in Scythia on the Pontic Sea, the two fragments are supposed to prove that the people lived in the steppes between Kuban, Don, and Volga, thus in about the same region as the *KSR* = Xasir or Xasar.

I am unable to accept Henning's conclusions. It must be emphasized that the two fragments were shortened by the scribes who put them together for the collection of Constantine Porphyrogenitus. For fragment 30 this has been proved by Moravcsik.[509] A comparison of fragment 30 and the beginning of fragment 37 shows clearly that the latter was also abbreviated. It refers to the battles in fragment 30, for it would be absurd to assume that in 463 the Saraguri subdued the Acatiri and three years later, before marching against the Persians, attacked them again. Fragment 30, as it stands, says nothing about the war between the Saraguri and other peoples beside the Acatiri, briefly referred to in fragment 37. In other words, the original Priscus text contained considerably more about the many fights of the Saraguri against the Acatiri and other peoples. It may also have been more specific about the region where those fights took place, although Priscus was apparently not well informed about

---

[508] Mommsen in the preface to his edition of *Jordanes*, lxx.
[509] 1930, 55-65.

the events in the vastness of European Sarmatia. Or should we really believe that the Herodotean griffins came from the river which encompassed the earth? Be that as it may, there is no reason to believe that in 463 the Acatiri had moved from the sites they had held in the last years of Attila's reign "in Scythia on the Pontic Sea," and after a few years under Attila's yoke had regained their freedom. For two or three years they were the subjects of the Saraguri, but by the middle of the sixth century Jordanes knew them as *fortissima gens*, subject to no one. Moravcsik thought it self-evident that at that time they were still where they were in the 460's, which, as I tried to demonstrate, was west of the Azov Sea.

Only by mistranslating the passage in fragment 37, which I quoted from Priscus' Greek text, could it be argued that the Acatiri followed the Saraguri on the march against the Persians. The editors of the Bonn edition and C. Müller in *Fragmenta Historicorum Graecorum* IV, 107, translated the passage *cum Acatiris aliisque gentibus coniuncti*. Doblhofer has *im Bunde mit den Akatziren*,[510] and Altheim *zusammen mit den Akatziren*,[511] although Moravcsik pointed out years[512] ago that these translations were wrong. Gordon correctly says "having attacked the Akatiri and other races."[513] I want to stress that Henning's views are not based on this mistranslation.

The East Romans tried to conclude an alliance with the Acatiri about 445 and actually concluded one with the Saraguri after the newcomers from the East had conquered the Acatiri. It is most unlikely that the Romans had contact with barbarians between Kuban, Don, and Volga, far beyond the ken of the government in Constantinople. In the wild melee of the early 460's, the Saraguri obviously pushed for a short time beyond the Don and Dnieper. All this speaks against the identification of the Acatiri with the *KSR* north of the Caucasus.

For Akatir I have no etymology to offer. Κουρίδαχος, the name of one of their rulers in the late 440's,[514] is possibly Turkish. Justi listed it as Iranian, probably because he relied upon a third-century inscription from the Crimea[515] which Latyshev restituted in analogy with Kuridachus.[516] *Ce nom*, says Sinor, *a une consonance turque, mais je n'ai pas réussi à l'identifier*.[517] Kuridachus might be *qurtaq, qurt*, "wolf," and the diminutive

---

[510] 1955, 74.
[511] Altheim 1962, 4, 277.
[512] 1930, 60, n. 1.
[513] Gordon 1960, 12.
[514] *EL* 130$_{15,19,23}$.
[515] Justi 1895, 167. Cf. also Zgusta 1955, 111, 133.
[516] *IOSPE* 1, 218.
[517] Sinor 1948, 2, n. 1.

suffix *q*; compare Gothic *Wulfila*. Németh maintained that *qurt*, "worm," acquired the meaning "wolf" only in recent times.[518] How recent is "recent"? In Qazwini's *Nuzhat al-qulub*, written in 1339, *qurt* already means wolf.[519] *Qurt* was apparently a general term for living beings, used for the wolf when its actual name was taboo.[520]

As long as the discussion of Akatir had to be, as briefly can the other tribal names of the Huns be dealt with.

Ultinčur

Ultzinzures, Οὐλτίνζουροι, is composed of *Ultin* and *čur*. Whatever *Ultin* may mean, it is probably as Turkish as *il* in *ilčur*.

Four names end certainly, one almost certainly, and another one possibly in *-gur*.

1. Κοντρίγουροι. Although the exact form hidden behind the various readings[521] cannot be determined, the name ends even in the most aberrant variants in *-gur*.

2. Hunuguri,[522] 'Ονόγουροι, is Turkish *On-Ogur*, "ten Ogur." Hamilton tried to prove that Onogur is a poor transcription of On-Uyghur. The Byzantines allegedly were unable to render the diphthong *uy* in their script.[523] But they wrote 'Ωηβάρσιος and 'Ωήχ;[524] there was nothing that could have prevented them from writing *'Ονωήγουροι.

3. Οὐτίγουροι. Except in two inferior codices, the readings, as manifold as those of Kutrigur,[525] all end in *-gur*.

4. The Bittugures, one of the tribes who acknowledged Dengizich as their leader, joined the Ostrogoths on their trek to Italy; Ragnaris was one of them. Agathias' Βίττορες is *ΒΙΤΓΟΡΡΕΣ.[526]

5. Τούσουρες. Priscus (*EL* 121₅) has Τούνουροι[dat], Jordanes (*Getica* 90₁₂) Tuncarsos[acc], *Tuncursos. Markwart emended Τούνσουρες to read Τούνγουρες.[527]

---

[518] *KCsA* 2, 44.

[519] *BSOAS* 6, 1931, 565.

[520] A. M. Shcherbak in *Istoricheskoe razvitie leksiki turetskikh iazykov*, 132-133.

[521] Moravcsik, *BT* 2, 171-172.

[522] *Getica* 63. Hunuguri is not Hun-uguri, in which case Jordanes would have written Hunnuguri, but Un-Uguri.

[523] 1962, 38.

[524] Menander, *EL* 452₂₉.

[525] Moravcsik, *BT* 2, 238.

[526] Zeuss 1837, 709.

[527] Markwart 1911, 11, note. Later (1932, 208), he changed his mind and took the name to be *Tunčur. But sigma could not render *č*.

In Koibal *ton* means "people"; see Pritsak (1952, 56) with reference to Castren. The Tongur, Dongur, Tongul were "bones" of the Altai Turks (Grum-Grzhimailo 1930, 19). If I remember correctly, Tongur was mentioned to me as a "bone" on the Dzhakul River in the Khoshun Kemchik in Tannu-Tuva.

6. *Σόροσγοι*. After signing the peace treaty of Margus, Bleda and Attila went to war against the Sorosgi, a people in Scythia.[528] Kulakovskii took the name, a *hapax legomenon*, for misspelled Saragur,[529] which was not a good guess. When one thinks of τὸ τῶν Σογὸς ἔθνος in Nicephorus Callistus,[530] which goes back to Theophylactus' τοὺς Ὀγώς, one is tempted to take the sigma at the beginning of the name for a dittography: προσσοροσγους <*προσοροσγους. *ΟΡΟΣΓΟΙ is possibly a distortion of ΟΡΟΥΓΟΙ. Priscus' Οὔρωγαι are misspelled Οὔγωροι.[531] The possibility that (Σ)οροσγοι stands for Ὀγουροι cannot entirely be ruled out.

Angisciri

The name occurs only in *Getica* 128₃: *angisciros^{acc}*, *angiscires*. The Angisciri were one of the four tribes which remained loyal to Dengizich. Vasmer took *angi-* to mean the same as OE *eng*, "grassland";[532] the Angisciri would, thus, be the "grassland Sciri." As, however, the other three tribes, Ultzinzures, Bittugures, and Bardores, have Turkish names, it seems more likely that Angisciri is also Turkish. The scribes may have assimilated an unfamiliar name to that of the Sciri, who in the *Romana* are named twice and in the *Getica* five times. *Angis-* is reminiscent of *äŋiz*, "field."[533] *Angisciri* might be *Angisgiri*.

Bardores

The name[534] is evidently compounded of *var*, as in Οὐαρχωνῖται, and -*dor*. This *dor-dur* is not only the second element in Ultzindur; it occurs also in *Bayundur*, the name of an Oghuz tribe, and the tribal names listed by Pritsak (1952, 77).[535] *Cegitur* is a Kirghiz clan.[536]

---

[528] Priscus, *EL* 122₂₂.

[529] 1913, 1, 265.

[530] *PG* 147, c. 385c.

[531] Moravcsik, *BT* 2, 227, 238.

[532] *Arkiv. f. nord. filol.* 58, 1944, 87-88.

[533] Kāshgharī, 22; Malov 1951, 206: 8, 15.

[534] *Getica* 128₂₃; v. l. *bardares*.

[535] Apparently none of them belongs to the group of names with the imperative suffix -*dur*, which L. Rásonyi discussed in *AOH* 15, 1962, 233-243.

[536] Vinnikov 1956, fig. 16.

Βαρσήλτ

This people is named together with Unugur and Sabir.[537] Markwart (1924, 324) took Barselt to be an Ossetic plural: *Barsel-t*. He identified the *Barsel with Menander's (*Βαρ)ζάλοι*; Basil-kᶜ in Ps. Moses Chorenacʿi; *B'grsyk*[538] in the list of 555; *Βερζίλια*, the old home of the Khazars; and Barčula, one of the three tribes of the Volga Bulgars. All this is highly hypothetical. For more speculations on these names, see Minorsky 1958, 94, and *Oriens* II, 1958, 125-126; Artamonov, index 498, s.v. Barsily. K. F. Smirnov (*KS* 45, 1952b, 95) thinks the graves at Agachkalinsk near Buinaksk on the northwestern shore of the Caspian Sea can be assigned to the Barsil. *Barsel* occurs in the legend of a Volga Bulgarian coin of the tenth century (see S. A. Ianina, *MIA* 111, 1962, 187, n. 41).

Καδισηνοί

John of Antioch (*EL* 139₆) is the only author to call the Cadiseni a Hunnic people. Seventy years ago Nöldeke proved that the Cadiseni, repeatedly named by Byzantine, Syriac, and Armenian authors, had nothing to do with the he Huns.[539]

Ζάλοι

Mentioned only by Menander (*EL* 443₉) as a Hunnic tribe. It is difficult not to think of Ptolemy's *Σάλοι* in European Sarmatia[540] and Pliny's *Salae* in Colchis,[541] but see *Βαρσῆλτ*.

Σάβιροι

On the various forms, see Moravcsik, *BT* 2, 262. For years the Sabirs were the favorite objects of name hunters. Pelliot was inclined to accept Németh's Turkish etymology;[542] the Sabirs were "the wanderers."[543] Henning (1952, 502, n. 5) thought he found the Sabirs in the Sogdian Naf-namak, which would place Sabir in the neighborhood of Turfan long after the fifth century. Moór offers a particularly unconvincing Iranian etymology.[544]

---

[537] Moravcsik, *BT* 2, 87.
[538] Restored as *B'RSYLQ* by Markwart; W. B. Henning (1952, 504, n. 4) suggests *B'RSYGQ*, Armenian *Barsilk'*.
[539] "Zwei Völker Vorderasiens," *ZDMG* 33, 1897, 157-163.
[540] *Geog.*
[541] *HN* VI, 14.
[542] 1950, 232.
[543] *MNy* 25, 1929, 81-88.
[544] *UJb* 31, 1959, 205-206.

After the collapse of Attila's kingdom, "Sciri and Sadagarii and certain of the Alans . . . received Scythia minor and Moesia inferior."[545] The Sadagarii cannot be separated from those *Sadages* who, at the same time, still loyal to Dengizich, "held the interior of Pannonia.[546] This has been pointed out by Zeuss as early as 1837[547] but did not prevent serious scholars, as well as a host of dilettantes, from offering the fanciest Iranian and Turkish etymologies. They either divided Sadagarii into Sada-garii[548] or Sadagarii;[549] Abaev preferred the reading Sadagarii because it gave him the chance to suggest an Ossetic etymology.[550] It is, or should be, obvious that -*es* is the Greek and -*arii* the Latin ending.[551] The name is obscure. It is not even known whether the tribe formed a part of the Hunnic confederacy in the narrow sense or was only loosely connected with it.

CONCLUSIONS

To judge by the tribal names, a great part of the Huns must have spoken a Turkish language. Ultinčur and Alpilčur are as Turkish as Bug-čor, the Pecheneg tribal names ending in τζουρ, and the Kirghiz tribal and clan names ending in *čoro*. Another common ending in Turkish tribal names, -*gur*, occurs in Kutrigur, Utigur, Onogur, Bittugur, *Tongur, and *Ugur. On the analogy with Ultinčur, Ultingir, ending in -*gir* like other definitely Turkish ethnic names, must likewise be Turkish. The same is true for Bardor = Var-dor and Ultindur.

The personal names give a different picture.

The names of the *Attilanic Huns* are as follows:

Turkish or probably Turkish: Basich, Berichos, Dengizich, Ellac, Emnetzur, Erekan, Eskam, Mundzucus, Oebarsios, Uldin, Ultzindur;

Germanic or Germanized: Attila, Bleda, Edekon, Laudaricus, Onegesius, Ruga;

Persian: Hormidac;

Hybrid: Kursich, Tuldila;

Unknown origin: Adamis, Charaton, Ernach, Esla, Mama, Octar, Skotta.

---

[545] *Getica* 265.
[546] *Ibid.*, 272-273.
[547] Zeuss 1837.
[548] Vasmer 1923, 49; Arnim 1936, 348-351; Harmatta 1947, 7-28.
[549] Markwart 1903, 44, and *Izv. russk. arkheol. inst. v Konst.* 15, 1911, 13, note.
[550] 1949, 179-180.
[551] Zgusta 1955, 263, § 533.

Akatir
Possibly Turkish: Kuridachos.

Bittugures
Germanic: Ragnaris

Utigur and Kutrigur
Turkish: Sandil, Sandilchos;
Iranian: Zabergan;
Of unknown origin: Anagaios, Chinialon.

Bosporan Huns
Of unknown origin: Gordas, Muageris.

Caucasian Huns
Iranian: Amazukes, Glones, Styrax;
Of unknown origin: Zilgibis.

Sabir
Probably Turkish: Balach, Iliger, Kutilzis;
Of unknown origin: Boarex.

Huns in the East Roman army
Turkish: Althias, Elminčur, Elmingeir, Zolbon;
Iranian: Aischmanos, Balas, Chorsomanos, Chorsomantis, Zartir;
Hybrid: Apsich, Apsikal;
Of unknown origin: Aigan, Akum, Argek, Askan, Bochas, Chalazar, Chelchal, Gubulgudu, Odolgan, Sigizan, Simmas, Sinnion, Sunikas, Tarrach, Turgun, Uldach.

The distribution of the Iranian and German or Germanized names is very instructive. No Germanic names occur among the non-Attilanic Huns. If any Germans in the East, outside the Crimea, survived the Hun storm, they either were too few or in a social position too low to allow their names to appear among those of the ruling groups or even in the ranks of those free warriors who took service in the Byzantine army. In contrast, no less than six of the Attilanic names are Germanic or pseudo-Germanic. The forms in Priscus and Jordanes are as Germanic as Alaric and Theoderic, not only because the real Hunnish names were transformed in Gothic pronunciation; they corroborate what Jordanes says about Attila's friendship with the Germanic leaders. The stress is on leaders. Thompson rightly emphasized the one-sidedness of the so-called Hunno-Gothic symbiosis. The generous and magnanimous Attila of German epic poetry shared with the Gothic and Gepidic chieftains the loot he brought back from his campaigns. If those wretched Goths who in the 460's were forced to march with the Huns had composed songs, they would have been very different from the poetry at the sites of the Germanic "kings."

Taken by themselves, Charaton and Ernac could be either Turkish or Iranian. In view of the absence of definitely Iranian and the preponderance of definitely Turkish names among the Attilanic Huns, they must be transferred from the column "of unknown origin" to the Turkish names. In a previous chapter I conjectured that the greater part of the Alans broke their alliance with the Huns about 400 A.D. and migrated west. This is now borne out by the analysis of the Attilanic names. In the fifth century the Alans played no political role in the life of the Huns. None of their nobles was accepted as equal, none rose to any prominence.

The absence of Iranian names before the sixth century speaks against strong relations between pre-Attilanic Huns and Parthians, Sasanian Persians, and Middle Asiatic Iranians. The Iranian names of the Caucasian Huns were no doubt borrowed either from Persians or from Armenians and Georgians under strong Persian influence. Of greater interest are the Iranian names in the Byzantine army, but they concern first of all the students of the proto-Bulgarians. Asparuch-Isperikh, Bezmer in the Princes' List, and Rasata in the list from Cividale are also of Iranian origin. To analyze the Iranian Hunnish names must be left to Iranian scholars. Some of these names, as, for instance, B(V)alas, are almost certainly Persian; others may be Sarmatian. Whereas there is very little archaeological evidence of Persian influence on the nomads between the Volga and the Crimea, the presence of Sarmatian elements in the culture of the proto-Bulgarians is well attested. The artificially deformed skulls in proto-Bulgarian graves cannot be separated from those in the graves of the Sarmatized Turks or Turkicized Sarmatians of the post-Attilanic graves in the South Russian steppes.

X. Early Huns in Eastern Europe

LITERARY, epigraphic, archaeological, and palaeoanthropological evidence indicate the presence of Huns near the Black Sea long before the Attilanic Huns broke into the Ukraine in the seventies of the fourth century.

No Greek or Roman knew where the Attilanic Huns came from. Ammianus Marcellinus placed their home beyond the Maeotis, the Sea of Azov, "near the ice-bound Ocean" (XXXI, 3, 1), which sheds some light on his geographic notions but none on the Huns. Eighty years later Priscus had nothing better to offer than the legend of the doe which showed the Huns the way across the Strait of Kerch into the Crimea.[1] Whether he read it in Eunapius or heard it at Attila's court cannot be determined. In any case, the legend is a variant of the widespread Eurasian story of the guiding animal.[2] A number of supposedly early Huns owe their existence to tamperings with the texts.

1. In *Nat. hist.* VI, 55, Pliny has: "After the Attacorsi, there are the Thuni and Focari tribes and — already belonging to the natives of India — the Casiri, situated in the interior in the direction of the Scythians. These are cannibals" (*Ab Attacoris gentes Thuni et Focari et, iam Indorum, Casiri introrsus ad Scythas versi humanis corporibus vescuntur*). This is the reading in the codex Leidensis Vossianus of the late ninth century, which

---

[1] Cf. Vasiliev 1936, 25-26.

[2] P. Pschmadt, *Die Sage von der verfolgten Hinde* (Greifswald, 1911); Gy. Moravcsik, *Egytemes Philologiai Közlöny* 1914, 280-293, 333-338 (French summary, *BZ* 23, 1923, 430); G. Hüsing, *Mitra* 1914, 42-45; J. Berze Nagy, *Ethnographia* 1927, 65-80, 145-164; W. Bang and G. R. Rachmati, *SB Berlin* 25:6, 1932, 693-695, 697, 701; J. Wiesner, *Pisciculi* (Münster, 1939), 18-19; K. Kerényi, *Anales de Historia Antigua y Medieval* (Buenos Aires, 1953), 76-89. I retract my consent (Maenchen-Helfen 1945c, 244) to Vasiliev's thesis on the Greek origin of the legend.

all editors agree is the best manuscript. It is also the reading in codices Vat. Lat. 3861 and Parisinus Lat. 6795 (both eleventh century), Vindo-bonensis 234 (twelfth or thirteenth century), and Parisinus Lat. 6797 (thirteenth century). The codex Florentinus Ricciardianus, full of many erratic readings, has *Chuni* instead of *Thuni*.

2. It has long been recognized that Orosius (*Hist. adv. Pag.* I, 2, 45) wrote *inter Funos, Scythas, et Gandaridas mons Caucasus*.[3] The codex Vat. Pal. 829 also has *Funos*, but a later hand added *Hunos*. In the codex Bobiensis Ambrosianus, we already read *Chunos* as in all later codices (*Chunos* or *Hunos*).

3. Another name so similar to that of the Huns that, independently from one another, Latin, Armenian, and Coptic scribes changed it into Huns was Uenni. Οὐεννοί in Hippolytus' *Chronicle*, written before 235 A.D.,[4] is itself a corruption of Οὐενετοί.[5] In the *Liber generationis mundi*, based on Hippolytus, the Οὐεννοί appear as *Uieni* or *Uenni*.[6] The *Barbarus Scaligeri* has instead *Hunni*.[7] Like the Western scribes, the Armenian translator of Hippolytus thought it his duty to correct the "error" of earlier copyists: He rendered Οὐεννοί by *Honkʿ*.[8]

4. The Greek original of Epiphanius' *Treatise on the Twelve Stones*, written about 394, is lost, but the greater part of an early Latin translation is preserved in the Collectio Avellana. In the "northern region which the ancients used to call Scythia" live *Gothi et Dauni, Uenni quoque et Arii usque ad Germanorum Amazonarumque regionem*.[9] Francesco Foggini, the first editor of *De Gemmis* (1743), thought the passage was corrupt and suggested the reading *Hunni* for *Uenni*. But he left the text as he found it. The man who translated the Greek original into Coptic was bolder—he simply altered a name that meant nothing to him to "Huns."[10]

5. A passage in Jordanes' *Getica* 30 seems to betray some knowledge of the Huns in their ancient sites in the East. Jordanes writes: "Scythia is formed like a mushroom, at first narrow and then broad and round in shape, extending as far as the Hunni, Albani, and Seres." As Mommsen noticed,[11] the simile points to Cassiodorus,[12] Jordanes' main source. Where

---

[3] Gutschmid 1889, p. vii.
[4] Hippolytus, *GCS* 4, 1929, 57, n. 28.
[5] Markwart 1903, 462, n. 2.
[6] *CM* I, 97, no. 58, 31.
[7] *Ibid.*
[8] Markwart 1903, 463, n. 28.
[9] *CSEL* 35, 753.
[10] Epiphanius, Blake and de Vis 1934, 257.
[11] In his edition of Jordanes, 61, n. 2.
[12] *Variae* III, 48.

did Cassiodorus read that the Huns were the neighbors of the Seres, supposedly the Chinese? There is little doubt that his source was one of the popular compendia which, directly or indirectly, went back to Dionysius' *Periegesis*. Cassiodorus recommended "the map of Dionysius" to his monks.[13] It is not particularly significant that in both the *Getica* and the *Periegesis* the Caspian Sea is a gulf of the ocean; this was a belief held and combatted since the time of the Ionian geographers. But it is striking that in the *Getica* Huns and Albani are named together as in some manuscripts of the *Periegesis*: "Along the shores of the Caspian Sea live the Scythians in the North, then Οὖννοι, followed by the Caspii and the martial Albani." These are the names in Müller's edition of the text,[14] still widely quoted.

Actually, none of the manuscripts used by Müller has Οὖννοι.[15] They have θοῦννοι, θοῦνοι, ὦνοι, and ὦννοι; codex *a*, by far the best, has θυνοι. As early as the later half of the fourth century there must have existed a variety of readings. Not knowing which one to chose, Avienus, who about 370 translated the popular primer into Latin, left the name out. He wrote: "Here, near the Caspian Sea the warlike Scythian is living and here the wild Albanians dwell" (*Hic uada propter |Caspia uersatur Scytha belliger, hicque feroces| degunt Albani*).[16]

Priscianus in the early sixth century has *Thynus*: "Then the Thyni follow, after them the audacious Caspian tribes. Then there are the Albani, rejoycing in fierce war" (*Hinc Thynus sequitur, Post fortis Caspia proles.| Hinc sunt Albani bellaces Marte feroci*).[17] In his scholion on the *Periegesis*, written before 1175, Eustathius of Thessalonica still knew of two readings: Οὖννοι and θοῦννοι.[18] As in the other above adduced "emendations," the well-known ethnic name prevailed).[19]

Dionysius concluded the catalogue of the peoples in the East with the Seres, ἔθνεα βάρβαρα Σηρῶν (v. 752), a name which, together with the preceding Phruni, he took from Strabo XI, 516, who had it from Apollodorus.[20]

The three peoples in the *Getica*, Huns, Albani, and Seres, are those with which the list in the "corrected" *Periegesis* begins—the Huns taking

---

[13] *Inst. div. litt.* c. 25.

[14] *GGM* 149.

[15] Cf. A. Ludwich, *Aristarchs homerische Textkritik* 2 (Leipzig, 1885), 594; E. Anhut, *In Dionysium periegetam quaestiones criticae* (Regiomonti, 1888); U. Bernays, *Studien zu Dionysius Periegetes* (Heidelberg, 1905), 66.

[16] *Orbis terrae*, vv. 905-908.

[17] Woestijne 1953, 77.

[18] *GGM*

[19] Kiessling's emendation Οὔιτιοι instead of Οὖννοι (*PW* VIII, 2953-2954) is incompatible with the readings in the manuscripts.

[20] Tarn 1951, 89.

the place of the Thyni—and *ends*. By radically shortening the list, leaving out all the names between the second, fourth, and last one, Cassiodorus or his source, followed by Jordanes, made the Huns and Albani the neighbors of the Chinese. The passage in the *Getica* does not go back to a lost ancient source. It is the product of telescoping a schoolbook into which the Huns had been smuggled. The passage is of some interest for the textual history of Dionysius' *Periegesis*. In the study of the Huns it has no place.[21]

It is a relief to turn from these fictitious Huns to Ptolemy's Χοῦνοι. In the third book of his geography, he lists them among the peoples of European Sarmatia—they live between the Basternae and the Rhoxolani.[22] Because these peoples are well known, it should be easy to locate the Chuni on the map of eastern Europe. However, we have to do with Ptolemy, not Strabo or another of the great Greek geographers.

Proceeding from west to east, Ptolemy puts the Peucini and Basternae "above Dacia" (III, 5, 7). He knows of a Peuce Mountain (III, 5, 5), but does not mention a "Basternon oros," so his Basternae were in the plains east of the mountain range which surrounds Dacia. He gives, furthermore, the bend of the Tyras (Dniester) as the boundary between Dacia and Sarmatia (III, 5, 6). Ptolemy's Basternae lived, thus, in Rumanian Moldova and, possibly, also east of the Prut River.

---

[21] Latyshev's translation of the verses in the *Periegesis*, *Scythica et Caucasica* I, 1, 186, based on Müller's edition, has been reprinted in *VDI* 1948, 1 (23), 241, without any change and with the same commentary. The Soviet historians, unaware of the philological work done since Latyshev's time, still make this obsolete text the cornerstone of their reconstruction of the history of the Huns, see, *e.g.*, Bernshtam 1951, 135; Trever 1959, 192; Artamonov 1962, 42; A. P. Smirnov in *Istoriia SSSR* 1 (Moscow, 1966), 323. Sometimes their ideas about the *Periegesis* are a little strange: Smirnov calls Dionysius, the contemporary of Ptolemy, a Byzantine author; G. B. Fedorov (*MIA* 83, 1960, 15) confuses him with Dionysius of Halicarnassus. L. N. Gumilev (*VDI* 1960, 4, 123-125) drew the most far-reaching conclusions from the Latyshev translation. In 155, under the pressure of the Hsien-pi, the Hsiung-nu fled from the Tarbagai westward. In 160, they were on the Volga. Under other circumstances the Hsiung-nu trekked in their wagons at a comfortable speed. This time they covered 2,600 kilometers in two or three years. Constantly fighting off the pursuing Hsien-pi, they could not take their children and old folk with them; they kept riding, day in, day out, until finally the enemy turned back. Only the sturdiest survived the desperate flight. The corpses of Hun women were scattered over Middle Asia. In these one thousand days all forms of higher social organization broke down, all the splendid cultural achievements of the past were lost. On the Volga the Hsiung-nu warriors had to find wives among an alien race. The Hsiung-nu turned into Huns. This is truly amazing story, but the most amazing thing is Gumilev's elementary miscalculation: 2,600 kilometers divided by 1,000 gives not 26 but 2.6 kilometers, a distance which should have not been too much for even the stoutest Hunnic ladies.

[22] Μεταξὺ δὲ Βαστερνῶν καὶ Ῥοξολάνων Χοῦνοι (*Geog.* III, 5, 10).

"Along the entire coast of the Maeotis are the Iazyges and Rhoxolani" (III, 5, 7), the former in the west, the latter in the east as far as the Tanais (Don), which separates European from Asiatic Sarmatia.

The middle of a line drawn from the Basternae to the Rhoxolani would be somewhere north of the Crimea. This seems to be the nearest the Chuni can be located.

However, the passage on the peoples along the Maeotis refers to a time long before Ptolemy wrote his *Geography*. As so often, he thoughtlessly copied earlier authors. By the middle of the second century, both the Iazyges and the Rhoxolani lived hundreds of miles away from the Sea of Azov.

Moving westward, the Iazyges had reached the Danube in the second decade of the first century;[23] in the first years of Claudius they trekked through Dacia to Hungary where they occupied the northwestern parts of the Alföld, gradually spreading over all of it and holding it for more than three hundred years. A few Iazyges may have stayed behind in the old sites, but these were not "the" Iazyges. It is true Ptolemy speaks about the "emigrant," *metanastai* Iazyges; he even names eight of their cities (III, 7, 1-2). And yet, slavishly copying his authorities, he puts the Iazyges east of the lower Dnieper.

The Rhoxolani, too, or, to be more cautious, most of them, had long left their old sites. Under Nero they came in contact with the Romans not on the Don but on the Danube. In the winter of 67/8 and again in 69, Rhoxolanic horsemen raided Moesia. In alliance with Diurpaneus, king of the Daci, the Basternae and Rhoxolani defeated a Roman corps in the southern Dobrogea.[24] In 101, Rhoxolani fought against Trajan on the lower Danube. A few years later the emperor concluded an alliance with them and they were paid subsidies; in return they pledged themselves to protect the Roman provinces from inroads of other Sarmatian tribes.[25]

There arises the question: Which Rhoxolani were the neighbors of the Chuni? Those of Ptolemy's text or those of Ptolemy's time?[26] The question may sound absurd, but one has to keep in mind how arbitrarily

---

[23] Cf. Diacoviciu 1960, 121.

[24] Whether the famous tropaeum at Adamclisi was erected on the battlefield is not as certain as it has been assumed; see A. Richmond, *SCIV* 19: 1, 1968, 3-29.

[25] Dessau 986; Tacitus, *Hist.* I, 79; Mommsen 1909, 1, 217-218; Patsch 1932, 164-166, 172-173; L. Halkin, *L'antiquité classique* 3, 1934, 121-161; M. Rostovtsev, *Gnomon* 10, 1934, 9; Patsch 1940, 152-163.

[26] He wrote his *Geography* between 135 and 143 (E. Šimek, *Historia Slovaca* 5, 1948, 111-121, 233).

Ptolemy handled his material, drawing indiscriminately from old and new sources.

It was only under Trajan and Hadrian that the regions bordering on Dacia to the east and Moesia inferior to the north became better known. After the conquest of Dacia the old trade route from the Greek cities on the Black Sea to Transylvania was much frequented. The road from Apulum in Dacia to Piroboridava on the Seret and, along its left bank, to the Danube[27] runs through the country of the Basternae. Although in the second century the steppe north of the Crimea was to the Romans as little known as before, southern Moldavia was no longer *terra incognita*. Had the Chuni lived north of the Crimea somewhere between Kakhovka and Melitopol, Ptolemy would hardly have known of them. But he could very well have learned of a formerly unknown people in Moldavia. He may have seen the name on a map or learned it from travelers; the Chuni could have been mentioned in military reports.[28] Whatever Ptolemy's source was, the Rhoxolani near whom he placed the Chuni were almost certainly those allied with the Romans.

On his map of Ptolemy's European Sarmatia, Kulakovskii placed the Chuni east of the Amadocian Mountains, east of the Borysthenes.[29] On Latyshev's map,[30] their sites are approximately in the same regions. The Russian scholars did not yet know the codex Ebnerianus. There, on the map of European Sarmatia, the Chuni are between the Ariaxes (Tiligul) and the Borysthenes (Dnieper), north of Ordessus,[31] a location which comes close to the one we assumed on the basis of the text. Whether we follow the map, or place the Chuni between the Basternae and Rhoxolani in Ptolemy's time, they lived either on the right or left bank of the Dniester near the northwestern shore of the Black Sea.[32]

Ammianus Marcellinus most probably had Ptolemy in mind when he said that the Huns were little known from ancient records (XXXI, 2, 1).

---

[27] See the map in E. Panaitescu, *Le grande strade romane in Romania* (Rome, 1938), 15.

[28] Rostovtsev 1931, 66-71.

[29] 1899.

[30] Minns 1913, map 2.

[31] Stevenson 1932, map 8.

[32] Although Ptolemy's Chuni lived in European Sarmatia, west of the Tanais, the river which separates European from Asiatic Sarmatia, Altheim (1:3-4, 1962, 419) places the people east of it, between the Manych and the upper Kuban; he supports this location by an allegedly Greco-Alanic inscription on a pebble from Apsheronsk which O. Kurz (*JAOS* 82, 1962, 553-554) proved to be a crude forgery produced by a man in Sebastopol about 1900. Altheim's pupil, R. Werner (1967, 487-488), likewise placed the Cis-Tanaitic Chuni across the river into Asia. O. Pritsak (*Der Islam* 15, 1960, 194) moves the people to the Volga and the Ural River. I pass over L. Bagrov's wild ideas (*Geografiska Annaler* 17, 1945, 380).

Loose as the term *monumenta vetera* may be, Ammianus would not have applied it to works written one or two generations before his time. It has been suggested that he referred to an old map[33] (which could have been one of Ptolemy's maps); he may have come across the name in a chorography of the type which became popular in the middle of the second century;[34] he may have found it in Solinus' unabridged *Collectanea Rerum Memorabilium*;[35] one could think of still other sources.[36] But to speculate about lost literature is futile. Ptolemy's *Geography* is the only extant work in which an ethnic name occurs so similar to that of the Huns that Ammianus, who knew his Ptolemy,[37] could identify the Chuni and the Huns.

Marcian of Heraclea did the same. His *Periplus of the Outer Sea*,[38] written before 550,[39] is in the main an excerpt from Ptolemy.[40] Writing a periplus, Marcian left out nearly all the ethnic names in his source. He named none of the twenty-six tribes in Lugdunensis, none of the twenty-four in Belgica Gallia, and only one of the sixty-eight in Germania Magna (II, 24-26, 27-29, 31-56). He listed three peoples in Sarmatia: Agathyrsi and "in the region of the Borysthenes beyond the Alani" οἱ καλούμενοι Χοννοὶ οἱ ἐν τῇ Εὐρώπῃ (II, 39), "the so-called Huns, those in Europe."

This is a strange selection. Ptolemy named as the "great nations" of European Sarmatia the Venetae, Peucini, Iazyges, Rhoxolani, Hamaxobii, and Alani (III, 3, 7). Marcian chose the last one. Ptolemy gave the names of forty-nine "minor" peoples, among which Agathyrsi took the twenty-seventh and the Chuni the forty-seventh place (III, 5, 8-10), in no way distinguished from the others. And yet, Marcian singled them out. The reason for such a seemingly arbitrary choice was obviously the importance these peoples had for the East Romans at Marcian's time. The qualification of the Chuni as "those of Europe" makes sense only if Marcian knew of Chuni elsewhere.

Marcian disregarded the Peucini and Hamaxobii and all the other queer names which meant nothing to him, but the Alans, though not those in Sarmatia, were until 534 very much alive. Their brothers were the allies of the Vandals in Africa. This, by the way, indicates the date of

---

[33] Kiessling, *PW* VIII, 2591-2592.

[34] Müllenhoff, *DA* III, 86.

[35] One of Ammianus' sources; cf. Th. Mommsen, *Hermes* 16, 1891.

[36] A. Romano, *Rivista di storia antica*, N.S. 8, 1904, 1-14.

[37] Malotet 1898, 9-12; Fischer 1932, 482-487.

[38] *GGM* I, 515-562; *Periplus of the Outer Sea*, Schoff 1927.

[39] Diller 1932, 34. The *misellus alienorum librorum breviator* (C. Müller, *GGM* I, CXXXX) is of course not the Marcian whom Synesius (*Ep.* 100, *PG* 66, 1472) called a philosopher and "more than a likeness to Hermes"; cf. also Fischer 1932, 447-452.

[40] Bunbury 1883, 660.

Marcian's *Periplus*: After Belisarius took Carthage and Justinian called himself *Alanicus* there was no longer any reason to speak of the Alans as an important people.

Why Marcian kept the Agathyrsi of Ptolemy's list is at first glance puzzling. Aristotle was the last author to mention them as a real people;[41] since then they had led a purely literary existence. Kaspar Zeuss tentatively identified them with the Hunnic Catir.[42] Validi Togan thought as late as 1939 that Zeuss was right.[43] When one considers that by the middle of the sixth century the Azatir were still *gens fortissima*,[44] it becomes understandable why Marcian named them together with the Chuni in Europe; he, too, took the Agathyrsi for another, older name of the Acatir.[45]

Whether this interpretation of Marcian's choice of the Alans and Agathyrsi be accepted or not is of no consequence for the main point: Marcian's identification of Ptolemy's Chuni with the Huns of his time. He apparently placed them more to the east than Ptolemy, presumably because he had those Huns in mind who in the first half of the sixth century repeatedly threatened the eastern Balkan provinces, the Huns in Europe, whom also Evagrius separated from "the other Hunnic peoples" in Asia.[46]

Ammianus' and Marcian's equation Chuni = Huns is not better and not worse than the many modern equations of this type: it is an equation of two names. What is the actual relationship between the Chuni and the Huns? Thompson's answer is—none; he takes the similarity of the names for a purely coincidental one.[47] Bussagli suspects Chuni to be an interpolation in Ptolemy's text,[48] which, I think, is most improbable. The scribe who is supposed to have smuggled the ethnic name into Ptolemy's list would, first, have used the usual form $O\tilde{v}vvoι$, and, second, he would have made them one of the great barbarian peoples of Sarmatia, not tucked away among forty-nine minor tribes.

The Chuni are not "the" Huns who (and in this respect Thompson is right) could not have survived in the Pontic area for two hundred years without becoming known to the Romans. They were not the "ancestors" of the Huns either. Most certainly they were not the descendants of Chih-

---

[41] Patsch 1925, 66-67; later (1937, 3, n. 3). Patsch thought some Agathyrsi might have lived in Dacia as late as the second century A.D.

[42] Zeuss 1837, 714.

[43] Ibn Fadlan 1939, p. XXX.

[44] *Getica* 36.

[45] On the Akatir, see O. J. Maenchen-Helfen 1966.

[46] VI, 41, Bidez, 145. In 515, they raided Cappadocia (*CM* I, 99, 15-16).

[47] Thompson 1948, 21.

[48] Bussagli 1950, 212, n. 1.

chih's Hsiung-nu, as Hirth[49] and Kiessling[50] thought. The myth of Chih-chih's "mighty Hsiung-nu empire in K'ang-chü" has been exploded by Teggart.[51] The Chinese annihilated Chih-chih's hordes to the last man.

Had Ptolemy's Chuni lived in Africa or the British Isles we could ignore them. But their sites were in a region where two and a half century later Huns did live. This still could be a coincidence, though a strange one. And yet, in order to prove that Chuni is more than an assonance to Hun more data would be welcome. I think they exist. In the 250's Goths, Borani, Carpi, and Οὐρουγοῦνδοι, peoples living beyond the lower Danube, broke into the Balkan provinces and made an expedition by sea to Asia Minor.[52] The Carpi were Dacians, the Borani possibly Sarmatians.[53] Who were the *Urugundi*? Historians and philologists have been discussing their nationality for more than a century. Some regard them as Germans, assuming that Οὐρουγοῦνδοι is a variant of Burgundi;[54] others see in them Strabo's Οὔργοι;[55] still others think they were a Hunnic people. The latter was the view of Kaspar Zeuss;[56] it is, I believe, the right one.

There are two arguments in its favor. There is, first, the name Burgundi in Mamertinus' *Panegyric on Emperor Maximian*. The rhetor praises the good fortune of the emperor. The barbarians are killing one another: "The Goths almost completely annihilated the Burgundi, and, in turn, for the defeated, the Alamanni and, likewise, the Tervingi, took up arms" (*Gothi Burgundos penitus excidunt rursumque pro victis armantur Alamanni itemque Tervingi*).[57] It has long been recognized that *Alamanni* is to be emended to read *Alani*; the Goths in South Russia could not have fought with the Alamanni on the Rhine. For the same reasons the *Burgundi* cannot be the Burgundians on the Roman *limes* in the West. To call them "east" Burgundians as if they were a splinter of the "west" Burgundians, somehow, sometime, somewhere chopped off from the mother folk, is sheer arbitrariness. Mamertinus himself clearly distinguishes between the *Bur-*

---

[49] *Keleti Szemle* 1901, 85.

[50] *PW* VIII, 2591.

[51] Teggart 1939, 153. Cf. also S. S. Sorokin, *KS* 64, 1956, 7, n. 1, and L. N. Gumilev in *Issledovaniia po istorii i kul'ture narodov vostoka* (Moscow and Leningrad, 1960), 161-166.

[52] Zosimus I, 27, 1, and 31, 1, Mendelssohn 1887, 19_{14} and 22_{13}. Cf. A. Alfoldi, *CAH* 11, 146.

[53] Some Slavomaniacs, *e.g.*, Remennikov, 1954, 10, take the Borani for Slavs. Their fantasies have been sharply rejected by V. V. Kropotkin (*Ocherki* 2, 128).

[54] For the older literature, see B. Rappaport 1899, 36, n. 4. Cf. L. Schmidt 1934, 130.

[55] A. D. Udal'tsov, *SE* 2, 1946, 41.

[56] Zeuss 1837, 280, 466, 694.

[57] XVII, 1, Galletier, 65.

gundi and the western *Burgundiones*. It is the same distinction which Zosimus makes between Οὐρουγοῦνδοι and Βούργουνδοι. Mamertinus' Burgundi and Zosimus' Οὐρουγοῦνδοι are obviously the same people. When one considers that in Latin transcriptions the initial *v-* in foreign names was frequently rendered by *b-*, as, for example, in Bandali or Bitheridus,[58] and that in Greek transcriptions the *v-* was often dropped (the best known example is Οὔλφιλας = Vulfila, the ethnic name must have been * *Vur(u)gund*.

It occurs in Agathias in a list of Hunnic tribal names: Κοτρίγουροι, Οὐτίγουροι, Οὐλτίτζουροι, and Βουρούγουνδοι.[59] Until Emperor Leo (died in 474), adds Agathias, the Βουρούγουνδοι and Ultizuri were well known and considered brave peoples; now they have disappeared, either because they were exterminated or had moved away.[60]

Zosimus' and Mamertinus' *Vur(u)gund* cannot be separated from Agathias' *Vurugund*. Their name is apparently related to Ὀνογούνδουροι or Οὐνογούνδουροι in Theophanes and Constantine Porphyrogenitus.[61]

The *Alpilčur lived on the Maeotis before the Attilanic Huns crossed the Don. As the name proves and as the context in which it appears shows, they were a Hunnic tribe. How long before the 370's they had lived in South Russia cannot be determined but their close and permanent association with the *Tungur, Itimari, and Boisci indicates that they were anything but newcomers.

*Tungur might be another Turkish name; the nationality of the Itimari is unknown;[62] the Boisci are supposed to be a branch of the people whom Ptolemy calls Ῥόβοισκοι, Orosius' Rhobasci: the Boisci on the Volga (*Ρᾶ* = Raha).[63] The personal name Βοισκος occurs three times in inscriptions in the Greek towns on the northern shore of the Black Sea:[64]

---

[58] Schönfeld 1911, p. xxiii.

[59] Agathias V, 11, 2, Keydell 1967, 177.

[60] Agathias V, 11, 4, Keydell 1967, 177.

[61] Moravcsik, *BT* 2. Pritsak's analysis of the name V(B)urugund (*UJB*, 1952, 56, 75, 77) contains nothing but wrong quotations. He divides Βουρούγουνδοι into Burugun+d; *-gun* is supposed to be the same collective suffic as in Οὐννουγοῦνοι, for which Pritsak refers to Moravcsik, *BT* 2, 189 (219 in the second edition). However, there the latter name is listed as an *erroneous* form of Ὀνόγουροι, recognized as such as early as 1774. This *-gun* is, furthermore, supposed to occur in Burgundiones, "the name of a proto-Bulgarian tribal group," *-dion* being the Turkish suffix *-d°n*. Pritsak refers to Moravcsik (*BT* 2, 102), who has nothing on these nonexisting proto-Bulgarians. The Burgundiones are, of course, the Germanic Burgundians.

[62] Tomaschek (1888, 17) thought the name was compounded of *Itil*, the Volga River, and Iranian *mar*, "men." Markwart (1903, 356) equated it with *Dirmar* in the Syriac list of 555.

[63] Markwart 1924, 269-270.

[64] It is not listed in Zgusta 1955.

twice in Chersonese in the second eentury[65] and in an inscription of the first or second century from Mangalia (Callatis) in the Dobrogea.[66] When one considers the many names in Euxine inscriptions which indicate the ethnic origin, like Daus, Callipides, Conapsus, Lazenus, Cholus, Reusinalus, Saius, Sauromates, Sindus, Sirachus, and Scythas, there can be no doubt that Boiscus means a man from the people or tribe of the Boisci. The Boii whom the Getic king Burebista defeated were, like the Taurisci, Celts. Boisci means the "little Boii," a name formed with the diminutive suffix common to Greek, Celtic, and Germanic; compare Basiliscus = regulus, Heracliscus, "little Heracles." In other words, there existed in South Russia a tribal confederacy of Hunnic, Celtic, and other tribes *before* the coming of the Attilanic Huns.

If there existed Turkish-speaking groups in eastern Europe before the fourth century A.D., they might have been Huns.[67] Attempts to find their traces have failed. Of the three not entirely dilettantish endeavors, one was made by the eminent Altaist W. Bang. He was inclined to derive *sagitta* from a Turkish word for vessel, which in the form *sayït* in Komanic meant "weapon." Although the origin of *sagitta* is obscure, it is unlikely that the Romans should have borrowed it from an obscure barbarian tribe in the East. The identification of θέγρι, an angel in the early Christian apocryphon *The Shepherd of Hermas*, with Turkish *teŋri* is equally untenable. There remains Yayïq, the name of the Ural River before it got its present name from the tsarina Elizabeth. Yayïq is supposed to be Turkish, a later form of Δάϊξ, as Ptolemy called the river. Turkologists and Altaists cannot agree on the word hidden behind Δάϊξ. Marquart assumed that the delta renders palatalized *d*; Pritsak thinks it stands for the fricative voiced dental; Menges takes it for the plosive voiced dental, and Poppe for the sibilant *ž*; even the possibility that delta transcribed *y* has been considered. Menges derives Yayïq from *yay-*, "to expand"; *yayïq* is supposed to mean "expanded." Ligeti points out that the verb has two variants; *yad* > *yaδ-*, *yas-*, *yai-*, and so forth, and *yań-* > *yai-*, *yan-*; he connects the name of the river with the second variant but denies that it ever was **dayïq*. In his opinion the initial *y-* became *d-* in the pronunciation of the word by Iranians who transmitted it to the Greek. Following Räsänen, Serebrennikov postulates an original *yayïq*, but the people in whose language *y-* turned into *d-* were in his opinion the Danube Bulgars. *Quot capita tot sensus.* Clauson rejects the Turkish etymology altogether. "The

---

[65] V. Latyshev, *IAK* 65, 1918, 10; A. K. Takhtai, *KS* 15, 1947, 59; *VDI* 3, 1960, 15.

[66] A. Radulescu, *SCIV* 14, 1963, 84.

[67] [*The text of the manuscript indicates that the author prepared footnotes from here to the end of the chapter; they are missing, however.—Ed.*]

most," he writes, "that can be claimed is that if the Ural river was called *yayik* instead of *dayik* when the local population became Turkish it was because the Turks could no longer pronounce initial *d-* and made it *y-* even in foreign words." Clauson, one of the few philologists who look beyond the pale of "pure linguistics," points out that in the second century A.D. the people on the Ural were Sarmatians. The archaeological and anthropological evidence is, indeed, unambiguous. From the seventh century B.C. to the third and fourth centuries A.D., the graves in the cis- and trans-Uralian steppes contain the goods of mounted Sarmatian herders; racially they were Europoids.

XI. Appendixes

1. THE CHRONICLE OF 452

The Gallic chronicle of 452 A.D., as it has come down to us, is both shortened and enlarged. Mommsen, who showed that the compiler of the Chronicle of 511 drew on a text that contained a number of entries missing in the present version of the earlier chronicle, did not notice that a later scribe added to it some material from Eastern sources. The author of the Chronicle of 452 reveals a knowledge of and interest in events in the East which one would not expect from a writer in southern Gaul. Under 438 he mentions the first publication of the *Codex Theodosianus*. He is the only Western author who knows of a Hun raid in Thrace in 445. The entry *s.a.* 447 is particularly unexpected: "A new disaster arose again for the East, in which no less than seventy cities were laid waste by a raid of the Huns, since no assistance was brought by the men of the West" (*Nova iterum Orienti consurgit ruina, qua septuaginta non minus civitates Chunorum depraedatione vastatae, cum nulla ab occidentalibus ferrentur auxilia*). It is at least conceivable that the chronicler learned somehow the number of the cities devastated by the Huns, although the exactness of his information is definitely unusual, but it is hard to imagine why he, on his own, should have criticized the inactivity of his own government. This is the voice of an East Roman we hear, not that of a man from Gaul. Thompson (1948, 93, 210) misunderstood the passage.

The prepenultimate entry is especially strange: "Attila invaded Gaul and demanded a wife as if she were his by right. There he inflicted one defeat, suffered another, and withdrew to his own territory" (*Attila Galliae ingressus quasi iure debitam poscit uxorem: ubi clade inflicta et accepta ad propria concedit*). This is all the chronicler of Marseilles is supposed to have said about a war that brought immeasurable misery not to Pisidia or the Thebais but to his own country, and not sometime in the past, but in the very

456

year in which he finished his work. If the terseness is strangely dispropor-
tionate to the importance of the events, the content of the entry, as it
stands, is unintelligible. Who is the woman whom Attila demanded as
if she were his by right? What is the connection between this demand
and the invasion of Gaul? No Western author shows any knowledge of
the alledged affair between Honoria and Attila to which the chronicler
alludes, a story which Priscus and those who copied him narrated with
such gusto. The entry clearly points to an Eastern source.

2. ARMENIAN SOURCES

In the present studies Armenian literature has been largely ignored.
I should justify what to some readers might seem to be a neglect.

It is now generally agreed that the work which for a long time went
under the name of Moses of Khorene was pieced together in the seventh,
if not the eighth or ninth century.[1] The *Life of St. Nerses*, formerly dated
in the fifth century,[2] turned out to be a late concoction.[3] The value of
Koriun as a historical source has become rather doubtful.[4] Until the complicated problem of the relationship between the various versions of Agathangelos is brought closer to a solution it seemed wiser not to touch this *fiction épique où le merveilleux le plus ahurissant alterne avec des prédictions
apocalyptiques*.[5] Elise Vardapet gives a detailed account of the war in
450-451 in which the Honkʿ played a prominent role. Or so it seemed
until Akinian proved that the book must be dated in the seventh century
and that the war is not the war between Yazdagird II and Vardan the
Great but the Armenian uprising of 572.[6] Akinian thought that the original was recast to fit the earlier war; Peeters[7] assumed that what we have
is the original and that the author transferred the recent fight for freedom
into the past in order to escape Persian censorship. In any case, Elise
Vardapet must be used with great caution, if he is used at all.

This leaves Faustus of Buzanta and Lazar of P'arb. Faustus' sources
are lives of saints, passions of martyrs, fragments of popular sagas, and

---

[1] M. Tarchnišvili, *Le Muséon* 60, 1947, 44; N. Akinian, *WZKM* 37, 1930, 204-217.
C. Tumanov (Toumanoff), in *Le Muséon* 73, 1960, 101 note, and *Handes Amsorya* 1961,
467, dates the literary activity of Moses of Khorene between 750 and 800; cf. M. van
Esbroeck, *Analecta Bollandiana* 80, 3-4, 1962, 428.

[2] J. R. Émine in Langlois 1869, 2, 18.

[3] Markwart 1932a, 153.

[4] Peeters, *Revue des études arméniennes* 9, 1929, 204-205.

[5] Peeters 1950, 79; cf. also M. Tarchnišvili, *Le Muséon* 60, 1947, 44.

[6] N. Akinian, *Elisaeus Vardapet und seine Geschichte des armenischen Krieges* 1,
German summary on pp. 371-393; see also W. Hengstenberg, *BZ* 38, 1938, 169-172.

[7] *Revue des études arméniennes* 9, 1929, 204-205; cf. Tarchnišvili, *Le Muséon* 60,
1947, 45.

half-religious, half-secular laments.[8] Like all Armenian histories the book abounds with wild exaggerations of Armenian victories over the vile fire worshippers. Faustus' account of the life of Grigoris,[9] "catholicus" of the Iberians and Albanians, is richly embroidered with pious inventions, but it is substantially true.[10] Grigoris suffered martyrdom in the land of Sanesan, king of the Mazʿkutʿkʿ or Mazʿkitʿkʿ, commander of an army of Honkʿ. Faustus describes their customs and speaks about their raids into Armenia.

In later Armenian literature Honkʿ [11] means doubtless Huns. Has it the same meaning in the works of the fifth and sixth centuries? This is at least doubtful. Markwart regarded the Mazʿkutʿkʿ as Massagetae whom he, in turn, equated with the Alans.[12] Peeters assumed that the Mazʿkutʿkʿ were rather the Μόσχοι, in Georgian the Meshketi of the Samtzkhe.[13] Orbeli[14] identified the Honkʿ with the ʿΗνίοχοι, Arrian's savage Heniochi, "a dangerous people when they shake their bridle."[15] It should be noted that none of the eleven peoples[16] whom Sanesan ruled besides the Honkʿ has a name even remotely similar to a Hun tribal name known from Western authorities.[17] As to the use of Honkʿ in Agathangelos, one also has to consider the possibility, which in one instance is almost a certainty,[18] that the author used the name "Hun" for earlier barbarians.[19]

For the period discussed in the present studies the Honkʿ in the *History of the Aluank*[20] need, I think, no justification. The last person to have a hand in it wrote at the earliest at the end of the eleventh or the beginning of the twelfth century.[21]

---

[8] P. Peeters, *R. Académie Belgique, Bull. classe de lettres*, ser. 5, vol. 17, 1931, no. 1, 35.

[9] The part of interest to us is best translated by Markwart [1932a?—*Ed.*], 211-212.

[10] Peeters 1932, 25.

[11] *-kʿ* is the plural suffix.

[12] Cf. Markwart [1932a?—*Ed.*], 218; cf. also Markwart 1929, 78.

[13] *Analecta Bollandiana* 50, 1932, 21.

[14] "Gorod bliznetsov *ΔΙΟΣΚΟΥΡΙΑΣ* i plemya vosnits *ΗΝΙΟΧΟΙ*," *Zhurnal ministerstva narodnago prosveshcheniia*, N.S. 33, May 1911, 195-215.

[15] Arrian, *Periplus Pont. Eux.* XI, 2; Lucan, *Pharsalia* III, 269-270.

[16] Orbeli (1911?—*Ed.*), 214. Cf. E. Honigmann, *BZ* 34, 1934, 145.

[17] Recently L. M. Melikset-Bek (*Doklady AN Azerbaĭdzh. SSR* 1957, no. 6, 712) pleaded again for the identification of the early Honkʿ with the Huns; Trever (1959, 191-194) and V. V. Struve (*VDI* 1960, 2, 182) take them to be a Caucasian people.

[18] A. Gutschmid 1894, 4, 382, 408.

[19] Cf. Artamonov 1962, 51-53.

[20] Movsēs Dasxurançi 1961.

[21] *Ibid.*, xx.

3. FIGURES IN OLYMPIODORUS

Thompson (1949, 8) praises Olympiodorus for his passion for statistics. Actually, most figures in Olympiodorus are dubious and some are outright fantastic. The following examples should suffice:

Ataulf mobilized ten thousand Goths against the twenty-eight men of Sarus (fr. 17).

Three hundred Huns killed eleven hundred Goths, losing themselves only seventeen men (Zosimus V, 45, 6).

In 408 the city of Rome paid Alaric 5, 000 pounds of gold, 30,000 pounds of silver, and delivered to him 4,000 silk garments, 3,000 scarlet-dyed skins, and 3,000 pounds of pepper, an amount which would have lasted the Visigoths for ten years (Zosimus V, 41, 4).

After the treacherous massacre of their wives and children in the summer of 408, the barbarian soldiers in Italy joined Alaric. They numbered more than thirty thousand (a favorite figure with Olympiodorus). In the confused situation after Stilicho's death, six or seven thousand soldiers could have made themselves the masters of Italy. But the government in Ravenna was not at all perturbed by this strengthening of Alaric's forces (Zosimus V, 35, 6).

The senator Maximianus was redeemed from the Visigoths with 30,000 solidi, which is more than the East Romans paid annually to the Huns in the 430's (Zosimus V, 45, 4).

"After the capture of Rome, Albinus, the city prefect, when the normal conditions of things were restored, reported [to the emperor] that the amount of grain distributed to the people was insufficient, for their number was increasing. He reported that as many as fourteen thousand children were born in one day" (fr. 25). Seeck (*Geschichte* 6, 60) and Sirago (1961, 130) accepted this figure. Stein (1959, 1, 394, n. 4) suggested emending τετέχ-θαι into δεδέχθαι; J. H. Freese (*The Library of Photius* 1, 141, n. 4) to τετάχθαι. The latter is the reading in codex Marcianus. Following it, R. Henry (*Photius* 1959, 1, 175) translates τετάχθαι ἀριθμὸν χιλιάδων δεκατεσσάρων as *on avait recensé quatorze mille personnes*. None of these scholars questioned the figure, which is impossible whatever the verb may be.

One could think that Photius misread Olympiodorus, but Zosimus has the same monstrous figures. All economic histories of the Roman Empire repeat Olympiodorus' account on the income of the rich families (fr. 44). I am afraid it is of questionable value.

4. THE ALLEGED LOSS OF PANNONIA PRIMA IN 395

The assertion, carried over from one book to the next,[1] that in 395 Germanic tribes, in particular the Marcomanni, made themselves masters

---

[1] Stein 1959, 1, 350; L. Schmidt 1934, 478; Swoboda 1958, 70, 224.

of Pannonia prima is based *solely* on the letter which in 396 Jerome sent to his friend Heliodorus. He wrote,

> I now come to the frail fortunes of human life, and my soul shudders to recount the downfall of our age. For twenty years and more the blood of Romans has every day been shed between Constantinople and the Julian Alps. Scythia, Thrace, Macedonia, Thessaly, Dardania, Dacia, Epirus, Dalmatia and all the provinces of Pannonia have been sacked, pillaged, and plundered by the Goths and Sarmatians, Quadi and Alans, Huns and Vandals and Marcomanni.[2]

This list of provinces and peoples is pure rhetoric. The vain littérateur could not even suppress his urge to show off his erudition in a letter of consolation. But even taken literally, the letter does not refer to 395. For twenty years and more, not just in the last twelve months, matrons, God's virgins, and ladies of gentle birth had been made "the sport of these beasts." It is, by the way, remarkable how Jerome, whenever he had a chance, dwelt on the rape of nuns and noble ladies.

In the list of provinces overrun by the barbarians in 395 Claudian named *plaga Pannoniae*.[3] He meant Pannonia secunda. Shortly after, Stilicho drove the enemy across the Danube;[4] *potor Savi* indicates precisely the liberated area.

Theodosius' death on January 17, 395, is supposed to have given the barbarians the signal to break into the border provinces. But a few lines in Claudian's panegyric on the third consulate of Honorius reflect some unrest in the northern Balkan provinces in the last months of 394.

When Theodosius fell ill in the fall of 394, he summoned his son Honorius to come to Milan as soon as possible.[5] The best and shortest communication between Constantinople and northern Italy was the road which ran through Adrianople, Philippopolis, Serdica, and Naissus to Singidunum, and from there through Emona to Aquileia. Theodosius' niece, with the young prince and little Galla Placidia,[6] took the longest route. In describing their journey[7] Claudian indulged in archaic names: Rhodope, Oeta, Pelion, Enipeus, Dodona, and Chaonia. Translated into the language of the time, it means that Serena hurried to Thessalonica and took the Via Egnatia, not to Dyrrhachium but to travel the poor road along the coast through Lissus, Narona, Burnum to Aquileia and Milan. She arrived

---

2 *Ep.* 60, 16.
3 *In Ruf.* II, 45.
4 *Cons. Stil.* II, 13, 191-201.
5 Socrates V, 26.
6 Seeck, *Geschichte* 5, 258, 544.
7 *3rd Cons. Hon.* 111-120.

there shortly before the death of the emperor, who had been anxiously waiting for his children.[8] The route over which Serena traveled makes sense only if the northern road was threatened by barbarians. Indeed, Claudian alluded to them at a later occasion: "Serena herself left the East and accompanied them [*sc.* Honorius] in the journey across Illyria, *fearless in the face of danger.*"[9]

For Pannonia prima the year 395 was no more "fateful" than any other year. There is no evidence that Carnuntum or any other Roman settlement between Vindobona and Brigetio was evacuated in that year.[10]

5. RELIGIOUS MOTIFS IN HUNNIC ART?

In the graves of the nomads of the fourth and fifth centuries heads of a bird of prey occur on numerous objects. Werner takes them for eagle heads.[1] Following Minns,[2] I would rather use the noncommittal term beak heads; the birds may be falcons, hawks, kites, vultures, or eagles. But Werner may be right. His interpretation, however, of the "eagle heads" as representations of the highest god of the Huns is unconvincing. First, there is no literary evidence that the Huns shared the belief of some Ugrian and Turkish tribes in the eagle god, creator of the universe. Second, it is unlikely that such humble objects as strap ends and horse bits should be decorated with the image of the highest god. Third, beak heads are known from Scythian and Sarmatian art long before the Huns. Fourth, the tendency to transform sharp corners, projections, the end of antlers, even cloud scrolls into beak heads can be followed throughout northern Eurasia, from Shantung[3] to the Ordos,[4] the Altai,[5] South Russia,[6] and the Balkans.[7] That the beak head is, besides the masks, the only pictorial motive in the metal work of the Attilanic period is merely significant for the general impoverishment of Hunnic art.

The scale motif, supposedly representing the feathers of the eagle god, is purely decorative. On saddle sheets it occurs side by side with rows

---

[8] Ambrose, *De obitu Theodosii* 34. Theodosius abstained from participation in the sacraments *donec Domini circa se gratiam filiorum experiretur adventu.*

[9] *6th Cons. Hon.* 92.

[10] Cf. H. Vetters 1963, 4. In Carnuntum sixty-seven coins, minted after 395, have been found.

[1] J. Werner 1956, 69-81.

[2] 1942, 5.

[3] Funerary stones from Wu Liang Tz'u.

[4] Salmony 1933, pl. 26: 4.

[5] Rudenko 1953, pl. 84.

[6] Borovka 1928, pl. 3b.

[7] *Wiener Beiträge zur Kunst- und Kulturgeschichte Asiens IX*, 1935, plates before pp. 49 and 53.

of triangles, hatched squares, and oblique lines of dots.[8] Besides, it is found in the art of civilizations in which an eagle god was neither worshipped nor represented. A few examples follow: bronze vessels of the middle Chou period in China; the Scythian rhyton from Karagodeuakhsh;[9] Parthian mountings from Nisa;[10] a Thracian gold pectoral;[11] a silver bottle from Boroczyce;[12] jewelry from Taxila;[13] a Nubian gold bracelet;[14] a Germanic bone handle of the fourth century;[15] Celtic metal work;[16] Visigothic things;[17] the ivory diptych from Monza;[18] gold plaques from the royal tombs at Byblos;[19] Sasanian quivers;[20] a Scythian gorytus.[21] I intentionally followed neither a chronological nor geographical order to emphasize the ubiquity of the motif. Whether the scales are fish scales or feathers can only in few cases be determined. On a gilt bronze pendant in the shape of a fish from a prehistoric grave at Chiba, Japan,[22] the scales are those of a fish; but on a Gepidic helmet, a fish, a bird, and quadrupeds have the same scales.[23] Werner drew attention to the scale pattern on a Sasanian Spangenhelm and the bands, segments, and cheek plates of most of the Spangenhelme of the Baldenheim type. An unexpected parallel occurs on the engraved stones from a grave at I-nan in Shantung. The helmets of the barbarians are decorated with scales. The occurrence of the same motif on the same objects in China and Germany is most probably a coincidence.

Finally, there is the tree with a bird on top, flanked by ibexes and deer, on a gold temple pendant from Verkhne Yablochno in the Don region.[24] Werner takes it for Hunnic; I would rather date it somewhat later. In

---

[8] Fettich, pl. 120.

[9] Often reproduced: *MAR* 13, 150, fig. 23; Minns 1945, 219, fig. 121; Ebert, *RV* 13, pl. 3b; Rostovtsev 1929, pl. 1:c.

[10] *Trudy iuzhno-turkmenstanskoĭ arkheologicheskoĭ kompleksnoĭ ekspeditsii* 8, 385, fig. 4. 5,

[11] Jacobsthal 1944, pl. 240c.

[12] Grünhagen 1954.

[13] Sir J. Marshall 1951, 2, 636; 3, pl. 191: x, y.

[14] *Amtl. Ber. aus Berliner Museen* 51, 1930, 129, fig. 7.

[15] *Wiener Prähist. Zeitschr.* 19, 1922, 214, pl. 2:2.

[16] Jacobsthal 1944, pl. 267, patterns 163-170.

[17] Jewelry from the necropolis de la Meseta Castellana in the Museo arqueologico, Barcelona.

[18] Delbrück, 1929, no. 63, p. 245.

[19] In the museum in Beirut.

[20] Sarre 1922, pl. 104.

[21] Vos 1963, pl. 9a.

[22] In the National Museum, Tokyo.

[23] *Germania* 32, 1954, 177, fig. 1:1-2; D. Csallány 1961, pl. 278.

[24] J. Werner 1956, pl. 69, 30:5.

any case, the motif is of ancient Near Eastern origin[25] and has nothing to do with the religion or mythology of the Huns. In passing, it should be noted that the motif of the tree flanked by horses, sometimes with a bird flying at the side of the tree, frequently occurs on Chinese semi-circular eavestiles of the late Chou and Han periods;[26] on a tile from Lin Tsu, the ancient capital of Ch'i in Shantung, the tree is flanked by horsemen wearing high pointed caps tilted forward, clearly barbarians.[27]

---

[25] Maenchen-Helfen, *Speculum* 33, 1958, 164.
[26] Sekino Takeshi 1956, pls. 5, 25, 26, fig. 110, 112.
[27] *Ibid.*, pl. 25.

XII. Background:
The Roman Empire at the
Time of the Hunnic Invasions

By Paul Alexander

DURING THE late fourth and early fifth centuries after Christ a people of Asiatic origin, the Huns, overran a number of tribes then living in eastern and central Europe. Their onslaught upset the military balance that had existed for centuries between the inhabitants of the Roman Empire with its Greco-Roman civilization and the nomadic and seminomadic peoples beyond the frontiers. The Huns thus ushered in the period of the Barbarian Invasions. They left no written records. A study of the Huns, therefore, must be based largely on historical sources composed by residents of the Roman Empire.

As a consequence, all information on the Huns and their subjects and allies is embedded in materials written by and for men viewing the movements and activities of barbarian peoples beyond the imperial frontiers from the vantage point of Greco-Roman political institutions, administrative geography, socioeconomic organization, and intellectual pursuits. The activities of the Huns and the structure of their society are therefore described in literary forms evolved by Greco-Roman historiography for the many barbarian peoples with whom the classical world had come in contact since the days of Herodotus in the fifth century B.C. Hunnic military operations are related to the system of Roman frontier fortifications and Roman army organization, which the Huns and their allies encountered in their sweep westward and southward. Their inroads into Roman provinces appear in the sources entangled with other issues facing the Roman Empire: the conflict between paganism and Christianity, the dogmatic controversies within the Christian Church, the Germanization of army, government, and society, and so on.

The sources thus present all information on the Huns intertwined in a thousand ways with the biographies of Roman statesmen, with Roman institutions, with issues and values of the Later Roman Empire. The author of this book, therefore, like all other students of Hunnic problems, was compelled to discuss his sources and the problems posed by them against a rich and complex background of Late Roman developments. To make his book more accessible, the publishers asked me, after the author's untimely death, to provide a background describing the Greco-Roman setting taken for granted in the sources on the Huns, as well as the situation and development of the Late Roman Empire and its civilization so deeply affected by the migrations and inroads of the Huns and their rulers. I was happy to comply with this request and thus to make a small contribution to the edition of Professor Maenchen's posthumous work. In this background essay I shall say little about the Huns themselves as this subject is set forth fully and in magisterial fashion in the body of the book. Furthermore, it hardly needs emphasizing that this chapter lays no claim to originality but is based on the standard works on Late Roman history.[1]

As Professor Maenchen explains in the first sections of his work, the classical authors were able to trace the movements of the Huns from the early seventies of the fourth century to the year 469, after which the Huns ceased to operate as organized units. It will therefore be convenient to begin this account with a survey of the Roman Empire during the joint reigns of three emperors: the Eastern Roman emperor Valens (364-378), his nephew, the West Roman emperor Gratian (367-383), and at least nominally another nephew, Valentinian II, who at the time of his proclamation (375) was four years old (†392). There were then several emperors, but only one empire. Indeed in the preceding decade it had been administered during several years by only one ruler, first by Julian "the Apostate" (360-363) and then briefly by Jovianus (363-364). After the latter, however, the Roman army had insisted on and obtained the appointment of two rulers jointly to govern the Roman world, Valentinian I (364-375, father of Gratian and Valentinian II), and his brother Valens. The notion of one empire, however, persisted, even in periods when the throne was occupied by more than one ruler. In later times the Empire was for long periods governed by a single ruler, for example by Theodosius the Great (379-395) and by Justinian I (527-565).

---

[1] Bury 1923; Stein 1959; and Jones 1964.

Geographically, the Empire stretched from the Atlantic Ocean in the West to the Rhine and along the Danube to the Eastern corner of the Black Sea, and from Hadrian's Wall in England and from the river Danube to the African desert, the northern boundaries of Nubia, and the Syrian desert. Beyond these frontiers lay what in Late Roman usage was called the *barbaricum*, areas inhabited by peoples who spoke neither Greek nor Latin ("barbarians"). East of the Rhine and north of the Danube in particular lived many Germanic tribes: Franks and Alamanni, including the Alamannic branch of the Juthungi, on the right bank of the Rhine, Lombards on the river Elbe, Vandals on the upper reaches of the rivers Oder and Vistula, still further to the East on both sides of the Dniestr the Visigoths (Tervingi) and Ostrogoths (Greutingi). The Ostrogoths had built a closely knit state ruled by King Ermanaric. The Visigoths were less firmly organized and had an alliance with Rome since 332. Large numbers of Goths had been won over to Christianity by a heretical (Arian) missionary, Ulfilas. From the Visigoths Christianity in its heretical form had spread to many other Germanic peoples, with the result that Arianism survived in the *barbaricum* long after it was condemned in the Empire (381). The Ostrogothic kingdom stretched eastward to the river Don, which separated it from the Iranian Alans. Since the late second century the Germanic tribes had furnished thousands of settlers and soldiers for the Roman Empire, and during the reign of Constantine the Great (305-337) the barbarization of the army had made considerable headway. The barbarian tribes were to be deeply involved in the Hunnic invasions of the Roman Empire.

Administratively, the Empire was normally divided into three praetorian prefectures: Britain, Gaul, Spain and northern Morocco formed one of them; another was made up by the rest of Roman North Africa, Italy and the Balkan Peninsula eastward about as far as the river Struma; the entire rest of the Empire, that is Europe from the Struma to the Bosporus, Asia Minor, Syria, Palestine, Egypt and Libya formed the gigantic praetorian prefecture of the East. In the late fourth century, the heads of these prefectures, the praetorian prefects, no longer commanded any troops, yet their wide civilian and fiscal powers gave the holders of this office a vice-regal status. In many legal cases their decisions were without appeal. They administered the largest part of the public revenue, and they paid the wages and stipends of the military personnel and of the huge bureaucracy brought into being at the beginning of the fourth century.

The praetorian prefectures were divided into "dioceses" (literally: administrative districts), most of them administered by a *vicarius*, in fact a subordinate of the praetorian prefect. The dioceses in turn were subdivided into provinces, the governors of which had various titles. The dioceses and provinces most immediately affected by the Hunnic invasions and consequently most frequently mentioned in this book were the following (from West to East): the Pannonian diocese comprising roughly lower Austria, western Hungary and Yugoslavia, that is, the two Roman provinces of Noricum, the two *provinces* of Pannonia (Pannonia prima and secunda), and the provinces of Valeria, Savia, and Dalmatia; (before Diocletian [284-305], the later provinces of Pannonia prima and Valeria had formed one province called Pannonia superior, the later provinces of Pannonia secunda and Savia another province called Pannonia inferior); the Dacian diocese, approximately eastern Yugoslavia and western Bulgaria, with the provinces of Moesia superior or Moesia prima, the two provinces of Dacia, and the provinces of Praevalitana and Dardania; the Macedonian diocese, approximately Greece; and the Thracian diocese, or eastern Bulgaria and the European part of Turkey, comprising the provinces of Lower Moesia, Scythia, Thrace, and others.

At the head of the official hierarchy stood the emperor or emperors. None of them resided any longer in the city of Rome. The ancient capital was still the seat of the Roman Senate, but by the late fourth century this body had lost its former functions, although individual senators frequently possessed considerable political and economic power. When the emperors were not campaigning, the imperial residences in the West were at Trèves on the Moselle or at Milan, in the East in the city of Constantinople walled and rebuilt by Constantine the Great and inaugurated in 330. The new capital in the East grew steadily in population throughout the fourth and fifth centuries and became the seat of a second senate comparable to that of Rome.

In the sixties and seventies of the fourth century the emperors spent much time and effort fighting external enemies, putting down a series of dangerous revolts and attempting to reconcile the Arian and anti-Arian factions within the Church. For many years Valentinian I waged war against the Alamanni on the Upper Rhine and against the Quadi and Sarmatians in Pannonia and Dacia. From 367 to 369 Valens battled the Visigoths. They had given military aid to a rebel, Procopius, who was captured and executed (366) after several months of civil warfare. In the end Valens was compelled to recognize Gothic independence, against a promise on the part of the Visigoths not to cross the Danube. Rome's most powerful and most dangerous enemy, however, was the Persian kingdom under the Sassanid dynasty. From 369 to 377 Valens campaigned against King Shapur II († 379) and was finally forced by the Gothic invasion of Dacia to abandon to him the Caucasian regions of Armenia and Iberia (Georgia). In the next decade a Moorish chieftain in North Africa, Firmus, rebelled against the government of Valentinian I and was suppressed only with the greatest difficulty and after a series of massacres (373). In addition, throughout much of the fourth and fifth centuries Gaul and Spain were harassed by bands of rebellious peasants, the *bacaudae*, and the emperors were frequently forced to send out expeditionary forces against them.

To defend the Empire against its foreign enemies the emperors of the fourth century were able to rely on a powerful military establishment. The total number of men under arms is difficult to estimate, but a sixth-century source lists 435,266 soldiers and sailors under Diocletian (284-305) and there is reason to believe that this figure, though somewhat exaggerated, is not far from the truth. The land forces were of two types. The best units made up mobile field armies called *comitatenses*, partly attached to one of the imperial courts, partly assigned to one of the more exposed provinces. Less effective yet by no means negligible were the *limitanei* or *ripenses* who were posted at the frontiers. The *limitanei* were named after the complex system of frontier fortifications, the *limes*, which dated back to the first century of the Christian era. It consisted of a long line of larger and smaller fortresses or ramparts built at regular intervals along the far-flung boundaries of the Empire. The fortifications of the Roman *limes* were maintained and expanded by successive emperors down to the time of Valentinian and Valens. The principal function of the frontier armies was to report on suspicious troop concentrations in the barbaricum and to hold back an invading force until reinforcements from the *comitatenses* could be rushed to the danger spot.

The largest numbers of soldiers in the Roman army were still infantry. However, since the middle of the third century warfare against the many barbarian tribes and against Sassanid Persia had placed a premium on rapid military movement. The emperors had therefore created new cavalry units or strengthened existing cavalry formations. These played an increasingly important role during the fourth century and became the decisive branch of the army in the fifth. Furthermore the Roman armies of the fourth and fifth centuries included so-called *federates*, or barbarian units supplied by barbarian tribes and fighting under their own chieftains. The armies also comprised large numbers of barbarians, especially German tribesmen, who were recruited individually. The Roman forces were commanded, since the days of Constantine the Great, by a corps of professional generals, the *magistri militum* or Masters of the Soldiers. Since in the fourth century the Mediterranean Sea enjoyed a period of tranquility from enemy attacks, the Roman navy did not receive the same attention from the emperors as did the land forces. The navy's principal harbors were situated at Ravenna on the Adriatic coast of Italy, at Misenum on the Tyrrhenian shore, and at Gesoriacum (Boulogne). In addition flotillas of light vessels existed on the Rhine and Danube. The latter in particular played an important role in the defense of the Empire against Germans and Huns.

The emperors, furthermore, had to wrestle with the manifold problems of religious policy. Ever since the days of Constantine the Great and his conversion to Christianity, the new religion had been gaining ground at an increasing pace. This conflict of religions was one of the most important aspects in the cultural development of the fourth century. However, during the sixties and seventies of that century the strength of the various pagan cults was far from spent as had been demonstrated by the revival of paganism during the reign of Constantine's nephew, Julian. Julian's successors on the imperial throne were all devout Christians, but such had been the impact of Julian's religious policy that for an entire generation paganism continued to be tolerated.

More complex was the attitude of Julian's successors to the adherents of the theology of Arius. This priest from Alexandria had maintained at the beginning of the century that Jesus Christ was, unlike God the father, a created being and at least implied that he was inferior to God. Although the Arian doctrine had been the subject of heated controversies, conciliar decisions, and compromises throughout the fourth century, Arianism in its different shades and factions still counted large numbers of adherents among both clergy and laity in the eastern provinces. The greatest opponent of Arianism was the Alexandrian bishop Athanasius who for almost half a century (328-373) fought the Arian doctrine by all means at his disposal, including a long series of theological treatises and pamphlets. In the West, Arianism was weakly represented, yet here too it encountered vigorous opposition from an outstanding writer, Hilary of Poitiers († 367). Because of the different political theological attitudes of West and East the western government was opposed to Arianism while the emperor Valens was favorably disposed toward it and appointed Arian clergy to important bishoprics in the eastern part.

Much of the secular and religious literature of the Empire was composed in the two dominant languages, Greek and Latin. The linguistic border divided the Latinized province of Tripolitania in North Africa from Greek-speaking Libya and Egypt in the south and the Romanized dioceses of Pannonia and Dacia from Hellenized Greece on the Balkan Peninsula. Territories to the west of this line spoke and wrote in Latin, those to the east, Greek. An advanced knowledge of the Greek language became rare in the western part of the Empire. In the East a familiarity with Latin was still indispensable in the fields of administration, law, and military affairs. Moreover, authors wishing to appeal to the senatorial nobility at Rome sometimes wrote in Latin. This was true, for example, for a historian and a poet frequently mentioned in this book: Ammianus Marcellinus of Antioch whose historical work composed in Latin reached to the year 378 and was probably completed not long after 390; and for Claudian of Alexandria († 404) whose Latin poems glorified the deeds of emperors and statesmen such as Honorius and Stilicho or reviled their opponents, notably the praetorian prefect of the East Rufinus or the imperial chamberlain, the eunuch Eutropius.

In some provinces of the Empire literary works were composed in languages other than Greek and Latin. Thus east of the Euphrates, in Osrhoene and Mesopotamia, and later in Syria, the Bible and theological works were translated into Syriac and a copious and original literature emerged in that language. It will be seen that Syriac sources preserved a good deal of historical information about the Huns. Similar developments took place in Egypt, where a popular literature in the Coptic language arose, and in Armenia.

The two decades ushered in by the accession of the two Pannonian emperors, Valentinian and Valens, closed with a catastrophe of the first magnitude, which was directly related to Hunnic history. The warfare of Emperor Valens against the Visigoths (367-369) had resulted in a peace treaty in which the Visigothic "judge" Athanaric had undertaken not to cross the Danube. Shortly afterward the imperial government had lent support to a rival Visigothic chieftain, Fritigern. At the beginning of the seventies the Huns attacked the Ostrogoths, subdued the majority of this people and forced the rest under their leaders Alatheus and Saphrax to cross the Dniestr. The Huns then drove Athanaric's Visigoths into the Pannonian provinces while the majority of the people under Fritigern appeared on the Lower Danube and in 376 asked for Valens' permission to cross into the Dacian diocese. Their request was granted, but the military officers entrusted by the imperial government with the task of supplying the fugitives with food embezzled part of the funds. Famine drove the Visigoths in 377 to commit acts of violence, and war ensued. This was all the more serious for the government as the Visigothic contingents were now joined by the Ostrogoths of Alatheus and Saphrax as well as by several groups of *federates*, slaves, and disgruntled elements from within the Empire, and later by bands of Huns and Alani. Of the two emperors, Gratian was prevented until the middle of 378, by warfare against the Alamanni on the Rhine, from coming to the aid of his uncle Valens. Several smaller or larger Roman armies suffered heavy losses in battles fought against the barbarian invaders, for example at Marcianople and in a place called Ad Salices ("near the willow trees") in the Dobrogea. In the end Valens himself appeared on the Balkans with the main army and decided not to wait for his nephew and the Western forces. On August 9, 378, he offered battle near the city of Adrianople. His large army was defeated, two-thirds of it were wiped out and the emperor himself perished during or after the battle. The victors attempted to capture the cities of Thrace, but were unable to do so. Marauding bands of Goths and other barbarians marched plundering through Dacia into Pannonia.

The defeat at Adrianople dealt a heavy blow to the military manpower of the eastern part of the Empire and opened the Balkans to the Germanic invaders. In this desperate situation the surviving ruler, Gratian, appointed as co-emperor a retired general, the Spaniard Theodosius I (379-395), and assigned to him the eastern part of the realm. The two emperors' first concern was to put an end to the Gothic raids of the Balkan Peninsula. In the years following the battle of Adrianople they waged war against the Goths with varying success. In the end they concluded separate peace treaties with individual Gothic groups (380-382). Some of the Goths entered the imperial army, other bands were settled on Roman soil, were granted autonomy and tax exemptions, and agreed to serve in the armed forces as *federates* under their own chieftains. As a consequence of these arrangements, the Roman army was rebuilt, but at the same time its Germanization was intensified and the demands of the Roman treasury upon the Roman taxpayers for the purpose of paying the Germanic troops increased significantly. In his relations with Persia, Theodosius was able to conclude a treaty of peace and friendship (387?). It divided Armenia in such a way that four-fifths of the country went to Persia and the rest to the Roman Empire.

The two emperors Gratian and Theodosius were also harassed by domestic uprisings especially in the western part of the Empire. In 383 a distant relative of Theodosius, Magnus Maximus, rebelled against Gratian and persuaded the emperor's army to join his side. Gratian was murdered, and the West was now ruled jointly by Maximus and (nominally) by the child emperor Valentinian II, Gratian's step-brother, in fact by his mother Justina assisted by a pagan general of Frankish descent, Bauto. Although Valentinian II had seniority, Theodosius acted as his protector and for a while prevented Maximus from seizing Italy. In 387, however, the government of Valentinian II asked Maximus for military aid against barbarian invaders of the Pannonian diocese. Maximus used this request as a pretext for an invasion of Italy and forced Valentinian and his mother to seek refuge in the East. In the next year Theodosius marched westward at the head of an army consisting largely of barbarian soldiers and defeated the usurper Maximus in two decisive engagements. Maximus was killed and Valentinian restored to office in the West. The pagan general Arbogast, like Bauto a German, now became Valentinian's chief minister.

Religious issues had played a considerable role during the rebellion of Maximus and were to be crucial in a later revolt during the reign of Theodosius. The emperor was a pious Christian determined to eradicate paganism and heresy without undue cruelty. In this endeavor he was supported, at the beginning of his reign, by Gratian. Gratian had been the first Roman emperor to resign the position of chief priest of the pagan cults and had met with opposition on the part of powerful pagan senators, such as the historian Virius Nicomachus Flavianus and the orator Q. Aurelius Symmachus. The pagan party retained its influence under Valentinian II and supplied a number of important officeholders. Thus in 384 Symmachus was appointed to the prestigious office of city prefect of Rome. In 389 Theodosius briefly visited Rome and in the next two years took several measures favoring paganism and its most prominent representatives. Meanwhile a conflict arose between Valentinian II and his chief minister, Arbogast, which ended in the death of the young emperor, either by murder or suicide. Since Arbogast was of barbarian origin, he could not himself aspire to the throne and in 392 proclaimed emperor a former professor of rhetoric, Flavius Eugenius, a nominal Christian who had strong sympathies for the pagan party at Rome. Theodosius now abandoned his moderate policy toward paganism and prepared for war against the usurper Eugenius and his supporters among the senatorial aristocracy. Eugenius openly allied himself with this pagan group, and the city of Rome in particular witnessed an intense pagan revival. Theodosius mustered an enormous army in the East. Most of the soldiers were once again of barbarian origin and included about 20,000 Visigoths led by their chieftain Alaric. In September 394 Theodosius won a decisive victory over Eugenius and his pagan supporters on the river Frigidus near the northeastern frontier of Italy. Since the war had been conducted on both sides as a test of strength between the Christian god and the pagan pantheon, Theodosius' victory on the Frigidus dealt a death blow to the defeated religion. Paganism now disappeared as a politically significant force from the ancient world.

In the Eastern Empire the Arian heresy had been liquidated by Theodosius at a much earlier date. Gratian had favored the cause of Nicene orthodoxy from the moment of his accession, and in the East the defeat and death of the pro-Arian emperor Valens at Adrianople thoroughly discredited the Arian cause. Moreover, both emperors, Gratian first and Theodosius later, were deeply influenced and impressed by the personality of St. Ambrose, bishop of Milan from 374 to 397, who was a passionate opponent of Arianism. Theodosius imposed the Nicene Creed upon his subjects. In 381 he convoked the Second Ecumenical Council at Constantinople, which reaffirmed the Nicene Creed. As a result Arianism ceased to play a politically or religiously important role within the Empire. As mentioned before, however, Arian clergy had been active in the area of ecclesiastical missions especially to the Germanic tribes. Hence, almost all these tribes had been converted to Arian Christianity. The conflict of Empire and Germanic barbarians, which dominated the history of the fifth century, was therefore deepened by a religious hostility between Nicene Romans and Arian Germans.

The reigns of Theodosius and his colleagues witnessed a literary renaissance of considerable proportions, and several works composed in this period figure in the present book as sources for the history of the Huns. Among the pagan literati in the Latin West the historian Ammianus Marcellinus, already mentioned, deserves a special place. Ausonius († 395), a native and long-time resident of Burdigala (Bordeaux), tutor of the emperor Gratian and a perfunctory Christian, wrote many poems, of which the most famous was a description of the river Moselle. One of his friends was the Roman orator Symmachus, already mentioned as one of the stanchest spokesmen of the pagan aristocracy of Rome. In 384 he addressed to the government of Valentinian II his passionate *Relatio* advocating the return of the statue of Victory to the Roman Senate house. Symmachus was also the author of an important historical work; it is lost but served as a source for several later accounts containing information on the Huns. Symmachus' plea regarding the statue of Victory was successfully opposed by the greatest Latin preacher and writer of the period, St. Ambrose, whose letters and other works also contain important contemporary references to the Huns.

Theodosius died at Milan only a few months after his victory over Eugenius and Arbogast. He was succeeded by his two sons, Arcadius, age eighteen, and Honorius, eleven. Arcadius was to govern the praetorian prefecture of the East advised by his praetorian prefect Rufinus, while Stilicho, son of an officer of Germanic descent and husband of a niece of Theodosius, was to administer the rest of the Empire for the child Honorius. Theodosius had mobilized most of the armed forces of the East for his campaign against Eugenius, and the majority of these troops were therefore still stationed in the West at the time of his death. Alaric and his Visigothic *federates*, however, had returned to the Balkans, had rebelled against the government, and were raiding the countryside to the very walls of Constantinople. In the spring of 395 Stilicho marched eastward against the Goths with a numerous army consisting largely of Eastern units that in the preceding year had fought for Theodosius on the river Frigidus. He confronted Alaric in northern Thessaly, but no battle was fought because the Eastern government ordered Stilicho to send the Eastern troops back to Constantinople. Stilicho complied with this request, and upon their return the soldiers assassinated the praetorian prefect Rufinus. The real power in the East now fell into the hands of the eunuch and imperial chamberlain Eutropius. The Visigoths under Alaric continued their depredations in Greece for more than a year. In the end Alaric and his people moved to Epirus and renewed their alliance with the Eastern government; Alaric was appointed Master of the Soldiers for Illyricum.

The warfare of both Eastern and Western governments against the Goths had been accompanied by a steadily deepening conflict between Stilicho and the Eastern government. Stilicho considered himself, with some justification, the executor of Theodosius' last will and policies and was intent upon extending the powers of his regency to the Emperor Arcadius and the East. Also involved in this conflict was the control of the dioceses of Dacia and Macedonia, the "Eastern Illyricum," which after 380 had belonged for certain periods to the West but which Arcadius now claimed because of his seniority. Stilicho had had a hand in the murder of Rufinus, and Rufinus' successor Eutropius, aware of Stilicho's intent of gaining influence over the Eastern court, was suspicious of his Western rival. In 397 Eutropius had Stilicho declared a public enemy by the Senate of Constantinople. For the next decade the two parts of the Empire were in a state of latent, and at times open, warfare, although as early as 395 Stilicho had agreed to cede eastern Illyricum to the East.

The internal policies of Eutropius, however, brought into being a strong opposition against the eunuch, which resulted in his deposition and execution (399). Part of this opposition came from rebellious Ostrogoths settled in Phrygia and their barbarian allies. For several months in 400 the Goths, under the former general Gainas, occupied Constantinople. This crisis gave a decisive impetus to an anti-Germanic movement which had been gathering momentum ever since Theodosius concluded peace treaties with the Goths and the subsequent intense penetration of government and army by barbarian elements. Now the bulk of the Gothic rebels were liquidated, partly by a mob in the capital, partly by an imperial army. The Eastern army was purged, at least temporarily, of some of its barbarian components, yet after Arcadius' death (408) Germanic soldiers were once again recruited as *federates* into the Roman army. These new *federates*, however, entered the Eastern Roman army as individuals rather than as tribes, were trained according to Roman discipline, served under Roman officers, and thus presented little political danger. In the western part of the Empire no such reorganization took place, and units of *federates* continued to serve as tribal units under their own chiefs. Furthermore, from that time on, in both halves of the Empire men of power and wealth, especially generals, often hired and employed considerable numbers of private cavalry soldiers, the *buccellarii*, who often were Huns, Germans, and other barbarians. Usually they were outstanding soldiers but occasionally they proved a source of political danger for the Western government as they normally were more loyal to their employers than to the emperor. In the East the regular army was strong enough to absorb the *federates* and to prevent the *buccellarii* from threatening political stability.

The anti-Germanic policies of the Eastern government naturally strained relations with the Western Empire administered by Stilicho who was of Germanic descent and remained loyal to the Germanophile policies of Theodosius. In 401 Alaric and his Visigoths left Illyricum and invaded Italy, which had not beheld a foreign enemy since the reign of the Emperor Aurelianus (270-275). In organizing the defense Stilicho withdrew troops from Britain and the Rhine frontier. He also incorporated contingents of Vandals and Alani in the Western army. With these forces Stilicho defeated the Visigoths in two battles at Pollentia and Verona (402), concluded with Alaric a treaty of alliance, and settled his people on the river Sava. It was during this period of Alaric's first invasion of Italy that the court of Honorius found refuge at Ravenna. This city remained the normal residence of Western emperors in the fifth century.

The defense of Italy against Alaric and his Visigoths had weakened significantly the provinces of the West. In 405 a huge army consisting of Goths and other barbarians commanded by Radagaisus crossed the Danube and the Alps into Italy. Stilicho was able to defeat them, but in the next year (406) Alani, Vandals, and Suebi crossed the Rhine into Gaul, soon to be followed by Alamanni and Burgundians, and the Gallic provinces suffered grievously from this barbarian onslaught. During these troubles Gaul and Spain fell into the hands of a usurper, Constantine, and were temporarily lost to Honorius. The crisis was deepened by the threat of a second Visigothic invasion of Italy. Stilicho favored continued collaboration with Alaric, but, as had been the case in Constantinople eight years earlier, an anti-Germanic policy prevailed at Ravenna. Stilicho was executed, and his family and supporters were harassed or killed (408). Thus the internal difficulties of the Empire, the conflicts between its Eastern and Western governments, and the different policies pursued toward barbarians within and outside the Empire, opened the frontiers to the barbarian invaders, both in the East and in the West. They also facilitated raids by groups of Huns and their subject peoples into the Empire, as well as the recruitment of Huns for Rome's civil and domestic wars.

Among the contemporaries of the early Hunnic entanglements with the Eastern Empire were two towering literary figures, St. Ambrose of Milan in the West, already mentioned, and John Chrysostom in the East. The latter had been a priest at Antioch and later became patriarch of Constantinople for six stormy years (397-403); he clashed with many important people, including Patriarch Theophilus of Alexandria (397-403) and the reigning empress, Eudoxia; he composed and delivered a large number of sermons and wrote many letters, some of which allude to imperial relations with the Huns. The poems of Claudian of Alexandria on Stilicho and other historical figures are also cited frequently in this book. While Claudian was an admirer of Stilicho and of his policies, his contemporary Claudius Rutilius Namatianus, in his poem on his return from Rome to his native Gaul, declared Stilicho a traitor; and as a fanatical pagan Namatianus condemned Stilicho's Germanophile and antipagan policies.

As stated, during the reign of Arcadius energetic measures had been taken in the East to undo the dangerous consequences of the Germanization of government and army. In the West the murder of Stilicho was partly inspired by similar anti-Germanic policies. Indeed, during the rest of Honorius' reign anti-Germanic officials frequently were in control of affairs, but they were rarely able to dispense with military aid given by Germanic or Hunnic groups from inside and outside the Empire. In fact, the anti-Germanic leaders of the Western government after the murder of Stilicho played into the hands of Alaric and his Visigoths then occupying the province of Noricum. The Visigoths were demanding monetary compensation for military services rendered to the government of Stilicho and formally acknowledged by the Roman Senate. This claim was repudiated by the new government. So in 408 Alaric invaded Italy for a second time. Twice his Visigoths laid siege to the city of Rome, in 408 and again in 410. On the second occasion the Eternal City, which had not seen an enemy inside its walls for eight centuries, was plundered by the Visigoths. On several occasions, during Alaric's stay in Italy, bands of Hunnic soldiers fought on the side of the government against the Visigoths. Alaric died at the end of the year 410 and his brother-in-law Athaulf was elected king of the Visigoths. They continued plundering the South and West of Italy in 411 and finally moved on to Gaul in the following year.

At that time the Gallic and Spanish provinces of the Empire witnessed both usurpations and barbarian invasions. Vandals, Alans, and Suebi had moved from Gaul into Spain (409). Other Alanic groups and the Burgundians supported a rebel emperor and threatened to invade Gaul. Under the impact of this threat the government in Ravenna gave the Visigoths permission to settle in Gaul. Already in 413, however, hostilities resumed between Visigoths and government troops, and the barbarians captured a number of important cities in southern France. In the end difficulties of supply forced Athaulf to leave Gaul and to cross the Pyrenees into Spain (414-415). There the Visigoths agreed to another treaty with Ravenna, which promised them annual supplies of grain in return for their entering the military service of the government as *federates* (416). In 418 they finally left Spain and were settled permanently as an autonomous body on lands in southwestern Gaul, in the provinces of Aquitania secunda, Novempopulana, and Narbonensis prima. A generation later the Gallic Visigoths were to play a decisive role in the great battle against the Huns in the *locus Mauriacus*, commonly called the Catalaunian Fields (near Troyes). After the Visigothic settlement in Gaul the Alani and Vandals in Spain were limited to the southwestern province of Baetica.

This last consolidation and pacification of the Western Empire, notably of Gaul and Spain, in the decade after the Visigothic sack of Rome, had been carried out by the first minister of Emperor Honorius, the general Flavius Constantius. He had married the Emperor's sister, the princess Galla Placidia, widow of the Visigothic leader Athaulf. He was elevated to the rank of co-emperor (Constantius III) in 421, but died at the end of that year. His widow was accused of intriguing against her brother and fled to Constantinople (423) together with her four-year-old son Valentinian. Later in that year her brother Honorius died, and his nephew, the Eastern emperor Theodosius II (408-450), thus became formally the sole ruler of the entire Empire.

During the last years of Arcadius and the early years of his son Theodosius II the Eastern Empire had been administered by the praetorian prefect of the East, Anthemius (404-414), under whom the new capital, Constantinople, received monumental land fortifications, the "Theodosian Walls." They enclosed a much larger area than the city built by Constantine the Great, the founder of the city, and their ruins still surround the city in the west and north. After the disappearance of Anthemius in 414, the regency for the child-emperor devolved upon his sister Pulcheria, then sixteen, who in 421 prevailed upon Theodosius to get married. The new empress, Eudocia, gradually established her influence over her weak husband at the expense of her sister-in-law. A few months after the marriage the Eastern armies attacked Persian Armenia but made peace with the Persian king when in 422 the Huns invaded Thrace.

When Galla Placidia and her son Valentinian arrived in Constantinople in 423, there was initially little inclination at the court to surrender Theo-

dosius' claim to the West by recognizing Valentinian as the heir of Honorius. Galla Placidia, however, had powerful allies in the West, notably
the commander in Roman North Africa, Bonifatius, who threatened to
block grain shipments to Italy unless Valentinian was made emperor. Moreover, the court at Ravenna, anxious to maintain its independence from
Constantinople, proclaimed a high official, John, emperor of the West.
Faced with this double threat the government of Theodosius II made up
its mind to support Valentinian's claim to the Western throne and to
recapture Italy from the usurper John by force of arms. The Eastern
armies were commanded by the Alan Ardabur and his son Aspar, the
latter of whom was to play an important role in Eastern politics for the
next three decades. The fortress of Ravenna fell by treachery, John was
executed, and Valentinian III was proclaimed Augustus at Rome by an
Eastern official (425). During the civil war in Italy John had been expecting the arrival of Hunnic *federates* from Pannonia recruited by a palace
official, Flavius Aetius, but Aetius and his 60,000 Huns arrived in Italy
several days after the usurper's execution and were sent back. Aetius
was dispatched to Gaul for whose defense against Germanic and later Hunnic invaders he was responsible from this time on.

Important evidence for the Hunnic raids and invasions of the late
fourth and early fifth centuries is contained in the works of two fathers
of the Western Church. The first is St. Jerome (circa 348-420), the translator of the Bible into Latin, who traveled widely especially over the eastern
part of the Empire and in 389 settled at Bethlehem in Palestine. Several
of his letters are testimony to the feelings of horror which the invaders
from the East instilled in the population of the Empire. An even more
important literary figure was the church father Augustine (354-430), bishop
of Hippo Regius in North Africa from 395 to his death. He wrote his most
influential work, the *City of God*, during 413-426 under the immediate
impact of the Visigothic sack of Rome. This work and other works of
his are cited in this book as a source for the history of the Huns. This is
true, likewise, of the historical-theological work completed probably in
418 by one of Augustine's disciples, the Spaniard Orosius, and written,
like the *City of God*, to explain the fall of Rome to the Visigoths.

The reign of Valentinian III in the West and the latter part of Theodosius II's rule in the East coincided with the climax of Hunnic power.
Their realm included many barbarian tribes, Germanic peoples as well
as others, for example the Acatiri on the northern shore of the Black Sea.
Theodosius II continued to be manipulated by his entourage, by his wife
Eudocia until 443, and after her eclipse by the chief eunuch Chrysaphius,
later once again by the emperor's sister, Pulcheria. In this period sea

walls were added to the Theodosian fortifications of the capital; these walls ran along the Golden Horn and the Sea of Marmara to protect the city against Vandal attacks. The Eastern Empire also conducted another indecisive war against its great neighbor to the East, Persia, in 441-442.

Under Theodosius II the Egyptian Olympiodorus wrote a history covering the years 407 to 425. More important for the history of the Huns was the sophist and historian Priscus from Panion in Thrace, who figures prominently in this book. In 448 he participated in an embassy to the court of the Hunnic ruler Attila and much later incorporated his account of his journey and his observations at the Hunnic court in a historical work on the years 411-472. Also important for the history of the Huns are the ecclesiastical histories of Socrates, of his contemporary Sozomen, and of Theodoret of Cyrrhus, all of which continued the *Ecclesiastical History* of Eusebius of Caesarea down to the reign of Theodosius II. The biography of St. Hypatius († 446), an Egyptian monk who became abbot of the monastery of Rufinianae near Chalcedon, was written by his disciple, Callinicus, and also contains some contemporary information on the Huns. It was in the latter half of Theodosius II's long reign that the government initiated the first official collection of imperial legislation, the *Codex Theodosianus*, was promulgated in both halves of the Empire (438). It contained all imperial laws issued since the year 312 and is frequently cited by the author of this book as an important source for the history of the Huns and related problems. Another official document of the late fourth and early fifth centuries was the *Notitia Dignitatum*, a list of civilian and military officials, their staffs, and their military units.

Apart from the Hunnic invasions and raids of the Balkans the principal developments of the early fifth century revolved around the Christological issue, that is, the problem how the divine and human aspects had been combined in the person of Jesus Christ. In the first half of the fifth century this question divided the Christian population of the Eastern Empire, where this theological issue was often complicated by ecclesiastical power struggles, especially between the patriarchal sees of Alexandria and Constantinople. On one extreme stood the Nestorians, the partisans of the Patriarch Nestorius of Constantinople (428-431) who followed the Antiochene school of theologians and insisted on a strict separation of divine and human natures in Christ. Their principal antagonists, the patriarchs Cyril (412-444) and Dioscorus (444-451) of Alexandria, held that in the incarnate Christ the two natures had been united in a single divine-human nature. This doctrine of a single nature, or monophysitism, triumphed over Nestorianism at the Third Ecumenical Council of Ephesus in 431 and again at the "Robber Council" of Ephesus in 449. Not long after the earlier of these councils Nestorius went into exile, during which he defended his life and doctrine in the *Book of Heraclides* preserved in a Syriac translation. After Theodosius II's death his successor Marcian (450-458), husband of the princess Pulcheria, reversed the trend. In consultation with Pope Leo I of Rome (440-461) a Fourth Ecumenical Council was convened at Chalcedon across the straits from Constantinople in 451. It reaffirmed the condemnation of Nestorianism, which survived only outside the Empire, and decreed that even after the incarnation Christ was one person in two natures. This compromise formula solved little, and for the next two centuries the struggle over the acceptance of Chalcedon and over monophysitism remained a burning religious and political issue in the East and in East-West relations.

Meanwhile the East, especially the Balkan Peninsula, had suffered gravely from the Hunnic invasions and from the large tribute payments made to the Huns in accordance with the various peace treaties concluded with them by the Eastern government. This government was strong enough, however, to prevent the Huns and their Germanic and other allies from founding barbarian kingdoms on its territory. The situation was different in the West during the reign of Valentinian III. Here the government was militarily too weak to defend itself against its countless barbarian foes without summoning Germanic or Hunnic auxiliaries. Here real power lay in fact not with the emperor but with the commander in chief of the armed forces, the *magister utriusque militiae*, normally distinguished from the other generals by the patrician title. At the beginning of Valentinian's reign the Western generalissimo was Felix, but in 430 Felix was murdered and succeeded by Aetius. As pointed out before, Aetius had been sent as a hostage to the Hunnic court during the reign of Honorius. After his release, Aetius was able to employ Hunnic troops where he needed them, even against the government in Ravenna. Thus when in 432 the regent Galla Placidia dismissed him, he was able, with the help of a Hunnic contingent, to force her to reappoint him to his post. On other occasions Aetius was able to call on the Huns for aid against the Germanic enemies of the Rmpire, against the Burgundians in 436, and against the Visigoths in the next year. Aetius' deeds were celebrated in several poems by his contemporary Merobaudes (fl. c. 440).

The Huns, however, were not the only barbarian nation to intervene in the internal affairs of the Western Empire. In 427 Bonifatius, commander in North Africa and a supporter of Galla Placidia and Valentinian, was driven by palace intrigues at Ravenna to rebel and felt threatened by the arrival of a superior imperial army in Africa. In this predicament he called upon the Vandals, then settled in the Spanish provinces of Baetica and Carthaginiensis, to come to his aid. Under their king Gaiseric († 477) they crossed the Straits of Gibraltar in 429, and after a series of conquests established a powerful and independent Vandal state in the richest of the African provinces, Proconsularis and Byzacena. Ominous for western Europe, and for Italy in particular, was the creation of a mighty Vandal navy after Gaiseric's capture of Carthage in 439. Simultaneously the British provinces were occupied by Angles, Saxons, and Jutes. Burgundians and Alani settled in the Gallic province of Viennensis, and Aremorica (Bretagne) seceded from the Empire.

In the following decade, however, even more dangerous developments threatened the government in Ravenna. The Vandal king Gaiseric felt endangered by an alliance between the Visigothic and Suebian occupants of Gaul and Spain. He decided, therefore, to persuade Attila, king of the Huns, to attack his enemies in western Europe. Simultaneously the princess Honoria, whom her brother, Emperor Valentinian, wished to give in marriage to a senator, offered her hand to Attila. The Hunnic ruler asked Ravenna to send him his fiancée, together with half of the Empire as her dowry. The government refused this demand. In 451 Attila marched toward Gaul, collecting on his way large military contingents from the subject tribes. Aetius was poorly prepared for this attack and had only small regular forces and *federates* at his disposal. Fortunately, however, for the Empire, the king of the Visigoths, Theoderic, realized that Attila's attack was directed as much against his kingdom as against the Roman Empire. The Visigoths therefore came to the aid of the Roman forces in Gaul. The Roman alliance with the Visigoths forced the Huns to lift the siege of Aureliani (Orléans) which they had begun, and to withdraw northeastward to the province of Belgica. There a great battle was fought at the *locus Mauriacus*, in which the Romans with their *federates* and their Visigothic allies were victorious. The casualties on both sides were staggering, but the Huns were allowed to march home. In 452 Attila invaded Italy, but a famine and epidemic forced him to withdraw after plundering the cities in the Po valley. He died suddenly in 453, and the empire, which he had founded, disintegrated rapidly. The Germanic tribes which he had incorporated into his realm rebelled against their Hunnic overlords or took service in the Roman armies. The latter was the case, for example, of a section of the Ostrogoths who under the leadership of Theoderic Strabo ("the Squinter") became *federates* in the Eastern military establishment and developed into one of the main supports for the power of the Eastern general Aspar. The chronicle composed by the Spanish bishop Hydatius, which covers the years 379 to 468, contains some useful information on Attila's last campaign.

In 454 the patrician Aetius, who was held responsible for the lack of military preparedness at the time of the Hunnic invasion of Italy and who moreover met determined opposition from the eunuchs surrounding the emperor, was massacred by Valentinian and his courtiers. Six months later the emperor himself became the victim of a palace conspiracy (455). Thus the last Western imperial dynasty founded by Valentinian I in 364 came to an end. The destruction of Gallic cities by barbarian invaders, the poverty of the Western Roman state under Valentinian III, and the suffering of the rural population are dramatically described in the work of a priest from Marseilles, Salvianus, who in 440 wrote his deeply pessimistic work, *Government of God*. It may also have been under Valentinian III that Vegetius composed two handbooks, one on military matters and another on veterinary discipline, which throw light on Hunnic history. Somewhat later Prosper of Aquitaine (ca. 390-after 455) composed at Rome under Pope Leo the Great a chronicle reaching from Adam to the Vandal sack of the city. Its most valuable part began in 412 and was based largely on the author's own observations. In 468 the Spanish bishop Hydatius completed another chronicle covering the period from 379 to 467.

During the later years of Valentinian III a rapprochement had taken place between the emperor and the Vandal king Gaiseric. In fact, the latter's son had been betrothed to the emperor's oldest daughter. In 455 Gaiseric used Valentinian's murder as a pretext for a surprise attack on Rome. For two weeks the Vandal soldiers plundered the city. The Eastern emperor, Marcian, carefully avoided an entanglement in Western affairs and sent no military aid. On the contrary, he assigned his Ostrogothic *federates* lands in Pannonia where only a few months before imperial authority had been reestablished by a Western army. Marcian's policies were influenced largely by Aspar, who in 423 had helped his father Ardabur to install Valentinian III on the Western throne. As a "barbarian" Aspar was disqualified from becoming emperor in his own right, but it was due to his influence that after Marcian's death the Senate and garrison troops at Constantinople proclaimed a military tribune, Leo I (457-474). Like his predecessor, the new emperor was an opponent of monophysitism and he therefore supported the decisions of the Council of Chalcedon, although somewhat less energetically than Marcian had done. As a result, monophysitism recovered from the blow that had been dealt to it in 451 and made considerable progress, especially in Egypt and Syria. The emperor and the kingmaker, however, did not always see eye to eye on matters of policy. Thus Leo was inclined to help the Western Emperor against his Vandal enemies while Aspar stood for an entente with the powerful ruler of North Africa. Against Aspar's advice Leo also refused the tribute payments promised by his predecessor to the Ostrogoths in Pannonia. The Ostrogoths responded by invading the prefecture of Illyricum (459) and Leo was thus compelled to resume the tribute payments. In connection with the peace negotiations the Ostrogothic king sent his young son, Theoderic, as a hostage to Constantinople. Almost thirty years later, in 488, this prince, by then the sole ruler of his people, was to lead them in an attack upon Italy where he established one of the most prosperous and enlightened of the barbarian kingdoms. Under Leo, too, Huns under Attila's son Dengizic invaded the Thracian diocese for the last time (469) and were defeated. This event marks the last military action of the Huns as an organized people.

In the West, the Vandal sack of Rome (455) had eliminated an emperor of three months' duration, Petronius Maximus. A few months later Gallic members of the senatorial order, in conjunction with the king of the Visigoths, Theoderic II, prevailed upon a former praetorian prefect of Gaul, Avitus, to take the purple (July 9, 455). During the last months of Valentinian's reign or shortly after his murder, Frankish tribes had annexed territory from the Rhine to the river Samara (Somme) in northeastern France and the Alamanni had settled permanently in Alsace and northern Switzerland. These tribes, as well as the Burgundians in the province of Viennensis (Savoy) and the Visigoths in the southwest of Gaul, now organized the territories under their occupation as barbarian kingdoms and at best recognized the nominal sovereignty of the Western emperor.

The main concern of the Emperor Avitus and his Gallic backers, however, was the Vandal peril. The imperial troops commanded by a general of Germanic descent, Ricimer, won a series of victories over Gaiseric's forces in Sicily and off the island of Corsica. Ricimer then availed himself of the discontent prevailing in Italy over the Gallic regime of Avitus to start a civil war. He was victorious (456) and Emperor Avitus ended his days as bishop of Piacenza. A similar fate was in store for Avitus' son-in-law, the poet Apollinaris Sidonius (ca. 430-479?). He belonged to the highest Gallic aristocracy and composed panegyrics on Avitus and later on the emperors Majorianus and Anthemius. In 469 he accepted a bishopric. In addition to his panegyrical poems he left a large collection of letters which are an important source for the history of western Europe in the fifth century and are cited repeatedly in this book for the light which they shed on Hunnic developments.

After Avitus' deposition the Eastern emperor Leo promoted Ricimer to the rank of patrician, and one of his associates, Majorianus, to that of general. Since Ricimer's Germanic origin disqualified him for the imperial office, Majorianus was proclaimed emperor (457-461) by his soldiers, but failed to win recognition from the East. The new emperor of the West did, however, act with surprising energy. He realized that an effective defense against Gaiseric's raids and invasions of Italy was impossible as long as the Western Empire did not dispose of an adequate fleet. He built a navy and recruited an army consisting largely of Hunnic and Ostrogothic mercenaries. In cooperation with the general Aegidius, Majorianus then restored imperial prestige in Gaul.

By 460 Majorianus' preparations for an attack on Vandal Africa were complete, and he was assured of military cooperation by the *de facto* ruler of Dalmatia, the *comes* Marcellinus, who was accompanied on the campaign by an army largely of Hunnic mercenaries. But Majorianus' navy was betrayed and destroyed in a naval battle off the southwestern shore of Spain. Not long afterward, peace was concluded, and the patrician Ricimer ordered the last energetic emperor of the West arrested and decapitated (461). Power was now in the hands of the patrician, and the puppet emperor whom he promoted to the throne, Libius Severus (461-465), possessed no independence whatever. Ricimer encountered, however, open hostility from the general commanding in Gaul, Aegidius, who conspired with Gaiseric to make an attack upon Italy. Ricimer managed to foil this plan by having Burgundians and Visigoths attack Aegidius. As a result, more Gallic and Spanish territory was lost, especially most of the province of Narbonensis prima to the Visigoths. Aegidius died (was murdered?) in 464 and Libius Severus in the next year. The Eastern government of Leo I now agreed to help defend Italy and Sicily against the Vandals. With Ricimer's approval he sent a new emperor to the West, the former Eastern emperor Marcian's son-in-law, Anthemius (467-472), who during the preceding winter had commanded Eastern units in a successful campaign against a Hunnic invasion. Anthemius was accompanied by a considerable Eastern army, and a fleet was commanded by Marcellinus, the ruler of Dalmatia. The enormous cost of the joint Eastern and Western campaign against Gaiseric was borne largely by the East. In 468 an army of 100,000 men and a navy of 1,100 ships were mobilized against the Vandals. The main force was commanded by Basiliscus, brother-in-law of Leo I, who by incompetence lost the fruits of an initially successful enterprise. In the aftermath of this debacle the Visigoths expanded further in Gaul, especially in the province of Aquitania prima, where the most important cities such as Turones (Tours) and Avaricum (Bourges) fell into their hands. Only the territory between the Samara on the Frankish frontier and the Liger (Loire), the northern boundary of the Visigothic dominions, continued to be administered by a Roman official, Aegidius' son Syagrius (470).

By that time the Huns had ceased to operate as organized military and political units. Six years later the last Western emperor, Romulus Augustulus (475-476), was deposed. Within the next two decades the remainders of the Roman Empire in the West—southern Gaul, Dalmatia, a few fortresses on the Danube, Italy—also were incorporated into Germanic kingdoms.

It remains to touch briefly on some historical sources frequently referred to in this book but composed after the fall of the Hunnic realm. A number of later chroniclers supply important information on Hunnic history. Under Justinian I in the sixth century an Illyrian, Marcellinus Comes, wrote a dry chronicle in Latin covering the years 379 to 534. A popular chronicle was written by the Syrian John Malalas of Antioch beginning with the biblical period and reaching to the second half of the sixth century, a highly uncritical compilation derived from a large variety of disparate sources. John Malalas' chronicle in turn served as a source for another similar compilation, the so-called Easter Chronicle or *Chronicon Paschale* composed not long after 628.

On a higher intellectual level are the historical works of Procopius of Caesarea, a contemporary of Justinian: the *History of the Wars*, the *Secret History*, and the treatise on Justinian's *Buildings*. Procopius' primary concern was the reign of Justinian I (527-565), but in excursuses and other parts of his works he often finds occasion to refer to events of the fourth and fifth centuries, in particular to the Huns and their Germanic subjects. A few decades earlier a high Western official in Ostrogothic Italy, Cassiodorus (487-583), composed a history of the Goths in Latin in which he attempted to construct for this Germanic people a past as noble as that of Rome. The work is lost, but in 551 a Goth from Italy, Jordanes, made excerpts from Cassiodorus' work, the so-called *Getica*, which are preserved. Jordanes also was the author of a world chronicle, the *Romana*, based for the fifth and sixth centuries largely on Marcellinus Comes. References are also made, in later parts of the present work, to a *History of the Lombards* composed at the court of Charlemagne by Paul the Deacon (ca. 720-797). Finally, a chronicle compiled in the ninth century at Constantinople by the abbot Theophanes preserves some information on Huns and their allies derived from sources now lost. Thus the literary evidence from which the history of the Huns must be reconstructed spans half a millennium, beginning with the historical work of Ammianus Marcellinus and reaching to the monastic chronicles of the mid-Byzantine era.

Bibliography

(Prepared by Jane Fontenrose Cajina)

I. ABBREVIATIONS

Many abbreviations set forth below are based on standards set by the *Oxford Classical Dictionary*, by Pugachenkova and Rempel' in *Istoriia iskusstv Uzbekistana*, and by a considerable body of German and Soviet scholars. These well-established norms, however, do not account for all abbreviations adopted.

A A	*Acta Antiqua*
A A H	*Acta Archaeologica Hungarica*
A A SS	*Acta Sanctorum*
Abh. Ak. Wiss.	*Abhandlungen der Deutschen Akademie der Wissenschaften (Klasse für Sprachen, Literatur und Kunst)*
Abh. Berlin	*Abhandlungen der Deutschen Akademie der Wissenschaften (Schriften der Sektion für Altertumswissenschaft)*
Abh. Göttingen	*Abhandlungen der Gesellschaft der Wissenschaften zu Göttingen*
Abh. München	*Abhandlungen der Bayerischen Akademie der Wissenschaften (Philosophisch-historische Klasse)*
Achil.	*Achilleis (Statius)*
ACO	*Acta Conciliorum Œcumenicorum*
Acta Phil. Scandin.	*Acta Philologica Scandinavica; Tidsskrift for Nordisk Sprogforskning*
ad a.	*ad annum*
Adv. Iovinian.	*Adversus Iovinianum (Jerome)*
Adv. Nationes	*Adversus Nationes (Arnobius)*
AÉ	*Archaeologiai Értesítö*
Aen.	*Aeneid (Virgil)*
AJ	*Antiquitates Judaicae (Josephus)*

486

Ak. Wiss.	Deutsche Akademie der Wissenschaften
A.M.	*anno mundi*
Amtl. Ber. aus Berliner Museen	*Amtliche Berichte aus Berliner Museen*
AN SSSR	Akademiia nauk Soiuza Sovetskikh Sotsialisticheskikh Respublik
Anab.	*Anabasis* (Xenophon)
Anecd.	*Anecdota* (Procopius)
Ann.	*Annals* (Tacitus)
Annales Acad. Scient. Fennicae	*Annales Academiae Scientarium Fennicae*
Anon. Vales.	*Anonymi Valesiani pars posterior* (Anonymus Valesianus)
Anz. f. DA	*Anzeiger für deutsches Altertum* (in *ZfDA*)
Anz. Wien	*Anzeiger der Akademie der Wissenschaften in Wien* (*Philosophisch-historische Klasse*)
AOH	*Acta Orientalia Hungarica*
APU	*Arkheologichni pam'iatki URSR*
Archiv	*Archiv für das Studium der neueren Sprachen und Literaturen*
Archiv f. latein. Lexicographie	*Archiv für lateinische Lexicographie und Grammatik*
Argon.	*Argonautica* (Valerius Flaccus)
Arkheol. issled.	*Arkheologicheskie issledovaniia v RSFSR 1934-1936 gg.*
Arkheol. sbornik	*Arkheologicheskiĭ sbornik gosudarstvennogo Ermitazha* (*Sibirskoe otdelenie*)
Arkiv f. nord. filol.	*Arkiv för nordisk filologi*
AS	*Arkheologicheskiĭ s"ezd*
BEFEO	*Bulletin de l'École française d'extrême orient*
Bell. Gild.	*Bellum Gildonicum* (Claudian)
Bell. Goth.	*Bellum Pollentinum* (*sive Gothicum*) (Claudian)
BJ	*Bellum Judaicum* (Josephus)
BMFEA	*Bulletin of the Museum of Far Eastern Antiquities* (*Ostasiatiska Samlingarna*)
BNJb	*Byzantinisch-neugriechische Jahrbücher*
Bonn. Jahrb.	*Bonner Jahrbücher*
Bp.	bishop
BSOAS	*Bulletin of the School of Oriental and African Studies*
BT	*Byzantinoturcica*
Bŭlg. akad. naukite	*Bŭlgarska akademiia na naukite, Izvestiia na arkheologicheski institut*
BZ	*Byzantinische Zeitschrift*
Caesar.	*Liber de caesaribus* (Aurelius Victor)

CAH	The *Cambridge Ancient History*
CAJ	*Central Asiatic Journal*
Carm.	*Carmina* (Horace)
Carm. min.	*Carmina minora* (Claudian)
CCSL	*Corpus Christianorum, Seria Latina*
Chron.	*Chronica* (Cassiodorus in *CM*)
Chron. Edess.	*Chronicon Edessenum* (in *CSCO*)
Chron. Maiora	*Chronica Maiora* (Isidorus in *CM*)
Chron. Pasch.	*Chronicon Paschale* (in *CM*, *PG*)
CIL	*Corpus Inscriptionum Latinarum*
CIRB	*Corpus Inscriptionum Regni Bosporani* (*Korpus bosporspikh nadpiseǐ*)
CM	*Chronica Minora* (in *MGH AA*)
CMH	The *Cambridge Medieval History*
Cod. Iust.	*Codex Iustiniani* (in *Corpus iuris civilis*)
Cod. Theodos.	*Codex Theodosianus*
Comm. in Danielem	*Commentarius in Danielem* (Jerome)
Comm. in Ezechielem	*Commentarius in Ezechielem* (Jerome)
Comm. in Isaiam (Jerome)	*Commentarius in Isaiam* (Jerome)
Commentationes hist. et philol.	*Commentationes historicae et philologicae*
Cons. Hon.	*De consulatii Honorii* (Claudian)
Cons. Stil.	*De consulatu Stilichonis* (Claudian)
Const. Sirmond.	*Constitutiones Sirmondianae* (in *Cod. Theodos. cum Constitutionibus Sirmondianis Leges*)
Cont. Prosp.	*Continuator Prosperi Hauniensis ad a. 455* (in *CM*)
CQ	*Classical Quaterly*
CSCO	*Corpus Scriptorum Christianorum Orientalium* (*Scriptores Syri*)
CSEL	*Corpus Scriptorum Ecclesiasticorum Latinorum*
CS Hist. Byz.	*Corpus Scriptorum Historiae Byzantinae*
Cyrop.	*Cyropaedia* (Xenophon)
DA	*Deutsche Altertumskunde*
De admin. imp.	*De adminstrando imperio* (Constantine Porphyrogenitus)
De aedif.	*De aedificiis Iustiniani* (Procopius)
De civ. Dei	*De civitate Dei* (Augustine)
De red. suo	*De redito suo* (Namatianus)
De vir. ill.	*De viris illustribus* (Jerome)
Descr. Graec.	*Descriptio Graeciae* (Pausanius)
der.	*derevnia* (village)
Dionys.	Dionysius "*Periegetes*"
Div. Inst.	*Divinae Institutiones* (Lactantius)

Doklady Azerbaĭdzh.   *Doklady akademii nauk Azerbaĭdzhanskoĭ SSR*

Doklady DPMKV   *Doklady dvadtsat' piatogo mezhdunarodnogo kongresa vostokovedov*

Ed. Bonn   Refers to *CS Hist. Byz.* 1929 (B. G. Niebuhr, ed.)

EI   *Excerpta de insidiis* (in *Exerpta Historica*)

EL   *Excerpta de legationibus* (in *Excerpta Historica*; all references to *EL* correspond to the pagination in C. de Boor's edition)

Ep.   *Epistulae* (*see* Ambrose, Basil the Great, Jerome, Leo I, Paulinus of Nola, Seneca the Younger, Sidonius Apollinaris, Symmachus, etc.)

Ep. mor.   *Epistulae morales* (Seneca)

Epigr.   *Epigram(mata)*

Epit.   *Epitome* (Justin)

Epit. de caes.   *Epitome de caesaribus* (Aurelius Victor in *Liber de caesaribus*)

Epit. rei milit.   *Epitoma rei militaris* (Vegetius Renatus)

Epithal.   *Epithalamium* (Claudian)

ES   *Excerpta de sententiis* (in *Excerpta Historica*)

ESA   *Eurasia Septentrionalis Antiqua*

Etym.   *Etymologiae* (Isidorus)

FHG   *Fragmenta Historicorum Graecorum*

fr.   Fragmenta (refers to the numeration in *FHG*)

g.   *god* (year); *gorod* (city)

GAIMK   Gosudarstvennaia Akademiia Istorii Material'noĭ Kul'tury

GCS   *Die griechischen christlichen Schriftsteller der ersten drei Jahrhunderte*

Geog.   *Geographia* (Ptolemy)

Georg.   *Georgics* (Virgil)

GGA   *Göttingische Gelehrte Anzeigen*

GGM   *Geographi graeci minores*

Graec. Aff. Cur.   *Graecorum Affectionum Curatio* (Theodoret)

Greg. Tur.   Gregory of Tours

GS   *Grammata Serica Recensa*

Herc. Oet.   *Hercules Oetaeus* (Seneca)

HGM   *Historici graeci minores*

Hist.   *Histories* (Tacitus)

Hist. adv. Pagan.   *Historiae adversum Paganos* (Orosius)

Hist. eccles.   *Historia ecclesiastica*

Hist. Franc.	*Historia Francorum* (Gregory of Tours)
Hist. Lang.	*Historia Langobardorum* (Paulus Diaconus)
Hist. relig.	*Historia religiosa* (Theodoret)
Hist. Rom.	*Historia Romana* (Paulus Diaconus)
Hist. Wand.	*Historia Gothorum, Wandalorum, Sueborum* (Isidorus)
HJAS	*Harvard Journal of Asiatic Studies*
HN	*Naturalis Historica* (Pliny the Elder)
IAK	*Izvestiia arkheologicheskoĭ komissii AN SSSR* (sometimes called *Izvestiia arkheograficheskoĭ komissii*)
IMKU	*Istoriia material'noĭ kul'tury Uzbekistana*
In Eutrop.	*In Eutropium* (Claudian)
In Ioannem homil.	*In Ioannem homiliae* (John Chrysostom)
In Psalm.	*Enarrationes in Psalmos* (Augustine)
In Ruf.	*In Rufinum* (Claudian)
Inscr. christ. Rom.	*Inscriptiones christianae urbis Romae*
Inst. div. litt.	*Institutiones divinarum et humanarum litterarum* (Cassiodorus)
IOSPE	*Inscriptiones Antiquae Orae Septentrionalis Ponti Euxini*
Iov. Trag.	*Iovis Tragoedus* (Lucian)
ISNIK	*Izvestiia saratovskogo nizhnevolzhskogo instituta kraevedeniia imeni M. Gor'kogo*
Ist. Rom.	*Istoria Romîniei*
Itin. Anton.	*Itinerarium Antonini* (Anonymus of Ravenna)
Iust.	Justinian
Izv. AN SSSR	*Izvestiia akademii nauk SSSR (seriia istorii i filosofii)*
Izv. GAIMK	*Izvestiia gosudarstvennoĭ akademii istorii material'noĭ kul'tury*
Izv. Kazakh.	*Izvestiia akademii nauk Kazakhskoĭ SSR (Seriia istorii, arkheologii i etnografii)*
Izv. Kirg.	*Izvestiia akademii nauk Kirgizskoĭ SSR (Seriia obshchestvennykh nauk)*
Izv. RAIMK	*Izvestiia rossiĭskoĭ akademii istorii* (Refers to the first 4 volumes of *Izv. GAIMK*)
Izv. russk. arkheol. inst. v Konst.	*Izvestiia russkogo arkheologicheskogo instituta v Konstantinopole*
Izv. UzFAN	*Izvestiia Uzbekskogo filiala AN SSSR*
JA	*Journal Asiatique*
JAOS	*Journal of the American Oriental Society*
Jahreshefte d. österr. archäolog. Inst.	*Jahreshefte des österreichischen archäologischen Instituts*

JHS	*Journal of Hellenic Studies*
JRAS	*Journal of the Royal Asiatic Society*
JRS	*Journal of Roman Studies*
JSFOU	*Journal de la société finno-ougrienne (see MSFOU)*
KCsA	*Körösi Csoma Archivum*
Khor. Mat.	*Materialy khorezmskoĭ Ekspeditsii*
KK	*K'ao-Ku*
KKHP	*K'ao-Ku Hsüeh-Pao*
KKTH	*K'ao-Ku T'ung-Hsün*
KS	*Kratkie soobshcheniia o dokladakh i polevykh issledovaniiakh instituta istorii material'noĭ kul'tury AN SSSR*
KSIA	*Kratkie soobshcheniia instituta arkheologii AN URSR*
KSIE	*Kratkie soobshcheniia instituta etnografii AN SSSR*
Leg. Burg.	*Leges Burgundionum in MGH (Salis, ed.)*
MAR	*Materialy po arkheologii Rossii*
mes.	*mestechko (small town)*
MGH AA	*Monumenta Germaniae Historica, Auctores Antiquissimi*
MGH EE	*Monumenta Germaniae Historica, Epistulae Karolini aevi*
MGH Scr. rer. Merov.	*Monumenta Germaniae Historica, Scriptores rerum Merovingicarum*
MIA	*Materialy i issledovaniia po arkheologii SSSR*
Mitteil. d. anthropolog. Ges. in Wien	*Mitteilungen der anthropologischen Gesellschaft in Wien*
MNy	*Magyar Nyelv*
Monatsschr. f. d. Gesch. u. Wiss. d. Judentums	*Monatsschrift für die Geschichte und Wissenschaft des Judentums*
MSFOU	*Mémoires de la société finno-ougrienne*
NA	*De natura animalium (Aelian)*
Nachr. Göttingen	*Nachrichten der Akademie der Wissenschaften zu Göttingen*
n. Chr.	*nach Christ*
n.e.	*nasheĭ ery* (A.D.; *do n.e.* means B.C.)
N.F.	*neue Folge*
Not. Dign. [or.] [occ.]	*Notitia Dignitatum in partibus orientis, in partibus occidentis*
Nov. Theodos.	*Novellae (Theodosianae)*
Nov. Val.	*Novellae (Valentinianae)*
N.S.	new series
Num. Közl.	*Numismatikai Közlöny*
Num. Zeitschr.	*Numismatische Zeitschrift*
OAK	*Otchet arkheologicheskoĭ Komisii AN SSSR*

obl.	*oblast'* (province)
Österr. Zeitschr. f. Kunst u. Denkmalpflege	*Österreichische Zeitschrift für Kunst und Denkmalpflege*
Or.	*Orationes* (*see* Themistius; Gregory of Nazianzen)
Ostasiat. Zeitschr.	*Ostasiatische Zeitschrift*
Paneg.	*Panegyric*: *Panegyric on Anthemius* (Sidonius); *Panegyric on Avitus* (Sidonius); *Panegyric on Maiorian* (Sidonius); *Panegyric on Theoderic* (Ennodius); *Panegyric to Theodosius* (Pacatus); *Panegyricus Messallae* (Tibullus); *Second Panegyric on Aetius* (Merobaudes)
Paneg. Prob.	*Panegyric on Probinus and Olybrius* (Claudian)
PBB	*Beiträge zur Geschichte der deutschen Sprache und Literatur*
Perieg.	*Periegesis* (Dionysius)
Periplus Pont. Eux.	*Periplus Ponti Euxini* (Arrian)
PG	*Patrologiae Cursus, seria Graeca*
PL	*Patrologiae Cursus, seria Latina*
PMLA	*Publications of the Modern Language Association of America*
PO	*Patrologia Orientalis*
Prähist. Zeitschr.	*Prähistorische Zeitschrift*
Probl. ist. sev. Prichernomor'ia	*Problemy istorii severnogo Prichernomor'ia v antichnuiu epokhu*
Proc. Brit. Acad.	*Proceedings of the British Academy*
PW	*Realencyclopädie der klassischen Altertumswissenschaft* (Pauly-Wissowa)
r.	*raĭon* (district); *reka* (river)
R. Académie Belgique, Bull. classe de lettres	*Royale Académie Belgique, Bulletin de la classe de lettres*
RANION	*Rossiĭskaia assotsiatsiia nauchnoissledovatel'skikh institutov obshchestvennykh nauk*
Rapt. Pros.	*De raptu Prosperpinae* (Claudian)
RÉA	*Revue des études anciennes*
Rel.	*Relationes* (Symmachus)
Revue d'hist. et de litt. religieuses	*Revue d'histoire et de littérature religieuses*
Röm.-germ. Kommission	*Römisch-germanische Kommission des Deutschen archäologischen Instituts* (source of *Germania*)
Röm. Limes in Österreich	Ak. Wiss. *Der Römische Limes in Österreich*
RV	*Reallexikon der Vorgeschichte*
s.	*selo* (village)
s.a.	*sub anno*

SA	Sovetskaia arkheologiia
SAI	Arkheologiia SSSR. Svod arkheologicheskikh istochnikov
SB	Sitzungsberichte (of an academy)
SB Berlin	Sitzungsberichte der Akademie der Wissenschaften in Berlin
SB Heidelberg	Sitzungsberichte der Akademie der Wissenschaften in Heidelberg (Philosophisch-historische Klasse)
SB München	Sitzungsberichte der Bayerischen Akademie der Wissenschaften
Scholia Apoll. Rhod.	Scholia Apolloniis Rhodiis (see Apollonius)
SCIV	Studii şi cercetări de istorie veche
Scr. Syri	Scriptores Syri (in CSCO)
SE	Sovetskaia etnografiia
SMAE	Sbornik muzeia antropologii i etnografii
Soobshcheniia Gos. Ermitazha	Soobshcheniia gosudarstvennogo Ermitazha
SPA	A Survey of Persian Art
st.	stanitsa (Cossack village)
Strateg.	(Strategy) Tactica (Mauricius)
s.v.	sub verbo
Synaxarium Eccles. Const.	Synaxarium Ecclesiae Constantinopolitanae
Tact.	Tactica (Arrian)
TDPMKV	Trudy dvadtsat' piatogo mezhdunarodnogo kongressa vostokovedov
Theoph. Byz.	Theophanes Byzantius
Theoph. Sim.	Theophylactus Simocatta
TIE	Trudy instituta etnografii imeni N. N. Miklucho Maklaia AN SSSR
TP	T'oung Pao
Trudy AS	Trudy arkheologicheskogo s"ezda
Trudy Gos. Ermitazha	Trudy gosudarstvennogo Ermitazha
Trudy Kazakh.	Trudy instituta istorii, arkheologii i etnografii akademii nauk Kazakhskoĭ SSR
Trudy Khor.	Trudy khorezmskoĭ arkheologo-etnograficheskoĭ ekspeditsii
Trudy Kirg.	Trudy kirgizskoĭ arkheologo-etnograficheskoĭ ekspeditsii
Trudy Tadzh.	Trudy instituta istorii, arkheologii i etnografii akademii nauk Tadzhikskoĭ SSR
Trudy Tuv.	Trudy tuvinskoĭ kompleksnoĭ arkheologo-etnograficheskoĭ ekspeditsii
TSARANION	Trudy sektsii arkheologii rossiĭskoĭ assosiatsii nauchno-issledovatel'skikh institutov obshchestvennykh nauk

TU	*Texte und Untersuchungen zur Ge-schichte der altchristlichen Literatur*
UJb	*Ungarische Jahrbücher* (also called *Ural-Altaische Jahrbücher*)
UUÅ	*Uppsala universitets Årsskrift*
UZSU	*Uchenye zapiski saratovskogo gosuniversiteta*
v.	*vek* (century); verse; volume
Var. Hist.	*Varia Historia* (Aelian)
VDI	*Vestnik drevneĭ istorii*
VO	*Vizantiĭskoe obozrenie*
vv.	*veká* (centuries); verses
VV	*Vizantiĭskiĭ vremennik*
WBKKA	*Wiener Beiträge zur Kunst und Kultur Asiens*
Wiener Prähist. Zeitschr.	*Wiener Prähistorische Zeitschrift*
WW	*Wên-Wu*
WWTK	*Wên-Wu Ts'an-K'ao Tzu-Liao*
WZKM	*Wiener Zeitschrift für Kunde des Mor-genlandes*
Zapiski inst. vostokoved.	*Zapiski instituta vostokovedeniia*
Zapiski vostochn., otd. russk. arkheol. obshchestva	*Zapiski vostochnye, otdelenie russkogo arkheologicheskogo obshchestva*
ZDMG	*Zeitschrift der Deutschen morgenlän-dischen Gesellschaft*
Zeitschr. f. d. österr. Gymnasien	*Zeitschrift für die österreichischen Gym-nasien*
Zeitschr. f. hist. Waffen- und Kostümkunde	*Zeitschrift für historische Waffen- und Kostümkunde*
Zeitschr. f. kl. Philologie	*Zeitschrift für klassische Philologie*
Zeitschr. f. Ortsnamenforschung	*Zeitschrift für Ortsnamenforschung*
Zeitschr. f. slav. Philologie	*Zeitschrift für slavische Philologie*
ZfDA	*Zeitschrift für deutsches Altertum und deutsche Literatur*
ZfDPh	*Zeitschrift für deutsche Philologie*
ZfN	*Zeitschrift für Numismatik*

II. Classical and Medieval Register of cited Names and Titles

Note: The editions listed in cross-references are those used by the author and can be found, for the most part, in the main bibliography.

Aelian (Claudius Aelianus), c. A.D. 170-235
    a. *De natura animalium*
    b. *Varia Historia*
Agathias Scholasticus of Myrina, sixth century A.D.
    History, inspired by Procopius and continued by Menander (*see* ed. Bonn; Keydell 1967)

Ambrose, Bp. of Milan, fourth century A.D.
  a. *Sancti Ambrosii opera* (*CSEL* 73, Faller, O., ed.)
    1. *De excessu fratris Satyri*
    2. *De fide*
    3. *De obitu Theodosii*
    4. *De Tobia*
    5. *Expositio evangelii secundum Lucam*
  b. In *PL*
    1. *Apologia Prophetae David*
    2. *Epistulae* (*PL* 16)
Ammianus Marcellinus, fourth century A.D.
  Res gestae, a history in thirty-one books, continuation of Tacitus to
    year 378 (English: *see* Rolfe 1939; for XXXI, 2, 1-2, the author
    follows the translation in Pighi 1948)
Andreas of Caesarea
  Commentarius in apocalypsin (*PG*)
Anna Comnena (*see* Comnena, Princess Anna)
Anonymus of Ravenna (*see* Cuntz, Otto [1929])
Anonymus Valesianus (*see* Cessi 1913)
Apollonius Rhodius, third century B.C.
  Scholia in Apollonii Rhodii Argonautica (*FHG*)
Arnobius, late third century A.D. and after
  Adversus Nationes, in seven books (*CSEL* 4)
Arrian (Flavius Arrianus), second century A.D.
  a. *Opera* (*see* Roos 1928)
  b. *Anabasis*
  c. *Periplus Ponti Euxini*
  d. *Tactica* (*see* Scheffer 1664)
Asterius of Amasea, c. A.D. 400
  Homilies (*PG* 40)
Augustine, Bp. of Hippo, A.D. 354-430
  a. *Opera* (*PL* 32-47)
    1. *De civitate Dei*
    2. *Enarrationes in Psalmos* (*PL* 37)
Aurelius Victor, Sextus, fourth century A.D.
  Caesares (*Liber de caesaribus*), from Augustus to Constantius (*see*
    Pichlmayr 1911)
Ausonius, fourth century A.D.
  a. *Opera* (*see* Toll 1671; English: *Loeb*; French: Jasinski 1935)
    1. *Ephemeris*
    2. *Epigrammata*
    3. *Epitome de caesaribus*
    4. *Gratiarum Actio ad Gratianum Imperatorem pro consulatu*
    5. *Mosella*
    6. *Praecatio consulis designati pridie Kal. Ian. fascibus Sumptis*
Avienus, fourth century A.D.
  Orbis terrae
Bar Hebraeus (*see* Wallis Budge 1932)
Barhadbeshabba Abbaya (Barhadbesabba Abbaia), Bp. of Halwan
  Historia ecclesiastica 25 (French: Nau 1913)

Basil the Great of Caesarea, fourth century A.D.
  Epistulae (*PG* 29-32)
Bede (Beda *Venerabilis*), A.D. 673-735
  Chronicon
Callimachus of Cyrene, c. 305 to c. 240 B.C.
  a. *Opera* (in *Anthologia Palatina*)
     1. *Aetia*
     2. *Epigrammata*
     3. *Vitae*
Callinicus, fifth century A.D.
  a. *Epigrammata*
  b. *De vita s. Hypatii*
Carpini, Giovanni de Piano, Abp. of Antivari, c. A.D. 1180-1252
  a. *The Journey of William Rubruck* (*see* Rockhill 1900)
  b. *The Mongol Mission* (*see* Dawson 1957)
Cassiodorus Senator, c. A.D. 490 to c. 583
  a. *Opera* (*PL* 69-70)
  b. *Chronica*, to year 519 (*see* Mommsen 1898a)
  c. *Epistulae* (English: Hodgkin 1886)
  d. A *History of the Goths*, in twelve books, nonextant, but summarized
     in *Getica* (*see* Mommsen 1882; English: Mierow 1915)
  e. *Historia tripartita* (*Hist. eccles.*, from A.D. 306 to 439, compiled from
     Theodoret, Socrates, and Sozomen)
  f. *Institutiones divinarum et humanarum litterarum*
  g. *Variae* I-II (*see* Mommsen 1898a, 12; English: Hodgkin 1886)
Cassius Dio Cocceianus, c. A.D. 40 to after A.D. 112
  History of Rome (*EL*, C. de Boor and Boissevain 1910)
Chrysostom, John, Bp. of Constantinople, c. A.D. 354-407
  a. *Opera* (*PG* 47-64)
     1. *Epistulae*
     2. *In Ioannem homiliae*
Claudian (Claudius Claudianus), late fourth century A.D. and after
  a. *Opera* (*MGH* 10; English: *see* Platnauer 1922*)
     1. *Bellum Gildonicum*
     2. *Bellum Pollentium* (*sive Gothicum*)
     3. *Carmina minora*
     4. *De consulatii Honorii* (3rd; 4th: *see also* Fargues 1933; 6th:
        see also K. A. Müller 1938)
     5. *De consulatu Stilichonis*
     6. *Epithalamium*
     7. *Fescennina de nuptiis Honorii Augusti*
     8. *In Eutropium*
     9. *In Rufinum*
     10. *Panegyric on Probinus and Olybrius*
     11. *Raptus Proserpinae* (*De raptu Proserpinae*)

---

* M. Platnauer's translation contains arbitrary changes and misinterpretations
of geographical names which I tacitly corrected.

Claudius Marius Victor of Marseille, d. A.D. 425
> *Aletheia* (in *CSEL* 16)

Clemens Alexandrinus, Titus Flavius, *floruit* c. A.D. 200
> *Protrepticus* (in *GCS* 12)

Comnena, Princess Anna, twelfth century A.D.
> *Alexiad* (English: Dawes 1928; French: Leib 1945)

Constantine VII, Porphyrogenitus, A.D. 905-959
> a. *De administrando imperio* (*see* Moravcsik 1949; English: Jenkins 1949)
> b. *Excerpta historica iussu Imp. Constantini Prophyrogeniti confecta* (*see* C. de Boor and Boissevain 1910)
> > 1. *Excerpta de legationibus*, including Cassius Dio Cocceianus, John of Antioch, Malchus, Menander, Petrus Patricius, and Priscus (English: 1931)
> > 2. *Excerpta de sententiis*, including Eunapius (English: 1936)
> > 3. *Excerpta de insidiis*, including John of Antioch and Malalas

Continuator Prosperi Hauniensis (a continuation of Prosper Tiro's *Chronica*)

Cyrillonas (Qurilona), *floruit* c. A.D. 400
> *Mamre on the Locusts* (English: Landersdorfer 1913)

Dion Cassius (*see* Cassius Dio Cocceianus)

Dionysius "Periegetes"
> *Periegesis, Scythica et Caucasica* (in *GGM*; Russian: Latyshev 1906)

Ennodius of Gaul, Bp. of Pavia, A.D. 473-521
> a. *Carmen* (*MGH AA* 7)
> b. *Panegyric on Theodoric* (*see* Vogel 1885)

Epiphanius, Bp. of Salamis, A.D. 315-403
> a. *De gemmis* (*see* Blake and de Vis 1934)
> b. *Treatise on the Twelve Stones* (in *Collectio Avellana*)

Eugippius, *floruit* A.D. 511
> *Vita s. Severini* (*see* Mommsen 1898b)

Eunapius of Sardis, c. A.D. 347-414.
> A history from A.D. 270-404, fragments in *ES* 4:84-85 (*see* C. de Boor and Boissevain 1910)

Eusebius Pamphili, Bp. of Caesarea, c. A.D. 260-340)
> *Historia ecclesiastica*, continued by Rufinus (*PG* 19-24; English: Mommsen and Eduard Schwarz 1956; French: Bardy 1952)

Evagrius Scholasticus, sixth century A.D.
> *Historia ecclesiastica*, from 431 to 594 (*see* Bidez and Parmentier 1898; English: Walford 1854)

Florus, Lucius Annaeus, second century A.D.
> *Epitome bellorum omnium annorum DCC* I-II (English: *Loeb* 1929)

Fredegar, seventh century A.D.
> *Chronicon* (*PL* 71)

Gregory I, Pope, c. A.D. 540-604
> *Dialogi de vita et miraculis patrum Italicorum* (*see* Moricca 1924)

Gregory of Nazianzen, A.D. 329-389
> a. *Opera* (PG 35-38)
> > 1. *De vita sua* (*PG* 37)
> > 2. *Orationes* (*PG* 35)

Gregory of Nyssa, fourth century A.D.
> In *PG* 46, 76

Gregory of Tours, A.D. 538-594
  a. *De miraculis s. Martini*
  b. *Dialogi* I
  c. *Historia Francorum*
Heliodorus, *floruit* 220-250 A.D.
    Aethiopica
Herodian of Syria, *floruit* early third century A.D.
    Histories of the Empire after Marcus, to year 238, in eight books
Hilarianus, Q. Julius
    De cursu Temporum (*PL*)
Hilary of Poitiers, fourth century A.D.
  a. *Opera* (PL 9-10)
    Contra Arianos
Hippocrates, fifth century B.C.
    De aere (English: *Loeb*)
Hippolytus (in *GCS* 4)
Historia tripartita (*see* Cassiodorus)
Honorius (in *Collectio Avellana, CSEL*)
Horace, 65-8 B.C.
    Carmina
Hydatius
    Consular Fasti (*CM* II)
Ioannes Kinnamos
    Epitome (*of Justin*)
Isaac of Antioch
    Homily on the Royal City (*Zeitschrift für Semitistik* 7; English: C.
    Moss, trans.)
Isidorus Hispalensis, Bp. of Seville, seventh century A.D.
  a. *Chronica maiora* (in *CM* II)
  b. *Etymologiae*, also called *Origines*
  c. *Historia Gothorum, Wandolorum, Sueborum* (*CM* II)
Itinerarium Antonini (*see* Cuntz 1929)
Jerome (Eusebius Hieronymus), c. A.D. 348-420
  a. *Opera* (PL 22-30)
    1. *Adversus Iovinianum*
    2. *Commentarius in Danielem*
    3. *Commentarius in Ezechielem* (*PL* 25)
    4. *Commentarius in Galatas* (*PL* 26)
    5. *Commentarius in Isaiam* (*PL* 24)
  b. *De viris illustribus* (Herding 1879)
  c. *Epistulae* (*CSEL* 14-16; English: F. A. Wright 1939; French: La-
    bourt 1954)
  d. *Hebraicae quaestiones in libro geneseos*
John of Antioch (In *EL, EI*, C. de Boor and Boissevain 1910)
John of Ephesus, sixth century A.D.
  a. *Ecclesiastical History* (Nau 1897; German: Markwart 1930, 97-99)
  b. *Lives of Eastern Saints* (*PO* 17)
John of Nikiu
    The Chronicle of John, Bishop of Nikiu (English: Charles 1916)

Jordanes, sixth century A.D.
> *Romana et Getica* (*see* Mommsen 1882; Closs 1866; Kalén 1934; English: Mierow 1915)

Josephus, Flavius, first century A.D.
> a. *Antiquitates Judaicae*, in twenty books
> b. *Bellum Judaicum*, in seven books

Joshua Stylites
> *The Chronicle of Johua Stylites* (*see* W. Wright 1882)

Justin (Justinus), Marcus Junianus, third century A.D. (?)
> *Epitome* (*of Trogus*)

Kézai, Simon (Simonis de Keza), late thirteenth century
> *Chronicon hungaricum* (Horányi, ed., 1782)

Kinnamos (*see* Ioannes Kinnamos)

Lactantius, c. A.D. 240 to c. 320
> a. *Opera* (*CSEL* 19, 27)
>> 1. *Divinae Institutiones*

Leo I, Pope, fifth century A.D.
> *Epistulae* (*ACO*; *PL* 54-56; German: Caspar 1933)

Liutprand (Liudprand), Bp. of Cremona, tenth century A.D.
> *Antapodosis* (English: F. A. Wright 1930)

Lucan, first century A.D.
> *Bellum Civile* (English: *Loeb* 1928)

Lucian of Samosata, second century A.D.
> a. *Iovis Tragoedus*
> b. *Toxaris*

Lydus, John (Ioannes), sixth century A.D.
> *De magistratibus populi Romani* (*see* Wünsch 1898)

Macarius Magnes
> *Apocritus* (English: Crafer 1919)

Malalas (Ioannes Rhetor), c. A.D. 491-598
> *Chronographia*, in eighteen books (L. A. Dindorf 1831; *EI*; *FHG* IV-V; *PG*)

Malchus of Philadelphia, *floruit* A.D. 500
> Continuation of Priscus (*EL*, C. de Boor and Boissevain 1910; *CS Hist. Byz.*; L. A. Dindorf 1877)

Mansi, Ioannes Dominicus
> *Sacrorum Conciliorum nova et amplissima collectio* VI

Marc le Diacre (Marcus Diaconus)
> *Vie de Porphyre, évêque de Gaza* (*see* Grégoire and Kugener 1930)

Marcellinus Comes, sixth century A.D.
> *Chronicon* (in *CM*)

Marcian of Heraclea
> *Periplus of the Outer Sea; East and West, and of the Great Islands Therein* (English: Schoff 1927)

Marco Polo (*see* Hambis 1955; Moule and Pelliot 1938)

Mauricius "The Tactician" (Maurice), Emperor of the East, c. A.D. 539-602
> *Artis militaris*, also called *Tactica*, and *Strategy* (*see* Scheffer 1664)

Menander "Protector", late sixth century A.D. and after
> a. (All quotations refer to *EL* 170-221, 442-447; also in *FHG* IV; *CS Hist. Byz.* 19)
> b. *Rhetores graeci* (*see* Spengel 1856)

Merobaudes, Flavius, fifth century A.D.
  a. *Flavii Merobaudes Reliquiae* (*see* Vollmer 1905)
  b. *Second Panegyric on Aetius*
Michael the Syrian
  Chronicle (French: Chabot 1904)
Moses of Khorene (Moses Chorenac'i, Moses Xorenac'i), *floruit* fifth century A.D.
  a. [History of Armenia, in Armenian], (French: trans. by P. E. Le Vaillant de Florival, Venice, 1841)
  b. [Geography, in Armenian], (French: trans. by P. Arsène Soukry, Venice, 1881)
Namatianus, Rutilius Claudius, *floruit* early fifth century A.D.
  De reditu suo (Woestijne, P. van de, ed.)
Nazarius
  Panegyric to Constantine
Nestorius
  The Bazaar of Heracleides (*see* Driver and Hodgson 1925; French: Nau 1910)
Nicephorus Callistus, A.D. 1256-1311
  Historia ecclesiastica (PG)
Nonnosus, sixth century A.D.
  Nonnosi Fragmenta (*FHG* and *HGM*)
Olympiodorus
  Codices (*see* Henry 1959; *The Library of Photius*; *CM* I)
Orosius of Tarraco, *floruit* early fifth century
  a. *Opera* (*see* Zangemeister 1889)
  b. *Historia adversum Paganos* (*CSEL* 5)
Pacatus Drepanius
  Panegyric to Theodosius (*Latini Pacati Drepanii Panegyricus Theodosio Augusto Dictus* in Galletier 1949)
Paulinus of Nola, A.D. 353-431
  a. *Opera* (*CSEL* 29-30)
    1. *Epistulae*
Paulinus of Pella
  Eucharistos (*CSEL* 16, 263-334)
Paulinus of Périgueux
  a. *De vita s. Martini episcopi* (CSEL 16)
  b. *Epigrammata* (*CSEL*)
Paulus Diaconus (Paul the Deacon), eighth century A.D.
  a. *Historia Langobardorum* (*see* Waitz 1878; English: Foulke 1906)
  b. *Historia Romana* (*see* Crivelluci 1914; reprint in Paredi 1937)
Pausanius, second century A.D.
  Descriptio Graeciae (English: Frazer 1898)
Philostorgius, c. A.D. 368 to after 433
  Historia ecclesiastica (*see* Bidez 1960; *PG* 65; English: *The Library of Photius*; Walford 1846)
Photius, ninth century A.D.
  Epiome (Henry 1959; English: *The Library of Photius*)
Pliny the Elder, A.D. 23-79
  Naturalis Historia, in thirty-seven books (English: *Loeb*)
Plutarch, c. A.D. 50 to c. 120

   a. *Lives*
     1. *Aemilius Paulus*
     2. *Galba*
Pomponius Mela of Tingentera, first century A.D.
   Cosmographia sive de situ orbis (*De chorographia*), (English: Golding 1585).
Priscus of Panium, fifth century A.D.
   Excerpta de legationibus Romanorum ad gentes (Quoted from *EL*, edition of C. de Boor and Boissevain 1910; *see also HGM* 1, 279; fr. refers to the numeration in *FHG*)
Procopius of Caesarea, sixth century A.D.
   a. *Opera* (*see* Haury, ed.; German: Rubin 1954; English: *Loeb*)
     1. *De aedificiis Iustiniani*
     2. *The History of the Wars of Justinian* (*De bello persico*, 1-2; *De bello vandalico*, 3-4; *De bello Gothico*, 5-7; Supplement, 8)
     3. *Anecdota* (Comparetti, ed.)
Prosper Tiro of Aquitaine, c. A.D. 390 to c. 455
   a. *Carmen de divina providentia* (PL 51)
   b. *Chronica*, to year 455 (*CM* II, Mommsen 1898a)
   c. *Epitome* (of the Chronicle)
   d. *De vocatione omnium gentium* (*PL* 51; English: De Letter 1952)
Prudentius, late fourth century A.D.
   Apotheosis
Pseudo-Caesarius (*see* Sulpicius Severus)
Ptolemy (Claudius Ptolemaeus), second century A.D.
   Geographia, also called *Cosmographia* (*see* Fischer 1932; English: Stevenson 1932)
Quodvultdeus
   Liber de promissionibus et praedicarionibus Dei (*PL*)
Rufinus of Aquileia, c. A.D. 345-410
   Historia ecclesiastica, to year 395 (*PL* 21)
St. Martin (*see* Sulpicius Severus)
Salvian, fifth century A.D.
   De gubernatione Dei, in eight books (*see* Sanford 1930)
Seneca the Younger, first century A.D.
   a. *Epistulae morales*
   b. *Hercules furens*
   c. *Hercules Oetaeus*
   d. *Oedipus*
Sidonius Apollinaris, fifth century A.D.
   a. *Letters* (English: Dalton 1915)
   b. *Poems* (English: W. B. Anderson 1965)
     1. *Panegyric on Anthemius*
     2. *Panegyric on Avitus*
     3. *Panegyric on Maiorian*
Silius Italicus, first century A.D.
   Punica
Simon of Kéza (*see* Kézai, Simon)
Socrates Scholasticus, c. A.D. 380 to c. 450
   Historia ecclesiastica, from 305 to 439 (*PG* 67; English: in *Nicene Fathers*, and in *Greek Ecclesiastical Historians* 3)

Solinus, *floruit* A.D. 200
  Collectanea Rerum Memorabilium (*see* Mommsen 1895)
Sozomen, *floruit* early fifth century A.D.
  Historia ecclesiastica, from 324 to 439 (*see* Bidez 1960; English: in
    Nicene Fathers, and in *Greek Ecclesiastical Historians*)
Statius, c. A.D. 45-96
  a. *Achilleis*
  b. *Thebais*
Strabo, 64 B.C. to c. A.D. 21
  Geographica, in seventeen books (English: *Loeb*; Thomson 1948)
Suidas (or *Suda*), Greek lexicon compiled c. A.D. 950 (*see* Adler 1938)
Sulpicius Severus, late fourth century A.D. and after
  a. *Opera* (in *CSEL*, Halm, ed.)
    1. *Chronicle*, to year 400
    2. *Dialogus* I (for St. Martin and Pseudo-Caesareus)
Symmachus, d. A.D. 525
  a. *Epistulae*
  b. *Relationes* (*MGH AA* 6)
  c. *Historia Romana* (lost)
Synesius of Cyrene, c. A.D. 370-413
  a. Essays and hymns (English: Fitzgerald 1930)
  b. *Catastasis* (*PG* 66)
  c. *De regno* (*PG*)
  d. *Egyptian Tale*
Tacitus, late first century A.D. and after
  a. *Annals*
  b. *Histories*
Themistius, fourth century A.D.
  Orationes (*see* K. W. Dindorf 1932; Harduin 1684)
Theodor Lector
  Historia ecclesiastica (*PG* 86)
Theodoret, c. A.D. 393-466
  a. *Graecorum Affectionum Curatio* (*see* Raeder 1904)
  b. *Historia ecclesiastica*, from Constantine to 428 (*GCS* 44; English:
    Walford 1854)
  c. *Historia religiosa* (*see* Lietzmann 1908)
Theophanes Byzantius, eighth century A.D.
  Chronographia I-II (*see* C. de Boor 1883; fragments in *FHG* IV,
    270-271 or *HGM* IV)
Theophylactus of Achrida (*PG* 126, 193c)
Theophylactus Simocatta (*see* C. de Boor 1887; Russian: Pigulevskaia 1957)
Tibullus, c. 50-19 B.C.
  Panegyricus Messallae
Trogus, Pompeius (*see* Justin)
Valerius Flaccus, *floruit* late first century A.D.
  Argonautica
Vegetius Renatus, late fourth century A.D. and after
  Epitoma rei militaris (*Mulomedicina*), in four books (*see* Lommatzsch
    1903; English: in J. K. Anderson 1961; Ridgeway 1906; German:
    in Hauger 1921; Hörnschmeyer 1929)

Venantius Fortunatus, sixth century A.D.
  Vita s. Germani (MGH AA 4)
Virgil, 70-19 B.C.
  a. *Aeneid*
  b. *Georgics*
Vita Olympiadis (in *Analecta Bollandiana*, ch. 7)
Xenophon, c. 428 to c. 354 B.C.
  a. *Anabasis*
  b. *Cyropaedia* (*see* L. Dindorf 1859)
  c. *Hellenica*
Zacharias Rhetor
  Church History (*see* Ahrens and Krüger 1899; interpretations by
    E. W. Brooks (in *CSCO*, third series)
Zonaras, Ioannes, twelfth century A.D.
  Epitome historiarum (*see* L. A. Dindorf 1875)
Zosimus, fifth century A.D.
  Historia nova, from Augustus to year 410 (see Mendelssohn 1887)

III. SOURCES

With few exceptions, only those books and articles are listed to which the author refers at least twice. It is understood that all serial publications of the great academies (*Abhandlungen, Izvestiia, Mémoires, Proceedings, Rendiconti, Sitzungsberichte, Zapiski,* and so on) referred to in abridged form are series which cover the humanities. Chinese dynastic histories are cited from the edition in *Po-na pen erh-shih-szu shih* (Shanghai, 1930-1937).

For many works the dates of the reprints are stated, not the dates of the original publication.

Aarbøger for nordisk Oldkyndighed og Historie (Copenhagen, 1885-).
Abaev, V. I.
  1949   *Osetinskiĭ iazyk i folk'lor* 1 (Moscow and Leningrad, 1949).
Åberg, N.
  1919   *Ostpreussen in der Völkerwanderungszeit* (Uppsala, 1919).
  1922   *Die Franken und Ostgoten in der Völkerwanderungszeit* (Uppsala,
             1922).
  1936a   *Til belysande a det gotinska kulturinslaget i Mellaneuropa och
             Skandinavien, Fornvännen* 31 (1936), 264-277.
  1936b   *Vorgeschichtliche Kulturkreise in Europa* (Copenhagen, 1936).
Abetekov, A. K.
  1967   "Arkheologicheskie pamiatniki kochevykh plemen v zapadnoĭ chas-
             ti Chuĭskoĭ doliny," *Drevniaia i rannesrednevekovaia kul'tura Kir-
             gizistana* (Frunze, 1967)
Abetekov, A. K. and Iu. D. Baruzdin
  1963   "Sako-usun'skie pamiatniki Talasskoĭ doliny," *Arkheologicheskie
             pamiatniki Talasskoĭ doliny* (Frunze, 1963), 17-31.
Abramova, M. P.
  1959   "Sarmatskaia kul'tura II v. do n.e.-I v. n.e.," *SA* 1 (Moscow,
             1959), 52-71.
  1961   "Sarmatskaia pogrebeniia Dona i Ukrainy," *SA* 1 (Moscow, 1961),
             91-110.
Abramzon, S. M.

1946   "K semantike kirgizskikh etnonimov," *SE* 3 (Moscow, 1946), 123-132.

1960   "Etnicheskiĭ sostav kirgizskogo naseleniia severnoĭ Kirgizii," *Trudy Kirg.* 4 (Moscow, 1960), 3-137.

Acker, W. R. B.
1965   *Japanese Archery* (Rutland, Vt. and Tokyo, 1965).

Acta Antiqua (Budapest).

Acta Archaeologia Hungarica, Moravcsik, Gy., ed. (Budapest, 1926).

Acta Conciliorum Œcumenicorum, Scwartz, Eduard, ed. (Berlin and Leipzig, 1924-40).

Acta Orientalia Hungarica, Ligeti, L., ed. (Budapest).

Acta Philologica Scandinavica; *Tidsskrift for Nordisk Sprogforskning* (Copenhagen).

Acta Sanctorum, Carnandet, J., ed. (Paris and Rome, 1867).

Adler, A., ed.
1938   *Suidae Lexicon* (Leipzig, 1928-38).

Ageeva, E. I. and A. G. Maksimova
1958   "Otchet Pavlodarskoĭ ekspeditsii," *Trudy Kazakh.* 7 (Alma Ata, 1958), 32-50.

Ahrens, K. and G. Krüger
1899   *Die sogenannte Kirchengeschichte des Zacharias Rhetor* in *Scriptores sacri et profani* (Leipzig, 1899).

Akhmerov, R. B.
1949   "Drevnie progrebeniia v g. Ufe.," *KS* 25 (1949), 113-117.
1955   "Mogil'nik bliz g. Sterlitamaka," *SA* 22 (Moscow, 1955), 153-176.

Akimova, M. S.
1961   "Anthropologicheskie dannye pro proiskhozhdeniiu narodov Volgo-Kam'ia," *Voprosy antropologii* 7 (1961), 29-40.
1964   "Materialy k antropologii rannikh Bolgar" in Gening and Khalikov 1964 (Moscow, 1964), 177-196.

Akishev, K. A. and G. A. Kushaev
1963   *Drevniaia kul'tura sakov i usuneĭ doliny r. Ili* (Alma Ata, 1963).

Alarcos, E.
1935   *El Toledano, Jordanes y San Isidro* (Santander, 1935).

Alekseenko, E. A.
1967   *Kety* (Leningrad, 1967).

Alekseev, V. P.
1954   "Paleoantropologiia lesnykh plemen severnogo Altaia," *KSIE* 21 (1954), 63-69.
1956   "Ocherki paleoantropologii Tuvinskoĭ avtonomnoĭ oblasti," *TIE* 23 (1956), 374-383.
1958   "Paleoantropologiia Altaia epokhi zheleza," *SA* 1 (1958), 45-49.
1960   English translation of Alekseev 1954 in *Contributions to the Physical Anthropology of the Soviet Union* (Cambridge, Mass., 1960), 238ff.
1963a   "Zaselenie territorii iuzhnoĭ Sibiri chelovekom v svete dannykh paleoantropologii," *Materialy i issledovaniia po arkheologii, etnografii i istorii Krasnoiarskogo kraia* (Krasnoiarsk, 1963), 5-10.
1963b   "Proiskhozhdenie khakasskogo naroda v svete dannykh antropologii," *Materialy i issledovaniia po arkheologii, etnografii i istorii Krasnoiarskogo kraia* (Krasnoiarsk, 1963), 135-164.

Alekseeva, E. P.
1955   "Arkheologicheskie raskopki v aula Zhako v Cherkesii," *KS* 60 (1955), 73-79.
Alföldi, A.
1926   *Der Untergang der Römerherrschaft in Pannonien* 2 (Berlin and Leipzig, 1926).
1928   "Les Champs catalauniques," *Revue des études hongroises* 6 (1928), 108-111.
1932   "Funde aus der Hunnenzeit und ihre ethnische Sonderung," *AAH* 9 (Budapest, 1932).
1938   *Tracce del christianesimo nell'epoca delle grandi migrazioni in Ungheria* (Rome, 1938).
1939a   "Antike Darstellungen zur Geschichte der Kultur der eurasischen Reiterhirten," *Folia Archaeologica* 1-2 (1939), 166-189.
1939b   "The Invasions of Peoples from the Rhine to the Black Sea," *CAH* 12 (1939), 146-150.
1944a   "Materialien zur Klassifizierung der gleichzeitigen Nachahmungen von römischen Münzen aus Ungarn und den Nachbarländern" (1944).
1944b   *Zu den Schicksalen Siebenbürgens im Altertum* (Budapest, 1944).
1949   "Der iranische Weltriese auf archäologischen Denkmälern," *Jahrbuch der schweizerischen Gesellschaft für Urgeschichte* (1949-50), 19-34.
1967   In *Gestalt und Geschichte, Festschrift Karl Schefold* (1967).
Alfs, J.
1944   "Der bewegliche Metallpanzer im römischen Heer," *Zeitschr. f. hist. Waffen-und Kostümkunde* 7 (1944), 69-126.
Allgemeine Geschichte (*see* L. Schmidt 1909).
Allwater, D.
1959   *Saint John Chrysostom* (London, 1959)
Altaner, B.
1960   *Patrology*, Graef, H. C., trans. (New York, 1960).
Altheim, F.
1951   *Attila und die Hunnen* (Baden-Baden, 1951).
1956a   "Greutungen," *Beiträge zur Namenforschung* 7 (1956), 81-93.
1956b   "Zum letzten mal: Greutungen," *Beiträge zur Namenforschung* 7 (1956), 241-246.
1962   *Geschichte der Hunnen* 1-4 (Berlin, 1959-62).
Altheim, F. and H. W. Haussig (*see* Haussig 1958)
Altheim, F. and R. Stiehl
1953   *Das erste Auftreten der Hunnen* (Baden-Baden, 1953).
1954   *Ein asiatischer Staat* (Wiesbaden, 1954).
Altschlesien; Mitteilungen des schlesischen Altertumsvereins und der Arbeitsgemeinschaft für oberschlesische Ur- und Frühgeschichte 9 (Breslau, 1940).
Amann, A.
1931   *Dictionnaire de théologie catholique* (1931).
Ambroz, A. K.
1966   *Fibuly iuga evropeĭskoĭ chasti SSSR* in *SAI* 1:30 (1966).
Amira, K. von and Cl. von Schwerin
1943   *Rechtsarchäologie* (Berlin, 1943).

Amiranashvili, Sh. Ia.
1950a "Dve serebrianye chashi iz raskopok v Armazi," *VDI* 31 (Moscow, 1950), 91-101.
1950b "Istoriia gruzinskogo iskusstva," *VDI* 1 (Moscow, 1950).
Analecta Bollandiana, suppl. to *AA SS*, Delehaye, H., ed. (Paris and Brussels, 1882-).
Anderson, J. K.
1961 *Ancient Greek Horsemanship* (Berkeley and Los Angeles, 1961).
Anderson, W. B., ed. and trans.
1965 *Sidonius, Poems and Letters* in *Loeb*; first print., 1936—title varies (Cambridge, Mass. and London, 1956-65).
Andrews, F. H.
1948 *Wall Paintings from Ancient Shrines in Central Asia* (London, 1948).
Anfimov, N. V.
1951 "Meoto-sarmatskiĭ mogil'nik u stanitsy Ust'-Labinskoĭ," *MIA* 23 (1951), 155-207.
1952 "Pozdnesarmatskoe pogrebenie iz Prikuban'ia," *Arkheologiia i istoriia Bospora* (Simferopol, 1952).
Annales Academiae Scientarium Fennicae (Helsinki).
Annibaldi, G. and J. Werner
1963 "Ostgotische Funde aus Acquasanta, Prov. Ascoli Piceno (Marche)," *Germania* 41:2 (Berlin, 1963), 356-373.
Annuaire de l'institut de philologie et d'histoire orientales et slaves (Brussels, 1932-).
Anthologica Palatina (Athologica Graeca Palatina), Dubner, Fr., ed. (1871-).
Anthropologie; časopis věnovaný fysickó anthropologii (Prague, 1923-).
Antichnye goroda severnogo Prichernomor'ia, Maksimova, M. I. (Moscow, 1955).
Antiquity (Gloucester, England).
Antonescu, I.
1961 "Săpăturile arheologice de la Gabăra," *Materiale* 7 (Bucharest, 1961), 449-459.
Anuchin, D. N.
1886 "O drevnikh iskusstvenno-deformirovannykh cherepakh, naĭden-nykh v predelakh Rossii," *Izvestiia obshchestva liubiteleĭ estest-voznaiia, antropologii i etnografii* 44:3 (Moscow, 1886), 367-414.
Appelgren-Kivalo, Hj., ed.
1931 *Alt-Altaische Kunstdenkmäler; Briefe und Bildmaterial von J. R. Aspelins Reisen in Sibirien und der Mongolei 1887-1889* (Helsingfors, 1931).
Arbman, H.
1937 *Schweden und das Karolingische Reich* (Stockholm, 1937).
Archaeologiai Értésitö (Budapest).
Archäologischer Anzeiger, supplement to *Archäologische Zeitung* (Berlin, 1889-).
Archäologische Funde in Ungarn, Thomas, B., ed. (Budapest, 1956).
Archiv für lateinische Lexicographie und Grammatik, Theilmann, Ph., ed. (Leipzig, 1884-1908).
Archiv für Religionswissenschaft (Freiburg, 1898-).
Archiv für slavische Philologie (Berlin, 1875-1928).
Archiv für Völkerkunde (Vienna, 1946-).

Archiv orientální (Prague, 1929-).

Arendt, W.

1932a "Ein alttürkischer Waffenfund aus Kertsch," *Zeitschr. f. hist. Waffen- u. Kostümkunde*, N.F. 4 (1932).

1932b "Beiträge zur Entstehung des Spangenharnisches," *Zeitschr. f. hist. Waffen- u. Kostümkunde*, N.F. 5 (1932).

Arkheologicheskie issledovaniia v RSFSR 1934-1936 gg. (Moscow and Leningrad, 1941).

Arkheologicheskie otkrytiia 1965 goda (Moscow, 1966).

Arkheologicheskie otkrytiia 1967 goda (Moscow, 1968).

Arkheologicheskiĭ sbornik gosudarstvennogo Ermitzha AN SSSR, Sibirskoe otdelenie (Leningrad, 1959-).

Arkheologiia (Ukrainskoĭ SSR), (Kiev, 1947-).

Arkheologiia i etnografiia Bashkirii (Ufa, 1962-).

Arkheologiia i etnografiia dal'nego vostoka (Novosibirsk, 1964).

Arkiv för nordisk filologei (Lund, 1883-).

Arnim, B. von

1933   *Turkotatarische Beiträge 2* in *Zeitschr. f. slav. Philologie* 10 (1933), 349-351.

1936   "Bermerkungen zum Hunnischen," *Zeitschr. f. slav. Philologie* 13 (1936), 100-109.

Ars Orientalis: the Arts of Islam and the East (Washington, 1954-).

L'Art mérovingien (Brussels, 1954).

Artamonov, M. I.

1962   *Istoriia Khazar* (Leningrad, 1962).

1969   *Treasures from Scythian Tombs*, Artamonov, M. I., ed. (London, 1969).

Artibus Asiae (Dresden, 1925/26-).

Arwidsson, G.

1954   *Die Gräberfunde von Valsgärde II* in *Valsgärde 8* (Stockholm and Copenhagen, 1954).

Arziutov, N. K.

1936   "Atkarskiĭ kurgannyĭ mogil'nik (raskopki 1928-1930 gg.)," *ISNIK* 7 (1936), 86-94.

Aspelin, J. R.

1877   *Antiquités du nord finno-ougrien* (Helsinki, 1877).

Attila (Attila és Hunjai), Németh, Gy., ed. (Budapest, 1940).

Auboyer, J.

1956   "L'arc et la flèche dans l'iconographie ancienne de l'Inde," *Artibus Asiae* 19:3-4 (1956), 173-185.

Avalichvili, Z.

1928   "Géographie et légende dans un écrit apocryphique de Saint Basile," *Revue de l'orient chrétien* (1927-28), 279-354.

Axelson, St.

1944   *Studia Claudianea* (Uppsala, 1944).

Azarpay, G.

1959   "Some Classical and Near Eastern Motifs in the Art of Pazyryk," *Artibus Asiae* 22:4 (1959), 314-315.

Babelon, E. B.

1901   *Traité des monnaies grecques et romaines* (Paris, 1901).

Babenchikov, B. P.
 1947 "Nekropol' Neapolia skifskogo," *Istoriia i arkheologiia drevnego Kryma* (Kiev, 1947), 94-141.

Bacon, E.
 1963 *Vanished Civilizations; Forgotten Peoples of the Ancient World* (London and New York, 1963).

Bacot, J.
 1940 *Documents de Touen-Houang relatifs à l'histoire du Tibet* (Paris, 1940).

Bader, O. N. and A. P. Smirnov
 1952 *Serebro zakamskoe pervykh vekov n.e.* (Moscow, 1952).

Baesecke, G.
 1940 *Vor- und Frühgeschichte des deutschen Schrifttums* (Halle, 1940).

Bailey, H. W.
 1939 "Turks in Khotanese Texts," *JRAS* (1939).
 1949 A Khotanese Text concerning the Turks in Kanṭṣou," *Asia Major*, N.S. 1 (1949), 28-52.
 1954 "L'Hārahūna," *Asiatica, Festschrift Friedrich Weller* (Leipzig, 1954), 13-21.
 1955 "Turkish Proper Names in Khotanese," *Togan Anniversary Volume* (1955), 200-203.
 1958 "Languages of the Saka," *Handbuch der Orientalistik* 1:4:1 (Leiden and Cologne, 1958), 130-154.
 1961 *Indo-Scythian Studies being Khotanese Texts* 4 (Cambridge, 1961).

Bang, W.
 1916 "Über die türkischen Namen einiger Grosskatzen," *Keleti Szemle* 17 (1916-17), 112-146.

Bang, W. and A. von Gabain
 1930 *Türkische Turfantexte* 1-4, *SB Berlin* (1929-30).

Banzarov, P.
 1891 *Chernia vera ili shamanstvo mongolov kirgiz* (St. Petersburg, 1891).

Bardy, G., ed. and trans.
 1952- *Histoire de l'église*, the *Historia ecclesiastica* of Eusebius, Bp. of Caesarea (Paris, 1952-).

Barkóczi, L.
 1959 "Transplantations of Samartians and Roxolans in the Danube Basin," *AA* 7 (Budapest, 1959), 443-453.

Barrière-Flavy, C.
 1893 *Étude sur les sépultures barbares du Midi et de l'ouest de la France* (Paris, 1893).
 1901 *Les arts industriels des peuples barbares de la Gaule* (Toulouse, 1901).

Bartoli, A.
 1948 "Il senato romano in onore di Ezio," *Rendiconti della Pontifica Accademia Romana di Archeologia* 22 (Rome, 1948), 267-273.

Bartucz, L. B.
 1936 "Die Gepidenschädel des Gräberfelds von Kiszombor," *Dolgozatok* 12 (Szeged, 1936), 204.
 1938 "A Szekszárdi húnkori sír csontvázának antropológiai vizsgálata, *Dissertationes Pannonicae*, ser. 2:10 (1938).

1939 "Die Geschichte der Rassen Ungarn und das Werden des heutigen hungarischen Volkskörpers," *UJb* 19 (1939), 281-303.

1940 "Geschichte der Rassen in Ungarn und das Werden des heutigen ungarischen Volkskörpers," in *Ungarische Rassenkunde*, Balogh, B. and L. Bartucz (Berlin, 1940), 281-320.

1961 "Anthropologische Beiträge zur I. und II. Periode der Sarmatenzeit in Ungarn," *AAH* 13:1-4 (1961), 157-229.

Baruzdin, Iu. D.

1956 "Kara-Bulakskiĭ mogil'nik (raskopki 1954 g.)," *Trudy Kirg.* 1 (Moscow, 1956), 57-69

1957 "Kara-Bulakskiĭ mogil'nik (raskopki 1955 g.)," *Trudy Kirg.* 3 (Moscow, 1957), 17-31.

1961 "Kara-Bulakskiĭ mogil'nik," *Izv. Kirg.* 3:3 (1961), 43-81.

Baruzdin, Iu. D. and G. A. Brykina

1962 *Arkheologicheskie pamiatniki Batkena Liaĭliaka*, AN Kirgizskoĭ SSR (Frunze, 1962).

Baskakov, N. A.

1951 *Karakalpakskiĭ iazyk* 1 (Moscow, 1951).

Battifol, L.

1919 *Étude de liturgie et d'archéologie chrétienne* (Paris, 1919).

Baur, C.

1930 *Der heilige Johannes Chrysostomus und seine Zeit* (Munich, 1930).

Bawden, C. R.

1958 "On the Practice of Scapulimancy among the Mongols," *CAJ* 4 (1958).

Baye, J. de

1892 *Mémoires de la Société des Antiquaires de la France* 51 (1892).

Baynes, N. H.

1955 In *Byzantine Studies and Other Essays*, first print., *JRS* 12, 1922 (London, 1955).

Baynes, N. H. and E. A. S. Dawes, ed. and trans.

1948 *Three Byzantine Saints* (Oxford, 1948).

Bazin, L.

1950 "Recherches sur les parlers T'o-pa," *TP* 39 (1950), 228-329.

Becatti, G.

1954 *Oreficeria antiche* (Rome, 1954).

Behmer, E.

1959 *Das zweischneidige Schwert der germanischen Völkerwanderungszeit* (Stockholm, 1939).

Behrens, G.

1924 *Aus der frühen Völkerwanderungszeit des Mittelrheingebietes* in *ZDMG* 17-19 (1921-24).

Beiträge zur Geschichte der deutschen Sprache und Literatur (Halle).

Belov, G. D.

1961 "Iz istorii ekonomicheskoĭ zhizni Khersonesa po II-IV vv. n.e.," *SA* 3 (1961), 322.

Beninger, E.

1929 "Germangräber von Laa an der Thaya (N.-Ö.)," *Eiszeit und Urgeschichte* 6 (1929), 143-155.

1931a "Der Wandalfund von Czéke-Cejkov, "*Annalen des Naturhisto-rischen Museums in Wien* 45 (1931), 217-219.

1931b "Der westgotisch-alanische Zug nach Mitteleuropa," Mannus-Bibliothek 51 (Leipzig, 1931).

1936 "Germanenfunde des 5. Jahrhunderts von Wien XXI—Leopoldau," *Mannus* 28 (Leipzig, 1936), 252-266.

1937 *Die germanischen Bodenfunde in der Slowakei* (Reichenburg, 1937).

1939 *Germanischer Grenzkampf in der Ostmark* (Vienna, 1939).

1944 "Die Kunstdenkmäler der Völkerwanderungszeit vom Wiener Bo-den," *Geschichte der bildenden Kunst in Wien I* (Vienna, 1944).

Berezovets, D. T. and V. P. Petrov
1960 "Lokhvitskiĭ mogil'nik," *MIA* 22 (1960), 84-99.

Berezovets, D. T., Pokrovs'ka, E. F. and A. I. Furmans'ka
1960 "Kurgany epokhy bronzy poblyzu s. Mar'ians'kogo," *APU* 9 (Kiev, 1960), 102-126.

Berg, L. S.
1950 *Natural Regions of the U.S.S.R.* (New York, 1950).

Bergmann, B. F.
1804 *Nomadische Streifzüge unter den Kalmüken* (Riga, 1804).

Bergman, F.
1939 *Archaeological Researches in Sinkiang* (Stockholm, 1939).

Berkhin, I.
1959 "Sarmatskoe pogrebenie u s. Salomatina," *Soobshcheniia Gos. Ermitazha* 15 (Leningrad, 1959), 37-41.

1961 "O trekh nakhodkax pozdnesarmatskogo vremeni v nizhnem Po-volzh'e, *Arkheol. sbornik* 2 (Leningrad, 1961), 141-153.

Bernshtam, A. N.
1935 "K voprosu o sotsial'nom stroe vostochnykh gunnov," *Problemy istorii dokapitalisticheskikh obshchestv* 5 (1935), 226-234.

1940 *Kenkol'skiĭ mogil'nik* (Leningrad, 1940).

1946 *Sotsial'no-ekonomicheskiĭ stroĭ orkhono-eniseĭskikh tiurok VI-VIII vekov* (Moscow and Leningrad, 1946).

1949 "Osnovnye etapy istorii kul'tury Semirech'ia i Tian'-shania," *SA* 11 (1949), 337-384.

1950 "Zolotaia diadema iz shamanskogo pogrebeniia na r. Kargalin-ka," *KS* 5 (1950).

1951a "Nakhodki u ozera Borovogo v Kazakhstane," *SMAE* 13 (1951), 216-229.

1951b *Ocherki po istorii gunnov* (Leningrad, 1951).

1952 "Istoriko-arkheologicheskie ocherki tsentral'nogo Tian'-shania i Pamiro-Alaia," *MIA* 26 (Moscow, 1952).

1953 "Ocherki po istorii gunnov," inquisition of 1951 article, *SA* 17 (1953), 320-326.

1954 *Po sledam drevnikh kul'tur* (Moscow, 1954).

1956 "Saki Pamira," *VDI* 1 (Moscow, 1956), 121-134.

Beshevliev, V.
1939 *Annuaire de l'Université de Sofia, Faculté Hist.-phil.* 35:1 (1939), 44-49.

1960 "Ein byzantinischer Brauch bei den Protobulgaren," *AA* 8:3-4

(Budapest, 1960), 17-21.
1963   *Die protobulgarischen Inschriften* (Berlin, 1963).
Besselaar, J. J. van den
1945   *Cassiodorus Senator en zijn Variae* (Utrecht, 1945).
Bichur, Gh.
1961   "Unele obserşţii cu privire la necropolele de tip Poieneşti din Moldova şi relaţiile acestor necropole cu lumea Sarmată," *SCIV* 12 (Bucharest, 1961), 253-289.
Bichurin, I. Ia.
1950   *Sobranie svedeniĭ o narodakh, obitavshikh v sredneĭ Azii v drevnie vremena* 1-2 (Moscow, 1950).
Bidez, J., ed.
1935   *Oratio* (Paris, 1935-).
1960   *Historia ecclesiastica* in *GCS* (Berlin, 1960).
Bidez, J. and L. Parmentier, ed.
1898   *Historia ecclesiastica* (Paris, 1898).
Bierbach, K.
1906   *Die letzten Jahre Attilas* (Berlin, 1906).

Bijdragen voor de Geschiedenis der Nederlanden (The Hague, 1946-).

Binyon, L.
1913   *Painting in the Far East* (London, 1913).
Birely, E.
1939   *Transactions of the Cumberland and Westmoreland Antiquarian and Archaeological Association* (1939).
Bishop, C. W.
1929   "Notes on the Tomb of Ho Ch'ü-ping," *Artibus Asiae* 1 (1928-29).
Blake, R. P. and H. de Vis, ed.
1934   *Epiphanius de Gemmis*, the Old Gregorian version and fragments of the Armenian version by R. P. Blake, and the Coptic-Sahidic fragments by H. de Vis (London, 1934).
Blavatskiĭ, V. D.
1951   "Razvedki v Anape," *KS* 37 (1951), 245-248.
1954   *Ocherki voennogo dela v antichnykh gosudarstvakh severnogo Prichernomor'ia* (Moscow, 1954).
1960   "Raskopki Pantikapeia v 1954-1958 gg.," *SA* 2 (1960), 168-192.
Blavatskiĭ, V. D. and D. B. Shelov
1955   "Razvedki na Kerchenskom poluostrove," *KS* 58 (1955).
Bleichsteiner, R.
1946   "Rossweihe und Pferderennen im Totenkult der kaukasischen Völker," *Wiener Beiträge zur Kulturgeschichte und Linguistik* 4 (Vienna, 1946), 419-455.
Blomgren, S.
1934   *Studia Fortunatiana* (Uppsala, 1934).
Bobrinskoĭ (Bobrinskiĭ), A. A.
1901   *Kurgany i sluchaĭnye arkheologicheskie nakhodki bliz" mes. Smely* 1-3 (St. Petersburg, 1887-1901).
Bönner Jahrbücher (Bonn, 1842-).

Bogdanova, I. A. and I. I. Gushchina
1967   "Novye mogil'niki II-III vv. n.e. u s. Skalistoe v Krymu," *KS*
        112 (1967), 132-139.
Boissevain, U. Ph., ed. (*see* de Boor, C. and U. Ph. Boissevain)
Bol'shaia Sovetskaia Entsiklopediia (Moscow).
Boodberg, P. A.
1936   "Two notes on the History of the Chinese Frontier," *HJAS* 1
        (Cambridge, Mass., 1936), 283-307.
1939   "Marginalia to the Histories of the Northern Dynasties," *HJAS* 4
        (Cambridge, Mass., 1939), 230-231.
1951   "Three Notes on the T'u-Chüeh Turks," *University of California
        Publications in Semitic Philology* 11 (1951).
Borovka, G. I.
1927   *Severnaia Mongolia* 2 (Leningrad, 1927).
1928   *Scythian Art* (London, 1928).
Brackman, C., Jr.
1909   *Ammianea et Anneana* (Leiden, 1909).
Brady, C.
1949   *The Legend of Ermanaric* (Berkeley, 1949).
Braĭchev'skaia, A. T.
1959   "Pyvdenna mezha cherniakhov'skoĭ kul'turi na Dnypru," *Arkheo-
        logiia* 11 (Kiev, 1959), 3-13.
1960   "Cherniakhovskie pamiatniki Nadporozh'ia," *MIA* 82 (1960).
Braĭchevskiĭ, M. Iu.
1956   "O nekotorykh spornykh voprosakh rannei istorii vostochnykh
        slavian," *KSIA* (1956), 6.
1957   "K istorii lesostepnoĭ polosy vostochnoĭ Evropy v I tysiacheletii
        n.e.," *SA* 1 (1957), 114-129.
1960   "Romashki," *MIA* 82 (1960), 100-147.
Braun, F. A.
1899   *Razyskaniia v oblasti goto-slavianskikh otnosheniĭ* (St. Petersburg,
        1899).
Brede, K. A.
1960   "Rozkopky Gavrylivs'kogo gorodyshcha rubezhu nashoĭ ery,"
        APU 9 (Kiev, 1960), 191-203.
Brenner, E.
1912   *Der Stand der Forschung über die Kultur der Merowingerzeit* in
        Berichte der Röm.-germ. Kommission 7 (Berlin, 1912).
Bretz, A.
1914   "Studien und Texte zu Asterios von Amasea," *TU* 40 (Leipzig,
        1914).
Brockelman, C., ed.
1928   *Mitteltürkischer Wortschatz nach Maḥmud Al-Kāšyarīs Dīvān Lu-
        γāt At-Turk* (Budapest and Leipzig, 1928).
Brooks, E.
1893   "The Emperor Zenon and the Isaurians," *The English Historical
        Review* 30 (London, 1893), 209-238.
Brown, Fr. E.
1936   *The Excavations at Dura-Europos; Report of the Sixth Season*
        (New Haven, 1936).

1937   "A Recently Discovered Composite Bow," *Seminarium Konda-kovianum* 9 (Prague, 1937), 1-10.

Bruns, G.
1935   *Der Obelisk und seine Basis auf dem Hippodrom zu Konstantinopel* (Istanbul, 1935).

Brusin, B.
1947   *Aquileia e Grado* (Udine, 1947).
1948   *La Basilica del Fondo Tullio alla Beligna de Aquileia* (Aquileia, 1948).
1959   *Limes-Studien* (Basel, 1959).

Budapest régiségei; régészeti es törteneti evkönyv (Budapest, 1889-).

Buddhaprakesh, D.
1957   "Kāl-idāsa and the Hūṇas," *Journal of Indian History* 35:1 (1957), 91-135.

Bugge, S.
1910   *Der Runenstein von Rök in Ostergötland, Schweden* (Stockholm, 1910).

Bugiani, C.
1905   *Storia di Ezio, generale dell'Impero sotto Valentiano III* (Florence, 1905).

Bŭlgarska akademiia na naukite, Izvestiia na arkheologicheski institut (Sofia).

Bulletin of the Museum of Far Eastern Antiquities (Stockholm).

Bulletin of the School of Oriental and African Studies (London).

Bulling, A.
1960   *The Decoration of Mirrors in the Han Period* (Ascona, 1960).

Bumie (Bun'ei), Ts.
1954   *Kodai hoppō bunka no kenkyū* (Kyoto, 1954).

Bunbury, E. H.
1883   *A History of Ancient Geography* (London, 1883).

Burkitt, F. C., ed.
1913   *Euphemia and the Goth, with the Acts of Martyrdom of the Confessors of Edessa* (Syriac), (London, 1903).

Burn, A. E.
1915   *Niceta of Remesiana* (Cambridge, 1915).

Bury, J. B.
1923   *History of the Later Roman Empire* (London, 1923).

Bussagli, M.
1950   "Osservazioni sul problema degli Unni," *Academia nazionale dei Lincei, Rendiconti*, third series, 5:3-4 (1950), 212-232.
1959   *Profili dell'India antica i moderna* (Turin, 1959).
1963   *Painting of Central Asia* (Geneva, 1963).

Byzantinisch-neugriechische Jahrbücher (Berlin, 1920-).

Byzantinische Zeitschrift (Munich and Leipzig).

Byzantinoslavica (Prague, 1929-).

Byzantinoturcica (see Moravcsik 1958).

Byzantion (Paris, 1924-).

Cahiers archéologiques; fin de l'antiquité et moyen âge, Grabar, A., ed. (Paris, 1945-59).

Calderini, A.
1930 "Aquileia Romana," *Pubblicazioni della Università Cattolica del Santo Cuore* 10, fifth series (1930).
The *Cambridge Ancient History* (Cambridge, 1961-).
The *Cambridge Medieval History*, Bury, J. P. and H. M. Gwatkin, ed. (Cambridge).
Canard, M., (*see* Ibn Fadlan 1958).
Cantacuzène, G.
1928 "Un papyrus relatif à la défense du Bas-Danube," *Aegyptus* 9 (Milan, 1928).
Capelle, W.
1940 *Die Germanen der Völkerwanderung* (Stuttgart, 1940).
Capitani d'Arzagno, A. de
1952 *La "Chiesa Maggiore" di Milano, Sancta Tecla* (Milan, 1952).
Carpini, Giovanni de Piano (*see* Bibliography II)
Carroll, T. D.
1953 *Account of the T'u-yü-hun in the History of the Chin Dynasty* in *Chinese Dynastic Histories Translations* 4 (Berkeley, 1953).
Caspar, E.
1933 *Geschichte des Papsttums* 1-2 (Tübingen, 1930-33).
Caucasica; *Zeitschrift für die Erforschung der Sprachen und Kulturen des Kaukasusvölker* (Leipzig, 1924-).
Cavallera, F.
1922 *Saint Jérôme, sa vie et son œuvre* (Louvain and Paris, 1922).
Červinka, I. L.
1936 "Germáni na Moravě," *Anthropologie* 14 (1936).
Cessi, R.
1913 *Anonymi Valesiani pars posterior* in *Rerum Italiarum Scriptores* 24:4, Cessi, R., ed. (Città di Castello, 1913).
1957 *Storia di Venezia* (Venice, 1957).
Chabot, J. B., trans.
1904 *Chronique de Michel le Syrien* (Paris, 1904).
Chadwick, N. K.
1955 *Poetry and Letters in Early Christian Gaul* (London, 1955).
Chambers, R. W., trans.
1912 *Widsith* (Cambridge, 1912).
Chang, Hung-shao
1921 *Shih ya* (Peking, 1921).
Ch'ang sha
1957 *Ch'ang sha fa chüeh pao kao* (Peking, 1957).
Chantre, E.
1887 *Recherches anthropologiques dans le Caucase* (Paris and Lyon, 1887).
Chapouthier, F.
1935 *Les Dioscures au service d'une déesse* (Paris, 1935).
Chard, C. C. and W. B. Workman
1965 "Soviet Archaeological Radio Carbon Date II," *Arctic Anthropology* 3:1 (1965).
Charles, R. H., trans.
1916 *The Chronicle of John, Bishop of Nikiu* (London, 1916).

Chavannes, E., ed.
1903   *Documents sur les Tou-kiue (Turcs) occidentaux* (St. Petersburg, 1903).
1906   In *T'oung Pao* (Leiden, 1906).
Chavannes, E., and P. Pelliot
1913   *Un traité manichéen retrouvé en Chine* (Paris, 1913).
Chêng Tê-k'un
1960   *Shang China* in *Archaeology of China* 2 (Cambridge, 1960).
1963   *Chou China* in *Archaeology of China* 3 (Cambridge, 1963).
Chernenko, E. V.
1964   "Shkiriani pantsyri skifs'kogo chasu," *Arkheologiia* 27 (1964), 144-152.
Chernetsov, V. N.
1953   "Bronza Ust'-Poluĭskago vremeni," *MIA* 35 (1953), 120-178.
1957   "Nizhnee Priob'e v I tysiacheletii nasheĭ ery," *MIA* 58 (1957), 136-245.
Chernikov, S. S.
1951a   "Otchet o rabotakh vostochno-kazakhstanskoĭ ekspeditsii 1948 g.," *Izv. Kazakh., seriia antropologii* 3 (Alma Ata, 1951), 64-80.
1951b   "Vostochno-kazakhstanskaia ekspeditsiia," *KS* 37 (1951), 144-150.
1965   *Zagadka zolotogo kurgana* (Moscow, 1965).
Chlenova, N. L.
1962   "Skifskiĭ olen'," *MIA* 115 (1962).
Christ, F.
1938   *Die römische Weltherrschaft in der antiken Dichtung* (Stuttgart, 1938).
Christensen, A.
1944   *L'Iran sous les Sassanids* (Copenhagen, 1944).
Chronicon Edessenum, Hallier, L., ed. (Leipzig, 1892).
Chronica Minora, *MGH AA* 9, 11, 13, Mommsen, Th. ed. (Berlin, 1892-98).
Cipolla, C.
1892   *Considerazioni sulle "Getica" di Jordanes* (Torino, 1892).
Classical Quaterly (London, 1907-).
Clauson, G.
1962   *Turkish and Mongolian Studies* (London, 1962).
1964   "A Postscript to Professor Sinor's Observations on a New Comparative Altaic Philology;" *BSOAS* 27:1 (London, 1964), 154-156.
Clemen, C.
1926   *Einige religionsgeschichtlich wichtige skythische Denkmäler, Festschrift Paul Clemen* (Bonn, 1926), 64-71.
Clemmensen, M.
1937   *Bulhuse* (Copenhagen, 1937).
Closs, C. A., ed.
1866   *De origine Actibusque Getarum (Jordanis De Getarum sive Gothorum origine et rebus gestis)*, (Stuttgart, 1866).
Codex Theodosianus (see Mommsen and Meyer 1954).
Collectanea Friburgensia, N.S. (Fribourg, 1893-1962).
Collectio Avellana, Günther, O., ed., in *CSEL* (Vienna and Leipzig, 1895-98).
Colledge, M. A. R.
1967   *The Parthians* (London, 1967).

Collinder, B.
1962   *Introduktion till de uraliska språkener* (Stockholm, 1962).
Comnena, Princess Anna (*see* Dawes 1928; Leib 1945).
Constitutiones Sirmondianae (*Leges*), (*see* Mommsen and Meyer 1954).
Cook, G. M., ed.
1942   *The Life of Epiphanius* (Washington, D. C., 1942).
Coon, C. S.
1930   *The Races of Europe* (New York, 1930).
Corpus Christianorum, Seria Latina (Turnhout, 1958-59).
Corpus Inscriptionum Regni Bosporani (*Korpus bosporskikh nadpiseĭ*), (Moscow and Leningrad, 1965).
Corpus Scriptorum Ecclesiasticorum Latinorum (Vienna and Leipzig, 1866-).
Corpus Scriptorum Historiae Byzantinae, Niebuhr, B. G., ed. (Bonn, 1829-).
Courcelle, P.
1948   *Histoire littéraire des grandes invasions germaniques* (Paris, 1948).
1953   "Sur quelques textes littéraires relatifs aux grandes invasions," *Revue belge de philologie et d'histoire* 31 (Brussels, 1953).
Courtois, C.
1955   *Les Vandales et l'Afrique* (Paris, 1955).
Coville, A.
1930   *Recherches sur l'histoire de Lyon de Ve siècle au IXe siècle* (Paris, 1930).
Crafer, T. W., trans.
1919   *Apocritus* (*Macarius Magnes*), (London and New York, 1919).
Critescu, M.
1964   "Studiul antropological scheletelor din secolul al III-lea e. n. descoperite la Pugorăşti," *Arheologia Moldovei* 2-3 (Bucharest, 1964), 329-339.
Crivelluci, A., ed.
1914   *Historia Romana* (*Paulus Diaconus*), (Rome, 1914).
Csallány, D.
1958   "Hamvasztásos és csontvázas hun temetkezések a Felsö-Tisza vidékén," *Annales Musei Miskolciensis de Herman Otto Nominati* 2 (1958), 83-97.
1961   *Archäologische Denkmäler der Gepiden im Mitteldonaubecken* in *AAH* 38 (Budapest, 1961).
Cuntz, O. ed.
1929   *Itineraria Romana* (Teubner, 1929). I: *Itineraria Antonini Augusti et Burdigalense*. II: *Ravennatis Anonymi Cosmographia et Guidonis Geographica*.
Curle, A. D.
1923   *The Treasure of Traprain* (Glasgow, 1923).
Czeglédy, K.
1966   "Das sakrale Königtum bei den Steppenvölkern," *Numen* 13 (1966), 14-26.
Dacia; revue d'archéologie et d'histoire ancienne (1929-).
Daffinà, P.
1967   *L'immigrazione dei Sakā nella Drangiana* (Rome, 1967).

Daicoviciu, C. and I. Nestor
1960   "Die menschliche Gesellschaft an der unteren Donau in vor- und nachrömischer Zeit," *XIe Congrès international de sciences historiques, Rapports 2, Antiquité* (Göteborg, Stockholm and Uppsala, 1960), 117-142.

Daicoviciu Anniversary Volume (Omagiu lui Constantin Daicoviciu), (Bucharest, 1960).

Dain, A., ed.
1938   *Sylloge Tacticorum* (Paris, 1938).

Dalton, O. M.
1915   *The Letters of Sidonius* (Oxford, 1915).
1964   *The Treasure of the Oxus* (London, 1964).

Darkó, E.
1935   "Influences touraniennes sur l'évolution de l'art militaire des grecs, des romains et des byzantins," *Byzantion* 10 (Paris, 1935), 443-469.

Dashevskaia, O. D.
1961   "Dva sbornika po istorii i arkheologii Kryma," *SA* 2 (1961), 282-288.

Davidovich, E. A. and B. A. Litvinskiĭ
1955   "Arkheologicheskiĭ ocherk Isfarinskogo raĭona," *Trudy Tadzh.* 35 (1955).

Davydova, A. V.
1956   "Ivolginskoe gorodishche," *SA* 25 (1956), 261-300.

Dawes, E. A. S., trans.
1928   *The Alexiad of Princess Anna Comnena* (London, 1928).

Dawson, C. H.
1957   *The Mongol Mission* (London, 1957).

Debets, G. F.
1936   "Materialy po paleoantropologii SSSR (N. Povolzh'e)," *Antropologicheskiĭ zhurnal* 1 (1936), 65-80.
1962   "On the Origin of the Kirgiz People in the Light of Anthropological Findings," *Studies in Siberian Ethnogenesis* (Toronto, 1962).

De Boor, C., ed.
1883   *Chronographia (Theophanes)* I-II (Leipzig, 1883).
1887   *Theophylactus Simocatta* (Leipzig, 1887).

De Boor, C. and U. Ph. Boissevain, ed.
1910   *Excerpta historica iussu Imperii Constantini Porphyrogeniti confecta* (Berlin, 1903-1910). Includes *Excerpta de legationibus* (Berlin, 1903-1906); *Excerpta de sententiis* (Berlin, 1906); *Excerpta de insidiis*, de Boor, C., ed. (Berlin, 1905). All Priscus sections are to be found in *EL*, de Boor, C., ed. (Berlin, 1903).

De Boor, H.
1932   *Das Attilabild in Geschichte, Legende und heroischer Dichtung* (Bern, 1932).

Degani, M.
1959   *Il tesoro romano barbarico di Reggio Emilia* (Florence, 1959).

Degrassi, A.
1949   "L'iscrizione in onore di Aezio e l'Atrium Libertatis," *Bolletino della commisione archeologica communale di Roma* 72 (1949), 33-44.

Delbrück, R.
1929   Die Consulardiptychen und verwandte Denkmäler (Berlin, 1929).
Delehaye, H.
1896   "Une épigramme de l'anthologie grecque," Revue des études grecques 9 (1896), 219-221.
1902   Synaxarium ecclesiae Constantinopolitanae, Delehaye, H., ed. (Brussels, 1902).
1933   Les origines du culte des martyrs (Brussels, 1933).
1940   Analecta Bollandiana, Delehaye, H., ed. (Paris, 1920-40).
De Lepper, J. L. M.
1941   De rebus gestis Bonifati, comitis Africae et magistri militum (Tilburg, 1941).
De Letter, P., trans.
1952   The Call of All Nations (Westminster, 1952).
Demiéville, P.
1952   Le concile de Ghasa (Paris, 1952).
Demougeot, E.
1947   "Les partages de l'Illyricum à la fin du ive siècle," Revue historique 198 (1947), 16-31.
1951   De l'unité à la division de l'Empire romain, 395-410 (Paris, 1951).
1952   "Saint Jérôme, les oracles sibyllins et Stilicho," RÉA 54 (1952), 38-92.
1958   "Attila et les Gaules," Mémoires de la société d'agriculture du département de la Maine (Paris, 1958).
De Rossi, J. B., ed.
1888   Inscriptiones christianae urbis Romae septima saecula antiquiores 1-2 (Rome, 1861-1888).
Dessau, H.
1916   Inscriptiones Latinae Selectae 1-3 (Berlin, 1882-1916).
1926   Geschichte der römischen Kaiserzeit (Berlin, 1924-26).
D'Eszlary, Th.
1962   "Les invasions hongroises en France à l'époque carolingienne," Schweizerische Zeitschrift für Geschichte 12:1 (1962), 63-78.
Detschev, D.
1927   "Der germanische Ursprung des bulgarischen Volksnamens," Zeitschr. f. Ortsnamenforschung 2 (1927), 199-216.
1952   Festschrift für Rudolf Egger 1 (Klagefurt, 1952).
Deutsche Altertumskunde, Müllenhoff, K. V., ed. (Berlin, 1870-1900).
Deutsches Archiv für Erforschung des Mittelalters (Marburg, 1937-).
Dewall, M. von
1964   Pferd und Wagen im frühen China (Bonn, 1964).
Diaconu, Gh.
1961   "Probleme ale culturii Sîntanacerneahov pe teritoriul R. P. R. în lumina cercetărilor din necropola de la Tîrgşor," with Russian and French summaries. SCIV 12:2 (1961), 273-288. Russian translation in Dacia, N.S. 5 (1961), 415-428.
D'iakonov, I. M. and A. Iu. Iakubovskiĭ, ed.
1954   Zhivopis' drevnego Piandzhikenta (Moscow, 1954).
D'iakonov, I. M. and V. A. Lifshits
1960   Dokumenty iz Nisy (Moscow, 1960).

Diculescu, C.
1922   Die Gepiden 1 (Leipzig, 1922).
1923   Die Wandalen und Goten in Ungarn und Rumänien (Leipzig, 1923).
Diekamp, Fr.
1938   Analecta Patristica (Orientalia Christiana Analecta) 117 (Rome, 1938).
Diénes, I.
1958   "A honfoglaló Magyarok fakengyele," Folia archaeologica 10 (Budapest, 1958), 125-142.
Diller, A.
1932   The Tradition of the Minor Greek Geographers (Lancaster, 1932).
Dindorf, K. W., ed.
1932   Themistii orationes (Leipzig, 1932).
Dindorf, L. A., ed.
1831   Chronographia (Malalas) in CS Hist. Byz. (Bonn, 1831).
1859   Cyropaedia (Xenophon), (1859).
1875   Epitome historiarum (Zonaras), (1868-75).
1877   Historici graeci minores (1870-77).
Dingwall, E. J.
1931   Artificial Cranial Deformation (London, 1931).
Doblhofer, E.
1955   Byzantinische Diplomaten und östlichen Barbaren (Graz, Vienna and Cologne, 1955).
Dobrovol'skiĭ, A. V.
1960   "Rozkopky dilianok A i G na mogyl'nyka zolotobalkivs'kogo poselennia na rubezhu nashoĭ eri v 1951 i 1952 rokakh," APU 9 (1960), 141-165.
Dobschütz, E.
1911   Die Akten der Edessenischen Bekenner Gurjas, Samonas und Abidos in TU 37:2 (Greek), (Leipzig, 1911), 150-199.
Dölger, F.
1932   Aus Antike und Christentum 3 (1932).
Doerfer, G.
1963   Türkische und mongolische Elemente im Neupersischen (Wiesbaden, 1963).
Dolgikh, B.
1934   Kety (Moscow, 1934).
Dorzhsuren, Ts.
1962   "Raskopki mogil khunnu v gorakh Noin-ula na r. Khuni-gol (1954-1957 gg.)," Mongol'skiĭ arkheologicheskiĭ sbornik (Moscow, 1962), 36-44.
Dremov, B. A.
1967   "Drevnee naselenie lesostepnogo Priob'ia v epokhu bronzy i zheleza po dannym paleoantropologii," SE 6 (1967), 53-66.
Driver, G. R. and L. Hodgson, trans.
1925   The Bazaar of Heracleides (Oxford, 1925).
Du Buisson, R. du Mesnil
1939   Les peintures de la synagogue de Doura-Europos 245-256 après J. C. (Paris, 1939).

Duchesne, L.
1924   *Early History of the Church* (New York, 1924).
Dudden, H.
1925   *Saint Ambrose* (Oxford, 1925).
Dümmler, E.
1888   *Geschichte des ostfränkischen Reiches* (Leipzig, 1888).
Duĭchev, I. (Dujčev, J.)
1938   "Protobulgares et Slaves," *Seminarium Kondakovianum* 10 (1938), 145-154.
1950   "Slaviano-bolgarskie drevnosti IX-go veka," *Byzantinoslavica* 11 (1950), 6-31.
1953   "Imia Asparuka v novootkrytykh nadpisiakh Gruzii," *Archiv orientální* 21 (Prague, 1953), 353-356.
Dumbarton Oaks Papers (Cambridge, Mass., 1941-).
Dumézil, G.
1948   *Jupiter Mars Quirinus* (Paris, 1948).
Dunlop, D. M.
1954   *The History of the Jewish Khazars* (Princeton, 1954).
Ebengreuth, A. L. von
1910   "Der Denar der Lex Salica," *SB Wien* 163 (1910).
Eberhard, W.
1949   *Das Toba-Reich Nordchinas* (Leiden, 1949).
Ebert, M.
1909a   "Die frühmittelalterlichen Helme vom Baldenheimer Typus," *Prähist. Zeitschr.* 1 (1909), 65-77.
1909b   "Ein Spangelhelm aus Aegypten," *Prähist. Zeitschr.* 1 (1909), 163-170.
1912   "Ein skythischer Kessel aus Südrussland," *Prähist. Zeitschr.* 44 (1912), 451-454.
1921   *Südrussland im Altertum* (Bonn, 1921).
Eckinger, K.
1933   "Bogenversteifungen aus römischen Gräbern," *Germania* 17 (1933), 289-290.
Edgerton, F.
1933   *Buddhist Hybrid Sanskrit Dictionary* (New Haven, 1933).
Edwards, C. B. and E. G. Heath
1962   *In Pursuit of Archery* (London, 1962).
Egami, Namio
1948   *Yurashia kodai hoppō bunka* (Tokyo, 1948).
1951   *Yurashia hoppō bunka no kenkyū* (Tokyo, 1951).
Egger, R.
1926   In *Röm. Limes in Österreich* 16 (1926), 106-112.
1929   "Civitas Noricum," *Wiener Studien* 47 (1929), 146-154.
1942   "Die Ostalpen in der Spätantike," *Das neue Bild der Antike* 2 (Leipzig, 1942), 394-411.
1948   *Der heilige Hermagoras* (Klagenfurt, 1948).
1955   "Von den letzten Romanen Vindobonas," *Anz. Wien* (1955), 76-81.
1962   *Römische Antike und frühes Christentum* (Klagenfurt, 1962).

Eisenberger, E. J.
1938   "Das Wahrsagen aus dem Schulterblatt," *Internationales Archiv für Ethnographie* 35 (1938), 49-116.
Eisner, J.
1933   *Slovensko v pravěku* (Bratislava, 1933).
1946   "Deux casques à côtes du type de Baldenheim, découverts à Dolnie Semerovce (Vallée de l'Ipel', Slovaquie)," *Historica Slovaca* 3-4 (1945-46), 30-43.
Elmer, R. P.
1926   *Archery* (Philadelphia, 1926).
1946   *Target Archery* (New York, 1946).
Emeneau, M. B.
1953   "The Composite Bow in India," *Proceedings of the American Philosophical Society* 97:1 (1953), 77-87.
Encyclopedia of Islam, new edition (Leiden, London and Leipzig, 1960-).
Engel, C.
1942   *Die ostgermanischen Stämme in Ostdeutschland, die gotische Ostseeherrschaft und das Gotenreich in Osteuropa, Deutschland und die osteuropäischen Quellen und Forschungen zur Geschichte ihrer Beziehungen* 20 (Leipzig, 1942).
Engels, Fr.
1959   *The Origin of the Family, Private Property and the State* (Moscow, 1959).
Ensslin, W.
1923   "Zur Geschichtschreibung und Weltanschauung des Ammianus Marcellinus," *Klio* 16 (Leipzig, 1923).
1927   "Maximinius und sein Begleiter, der Historiker Priskos," *BNJb* 5 (1926-27), 1-9.
1947   *Theoderich der Grosse* (Munich, 1947).
1948   "Des Symmachus Historia Romana als Geschichtsquelle für Jordanes," *SB München* 3 (1948; also 1949).
Epigraficheskie nakhodki (*Novye epigraficheskie nakhodki v Kirgizii* (*1961 g.*), (Frunze, 1962).
Epigrafika Kirgizii 1 (Frunze, 1963).
Erdély, I.
1962   "Raskopki v Noin-Ule," *AAH* 14:3-4 (1962), 231-247.
Erdély, I., Dorjsüren, C. and D. Navan
1967   "Results of the Mongolian-Hungarian Archaeological Expeditions 1961-1964," *AAH* 19:3-4 (1967), 335-370.
Ethnographia; a Magyar néprajzi társaság értesítöje (Budapest, 1890-).
Eurasia Septentrionalis Antiqua (Helsinki, 1926).
Evelein, M. A.
1911   "Ein römischer Helm des Leidener Museums," *Prähist. Zeitschr.* 3 (1911), 144-156.
Evtiukhova, L. A.
1948   *Arkheologicheskie pamiatniki eniseĭskikh kyrgyzov* (Abakan, 1948).
Fargues, P.
1933   *Claudian* (*Paneg. de quarto Cons. Hon.*), (Paris, 1933).
Fasoli, G.
1945   *Le incursioni Ungare in Europa nel secolo X* (Florence, 1945).

Fedorov, G. B.
1954 "Itogi trekhletnikh rabot v Moldavii v oblasti slaviano-russkoĭ arkheologii," *KS* 56 (1954), 8-23.
1960a "Malaeshtskiĭ mogil'nik," *MIA* 82 (1960), 253-302.
1960b "Naselenie Prutsko-Dnestrovskogo mezhdurech'ia," *MIA* 89 (1960).
1960c "Rimskie i rannevizantiĭskie monety na territorii Moldavskoĭ SSR," *Omagiu lui Constantin Daicoviciu* (Bucharest, 1960), 179-191.

Fedorov, Ia. A.
1960 "Nekotorye voprosy etnogeneza narodov Dagestana v svete dannykh arkheologii," *SA* 3 (1960), 17-28.

Ferguson, J. C.
1929 "The Tomb of Ho Ch'ü-ping," *Artibus Asiae* (1928-29).

Fersman, A. E.
1922 *Dragotsennye i tsvetnye kamni Rossii* (Petrograd, 1922).

Fettich, N.
1930 "Der Schildbuckel von Herpály," *AAH* 1 (1930).
1931 "Bestand der skytischen Altertümer Ungarns" in Rostovtsev 1931 (Berlin, 1931), 454-527.
1940 "A hunok régészeti emlékei" in *Attila és Hunjai* (1940), 227-264.
1941 "Antikes Gut in der Hinterlassenschaft der alten südrussichen Steppenvölker," *Folia archaeologica* (Budapest, 1941).
1953 "La trouvaille de tombe princière hunnique à Szeged-Nagyszéksós, *AAH* 32 (Budapest, 1953).

Fiebiger, O.
1939 "Inschriftensammlung zur Geschichte der Ostgermanen," *Denkschriften Wien* 70:3 (Vienna, 1939).

Fiebiger, O. and L. Schmidt
1939 "Inschriftensammlung zur Geschichte der Ostgermanen," *Denkschriften Wien* 60:3 (Vienna, 1939).

Fischer, J.
1932 *Claudii Ptolemaei Geographiae, Codex urbinas graecus* (*Tomus Prodromus*) 82 (Leiden and Leipzig, 1932).

Fischer, J. E.
1803 *Recherches historiques sur les principales nations établies en Sibérie* (Paris, 1803).

Fitzgerald, A., trans.
1930 *The Essays and Hymns of Synesius of Cyrene* (Oxford, 1930).

Flinders-Petrie, W. M., Sir
1917 *Tools and Weapons* (London, 1917).

Florescu, A. K.
1960 "Diadema iz zolotoĭ plastinki epokhi pereseleniia narodov, naĭdennaia v Bukheni," *Dacia*, N.S. 4 (1960), 561-567.

Focke, F.
1941 *Ritte und Reigen* (Stuttgart and Berlin, 1941).

Folia archaeologica in *AAH* (Budapest, 1939-).

Forcella, V. and E. Selotti
1897 *Iscrizioni cristiane in Milano anteriori al IX secolo* (Codogno, 1897).

Forrer, R.
1935   L'Alsace romaine (Paris, 1935).
Foulke, W., trans.
1906   History of the Langobards by Paul the Deacon (New York, 1906).
Fragmenta Historicorum Graecorum 4, Müller, C., ed. (Paris, 1885).
Frankle, E.
1948   Word Formation in the Turkish Languages (New York, 1948).
Frazer, J. G.
1898   Description of Greece (Pausanius), Frazer, J. G., trans. (London, 1898).
1915   The Golden Bough (London, 1911-1915).
Freeman, E. A.
1964   Western Europe in the Fifth Century (London, 1964).
Freiman, A. A.
1951   "Khorezmiĭskiĭ iazyk," Zapiski inst. vostokoved. (Moscow, 1951).
Friedrich, J.
1954   Die Entzifferung verschollener Schriften und Sprachen (Berlin, 1954).
Friesen, O. von
1912   Rökstenen (Stockholm, 1912).
Frye, R. N.
1952   Archaeologia orientalis in memoriam Ernst Herzfeld (New York, 1952).
1962   The Heritage of Persia (London, 1962).
Fuchs, S.
1944   Die Kunst der Ostgotenzeit (Berlin, 1944).
Fundamenta (Philologiae Turcicae Fundamenta I), Deny, J., ed., (Wiesbaden, 1959). Other volumes of this series have appeared since author's death.
Furmans'ka (Furmanskaia), A. I.
1953   "Fibuli z rozkopok Ol'biĭ," Arkheologiia 8 (Kiev, 1953), 76-94.
1960a   "Doslidzhennia na diliantsi V Zolotobalkivs'kogo poselennia v 1952 rotsi," APU 9 (Kiev, 1960), 180-190.
1960b   "Kurhan bilia s. Dolyny," APU 8 (Kiev, 1960).
Gabain, A. von
1950a   Alttürkische Grammatik, second ed., (Leipzig, 1950).
1950b   Über Ortsbezeichnungen im Alttürkischen (Helsinki, 1950).
1955   Zeki Velidi Togan'a Armağan (Istanbul, 1950-55).
Gaĭdukevich, V. F.
1940   "Pamiatniki rannego srednevekov'ia v Tiritake," SA 69 (1940), 190-204.
1947   "Nekotorye itogi raskopok Tiritaki i Mirmekiia," VDI 3 (1947), 187-204.
1949   Bosporskoe tsarstvo (Moscow and Leningrad, 1949).
1955   "Istoriia antichnykh gorodov severnogo Prichernomor'ia," Antichnye Goroda (1955), 23-147.
1958   "Raskopki Tiritaki i Mirmekiia v 1946-1952 gg.," MIA 85 (1958), 149-218.
1959   "Nekropoli nekotorykh vosporskikh gorodov," MIA 69 (1959), 154-238.

Gallay, R.
1943   *La vie de Saint Grégoire de Nazianze* (Paris, 1943).
Galletier, E., ed. and trans.
1949   *Oratores panegyrici* 1 (Paris, 1949).
1955   *Panégyriques latins* 3 (Paris, 1955).
Gamburg, B. Z. and N. G. Gorbunova
1956   "Mogil'nik epokhi bronzy v Ferganskoĭ doline," *KS* 63 (1956), 85-93.
1957a   "Ak-tamskiĭ mogil'nik," *KS* 69 (1957), 78-90.
1957b   "Mogil'nik Khangiz," *Izv. Tadzh.* 14 (1957), 33-44.
1959   "Arkheologicheskie raboty Ferganskogo oblastnogo kraevedcheskogo muzeia v 1953-1954 gg.," *IMKU* 1 (Tashkent, 1959).
Gamillscheg, E.
1936   *Romania Germanica* 1-3 (Berlin, 1934-36).
Gardthausen, V.
1869   *Collectanea Ammianea* (Kiel, 1869).
Garscha, F.
1936   In *Germania* 20 (Berlin, 1936), 191 ff.
1960   "Zum Grabfund von Altlussheim," *Jahrbuch des römisch-germanischen Zentralmuseums* 7 (Mainz, 1960), 315-318.
Garutt, V. E. and K. B. Iur'ev
1959   "Paleofauna Ivolginskogo gorodishcha po dannym arkheologicheskikh raskopok 1949-1956 gg.," *Arkheol. sbornik* 1 (Leningrad, 1959).
Gening, V. F.
1955   "Pamiatki kharinskogo vremeny v Prikam'e," *KS* 57 (1955), 115-123.
Gening, V. F. and A. Kh. Khalikov
1964   *Rannie bolgary na Volge*; *Bol'she-Tarkhanskiĭ mogil'nik* (Moscow, 1964).
Geographi graeci minores, Müller, C., ed. (Paris, 1882).
Geographical Journal (London).
Gerasimov, M. M.
1949   *Osnovy vosstanovleniia litsa po cherepu* (Moscow, 1949).
Gerke, F.
1952   "Die Wandmalereien in der neugefunden Grabkammer in Pécs (Fünfkirchen)" *Forschungen zur Kunstgeschichte und christlichen Archäologie* 1:1 (1952), 115-122.
Germanen-Erbe; *Monatschrift für deutsche Vorgeschichte* (Leipzig, 1936-).
Germania (*Anzeiger der röm.-germ. Kommission des deutschen archäologischen Instituts* (Berlin, 1917).
Germanoslavica (Brünn, 1931/32-).
Geschichte 1-4 (*see* (Altheim 1962).
Geschichte 5 (*see* Seeck 1913).
Geschichte 6 (*see* Seeck 1920).
Gesner, J. M., ed.
1759   *Claudian* (Leipzig, 1759).
Getica (*see* Mommsen 1882).
Geyer, E.
1932   "Wiener Grabfunde aus der Zeit des untergehenden Limes II," *Wiener Prähist. Zeitschr.* 19 (Vienna, 1932), 259-266.

Ghirshman, R.
1945   *Bégram* (Cairo, 1945).
1962   *Persian Art: The Parthian and Sassanian Dynasties* (New York, 1962).
Gianelli, G. and S. Mazzarino
1956   *Trattato di storia romana* (Rome, 1956).
Gibbon, E.
1900   *The History of the Decline and Fall of the Roman Empire*, Bury, J. B., ed. (London, 1897-1900).
Gimpū, Uchida
1953   *Gakugei* 36 (1948), 28-32 and *Yūboku minzoku no shakai to bunka* (1952) 49-66, reprinted in *Kyōdo shi Kenkyū* (Tokyo, 1953), 177-194.
Ginters, W.
1928   *Das Schwert der Skythen und Sarmaten in Südrussland* (Berlin, 1928).
Ginzburg, L.
1899   *Monatschrift für die Geschichte und Wissenschaft des Judentums* (1899).
Ginzburg, V. V.
1946a   "Materialy k antropologii gunnov i sakov," *SE* 4 (1946), 207-210.
1946b   "Antropologicheskie materialy iz kurganov u goroda Yangi-iul' bliz Tashkenta," *SE* 4 (1946).
1949   "Cherepa iz zoroastriĭskogo kladbishcha XIII v. v Frinkente," *SMAE* 9 (1949).
1950a   "Materialy k paleoantropologii vostochnykh raĭonov sredneĭ Azii," *KSIE* 11 (1950), 83-96.
1950b   "Pervye antropologicheskie materialy k probleme etnogeneza Baktrii," *MIA* 15 (1950), 241-250.
1954   "Drevnee naselenie tsentral'nogo Tian-shania i Alaia po antropologicheskim dannym," *Sredneaziatskiĭ etnograficheskiĭ sbornik* 1 (Moscow, 1954), 354-412. Also in *TIE* 31 (1954).
1956a   "Drevnee naselenie vostochnykh i tsentral'nykh raĭonov Kazakhskoĭ SSR po antropologicheskim dannym," *Antropologicheskiĭ sbornik* 1 (Moscow, 1956), 238-298.
1956b   "Materialy k antropologii drevnego naseleniia Ferganskoĭ doliny," *Trudy Kirg.* 1 (Moscow, 1956), 85-102.
1957   "Antropologicheskie materialy iz Vuadil'skogo i Ak-tamskogo mogil'nikov," *KS* 69 (1957), 91-93.
1959a   "Etnogeneticheskie sviazi drevnego naseleniia Stalingradskogo Zavolzh'ia," *MIA* 60 (1959), 524-594.
1959b   "Materialy k antropologii drevnego naseleniia iugo-vostochnogo Kazakhstana," *Trudy Kazakh.* 7 (1959), 266-269.
1959c   "Osnovye voprosy paleantropologii sredneĭ Azii v sviazi s izucheniem etnogeneza ee narodov," *KSIE* 31 (1959), 27-35.
1960a   "Materialy k antropologii drevnego naseleniia iuzhnoĭ Kirgizii," *Izv. Kirg.* 2:3 (1960), 151-162.
1960b   "Antropologicheskie dannye k istorii narodov sredneĭ Azii," *Doklady DPMKV* (Moscow, 1960).

1962a "K antropologii naseleniia Ferganskoĭ doliny v epokhu bronzy," *MIA* 118 (1962), 201-218.

1962b "Kraniologicheskie materialy iz severnogo Kazakhstana i vopros o proizkhozhdenii rannikh tiurskikh kochevnikov," *KSIE* 36 (1962), 95-99.

1963a "Antropologicheskie dannye k istorii narodov sredneĭ Azii," *TDPMKV* 3 (1963), 40-46.

1963b "Antropologicheskiĭ sostav naseleniia Sarkela-Beloĭ Vezhi i ego proizkhozdenie," *MIA* 109 (1963), 260-281.

1963c "Materialy k antropologii drevnego naseleniia severnogo Kazakhstana," *SMAE* 21 (1963).

Ginzburg, V. V. and B. V. Firsteĭn
1958 "Materialy k antropologii drevnego naseleniia zapadnogo Kazakhstana," *SMAE* 18 (1958), 390-427.

Ginzburg, V. V. and E. V. Zhirov
1949 "Antropologicheskie materialy iz kenkol'skogo katakombnogo mogil'nika v doline r. Talas Kirgizskoĭ SSR," *SMAE* 10 (1949), 213-265.

Giraud, L.
1960 *L'empire des Turcs célestes* (Paris, 1960).

Gitti, A.
1953 *Ricerche sui rapporti tra i Vandali e l'impero romano* (Bari, 1953).

Giunta, F.
1952 *Jordanes e la cultura del alto medio evo* (Palermo, 1952).
1958 *Genserico e la Sicilia* (Palermo, 1958).

Glazkova, V. M. and V. P. Chtentsov
1960 "Paleoantropologicheskie materialy Nizhnevolzhkogo otriada Stalingradskoĭ ekspeditsii," *MIA* 78 (1960), 285-292.

Götze, A.
1909 *Ostgotische Helme und symbolische Zeichen* in *Mannus* I (Würzburg, 1909).

Gokhman, I. I.
1958 "Antropologicheskie materialy iz plitochnykh mogil Zabaĭkal'ia," *SMAE* 18 (1958), 428-443.
1960 *Antropologicheskaia kharakteristika cherepov iz Izvolginskogo gorodishcha* (Ulan-Ude, 1960).

Golding, A., trans.
1585 *The Worke of Pomponius Mela* (*The Cosmographer*) (London, 1585).

Golenko, K. V.
1957 "Klad monet naĭdennyĭ v 1951 g. v Patree," *SA* 2 (1957), 197-204.
1960 "Vtoroĭ patreĭskiĭ klad monet," *Numismatika i epigrafika* 1 (1960).

Golenko, K. V. and N. I. Sokol'skiĭ
1968 "Klad 1962 g. iz Kepi," *Numismatika i epigrafika* 7 (1968), 72-126.

Gol'msten, V. V.
1928 "Arkheologicheskie pamiatniki Samarskoĭ gubernii," *TSARANION* 4 (1928), 125-137.

Golubeva, L. A.
1957 "Soveshchanie, posviashchennoe problemam cherniakhovskoĭ kul'tury i ee roli v ranneĭ istorii slavian," *SA* 4 (1957).

Gombocz, Z.
1924   Streitberg Festgabe (Leipzig, 1924).
Gordon, C. D.
1960   The Age of Attila (Ann Arbor, 1960).
Goriunova, E. I.
1961   "Etnicheskaia istoriia Volgo-Okskogo mezdurech'ia, MIA 94 (1961).
Gorodtsov, V. A.
1905   "Resul'taty arkheologicheskikh issledovaniĭ v Iziumskom uezde,
        Khar'kovskoĭ gubernii 1901 g.," Trudy XII AS 1 (Moscow, 1905).
1907   "Resul'taty arkheologicheskikh issledovaniĭ v Bakhmutskom uez-
        de, Ekaterinoslavskoĭ gubernii 1903 g.," Trudy XIII AS 1 (Mos-
        cow, 1907).
Goubert, P.
1951   "Le rôle de Saint-Pulchérie et de l'eunuque Chrysaphios," Das
        Konzil von Chalcedon (Würzburg, 1951).
Graevius, J. G.
1722   Thesaurus antiquitatum et historiae Italiae (Lugduni Batavorum,
        1722).
Graf, A.
1936   Übersicht der antiken Geographie von Pannonien (Budapest, 1936).
Graf, G.
1944   Geschichte der christlichen arablichen Literatur (Città del Vaticano,
        1944).
Grakov, B. N.
1929   "Deux tombeaux de l'époque scythique aux environs de la ville
        d'Orenbourg," ESA 4 (1929).
1947   "Γυναιχοϰϱατόυμενοι, Perezhitki matriarkhata u sarmatov,"
        VDI 3 (1947).
1950   "Skifskiĭ Gerakl," KS 34 (1950), 7-18.
Grammata Serica Recensa, Karlgren, B. (Stockholm, 1957).
Grancsay, S. V.
1949   "A Barbarian Chieftain's Helmet," Bulletin of the Metropolitan
        Museum of Art (June 1949), 272-281.
Grebnev, A. V.
1966   Tuvinskiĭ geroicheskiĭ epos (Moscow, 1966).
The Greek Ecclesiastical Historians of the First Six Centuries of the Christian
        Era (London, 1843-46).
Greenslade, S. L.
1945   "The Illyrian Churches and the Vicariate of Thessalonica 378-
        395," Journal of Theological Studies 44 (1945), 17-30.
Grégoire, H. and M. A. Kugener, ed. and trans.
1930   Vie de Porphyre, évêque de Gaza (Paris, 1930).
Griaznov, M. P.
1951   "Arkheologicheskoe issledovanie territorii odnogo drevnego posel-
        ka (Raskopki severo-altaĭskoĭ ekspeditsii 1949 g.)," KS 40 (1951).
1956   "Istoriia drevnikh plemen verkhneĭ Ob'i po raskopkam bliz s.
        Bol'shaia Rechka," MIA 48 (1956).
1958   Drevnee iskusstvo Altaia (Leningrad, 1958).
1961   "Drevneĭshie pamiatniki geroicheskogo eposa narodov iuzhnoĭ
        Sibiri," Arkheol. sbornik 3 (1961), 7-31.

Dei griechischen christlichen Schriftsteller der ersten drei Jahrhunderte, Ak. Wiss. (Leipzig, 1897-).

Grigor'ev, G. V.
1940   *Kaunchi-Tepa* (*raskopki 1934 g.*), (Tashkent, 1940).
1948   "Kelesskaia step' v arkheologicheskom otnoshenii," *Izv. Kazakh.* 1 (1948).

Gröbbels, I. W.
1905   *Der Reihengräberfund von Gammertingen* (Munich, 1905).

Grønbech, V.
1931   *The Culture of the Teutons* (London and Copenhagen, 1931).

Groot, J. J. M. de
1921   *Die Hunnen der vorchristlichen Zeit in chinesische Urkunden zur Geschichte Asiens* 1 (Berlin and Leipzig, 1921).
1926   *Die Westlande Chinas in vorchristliche Zeit* in *Chinesische Urkunden zur Geschichte Asiens* 2 (Berlin and Leipzig, 1926).

Grosse, R.
1920   *Römische Militärgeschichte von Gallienus bis zum Beginn der byzantinischen Themenverfassung* (Berlin, 1920).

Grünhagen, W.
1954   *Der Schatzfund von Gross Bodungen* (Berlin, 1954).

Grützmacher, G.
1913   *Synesios von Kyrene* (Leipzig, 1913).

Grum-Grzhimaĭlo, G. E.
1930   *Zapadnaia Mongoliia i Uriankhaĭskiĭ kraĭ* 1-3 (St. Petersburg, 1914-30).

Grumel, V.
1952   "L'Illyricum de la mort de Valentian Ier à la mort de Stilicon," *Revue des études byzantines* 9 (1952), 5-46.

Grundtvig, S.
1870   "Om de gotiske folks vabenéd," *Oversigt over det Kongelike Danske Videnskabernes Selskabs Forhandlinger* (1870).

Güldenpenning, A.
1885   *Geschichte des römischen Reiches unter den Kaiser Arcadius und Theodosius II* (Halle, 1885).

Güldenpenning, A. and J. Ifland
1878   *Der Kaiser Theodosius der Grosse* (Halle, 1878).

Gushchina, I. I.
1962   "Nakhodki iz Krasnodarskogo kraia," *SA* 2 (1962).
1967   "O Sarmatakh v iugo-zapadnom Krymu," *SA* 1 (1967), 40-51.

Gutschmid, A. von
1888   *Geschichte Irans und seiner Nachbarlände von Alexander dem Grossen bis zum Untergang der Arsaciden* (Tübingen, 1888).
1889   *Orosius*, Zangemeister, C., ed. (Leipzig, 1889).
1894   *Kleine Schriften* (Leipzig, 1889-94).

Hambis, Louis, ed.
1955   *La description du monde* (*Marco Polo*), in French translation (Paris, 1955).

Hamilton, J. R.
1955   *Les Ouïghours à l'époque des cinq dynasties* (Paris, 1955).
1962   "*Toquz-Oγuz et On-Uyγur*," *JA* 250 (1962), 23-63.

Hampel, J.
1897   "Skythische Denkmäler aus Ungarn," *Etnologische Mitteilungen* (1897).
1905   *Alterthümer des frühen Mittelalters in Ungarn* 1-3 (Braunschweig, 1905).

Han, Ju-lin
1941   "T'u chüe Kuan-hao yen-chiu," *Studia Serica* 1, based on the *T'ung-tien of Tu You*, ch. 197 (1940-41).

Hančar, F.
1955   *Das Pferd in prähistorischer und früher historischer Zeit* (Vienna, 1955).

Harduin, J., ed. and compiler
1684   *Themistii Orationes* (Leipzig, 1684). (*See also* K. W. Dindorf 1932).

Harmatta, J.
1947   "Das Volk der Sadagaren," *Analecta Orientalia memoriae Alexandri Csoma de Körös dicata* (Budapest, 1947).
1950   *Studies on the History of the Samartians* (Budapest, 1950).
1951   "The Golden Bow of the Huns," *AAH* 1 (1951), 114-149.
1952   "The Dissolution of the Hun Empire" 1, *AAH* 2 (1952), 277-304.
1955   "Problème de la détermination et l'appréciation historique du matériel archéologique hunnique," *Conférence archéologique de l'Académie hongroise de science* (Budapest, 1955).
1958   "La société des Huns à l'époque d'Attila," *Recherches internationales à la lumière du marxisme* 2 (1958), 179-238.
1962   "Byzantinoturcica," *AAH* 10 (1962), 131-150.

Hartke, W.
1940   *Geschichte und Politik im spätantiken Rom* (Leipzig, 1940).
1951   *Römische Kinderkaiser* (Berlin, 1951).

Harva, U.
1938   *Die religiösen Vorstellungen der altaischer Völker* (Helsinki, 1938).
Harvard Journal of Asiatic Studies (Cambridge, 1936-).

Hatt, J.-J.
1966   "Découverte à Hochfelden d'une tombe barbare du ve siècle," *Académie des Inscriptions et Belles-Lettres, comptes rendus* 1965, Janvier-Juin (1966), 254-264.

Hauger, A.
1921   *Zur römischen Landwirtschaft und Haustierzucht* (Hannover, 1921).

Hauptmann, L.
1935   "Kroaten, Goten und Sarmaten," *Germanoslavica* 3 (1935), 95-127, 315-353.

Haussig, H. W.
1954   "Theophylakts Exkurs über die skythischen Völker," *Byzantion* 23 (1953-54), 275-462.
1958   "Die protobulgarische Fürstenliste," in Altheim, F. and H. W. Haussig, *Die Hunnen in Osteuropa* (Baden-Baden, 1958), 9-29.

Heikel, H. J.
1894   "Antiquités de la Siberie orientales," *MSFOU* 6 (1894).
1918   *Altertümer aus dem Tale des Talas in Turkestan* (Helsinfors, 1918).

Heinzel, W.
1887   "Über die Hervararsaga," *SB Wien* 114 (1887), 415-519.
Helm, K.
1937   *Altgermanische Religionsgeschichte* (Heidelberg, 1937).
Helm, R.
1932   "Untersuchungen über den auswärtigen diplomatischen Verkehr des römischen Reiches im Zeitalter der Spätantike," *Archiv für Urkundenforschung* 12 (Berlin and Leipzig, 1932), 375-436.
Henning, R.
1907   *Der Helm von Baldenheim und die verwandten Helme des frühen Mittelalters* (Strassburg, 1907).
Henning, W. B.
1952   "A Farewell to the Khagan of the Aq-Aquatärän," *BSOAS* 14:3 (1952), 501-522.
Henry, R., ed. and trans.
1959   "Codices" 1-84 (Olympiodorus) in *Photius, Bibliothèque* (Paris, 1959).
Herding, W., ed.
1879   *Hieronymi De viris illustribus liber* (1879).
Hermes; *Zeitschrift für klassische Philologie* (Berlin, 1866-).
Herzfeld, E.
1924   *Paikuli* (Berlin, 1924).
1930   *Kushano-Sassanian Coins* in *Memoirs of the Archaeological Survey of India* 38 (Calcutta, 1930).
1947   *Zoroaster and His World* (Princeton, 1947).
Heukemes, B., Hoepke, H. and W. Kindler
1956   "Künstliche Schädelmissbildung ungewöhnlicher Art aus einem fränkischen Grabfund des 7. Jahrhunderts aus Heidelberg," *Ruperto-Carola, Sonderband* (June 1956), 94-101.
Heusler, A. and W. Ranisch, ed.
1903   *Eddica minora* (Dortmund, 1903).
Hinks, R. P.
1933   *Catalogue of the Greek, Etruscan and Roman Paintings and Mosaics* (London, 1933).
Hirth, Fr.
1899   *Nachworte zur Inschrift des Tonjukuk* in Radlov 3 (St. Petersburg, 1899).
1900   "Über Wolga-Hunnen und Hsiung-nu," *SB München* 2 (1900), 245-278.
1901   "Hunnenforschungen," *Keleti Szemle* (1901), 81-91.
1909   "Mr. Kingsmill and the Hsiung-nu," *JAOS* (1909), 32-45.
Histoire de l'église, Fliche, A. and V. Martin, ed., 4 (Paris, 1948).
Historia ecclesiastica, Bidez, J. and L. Parmentier, ed. (Paris, 1898); also in *GCS*.
Historici graeci minores, Dindorf, L. A., ed. (Leipzig, 1870-77).
Hjörtsjö, C. H. and A. Walander
1947   *Das Schädel- und Skelettgut der archäologischen Untersuchungen in Ost-Turkistan* (Stockholm, 1947).
Hodgkin, Th.
1886   *The Letters of Cassiodorus*, Hodgkin, Th., trans. (London, 1886).

1889   The Dynasty of Theodosius (Oxford, 1889).
1898   Italy and Her Invaders (Oxford, 1898).
Hörnschemeyer, R.
1929   Die Pferdezucht im klasisschen Altertum (Giessen, 1929).
Hoffiller, V.
1911   "Oprema rimskogo vojnika u prvo doba carstva," Vjesnik hrvat-
        skoga arheoloskoga društva, N.S. 11, 1910-11 (Zagreb, 1911), 240.
Holder, A.
1896   Alt-celtischer Sprachschatz (Leipzig, 1896).
Hollander, L. M., trans.
1936   Old Norse Poems (New York, 1936).
Holmqvist, W.
1939   Kunstprobleme der Merowingerzeit in Kgl. Vitterhets historie och
        antikvitets Akademiens Handlingar 47 (Stockholm, 1939).
1951   Tauschierte Metallarbeiten des Nordens in Kgl. Vitterhets historie
        och antikvitets Academiens Handlingar 70:2 (Stockholm, 1951).
Holthausen, F.
1934   Gotisches etymologisches Wörterbuch (Heidelberg, 1934).
Homeyer, H.
1951   Attila: der Hunnenkönig von seinen Zeitgenossen dargestellt. Ein
        Beitrag zur Wertung geschichtlicher Grösse (Berlin, 1951).
Honigmann, E.
1944   "The Original Lists of the Members of the Council of Nicaea,
        the Robber-Synod and the Council of Chalcedon," Byzantion 16,
        1942-43 (1944), 20-80.
Honigmann, E. and A. Maricq
1953   Recherches sur les Res gestae Saporis (Brussels, 1953).
Horedt, K.
1958   Contribuţii la istoria Transilvaniei în secolele IV-XIII (Bucha-
        rest, 1958).
1960   "Gepizii," Ist. Rom., (1960), 702-714.
Houtsma, M. Th.
1894   Ein türkisch-arabisches Glossar (Leiden, 1894).
Hutton, E.
1915   Attila and the Huns (London, 1915).
1926   The Story of Ravenna (London, 1926).
Iakobson, A. L.
1959   "Rannesrednevekovyĭ Khersones," MIA 63 (1959). "Rannesred-
        nevekovye poseleniia vostochnogo Kryma," MIA 85.
Iakovlev, E. K.
1900   Etnograficheskiĭ obzor inorodcheskago naseleniia doliny iuzhnago
        Eniseia (Minusinsk, 1900).
Iamgerchinov, B. D. et al.
1963   "The History of Cultural Relations of Kirgizstan with Some
        Countries of Asia in Connection with the Latest Archaeological
        Data," TDPMKV 3 (Moscow, 1963), 5-15.
Ibn Fadlan
1939   A. Zeki Validi Togan: Ibn Fadlan's Reisebericht, Zeki Validi,
        A. (Leipzig, 1939).

1956   A. P. Kovaleskiĭ: *Kniga Akhmeda Ibn-Fadlana o ego puteshestvii na Volgu v 921-922 gg.*, Kovalevskiĭ, A. P. (Kharkov, 1956).

1958   M. Canard: *La relation du voyage d'Ibn Fadlan chez les Barbares de la Volga* in *Annales de l'institut d'études orientales* 16 (Algiers, 1958), 41-145.

Ikeuchi, Hiroshi
    1930   "A Study of the Su-shên," *Memoirs of the Toyo Bunko* 5 (1930).
    1932   "A Study of the Fu-yü," *Memoirs of the Toyo Bunko* 9 (1932).

Il'inskaia, V. A.
    1957   "Pamiatniki skifskogo vremeni v basseĭne r. Psel," *SA* 27 (1957), 232-249.

Illins'ka (Il'inskaia), V. A., Kovpanenko, G. T. and E. O. Petrovs'ka
    1960   "Rozkopky kurganiv epokhy bronzy poblyzu s. Pervomaĭs'ky," *APU* 9 (1960), 127-140.

Inner Mongolia (Inner Mongolia and the Region of the Great Wall), Mizuno, Seiichi and Namio Egami in *Archaeologia Orientalis*, Series B:1 (Tokyo and Kyoto, 1935).

Inostrantsev, K.
    1926   *Khunnu i gunny* (Leningrad, 1926).

Inscriptiones Antiquae Orae Septentrionalis Ponti Euxini, Latyshev, V. V., coll., 1 (1885), 2 (1890), 4 (1901).

Inscriptiones christiane urbis Romae septimo saeculo antiquiores 1, 2:1, de Rossi, J. B., ed. (Rome, 1861-88; N.S. 1922-56).

Intercisa 2 in *AAH*, N.S. 36 (Budapest, 1957).

Ioniță, I.
    1964   "Noi descoperire sarmatice pe terituriul Moldovei," *Arheologia Moldovei* 2-3 (Bucharest, 1964), 311-325.

Ishcherikov, P. F.
    1959   "Gorodishche Ufa-II," *Bashkirskiĭ arkheologicheskiĭ sbornik* (Ufa, 1959), 97-99.

Ismagulov, O.
    1962   "Antropologicheskaia kharakteristika usuneĭ Semirech'ia," *Trudy Kazakh.* 16 (Alma Ata, 1962), 168-191.

Istoria Romîniei (Bucharest, 1960).

Istoricheskoe razvitie leksiki turetskikh iazykov (Mocow, 1961).

Istoriia drevnego Kryma (Istoriia i arkheologiia drevenego Kryma), (Kiev, 1957).

Istoriia material'noĭ kul'tury Uzbekistana (Tashkent).

Istoriia Sibiri 1 (Leningrad, 1968).

Istoriia sredneĭ Azii (Istoriia, arkheologiia i etnografiia sredneĭ Azii), (Moscow, 1968).

Istoriia srednevekovogo Kryma (Istoriia i arkheologiia srednevekovogo Kryma) (Moscow, 1958).

Itineraria Romana, Cuntz, O., ed. (Leipzig, 1940).

Iudakhin, K. K.
    1948   *Kirgiz sözlüğü* (Ankara, 1945-48).
    1965   *Kirgizsko-russkiĭ slovar'* Moscow, 1965).

Ivanov, S. V.
    1955   "K voprosu o znachenii izobrazheniĭ na starinnykh predmetakh kul'ta u narodov Saiano-altaĭskogo nagor'ia," *SMAE* 16 (1955).

Ivanova, A. P.
1951   "Kerchenskaia stela s izobrazheniem vsadnika i sidiashcheĭ zhensh-
        chiny," *KS* 39 (1951), 27-34.
1953   *Iskusstvo antichnykh gorodov severnogo Prichernomor'ia* (Lenin-
        grad, 1953).
1954   "Bosporskie antropomorfnye nadgrobiia," *SA* 13 (1954), 242-244.
Jacobsthal, P.
1944   *Early Celtic Art* (Oxford, 1944).
Jänichen, H.
1956   *Die Bildzeichen der königlichen Hoheit bei den iranischen Völkern*
        (Bonn, 1956).
Jahrbuch der Preussichen Kunstsammlungen (Berlin, 1880-).
Jahrbuch für fränkische Landesforschung (Kallmünz, 1935-).
Jahrbücher für Geschichte Osteuropas (Breslau, 1936-).
Jahreshefte des österreichischen archäologischen Instituts (Vienna).
Jalland, T.
1941   *The Life and Times of St. Leo the Great* (London, 1941).
Janin, R.
1953   *La géographie écclesiastique de l'empire byzantin* (Paris, 1953).
Jasinski, M., trans.
1935   *Ausone, Traduction nouvelle de Max Jasinski* (Paris, 1934-35).
Jażdżewski, K.
1959   "Das gegenseitige Verhältnis slawischer und germanischer Ele-
        mente in Mitteleuropa seit dem Hunneneinfall bis zur awarischen
        Landnahme an der mittleren Donau," *Archaeologia Polona* 2
        (1959), 51-70.
Jenkins, R. J. H., trans.
1949   *De administrando imperio (Constantine Porphyrogenitus)* in Eng-
        lish translation (Budapest, 1949).
Jettmar, K.
1953   "Hunnen und Hsiung-nu: ein archäologisches Problem," *Archiv
        für Völkerkunde* 617 (1953), 166-180.
Joki, A. J.
1952   *Die Lehnwörter des Sajansamojedischen* (Helsinki, 1952).
Jones, A. H. M.
1964   *The Later Roman Empire 284-602* 1-2 (Norman, Okla., 1964).
Jonsson, Finnur, ed.
1915   *Den norsk-islandske skjaledigtning* (Copenhagen, 1915).
Jordanes (see Mommsen 1882).
Jouai, L. A. A.
1938   *De magistraat Ausonius* (Nijmegen, 1938).
Journal asiatique (Paris).
Journal de la société finno-ougrienne (Suomalais-ugralainen seura aikakauskirja),
        (Helsinki, 1886-).
Journal of Hellenic Studies (London, 1880-).
Journal of Roman Studies (London, 1911-).
Journal of the American Oriental Society (Boston, 1843/49-).
Journal of the Royal Asiatic Society of Great Britain and Ireland (London).
Jung, J.
1887   *Römer und Romanen in den Alpenländern* (Innsbruck, 1887).

Jungandreas, W.
1934 "Umlokaliesierung in der Heldendichtung," *ZfDPh* 59 (1934).
Justi, F.
1895 *Iranisches Namenbuch* (Marburg, 1895).
Kadyrbaev, M. K.
1959 "Pamiatniki rannikh kochevnikov tsentral'nogo Kazakhstana," *Trudy Kazakh.* 7 (1959), 162-202.
1962 "Novye materialy po istorii rannikh kochevnikov Kazakhstana," *Trudy Kazakh.* 18 (1962).
Kalén, H.
1934 *Studia in Iordanem philologica* (Uppsala, 1934).
Kamenetskiĭ, I. S. and V. V. Kropotkin
1962 "Pogrebenie gunnskogo vremeni bliz Tanaisa," *SA* 3 (1962), 235-240.
Kantorowicz, E.
1927 *Kaiser Friedrich der Zweite* (Berlin, 1927).
Kao, Chü-hsün
1960 "The Ching Lu Shen Shrines of Han Sword Worship in Hsiung Nu Religion," *CAJ* 5:3 (1960), 221-232.
Kaposhina, S. I.
1950 "Pamiatniki zverinogo zhilia iz Ol'vii," *KS* 34 (1950), 42-52.
1962 "Raskopki Kobiakova gorodishcha i ego nekropolia," *Arkheologicheskie raskopki na Donu* (Rostov, 1962), 95-112.
Karlgren, B.
1934 "Early Mirror Inscriptions," *BMFEA* 6 (1934), 9-79.
1950 *The Book of Odes* (Stockholm, 1950).
1952 *A Catalogue of the Chinese Bronzes in the Alfred F. Pilsbury Collection* (Minneapolis, 1952).
1957 *Grammata Serica Recensa* (Stockholm, 1957).
Karutz, R.
1911 *Unter Kirgisen und Turkmenen* (Leipzig, 1911).
Kāshgharī, M.
1928 *Mitteltürkischer Wortschatz nach Maḥmūd Al-Kāšyarī's Dīvān Luγāt At-Turk*, Brockelmann, C., ed. (Budapest, 1928).
Kazamanova, L. N.
1958 "Klad rimskikh denariev I-III vv. n.e. iz Turia, Zlatopol'skogo raĭona, Cherkasskoĭ oblasti," *SA* 1 (1958), 182-186.
Kent, R. G.
1940 *The Sounds of Latin* (Baltimore, 1940).
Keramopoulos, A.
1953 Πρόσφορα εἰς Στ. Κυριακίδην (Thessalonica, 1953).
Keydell, R., ed.
1967 *Agathiae Myrinaei Historiarum libri quinque* (Berlin, 1967).
Kharko, L. P.
1949 "Tiritakskiĭ monetnyĭ klad 1946 g.," *VDI* 2 (1949), 73-86.
Khazanov, A. M.
1963 "Genezis sarmatskikh bronzovykh zerkal," *SA* 4 (1964), 58-71.
1964 "Religiozno-magicheskoe ponimanie zerkal u sarmatov," *SE* 3 (1964).

1966   "Slozhnye luki evraziĭskikh stepeĭ i Irana v skifo-sarmatskuiu epokhu," *Material'naia kul'tura narodov sredneĭ Azii i Kazakhstana* (Moscow, 1966), 29-44.

Khersonesskiĭ sbornik (*Bulletin du Musée d'état de Chersonèse taurique*) 2 (Sevastopol, 1927).

Khodzhaĭov, T. K.
1966   "O prednamerennoĭ deformatsii golovy u narodov sredneĭ Azii v drevnosti," *Vestnik Karakalpakskogo filiala AN SSSR* 4 (1966), 60-67.

Khorezm (*Arkheologicheskie i etnograficheskie raboty khorezmskoĭ ekspeditsii 1945-1948*), (Moscow, 1952). See also *Trudy Khor.*

Kiatkina, T. P.
1964   "Kraniologicheskiĭ material iz katakombskikh zakhoroneniĭ vremeni u iuzhnoĭ Turkmenii," Tashkentskiĭ universitet, *Nauchnye trudy* 235 (Tashkent, 1964), 52-66.

Kibirov, A. K.
1959a   "Arkheologicheskie pamiatniki Chatkala," *Trudy Kirg.* 2 (1959), 3-62.
1959b   "Arkheologicheskie raboty v tsentral'nom Tian'-shane," *Trudy Kirg.* 2 (1959), 63-138.

Kieseĭtzky, G. and C. Watzinger
1909   *Griechische Grabreliefs aus Südrussland* (Berlin, 1909).

Kim, Chewon
1948   *Two Old Silla Tombs: Ho-U Tomb and Silver Bell Tomb* (Seoul, 1948).

King, N. Q.
1960   *"There's such Divinity doth hedge a King"* (Edinburgh, 1960).

Kinzhalov, R. V. and V. G. Lukonin
1960   *Pamiatniki kul'tury sasanidskogo Irana* (Leningrad, 1960).

Kiselev, S. V.
1948   "Drevne-khakasskiĭ *el*," *Khakasskiĭ nauchno-issledovatel'skiĭ institut iazyka, literatury i istorii* 1 (1948), 31-34.
1951   *Drevnaia istoriia iuzhnoĭ Sibiri* (Moscow and Leingrad, 1951).

Kiuner, N. V.
1961   *Kitaĭskie izvestiia o narodakh iuzhnoĭ Sibiri, tsentral'noĭ Azii i dal'nego vostoka* (Moscow, 1961).

Klebel, E.
1939   "Langobarden, Bajuwaren, Slawen," *Mitteilungen der anthropologischen Gesellschaft in Wien* 69 (1939), 41-116.
1957   *Probleme der bayerischen Verfassungsgeschichte* (Munich, 1957).

Kliastornyĭ, S. G.
1964   *Drevnetiurkskie runicheskie pamiatniki* (Moscow, 1964).

Klio: Beiträge zur alten Geschichte (Leipzig, 1911-).

Klopsteg, P. E.
1947   *Turkish Archery and the Composite Bow* (Evanston, Ill., 1947).

Kluge, F.
1911   "Der Tod des Attila, eine altgermanische Dichtung," *Deutsche Rundschau* 146 (1911), 451-455.
1921   "Zur Totenklage auf Attila," *PBB* 37 (1921), 157-159.

Knipovich, T. N.
1949   Tanais (Moscow and Leningrad, 1949).
Kobylina, M. M.
1956   "Phanagoria," *MIA* 57 (1956), 5-101.
1963   "Issledovaniia Fanagorii v 1959-1960 i 1962 gg.," *SA* 4 (1963), 129-138.
Köhalmi Katalin, U.
1958   "Fakengyel és egyéb Fatárgyak egy nyugat-mongóliai múzeum-ban," *Folia archaeologica* 10 (1958), 143-147.
Körösi Csoma Archivum; a Köröso Csoma—társaság folyóirata (Budapest 1921-24; Hannover, 1921-).
Kogel, R.
1894   *Geschichte der deutschen Literatur bis zum Ausgang des Mittelalters* (Strassburg, 1894).
Kollwitz, J.
1941   *Oströmische Plastik der Theodosianischen Zeit* (Berlin, 1941).
Komarova, M. N.
1952   "Tomskiĭ mogil'nik," *MIA* 21 (1952).
Kondakov, N.
1896   *Russkie klady* (St. Petersburg, 1896).
Kondakov, N. and I. Tolstoĭ
1889   *Russkie drevnosti v pamiatnikakh iskusstva* (1889-99).
Konduktorova, T. S.
1956   "Materialy po paleoantropologii Ukrainy," *TIE* 33 (1956), 166-203.
1958   "Paleoantropologicheskiĭ material iz mogil'nika poleĭ pogrebal'-nykh urn Khersonskoĭ oblasti," *Sovetskaia Antropologiia* 2 (1958), 69-79.
Kononov, A. N.
1949   "Opyt analiza termina Türk," *SE* 1 (1949), 40-47.
1958   *Rodoslovnaia Turkmen* (Moscow and Leningrad, 1958).
Konzil von Chalcedon (Das Konzil von Chalcedon), Grillmeier, A. and H. Bacht, ed. (Würzburg, 1951/53).
Koriun (bishop)
1927   "Beschreibung des Lebens und Sterbens des hl. Lehrers Mesrop" in *Ausgewählte Schriften der armenischen Kirchenväter*, Weber, S., ed. and trans. (Munich, 1927).
Korzukhina, G. F.
1955   "K istorii srednego Podneprov'ia v seredine I tysiacheletiia n.e.," *SA* 22 (1955), 61-82.
Kotliarevskiĭ, A. A.
1863   *O pogrebal'nykh obychaiakh iazycheskikh slavian* (Mocsow, 1863).
Kotsevalov, A.
1959   "Borysthenes-Borysthenites and Tanais-Tanaites," *Annals of the Ukrainian Academy of Arts and Sciences in the U.S.A.* 7 (1959).
Kotwicz, Wl.
1945   "Contributions à l'histoire de l'Asie centrale, *Rocznik orjenta-listyczny* 20 (1939-45), 159-195.
Kotwicz, Wl. and A. Samoĭlovitch
1926   "Le monument turc d'Ikhe-Khuchotu en Mongolie Centrale," *Rocznik orjentalistyczny* 4 (1926), 60-107.

Kovacs, J.
1913 "Les fouillages de Mezäband," *Dolgozatok* 4 (1913), 390-429.
Kovaleskiĭ, A. P. (*see* Ibn Fadlan 1956).
Kovrig, I.
1959 "Nouvelles trouvailles du ve siècle découvertes en Hongrie," *AA* 10 (1959), 209-225.
1963 "Das Awarenzeitliche Gräberfeld von Alattyan," *AAH* 40 (1963).
Kozhomberdiev, I.
1960a "Mogil'nik Akchiĭ-Karasu v doline Ketmen'-Tiube," *Izv. Kirg.* 1:3 (1960), 109-123.
1960b "Novye dannye o Kenkol'skom mogil'nike," *KS* 80 (1960), 70-75.
1963 "Katakombnye pamiatniki Talasskoĭ doliny," *Arkheologicheskie pamiatniki Talasskoĭ doliny* (Frunze, 1963), 33-77.
Krahe, H.
1942 "Beiträge zur illyrischen Wort- und Namenforschung 17; Der Flussname Nedao und Verwandtes," *Indogermanische Forschungen* 58 (1942), 208-218.
Krasheninnikov, M.
1915 "Novaia rukopis' izvlechenii περὶ πρέσβεων ʿΡωμαίων," *Vizantiĭskoe obozrenie* 1:1-2 (1916).
Krause, E.
1904 "Der Fund von Höckricht, Kreis Ohlau," *Schlesiens Vorzeit in Bild und Schrift*, N.S. 3 (1904), 46-50.
Krause, W.
1954 *Quatrième congrès internationale des sciences onomastiques* (Uppsala, 1954).
1955 *Handbuch des Gotischen* (München, 1955).
Kravchenko, N. M.
1967 "Kosanovskiĭ mogil'nik," *MIA* 139 (1967), 77-135.
Kris, Kh. I. and E. V. Veĭmarn
1958 "Kurgan epokhi bronzy bliz Bakhchisaraia," *KS* 71 (1958), 65-71.
Kropotkin, V. V.
1956 "Review of 'Materialy po arkheologii iugo-zapadnogo Kryma'," *SA* 25 (1956), 345-348.
1957 "Review of A. L. Mongaĭt, *Arkheologiia v SSSR*," *SA* 3 (1957), 297-298.
1958 "Iz istorii denezhnogo obrashcheniia v vostochnoĭ Evrope v I tysiacheletii n.e.," *SA* 2 (1958), 279-285.
1959 "Mogil'nik Suuk-su i ego istoriko-arkheologicheskoe znachenie," *SA* 1 (1959), 181-194.
1961 *Klady rimskikh monet na territorii SSSR* (Moscow, 1961).
Kruglikova, I. T.
1956 "Pozdneantichnye poseleniia Bospora na beregu Azovskogo moria," *SA* 25 (1956).
1957 "Pogrebenie IV-V vv. der. Aĭbazovskoe," *SA* (1957), 253-257.
1961 "Poselenie derevni Semenovski," *KS* 83 (1961).
1962 "Issledovaniia Sel'skikh poselenii antichnykh gosudarstv na iuge SSSR," *AA* 14:3-4 (Budapest, 1962), 217-230.
1965 "Bospor III-IV vv. n.e. v svete novykh arkheologicheskikh issledovaniĭ," *KS* 103 (1965), 3-10.

1966   *Bospor v pozdneantichnoe vremia* (Moscow, 1966).
Krupnov, E. I.
1948   "Arkheologicheskie pamiatniki verkhov'ev Tereka i basseĭna r. Sunzhi," *Trudy gosudarstvennogo istoricheskogo muzeia* 17 (Moscow, 1948).
1949   "Arkheologicheskie raboty na severnom Kavkaze," *KS* 27 (1949), 11-20.
1957   "Pervye itogi izucheniia vostochnogo Predkavkaz'ia," *SA* 2 (1957), 154-173.
Kukhraneko, Iu. V.
1954   "K voprosu o slaviano-skifskikh i slaviano-sarmatskikh otnosheniiakh," *SA* 19 (1954), 111-120.
1955   "Poselenie i mogil'nik poleĭ pogrebeniĭ v sele Privol'nom," *SA* 22 (1955), 125-152.
1958   "Ekonomicheskiĭ stroĭ i byt vostochnykh slavian v pervoĭ polovine I tysiacheletiia," *Ocherki* (Moscow, 1958), 52-89.
Kulakovskiĭ, Iu. A.
1891   "Kerchenskaia khristianskaia katakomba 491 g.," *MAR* 6 (1891).
1899a   *Alany po svedeniiam klassicheskikh i vizantiĭskikh pisateleĭ* (Kiev, 1899).
1899b   *Karta evropeĭskoĭ Sarmatii po Ptolemeiu* (Kiev, 1899).
1913   *Istoriia Vizantii* (Kiev, 1913).
Die Kunst der Spätantike im Mittelmeerraum, Kaiser-Friedrich-Museum (Berlin, 1939).
Kurz, O.
1962   "The Pebble from Ashperonsk and Its Alleged Greco-Alanic Inscription," *JAOS* 82 (1962).
Kuznetsov, V. A.
1962   "Alanskie plemena severnogo Kavkaza," *MIA* 106 (1962).
Kuznetsov, V. A. and V. K. Pudovin
1961   "Alany v zapadnoĭ Evrope v epokhu 'velikogo pereseleniia narodov'," *SA* 2 (1969), 79-95.
Kyzlasov, L. P.
1951a   "Pamiatniki pozdnikh kochevnikov tsentral'nogo Kazakhstana," *Izv. Kazakh.* 3 (1951), 53-63.
1951b   "Roznaia kostianaia rukoiatka pleti iz mogily Ak-Kiuna (Altaĭ)," *KS* 36 (1951), 50-55.
1958   Etapy drevneĭ istorii Tuvy," *Vestnik Moskovskogo universiteta* 4 (1958), 71-99.
1960   *Tashtykskaia epokha* (Moscow, 1960).
Labourt, J., ed. and trans.
1954   *Lettres* (*Jerome*) 1-4 (Paris, 1949-54).
Lamy, Th. J., trans.
1889   *S. Ephraem Syri Hymni et Sermones* (Malines, 1889).
Landersdorfer, S., trans.
1913   *Mamre on the Locusts* (Cyrillonas) in *Bibliothek der Kirchenväter* 6 (1913).
Langen, P.
1867   *Programm Gymnasium Düren* (Düren, 1867).
Langlois, V., ed.
1869   *Collection des historiens de l'Arménie* (1867-69).

Latouche, R.
1946   *Les grands invasions et la crise de l'occident au Ve siècle* (Paris, 1946).
Lattimore, O.
1940   *Inner Asian Frontiers of China* (London and New York, 1940).
Latynin, B. A. and T. G. Oboldueva
1959   "Isfarinskie kurgany," *KS* 76 (1959), 17-27.
Latyshev, V. V., ed. and trans.
1906   *Scythica et Caucasica e veteribus scriptoribus graecis et latinis* (*Dionysius*), in Russian translation (St. Petersburg, 1904-1906).
Laufer, B.
1913   *Notes on the Turquoise in the East* (Chicago, 1913).
1914   *Chinese Clay Figures* 1 (Chicago, 1914).
Laurent, V.
1945   "Note d'histoire écclesiastique," *Revue des études byzantines* 3 (1945), 115-123.
Laute-Cirtautas, I.
1961   *Der Gebrauch der Farbbezeichnungen in den Turkdialekten* (Wiesbaden, 1961).
Lebeau, Ch.
1820   *Histoire du Bas-Empire* (Paris, 1819-20).
Lebzelter, V. and G. Müller
1935   "Über die Rassengliederung der Langobarden," *Forschungen und Fortschritte* 11 (Berlin, 1935), 318ff.
Le Coq, A. von
1924   *Die Buddhistische Spätantike in Mittelasien* 3 (Berlin, 1924).
1925   *Bilderatlas zur Kunst- und Kulturgeschichte Mittel-Asiens* (Berlin, 1925).
Ledevev, Ph.
1931   "Die Staterprägungen der Stadt Nagidos," *ZfN* 41 (1931), 153-276.
Leib, B., trans.
1945   *Alexiade; règne de l'empereur Alexis I Comnène*, Comnena, Princess Anna (Paris, 1937-45).
Leicher, R.
1927   *Die Totenklage in der deutschen Epik von der ältesten Zeit bis zur Nibelungenklage* (Breslau, 1927).
Lemerle, P.
1954   "Invasions et migrations dans les Balkans depuis la fin de l'époque romaine jusqu'au IIIe siècle," *Revue historique* 211 (1954), 265ff.
Levasheva, V. P. and E. R. Rygdylon
1952   "Shalabolinskiĭ klad bronzovykh kotlov, khraniashchiĭsia v Minusinskom muzee," *KS* 43 (1952), 132-137.
Levin, M. G.
1962   *Ethnic Origins of the Peoples of Northeastern Asia* (Toronto, 1963).
1963   *Physical Anthropology and Ethnographic Problems of the Peoples of the Far East* (Toronto, 1963).
Levina, L. M.
1966   "Keramika i voprosy khronologii pamiatnikov Dzhety-Asarskoĭ kul'tury," *Material'naia kul'tura narodov srednei Azii i Kazakhstana* (Moscow, 1966), 45-90.

Levison, W.
1903   "Bischof Germanus von Auxerre und die Quellen zu seiner Geschich-
        te," *Neues Archiv für altere deutsche Geschichtskunde* 29 (1903), 97-
        175.
Levy, H. L.
1948   "Claudian's *In Rufinum* and an Epistle of Saint Jerome," *Ameri-
        can Journal of Philology* 69 (Baltimore, 1948), 62-68.
Li, Chi
1957   *The Beginnings of Chinese Civilization* (Seattle, 1957).
Li, I-yu
1963   *Nei Mêng-ku ch'u-t'u wên-wu hsüan chi,* text in Chinese and Mon-
        golian (Peking, 1963). Approximate translation of title: *Exca-
        vated cultural relics of Inner Mongolia; selected works.*
Liang, Shang-ch'un
1942   *Yen ku ts'ang ching* (Peking, 1942).
Liapushkin, I. I.
1947   "Poseleniia epokhi zheleza v basseĭne r. Vorskly," *KS* 21 (1947).
1950a   "Pamiatniki kul'tury poleĭ pogrebeniĭ levoberezh'ia Dnepra," *KS*
        33 (1950), 29-38.
1950b   "Pamiatniki kul'tury poleĭ pogrebeniĭ pervoĭ poloviny I tysiacheleti-
        ia n.e. dneprovskogo lesistepnogo levoberezh'ia," *SA* 13 (1950), 7-32.
1961   "Dneprovskoe lesostepnoe levoberezh'e v epokhu zheleza," *MIA*
        104 (1961).
Liberov, P. D.
1949   "Skifskie kurgany Kievshchiny," *KS* 30 (1949), 93-104.
1951   "Kurgany u sela Konstantinovki," *KS* 37 (1951), 137-143.
1965   *Pamiatniki skifskogo vremeni na srednem Donu* (Moscow, 1965).
The Library of Photius 1, Freese, J. H., trans. (London, 1920).
Lietzmann, H. von, ed.
1908   *Das Leben des heiligen Symeon Stylites* in *TU* 32 (Leipzig, 1908).
Lifshits, V. A.
1962   *Sogdiĭskie dokumenty s gory Mug* (Moscow, 1962).
Ligeti, L.
1961   "A propos des éléments 'Altaïques' de la langue hongroise,"
        Acta Linguistica 11:1-2 (Budapest, 1961), 15-41.
Lindqvist, S.
1926   *Vendelkulturens alder och ursprung* in *Kgl. Vitterhets historie
        och antikvitets Akademiens Handlingar* 36:1 (Stockholm, 1926).
Lipták, E.
1957   "Awaren und Magyaren im Donau-Thiess Zwischenromgebiet,"
        AAH 8 (1957), 199-267.
1959   "The 'Avar Period' Mongoloids in Hungary," *AAH* 10 (1959),
        251-279.
1961   "Germanische Skelettreste von Hács-Béndekpuszta," *AAH* 13
        (1961), 231-246.
Litvinskiĭ, B. A.
1956   "Ob izuchenii v 1955 g. pogrebal'nykh pamiatnikov kochevnikov
        v Kara-Mazarskikh gorakh," *Trudy Tadzh.* 63 (1956), 37-46.
1959   "Izuchenie kuramov v severo-vostochnoĭ chasti Leninabadskoĭ
        oblasti v 1957 g., *Trudy Tadzh.* 103 (1959), 109-129.

1961 "Issledovanie mogil'nikov Isfarinskogo raĭona," *Trudy Tadzh.* 27 (1961), 59-80.

1964 "Zerkalo v verovaniiakh drevnikh fergantsev," *SE* 3 (1964), 97-104.

1966 "Slozhnostavnoĭ luk v drevneĭ sredneĭ Azii," *SA* 4 (1966), 51-69.

1967 "Dzunskiĭ mogil'nik i nekotorye aspekty kangiuĭskoĭ problemy," *SA* 2 (1967), 29-37.

Litvinskiĭ, B. A. and E. A. Davidovich

1956 "Predvaritel'nyĭ otchet o raskopkakh kurganov v Vorukhe (Isfarinskiĭ raĭon) v 1954 g.," *Trudy Tadzh.* 37 (1956), 61-68.

Liu, Mau-Tsai

1958 *Die chineseschen Nachrichten zur Geschichte der Ost-Türken (T'uküe)* in *Göttinger asiatische Forschungen* 10 (Wiesbaden, 1958).

Lizerand, G.

1910 *Aetius* (Paris, 1910).

Lo-yang ching (Lo-yang ch'u t'u ku ching); Wên-wu kuan li wei yüan hui (1959).

Loeb Classical Library (Cambridge, Mass.).

Loehr, M.

1955 "The Stag Image in Scythia and the Far East," *Archives of the Chinese Art Society* 9 (1955), 63-71.

1956 *Early Chinese Bronze Weapons* (Ann Arbor, 1956).

Loewe, R.

1923 "Gothische Namen in hagiographischen Texten," *PBB* 47 (Halle, 1923), 407-433.

Lommatzch, H. P., ed.

1903 *Digestorum artis mulomedicinae libri quatuor (Vegetius)*, (Leipzig, 1903).

L'Orange, H. P.

1953 *Studies on the Iconography of Cosmic Kingship in the Ancient World* (Oslo, 1953).

Lot, F.

1935 *Les invasions germaniques* (Paris, 1935).

1936 "La 'Notitia dignitatum utriusque imperii'," *RÉA* 38 (1936).

Lot, F., Pfister, Chr. and F. L. Ganshof

1928 *Histoire du moyen âge* 1 (Paris, 1928).

Loyen, A.

1942 *Recherches historiques sur les panégyriques de Sidoine Apollinaire* (Paris, 1942).

Lü Kuang (*Biography of Lü Kuang*), Mather, R. B., trans. and annotator (Berkeley and Los Angeles, 1959).

Lubo-Lesnichenko, E.

1961 *Drevnie kitaĭskie shelkovye tkani i vyshivki v sobranii gosudarstvennogo Ermitazha* (Leningrad, 1961).

Ludwig, A., ed.

1897 *Eudociae Augustae, Procli Lycii, Claudiani carminum reliquiae* (Leipzig, 1897).

Luebeck, E.

1872 *Hieronymus quos noverit scriptores et ex quibus hauserit* (Leipzig, 1872).

Lüttich, R.
1910   *Ungarnzüge in Europa im zehnten Jahrhundert* (Berlin, 1910).
Lutskevich, I. N.
1948   "Materialy do karty poshyrennia pam'iatok kul'tury poliv pok-
        hovan' na territorii Khar'kiv'skoï oblasti," *Arkheologiia* 2 (Kiev,
        1948), 164-178.
1952   "Sarmats'ki kurgany u s. Nesherotove Voroshilovograds'koï ob-
        lasti," *Arkheologiia* 7 (Kiev, 1952), 136-141.
Macartney, C. A.
1934   "The End of the Huns," *BNJb* 10 (1934), 106-114.
1951   *The Origin of the Hun Chronicle and Hungarian Historical Sour-
        ces* (Oxford, 1951).
1953   *The Medieval Hungarian Historians* (Cambridge, 1953).
Macrea, M.
1958   "Une nouvelle inscription latine de Dacie datant du IVe siècle,"
        Dacia, N.S. 2 (1958), 467-472.
Maenchen-Helfen, O. J.
1931   *Reise ins asiatische Tuwa* (Berlin, 1931).
1939   "The Ting-Ling," *HJAS* 4 (1939), 77-86.
1941   "A Chinese Bronze with Centralasiatic Motives," *BMFEA* 13
        (Stockholm, 1941).
1945a   "Are Chinese *hsi-p'i* and *kuo-lo* IE Loan Words?" *Language* 21
        (1945), 256-260.
1945b   "Huns and Hsiung-nu," *Byzantion* 17 (1944-45), 222-243.
1945c   "The Legend of the Origin of the Huns," *Byzantion* 17 (1944-45),
        244-251.
1945d   "The Yueh-chi Problem Re-Examined," *JAOS* 65 (1945), 71-
        82.
1947   "Odoacer," *American Historical Review* 52 (New York, 1947),
        836-841.
1951   "Manichaeans in Siberia," *Semitic and Oriental Studies Presented
        to William Popper* (Berkeley, 1951), 311-326.
1955a   "The Date of Ammianus Marcellinus' Last Book," *American
        Journal of Philology* 76 (Baltimore, 1955), 384-399.
1955b   "Pseudo-Huns," *CAJ* 1 (1955), 101-106.
1957a   "Crenelated Mane and Scabbard Slide," *CAJ* 3 (1957), 85-138.
1957b   "Germanic and Hunnic Names of Iranian Origin," *Oriens* (1957),
        280-283.
1957c   "Review of D. Carter's *The Symbol of the Beast*," *JAOS* 77:4
        (1957).
1957d   "Review of Two Russian Works on the Archaeology of Central
        Asia," *CAJ* 2 (1957), 305-306.
1958   "A Chinese Bronze with Central Asiatic Motives," *BMFEA* 30
        (Stockholm, 1958), 165-175.
1959   "The Ethnic Name Hun," *Studia Serica Bernhard Karlgren de-
        dicata* (Copenhagen, 1959), 223-238.
1964   "The Date of Maximus of Turin's Sermo XVIII," *Vigiliae Christia-
        nae* 18:2 (1964).
1966   "Akatir," *CAJ* 11:4 (1966), 277-286.
Magyar Nyelv (Budapest, 1905-).

Maksimov, E. V.
1956a "Obsuzhdenie voprosov rannei istorii vostochnykh slavian v Institute arkheologii AN SSSR," *KSIA* 6 (1956), 72-78.
1956b "Pozdneischie sarmato-alanskie pogrebeniia V-VIII vv. na territorii Nizhnego Povolzh'ia, *Trudy Saratovskogo oblastnogo muzeia kraevedeniia* 1 (Saratov, 1956), 65-85.
1966a "Sarmatskie bronzovye kotly i ikh izgotovlenie," *SA* 1 (1966), 51-60.
1966b "Sarmatskie diagonal'nye pogrebeniia vostochnoi Evropy," *Arkheol. sbornik* (Saratov, 1966), 98-115.

Malikov, K. M.
1961 "Zhertvennik iz pregorodnogo zdaniia Neapolia skifskogo," *KSIA* 11 (1961), 65-68.

Malone, K.
1925 "Widsith and the Hervararsaga," *Publications of the Modern Language Association of America* 40 (1925).
1959 *Studies in Heroic Legend and in Current Speech* (Copenhagen, 1959).
1962 *Widsith* in *Anglistica* 13 (Copenhagen, 1962).

Malotet, A.
1898 *De Ammiani Marcellini disgressionibus quae ad externas gentes pertineant* (Paris, 1898).

Malov, S. E.
1929 "Drevneturetskie nadgrobiia s nadpisiami basseina r. Talas," *Izv. AN SSSR, otdelenie gumanitarnykh nauk* (1929), 799-802.
1951 *Pamiatniki drevnetiurskoi pis'mennosti* (Moscow and Leningrad, 1951).
1952 *Eniseiskaia pis'mennost' tiurkov* (Moscow and Leningrad, 1952).
1959 *Pamiatniki drevnetiurskoi pis'mennosti Mongolii i Kirgizii* (Moscow and Leningrad, 1959).

Mamonova, N. N. and R. F. Tugutov
1959 "Raskopki gunnskogo mogil'nika v cheremukhovnoi padi," *Arheol. sbornik* 1 (1959), 74-79.

Manas; Kirgizskii epos Velikii pokhod (Moscow, 1946).

Mandelshtam, A. M.
1959 "Mogil'nik Aruk-tau v Bishkendskoi doline (iuzhnyi Tadzhikistan)," *KS* 76 (1959), 73-82.
1963 "Nekotorye novye dannye o pamiatnikakh kochevogo naseleniia iuzhnogo Turkmenistana v antichnuiu epokhu," *Izv. AN Turkmenskoi SSR, seriia obshchestvennykh nauk* 2 (1963), 27-33.

Mannus; Zeitschrift für Vorgeschichte (Würzburg, 1909-).

Mannus-Bibliothek (Leipzig, 1910-).

Marchenko, I. D.
1956 "Raskopki vostochnogo nekropolia Fanagorii," *MIA* 57 (1956), 102-127.

Marco Polo (*see* Hambis 1955; Moule and Pelliot 1938).

Margulan, A. Kh., Akishev, K. I., Kadyrbaev, M. K. and A. M. Orazbaev
1966 *Drevniaia kul'tura tsentral'nogo Kazakhstana* (Alma Ata, 1966).

Marquart (Markwart), J.
1898a *Die Chronologie der allttürkischen Inschriften* (Leipzig, 1898).

1898b   "Historische Glossen zu den alttürkischen Inschriften," *WZKM* 12 (1898), 157-200.

1901   "Ērānšahr nach der Geographie des Ps. Moses Xorenac'i," *Abh. Göttingen*, N.F. 3:2 (1901).

1903   *Osteuropäische und ostasiatische Streifzüge* (Leipzig, 1903).

1914   "Über das Volkstum der Komanen," *Abh. Göttingen*, N.F. 13:1 (1914).

1915   "Das Reich Zābul und der Gott Žūn, vom 6.-9. Jahrhundert," *Festschrift Ed. Sachau* (Berlin, 1915), 248-292.

1920   "Skizzen zur geschichtlichen Völkerkunde von Mittelasien und Siberien," *Ostasiatische Zeitschrift* 8 (Berlin, 1919-20), 289-299.

1924   "Ein arabischer Bericht über die arktischen (uralischen) Länder aus dem 10. Jahrhundert," *UJb* 4 (1924), 262-334.

1929   "Kultur- und sprachgeschichtliche Analekten," *UJb* 9 (1929), 68-103.

1930   *Südarmenien und die Tigrisquellen nach griechischen und armenischen Geographen* (Vienna, 1930).

1931   *A Catalogue of the Provincial Capitals of Ērānšahr, Analecta Orientalia* 3 (Rome, 1931).

1932a   *Die Entstehung der armenischen Bistümer* in *Orientalia Christiana* 27:2:80 (1932).

1932b   "Die Sigynnen," *Caucasica* 10 (Leipzig, 1932).

1938   *Wehrot und Arang* (Leiden, 1938).

Marshall, F. A.

1911   *Catalogue of the Jewellery, Greek, Etruscan and Roman, in the British Museum* (London, 1911).

Marshall, Sir J.

1951   *Taxila* (Cambridge, 1951).

Martin, F.-R.

1893   *L'âge du bronze au Musée de Minoussinsk* (Stockholm, 1893).

Martin, K.

1888   *Theodorich der Grosse bis zur Eroberung Italiens* (Freiburg, 1888).

Martynov, G. I.

1958   "Issykskaia nakhodka," *KS* 59 (1958), 150-156.

Materiale (*Materiale arheologice privind istoria veche* 4) from *Materiale si cercetări arheologice* 2, Academia Republicii Populare Romînei, Institutul de Arheologie (Bucharest, 1953-).

Materialy i issledovaniia po arkheologii SSSR (Moscow, 1918-).

Materialy khorezmskoǐ ekspeditsii 1-4 (Moscow).

Materialy po arkheologii Rossii (Moscow, 1866-1918).

Mather, R. B., trans. and annotator

1959   *Biography of Lü Kuang* (Berkeley and Los Angeles, 1959).

Matsulevich, L. A.

1929   *Byzantinische Spätantike* (1929).

1933   "K voprosu o stadial'nosti v gotskikh nadstroechnikh iavleniiakh," *Izv. GAIMK* 100 (1933).

1934   "Pogrebenie varvarskogo kniazia v vostochnoǐ Evrope," *Izv. GAIMK* 112 (1934).

1947   "Bliakhi-oberegi sarmatskogo pantsyria," *Soobshcheniia Gos. Ermitazha* 4 (1947).

Matthews, W. K.
1951   *Languages of the U.S.S.R.* (Cambridge, 1951).
Mayer, L. A.
1933   *Saracenic Heraldry* (Oxford, 1933).
Mazhitov, N. A.
1959   "Kurgannyĭ mogil'nik v derevne Novo-Turbasly," *Bashkirskiĭ arkheologicheskiĭ sbornik* (Ufa, 1959), 114-142.
Mazzarino, S.
1942   *Stilicone: la crisi imperiale dopo Teodosio* (Rome, 1942).
1956   *Trattato di storia romana* in Gianelli, G. and S. Mazzarino 2 (Rome, 1956).
McGeachy, J. A.
1942   *Quintus Aurelius Symmachus and the Senatorial Aristocracy of the West* (Chicago, 1942).
McLeod, W.
1965   "The Range of the Ancient Bow," *Phoenix* 19:1 (1965), 1-14.
Medinger, P.
1933   "L'arc turquois et les archers parthes à la bataille de Carrhes," *Revue archéologique* 7:2 (1933), 227-234.
Medvedev, A. F.
1959   "K istorii plastinchatogo dospekha na Rusi," *SA* 2 (1959), 119-134.
Melioranskiĭ, P.
1899   "Po povodu novoĭ arkheologicheskoĭ nakhodki v Aulieatinskom uezde," *Zapiski vostochn., otd. russk. arkheol. obshchestva* (1899), 271-272.
Meliukova, A. I.
1962   "Sarmatskoe pogrebenie iz kurgana u sela Oloneshty," *SA* 1 (1962), 195-208.
1964   *Vooruzhenie skifov, SIA* 1-4 (Moscow, 1964).
Mémoires de la socitété finno-ougrienne (Suomalais-ugrilainen seura toimituksia), (Helsingfors, 1890-).
Mendelssohn, L., ed.
1887   *Zosimi comitis et exadvocati fisci historia nova* (Leipzig, 1887).
Menges, K. H.
1945   Etymological Notes on Some Päčänäg Names," *Byzantion* 17 (1944-45), 256-280.
1951a   "Altaic Elements in the Proto-Bulgarian Inscriptions," *Byzantion* 21 (1951), 85-118.
1951b   "Oriental Elements in the Vocabulary of the Oldest Russian Epos," *Word* 7, monograph 1, supplement.
1954   *Glossar zu den volkskundlichen Texten aus Ost-Türkistan* (Wiesbaden, 1954).
Merpert, N. I.
1951   "O genezise Saltovskoĭ kul'tury," *KS* 36 (1951), 14-30.
1953   "Voprosy proiskhozhdeniia bulgar v knige A. P. Smirnova « Volzhkie bulgary »," *SA* 27 (1953), 274-284.
Mets, N. D.
1953   "Klady monet," *KS* 52 (1953), 113-120.
Meyer-Plath, B. and A. M. Schneider
1943   *Die Landmauer von Konstantinopel* 2 (Berlin, 1943).

Mierow, C. C., trans.
1915 *The Gothic History of Jordanes* (Princeton, 1915).
Migne, J. P.
1890 *Patrologiae Cursus, seria Latina* (Paris, 1854-90).
1899 *Patrologiae Cursus, seria Graeca* (Paris, 1857-99).
Milashevskaia, N. N.
1957 "Novye paleoantropologicheskie materialy iz Kenkol'skogo mogil'-nika," *Sovetskaia antropologiia* 2\(1957), 211-214.
1959 "Rezul'taty paleoantropologicheskikh issledovanii v Kirgizii," *Trudy Kazakh.* 2 (1959), 295-331.
1964 "Istoriia rasprostraneniia mongoloidnogo tipa na territorii Kir-gizii," *Tashkentskiĭ Universitet, Nauchnye trudy* 235 (Tashkent, 1964), 67-85.
Miller, Vs.
1886 Epigraficheskie sledy iranstva na iuge Rossii," *Zhurnal minis-terstva narodnogo prosveshcheniia* (October 1886).
Minaeva, T. M.
1927 "Pogrebeniia s sozhzheniem bliz g. Pokrovska," *UZSU* 6 (Sara-tov, 1927), 91-123.
1929 "Zwei Kurgane aus der Völkerwanderungszeit bei der Station Šipovo," *ESA* 4 (1929), 194-209.
1951 "Arkheologicheskie pamiatniki na r. Giliach v verkhoviakh Ku-bani," *MIA* 23 (1951), 273-301.
1956 "Mogil'nik Baĭtal-Chapkan v Cherkessii," *SA* 26 (1956), 236-261.
1960 "Poselenie v ust'e r. Uzun-kol," *SA* 2 (1960), 193-207.
Minns, E. H.
1913 *Scythians and Greeks* (Cambridge, 1913).
1945 *The Art of the Northern Nomads* in *Proc. Brit. Acad.* 1942 (London, 1945).
Minorsky, V.
1937 *Hudud al ʿAlam* (London, 1937).
1958 *A History of Sharvan and Darband* (Cambridge, 1958).
Mitrea, B.
1961 "Beiträge zum Studium der hunnischen Altertümer. Zwei neue hunnische Kesselgriffe aus dem südlichen Muntenien," *Dacia*, N.S. 5 (1961), 549-558.
Mitrea, B. and N. Anghelescu
1960 "Fragmente de Cazan Hunic descoperite în sud-estul Munteniei," *SCIV* 11 (1960).
Mitrea, B. and C. Preda
1966 *Necropole din secolul IV^lea E.N. în Muntenia* (Bucharest, 1966).
Mitscha-Märheim, H.
1953 "Neue Bodenfunde zur Geschichte der Langobarden und Slawen im österreichischen Donauraum," *Festschrift für Rudolf Egger* (Klagenfurt, 1953), 355-376.
1962 "Knochenbeschlag eines Reflexbogens," *Akten zum VII. inter-nationalen Kongress für Frühmittelalterforschung* (Graz and Co-logne, 1962), 350ff.
1963 *Dunkler Jahrhunderte goldene Spuren* (Vienna, 1963).

Mizuno, Seiichi and Namio Egami
1935 "Sui-yüan Bronzes" (Japanese) in *Inner Mongolia* (Tokyo and Kyoto, 1935), English summary 6-13.
Mnemosyne; Bibliotheca classica Batava, third series (Lugduni Batavorum, 1933/34-47).
Mogil'nikov, G. M.
1968 "Lesnye plemena Priirtysh'ia i nizhnego Priob'ia v I k nachale II tysiacheletii n.e.," *Istoriia Sibiri* (1968), 303-306.
Mohr, W.
1938 *Altgermanische Altertumskunde* (Munich, 1938).
Momigliano, A.
1955 "Cassiodorus and Italian Culture of His Time," *Proc. Brit. Acad.* (1955).
Mommsen, Th.
1882 *Jordanes (Jordanis Romana et Getica)*, Mommsen, Th., ed. (Berlin, 1882).
1894 *Variae I-II (Cassiodorus)*, Mommsen, Th., ed. (Berlin, 1894).
1895 *Collectanea Rerum Memorabilium*, Mommsen, Th., ed. (1895).
1898a *Chronica Minora*, Mommsen, Th., ed. in *MGH AA* 9, 11, 13 (Berlin, 1892-98).
1898b *Vita s. Severini* (Eugippius), Mommsen, Th., ed. (Berlin, 1898).
1901 "Aetius," *Hermes* 46 (1901), 516-547.
1905 *Reden und Aufsatze* (Berlin, 1905).
1906 *Historische Schriften* 1 (Berlin, 1906).
1909 *The Provinces of the Roman Empire* (London, 1909).
1913 *Gesammelte Schriften* 1-8 (1905-1913).
Mommsen, Th. and P. Meyer, ed.
1954 *Codex Theodosianus cum Constitutionibus Sirmondianis Leges* (Berlin, 1954).
Mommsen, Th. and Eduard Schwarz, ed.
1956 *Werke (Eusebius of Caesarea)*, suppl. to *GCS* (Leipzig, 1902-1956).
Monatsschrift für die Geschichte und Wissenschaft des Judentums, Ginzburg. L. (1899).
Il Mondo Classico; revista bimestrale bibliografica-scientifica-umanistica (Turin, 1931).
Mongaït, A. L.
1955 *Arkheologiia v SSSR* (Moscow, 1955).
Monneret de Villard, U.
1938 *Storia della Nubia christiana* in *Orientalia Christiana Analecta* 118 (Rome, 1938).
Montell, G.
1945 *History of the Sino-Swedish Expedition in Asia 1927-1937* (Stockholm, 1945).
Monumenta Germaniae Historica, Auctores Antiquissimi (Berlin, 1877-1919).
Monumenta Germaniae Historica, Scriptores rerum Merovingicarum, revised edition 1951 (1885-1919).
Monumenta Serica; Journal of Oriental Studies of the Catholic University of Peking (Peking, 1935/36-).
Moravcsik, Gy.
1930 "Zur Geschichte der Onoguren," *UJb* 10 (1930), 53-90.

1932   "Attilas Tod in Geschichte und Sage," *KCsA* 2 (1926-32), 83-116.

1933   "Die Namenliste der Gesandten am Konzil vom Jahre 869/70," *Izvestiia na istoricheskoto druzhestvo v Sofiia* 13 (1933), 8-23.

1946   "Byzantine Christianity and the Magyars in the Period of Their Migration," *The American Slavic and East European Review* (*Slavic Review*) 5 (1946), 29-45.

1949   *De administrando imperio* (*Constantine Porphyrogenitus*), (Greek), Moravcsik, Gy., ed. (Budapest, 1949).

1958   *Byzantinoturcica* 1-2 (*BT* 1: *Die byzantinische Quellen der Geschichte der Türkvolker; BT* 2: *Sprachreste der Türkvolker in den byzantinische Quellen* (Berlin, 1958).

Moricca, V., ed.

1924   *Dialogi de vita et miraculis patrum Italicorum* (*Gregory I,*) (Rome, 1924).

Morintz, S.

1959   "Nekotorye voprosy sarmatskogo naseleniia v Moldove i Muntenii v sviazi s Fokshanskim pogrebeniem," *Dacia* 3 (1959), 451-470.

1960   "Ein sarmatisches Grab aus Căscioarale," *Dacia* 4 (1960), 553-560.

Morrison, S. E.

1965   *The Oxford History of the American People* (Oxford, 1965).

Mosberg, G. I.

1946   "K izucheniiu mogil'nikov rimskogo vremeni iugo-zapadnogo Kryma," *SA* 8 (1946), 113-119.

Moshinskaia, V. I.

1953a   "Gorodishche i kurgany Potchevash," *MIA* 35 (1953), 189-220.

1953b   "Material'naia kul'tura khoziaĭstvo Ust'-Poluia," *MIA* 35 (1953), 72-106.

1965   *Arkheologicheskie pamiatniki severo-zapadnoĭ Sibiri* (Moscow, 1965).

Moshkova, M. G.

1960   "Rannesarmatskie bronzovye priazhki," *MIA* 78 (1960), 293-307.

1963   *Pamiatniki prokhorovskoĭ kul'tury* in *SAI* 1-10 (Moscow, 1963).

Moule, A. C. and P. Pelliot, ed. and trans.

1938   *The Description of the World* (*Marco Polo*), (London, 1938).

Movsēs Dasxurançi

1961   *The History of the Caucasian Albanians*, Dowsett, C. J. F., trans. (London, 1961).

Müllenhoff, K. V.

1847   *De antiquissima Germanorum poesi chorica* (Kiel, 1847).

1900   *Deutsche Altertumskunde* (Berlin, 1807-1900).

Müller, C., ed.

1882   *Geographi graeci minores* 2 (Paris, 1882).

1885   *Fragmenta Historicorum Graecorum* 4 (Paris, 1885).

1894   *Disserationes philologicae Vindobonenses* 4 (1894).

Müller, F. W. K.

1912   "Doppelblatt aus einem manichäischen Hymnenbuch (Mahrnâmag)," *Abh. Berlin* 5 (1912).

1915   "Zwei Pfahlinschriften aus den Turfanfunden," *Abh. Berlin* 3 (1915).

1920   *The Chronicle of Zacharias of Mytilene*, Müller, F. W. K., trans.,
        Ostasiat. Zeitshr. 8 (1919-20).

Müller, G.
1935   "Die gotische Fibel von Gátér in Ungarn," *Mannus* 27 (1935).

Müller, K. A., ed.
1938   *Claudian, De consulatii Honorii, in libro sexto* in *Neue deutsche
        Forschungen, Klassische Philologie* 7 (1938), 17-22.

Murphy, F. X.
1945   *Rufinus of Aquileia* (Washington, D. C., 1945).

Mutafčiev, P.
1932   *Bulgares et Roumains dans l'histoire des pays panubiens* (Sofia,
        1932).

Nakhodki v Kirgizii (Novye epigraficheskie nakhodki v Kirgizii—1962 g.),
        Batmanov, I. A., ed. (Frunze, 1962).

Narysy (Narysy starodavn'oĭ istoriĭ Ukraĭns'koĭ RSR), (Kiev, 1957).

Nash-Williams, V. E.
1932   "The Roman Legionary Fortress at Carleon in Monmouthshire,"
        Archaeologia Cambrensis 87:1 (1932), 48-104.

Nau, F.
1897   "Étude sur les parties inédites de la chronique ecclésiastique
        attribuée à Denys de Tellmahré," *Revue de l'orient chrétien* 2
        (1897). Also found in Markwart 1930.
1910   *Le Livre d'Héraclide de Damas*, Nau, F., trans. (Paris, 1910).
1913   *Histoire de l'église nestorienne (Barhadbeshabba Abbaia)*, Nau, F.,
        ed. and trans., *Hist. eccles.* 25 in *PO* 9:5 (Paris, 1913).

Negmatov, N.
1957   *Usrushana v drevnosti i rannem srednevekov'e* (Dushanbe, 1957).

Nehring, A.
1917   *Seele und Seelenkult bei den Griechen, Italikern und Germanen*
        (Breslau, 1917).

Nemeskéri, J.
1945   "Anthropological Examination of the Skull from Gyöngyosapáti,"
        AÉ (1945), 308-311.
1952   "An Anthropological Examination of Recent Macrocephalic Finds,"
        AAH 2 (1952), 223-232.

Németh, Gy.
1926   "Die Köktürkischen Grabinschriften aus dem Tale des Tala in
        Turkestan," *KCsA* 2 (1926), 134-143.
1929   "Szabirok és magyarok," *MNy* 25 (1929), 81-88.
1930   "Die Petschenegischen Stammesnamen," *UJb* 10 (1930), 27-34.
1940   *Attila és Hunjai*, Németh, Gy., ed. (Budapest, 1940).

Nerazik, E. E.
1958   "Arkheologicheskoe obsledovanie gorodischcha Kunia-Uaz v 1952
        g.," *Trudy Khor*, 3 (1958), 367-396.
1959   "Keramika Khorezma afrigidskogo perioda," *Trudy Khor.* 4 (1959),
        221-260.
1963   "Raskopki Iakke-Parsana," *Khor. Mat.* 7 (1963), 3-40.

Nerman, B.
1940   "Ännu en Konisk prakthjähn ifrån ett svenskt fynd," *Fornvännen*
        35 (1940).

Nestor, I. and C. S. Nicolăescu-Plopşor
1937   "Hunnische Kessel aus der kleinen Wallachei," *Germania* 21 (1937), 178-182.
Neuss, W.
1933   *Die Anfänge des Christentums im Rheinlande* (Bonn, 1933).
Nicene Fathers (*A Select Library of Nicene and Post-Nicene Fathers of the Christian Church*), second series, 2 (New York, 1890).
Nicolăescu-Plopşor, D.
1961   "Anthropologische Befunde über die Skelettreste aus dem Hunnengrab von Dulceanca (Rayon Rosiori)," *Dacia*, N.S. 5 (1961).
Nicolai Responsa (*Nicolaus I, Papa capitulis 106 ad consulta Bulgarorum respondet*), Perels, E., ed., *MGH EE* 6:4, 568-600.
Niebuhr, B. G., ed.
1829   *Corpus Scriptorum Historiae Byzantinae* (Bonn, 1829-).
Niederle, J.
1926   *Manuel de l'antiquité slave* (Paris, 1926).
Nikitina, G. F.
1964   "Poseleniia cherniakhovskoĭ kul'tury na srednem Dnestre," *SA* 2 (1964), 140-150.
Nil'sen, V. A.
1959   "Kyzyl-Kyr," *IMKU* 1 (1959), 60-78.
Nischer-Falkenhof, E.
1947   *Stilicho* (Vienna, 1947).
Nöldeke, Th., trans.
1879   *Geschichte der Perser und Araber zur Zeit der Sasaniden*, translated from the Arabian Chornicle of Tabari (Leiden, 1897).
Norden, E.
1927   *Die germanische Urgeschichte in Tacitus Germania* (Berlin, 1927).
1934   *Alt-Germanien* (Leipzig, 1934).
Norsk Tidsskrift for Sprogvidenskap (Oslo, 1928-).
Notitia dignitatum in partibus Occidentis Orientis (1839-1853; 1876).
Nouvelle Revue d'Hongrie (Budapest, 1908-).
Novye epigraficheskie nakhodki v Kirgizii (1961 *g.*), (Frunze, 1962).
Numismatic Chronicle (London, 1861-).
Numismatische Zeitschrift (Vienna, 1967-).
Nuovo Didaskaleion (Catania, 1947-).
Nurmukhammedov, Nagim-Bek
1970   *Iskusstvo Kazakhstana*, Veĭmarn, B. V., ed. (Moscow, 1970).
Obel'chenko, O. V.
1956   "Luiu-Mazarskiĭ mogil'nik," *Trudy instituta istorii i arkheologii AN Uzbekskoĭ SSR* 8 (1956), 205-227.
1957   "Kurgannye pogrebeniia pervykh vekov n.e. i kenotafy kuiumazarskogo mogil'nika v Bukharskoĭ oblasti," *Trudy sredneaziatiskogo gosudarstvennogo universiteta*, N.S. 111, *Istoriia nauki* 25 (1957).
1961   "Liavandakskiĭ mogil'nik," *IMKU* 2 (Tashkent, 1961), 97-174.
Oboldueva, T. G.
1948   "Kurgany kauchinskoĭ i dzhunskoĭ kul'tury v Tashkentskoĭ obl.," *KS* 23 (1948).
Obolensky, D.
1948   *The Bogomils* (Cambridge, 1948).

Oborin, V. A. and O. N. Bader
1958   Na zare istorii Prikam'ia (Perm, 1958).
Ocherki (Ocherki istorii SSSR. Krizis rabovladel'cheskoĭ sistemy i zarozhdenie
        feodalizma na territorii SSR III-IX vv. (Moscow, 1958).
Odobescu, A.
1906   Le Trésor de Petrossa (Paris, 1889-1906).
Österreichische Zeitschirft für Kunst und Denkmalpflege (Vienna, 1947-).
Okladnikov, A. P.
1940   "Pogrebenie bronzovogo veka v angarskoĭ taĭge," KS 8 (1940),
        106-112.
1950   "Neolit i bronzovyĭ vek Pribaĭkal'ia I-II," MIA 18 (1950).
1954   "Oleniĭ kamen' s r. Ivolgi," SA 19 (1954), 207-220.
1955a   Istoriia iakutskoĭ ASSR (Moscow and Leningrad, 1955).
1955b   "Neolit i bronzovyĭ vek Pribaĭkal'ia III," MIA 43 (1955).
Okladnikov, A. P. and V. D. Zaporozhskaia
1959   Lenskie pisanitsy (Moscow and Leningrad, 1959).
Omagiu lui Constantin Daicoviciu (Bucharest, 1960).
Oratio, Bidez, J., ed. (Paris, 1935-).
Orationes Themistii (see K. W. Dindorf 1928).
Orbeli, I. A. and K. V. Trever
1925   Sasanidskiĭ metall (Leningrad and Moscow, 1935).
Orbeli Anniversary Volume (Issledovaniia po istorii kul'tury narodov vostoka;
        sbornik v chest' akademika I. A. Orbeli (Moscow and Leningrad,
        1960).
Orkun, H. N.
1941   Eski türk yazitlari 1-4 (Istanbul, 1936-41).
Oshanin, L. V.
1954   "Etnogenez tadzhikov po dannym sravitel'noĭ antropologii tiurskikh
        i iranskikh narodov sredneĭ Azii," Trudy Tadzh. 27 (1954), 13-24.
1959   Antropologicheskiĭ sostav naseleniia sredneĭ Azii i etnogenez ee
        narodov 1-3 (Erevan, 1957-59).
Palanque, J.-R.
1931   "Famines à Rome à la fin du ive siècle," RÉA 33 (1931), 346-
        356.
1933   Saint Ambroise et l'empire romain (Paris, 1933).
1951   "La préfecture de prétoire de l'Illyricum au ive siècle," Byzantion
        31 (1951), 5-14.
Pamiatniki kul'tury sasanidskogo Irana (Leningrad, 1960).
Panciera, S.
1957   Vita economica di Aquileia in età Romana (Aquileia, 1957).
Pando, J. C.
1940   The Life and Time of Synesius of Cyrene as Revealed in His Works
        (Washington, D. C., 1940).
Papabasileos, G. A.
1896   'Αθηνα (1896).
Párducz, M.
1944   Denkmäler der Sarmatenzeit Ungarns I-III, AAH 25 (1941); AAH
        28 (1944).
1949   "Dom v g. Mokhach iz vremen pereseleniia narodov," AÉ 76
        (1949).

1959   "Archäologische Beiträge zur Geschichte der Hunnenzeit in Ungarn," *AAH* 11:1-4 (1959), 309-398.
1963   *Die ethnischen Probleme der Hunnenzeit in Ungarn* (Budapest, 1963).

Párducz, M. and J. Korek
1948   "Éléments germaniques dans la civilisation sarmatique récente de la région limitée par les fleuves Maros, Tisza et Körös," *AÉ* 7-9 (1946-48), 299-312.

Paredi, A.
1937   *I prefazi Ambrosiani* (Milan, 1937).

Patrologia Orientalis, Graffin, R., ed. (Paris, 1907-).

Patrologiae Cursus, seria Graeca, Migne, J. P., ed. (Paris, 1857-99).

Patrologiae Cursus, seria Latina, Migne, J. P., ed. (Paris, 1854-90).

Patsch, C.
1925   "Banater Sarmaten," *Anz. Wien* 66 (1925), 181-216.
1928   "Die Völkerbewegung an der unteren Donau in der Zeit von Diokletian bis Heraklius. I: Bis zur Abwanderung der Goten und Taifalen aus Transdanuvien," *SB Wien* 208:2 (1928).
1931   "Die quadisch-jazygische Kriegsgemeinschaft im Jahre 374/5," *SB Wien* 209:5 (1931).
1932   "Aus 500 Jahren vorrömischer und römischer Geschichte Südosteuropas. I: Bis zur Festsetzung der Römer in Transdanuvien," *SB Wien* 214:1 (1932).
1940   "Der Kampf um den Donauraum unter Domitian und Trajan," *SB Wien* 217:1 (1940).

Paudler, F.
1933   "Dātrākarna," *Festschrift für M. Winternitz* (Leipzig, 1933).

Pauly-Wissowa-Kroll (*Realencyklopädie der klassischen Altertumswissenschaft*), (Stuttgart, 1893-).

Pearce, J. W. E.
1938   "The Reign of Theodosius I," *Transactions of the International Numismatic Congress* (London, 1938), 235-237.

Peeters, P.
1914   "La canonisation des saints dans l'église russe," *Analecta Bollandiana* 33 (1914).
1932   "Un colophon gèorgien de Thornik le Moine," *Analecta Bollandiana* 50 (1932).
1950   *Le tréfonds oriental de l'hagiographie byzantine* (Brussels, 1950).
1951   *Recherches d'histoire et de philologie orientales* 1 (Brussels, 1951).

Pelliot, P.
1950   *Notes sur l'histoire de la horde d'or* (Paris, 1950).

Pelliot, P. and L. Hambis
1951   *Histoire des campagnes de Gengiz-Khan I* (Leiden, 1951).

Perels, E., ed. (*see Nicolai Responsa*).

Perets, V. N.
1926   *Slovo o polku Igorevi* (Kiev, 1926).

Pervonaoglu, J.
1904   *Greek-English Lexicon* (Athens, 1904).

Peshanov, V. F.
1961   "Metropol'skaia diadema," *KSIA* 11 (1961), 70-74.

Petersen, E.
1939   Der ostelbische Raum als germanisches Kraftfeld im Lichte der Bodenfunde des 6.-8. Jahrhunderts (Leipzig, 1939).
Petri, B. E.
1928   Dalekoe proshloe Pribaĭkal'ia (Irkutsk, 1928).
Petrov, K. I.
1963   In Ocherk proiskhozhdeniia kirgizskogo naroda (Frunze, 1963).
Petrov, V. P.
1964a   "Cherniakovskiĭ mogil'nik," MIA 116 (1964), 53-117.
1964b   "Maslovskiĭ mogil'nik na r. Tovmach," MIA 116 (1964), 118-167.
Petrov, V. P. and A. P. Kalshchuk
1964   "Skarb skribnikh recheĭ z s. Kachyn, Volynskoĭ oblasti," Materialy i doslidzhennia z arkheolohii Prykarpattia i Volyni 5 (1964), 88-93.
Piatysheva, N. V.
1956   Iuvelirnye izdeliia Khersonesa (Moscow, 1956).
Pichlmayer, F., ed.
1911   Sexti Aurelii Victoris Liber de caesaribus (Leipzig, 1911).
Pichon, R.
1906   Les derniers écrivains profanes (Paris, 1906).
Pick, B. and G. Rigling
1910   Die antiken Münzen Nord-Griechenlands (Berlin, 1898-1910).
Pighi, J. B., ed.
1948   Ammiani Marcellini rerum gestarum capita selecta (Neuchâtel, 1948), 68-71.
Pigulevskaia, N.
1939   "Siriĭskiĭ istochnik VI v. o narodakh Kavkaza," VDI 1:6 (1939), 107-115.
1940   Mesopotamia na rubezhe V-VI vv. n.e. (Moscow and Leningrad, 1940).
1957   Feofilakt Simokatta, Pigulevskaia, N. V., trans. (Moscow, 1957).
Pinder, M. E. and G. Parthey, ed.
1848   Itinerarium Antonini Augusti et Hierosolymitanum (Berlin, 1848).
Piotrovskiĭ, B. B.
1949   "Raskopki urartskoĭ kreposti na kholme Kamir-Blur (Teishe-baini)," KS 27 (1949), 3-10.
1955   Kamir-Blur (Erevan, 1955).
1959   Vanskoe tsarstvo (Moscow, 1959).
Pipidi, D. M.
1959   Contribuţii la istoria veche a Rominiei (Bucharest, 1958).
Platnauer, M., ed. and trans.
1922   Claudian in The Loeb Classical Library (Cambridge, Mass., 1922).
Pleidell, A.
1934   "Das erste Kapitel der ungarischen Städtegeschichte," Századok 58 (1934), 1-9.
Pletneva, S. A.
1958   "Pechenegi, torki i polovtsy v iuzhnorusskikh stepiakh," MIA 62 (1958), 200-204.
1960   "Srednevekovye poseleniia verkhov'ev Severskogo Dona," KS 3? (1960).

Po sledam (*Po sledam drevnikh kul'tur, Ot Volgi do tikhogo okeana*), Bernshtam, A. N. (Moscow, 1954).

Pochettino, I. G.
1930   *I Langobardi nell'Italia meridionale* (Caserta 1930).

Pogrebova, N. N.
1958   "Pozdneskifskie gorodishcha na nizhnem Dnepre," *MIA* 64 (1958), 103-247.

Pokoshev, N. A.
1948   "Iz materialov po izucheniiu ananinskoĭ epokhi," *SA* 10 (1948), 183-202.

Pokrovskaia, L. A.
1961   "Terminy rodstva v tiuretskikh iazykakh" in *Istoricheskoe razvitie leksiki tiuretskikh iazykov* (Moscow, 1961).

Polevoĭ, L. L.
1965   In *Istoriia Moldavskoĭ SSR* (Kishinev, 1965).

Polivanova, V.
1890   "Zametka o proiskhozhdenii mednago sosuda iz Sengileevskago uezda, Simbirskoĭ gubernii," *Trudy VII AS* 1 (Iaroslavl'); 39 (Moscow, 1890).

Pope, S. T.
1962   *Bows and Arrows* (Berkeley and Los Angeles, 1962).

Popović, I.
1961   "Quel était le peuple pannonien qui parlait $\mu\varepsilon\delta o\varsigma$ et strava?," *Sbornik radova Vizantoloshkog instituta* (1961), 197-226.

Porada, E.
1963   *Iran ancien* (Paris, 1963).

Post, P.
1953   "Der kupferne Spangelhelm," *34. Bericht der römisch-germanischen Kommission 1951-1953*, (Berlin, 1951-53), 115-150.

Posta, B.
1905   *Archäologische Studien auf russischem Boden* (Budapest, 1905).

Potapov, A. P.
1949   "Osobennosti material'noĭ kul'tury kazakhov, obuslovlennye kochevym obrazom zhizni," *SMAE* 12 (1949), 43-70.

Poucha, P.
1955   *Thesaurus linguare tachariae dialecti A* (Prague, 1955).
1956   *Die geheime Geschichte der Mongolen* (Prague, 1956).

Poulik, J.
1950   *Jižní Murava—zemé davnych Slovanů* (Brno, 1950).

Povest' vremennykh let (Moscow and Leningrad).

Prähistorische Zeitschrift (Berlin, 1909-).

Preda, C.
1961   "Săpăturile de salvare de la Olteni," *Materiale* 7 (1961), (French summary) 510-511.

Preger, Th., ed.
1907   *Patria Constantinopolis* (*Scriptores originum Constantinopolitarum*), (Leipzig, 1907).

Preisigke, F.
1922   *Namenbuch* (Heidelberg, 1922).

Pridik, E.
1914　"Novye kavkazskie klady," *MAR* 34 (1914).
Pritsak, O.
1952　"Stammesnamen und Titulaturen der altaischen Völker," *UJb* 24 (1952), 49-104.
1954a　"Kultur und Sprache der Hunnen," *Festschrift für Dmytro Čyševs'kyj zum 60. Geburtstag* (Berlin, 1954), 238-249.
1954b　"Ein hunnisches Wort," *ZDMG* 104 (1934), 124-136.
1955　*Die bulgarische Fürstenliste und die Sprache der Protobulgaren* (Wiesbaden 1955).
1956　"Der Titel Attila," *Festschrift für Max Vasmer; Veröffentlichungen der Abteilung für slavische Sprachen und Literaturen des Osteuropa-Instituts an der freien Universität Berlin* (Berlin, 1956), 404-419.
Problemy istorii severnogo Prichernomor'ia v antichnuiu epokhu (Moscow, 1959).
Protase, D.
1960　"Ein Grab aus dem 5. Jahrhundert aus Cepari (Transilvanien)," *Dacia*, N.S. 4 (1960), 569-575.
Przyluski, J.
1950　*La grande Déesse* (Paris, 1950).
Pugachenkova, G. A. and L. I. Rempel'
1965　*Istoriia iskusstv Uzbekistana* (Moscow, 1965).
Pulleyblank, E. G.
1962　"The Consonantal System of Old Chinese," *Asia Mayor* 9:1:2 (1962), 57-144.
1963　"The Consonantal System of Old Chinese," *Asia Mayor* (1963), 205-265.
1966　"Chinese and Indoeuropeans," *JRAS* (1966), 9-39.
Radin, M.
1919　*Studies on Uncomposed Names in Old English* (Uppsala, 1919).
Radlov, V. V.
1893　*Aus Sibirien* (Leipzig, 1893).
1894　*Sibiriskie drevnosti* in *MAR* 15 (1894).
1899　*Die alltürkischen Inschriften der Mongolei* 1-3, zweite Folge (St. Petersburg, 1889).
Raeder, J., ed.
1904　*Theodoreti Graecorum affectionum curatio* (Leipzig, 1904).
Räsänen, M.
1949　*Materialen zur Lautgeschichte der türkischen Sprachen* (Helsinki, 1949).
Raevskiĭ, K. A.
1955　"Nazemnye sooruzheniia zemledel'tsev mezhdurech'ia Dnepra-Dnestra v I tysiacheletii n.e.," *SA* 23 (1955), 250-276.
Rakhimov, M.
1959　*Materialy vtorogo soobshcheniia arkheologov i etnografov srednei Azii* (Moscow and Leningrad, 1959).
Ramstedt, G. I.
1951　"Alte türkische und mongolische Titel," *JSFOU* 55 (1951).
Rapoport, Iu. A.
1958　"Raskopki gorodishcha Shakh-Senem," *Trudy Khor.* 2 (1958), 397-420.

Rapoport, Iu. A. and S. A. Trudnovskaia
1958   "Gorodishche Giaur-Kala," *Trudy Khor.* 2 (1958).
Rappaport, B.
1899   *Die Einfälle der Goten in das römische Reich* (Leipzig, 1899).
Raschke, G.
1940   "Zum Bronzekessel von Raase-Bennisch," *Altschlesien* 9 (1940), 114-119.
Rásonyi, L.
1932   "A honfoglaló magyarsággal Kapcsolators török tulajdonnevek-herz," *MNy* 18 (1932), 100-105.
1953   "Sur quelques catégories des noms de personnes en turc," *Acta Linguistica* 3 (1953), 323-350.
1961   "Les noms de nombre dans l'anthroponymie turque," *AOH* 12:1-3 (1961), 45-71.
Rattisti, C.
1956   *I Goti in Occidente* (Spoleto, 1956).
Rau, P. D.
1926   *Die Hügelgräber römischer Zeit an der unteren Wolga. Mitteilungen des Zentralmuseums der Autonomen Sozialistischen Räterepublik der Wolgadeutschen* 1 (Pokrovsk, 1926).
1927   *Prähistorische Ausgrabungen auf der Steppenseite des deutschen Wolgagebiets im Jahre 1926. Mitteilungen des Zentralsmuseums der Autonomen Sozialistischen Räterepublik der Wolgadeutschen* 2 (Pokrovsk, 1927).
1928   *Kurgany s kostrishchami i kostrishcha v kurganakh nizhnego Povolzh'ia, TSARANION* 4 (1928), 431ff.
Rauschen, G.
1897   *Jahrbücher der christliche Kirche unter Kaiser Theodosius* (Freiburg, 1897).
Realencyclopädie der klassischen Altertumswissenschaft (see Pauly-Wissowa).
Realencyclopädie für protestantische Theologie und Kirche (Leipzig, 1896-1913).
Reallexikon der Vorgeschichte, Ebert, M., ed. (Berlin).
Regling, K.
1932   "Dynastenmünzen von Tyana, Morima und Anisa in Kappadokien," *ZfN* 42 (1932), 1-23.
Reichel, W.
1942   *Griechisches Goldrelief* (Berlin, 1942).
Reinelt, P.
1903   *Studien über die Briefe des hl. Paulinus von Nola* (Breslau, 1903).
Remmenikov, A. M.
1954   *Bor'ba plemen severnogo Prichernomor'ia v III veke n.e.* (Moscow, 1954).
Res gestae Saporis (Recherches sur les Res gestae Saporis), by Honigmann, E. and A. Maricq (Brussels, 1953).
Responsa Nicolai (see *Nicolai Responsa*).
Revista istorică română (Bucharest, 1931-).
Revue archéologique, third series (Paris, 1883-).
Revue belge de philologie et d'histoire (Brussels, 1922-).
Revue Charlemagne; consacrée à l'archéologie et à l'histoire du haut moyen âge (Paris, 1911-12).

Revue d'histoire ecclésiastique (Louvain, 1900-).
Revue d'histoire et de littérature religieuses, N.S. (1910-22).
Revue des études anciennes (Bordeaux, 1899-).
Revue des études byzantines (Saint-Cloud, 1943-).
Revue des études grecques (Paris, 1888-).
Revue des études hongroises (*Revue d'histoire comparée*), (Paris, 1923-).
Revue des études slaves (Paris, 1921-).
Revue des sciences philosophiques et théoriques (Paris, 1907-).
Revue historique (Paris, 1876-).
Revue historique du sud-est européen (Bucharest, 1924-).
Revue internationale d'histoire militaire (Paris, 1939-).
Revue internationale des études balkaniques (Belgrade,1934-).
Rheinische Forschungen zur Vorgeschichte 2, Kühn, H., ed. (1937).
Ridgeway, W.
   1906   *The Origin and Influence of the Thoroughbred Horse* (Cambridge, 1906).
Rikman, E. A.
   1957   "Raskopki selishcheĭ pervykh vekov nasheĭ ery v Podnestrov'e," *KS* 68 (1957), 75-83.
   1958   "Mogil'nik pervykh stoletiĭ novoĭ ery u s. Budeshty v Moldavii," *SA* (1958), 187-200.
   1960   "Zhilishcha budeshtskogo selishcha," *MIA* 82 (1960), 303-327.
   1967   *Pamiatnik epokhi velikogo pereseleniia narodov* (Kishinev, 1967).
Rockhill, W. W.
   1900   *William of Rubruk* (London, 1900).
Römisch-germanische Kommission des Deutschen archäologischen Instituts, source of *Germania* (Berlin and Leipzig).
Roginskiĭ, Ia. Ia. and M. G. Levin
   1955   *Osnovy antropologii* (Moscow and Leningrad, 1955).
Rolfe, J. C., ed. and trans.
   1939   *Ammianus Marcellinus* in *Loeb* (Cambridge, Mass., 1939).
Romana (see Mommsen 1882).
Romano, G. and A. Solmi
   1940   *Le dominazioni barbariche in Italia* (*395-888*), (Milan, 1940).
Roos, A. G., ed.
   1928   *Flavii Arriani quae exstant omnia* (Leipzig, 1907-1928).
Rosenfeld, H.
   1956   "Goten und Greutungen," *Beiträge zur Namenforschung* (1956), 195-206.
   1957a "Goten und Greutungen," *Beiträge zur Namenforschung* (1957), 36-43.
   1957b "Ost- und Westgoten," *Die Welt als Geschichte* (1957), 245-258.
Rostovtsev, M. I.
   1914   *Antichnaia dekorativnaia zhivopis' na iuge Rossii* (St. Petersburg, 1913-14).
   1921   "Le culte de la grande déesse dans la Russie mériodionale, *Revue des études grecques* 32 (1921), 462-481.
   1922   *Iranians and Greeks in South Russia* (Oxford, 1922).
   1923   "Une trouvaille de l'époque greco-sarmate de Kertch," *Fondation E. Piot. Monuments et mémoires* 26 (1923), 99-163.

1929   *Le centre de l'Asie, la Russie, la Chine et le style animal* (Prague, 1929).

1930   *A History of the Bosporus*, second ed. (Oxford, 1930).

1931   *Skythien und der Bosporus* (Berlin, 1931).

Roux, J. P.
1959   "L'origine céleste de la souveraineté dans les inscriptions paléo-turques de Mongolie et de Sibérie," *La regalità sacrà. The Sacral Kingship* (Leiden, 1959).

Roy, P. Ch., trans.
1887   *Mahābhārata* (Calcutta, 1887).

Rubin, B.
1954   *Prokopios von Kaisareia* (Stuttgart, 1954).

1960   *Das Zeitalter Justinians* (Berlin, 1960).

Rudenko, S. I.
1953   *Kul'tura naseleniia gornogo altaia v skifskoe vremia* (Moscow and Leningrad, 1953).

1960   *Kul'tura naseleniia tsentral'nogo altaia v skifskoe vremia* (Moscow, 1960).

1962a   *Kul'tura khunnov i noinulskie kurgany* (Moscow and Leningrad, (1962).

1962b   *Sibirskaia kollektsiia Petra I* (Moscow and Leningrad, 1962).

Rudinskiĭ, M. Ia.
1930   "Kantemyrivs'ky mohyly ryms'koĭ doby," *Zapiski vseukraïns'kogo arkheologichnogo komitetu* 1 (1930), 127-126; (French summary) 156-158.

Rudolph, R. C.
1951   *Han Tomb Art of West China* (Berkeley and Los Angeles, 1951).

Runciman, S.
1930   *A History of the First Bulgarian Empire* (London, 1930).

Rupp, H.
1937   *Die Herkunft der Zelleneinlage und die Almandinscheibenfibeln im Rheinland* in *Rheinische Forschungen zur Vorgeschichte* 2 (1937).

Rybakov, B. A.
1957   "Mesto slaviano-russkoĭ arkheologii v sovetskoĭ istoricheskoĭ nauke," *SA* 4 (1957), 55-65.

1958   "Slaviane v Evrope v epokhu rabovladel'cheskogo stroia," *Ocherki* (1958), 30-52.

Rygdylon, E. R. and P. P. Khoroshikh
1959   "Kollektsiia bronzovykh kotlov Irkutskogo muzeia," *SA* 1 (1959), 253-258.

Rykov, P. S.
1925   "Suslovskiĭ kurgannyĭ mogil'nik," *UZSU* 4 (1925), 28-81.

1926   "Arkheologicheskie raskopki i razvedki v Nizhnem Povolzh'e i uralskom krae letom 1925 g.," *Izvestiia kraevedcheskogo instituta izucheniia Iuzhno-Volzhskoĭ oblasti pri Saratovskom gosudarstvennom universitete* 1 (1926), 89-134.

1929   "Izvestiia razvedki i raskopki v Nizhnevolzhskom krae, proizvedennye v 1928 g.," *ISNIK* 3 (1929), 131-155.

1931   "Otchet ob arkheologicheskikh rabotakh, proizvedennykh v Nizhnem Povolzh'e letom 1929 g.," *ISNIK* 4 (1931), 49-79.

1936a "Arkheologicheskie raskopki kurganov v urochishche 'Tri Brata' v Kalm. oblasti, proizvedennye v 1933 i 1934 gg.," *SA* 1 (1936), 115-157.
1936b *Ocherki po istorii Nizhnego Povolzh'ia po arkheologicheskim materialam* (Saratov, 1936).
1936c "Raskopki kurgannogo mogil'nika v raĭone g. Elisty," *ISNIK* 7 (1936), 57-70.

Sadée, E.
1938 "Frühgermanische Wagenzüge und Wagenburgen," *Festschrift für August Oxé* (Darmstadt, 1938).

Sadykova, M. Kh.
1962a "Novye pamiatniki zheleznogo veka Bashkirii," *Arkheologiia i etnografiia Bashkirii* (Ufa, 1962), 88-122.
1962b "Sarmatskie pamiatniki Bashkirii," *MIA* 115 (1962), 242-273.
1962c "Sarmatskiĭ mogil'nik v der. Starye Kiishki," *Arkheologiia i Etnografiia Bashkirii* (Ufa, 1962), 88-122.

Saeculum; SS. patrum aegyptiorum opera omnia 4, Migne, J. P., ed. (Paris, 1858).

Salin, E.
1950 *La civilisation mérovingienne* (Paris, 1950).
1968 *Académie des inscriptions et belles-lettres. Comptes rendus des séances de l'année 1967* (Paris, 1968).

Salin, E. and France-Lanord, A.
1949 "Le trésor d'Arian en Calvados," *Fondation E. Piot, Monuments et mémoires* 42 (1949), 119-135.

Salmony, A.
1933 *Sino-Siberian Art in the Collection of C. T. Loo* (Paris, 1933).
1935 *Sino-Siberian Art* (Paris, 1935).

Sal'nikov, K. V.
1940 "Sarmatskie kurgany bliz g. Orska," *MIA* 1 (1940), 121-238.
1948 *Drevneĭshie naselenie Cheliabinskoĭ oblasti* (Cheliabinsk, 1948).
1950 "Sarmatskie pogrebeniia v raĭone Magnitogorska," *KS* 34 (1950), 115-121.
1951 "Arkheologicheskie issledovaniia v kurganskoĭ cheliabinskoĭ oblastiakh," *KS* 37 (1951), 88-96.
1952 *Drevneĭshie pamiatniki istorii Urala* (Sverdlosk, 1952).

Sammlung Trau (Vienna, 1935).

Samokvasov, D. Ia.
1908 *Mogily russkoĭ zemli* (Moscow, 1908).

San Lazzaro, Cl. di
1938 "Missis etiam per Marcianum principem Aetio duce caeduntur auxiliis," *Convivium* 10 1(938), 338-389.

Sanford, E. M., trans.
1930 *On the Government of God* (New York, 1930).

Saria, B.
1939 "Der spätrömische Limes im westlichen Jugoslawien," *Studi Bizantini e Neoellenici* 5 (1939), 308-316.

Sarre, F.
1922 *Die Kunst des alten Persien* (Berlin, 1922).

Satterer, J. Ch.
1798   Göttingen, Commentationes historica et philologica (1797-98).
Sauter, Marc-R.
1961   Quelques contributions de l'antropologie à la connaissance du haut moyen âge," Mémoires et documents publiés par la société d'histoire et d'archéologie de Genève 40 (Geneva, 1961), 1-18.
Sauvaget, J.
1950   "Noms et surnoms de Mamelouks," JA 228 (1950), 31-38.
Schaeffer, C. F. A.
1968   Ugarica 1-5, Bibliothèque archéologique et historique 31, 47, 64, 74, 80 (Paris 1939-68). At head of title: Mission de Ras Shamra 3, 5, 8, 15, 16.
Schafer, E. H.
1950   "The Camel in China down to the Mongol Dynasty," Sinologica 2 (1950).
1963   Golden Peaches of Samarkand (Berkeley and Los Angeles, 1963).
Scheffer, J., ed.
1664   Arriani Tactica et Mauricii artis militaris libri duodecim (Uppsala, 1664).
Schiltberger, H.
1885   Hans Schiltbergers Reisebuch, Bibliothek des litterarischen Vereins zu Stuttgart 172 (Tübingen, 1885).
Schirren, C.
1846   De ratione quae inter Iordanem et Cassiodorum intercedat commentatio (Dorpat, 1846).
Schmidt, A. V.
1927   "Kačka," ESA 1 (1927), 18-50.
Schmidt, B.
1961   Die späte Völkerwanderungszeit in Mitteldeutschland (Halle, 1961).
Schmidt, K. D.
1939   Die Bekehrung der Germanen zum Christentum (Göttingen, 1939).
Schmidt, L.
1909   Allgemeine Geschichte der germanischen Völker bis zur Mitte des sechsten Jahrhunderts (Munich and Berlin, 1909).
1927   "Die Ostgoten in Pannonien," UJb 6 (1927), 459-460.
1934   Geschichte der deutschen Stämme bis zum Ausgang der Völkerwanderung. Die Ostgermanen (Munich, 1934).
1942   Die Wandalen (Munich, 1942).
Schneider, A. M. (see Meyer-Plath and Schneider 1943).
Schneider, H.
1934   Germanische Heldensage II (Berlin, 1934).
1954   Geistesgschichte des antiken Christentums (Munich, 1954).
Schönemann, K.
n.d.   Die Entstehung des Städtwesens in Südosteuropa (Breslau, n.d.).
1925   "Hunnen und Ungarn," UJb 5 (1925), 293-303.
Schönfeld, M.
1911   Wörterbuch der altgermanischen Personen- und Völkernamen (Heidelberg, 1911).
Schoff, W. H., trans.
1927   Periplus of the Outer Sea (Philadelphia, 1927).

Schoppa, H.
1933   *Die Darstellungen der Perser in der griechischen Kunst bis zum Beginn des Hellinismus* (Heidelberg, 1933).

Schott, L.
1961   "Derformierte Schädel aus der Merowingerzeit Mitteldeutschlands in antropologischer Sicht," in B. Schmidt (1961), 211-226.

Schramm, G.
1960   "Eine hunnisch-germanische Namenbeziehung?" *Jahrbuch für fränkische Landesforschung* 20:1 (1960), 129-155.
1965   "Horizonte geschichtlichen Wissens von Osteuropas im Spiegel der Nameüberlieferung," *Jahrbücher für Geschichte Osteuropas*, N.F. 13:1 (1965).

Schramm, P. E.
1955   *Herrschaftszeichen und Staatssymbolik I-II* (Stuttgart, 1954-55).

Schröder, E.
1922   "Die Leichenfeier für Attila," *ZfDA* 59 (1922), 240-244.

Schubert, H. von
1911   "Die Anfänge des Christentums bei den Burgundern," *SB Heidelberg* 3 (1911).

Schück, H.
1918   *Studien i Hervararsagen* in *Uppsala Universitets Årsskrift* 3:2 (Uppsala, 1918).

Schulz, W.
1939   *Vor- und Frühgeschichte Mitteldeutschlands* (Halle, 1939).
1940   *Die thüringer* in *Vorgeschichte der deutschen Stämme*.
1942   "Funde der spätgermanischen Zeit (7. Jahrhundert) von Stossen, Kreis Weissenfelds," *Nachrichtenblatt für deutsche Vorzeit* 18 (1942), 21-23.

Schwarz, Eduard, ed.
1932   *Acta Conciliorum Œcumenicorum* (Berlin and Leipzig, 1932).

Schwarz, Ernest
1929   "Die Frage der slavische Landnahme in Ostgermanien," *Mitteilungen des österreichischen Instituts für Geschichtsforschung* 43 (1929), 187-260.
1934   "Publizistische Sammlungen zum Acaciaschen Schisma," *Abh. München* 10 (1934).
1936   *Germanische Stammeskunde* (Heidelberg, 1936).
1939   "Kyrillos von Scythopolis," *TU* 49:2 (IV :4:2).
1951   *Goten, Nordgermanen, Angelsachsen* (Bern, 1951).
1954   "Das Problem der Herkunft der Baiern," *Forschungen und Fortschritte* 28:9 (1954).
1956   *Germanische Stammeskunde* (Heidelberg, 1956).

Schwidetzky, I.
1963   "Europide und Mongolide in Russisch-Asien seit dem Jungpaläolithikum," *Homo* 14:3 (1963), 151-167.

Schwyzer, E.
1914   "Die sprachlichen Interessen des Prokops von Cäsarea," *Festgabe Hugo Blümner* (Zürich, 1914), 303-327. Also in *ZfDA* 66 (1929), 94-100.

Seeck, O.
1913   *Geschichte des Untergangs der antiken Welt* 5 (Berlin, 1913).
1919   *Regesten der Kaiser und Päpste* (Stuttgart, 1919).
1920   *Geschichte des Untergangs der antiken Welt* 6 (Stuttgart, 1920).
1923   *Geschichte des Untergangs der antiken Welt* (Stuttgart, 1921-23).
Segalen, V., de Voisins, G. and J. Lartigue.
1924   *Mission archéologique en Chine* (Paris, 1923-24).
Sekino, Tadashi et al.
1927   *Rakuro-gun jidai no iseki* (*Archaeological Researches on the An-
       cient Lolang District*) 4: *Koseki chōsa tokubetsu hōko* (*Archaeological
       Survey; special report*), text volume and 200 plates (Seoul?, 1925-27).
Sekino, Takeshi
1956   *Chūgoku kōkogaku kenkyū* (*A Study of Chinese Archaeology*), (To-
       kyo, 1956).
Semeniuk, G. I.
1958   "K probleme rabstva u kochevykh narodov," *Izv. Kazakh.* 1:6
       (1958), 55-82.
Seminarium Kondakovianum, Institut Kondakov (Prague, 1927-).
Senigova, T. N.
1956   "Otchet o rabote zapadno-kazakhstanskoĭ arkheologicheskoĭ ek-
       speditsii 1953 g.," *Trudy Kazakh.* 1 (1956), 140-156.
1959   "K izucheniiu tekhnicheskikh osobennosteĭ keramiki nizov'ia Syr-
       Dar'i," *Trudy Kazakh.* 7 (1959), 215-231.
Serebrennikov, B. A.
1960   "O nekotorykh spornykh voprosakh sravnitel'no-istoricheskoĭ fo-
       netiki tiurskikh iazykov," *Voprosy russkogo iazykoznaniia* 4 (1960),
       62-72.
Settegast
1904   *Quellenstudien zur gallo-romanischen Epik* (Leipzig, 1904).
Seyrig, H.
1937   "Armes et costumes iraniens de Palmyre," *Syria* 18 (1937).
Shakhmatov, A. A.
1919   *Drevneĭshie sud'by russkago plemeni* (Petrograd, 1919).
Shcherbak, A. M.
1959   *Oguz-nāme* (Moscow, 1959).
Shelov, D. B.
1950   "K voprosu o vzaimodeĭstvii grecheskikh i mestnykh kul'tov
       v severnom Prichernomor'e," *KS* 34 (1950), 62-69.
1961   *Nekropol' Tanaisa* in *MIA* 98 (1961).
1962   "Novye dannye o Tanaise," *Arkheologicheskie raskopki na Donu*
       (Rostov, 1962), 70-77.
1965   "Raskopki severo-vostochnogo uchastka Tanais," *MIA* 127 (1965),
       56-129.
1966   "Nizhne-Donskaia ekspeditsiia v 1962-63 gg.," *KS* 107 (1966).
1967   *Tanais* (Moscow, 1967).
Shilov, V. P.
1950   *Pogrebeniia sarmatskoĭ znati* (1950?).
1959   "Kalinovskiĭ kurgannyĭ mogil'nik," *MIA* 60 (1959), 323-523.
Shleev, V. V.
1950   "K voprosu o skifskikh navershiiakh," *KS* 34 (1950), 53-61.

Shovkoplyas, I. G.
1957   *Arkheologichni doslidzhennia na Ukraini* (1917-1957), (Kiev, 1957).
Shul'ts, N. P.
1953   *Mavzoleĭ Neapolia skifskogo* (Moscow, 1953).
1957   "Issledovaniia Neapolia skifskogo (1945-1950 gg.)," *Istoriia i arheologiia drevnego Kryma* (Kiev, 1957), 61-93.
Sickman, L. and A. Soper
1956   *The Art and Architecture of China* (Baltimore, 1956).
Sieg, E., Siegling, W. and W. Schultze
1931   *Tocharische Grammatik* (Göttingen, 1931).
Sigonoa, C.
1732   *De occidentali imperio* (Milan, 1732).
Šimek, E
1935   *Velká Germanie Klaudia Ptolemaia II* (Brno, 1935).
Simmons, P.
1948   *Chinese Patterned Silk* (New York, 1948).
Simonyi, D.
1955   "Das Kontinuitätsproblem und das Erscheinen der Slawen in Pannonien," *Studia Slavica* 1 (1955), 333-361.
1959   "Die Bulgaren des 5. Jahrhunderts im Karpatenbecken," *AAH* 10 (1959), 227-250.
Sinica; Zeitschrift für Chinakunde und Chinaforschung (Heidelberg, 1925-).
Sinica Franciscana (Florence, 1929-).
Sinitsyn, I. V.
1932   "Sarmatskie kurgannye pogrebeniia v severnykh raĭonakh Nizhnego Povolzh'ia," *Sbornik Nizhnevolzhskogo kraevogo muzeia* (Saratov, 1932), 56-75.
1936   "Pozdne-sarmatskie pogrebeniia Nizhnego Povolzh'ia," *ISNIK* 7 (1936), 71-84.
1946   "K materialam po sarmatskoĭ kul'ture na territorii Nizhnego Povolzh'ia," *SA* 8 (1946), 73-95.
1947   *Arkheologicheskie raskopki na territorii Nizhnego Povolzh'ia* (Saratov, 1947).
1950   "Arkheologicheskie pamiatniki po reke Malyĭ Uzen," *KS* 32 (1950), 101-112.
1952   "Arkheologicheskie issledovaniia v Saratovskoĭ oblasti i zapadnom Kazakhstane," *KS* 45 (1952), 62-73.
1954a   "Arkheologicheskie issledovaniia zavolzhskogo otriada Stalingradskoĭ ekspeditsii," *KS* (1954), 77-94.
1954b   "Arkheologicheskie pamiatniki v nizov'iakh r. Ilovli," *UZ U* 39 (1954), 218-253.
1956a   "Arkheologicheskie issledovaniia v zapadnom Kazakhstane," *Arkheologiia Kazakhstana* 1 (1956), 87-139.
1956b   "Pamiatniki Nizhnego Povolzh'ia skifo-sarmatskogo vremeni," *Trudy Saratovskogo oblastnogo muzeia kraevedeniia* 1 (1956), 22-63.
1959   "Arkheologicheskie issledovaniia Zavolzhskogo otriada," *MIA* 60 (1959), 39-205.
1960   "Drevnie pamiatniki v nizov'iakh Eruslana," *MIA* 78 (1960), 10-167.

Sinitsyn, I. V. and U. E. Erdniev
1963 "Arkheologicheskie raskopki v Kalmykskoĭ ASSR v 1961 godu," *Trudy Kalmykskogo respublikanskogo kraevedcheskogo muzeia* 1 (Elista, 1963).
1966 "Novye arkheologicheskie pamiatniki na territorii Kalmykskoĭ ASSR," *Trudy Kalmykskogo respublikanskogo kraevedcheskogo muzeia* 2 (Elista, 1966).
Sinologica; Zeitschrift für chinesische Kultur und Wissenschaft (Basel, 1948-).
Sinor, D.
1948 "Autour d'une migration de peuples au ve siècle," *Extrait du journal asiatique* (1946-1947), (Paris, 1948).
Sirago, V. A.
1961 *Galla Placidia* (Louvain, 1961).
Sivieo, G.
1954 *Gli ori del Museo Nazionale de Napoli* (Naples, 1954).
Skalon, K.
1962 "Izobrazhenie drakona v iskusstve IV-V vekov," *Soobshcheniia Gos. Ermitazha* 22 (1962), 40-43.
Skard, E.
1940 "Asterius von Amasea und Asterius der Sophist," *Symbolae Osloenses* 20 (1940), 86-132.
Skrzhinskaia, E. Kh., trans.
1960 *Iordan, O proiskhozhdenii i deianiiakh getov*, vstupitel'naia stat'ia perevod, kommentarii E. Kh. Skrzhinskoĭ (Moscow, 1960).
Slovenská archeologia (Bratislava, 1953-).
Smirnov, A. P.
1952 *Ocherki drevneĭ i srednevekovoĭ istorii narodov srednego Povolzh'ia i Prikam'ia* in *MIA* 28 (1952).
1957 "Zhelesnyĭ vek Bashkirii," *MIA* 58 (1957), 5-113.
1958 *Istoriia arkheologiia srednevekovogo Kryma* (Moscow, 1958).
1967 *O proiskhozhdenii chuvashskogo naroda* (Cheboksary, 1967).
Smirnov, Ia. I.
1909 *Vostochnoe serebro* (St. Petersburg, 1909).
Smirnov, K. F.
1947 "Sarmatskie kurgannye pogrebeniia v stepiakh Povolzh'ia i iuzhnogo Priural'ia," *Doklady i soobshcheniia istoricheskogo fakulteta Moskovskogo gosudarstvennogo universiteta* 5 (1947).
1948a "O pogrebeniiakh Roksolanov," *VDI* (1948), 213ff.
1948b "Sarmatskie pogrebeniia iuzhnogo Priural'ia," *KS* 22 (1948), 80-86.
1950a "Novye dannye po sarmatskoĭ kul'ture severnogo Kavkaza," *KS* 32 (1950), 113-125.
1950b "Sarmatskie plemena severnogo Prikaspiia," *KS* 34 (1950), 97-114.
1951a "Arkheologicheskie issledovaniia v raĭone dagestanskogo selenia Tarki v 1948-1949 gg.," *MIA* 23 (1951), 226-272.
1951b "O nekotorykh itogakh issledovaniia mogil'nikov meotskoĭ i sarmatskoĭ kul'tury Prikuban'ia i Dagestana," *KS* 37 (1951), 226-272.
1952a "Osnovnye puti razvitiia meoto-sarmatskoĭ kul'tury srednego Prikuban'ia," *KS* 46 (1952), 3-18.
1952b "Arkheologicheskie issledovaniia v Dagestane v 1948-1950 godakh," *KS* (1952), 83-96.

1953   "Itogi i ocherednye zadachi izucheniia sarmatskikh plemen i kul'tury," *SA* 17 (1953), 133-148.
1954a   "Rabota pervogo nizhnevolzhkogo otriada Stalingradskoĭ ekspeditsii," *KS* 55 (1954), 64-76.
1954b   "Voprosy izucheniia sarmatskikh plemen i ikh kul'tury v sovetskoĭ arkheologii," *Voprosy* (1954), 195-219.
1958   "Meotskiĭ mogil'nik u Stanitsy Pashkovskoĭ," *MIA* 64 (1958), 272-312.
1959   "Kurgany u sel Ilovatka i Politodel'skoe Stalingradskoĭ oblasti," *MIA* 60 (1959), 206-322.
1960   "Kurgany bĭlia m. Velykogo Tomaka," *APU* 8 (1960), 164:189.
1961   *Vooruzhenie savromatov* in *MIA* 101 (1961).
1964   *Savromaty* (Moscow, 1964).
1966   "Sarmatskie pogrebeniia v basseĭne r. Kindelia Orenburgskoĭ oblasti," *KS* 107 (1966), 33-43.

Smirnov, K. F. and B. G. Petrenko
1963   *Savromaty Povolzh'ia i iuzhnogo Priural'ia* in *Arkheologiia* 19 (1963).

Smirnov, K. F. and S. A. Popov
1968   "Raboty v Orenburskoĭ oblasti," *Arkheologicheskie otkrytii* 1967 *goda* (Moscow, 1968), 113-114.

Smirnova, O.
1962   *Drevniĭ mir* (Moscow, 1962).

Snodgrass, A.
1964   *Early Greek Armour and Weapons* (Edingburgh, 1964).

Sofer, J.
1937   "Das Hieronymuszeugnis für die Sprachen der Galater und Trevener," *Wiener Studien* 55 (1937), 148-158.

Sokolova, K. F.
1958a   "Antropologicheskie materialy iz rannesrednevekovykh mogil'nikov Kryma," in A. P. Smirnov 1958 (1958), 63-87.
1958b   "Antropologicheskiĭ material iz Alushtinskogo mogil'nika," *Sovetskaia antropologiia* 2 (1958), 55-67.

Sokol'skiĭ, N. I.
1955   "O bosporskikh shchitakh," *KS* 58 (1955), 14-25.

Solari, A.
1938   *Il rinnovamento dell'impero romano* (Milan, 1938).

Solomonik, E. I.
1957   "O tavrenii skota v severnom Prichernomor'e," *Istoriia i arkheologiia drevnego Kryma* (Kiev, 1957), 210-218.
1959   *Sarmatskie znaki severnogo Prichernomor'ia* (Kiev, 1959).

Solymossy, A.
1937   "La légende de la viande amortie sous la selle," *Nouvelle Revue de Hongrie* (August 1937), 134-140.

Sommerström, B.
1959   *Archaeological Researches in the Edsen-Gol Region* 1-2 (Stockholm, 1956-58).

Sorokin, S. S.
1956a   "O datirovke i tolkovanii kenkol'skogo mogil'nika," *KS* 64 (1956), 8-14.
1956b   "Sredneaziatskie podboĭnye i katakombnye zakhoroneniia," *SA* 20 (1956), 97-117.

1958 "Arkheologicheskie pamiatniki severo-zapadnoĭ chasti Aktiubin-skoĭ oblasti," *KS* 71 (1958), 78-85.
1961a "Borkorbazskiĭ mogil'nik," *Trudy gos. Ermitazha* 5 (1961), 117-161.
1961b "Zheleznye izdeliia iz kenkol'skoi kollektsii," *Soobshcheniia gos. Ermitazha* 20 (1961), 51ff.

Sosnovskiĭ, G. P.
1935 "Deretuĭskiĭ mogil'nik," *Problemy istorii dokapitalisticheskikh obshchestv* 1-2 (1935), 168-176.
1946 "Raskopki Il'movoĭ padi," *SA* 8 (1946), 51-66.
1947 "O poselenii gunnskoĭ epokhi v doline r. Chikoia (Zabaĭkal'e)," *KS* 14 (1947).

Soveshchanie ("Soveshchanie posviashchennoe problemam cherniakhovskoĭ kul'tury i ee roli v ranneĭ istorii slavian"), *SA* 4, (Kiev, 1957), 274-277.

Sovetskaia antropologiia (Moscow, 1957-59); superseded by *Voprosy antropologii.*

Spasskaia, E. Iu.
1956 "Mednye kotly rannikh kochevnikov Kazakhstana i Kirgizii," *Uchenie zapiski Alma-atinskogo gosudarstvennogo pedagogicheskogo instituta* 11 (1956), 155-169.

Speculum; a Journal of Medieval Studies (Cambridge, Mass., 1926-).

Spengel, L., ed.
1856 *Rhetores graeci* (Leipzig, 1853-56).

Spitsyn, A.
1902 "Drevnosti kamskoĭ chudi po kollektsii Teploukhovykh," *MAR* 26 (1902).
1905 "Veshchi s inkrustatsieĭ iz kerchenskikh katakomb 1904 g.," *IAK* (1905), 115-126.
1915 *Arkheologicheskiĭ al'bom* in *Zapiski vostochn., otd. russk. arkheol. obshchestva* 11 (1915).
1948 "Polia pogrebal'nykh urn," *SA* 10 (1948), 53-72.

Spuler, B.
1943 *Die goldene Horde* (Leipzig, 1943).
1952 *Iran in frühislamischer Zeit* (Wiesbaden, 1952).

Stade, K.
1933 "Beinplatten zur Bogenversteifung aus römischen Waffenplätzen," *Germania* 17 (1933), 110-114.

Stein, A.
1928 *Innermost Asia* (Oxford, 1928).

Stein, E.
1925 "Untersuchungen zur spätrömischen Verwaltungsgeschichte," *Rheinische Museum* 74 (1925), 347-394.
1959 *Histoire du Bas-Empire* 102 (Paris and Brussels, 1959).

Stevens, C. E.
1933 *Sidonius Apollinaris and His Age* (Oxford, 1933).
1940 "The British Sections of the Notitia Dignitatum," *Archaeological Journal* (London, 1940).

Stevenson, E. L., trans.
1932 *Geography of Claudius Ptolemy* (New York, 1932).

Stoliar, A. D.
1958 "Raskopki kurganov u khutorianina Popova v 1950-1951 gg.," *MIA* 62 (1958), 348-416.

Straub, J.
1952   *Studien zur Historia Augusta* (Bern, 1952).
Ström, H.
1939   *Old English Personal Names in Bede's History* (Lund, 1939).
Stroheker, K. F.
1965   *Germanentum und Spätantike* (Zürich and Stuttgart, 1965).
Stuchi, S.
1945   "Le difese romane alle porta orientale d'Italia e il vallo delle
        Alpe Giule," *Aevum* 19 (1945).
Stumpfl, R.
1936   *Kultspiele der Germanen* (Berlin, 1936).
Sturenberg, N.
1932   *Relative Ortsbezeichnungen* (Leipzig, 1932).
Sturtevant, E. H.
1940   *The Pronunciation of Greek and Latin* (Philadelphia, 1940).
Suidas (*Suidae Lexicon*), Adler, A., ed. (Leipzig, 1928-38).
Sulimirski, T.
1964   "Sarmatians in the Polish Past," *Polish Review* 9:1 (1964), 13-66.
Sullivan, M.
1962   *The Birth of Landscape Painting in China* (Berkeley, 1962).
Sun, Shou-tao
1957   "Hsi-ch'a-kou ku-mu-chün pei chüeh shih-chien ti chiao-hsün,"
        (Report on the excavation of ancient tombs at Hsi-ch'a-kou)
        in *WWTK* 1 (1957), 53-56.
Sundwall, J.
1915   *Weströmische Studien* (Berlin, 1915).
A Survey of Persian Art, 1-6 Pope, U. A., ed. (London and New York, 1938-39).
Svoboda, B.
1966   "Zum Problem antiker Traditionen in der ältesten slawischen
        Kultur," *Origine et débuts des Slaves* 5 (Prague, 1966), 87-114.
Svoboda, B. and D. Concev
1956   *Neue Denkmäler antiker Toreutik* (Prague, 1956).
Swoboda, E.
1958   *Carnuntum* (Graz and Cologne, 1958).
Sylloge Tacticorum, Dain, A., ed. (Paris, 1938).
Symonovich, E. A.
1955   "Pamiatniki cherniakhovskoĭ kul'tury stepnogo Podneprov'ia,"
        SA 24 (1955), 282-316.
1956   "O nekotorykh tipakh poseleniĭ pervykh vekov n.e. v severnom
        Prichernomor'e," *KS* 65 (1956), 131-135.
1957a   "Lepnaia posuda pamiatnikov cherniakhovskoĭ kul'tury nizhnego
        Dnepra," *KS* 68," (1957), 14-19.
1957b   "Stekliannaia posuda serediny I tysiacheletiia n.e. s nizhnego
        Dnepra," *KS* 69 (1957), 22-30.
1958   "K voprosu o rannecherniakhovskikh poseleniiakh kul'tury po-
        leĭ pogrebeniĭ," *SA* 1 (1958), 248-252.
1964a   "Ornamentatsiia cherniakhovskoĭ keramiki," *MIA* 116 (1964),
        270-361.
1964b   "Severnaia granitsa pamiatnikov cherniakhovskoĭ kul'tury," *MIA*
        116 (1964), 7-43.

Synaxarium ecclesiae Constantinopolitanae, Delehaye, H., ed. (Brussels, 1902).

Széleky, Gy.
    1961   "Le sort des agglomérations pannoniens au début du Moyen Âge et les origines de l'urbanisme en Hongrie," *Annales Universitatis Scientiarum Budapestiensis, sectio historica* 3 (Budapest, 1961), 59-96.

Takáts, Z.
    1925   "Chinesisch-hunnische Kunstformen," *Bulletin de l'institut archéologique bulgare* 3 (1925).
    1927   "Kinai-Hunn Kapcsolatok," *AÉ* (1927), 146ff.
    1955   "Catalaunischer Hunnenfund und seine ostasiatischen Verbindungen," *AOH* 5 (1955), 143-173.
    1959   "Neuendeckte Denkmäler der Hunnen in Ungarn," *AOH* 9:1 (1959), 85-96.
    1960   "Some Chinese Elements in the Art of the Early Middle Ages of the Carpathian Basin, *East and West* (1960), 121-134.

Talitskaia, I. A.
    1952   "Materialy k arkheologicheskoĭ karte basseĭna r. Kamy," *MIA* 27 (1952).

Tallgren, A. M.
    1929   "Zur osteuropäischen Archäologie," *Finnisch-Ugrische Forschungen* 20 (Helsingfors, 1929).
    1937   "The South Siberian Cemetery of Oglakty from the Han Period," *ESA* 11 (1937).

Tarn, W. W.
    1951   *The Greeks in Bactria and India* (Cambridge, 1951).
    1952   *Alexander the Great* (Cambridge, 1950).

Teggart, Fr. J.
    1939   *Rome and China* (Berkeley, 1939).

Teploukhòv, S. A.
    1929   "Opyt klassifikatsii drevnikh metallicheskikh kul'tur Minusinskogo kraia," *Materialy po etnografii* 4:2 (1929), 41-62.

Terenozhkin, A.
    1940   "Pamiatniki material'noĭ kul'tury na Tashkentskom kanale," *Izv. UzFAN* 9 (1940).
    1950   "Sogd i chash," *KS* 33 (1950), 152-169.

Texte und Untersuchungen zur Geschichte der altchristlichen Literatur (Berlin, 1883-).

Thierry, A.
    1856   *Histoire d'Attila et de ses successeurs* (Paris, 1856).

Thiersch, H.
    1935   *Artemis Ephesia I* in *Abh. Göttingen*, dritte Folge 12 (1935).

Thomas, F. W.
    1951   *Tibetian Literary Texts and Documents Concerning Chinese Turkestan* (London, 1951).

Thompson, E. A.
    1944   "Olympiodorus of Thebes," *CQ* 38 (1944), 43-52.
    1945a   "The Camp of Attila," *JHS* 65 (1945), 112-115.
    1945b   "Priscus of Panium, Fragment 1b," *CQ* 39 (1945).
    1946   "Christian Missionaries among the Huns," *Hermathena* 67 (1946), 73-79.

1947a   The Historical Work of Ammianus Marcellinus (Cambridge, 1947).
1947b   "Notes on Priscus Panites," CQ 41 (1947), 61-65.
1948   A History of Attila and the Huns (Oxford, 1948).
1956   "Zosimus on the End of Roman Britain," Antiquity 119 (September 1956), 163-167.
1957a   "Christianity and the Northern Barbarians," Nottingham Medieval Studies 1 (1957).
1957b   "A Chronological Note on St. Germanus of Auxerre," Analecta Bollandiana 75 (1957).
1961   "The Visigoths in the Time of Ulfila," Nottingham Medieval Studies 5 (1961), 3-32.
Thomsen, V.
1912   "Dr. M. A. Stein's Manuscripts in Turkish 'Runic' Script from Miran and Tun-Huang," JRAS (1912), 181-227.
1924   "Alttürkische Inschriften aus der Mongolei," ZDMG 78 (1924), 121-175.
Thomson, J. O.
1948   History of Ancient Geography (Cambridge, 1948).
Thordeman, B.
1940   Armour from the Battle of Wisby 1361 (Stockholm, 1939-40).
Tihelka, K.
1963   "Das Fürstengrab bei Blučina, Bez. Brno-Land, aus der Zeit der Völkerwanderung," Památky archeologické 54 (1963), 467-498.
Tihanova, M. A.
1941   "Kul'tura zapadnykh oblastei ukrainy v pervye veka n.e.," MIA 6 (1941), 276ff.
1956   "Borochitskiĭ klad," SA 25 (1956), 301-317.
1957   "O lokal'nykh variantakh cherniakhovskoĭ kul'tury," SA 4 (1957), 168-194.
1960   "Laskovskiĭ klad," SA 1 (1960), 196-204.
1963   "Raskopki na poselenii III-IV vv. u s. Lepesovka v 1957-1959 gg.," SA 2 (1963), 178-191.
Tillemont, L. S. Le Nain de
1738   Histoire des empereurs (Paris, 1670-1738).
Tiratsian, G. A.
1960   "Utochnenie nekotorykh detaleĭ sasanidskogo vooruzheniia," Orbeli Anniversary Volume (1960), 474-486.
Togan (see Ibn Fadlan).
Toll, J., ed.
1671   Ausonii Opera (Amsterdam, 1671).
Toll, N.
1927   "Zametki o kitaĭskom shelke na iuge Rossii," Seminarium Kondakovianum 1 (1927).
Tolstov, S. P.
1948   Po sledam drevnekhorezmskoĭ tsivilizatsii (Moscow, 1948).
1949   "Khorezmskaia arkheologo-etnograficheskaia ekspeditsiia AN SSSR v 1948 g.," Izv. AN SSSR 6:3 (1949), 236-262.
1952   "Khorezmskaia arkheologo-etnograficheskaia ekspeditsiia AN SSSR (1945-48 gg.)," Trudy Khor. 1(1952), 7-46.

1954 "Arkheologicheskie raboty khorezmskoĭ arkheologo-etnograficheskoĭ ekspeditsii AN SSSR v 1951 g.," *SA* 19 (1954), 239-262.

1957 "Itogi dvadtsati let raboty khorezmskoĭ arkheologo-etnograficheskoĭ ekspeditsii (1937-1956 gg.)," *SE* 4 (1957), 31-59.

1958a "Khorezmskaia arkheologo-etnograficheskaia ekspeditsiia 1955-1956 gg.," *SA* 1 (1958), 106-133.

1958b "Raboty khorezmskoĭ arkheologo-etnograficheskoĭ ekspeditsii AN SSSR v 1949-1953 gg.," *Trudy Khor.* 2 (1958), 7-258.

1962 *Po drevnim del'tam Oksa i Iaksarta* (Moscow, 1962).

Tolstov, S. P., Zhdanko, T. A. and M. A. Itina

1963 "Raboty khorezmskoĭ arkheologo-etnograficheskoĭ ekspeditsii AN SSSA v 1958-1961 gg.," *Khor. Mat.* 6 (1963), 3-90.

Tončeva, G.

1952 "Contribution à l'iconographie du grand dieu d'Odessos," *Bulletin de l'Institut archéologique* 28 (1952), 83-90.

Tóth, T. A.

1962 "Palaeoanthropological Finds from the Valley of Hudjirte (Noin-Ula, Mongolia)," *AAH* 14:3-4 (1962), 249-253.

1967 "Some Problems in the Palaeoanthropology of Northern Mongolia," *AAH* 19:3-4 (1967), 377-390.

T'oung Pao (*Archives concernant l'histoire, des langues, la géographie et l'ethnographie de l'Asie orientale*), (Leiden).

Transactions of the Royal Historical Society (London, 1872-).

Trautman, R.

1944 *Die slavischen Völker und Sprachen* (Göttingen, 1944).

Tretiakov, P. N.

1948 *Vostochnoslavianskie plemena*, second ed. 1953 (Moscow, 1948).

1953 *Po sledam drevnikh kul'tur. Drevniaia Rus'* (Moscow, 1953).

1954 "Ranneslavianskaia kul'tura v verkhnem Podneprov'e," *KS* 55 (1954), 11-16.

Trever, K. V.

1935 *See* Orbeli and Trever 1935.

1940 *Pamiatniki greko-baktriĭskogo iskusstva* (Moscow and Leningrad, 1940).

1959 *Ocherki po istorii i kul'ture kavkazskoĭ Albanii* (Moscow and Leningrad, 1959).

Trofima, T. A.

1957 "Palaeoanthropological Remains Coming from the Territory of Ancient Xorezm." *East and West* 8:3 (1957).

1958a "Kraniologicheskie materialy iz antichnykh kreposteĭ Kalaly-Gir 1 i 2," *Trudy Khor.* 2 (1958), 543-630.

1958b "Materialy po paleoantropologii Khorezma i sopredel'nykh oblasteĭ," *Trudy Khor.* 2 (1958), 639-701.

1959 *Drevnee naselenie Khorezma po dannym antropologii* in *Khor. Mat.* 2 (1959).

1960 "Osnovnye itogi i zadachi paleoantropologicheskogo izucheniia sredneĭ Azii," *SE* 2 (1960), 110-122.

1963 "Priaral'skie Saki (Kraniologicheskiĭ ocherk)," *Khor. Mat.* 6 (1963), 221-247.

Troplong, E.
1908   *La diplomatie d'Attila* in *Revue d'histoire diplomatique* 22 (1908).
Trudy Dvadtsat'-piatogo (XXV) mezhdunarodnogo kongressa vostokovedov 1-4 (Moscow, 1963).
Trudy instituta istorii, arkheologii i etnografii Kazakhskoĭ SSR (Alma Ata).
Trudy iuzhno-turkmenistanskoĭ arkheologicheskoĭ kompleksnoĭ ekspeditsii (Ashkhabad, 1949-).
Trudy khorezmskoĭ arkheologo-etnograficheskoĭ ekspeditsii 1-2 (Moscow, 1956-58); 2: *Arkheologicheskie i etnograficheskie raboty khorezmskoĭ ekspeditsii* 1949-1953 gg. (Moscow, 1958).
Trudy kirgizskoĭ arkheologo-etnograficheskoĭ ekspeditsii 1-2 (Moscow, 1956-59).
Trudy Saratovskogo oblastnogo muzeia kreavedeniia (Saratov).
Trudy tuvinskoĭ kompleksnoĭ arkheologo-etnograficheskoĭ ekspeditsii (Moscow and Leningrad).
Tsalkin, K. V.
1960   "Istoriia skotovodstva v severnom Prichernomor'e," *MIA* 53 (1960).
Tudor, D.
1948   "Sucidava III," *Dacia* 11-12, 1945-1947 (1948), 141-208.
1958   *Oltenia romană* (Bucharest, 1958).
1965   *Sucidava; une cité daco-romaine et byzantine en Dacie* (Brussels, 1965).
Turfan-Texte (Türkische Turfantexte) 1-4 (*see* Bang and Gabain 1930).
Uigurica (Ugurica) 1-5 (*see* Schaeffer 1968).
Ulrich, H.
1957   "Trois cranes artificiellement déformés du Bas-Rhin," *Bulletin et mémoires de la société d'anthropologie de Paris* 5-6 (Paris, 1957), 276-283.
Ulrich-Bansa, O.
1949   *Moneta Mediolanensis* (Venice, 1949).
Umehara, S.
1931   *Ō bei ni okeru shina kokyo* (Kyoto, 1931).
1935   *Shina kodō seikwa* 4 (Osaka, 1935).
1938   *Kodai hoppō kei bumbutsu no kenkyū* (Kyoto, 1938). Includes *Tōhō gakuhō* 1 (Kyoto, 1931), 49-90.
1960   *Mōko Noin Ura hakken no ibutsu* (Tokyo, 1960).
Ungarische Jahrbücher (Ural-Altaische Jahrbücher), (Berlin, Leipzig and Wiesbaden, 1921-).
Untaru, G.
1962   "Mormînt sarmatic desoperit în orasul Focşani," *SCIV* 13:1 (1962), 157-162.
Uspenskiĭ, K. N.
1950   "Theophanes und seine Chronographie," *VV* 3 (1950), 396-438.
Uzmanova, Z. I.
1963   "Raskopki masterskoĭ remeslennika parfianskogo vremeni na gorodishche Giaur-Kala," *Trudy iuzhno-turkmenskoĭ arkheologicheskoĭ kompleksnoĭ ekspeditsii* 12 (1963).
Vaĭnshteĭn, S. I.
1964   "Tuva v period razlozheniia pervobytnoobshchinnogo stroia i voznyknoveniia klassovogo obshchestva," *Istoriia Tuvy* (Moscow, 1964), 35-54.

1966   "Nekotorye voprosy istorii drevnetiurskoĭ kul'tury," *SE* 3 (1966),
        60-81. English translation in *Soviet Anthropology and Archaeology*
        6:4 (1968), 3-24.

Vaĭnshteĭn, S. I. and V. P. D'iakonova
1966   "Pamiatnik v mogil'nike kokel' kontsa I tysiacheletiia do nasheĭ
        ery-pervykh vekov nasheĭ ery," *Trudy Tuv.* 2 (1966), 185-291.

Vámbéry, A.
1882   *Der Ursprung der Magyaren* (Leipzig, 1882).

Vamos, F.
1932   "Attilas Hauptlager und Holzpaläste," *Seminarium Kondakovia-
        num* 5 (1932), 131-148.

Vance, M.
1907   *Beiträge zur byzantinischen Kulturgeschichte* (Jena, 1907).

Van Millingen, A.
1899   *Byzantine Constantinople* (London, 1899).

Vasiliev, A. A.
1936   *The Goths in the Crimea* (Cambridge, Mass., 1936).
1950   *Justin the First* (Cambridge, Mass., 1950).

Vasiutkin, S. M.
1968   "Nekotorye voprosy arkhologii Bashkirii I tysiacheletiia nasheĭ
        ery," *SA* 1 (1968), 56-72.

Vasmer, M.
1923   *Untersuchungen über die ältesten Wohnsitze der Slaven. I: Die
        Iraner in Südrussland* (Leipzig, 1923).
1955   *Russisches etymologisches Wörterbuch* (Heidelberg, 1955).

Veeck, W.
1931   *Die Alamannen in Württemberg* (Berlin and Leipzig, 1931).

Veĭmarn, B. V.
1957   "Raskopki Inkermanskogo mogil'nika v 1948 g.," *Istoriia i arkheo-
        logiia drevnego Kryma* (Kiev, 1957), 219-237.
1958   "Peshchernye goroda Kryma v svete arkheologicheskikh issledo-
        vaniĭ 1954-1955 g.," *SA* 1 (1958), 71-79.

Velikhanova, M. S.
1965   "K etnograficheskoĭ antropologii Prutsko-Dnestrovskogo mezh-
        durech'ia v I tysiacheletii n.e.," *KS* 105 (1965), 59-67.

Velkov, V. I.
1959   *Gradŭt v Trakiia i Dakiia prez kŭsnata antichnost* (Sofia, 1959).

Vernadsky, G.
1943   *Ancient Russia* (New Haven, 1943).
1959   *The Origins of Russia* (Oxford, 1959).

Vestnik drevneĭ istorii (Moscow, 1937-).

Vetter, G.
1938   *Die Ostgoten und Theoderich* (Stuttgart, 1938).

Vetters, H.
1950   "Dacia ripensis," *Österreichische Akademie der Wissenschaften,
        Schriften der Balkankommission, Antiquarische Abteilung* 11
        (1950).
1963   "Zur Spätzeit des Lagers Carnuntum," *Österr. Zeitschr. f. Kunst
        und Denkmalpflege* 17:4 (1963).

Viazmitina, M. I.
1953   "Izuchenie sarmatov na territorii Ukraïnskoï RSR," *Arkheologiia* 8 (1953), 56-75.
1959   "Sarmatskie plemena," *Narysy starodavn'oï istoriï Ukraïns'koï RSR* (Kiev, 1959), 215-242.
1962   *Zolota Balka* (Kiev, 1962).
Vigiliae Christianae (Amsterdam, 1947-).
Vinnikov, Ia. R.
1956   "Rodo-plemennoï sostav i rasselenie kirgizov na territorii iuzhnoï Kirgizii," *Trudy Kirg.* 1 (1956), 136-181.
Vinogradov, V. B.
1963   *Sarmaty severo-vostochnogo Kavkaza* (Groznyï, 1963).
1966a   "Figurki 'Skifov' iz Chechenoingushetii," *SA* 2 (1966).
1966b   *Taïny minavskikh vremen* (Moscow, 1966).
Vitt, V. O.
1952   "Loshadi pazyrykskykh kurganov," *SA* 16 (1952), 163-205.
Vives, I.
1942   *Inscripciones cristianas de la España cristiana y visigoda* (Barcelona, 1942).
Vizantiïskiï vremennik (Moscow, 1947-).
Vladimirtsov, B. Ia.
1934   *Obshchestvennyï stroï Mongolov* (Leningrad, 1934).
Vlček, E.
1957   "Antropologický material z období stěhováui národů na Slavensku," *Slovenská Archaeologia* 5:2 (1957), 402-423; (German summary) 423-424.
Voedvodskiï, M. V. and M. P. Griaznov
1930   "Usunskie mogil'niki na territorii Kirgizskoï SSR," *VDI* 3 (19-38).
Vogel, Fr., ed.
1885   *Magni Felicis Ennodii Opera* in *MGH AA* 7 (Berlin, 1885).
Volkov, V.
1962   "Bronzovye nakonechniki strel iz muzeev MNR," *Mongol'skiï arkheologicheskiï sbornik* 18-26 (1962).
Vollmer, Fr., ed.
1905   *Fl. Merobaudis reliquiae, MGH AA* 14 (1905).
Voprosy antropologii (Moscow, 1960-); supersedes Sovetskaia Antropologiia.
Voprosy iazykoznaniia, Institut iazykoznaniia AN SSSR (Moscow, 1952-).
Voprosy istorii (Moscow, 1945-).
Voprosy skifo-sarmatskoï arkheologii, AN SSSR (Moscow, 1954).
Vordemfelder, H.
1923   *Die germanische Religion in den deutschen Volksrechten* (Giessen, 1923).
Vorgeschichte (*Vorgeschichte der deutschen Stämme*) 3 (Leipzig and Berlin, 1940).
Vorob'ev, M. V.
1961   *Drevniaia Koreia* (Moscow, 1961).
Vorob'eva, M. G.
1959   "Keramika Khorezma antichnogo perioda," *Trudy Khor.* 4 (1959), 63-220.

Voronets, M. E.
 1940 "Arkheologicheskie issledovaniia 1937-1939 gg. v Uzbekistanskoĭ
      SSR," *VDI* 3-4 (12-13), (1940), 324-339.
 1951 "Otchet arkheologicheskoĭ ekspeditsii Muzeia istorii AN Uzbe-
      kistanskoĭ SSR o raskopkakh pogrebal'nykh kurganov vozle st.
      Vrevskaia," *Trudy muzeia istorii Uzbekistana* (Tashkent, 1951).
Vos, M. F.
 1963 *Scythian Archers in Archaic Attic Vase-Painting* (Groningen, 1963).
Vostrov, V. V.
 1961 "Rodoplemennoĭ sostav i rasselenie kazakhov na territorii Se-
      mirechenskoĭ oblasti," *Trudy Kazakh.* 12 (1961), 119-135.
Vulpe, R.
 1961 "La Valachie et la Basse-Moldavie sous les Romains," *Dacia*,
      N.S. 6 (1961), 365-393.
Vysotskaia, T. N. and E. N. Cherepanova
 1966 "Nakhodki iz pogrebeniĭ IV-V vv. v Krymu," *SA* 3 (1966), 187-
      196.
Wagner, N.
 1967 *Getica; Untersuchungen zum Leben des Jordanes und zur frühen
      Geschichte der Goten* (Berlin, 1967).
Wais, I. G.
 1940 *Die Alamannen in ihrer Auseinandersetzung mit der römischen Welt*
      (Berlin, 1940).
Waitz, G., ed.
 1878 *Historia Langobardorum* (Hannover, 1878).
Waley, A.
 1931 *The Travels of an Alchemist* (London, 1931).
 1946 *Chinese Poems* (London, 1946).
Walford, E., ed. and trans.
 1846 *Ecclesiastical History (containing fragments from Philostorgius)*,
      (1846).
 1954 *History of the Church from* A.D. *322 to the Death of Theodore of
      Mopsuestia,* A.D. *427, by Theodoret, bp. of Cyrus and from* A.D. *431
      to* A.D. *594 by Evagrius* (London, 1854).
Walke, N.
 1965 "Das römische Donaukastell Straubing-Sorviodūrūm," *Limes-
      forschungen* 3 (Berlin, 1965).
Wallis Budge, E. A., trans.
 1932 *The Chronography of Gregory Abû'l Faraj (Bar Hebraeus)*, (Lon-
      don, 1932).
Walser, G.
 1951 *Rom, das Reich und die fremden Völker in der Geschichtsschreibung
      der frühen Kaiserzeit* (Baden-Baden, 1951).
Watson, W.
 1962 *Early Chinese Bronzes* (Rutland, Vt., 1962).
Weber, L.
 1936 "Die katalaunische Geisterschlacht," *Archiv für Religionsgeschichte*
      33 (1936), 162-166.
Wedemeyer, A.
 1930 *Japanische Frühgeschichte* (Tokyo, 1930).

Weerd, H. van de and P. Lambrechts
1938   "Note sur le corps d'archers au haut empire," *Dissertationes Pannonicae* 10, second series (Budapest, 1938).

Weibel, A. C.
1952   *Two Thousand Years of Textiles* (New York, 1952).

Wên-Wu (*Cultural Relics*), (Peking, 1950-).

Wên-Wu Ts'an-K'ao Tzu-Liao (*Reference Materials on Cultural Relics*), variant title of *Wên-Wu* 1950-1958.

Wenley, A. G.
1949   "The Question of the Po-Shan-Hsiang-Lu," *Archives of the Chinese Art Society of America* 3 (1946-49).

Wenskus, R.
1961   *Stammesbildung und Verfassung* (Cologne and Graz, 1961).

Werner, Joachim
1932   "Bogenfragmente aus Carnuntum und von der unteren Wolga," *ESA* 7 (1932), 33-58.

1935   *Münzdatierte austrasische Grabfunde* (Berlin, 1935).

1950   "Zur Herkunft der frühmittelalterlichen Spangenhelme," *Prähist. Zeitschr.* 34-35 (1949-50), 178-193.

1956   "Beiträge zur Archäologie des Attila-Reiches," *Abh. München*, N.F. 4:38:a-b (Munich, 1956).

1958   "Neue Daten zur Verbreitung der artifiziellen Schädeldeformation im 1. Jahrtausend n. Chr.," *Germania* 36:1-2 (1958), 162-164.

1959   "Studien zu Grabfunden des 5. Jahrhunderts aus der Slovakei und der Karpathenukraine," *Slovenská Archeologia* (Bratislava, 1959), 422-438.

1960   "Die frühgeschichtlichen Grabfunde vom Spielberg bei Erlbach, Ldkr. Nördlingen, und von Fürst, Ldkr. Laufen a. d. Salzach," *Bayerische Vorgeschichtsblätter*, 25 (1950), 164-179.

1962a   *Das erste Jahrtausend*, Tafelband (Düsseldorf, 1962).

1962b   "Die Langobarden in Pannonien," *Abh. München*, N.F. 55a (Munich, 1962).

Werner, J. and G. Annibaldi
1963   "Ostgotische Funde aus Acquasanta, Prov. Ascoli Piceno (Marche)," *Germania* 41:2 (1963), 356-373; (Annibaldi 356-365; Werner 365-373).

Werner, Robert
1967   "Das früheste Auftreten des Hunnennamens Yüe-či und die Hephthaliten," *Jahrbücher für Geschichte Osteuropas* 15:4 (1967), 487-558.

Wheeler, J.
1951   *Taxila* 1-3 (Cambridge, 1951).

White, L.
1962   *Medieval Technology and Social Change* (Berkeley and Los Angeles, 1962).

White, W. C.
1939   *Tomb Tile Pictures of Ancient China* (Toronto, 1939).

Wiener Beiträge zur Kulturgeschichte und Linguistik (Vienna).

Wiener Prähistorische Zeitschrift (Vienna, 1914-39).

Wiener Zeitschrift für Kunde des Morgenlandes (Vienna, 1887-).

Wiener Studien; Zeitschrift für Klassische Philologie (Vienna, 1879-).

Wietersheim, E. K. von
1881   Geschichte der Völkerwanderung 1-2 (Leipzig, 1880-81).
Wikander, St.
1946   Feuerpriester in Kleinasien und Iran (Lund, 1946).
Windischmann, Fr.
1858   Die persische Anphita oder Anaitis in Abh. München 8 (1858), 86ff.
Witsen, N. C.
1962   Noord en Oost Tartarye, Rudenko, S. I., ed. (1962).
Wittfogel, K. A. and Fêng Chia-shêng
1949   History of Chinese Society. Liao (New York, 1949).
Woestijne, P. van de
1950   "Les scolies à la Thébaide de Stace," L'antiquité classique 19 (1950), 149-169.
1953   La Périégèse de Priscien (Bruges, 1953).
Wolff, F.
1935   Glossar zu Firdosis Schahname (Berlin, 1935).
Wright, F. A., trans.
1930   The Works of Liudprand of Cremona (London and New York, 1930).
1939   Letters of Jerome in Loeb (Cambridge, Mass., 1939).
Wright, W., trans.
1882   The Chronicle of Joshua Stylites (Cambridge, 1882).
Wünsch, R., ed.
1898   Joannis Laurentii Lydi Liber de mensibus (1898).
Wurm, G., ed.
1844   De rebus gestis Aetii dissertatio (Bonn, 1844).
Yamgerchino, B. D. (see Iamgerchinov, B. D.).
Yao Wei-yüan
1958   Pei chao hu hsing k'ao (Peking, 1958).
Yetts, W. P.
        The George Eumorfopoulos Collection Catalogue of the Chinese and Corean Bronzes (London, 1929-32).
Zabelina, N. N. and L. N. Rempel'
1948   Sogdiĭskiĭ vsadnik (Tashkent, 1948).
Zadneprovskiĭ, Iu. A.
1956   "Ob etnicheskom sostave naseleniia drevneĭ Fergany," KS 61 (1956), 39-44.
1958   "Gorodishche Shurashshabat," KS 71 (1958), 99-108.
1960   "Arkheologicheskie raboty v iuzhnoĭ Kirgizii v 1957 godu," KS 78 (1960), 43-52.
1962   Drevnezemledel'cheskaia kul'tura Fergany in MIA 118 (1962).
Zahn, R.
1911   Amtliche Berichte aus den Preussischen Kunstsammlungen (1911).
Zalkind, N. G.
1952   "Kraniologicheskie materialy s territorii drevnego Khorezma," Trudy Khor. 1 (1952), 197-204.
Zambaur, A.
1927   Manuel de généalogie et chronologie pour l'histoire de l'Islam (Hannover, 1927).

Zasetskaia, I. P.
1968   "O khronologii pogrebeniĭ epokhi pereseleniia narodov Nizhnego Povolzh'ia," *SA* 2 (1968), 52-62.

Zbrueva, A. V.
1952   "Istoriia naseleniia Prikam'ia v anan'skuiu epokhu," *MIA* 30 (1952).

Zeest, I. B.
1951   "Zhilye doma drevnego Kimmerika," *KS* 37 (1951), 191-195.
1958   "Raskopki Germonassy," *KS* 58 (1955), 114-121.

Zeiller, J.
1918   *Des origines chrétiennes dans les provinces danubiennes de l'empire romain* (Paris, 1918).
1935   *Comptes rendus de l'académie des inscriptions* (1935), 238-250.

Zeiss, H.
1933   "Ein hunnischer Fund aus dem Elsass," *Germania* 17 (1933).
1934   *Die Grabfunde aus dem spanischen Westgotenreich* (Berlin and Leipzig, 1934).
1938   "Grabfunde aus dem Burgundenreich an der Rhône," *SB München* 7 (1938).

Zeitschrift der deutschen morgenländischen Gesellschaft (Leipzig, 1847-).
Zeitschrift für deutsche Philologie (Halle, 1869-).
Zeitschrift für deutsches Altertum und deutsche Literatur (Leipzig, 1841-)
Zeitschrift für die österreichischen Gymnasien (Vienna, 1850-1920).
Zeitschrift für Ethnologie (*und Urgeschichte*), Berliner Gesellschaft für Anthropologie (Berlin, 1969-).
Zeitschrift für historische Waffen- und Kostumkünde (Dresden and Berlin, 1894-).
Zeitschrift für klassische Philologie (*see Wiener Studien*).
Zeitschrift für Numismatik (Berlin, 1879-).
Zeitschrift für Ortsnamenforschung (Munich and Berlin, 1925-).
Zeitschrift für Semitistik und verwandte Gebiete im Auftrage der deutschen morgenländischen Gesellschaft (Leipzig, 1922-).
Zeitschrift für vergleichende Sprachforschung, Dümmler, F., ed. (Berlin).

Zeuss, K.
1937   *Die Deutschen und die Nachbarstämme* (München, 1837).

Zezenkova, V. Ia.
1961   "Cherep iz Kyzyl-Kyra," *IMKU* 2 (Tashkent, 1961), 302-306.
1963   "Kraniologicheskiĭ material iz mogil'nikov Bukharskoĭ oblasti, *IMKU* 4 (Tashkent, 1963), 66-72.

Zgusta, L.
1955   *Die Personennamen griechischer Städte der nördlichen Schwarzmeerküste* (Prague, 1955).

Zhirov, E. V.
1940   "Ob iskusstvennoĭ deformatsii golovy," *KS* 8 (1940), 81-88.
1949   "Cherepa iz zoroastriĭskikh pogrebeniĭ v sredneĭ Azii," *SMAE* 10 (1949).

Zhivopis' drevnego Piandzhikenta (*see* D'iakonov, M. M. and A. Iu. Iakubovskiĭ).

Ziegel, K.
1939   Die Thüringe der späten Völkerwanderungszeit im Gebiet östlich
       der Saale in Jahresschrift für die Vorgeschichte der sächsisch-thü-
       ringischen Länder 31 (1939).
Zimmer, E.
1947   Myth and Symbol in Indian Art and Civilization (New York,
       1947).
1956   The Philosophies of India (Berkeley and Los Angeles, 1956).
Zolotarev, I. M.
1957   "Cherepa iz pereĭminskogo i kozlovskogo mogil'nikov (sredniaia
       Ob')," MIA 58 (1957), 246-250.
Zuev, Iu. A.
1960a "K etnicheskoĭ istorii usuneĭ," Trudy Kazakh. 8 (1960), 5-23.
1960b "Tamgi loshadeĭ iz vassal'nykh kniazhestv," Trudy Kazakh. 8
       (1960), 93-140.

Index

Prepared by Gladys Crofoot Castor

DIOCESES AND PROVINCES
OF THE ROMAN EMPIRE,
5TH CENTURY A.D.

DIOCESES IN BOLD CAPITALS (e.g., D. DACIAE)
PROVINCES IN LIGHTER CAPITALS (e.g., DALMATIA)